TEAR GAS EPIPHANIES

McGILL-QUEEN'S/BEAVERBROOK CANADIAN FOUNDATION STUDIES IN ART HISTORY

Martha Langford and Sandra Paikowsky, series editors

Recognizing the need for a better understanding of Canada's artistic culture both at home and abroad, the Beaverbrook Canadian Foundation, through its generous support, makes possible the publication of innovative books that advance our understanding of Canadian art and Canada's visual and material culture. This series supports and stimulates such scholarship through the publication of original and rigorous peer-reviewed books that make significant contributions to the subject. We welcome submissions from Canadian and international scholars for book-length projects on historical and contemporary Canadian art and visual and material culture, including Native and Inuit art, architecture, photography, craft, design, and museum studies. Studies by Canadian scholars on non-Canadian themes will also be considered.

The Practice of Her Profession
Florence Carlyle, Canadian Painter in the Age of Impressionism
Susan Butlin

Bringing Art to Life
A Biography of Alan Jarvis
Andrew Horrall

Picturing the Land
Narrating Territories in Canadian Landscape Art, 1500 to 1950
Marylin J. McKay

The Cultural Work of Photography in Canada
Edited by Carol Payne and Andrea Kunard

Newfoundland Modern
Architecture in the Smallwood Years, 1949–1972
Robert Mellin

The Codex Canadensis *and the Writings of Louis Nicolas*
The Natural History of the New World, Histoire Naturelle des Indes Occidentales
Edited and with an Introduction by François-Marc Gagnon, Translation by Nancy Senior, Modernization by Réal Ouellet

Museum Pieces
Toward the Indigenization of Canadian Museums
Ruth B. Phillips

The Allied Arts
Architecture and Craft in Postwar Canada
Sandra Alfoldy

Rethinking Professionalism
Essays on Women and Art in Canada, 1850–1970
Edited by Kristina Huneault and Janice Anderson

The Official Picture
The National Film Board of Canada's Still Photography Division and the Image of Canada, 1941–1971
Carol Payne

Paul-Émile Borduas
A Critical Biography
François-Marc Gagnon
Translated by Peter Feldstein

On Architecture
Melvin Charney: A Critical Anthology
Edited by Louis Martin

Making Toronto Modern
Architecture and Design, 1895–1975
Christopher Armstrong

Negotiations in a Vacant Lot
Studying the Visual in Canada
Edited by Lynda Jessup, Erin Morton, and Kirsty Robertson

Visibly Canadian
Imaging Collective Identities in the Canadas, 1820–1910
Karen Stanworth

Breaking and Entering
The Contemporary House Cut, Spliced, and Haunted
Edited by Bridget Elliott

Family Ties
Living History in Canadian House Museums
Andrea Terry

Picturing Toronto
Photography and the Making of a Modern City
Sarah Bassnett

Architecture on Ice
A History of the Hockey Arena
Howard Shubert

For Folk's Sake
Art and Economy in Twentieth-Century Nova Scotia
Erin Morton

Spaces and Places for Art
Making Art Institutions in Western Canada, 1912–1990
Anne Whitelaw

Narratives Unfolding
National Art Histories in an Unfinished World
Edited by Martha Langford

Canadian Painters in a Modern World, 1925–1955
Writings and Reconsiderations
Lora Senechal Carney

Sketches from an Unquiet Country
Canadian Graphic Satire, 1840–1940
Edited by Dominic Hardy, Annie Gérin, and Lora Senechal Carney

I'm Not Myself at All
Women, Art, and Subjectivity in Canada
Kristina Huneault

The Global Flows of Early Scottish Photography
Encounters in Scotland, Canada, and China
Anthony W. Lee

Tear Gas Epiphanies
Protest, Culture, Museums
Kirsty Robertson

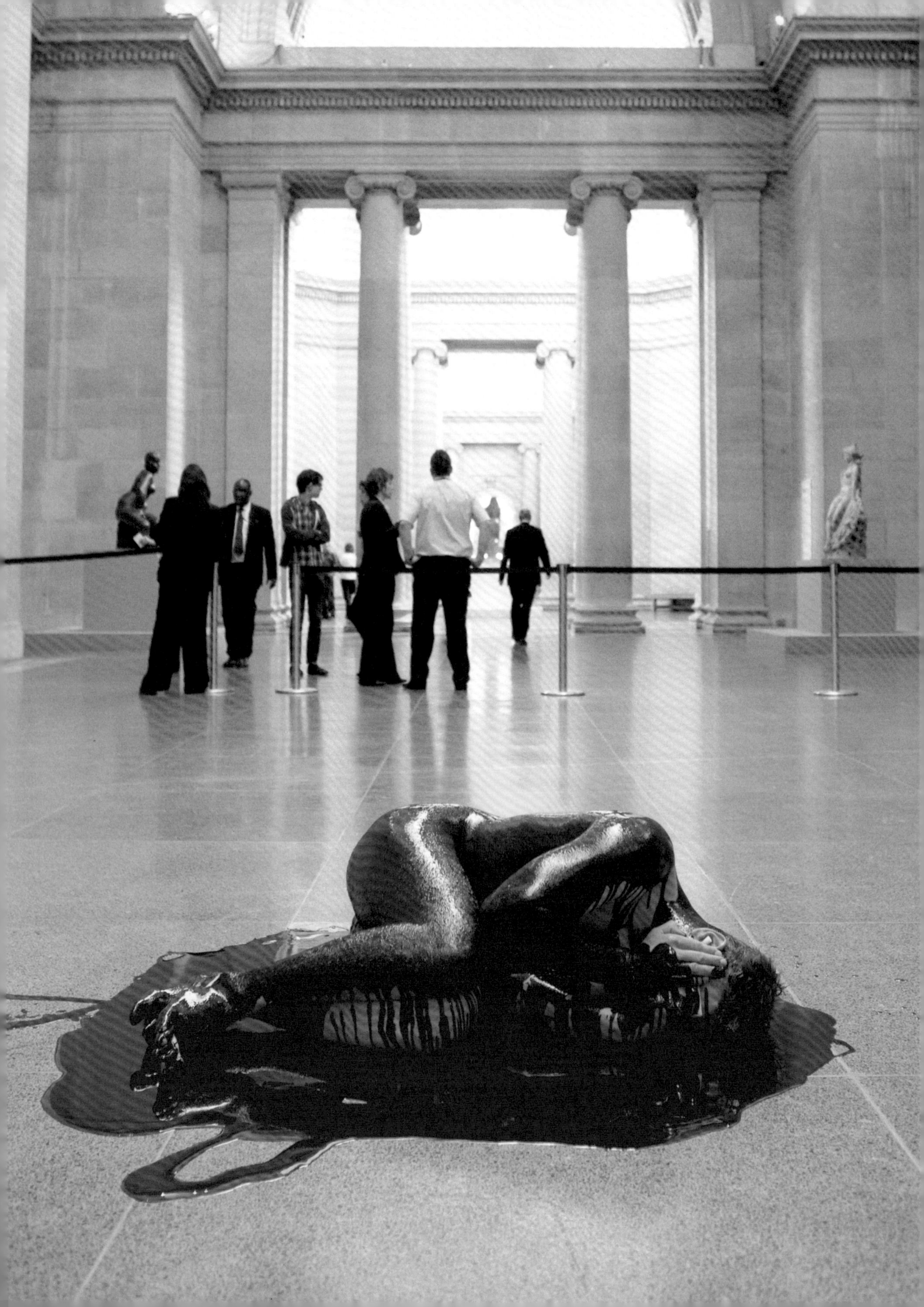

Kirsty Robertson

TEAR GAS EPIPHANIES

Protest, Culture, Museums

McGill-Queen's University Press
Montreal & Kingston | London | Chicago

ISBN 978-0-7735-5700-0 (cloth)
ISBN 978-0-7735-5701-7 (paper)
ISBN 978-0-7735-5829-8 (ePDF)

Legal deposit second quarter 2019
Bibliothèque nationale du Québec

Printed in Canada on acid-free paper

This book has been published with the help of a grant from the Canadian Federation for the Humanities and Social Sciences, through the Awards to Scholarly Publications Program, using funds provided by the Social Sciences and Humanities Research Council of Canada.

Funded by the Government of Canada | Financé par le gouvernement du Canada | Canada
Canada Council for the Arts | Conseil des arts du Canada

We acknowledge the support of the Canada Council for the Arts, which last year invested $153 million to bring the arts to Canadians throughout the country.

Nous remercions le Conseil des arts du Canada de son soutien. L'an dernier, le Conseil a investi 153 millions de dollars pour mettre de l'art dans la vie des Canadiennes et des Canadiens de tout le pays.

Library and Archives Canada Cataloguing in Publication

Title: Tear gas epiphanies : protest, culture, museums / Kirsty Robertson.
Names: Robertson, Kirsty, 1976– author.
Series: McGill-Queen's/Beaverbrook Canadian Foundation studies in art history.
Description: Series statement: McGill-Queen's/Beaverbrook Canadian Foundation studies in art history | Includes bibliographical references and index.
Identifiers: Canadiana (print) 20190064633 | Canadiana (ebook) 20190064684 | ISBN 9780773557017 (softcover) | ISBN 9780773557000 (hardcover) | ISBN 9780773558298 (ePDF)
Subjects: LCSH: Museums—Political aspects—Canada—History—20th century. | LCSH: Museums—Political aspects—Canada—History—21st century.
Classification: LCC AM21.A2 R63 2019 | DDC 069.0971—dc23

For Tim, Caroline, and Liz

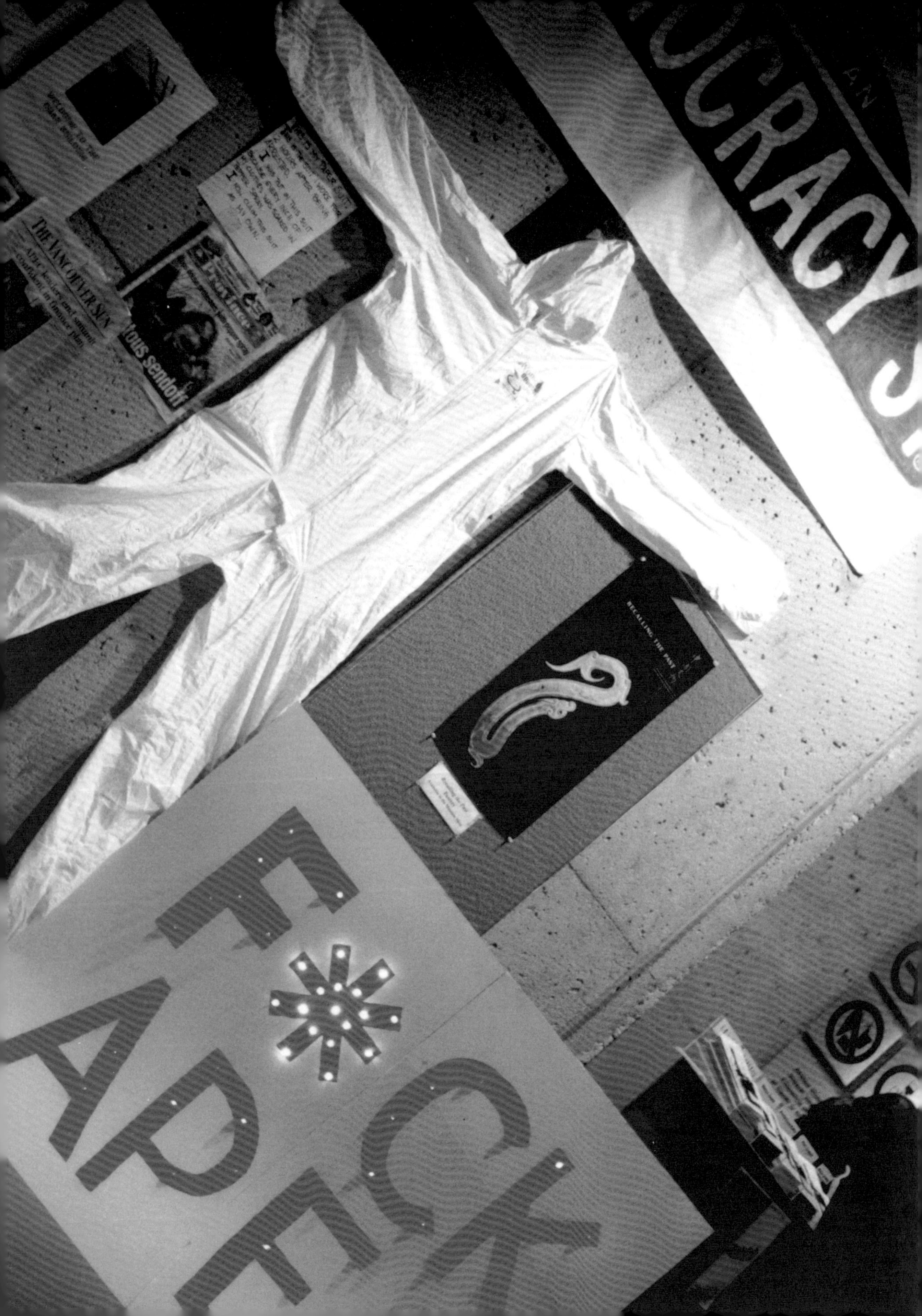
THE VANCOUVER SUN
RECALLING THE PAST

Contents

Preface | xi

1 Introduction: Museums, Protest, and Cities | 3

1a Of Directors, Museums, and National Identity | 31

Part 1 Context

2 Protest at the Threshold: A Short History of Contentious Politics at Canadian Museums, 1900–96 | 39

2b The UBC *Museum of Anthropology as Model* | 71

3 Crossing the Threshold: Counter-Histories, Museum Exteriors, Interiors, and Archives | 76

3c "She walked in and removed her work from the wall": Artists against Reed Paper at the Art Gallery of Ontario, 1976 | 103

Part 2 Case Studies

4 Reactionary Protest: The Warrior Nation and the Canadian War Museum | 111

4d The Postponement of The Lands within Me: *Expressions by Canadian Artists of Arab Origin, 2001* | 142

5 "It takes a lot of wrongs to make a museum of rights": Indigenous Resistance and the Canadian Museum for Human Rights | 145

5e Wendy Coburn: Anatomy of a Protest | 178

6 When the Land Comes First: Oil, Museums, and (Missing) Protest | 182

6f Reversing the Flow: Yes Men Tackle the Canadian Government | 219

7 "Intellectual Properties": Real Estate, Occupy Vancouver, and the Vancouver Art Gallery | 223

7g Stan Douglas and the Woodward's Redevelopment | 261

8 Conclusion | 267

Figures | 273

Notes | 277

Bibliography | 339

Index | 389

Preface

In the early 2000s, when I had the initial idea for *Tear Gas Epiphanies*, my aim was to write about connections among anti-capitalist protest, emotion, and the emotional or affective labour that undergirds what is variously called the new economy or the creative industries.[1] I expected to do this through an analysis of the role of artists in a changing economy in Canada. During my research, however, I kept coming across museums as sites and sources of protest. Globally, museums at the time were going through a period of transformation, primarily through building projects and renovations characterized by increasingly glitzy exteriors. The expansion and makeover of museums was bound up with the growth of creative industries, and as such, cultural institutions already played a role in my research project. But museums insistently pressed forward, particularly as every protest in the street seemed to be accompanied by one at a museum. It was in 2008, as a series of well-organized protest/art/performance actions took place at museums in the United Kingdom and United States, that I turned my attention fully to these events and institutions.

Tear Gas Epiphanies thus begins in two places: at a protest and in a museum. If those two locales seem utterly distinct, it is the goal of this book to show that they are not. The book concentrates on the years 1988 to 2017. During that time period, the carnivalesque alterglobalization movement that emerged in North America in 1999 gave way to a faltering anti-war movement after 2003.[2] A period of relative quiet characterized the first decade of the 2000s, with the exception of a growing global movement resisting climate change. Visible collective action reappeared powerfully following the global economic crisis of 2008, beginning with the Arab Spring in 2010, spilling into the Occupy movement the following year, and the Maple Spring/Quebec student strike in 2012. Idle No More emerged in late 2012 as did Black Lives Matter, the two profoundly challenging systemic and often invisible white supremacy and, by extension, unsettling the status quo of activism in North America and beyond. These were large social movements, many of them with deep roots that stretched back decades. Alongside them, innumerable other political actions, small and large, also took place. During the same period, security forces confronting direct action in Canada and elsewhere became progressively more militarized, and interventionist events were rendered ever more dangerous for those engaged in political action. Terrorist attacks in New York and Washington in 2001 led to the passage of the Patriot Act in the United States and its corollary, Bill C-36 (the Anti-Terrorism Act) in Canada, both of which brought with them increased police powers.[3] Municipal, provincial, and federal legislation additionally made protest more difficult, for example by forcing organizers to register march routes in advance and by banning the wearing of face masks.[4]

It was in this challenging environment that museums increasingly became targets for a variety of actions, both connected to and distinct from the large movements outlined above. Interventions at and outside museums ranged from anti-oil performances and awareness campaigns on drone warfare to anti-racism initiatives, battles over representation, and resistance to gentrification. It should be noted that museums have long been used as sites for protests, interventions, and even as collaborators in political action. One of the goals of this book is to fill in what is largely an occluded history. Nevertheless, from the middle of the first decade of the 2000s through to the present, there has been a definite uptick in action at and against museums, and I wanted to know why.

Therefore, the book I ultimately wrote – *Tear Gas Epiphanies* – is a book about museums. But to get at museums and how they deal with the actions that take place at their thresholds, I need to first explain the book's title and second to look briefly at *why* people protest. In the early days of research, I spent a great deal of time reading first-person accounts of participation in collective action. I was also, at the time, attending a number of demonstrations, some of them large, some of them small. I was not and am not an organizer, but I remain committed to a number of political causes. And I remain aware that protest occupies numerous registers. Activism encompasses many strategies, among them marches in the street, squats, meetings in living rooms and community centres, presentations at city councils and courtrooms, interventions in board rooms, hacking, research, writing, social media, and many, many other forms of long-term organization. Sometimes a protest is not a protest but a sit-in, an occupation, a march, a demonstration, a blockade, a vigil, a sacred fire.[5] Sometimes a protest is a small procession of people walking awkwardly together trying not to catch one another's eyes. Sometimes political action is a dour and depressing thing. Sometimes there are long, weighty speeches that sap the life from the milling crowd. Often there is whining or judgment. Always there are more people handing out flyers than there should be. Often protesters are hurt, arrested, and bullied. Sometimes protest is a cacophonous, carnivalesque takeover of public space. And sometimes, within each of these scenarios, with glaring, blazing optimism, protest is epiphanal.

Protest is fiercely embodied. And although people experience it differently, the conditions of the event – the threatening presence of forces of security, the potential use of tear gas, pepper spray, and other forms of suppression, the press of the crowd, the sound of chanting, or at smaller actions, the sense of togetherness, of accomplishment – are necessarily acted out on, and through, the body. The accounts I was reading were littered with what I came to call "tear gas epiphanies," stories of people caught up in political actions large and small and changed by them.[6] Such accounts are, in fact, *so common* that one is hard pressed to find a participant-observer description of protest that does not include a moment of awareness and, often, of flourishing.

For example: John Lewis, remembering his arrest following a sit-in during the civil rights movement, wrote, "As we were led out of the store single file, singing 'We Shall Overcome,' I felt exhilarated. As we passed through a cheering crowd gathered on the sidewalk outside, I felt high, almost giddy with joy. As we approached the open rear doors of a paddy wagon, I felt elated."[7] Describing the "roar of unqualified joy" that greeted word of President Mubarek's flight from Cairo during the occupation of Tahrir Square in February 2011, journalist Jason Koutsoukis wrote, "In an instant the street outside the presidential office was convulsed with a wild surge of energy."[8] "What an incredible joy!" said youth leader and activist Brigette DePape after participating in an Idle No More action.[9] The collective Notes from Nowhere, reminiscing about anti-WTO protests in Seattle in 1999, wrote, "all we could see was people – our people – spilling out of the streets and onto the sidewalks, a cacophony of colour and exhilaration."[10] These quotes are but a small sampling of the heightened emotions and togetherness that I have also experienced, most notably in 2001, in the tear gas at anti-FTAA protests in Quebec City where the non-stop drumming, chanting, and dancing, combined with our unified presence made it feel like another world was not just possible but was present. Though this book has changed greatly over the years, the kernel can be found in that moment, now some seventeen years ago. By 2012, social psychologist John Drury, who has studied emotions in protest for well over a decade, concluded, "[r]esearch on activists' experiences shows that collective actions that shift or challenge existing power relations feel joyful, exhilarating and even euphoric ... They feel good."[11]

Unruly though it is, protest often offers a moment of great clarity, perhaps because the event is usually experienced as a trenchant binary – power versus the people.[12] Such deeply felt and potentially life-altering occurrences are found across history, class, race, gender, and geography and are recorded in the work of many writers, scholars, activists, and others.[13] Émile Durkheim called the moment of emotional togetherness in the crowd "collective effervescence,"[14] Victor Turner called it "communitas."[15] Gustav LeBon infamously feared the "mob mentality"[16] of the emotional crowd yet nevertheless acknowledged its power. More recently, the "bonding properties of tear gas" became central to Naomi Klein's analysis of social movements at the turn of the millennium, and elsewhere she has referred to the "effervescence" of protest.[17] Marina Vishmidt describes the "optimism on the waste ground" created by protests against education cuts in Britain.[18] Judith Butler writes about "bodies in alliance";[19] Mikhail Bahktin, writing about the carnivalesque, refers to "bodily participation in the potentiality of another world";[20] Francesca Polletta's recent book, *It Was Like a Fever*, describes the way that emotional solidarity spread amongst young Black students in the 1960s civil rights movement,[21] and others write about "collective emotions"[22] and "collective joy."[23] Anarchist Murray Bookchin writes, "Nearly every revolutionary uprising in the history of our time has been initiated ... by a joyousness and solidarity that turned everyday life into a festival."[24] Nick Crossley and Ron Eyerman write, "the force of emotion is an essential part of what keeps a movement moving and its lack helps explain its decline."[25] Importantly, the experience is not just exhilarating; often it is empowering. Talking about the Grassy Narrows blockade (Interstice 3c), Judy DaSilva notes that when youth in the community began to use their bodies as shields to stop the logging trucks, "that's how our people became empowered. It was that simple."[26]

Clearly, in many circumstances, protest is a powerful, empowering, and often extremely positive experience. But it is not quite that simple. Diana Taylor talks about the contagion of social movements, the way they seem to appear out of nowhere and spread far and wide.[27] In her research she looks for "affects that transcend individual feelings to form transnational conditions (perhaps unspoken coalitions) of resistance or even revolt."[28] Not surprisingly, she finds them. But Taylor's argument also shows the double-sided nature of such "politics of passion," noting "unruly acts and passions ... cross ideological bounds, showing the fears, anxieties, prejudices, and hopes that animate the attitudes and actions of the State itself."[29] When protest challenges the accepted status quo, moral panic typically follows, and social movements are quashed, often violently. Judith Butler has also recently written eloquently about the instability of social movements, noting the euphoria of participation but remarking equally that "bodies in the street" are neither "intrinsically good nor intrinsically bad" and that the tear gas epiphany, as I describe it, is not necessarily indicative of progressive politics.[30] Butler notes the joy of assembly but also cautions against its limits, observing that public assembly presupposes that one can assemble and is not imprisoned or actively under surveillance.

In short, first-person accounts of protest are frequently characterized by descriptions of joyous togetherness. But these statements are often followed either by equally firm disavowals of the potential of such moments and/or by descriptions of violent suppression. In the aftermath, almost every aspect of protest action is critiqued, from its efficacy to its aesthetics.[31] Often the epiphanal experience is linked to trauma, and protesters emerge burned out, with arrests and records that can prevent their employment. Taking into account both the joy and the aftermath, long-time activist Micah White's much-read book *The End of Protest* calls for an end to protest in the streets, which he suggests has become ineffective and predictable and largely only symbolic.[32]

While many dismissals come from people who appear never to have attended a political gathering,[33] others, like White's, are thoughtful provocations, questioning the role of protest action. Protest is not all things to all people. It is often cut through with racist undertones and sexist overtones.[34] Collective action is easier for some people than for others.[35] Take, for example, the extreme police response to primarily African-American demonstrators in Ferguson, Missouri, in the wake of the 2014 shooting of the unarmed Mike Brown versus the relatively limited police presence at mostly white anti-abortion demonstrations (despite the murder of a number of abortion-providing doctors and bombings of several clinics).[36] Long-time activists are also aware of the seductive charm of the protest and note that it can take away from the everyday labour of working for change. "Activism is a form partly forced upon us by weakness," wrote Andrew X in a much-circulated piece from 1999 called "Give Up Activism."[37]

Not surprisingly, the intense experience – the tear gas epiphany – often followed by dismissal or deep questioning, results in the extreme ebbs and flows of social movements. It also results in a process of erasure – protest movements seem to emerge anew every decade or so, with previous actions largely forgotten. Protest movements are quick to overwrite and erase their own histories, often seeing each event as disconnected and each cause as starting anew.

I would add that the experience of protest – the tear gas epiphany – is excessive; it is *too much* for academic writing. To use it as evidence seems to foreground the irrational and pleasurable. In short, it is *easier* to write critically and dispassionately – the epiphanal, emotional moment is anecdotal, and scholarly writing abhors anecdotes as evidence.[38] I make no judgment here as I do the same thing. But when epiphanal moments show up across history in so many different kinds of protests and in myriad geographic locations, in ebbs and flows, never seeming to entirely disappear, to discount them as generational, narcissistic self-satisfaction seems short-sighted, particularly as people keep showing up, keep putting their bodies on the line, and keep protesting. My conclusion ultimately is that the process of erasure and dismissal is partly normative thinking and partly what keeps social movements going. Re-emergence is a constant and perhaps a necessity.

In recounting the importance of the experience of the tear gas epiphany as a precursor to research on museums and protest, I aim to remind readers of the power of action and to acknowledge that what those targeting and intervening in museums experience is fleeting and largely absent from my scholarly analysis. My goal in the rest of the book is not to show how each protest at a museum called into being a special or joyful uprising. Rather, I foreground the experience of collective action in the preface (and in the title) before the rest of the book turns to the multiple ways that museums are implicated in social movements and political action. In the book, I call repeatedly for museums to build sustainable relationships with oppositional movements. I do so cognizant of the fact that in most cases, what museums can collect, display, or study is largely the detritus, the lingering aftereffects of actions. Nonetheless, I argue strongly for museums to engage and to do so acknowledging their compromised position. So, too, I am aware that the documents I work with – scholarly analysis, images, artworks, ephemeral objects and detritus, media coverage, interviews, etc. – cannot capture the epiphanal moment, and because of that they indicate the fragility of recording and remembering protest, where the collecting of its memories and material culture is fraught, partial, and fragmented.

As I noted above, museums are targeted for many reasons. And in turn, museums engage with protest in many ways. Sometimes they resist it; sometimes they welcome it. In the case studies in this book, museums apologize for their actions toward protesters, they organize exhibitions to welcome activists into their halls, they work with Indigenous communities to enact change outside of the museum, they rehang permanent collections in response to critique, they help to protect artists whose shows have been censored, they work hard to open archives to various parties whose histories are contained therein. And on the other hand, museums (sometimes the same museums) work closely with the oil and gas sector against activist demands, maintain parochial relationships with narrowly defined norms of settler nationalism, refuse the repatriation of certain objects, and actively rebuff and repudiate critiques. Museums are multifaceted, and it is precisely the contradictory nature of museums that makes them such tempting objects of study.

As with all books, numerous people helped to bring this final work to fruition. First and foremost, I would like to thank the activists, organizers, land and water protectors, and many others who stand strong for a better world and without whom this book would simply not exist.

I am extremely grateful to friends who helped this project along in so many ways over the years. Alex Boutros, Kaarla Sundström, Amanda Boetzkes, Susan Cahill, Keri Cronin, Ayesha Hameed, Kristy Holmes, Claudette Lauzon, Deirdre Martin, Erin Morton, Sarah E.K. Smith, Andrea Terry, Tamara Vukov, and Kim Wahl provided friendship, conversation, and good times from the first inkling of an idea to the final book. At McGill and Queen's Universities several faculty members provided support and thoughtful counsel, among them Lynda Jessup, Susan Lord, Janice Helland, Christine Ross, William Straw, Clive Robertson, and Jan Allen, as well as Imre Szeman, Janine Marchessault, and Martha Langford at other institutions. Colleagues in the Department of Visual Arts at Western University have been impressive interlocutors, and I thank the Old East crew – Kelly Wood, Steven Heighington, Kelly Jazvac, Patrick Howlett, David Merritt, Dawn Merritt, and Tim Pearson (as well as Lucy, Scout, and Angus) – for numerous feasts and discussions of the pros and cons of poutine; Christine Sprengler, for beer and roller derby; and Patrick Mahon, Bridget Elliott, Sarah Bassnett, John Hatch, Christof Migone, and Cody Barteet for their collegiality and friendship. The front office administrators in the Department of Visual Arts, including Marlene Jones, Paula Dias, Meghan Edmiston, and Joanne Gribbon, were invaluable and instrumental in the book's completion.

I'd also like to acknowledge the many upper-year undergraduate students at Western in a number of my classes who were willing to talk endlessly about museums and all of my graduate students (some now colleagues), among them Samantha Angove, Christina Battle, Genevieve Flavelle, Amy Freier, Helen Gregory, Ellen Groh, Keely McCavitt, Ahlia Moussa, Rehab Nazzal, Katie Oates, Kelsey Perreault, Stephanie Radu, Laura Ritchie, Jon Sarma, Jessica Sealey, and Sarah Smith, who worked as RAs or whose work is cited in these pages. Stephanie Anderson in particular has been an irreplaceable research assistant on this project and an excellent scholar and colleague.

Meals and conversations with Max Haiven, Emma Dowling, and Susan Schuppli came at critical junctures in the project. Lisa Vinebaum, Luanne Martineau, Shannon Stratton, Maria Elena Buszek, Kelly Thompson, Janis Jefferies, and Namita Gupta Wiggers supported one significant detour in my research and Laura Murray and Tina Piper another. Thank you for your friendship, conversations, and laughter.

As *Tear Gas Epiphanies* came together, comments and feedback from several conferences and workshops helped to guide it toward completion. I am especially grateful to the Museum Futures symposium (Montreal, 2017), notably to Christina Kreps and Monica Patterson, who read a chapter of my book for an inspirational round table, to those in the Curatorial Dreaming workshop organized by Shelley Butler (especially Eugenia Kisin), to many people who took part in hallway conversations (especially Erica Lehrer, Steve Lyons, Jason Jones, and Beka Economopoulos), as well as to Jenny Burman who encouraged me to attend. An invitation from Mariane Bourcheix-Laporte to speak in the Spaces of Contestation series at Simon Fraser University in 2014 led to a walk along the proposed site of the Trans-Mountain pipeline with Gabriel Saloman and Stephen Collis that profoundly influenced chapter 6. And finally, numerous participants at the Museum Openings workshop in Winnipeg, particularly Angela Failler, Nadine Blumer, Amber Dean, Erika Lehrer, Heather Igloliorte, and Jennifer Carter, helped me to craft the chapter on the Canadian Museum for Human Rights.

Tear Gas Epiphanies would not have been possible without the help of numerous archivists, curators, and librarians who generously responded to my queries and helped me to find the objects and files that enabled the project to take shape. There are too many to mention here, but I single out Karine Duhamel (CMHR), Katie Ferrante (MOA), Xavier Gélinas (CMH), Lorne Hammond (RBCM), Melanie Hardbattle (SFU), Jane Devine Mejia (VAG), Marilyn Nazar (AGO), Jillian Povarchook (MOV), Moya Waters (MOA), and an unknown archivist at the CWM who tracked down a file number I had lost. Charles McFaddin, whom I never met but who started a file on protests at the AGO that helped me out more than forty years later, and Ruth Phillips, who ensured that an archive of dissent against the 1997 APEC conference be held at the MOA, made the content of this book much richer than it would otherwise have been.

I'd also like to thank a group of people I've never actually met, or have only met in passing, but who undertake a serious amount of intellectual and emotional labour to share their ideas over social media. This is not a frivolous acknowledgment. In many cases, these people have transformed my thinking on current events and my ways of being in the world. Often this online labour goes entirely unremarked. While I have cited specific tweets and posts, the overall influence far exceeds those citations, and thus, I would like to thank Clayton Thomas Müller (@CreeClayton), Rinaldo Walcott (@blacklikewho), Sara Ahmed (@SaraNAhmed), Kim TallBear (@KimTallBear), Eve Tuck (@tuckeve), Christi Belcourt (@christibelcourt), and especially Zoe Todd (@zoestodd), Desmond Cole (@DesmondCole), and Chelsea Vowel (@apihtawikosisan).

I would like to acknowledge the help of numerous grants from Western University that generously funded travel, research, and presentations. A SSHRC grant funded much of the initial research. This book has been published with the help of a grant from the Federation for the Humanities and Social Sciences through the Awards to Scholarly Publications Program, using funds provided by the Social Sciences and

Humanities Research Council of Canada. My experience with McGill-Queen's University Press, led by Jonathan Crago, made the process of publication a pleasant one, as did two anonymous readers who invested their time and interest in the book. It was a pleasure to read the comments.

Finally, I would like to thank my family, in Vancouver and in Nova Scotia, who have supported me in all of my endeavours and who have just as often provided places for me to stay while researching and writing. I often think about the fact that this book, and my academic career, would not have been possible had my brother and my partner not replaced my laptop in 2005 when it was stolen and I had no insurance and no money. That was a turning point in my academic life, and I think of it often and remain thankful for it always. And most important, I express my unending gratitude and love to Caroline, Liz, and Tim, my affinity group. When we travelled together to the anti-FTAA protests in Quebec City in 2001, I had no idea that that day would change my life. The experience of that protest led to my dissertation and eventually, indirectly, to this book (which remains the same only in title). Caroline died suddenly in 2007, an event that still feels raw and new. Liz is too far away but always close to my heart. And Tim is everything, every day. I could not ask for more.

This book was written primarily in London, Ontario, on the traditional territories of the Anishinaabeg, Haudenausaune, Lenaapeewak, and Attawandaron peoples, all of whom have long-standing relationships to the land of southwestern Ontario and the City of London, and on the south shore of Nova Scotia, in Mi'kma'ki, the ancestral and unceded territory of the Mi'kmaq People.

TEAR GAS EPIPHANIES

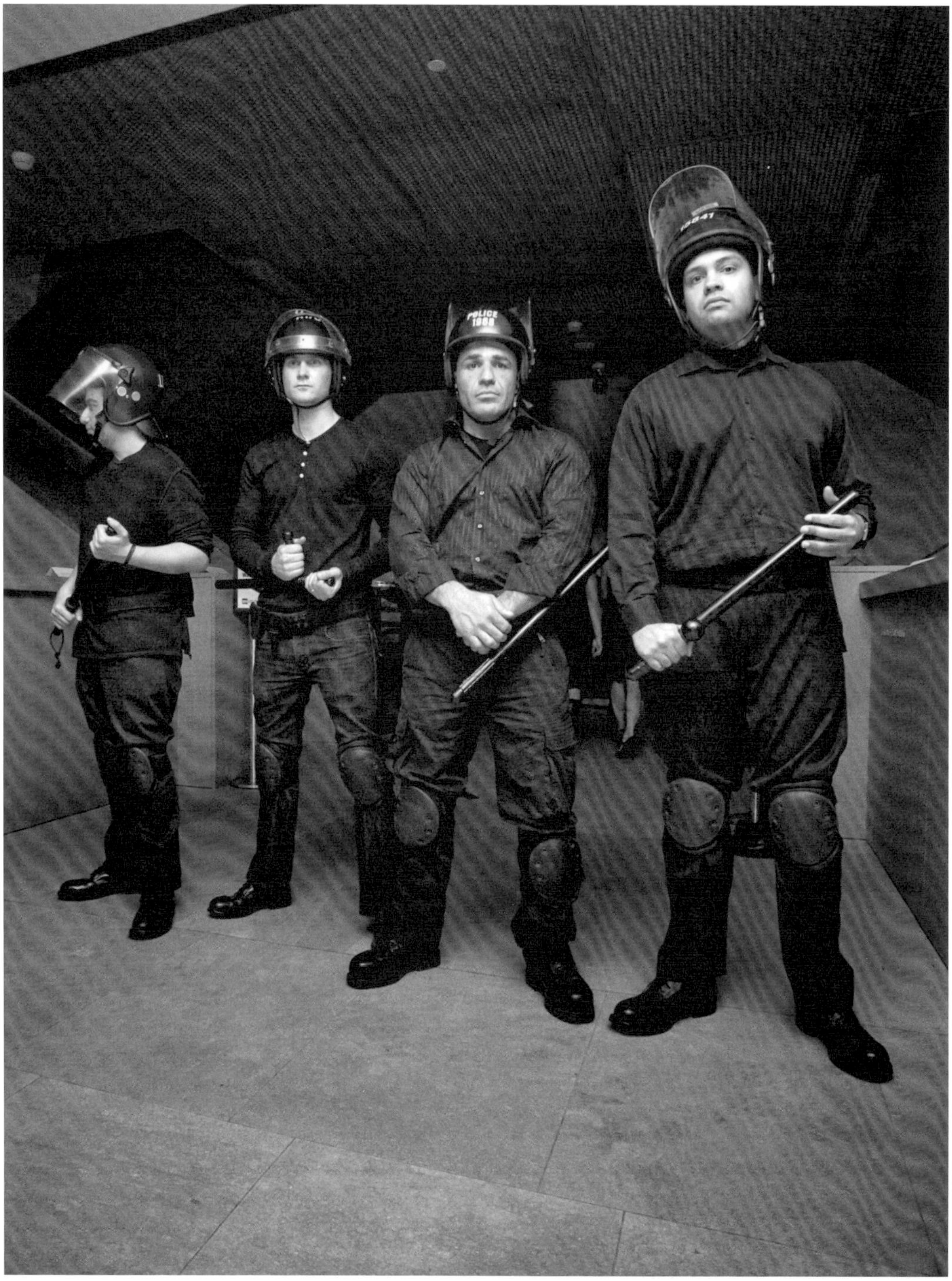

Figure 1.1
Volunteers dressed as riot police greet invitees at "Massive Uprising," Art Gallery of Ontario, Toronto, March 2009.

1

Introduction: Museums, Protest, and Cities

> Songs like "We're Not Gonna Take It" by Twisted Sister played as guests arrived for the party, which was dubbed "Massive Uprising" … Riot police wielding billy clubs greeted attendees as they entered Walker Court, where a group of models dressed as hippies conducted a sit-in in the middle of the floor. Placards with logos like "Fight for Your Right to Party" and "Join the Up Rising" were placed in black metal bins around the venue, and black linens and camouflage netting topped bars throughout the space. Red lighting filled Baillie Court, where actors dressed as John Lennon and Yoko Ono re-enacted the couple's famous bed-in for peace atop a bed on a riser in the centre of the room. Video footage of the couple was broadcast on the walls, and linens with graffiti tags topped tables. Specialty cocktails … called the Capitalist Cocktail and Moscow Mules – added to the theme
>
> Susan O'Neill, "What a Riot."[1]

In March 2009, the Art Gallery of Ontario (AGO), one of Canada's largest galleries, reopened after an extensive renovation by "starchitect" Frank Gehry.[2] On that night, as partygoers traipsed amid fake riot police and hipster hippies sipped "Capitalist Cocktails" and nibbled on hors d'oeuvres off napkins emblazoned with "AGO" on which the "A" had been replaced by the anarchist symbol, it might have seemed as if the co-option and corruption of recent protest was complete. At the

"Massive Uprising" party, radical protest was neither scathingly critiqued nor dismissed. Rather, an image of "anti-capitalist" protest was pasted onto 1960s counter-culture, communist revolution, and anarchist uprising and then translated into a successful fundraiser for the arts.[3]

There are several ways this event could be interpreted. First, one might look to the museum itself. In parodying protest, "Massive Uprising" dismissed its radical potential and in so doing revealed an accepted relationship between the art world and protest. In this reading, when it comes to protest, museums act vampirically, encouraging the creation of subversive work, then sucking the active opposition out of it, leaving an empty shell that nevertheless confers a sense of edginess upon the institution.[4]

Second, one might take a different approach, noting how, despite the knotty relationship with dissent, museums remain remarkably popular venues for staging protests. Though "Massive Uprising" caricatured this liaison, pickets, protests, and demonstrations on the steps and thresholds of museums are not an uncommon sight. As public institutions representative of the state, with links to corporate and art worlds and to government, museums are peculiarly evocative locations for performative politics. One could also develop this analysis to look at how a number of museums have self-reflexively understood their multifaceted social roles and have resisted the first interpretation, inviting activists inside and offering their spaces for expansive political thought and action.[5]

Third, one might expand the frame to see the larger context of the event. On the evening of the "Massive Uprising" opening, as patrons wandered through the contemporary art exhibit watching a roller-skating "Guerrilla Girl," news spread across the Internet that twenty-three workers from the AGO had been laid off the very same day, while forty-three more were left without contracts.[6] Underlying critiques that museum administration lacked tact in firing workers on the same day it invited in 1,600 benefactors at $125 a head was a distinct bitterness.[7] The only people who had gained from the recently completed extensive renovations to the museum, it seemed, were the partygoers – not the artists and not the employees.

Thus, at play in what on the surface appeared to be a party was a strangely comprehensive visioning of the relationships between protest and museums. As "riot police" (likely indebted art school students in disguise) gently pushed potential donors and benefactors through the spectacular Gehry-designed front entrance, multiple interconnected stories emerged. Here was the rise of finance capitalism, anti-capitalist protest, and increased security, the celebration of creative industries as an economic boon for faltering post-industrial economies, all performatively worked into a party for the city's economic and artistic elite held in an expensively renovated cultural institution.[8] Indeed, the very event was a celebration of this transformation, exemplary of a spate of museum building tied up with the econo-

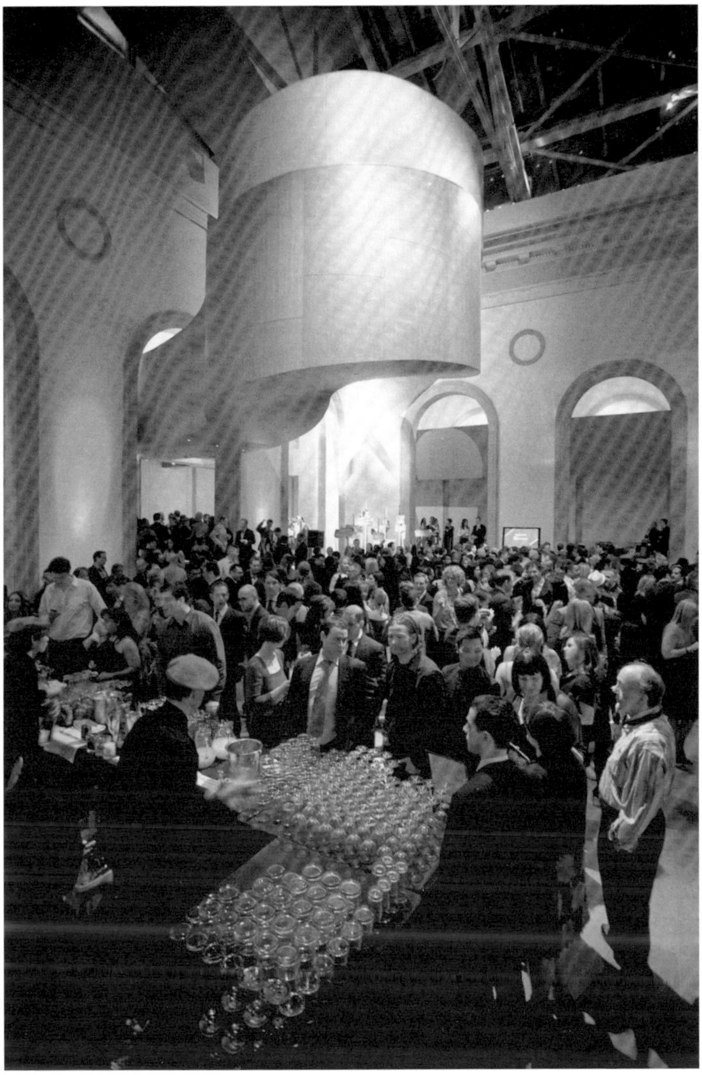

Figure 1.2
Bartenders serve "Capitalist Cocktails" and "Moscow Mules" at "Massive Uprising," Art Gallery of Ontario, Toronto, March 2009.

mization of culture and development of "Creative Cities,"[9] where knowledge workers like to live and tourists like to tour. And just a few months later, the streets outside the gallery would erupt in real protest as police faced off with activists who had gathered against G20 meetings held behind heavily guarded barricades just blocks away.[10] It would be one of the most brutal suppressions of protesters in the city's, and indeed the country's, history.

Tear Gas Epiphanies focuses on the tension and friction created at the intersections of protest, museums, cities, and culture that "Massive Uprising" illustrates. The book regards museums as key institutions that occupy the uncomfortable space between the state, the private sector, the arts, and the economy, while also being both targets of, and occasionally providing encouragement for, contentious politics. Through an examination of actions outside and inside museums in Canada from the

Figure 1.3
Exterior of the closed AGO during the G20 meetings, 26 June 2010.

Figure 1.4 *Opposite*
Gophers Against Getting Stuffed, a tongue-in-cheek exhibit at the Torrington Gopher Museum in Torrington, Alberta.

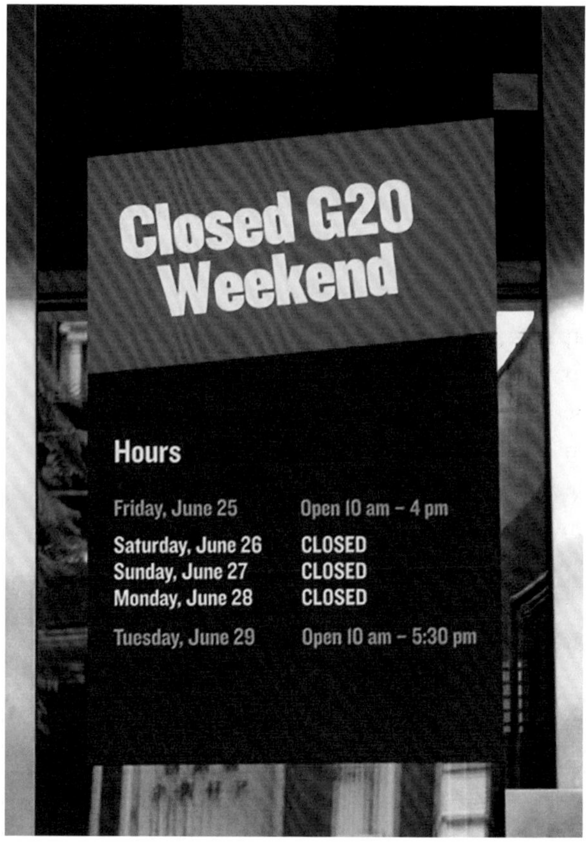

1900s to the present, with a focus on the late 1990s to 2017, this book sutures together demonstrations at museums with the larger movements of which they are a part. My perspective moves from the museum to the protest, spilling out into analysis of the cities and cultural policy that inflect the way museums interact with the everyday lives of urban citizens. Throughout, I acknowledge that museums are complex and multifaceted institutions and that activists often have multiple reasons for targeting such establishments. In this book, examples are drawn from actions and responses at two major art galleries, a universal museum, a war museum, a history museum, and a museum for human rights. I draw from museum anthropology and art history studies, social movements studies, as well as from mainstream media and popular culture sources, archives, interviews, and even social media to try to understand how contentious politics functions as a part of museums. As Wayne Modest, head of the Research Center for Material Culture, the research institute of the Tropenmuseum, asked at 2017 Museum Futures conference in Montreal, referring to curators and museums, "How are we implicated in the politics of the present?" – a query that I use as a guiding principle.[11]

Museums and Contentious Politics

Museums have long provided sites for the performance and mobilization of contentious politics.[12] From Canadian ex-pat Mary Richardson's 1914 attack on Velazquez's *Rokeby Venus* in London's National Gallery to protest the imprisonment of suffragist Emmeline Pankhurst[13] to the occupation of the Vancouver Art Gallery by unemployed workers in 1938[14] and from actions staged by the Art Workers' Coalition in New York in the late 1960s[15] to the very recent closure of an anti-apartheid museum in Port Elizabeth, South Africa, under community pressure,[16] examples abound of museums as the stages for political action. From the first museums through to the present moment, they have been sites of conflict. Beginning in the 1980s, museum studies scholarship began to pick up on voices that had long been criticizing the colonial history of collections, coupled with pressure to revisit the representation of Indigenous and non-mainstream groups in museum displays and to repatriate certain objects.[17] In the same period, museums faced critique from the left for accepting corporate sponsorships and becoming more market-driven and from the right for showing work perceived to be controversial or overly costly and occasionally for existing at all.[18]

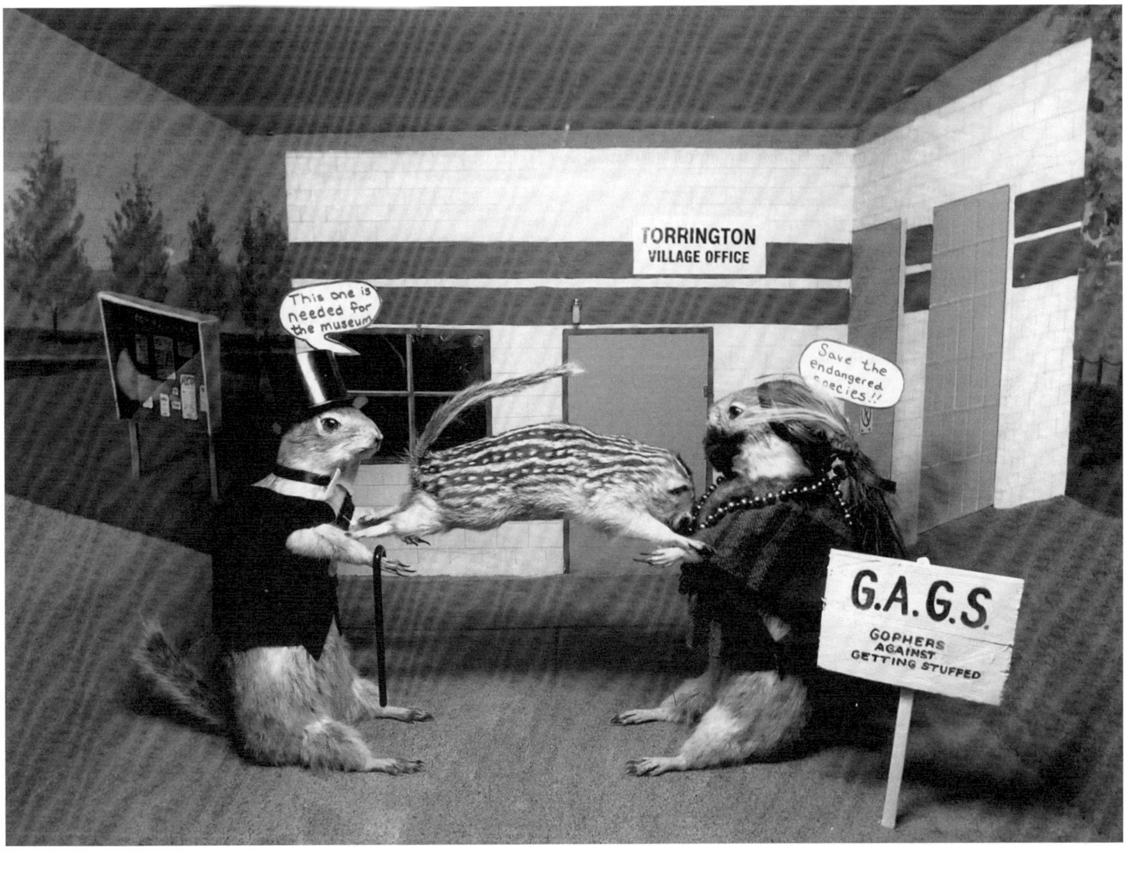

Protesters gather outside museums large and small. At one end of the scale, People for the Ethical Treatment of Animals (PETA) and other international animal rights activists have repeatedly targeted the Torrington Gopher Museum in Torrington, Alberta, (population 179), for its displays of stuffed gophers (the museum, in fact, has a display dedicated to the protests).[19] And at the other end, I could point to any number of examples such as the immensely creative actions undertaken recently by climate change activists against British Petroleum's sponsorship of the Tate Museum or David Koch's (of Koch Industries) support of the Metropolitan Museum (see chapter 6).[20]

In addition to being targets of actions, museums also often provide convenient and photogenic backdrops for protests over any number of issues: Trafalgar Square outside the National Gallery of Art in London, the National Mall in front of the Smithsonian, the courtyard in front of the Vancouver Art Gallery, and Tiananmen Square in front of the Forbidden City, the Mao Zedong Mausoleum, and the National Museum of China are all examples of important cultural sites where gatherings of people have been variously encouraged, tolerated, and outright suppressed.

These are just a tiny sampling of the protests, interventions, resistances, and negotiations at museums. In chapter 2, I present an overview of such actions in Canada, from the 1900s through to the present. The sheer number of instances of protest at, outside, and against museums suggests that such actions are not anomalous but rather are part and parcel of the very being of museums. As such, I suggest that protest should draw the attention of those interested in studying and working with/in institutions.

Together, such incidents and interactions prompt the question: why the museum? As Lucy Lippard notes, "the museum remains both the hand that feeds and the citadel to be stormed."[21] Occasionally, actions are aimed at specific collections or exhibitions, but just as often, museums are markers or nodes – sites that connect government, corporate interests, philanthropists, communities, and others.[22] Museums are cultural institutions embedded within the political, social, economic, architectural, and ideological networks of the city and often of the nation. They are contested spaces – a term much used in museum studies to describe the way museums are perceived as neutral when in fact they are anything but. Moreover, they are contestable spaces and are frequently used as such by a variety of groups to mobilize viewpoints that might otherwise be lost. To be blunt, it is easier to target a museum than a bank, and it is perhaps easier to encourage change on the part of museums than it is on the part of the oil industry. Museums are places where the rich network, wine, and dine.[23] They are places where dirty records are greenwashed. But they are also, often, places where critical thinking is encouraged and nurtured. Though museums come in for their fair share of deserved critique, they nevertheless engage with difficult topics, activist positions, and controversial material.[24] In fact, it is occasionally these progressive policies that draw pickets and demonstrations, this time from groups intent on maintaining the museum as a bastion of tradition (that is, as a location for the celebration of white Eurocentric culture in North America and Europe).[25] From all perspectives, museums tend to be targets for interventionist action because they are perceived as public spaces. Perhaps museums are places where the public still feels it has a stake.

How have museums responded? On the one hand, Robert Janes and Richard Sandell suggest, "Most museum practitioners and their governing bodies are cautious about their engagement with contemporary issues and wary about being perceived to be biased, or to be lending support to particular moral or political standpoints."[26] But on the other hand, drawing on his long experience directing the Glenbow Museum, Janes writes more openly, suggesting that museums are as yet "unique and valuable social institutions that have no suitable replacement, irrespective of their shortcomings."[27] For Janes, the possibility of an engaged museum is a near reality. I agree with this perspective. Though I began from a place highly critical of museums, I have come to see (some of) them as important spaces for working through contentious topics, though I also suggest that this responsiveness is, in many cases, a future goal rather than a present reality.[28]

In the introduction to her book *Museum Pieces*, Ruth Phillips notes,

> Most Canadians have become more accustomed to hearing about the activities of their museums when the latest protest or demonstration hits the national media. The furor of the moment might surround a demand to remove a familiar piece of art whose colonial content has come to seem offensive, an exhibition accused of misrepresenting a particular constituency, or the spending of public funds on a new museum or work of art that, some feel, does not adequately serve the nation as a whole.[29]

Phillips suggests that "Canada has seen a disproportionately large number of such museum-based contestations and ... they receive an exceptional amount of coverage in the national media."[30] She continues, "the challenge posed to the traditional construct of Canada as a settler nation rooted in French and British colonial histories by increasingly effective Aboriginal activism and the growth of diasporic communities provides not just the backdrop to a history of museum change but, rather, its enabling conditions." [31] Phaedra Livingston agrees, noting that "exhibition controversies ... [have] been catalyst for significant progress in Canadian museum administration."[32]

Phillips's comments refer primarily to two exhibitions that faced extensive demonstrations: *Spirit Sings: Artistic Traditions of Canada's First Peoples* at the Glenbow Museum in 1988 and *Into the Heart of Africa* at the Royal Ontario

Museum (ROM) in 1989. These two very well-known altercations (covered in more detail in chapters 2 and 6) resulted in deep changes to Canadian museum operations, many stemming from the 1994 Task Force on Museums and First Peoples (itself a response to the reaction to *Spirit Sings*). *Spirit Sings* and *Into the Heart of Africa* have entered the record as a part of a series of upheavals in museums in the 1990s as controvery after controversy seemed to dog mainstream institutions.

I both agree with and disagree with Phillips that Canadian museums in particular are targeted by "museum-based contestation." In fact, while there are a large number of interruptions to the daily work of museums in Canada (see chapter 2), many other countries have seen large and well-organized performative interventions, most recently focused on the presence of fossil fuel corporations as sponsors of cultural events. In the UK, France, Norway, the US, and Australia, for example, broad-based social movements (for reform of immigration and detention policies[33] or against oil sponsorship of the arts) have used museums as one place among many to make their cases. Groups such as Liberate Tate, Not An Alternative, Occupy Museums, and Gulf Labor have organized numerous theatrical protest interventions into museums. Such events are largely missing in Canada. Nevertheless, I throroughly agree with Phillips that activism is an "enabling condition" in museums in Canada. There is a clear trajectory of contestation in and against museums in Canada, and most actions are focused on specific museums and on issues of representation, collections, and repatriation. Indigenous issues are front and centre. Thus, I follow activist Harsha Walia in arguing that "Indigenous self-determination must become the foundation for all our broader social justice mobilizing."[34] Protests at museums in Canada offer a way of thinking through how "Indigenous self-determination is increasingly understood as intertwined with struggles against racism, poverty, police violence, war and occupation, violence against women and environmental justice."[35] In short, I treat the presence of some actions and the absence of others as a question rather than a critique and ask whether museums can provide the venues for working through the complexities of intersectionality and decolonization – both absent from many (but not all) of the spectacular actions that have taken place at museums in Europe and the US. Canadian museums *have* responded to intervention and have changed policy and approach to display, collection, and storage because of outside action.

As will become apparent, however, museums in Canada have an uneven relationship with protest, often actively resisting the presence of activists and land and water protectors. Canadian museums are also particularly savvy when it comes to distancing themselves from intervention, accepting change only when it fits with already accepted directions of museum policy. As important cultural sites, museums are tasked with creating commentary on contemporary and historic events, artefacts, and artworks. They are *also* places with responsibilities for housing and archiving the material evidence of those events. As numerous theorists remind us, archives, like museums, cannot be neutral, nor can they be complete.[36] Thus it is that the process of archiving protest is nearly as complex as the decisions made whether to ignore, support, or suppress actions within museums themselves. As I show in chapter 3, Canadian museums have been lax in collecting the ephemera of protests or even political objects in general (although this too appears to be changing).

In short, while this book fills in a missing history of protest against cultural institutions, placing well-known actions outside *Spirit Sings* and *Into the Heart of Africa* into a much longer trajectory, I also argue that the period after those two famous events has been one of continued pressure and reaction. While big movements have emerged spectacularly outside of Canada – for example, in Liberate Tate and Occupy Museums – I suggest that the slow work that has taken place in Canada has had a deep impact on museum operations in a way that other movements might do well to note. However, I nonetheless suggest that in Canada as well it is high time to look both at the period following those two singular events (which are often seen as the *only* such actions at Canadian institutions) and to understand in a larger sense the impact of contentious politics at museums. In the remainder of this introduction, I flesh out some of these claims, looking first at the particular period covered by the book and second at what is happening at museums and archives elsewhere, before providing a summary of the chapters.

Creative Industries, Protest, Museums

Though beginning with an overview of protests at museums in Canada since 1900, this book focuses on the period from the very late 1990s to 2017. It was a period of great transition both for museums and for activism.[37] At the end of the section, I return to traditional museums (history, natural history, war museums, and so on), but I look first to art galleries, and particularly to large-scale contemporary art galleries, as they were foregrounded in the period as indicative of the potential of cultural institutions within global cities.[38] The mid-to-late 1990s saw a rise in rhetoric of knowledge, intellectual property, and innovation being used to promote growth in de-industrializing economies. In 1998, such strategies were normalized in a UK Mapping Document on the creative industries, which suggested that, among other things (such as software, pharmaceutical research and development), arts and culture could be exploited for economic growth.[39] Arts, culture, and museums, the report's authors contended, contribute to the formation of vibrant urban spaces that attract the real money-makers, typically IP developers, finance, and R&D. Gradually, the ideas contained in the document filtered into policies in cities around the globe, often translating into refurbishments of city centres, the erection of "starchitect"-designed cultural institutions, and widespread gentrification.[40] As a corollary, marketing models were applied to the arts, drawing out what George Yúdice calls "the expediency of culture."[41] Importantly, artists, the arts, and culture all benefitted and lost during this period, riding a wave of celebratory creative industries language and crashing when the rhetoric could not keep up with actual needs.[42]

In Canada, as I show in chapter 3, creative industries rhetoric met with mixed reception, in part because it conflicted with deeply held views on the national importance of culture. Nevertheless, by the early years of the 2000s, the marketable rhetoric of the UK Mapping Document had caught on in Canada, particularly as urban guru Richard Florida's work gained traction, aided by his move to Toronto in 2007. In Florida's theory of "Creative Cities" and the "creative class," cities that attracted a diverse group of "creatives," who ranged from health care workers to artists, could succeed even in the direst of economic circumstances.[43] The theories, and the statistics that Florida used to promote them, made the creative industries rhetoric coming from the UK irresistible to many North American policy-makers, and in all of the cities written about in this book, programs to revitalize city centres and attract knowledge workers and tourists were quickly introduced (their success, or lack thereof, is a different story).

As Imre Szeman notes, "One of the signal developments of neoliberalism was to produce a situation in which it appeared that art and life had been folded together."[44] At the turn of the millennium, artists and other cultural workers were repeatedly held up as models of the new economy, as resourceful, creative entrepreneurs producing the immaterial goods of the new economy: intellectual property, design, innovation.[45] Work came to be described less in terms of alienated labour and more as a site for self-transformation and creativity.[46] According to many commentators and theorists, the resulting blurring of boundaries between work and leisure meant that effectively all time was now work time.[47] Coupled with this was the fact that in the creative industries, work is often informal, irregular, and insecure and thus often dependent on willpower and self-motivation. Not surprisingly then, a "profoundly effective form of new disciplinarity, a technology of the self," developed.[48] A plethora of labels emerged: post-Fordism, post-industrialization, network society, liquid modernity, information society, new economy, new capitalism, risk society, and creative labour, network labour, cognitive labour, affective labour, immaterial labour – all essentially indicating that late neoliberal capitalism has produced new habits, new ways of being, new embodiments, and new affects under an umbrella of precarious labour.[49]

There was a distinct connection to the arts. For example, in the late 1990s proponents of an "experience economy" began to push the search for profit-generating, yet somehow authentic, experiences to the foreground. Participatory and social art practices were a part of this push, linked to the new economy and the marketing of creativity but also to resistance to those economies.

Shannon Jackson writing in the *En Mas'* catalogue asks:

> Why are we seeing a renewed art-world interest in performance at this particularly [*sic*] moment of the twenty-first century? One kind of answer would position this interest within an overall socioeconomic shift, a shift from a Fordist economic emphasis in the production of objects to a post-Fordist emphasis on the production of services … The spirit of performance is both a symptom of and a canny response to a globalizing world.[50]

While Jackson critiques some of the shortcomings in the theorization of an experience economy in which service workers are asked "to perform," she nonetheless draws attention to the way festivals, interventions in the street, and event-based programming all seem to encourage an emancipatory form of participatory action that nonetheless "heed[s] the call of an event-based service economy." She concludes, "Is performance being channeled to encourage our cathexis to – rather than our resistance of – an experience economy that has been propelling us along?"[51] Importantly, while Jackson's comments are related primarily to art production, and while this section concentrates on the relationship between art production and art galleries, the same was true of other kinds of cultural institutions (science museums, natural history museums, and so on) that reworked displays into more user-friendly and participatory frameworks. Jackson concludes that some artworks *can* be radically interventionist; for her, the art world was not infinitely compromised nor entirely an anaesthetic to the politics of any radical art.[52]

Nevertheless, an "anti-art" argument was popular at the turn of the millennium and was connected to a critique of neoliberalism, which had, in the late 1990s and early 2000s, downloaded a great deal of social responsibility onto the arts. The arts were expected to in-fill for the missed presence of the state, providing mental health support, inner-city clean-up, and participatory projects intended to "improve" communities.[53] Angela McRobbie, for example, details how the dismantling of the welfare state found its corollary in the marketization of arts funding – public funding became instrumental, tied to outcomes, results, and social "amelioration."[54] Museums were recast as social centres, capable not just of attracting diverse audiences but also of parceling out therapeutic programming. Though arguably educating the masses had always been a prime goal of cultural institutions, the role of programming was, at this time, almost completely disconnected from the role of collecting, a process that was both lauded and bemoaned in museums literature.[55] For some, culture and, by proxy, art were just resources to be exploited and as such were inevitably enveloped, co-opted, and compromised.[56] Plenty of anecdotal evidence exists to suggest that the seductive logic of the creative industries had also immured the art world – artists scrambling for a piece of the pie, or too busy trying to survive, could find little time or space for resistance.[57]

Taking up this kind of question, the first decade and a half of the new millennium saw a number of scholars writing extensively on the histories and legacies of participatory, collaborative, and collective art practices.[58] Despite occasionally intense disagreements, most agree that new forms of "participatory art" and post-studio art emerged in the 1990s. Central to this emergence was French curator Nicolas Bourriaud's now well-worn definition of relational aesthetics, or art that is interactive, collaborative, and takes as its starting point human relations and encounters.[59] Influenced by or writing against Bourriaud's definition, scholars were interested, to a greater or lesser extent, in the potential of art as a radical gesture or intervention.[60] Not all activists are artists, and certainly not all artists are activists, but art and activism enjoy a peculiarly close, though often fraught, relationship through the twentieth century to the present moment.[61] Socially engaged art practices draw from, imitate, and occasionally participate in social movements. Museums provided the backdrop to many of these analyses, though only rarely were they in the foreground. Similarly, protest action in the streets was seldom mentioned in the above texts, although in-depth analyses could be found in the writing of Julia Bryan-Wilson, Gregory Sholette, Yates McKee, Rebecca Zorach, and others.

In 1999, just a few months after the introduction of the UK Mapping Document on the Creative Industries, a protest movement already well established in the Global South made its first two major appearances in the Global North: in Seattle (in the now infamous "Battle for Seattle") and in London in the J18 Carnival Against Capital. Loosely organized against the fallout of corporate capitalism, what came to be popularly known as the "anti-globalization" or alterglobalization movement brought hundreds of thousands of people into the streets, often for disparate but nevertheless connected reasons (the phrase "from teamsters to turtles" was a popular one in 1999, reflecting the sometimes uncomfortable coming together of environmentalists with anti-capitalists and big labour).[62] Images in the mainstream media tended to show the movement's purported violence, while on the street protests continued to grow through an anarchist-inspired horizontalism that favoured a leaderless "movement of movements" rather than single-cause interventions. Then, following massive protests against the war in Iraq in 2003, the alterglobalization movement seemed to lose its impetus. As Emma Dowling, Rodrigo Nunes, and Ben Trott noted in 2007, "the most optimistic ideas put forward [in 2001][63] were partly the product of a moment of intensification of struggle in the late 1990s. That many today should take a more sober – sometimes somber – note reflects a less hospitable environment, where many of the advances of that period seemed to have been stalled or reached dead-ends."[64]

At the time, despite the growing body of literature and analysis about the arts, economics, and resistance, the alterglobalization movement really did not consider culture. On one level this is surprising: both creative industries rhetoric and alterglobalization protest emerged partly in response to changes in the global economy that shifted manufacturing south and east, opening the way for the post-industrial "weightless capitalism" of neoliberal economies in the Global North.[65] But in 1999–2000, anti-capitalist protest tended to focus on increasing corporate power, fear of environmental destruction, labour exploitation (particularly through outsourcing and sweatshops), and the ways that these outcomes could be exacerbated through international trade agreements that moved power away from local and even national governments and into the hands of vast extra-national bodies such as the World Trade Organization, the International Monetary Fund, and the G8.[66] If alterglobalization protest dealt with the global, it was later movements, such as Occupy, that dealt with the local (see chapter 7). The years from 2003 to 2010 saw few large-scale actions, though a period of quiet should not be mistaken for a period of apathy (see in particular chapters 5, 6, and 7).

In 2010, in the wake of a global recession, the new UK Conservative government was the first to dismiss the economic potential of creative industries.[67] The hope that creativity and innovation could save post-industrial economics was laid to waste, leaving in its wake global cityscapes changed dramatically by extensive cultural building projects now replaced by austerity measures that affected all but that most creative of industries: the financial sector, which remained largely untouched despite the 2008 global economic crisis. And this was the moment protest returned.

At the end of 2011, *Time Magazine* named "The Protester" the person of the year. In the introduction to the issue, Kurt Andersen writes of the 2000s, "credit was easy, complacency and apathy were rife, and street protests looked like pointless emotional sideshows – obsolete, quaint, the equivalent of cavalry to mid-twentieth-century war. The rare large demonstrations in the rich world seemed ineffectual and irrelevant (see the Battle for Seattle, 1999)."[68] As noted in the preface, I suggest that such overwriting is an unfortunate part of the ebb and flow of social movements, though I do not agree with the sentiment. While it might be true that in 2011 the protester became "a maker of history" and "the defining trope of our times,"[69] the Arab Spring, the Occupy movement, and actions elsewhere would not have been possible without the decade-long global struggle that came beforehand, which in turn would not have been possible without the Zapatista uprising in Chiapas, Mexico, and global resistance against IMF policies in the 1990s. A two-decade-long struggle against neoliberal policies cannot be erased for the media-friendly images of 2008 on. Nevertheless, movements organized around interconnected issues (such as migrant rights, anti–climate change, and anti-austerity) gained strength. The Arab Spring led eventually to the Occupy movement in 2011 after the financial crash of 2008. In North America, Idle No More and Black Lives Matter emerged strongly shortly thereafter, both of them part of long-term Indigenous and anti-racist resistance.

The alterglobalization movement rarely targeted museums, unless they were being used as meeting places for trade negotiations. But as the movement waned, two major developments did occur. In the UK, a series of actions against the fossil fuel sponsorship of cultural events emerged shortly after the economic crash in 2008. And in the US in 2011, Occupy Wall Street (OWS), a large social movement, turned its attention to the impact of creative industries rhetoric on precarious workers, often taking their struggles to museums.[70]

Reflecting on his role in Occupy Museums (OM), which emerged from Occupy Wall Street in 2011 and staged numerous interventions into museums in 2011 and 2012, Noah Fisher argues in the online journal *Field* that "when the squares were evicted, the movements brought the strategy of occupation into cultural spaces and, perhaps most prominently, into art institutions."[71] Though OM was invited inside the art system to stage interventions at Documenta 13 and the Berlin Biennale 7 in 2012 and at the Whitney Biennale in 2016, Fisher's overview is a no-holds-barred takedown of the elitism of art institutions (including museums, biennales, and auction houses), which he refers to as "core components of the Capitalist motherboard."[72] For Fisher and activists who had been evicted from Zuccotti Park (where OWS was located),

> Upscale art milieus – from upscale art fairs to major museums – in their surging economic significance and the popular fascination they arise, are being hacked to reveal a massive new wave of social, racial, and economic inequality at the epicenter of high-art luxury. In some cases this is meant to apply pressure on the 1%, with a leverage that would be nearly impossible to access in other spheres.[73]

Gulf Labor (of which Fisher was a part) agreed, writing, "We see monuments to 'culture' woven into a monstrous assemblage of fossil fuels, financial power, and imperial geopolitics."[74] Drawing possibly on Chin Tao Wu's 2002 intensely detailed research of the composition of museum boards in the US and the UK or possibly on earlier movements such as the late-1960s Art Workers' Coalition (chapter 2), both groups noted the ties between board membership and wealth derived from the contemporary art market, resource extraction, and poor labour practices (particularly in the building of the Guggenheim Abu Dhabi).[75] Actions were theatrical and performative and reflected deeply on the compromised position of artists, who were both of the system and outside of it.[76]

OM emerged at a time when museums were regarded as compromised institutions, not just in terms of the constitution of boards but also in terms of the way that museums were perceived to stymie the impact of political work. Writing in 2006, *Guardian* art critic Adrian Searle made a typical comment: "one of the problems with art that attempts to make statements … it gets assimilated," he said.[77] It seemed to many that, between the late 1990s and the first few years of the twenty-first century, no space at all remained for activist, radical, or political art.[78] For Fisher,

> Generations have witnessed the absorption of political dissent by soft and cooptive, rather than antagonistic, responses from capitalist institutions – including advertising corporations, private academies, and art institutions. Therefore, it makes sense to take a hard look at whether art institutions only serve as traps set by the elite to absorb dissent or if they can contribute to the shift away from late capitalism that these political movements demand.[79]

A less radical stance than Fisher's is found in a lengthy article in the *New York Times*. Trying to explain the spread of activism at European and American institutions, *New York Times* art critic Holland Cotter writes, "That museums are now targets says something about their newly perceived status. Once considered standoffish, genteel and politically marginal, they are now viewed as being emblematically engaged players within the power network of global capitalism."[80] Cotter argues that museums are tightly connected to "the exchange of cultural and corporate capital," and he agrees with Gulf Labor and with Fisher that a reflection of the twenty-first-century accumulation of wealth in the hands of fewer and fewer people is reflected in the art world, both in terms of how the wealthy "[snap up] investment-worthy contemporary art" and in the way that museums appear to benefit from this through tax-break-encouraged donation. For Cotter, museums have come to use corporate strategies such as "relentless expansion, user-friendliness, slick advertising." He notes also that such strategies have been successful. At least some museums have become immensely popular "destination brands; busy, event-driven entertainment centers." He concludes that this is not a positive development: "as generators of life lessons, shapers of moral thinking, explainers of history, [museums] no longer matter, because they're not asking people to look for any of that."[81]

Both Fisher and Cotter condemn museums for their relationship to "the 1%" and for their seeming unwillingness to engage with their own compromised positions. Cotter outlines protests going back to the 1960s and argues compellingly that many of these interventions "exposed" the inner workings of the museum. He calls for museums to engage in "exploratory truth-telling." He is essentially calling for museums to engage with the now-central term in museum studies, "difficult knowledge," a term popularized by Deborah Britzmann and used in museum studies to explore how certain museum exhibits can shake visitors to the core, creating lasting learning opportunities that can unsettle long-held assumptions.[82] Cotter argues that museum exhibits "could wake people up; compel them to stop, look and read when they might have passed by; and prompt them to see that art isn't just about objects – it's about ideas, histories and ethical philosophies that they may have a stake in, and an opinion about." To be glib, he hopes that museums can encourage epiphanal moments in much the same way that I argue that performative protest can. He concludes, writing of the impact of museum renovation and expansion projects, "Gentrification makes for a ruinous moral ecology. When the artists go, resistance goes, and rebellion is the foundation of interesting art and a moral life."[83] Interestingly, he concludes by pointing to protest actions at museums, referring to them as a new form of art, and reflecting, "I savor the prospect, any day now, of glancing out a window at the new Whitney, or gazing across MOMA's atrium, or walking through one of the Met's little-traveled permanent-collection galleries, and, suddenly, there they [OM activists] are."[84]

Cotter's concluding remarks point to a developing tension in terms of how the relationship between interventionist groups and museums should be conceived. Can museums be allies, or are they so compromised that any kind of rapport is impossible? At the end of his article, Fisher reflects on the invitation of Occupiers to the Berlin Biennale 7 and to Documenta 13 and argues that museums, even though they may co-opt resistance, nonetheless have a relationship to it, thus making them impactful spaces wherein to work through, explore, and share political viewpoints. He writes, "Museums, as institutions well regarded in social life, are hence useful in exposing the contradictions between democracy and capitalism."[85] It is useful to explore these contradictions in more detail.

Midway through his article, Cotter quotes David J. Skorton of the Smithsonian, who notes, "At a time when public trust in many other institutions seems to be declining … the Smithsonian's role is to stay neutral and provide careful, fact-based information and education 'that we need to make informed decisions.' 'We can't be seen as partisan, political.'"[86] Cotter reads this as museums refusing to engage with activism, but I suggest a slightly different reading, particularly given the recent opening of the Smithsonian National Museum of African American History Culture, which has a direct and vocal relationship to historical and current activism. It is now well known that museums are not neutral spaces.[87] And Skorton's comment might equally apply to the Smithsonian's long history, outlined by Kylie Message, of collecting protest ephemera.[88] To be partisan would, arguably, be to *never* collect the material culture representing dissenting opinions. One might point to a number of recent important exhibitions (key among them *Disobedient Objects*, an exhibition that gathered together the material culture of dissent at the Victoria and Albert in 2014, and *En Mas': Carnival and Performance Art of the Caribbean*, a multi-sited exhibition with performances in eight cities in six countries around the world that "considers the connections between Carnival and performance, masquerade and social criticism, diaspora and transnationalism") that have grappled with and answered many of the questions raised by critics above (see also chapter 3).[89] Gavin Grindon, one of the curators of *Disobedient Objects*, notes in the catalogue, "Social movements, though they may appear chaotic, are one of the principal sites where culture grows ... What happens when you place disobedient objects at the heart of a building that was conceived for such obedient purposes?"[90] And Claire Tancons has articulated some of the difficulties of translating the movement of live performance, specifically of carnival, into "a conservative exercise in arranging objects in space."[91] In short, curators and museums were and are starting to think deeply about a number of questions: how to keep the spirit of protest, the epiphanal moments, alive in the gallery; how to showcase artefacts from movements that might see museums as elite and conciliatory institutions; how to include and indeed foreground those who have been left out; and how museums and galleries can themselves contribute to political movements (see also chapter 3). Simultaneously, a number of theorists began to argue that art held great political potential as a part of, and a corollary to, activist movements.[92] As Szeman writes, "art practices might well have the power to activate deadened sensibilities and faded political will by reminding publics that social life is something to be created and celebrated rather than feared or endured."[93]

A veritable explosion of recent books and articles documenting and analyzing these practices suggests that political art can encourage, teach, or lead to action.[94] Increasingly, such texts argue for the affective impact of certain types of politicized and participatory art, a kind of experiential moment that, if it does not replicate the tear gas epiphany, certainly has something in common with it.[95] Gregory Sholette, for example, uses activists Dara Greenwald and Josh MacPhee's term "social movement culture" to describe "Banner drops, giant puppets, street stencils, agitational graphics, protest posters, cardboard signs, demonstration flags and pendants, comic book zines, anti-capitalist graffiti and public performances," a kind of contemporary art activism that takes place within social movements, that often actively resists institutionalization, but, according to Sholette, has deeply affected more mainstream art production.[96] Moving closer to the institution, Claire Bishop, though often critical of activist art, summarizes the argument for socially engaged art, suggesting that supporters feel that "the creative energy of participatory practices rehumanizes – or at least de-alienates – a society rendered numb and fragmented by the repressive instrumentality of capitalism"[97] and that participatory projects work "to restore and realize a communal collective space of shared social engagement."[98] When art crosses a boundary and instigates action, there is often backlash.[99] It is also worth noting that most of these texts separate the creation of artwork from its display. Political projects tend to be described as if they emerged already complete: processes of applying for grants, negotiating with curators and museums, extracting payment for the labour of creating and exhibiting the work, and selling the work are rarely considered worthy of attention, even when the works themselves are about changing patterns of labour.

Thus, even as museums were and are heavily criticized, at the same time, in art historical literature, museums and galleries are underscored as one location where the development of a performative language critical of the creative industries takes place. Shannon Jackson gives a way into the critique: "If progressive artists and critics unthinkingly echo a routinized language of anti-institutionalism and anti-statism, we can find ourselves unexpectedly colluding with neoliberal impulses that want to dismantle public institutions of human welfare."[100]

After the election of Donald Trump to the US presidency, many museums, ranging from the United States Memorial Holocaust Museum to the Museum of Modern Art resisted in ways small and large that together were quite unique for mainstream institutions.[101] The #J20 art strike, for example, called on artists, critics, art historians, dealers, curators, and museums to stop work on Inauguration Day to protest "the incoming administration of Donald Trump. The J20 Art Strike is an opportunity to reflect on what the new administration portends for art."[102] The action recalled the 1970 Art Strike against Racism, Sexism, Repression and War, which was an "expression of shame and outrage at our government's policies of racism, war and repression."[103] Although the Queen's Museum was the only major museum closed for the 2017 strike, several altered their programming and displays. Most notably, "the Museum of Modern Art replaced seven works in its sacrosanct fifth-floor galleries – the domain of van Gogh, Picasso, and Pollock – with pieces by artists from three of the seven targeted Muslim-majority nations."[104] Shortly after #J20, Graham Bowley asked in the *New York Times:*

> Times of political change and social upheaval raise questions about what a museum is for. When an institution like the Guggenheim is confronted by such tumult, should it respond? And how? Should a museum change with the events around it, or should it stand true, like an immovable rock, as political storms come and go? Is a museum's job to explain the historical past, or is its presentation of the past really about understanding the present? Even the future?[105]

Bowley covers a number of actions that have taken place in the museum since the election of Trump, but his article expresses sympathy for the argument that museums should rise above the maelstrom, providing a longer view on events rather than responding immediately to changing circumstances. His questions, at this particular moment, are useful and are reflected in the work of a number of museum studies scholars who offer a slightly different take on museums than do the art historians and critics looking at art galleries and contemporary art.

Robert Janes and Richard Sandell, for example, note that museums tend to be timid in undertaking political action, but there is

> a small but growing number of museums, galleries and heritage organisations experimenting with new ways of working that seek to not only engage with and explore, but also to act upon social inequality, political injustice and the causes of environmental destruction. These institutions are key intellectual and civic resources, as well as uniquely trusted public spaces where substantive issues can be explored, debated and acted upon, and where ethical behaviours can be modelled. This work can be understood as a form of activist practice that seeks to harness the museum's unique resources towards more sustainable, fair and just societies.[106]

Fiona Cameron agrees (at least partially). In the introduction to her edited volume *Hot Topics*, Cameron argues:

> Previously considered off-limits, the introduction of these subjects and their representation in museums has been problematic. While some museums have successfully and meaningfully engaged hot topics, in reality few are willing to do so because they are seen as high risk due to a fear of political and social repercussions, such as funding withdrawal or the alienation of audiences.[107]

Janes and Sandell's and Cameron's care in dealing with the role of political action in museums reflects the fact that museums themselves have little to no consensus on how to deal with contentious politics, though the questions being asked suggest a growing interest in the topic.

In 2017, the Museums Association conducted a poll of its membership, asking "Do sponsorship protests damage relations with sponsors and philanthropists?" Sixty-seven per cent answered yes.[108] Voicing a well-rehearsed argument, and speaking specifically to BP's sponsorship of cultural events in the UK, theatre critic and historian Kate Maltby suggests that in a climate of government funding cuts, "if protest pushes BP away from its philanthropic commitments, we will all be the losers." She suggests that anything disrupting the flow of money to the arts is bad news for all, ultimately making the arts less accessible.[109] Jonathan Jones, writing in *The Guardian* agrees: "The critics of business sponsorship are playing fantasy politics against the softest of targets. Museums are not anyone's enemy. But they are vulnerable precisely because they are run by decent people. Let's guilttrip them! So much easier than taking on the heartless corporations themselves."[110]

MuseumNext USA conducted a poll of 1,000 Americans, asking, "do you believe that museums should have something to say about social issues?" Overall, only 27.5 per cent of respondents said yes to this question, with 31 per cent saying no and 40.5 per cent saying maybe.[111] However, when the answers were divided by age, a clear distinction was found: "When asked if museums should actively campaign on issues such as homelessness, inequality and the environment, 47% of the under 30 age group said yes, while a further 28% said maybe. This would further point to a real hunger in the under 30 age group for museums to be more activist."[112] According to an article in the *New Statesman*, protests at UK art galleries are now so common that Arts Council England has released new guidelines for galleries on managing disturbances. The guidelines say that governing bodies are becoming increasingly risk-averse because of fear of demonstrations.[113]

Jenny Ellison's extensive interviews with several museums in Canada clearly showed that in 2003 museum staff and curators were very concerned with consulting community stakeholders and very unwilling to deal with controversial content[114] (even though, it should be noted, neither *Spirit Sings* nor *Into the Heart of Africa* had been conceived as even remotely political or contentious exhibitions). Ellis concludes that the reception of both exhibitions "did not seem to catalyse debate within museums in Canada so much as create a chilly climate among curatorial staff."[115] A fear of losing funding, losing sponsors, or facing ruined reputations was profoundly influential, according to Ellis, even though she additionally notes that her study showed that museum audiences were actually very open to having museums deal with controversial subject matter and, in fact, willing to allow museums to take the lead on public opinion – fully 84 per cent of respondents felt that museums are sources of reliable information. But the museums themselves were also shown, in the study, to largely ignore audience feedback. One of the outcomes of greater community consultation at the outset of exhibitions has been the loss of time or willingness to follow up on how the shows were received, in turn creating a feedback loop – audience willingness to view controversial shows does not really translate into museums wading into political topics.[116] Ellis's study presents a nice counterpoint to those undertaken by the Museums Association. And interestingly, in the decade and a half since the study was undertaken, an avoidance of controversial material has arguably translated into accepting many of the demands made by demonstrators in the 1990s.

When protests erupted at *Spirit Sings* and *Into the Heart of Africa* (and a number of other exhibitions around the globe), often the issue was not the earnest approach of the curator but rather the appropriation of the act of storytelling, the telling of someone else's story. As Shelley Butler notes, in the 1980s and 1990s the idea that museums conferred prestige and authority to "particular notions of heritage, history, art, and taste" led to communities being "deeply concerned with the way in which they are, or are not, represented by museums. These issues regarding the politics of representation become particularly intense in the context of contemporary multicultural and postcolonial societies."[117]

In major Canadian institutions, appropriative approaches have changed slowly but significantly, despite Ellis's findings, and often as a result of pressure from outside the museum. While a number of recent controversies over appropriation of Indigenous and Black culture by white artists erupted into responsive action in museums in the United States,[118] many authoritative galleries and museums in Canada appeared to have learned a lesson from protests in earlier decades. For example, in July 2017 *Every.Now.Then* opened at the AGO in response to Canada 150 celebrations.[119] Not only was the exhibition immensely diverse in its interpretation of Canadian history, it foregrounded stories that had been erased, suppressed, or overshadowed in settler culture. The show also included "Powerful, precisely rendered graphite portraits of key activists in Black Lives Matter Toronto," drawn by Syrus Marcus Ware, a BLM organizer and core member.[120] Also in July 2017, when a giant Canadian flag (installed for 150 celebrations) outside Themuseum in Kitchener, Ontario, was painted black and a banner graffitied with "150+ years of resistance #unsettling 150" hung on the gallery, workers at first called the police and arranged for the flag to be cleaned but kept the banner, installing it in an exhibition ongoing at the time called *A Cause for Celebration? First Things First*, "which examines injustices by Canada's prime ministers against Indigenous people and incorporates the work of indigenous artists." David Marskell, CEO of Themuseum, was quoted as saying he was pleased that the museum had been chosen for the intervention.[121] The police, nonetheless, were still called. Museums are still institutions tied to their pasts and aimed only partially toward the future (if the institution is engaged with the process of looking back).

One of the key questions raised in this book is: how can we understand long-term negotiations with and interventions into museums – primarily by Indigenous peoples and other communities marginalized by mainstream institutions – in relation to spectacular uprisings that erupt at the thresholds of the same museums? On the one hand, the relationship between OWS, creative industries rhetoric, and art criticism focused on participatory practices does much to explain the emergence of performative groups targeting museums for their sponsorships, but such analyses inadvertently sideline many of the long-term efforts to decolonize and/or Indigenize museum collections, art exhibitions, and the larger cultural systems that contain them. On the other hand, often disparate groups come together in powerful trans-issue movements that use the museum to mobilize around other issues (chapters 5 and 6). I argue that in order to understand any relationship between museums and contentious politics, a wide lens must be employed and, in fact, the long-term struggles must be highlighted beside, and potentially above and beyond, those that have recently and spectacularly emerged. Such histories are carefully outlined in the massive literature on Indigenous representation in museums and galleries, in critical museums studies in general, and in books by scholars such as Susan Cahan, Aruna D'Souza, Kylie Message, Shelley Butler, and Julia Bryan-Wilson, who have looked specifically at instances where marginalized groups have targeted museums.

To conclude this section, I turn to the words of Not An Alternative, an activist group that has focused specifically on museums. They note:

> Institutions are not monolithic unities. They are complex multiplicities, split within themselves and between themselves and their settings. Museums have custodial staff, administrators, curators, IT personnel, fundraisers, directors, donors, trustees, and visitors. They also have their broader cultural position, their reputation as sites of authoritative knowledge. This makes them sites worth seizing. When art activists commandeer a museum, they split it from within. The already existent divisions within the institution are activated. Anyone affiliated with the museum is forced to take a side: few or many, rich or poor, past or future? By occupying institutions, identifying allies on the inside, empowering employees, working with whistle-blowers, leveraging legal grey zones, and strategically mobilizing the symbolic power of key constituencies, activist art collectives redeploy the arsenals of power that have already been stored. The institution is liberated.[122]

Canadian Museums, Creative Industries, Protest

In this book, the examples and case studies are all Canadian – focusing on specific museums, protest, and the influence of creative industries rhetoric primarily at major, authoritative establishment institutions. In focusing on Canada, a middle state at the margins of global power, the examples in *Tear Gas Epiphanies* speak to the continued importance of the national as a part of globalization where, as Saskia Sassen notes, "the national is also often one of the key enablers and enactors of the emergent global scale."[123] Thus, while museums participate in global initiatives (such as the International Council of Museums [ICOM]) and are a part of international tourism routes, they are also grounded by their geographic attachments. While Johanne Sloan argues convincingly that "contemporary art in Canada has not, for the most part, become embedded in nationalist narratives; nor do contemporary art and artists often figure in the imaginative work of nationhood,"[124] the same is definitely not true of many of the museums covered in this book and the exhibitions they mount. For instance, Carl Good argues that "nationness is not disappearing if what is obliging us to shape our work around the increasing fluidity of national borders is itself a nation – the very nation that cradles our institutions in its ever-increasing complexity, transformation, and juridical decentering."[125] Many of the museums covered in this book are federal institutions that have the representation of nation written right into their mandates. Thus, I write cognizant of the fact that Canada is a settler nation and that processes of decolonization are stymied by projects of nation-building. In the exhibitions covered in Part 2 of this book, competing narratives of Canada as a Warrior Nation, a Peacekeeping Nation, and a petro-state overlap and intersect with cultural policy that is then presented in museums as a seamless narrative told through objects, artefacts, and artworks. But museums are the same spaces where many of these narratives are resisted, both inside and at the threshold of the institution. Throughout the book, attempts to unsettle nation and the ways that the settler nation is constructed are repeatedly juxtaposed. Museums are both implicit and explicit participants in creating and undermining these narratives.

In the period covered by this book, most major institutions, particularly federally funded ones, oscillated between the illustration of settler narratives of nationhood and strong attempts to decolonize collections, particularly around concerted attempts at reconciliation. These struggles are ongoing. Kelsey R. Wrightson argues that "museums as authoritative spaces are both reflective and active hubs in a matrix of explicitly settler colonial power and knowledge ... museums remain implicated in the perpetuation of explicitly settler colonial regimes of power, and the settler colonial politics of recognition, specifically."[126] She argues that even when museums seemingly engage with reconciliation, they remain implicated in a colonial politics of recognition, one that is conciliatory "but still fundamentally colonial."[127] I am both sympathetic to her argument (chapters 2, 5, 6, and 7) and aware that there are processes at work in some Canadian institutions to move beyond impasse, and beyond the museum as "contact zone," into real reciprocal arrangements (see Interstice 2b).

Importantly for this book, I argue that what has happened and is happening at museums in Canada (many of them Indigenous-run, such as the U'Mista Cultural Centre and the Nisga'a Museum/Hli G̲oothl Wilp-Adok̲shl Nisga'a) actively unsettles any idea that museums are monolithic. In addition, the presence of such institutions can complicate celebratory coverage of museum interventionist movements that overlook or erase the resistance of Indigenous peoples and peoples of colour.[128] Similarly, the application of creative industries rhetoric in Canada, so important to the OM resistance, operates differently in Canada and challenges action against institutions, which often combine public funding with private philanthropy and sponsorships. Any idea of a "knowledge economy" in Canada was and is complicated by the realities of Canadian cultural policy: creative industries were and are as often military research and development or software applications enabling resource extraction as they are the arts and culture.

How to Read This Book

This book is informed by critical museum studies and critical curatorial studies, both from anthropological and art historical perspectives. I also draw on social movement theory, on manifestos, articles, and announcements emerging from activist movements, and on texts considering the emergence and impact of creativity as an economic pursuit. In bringing together an art criticism perspective with a museums anthropology one, and reading those alongside activist literature, I will inevitably step on a few toes. But I also follow Erika Lehrer in arguing that a "more 'distributed' view of the museum allows sites of resistance to come into view as well, highlighting museums as *processes*: monumental gestures that catalyze broader conversations in multiple directions and spur the development of an array of other social spaces that form their own frames of meaning, resulting in productive tensions that have ongoing impact over time."[129] Overall, I am inspired by anthropologist Christina Krep's assertion that museum studies is inherently interdisciplinary[130] and by Kylie Message, who argues that museum studies is a "boundary discipline" that can encourage a kind of intellectual activism (what she calls the "disobedient museum"), that can "transgress traditional disciplinary models and highlight new connections or reframe existing or new sites of conflict."[131]

I have visited all of the museums covered in this book, most of them multiple times. In places where interviews are included, interviewees were given the opportunity to speak anonymously or by name and to edit comments they made once the text and analysis were complete. Archival research was conducted where possible. An overwhelming fact, however, was that a lot of the material simply did not exist in traditional archives. While most museums collect newspaper clippings pertaining to their exhibitions, most do not collect ephemera from protests that take place against them. As noted in the preface, defiant social movements have a tendency to drop out of official histories except as footnotes. One of the major conclusions drawn by this book is that major museums in Canada *should* collect material from protests, certainly when the protests take place at or in relation to the institution. In the United States and Britain in particular, there is evidence that the processes of collection documented by Message at the Smithsonian National Museum of American History and Susan Cahan at the Whitney Museum of American Art as well as by Greg Sholette at MOMA have taken off.[132] To my knowledge, the same is not currently true in Canada, with a few exceptions such as the Museum of Vancouver (which I discuss in further detail in chapters 3 and 7).[133] I researched the protests, many of which have been forgotten, through the Canadian newsstand database with a number of keywords (among them protest, museums, controversy, gallery, activism). I also searched in publications such as *artscanada*, *Canadian Forum*, *Fuse Magazine*, and others. I am sure that I nonetheless missed finding many actions that were not covered in the mainstream press or that were too small to attain coverage. I was, at one point, interested in creating a timeline of actions, but it proved beyond the scope of this project. I am also trained as a historian of visual and material culture and work as a museum studies professor in a visual arts department. Though I have been profoundly influenced by the anthropological and ethnographic approaches taken in many museum studies texts, my training shows through in my interest in contemporary art practices.

Tear Gas Epiphanies is divided into two parts. Part 1 of the book builds up the background context for the case studies through chapters that deal with protest, cultural policy, and museums. Part 2 brings these strands together through a series of case studies, each focused on a particular issue-based protest/ movement and a museum.

In Part 1, chapters 2 and 3, I lay out the groundwork, establish the theoretical framework, and illustrate the economic and political backdrop against which people organized. Chapter 2 provides a history of protest in, outside, and against Canadian museums, from the 1900s through to the 1990s. Chapter 3 looks at thresholds, interiors, and behind the scenes at museums. I analyze the way that museum architecture and exteriors are caught up in processes of gentrification and downtown regeneration; by contrast, the way that critical curatorial programs have disrupted such developments and have occasionally reimagined gallery space as radical and interventionist; and finally, the difficulties and challenges faced by archives and archivists trying to collect protest ephemera.

The chapters in Part 2 fill in the history of protest and museums in Canada following on the two major events of the late 1980s and early 1990s, the demonstrations outside *Spirit Sings* and *Into the Heart of Africa*. Chapter 4 investigates the links between anti-war protest, veteran activism, military investment, and the opening of the new Canadian War Museum building in Ottawa in 2005. Chapter 5 examines the building of a Canadian Museum for Human Rights in Winnipeg through a public–private partnership and looks closely at the way that Shoal Lake 40 First Nation was able to use the museum in their struggle to secure funding for a road that would connect the reserve to the mainland, thus allowing access to clean water. Chapter 6 considers a "missing" protest in Canada, focusing on the numerous actions against oil sponsorship at museums in the US and UK and the lack of similar undertakings in Canada despite extensive corporate sponsorship of the arts in Canada by the resource sector. And finally, chapter 7 reveals the associations between real estate development, homelessness, and the contemporary art scene in Vancouver, looking closely at how Occupy Vancouver set up their encampment in the courtyard of the gallery, drawing together issues of culture, museums, and also Indigenous rights and land claims. A brief conclusion examines an actual protest archive, one held by the UBC Museum of Anthropology, dedicated to anti-capitalist demonstrations that took place during the Asia Pacific Economic Cooperation (APEC) meetings at the museum and UBC in 1997.

In between the chapters can be found a series of short interstices. Each introduces an action, exhibition, artwork, or event that further illuminates the argument made in *Tear Gas Epiphanies*. While the chapters concentrate primarily on institutions, the interstices should be seen more as a textual curatorial undertaking, an attempt to bring together a series of interventions that, in the words of Lucy Lippard, "work ... into the cracks of the system."[134] The interstices are organized roughly chronologically, with the first three dedicated to sit-ins, protests, and actions that pre-date *Spirit Sings* and *Into the Heart of Africa* and the last four devoted to interventions and artworks from after 2000. The interstices comprise a chronology of activist actions at museums and galleries that have gone largely unmarked in the history of Canadian visual culture. They can be read separately or alongside the chapters.

I include here a note on terminology. The term protest often assumes that those engaged in action are solely *against* something, which by proxy grants that something legitimacy. Most people putting their bodies on the line are also very much *for* something: clean water, clean air, accessible health care, a better world. Protest and even activism have come to be contested terms. Some prefer the term direct action because it assumes that one is engaging rather than complaining.[135] Keeping these critiques in mind, in analysis of anti-capitalist, anti-gentrification, pro-environment actions, I have used terms such as protest, direct action, and activism. However, in analysis of actions undertaken by First Nations, Métis, and Inuit, I employ words that are used by the community. Names such as land and water protectors and defenders or terms such as following traditional laws are often used in lieu of protest or activism. In each case, I try to follow the lead of the organizers.

In this book, I also use different terminology to distinguish between actions at museums that are connected to larger movements and those that are not. In the literature around political museum interventions, the word controversy is used frequently, in fact almost ubiquitously, particularly to describe the largest and most famous demonstrations.[136] This is true of Canada and elsewhere. The term has been a go-to in the literature, particularly in the late 1990s, as seen in the emergence of critical museums studies literature that addressed the numerous "controversies" that erupted around issues of race and representation. But the word controversy is also often used to downplay the importance and impact of such actions, often spinning altercations as overwrought and suggesting that targeted exhibitions, sponsors, or artworks have been misread and misrepresented. In short, while I outline above the reasons the term protest is problematic, and where possible I do not use it to refer to Indigenous interventions into museums and collections, I nonetheless find the word controversy equally compromised.[137]

I use the term controversy only to refer to complaints that are specific to museums and are not tied to larger social movements. The controversy over the National Gallery of Canada's 1991 acquisition of abstract expressionist Barnett Newman's *Voice of Fire* painting (which is essentially two blue and one red stripe, the simplicity of which caught the attention of the public, the media, and several politicians) is a key example of the distinction that I am getting at. While John O'Brian, Bruce Barber, and others have argued convincingly that there is a wide context to be considered in dealing with complaints aimed at the gallery's purchase, these complaints are not linked to more widespread political movements.[138] In short, controversy is a useful term in some cases, particularly when issues of free speech and artistic freedom and cultural appropriation are raised and even more specifically when those issues accrue to works of contemporary art. Controversies over artworks have not, however, been as prevalent in Canada as in the United States, and thus I have largely avoided the term in most of my case studies.

In sum, *Tear Gas Epiphanies* analyzes how museums in Canada, caught up in multiple influences and representing multiple constituencies, deal with, resist, benefit from, and endure protests that take place at their thresholds and within their halls. I build on the work of Shelley Butler, Susan Cahan, Aruna D'Souza, Kylie Message, and a few others to further understand the relationship between cultural institutions and resistance. I try to bring together the academic work of critical museum studies with what Yates McKee terms "militant research."[139] I also look beyond the museum to see how culture and museums were influenced by international economic policy, municipal culture and creative cities policy, and ongoing attempts to implement often parochial understandings of nation. Missing in this book are some of the most famous works associated with activist or interventionist art in Canada, among them the work of General Idea, Carole Condé and Karl Beveridge, Joane Cardinal-Schubert, Ian Wallace, Istvan Kantor, Jamelie Hassan, Rebecca Belmore, Camille Turner, and many others. Many of those are present in my co-edited volume, *Imagining Resistance*. Absent also are the artist-run centres that have themselves had an agonistic relationship with mainstream museums, as well as some of the newer small-scale semi-commercial or artist project spaces that are deeply antagonistic toward the "social grooming and cultural elitism" of authoritative institutions.[140] I've written elsewhere about the political currency of small institutions and turn here rather to the much larger and more multifaceted major institutions. This book refuses the separation between protest and status quo – in almost all cases, scholarly works are about protest *or* economy, art, nation, and so on. Rarely do they look at the messy intersections, the tangles and overlaps. I argue that museums provide a way of revealing these overlaps and making them clear. *Tear Gas Epiphanies* does two things: it fills in a missing history of contentious politics at Canadian museums, and it takes four case studies and reads them deeply against a part of wider narratives of museum renovation projects, changing museum approaches to certain difficult topics, and the expansion of the interrogatory museum.

Interstice 1a

Of Directors, Museums, and National Identity

In 1972, a battle erupted over the Art Gallery of Ontario's (AGO) hiring of a new chief curator, American Richard Wattenmaker, former director of the Rutgers University Art Gallery. Those reacting, who were primarily Ontario-based artists and their supporters gathered in the Committee to Strengthen Canadian Culture, were frustrated that Canadian museums offered few opportunities for Canadian artists. In the late 1960s, anti-Americanism had developed into Canadian nationalism as a left-wing standpoint. It was a peculiarly vital thread of activism within the arts and cultural scenes in the late 1960s and 1970s. Simmering resentment at the control of the cultural establishment by those who were unfamiliar with Canadian arts and artists coalesced around the hiring of Wattenmaker. That one of the major institutions in the country would be helmed by an American who (apparently) showed little interest in Canadian artists and showcasing their work erupted into a series of demonstrations and other interventions.[1]

The AGO claimed that the hiring committee was "unable to find a sufficiently qualified Canadian who was willing to take the job" and that to hire a Canadian "we may have to lower our standards in terms of academic qualifications and professional museum experience," a statement that produced significant backlash in letters to the editor and other media coverage.[2] Furthermore, Canadian Artists' Representation (CAR), the artists' union that had been formed in 1967, had been corresponding with the AGO, sending lists of possible candidates and receiving supportive comments back from gallery administrators. The announcement of

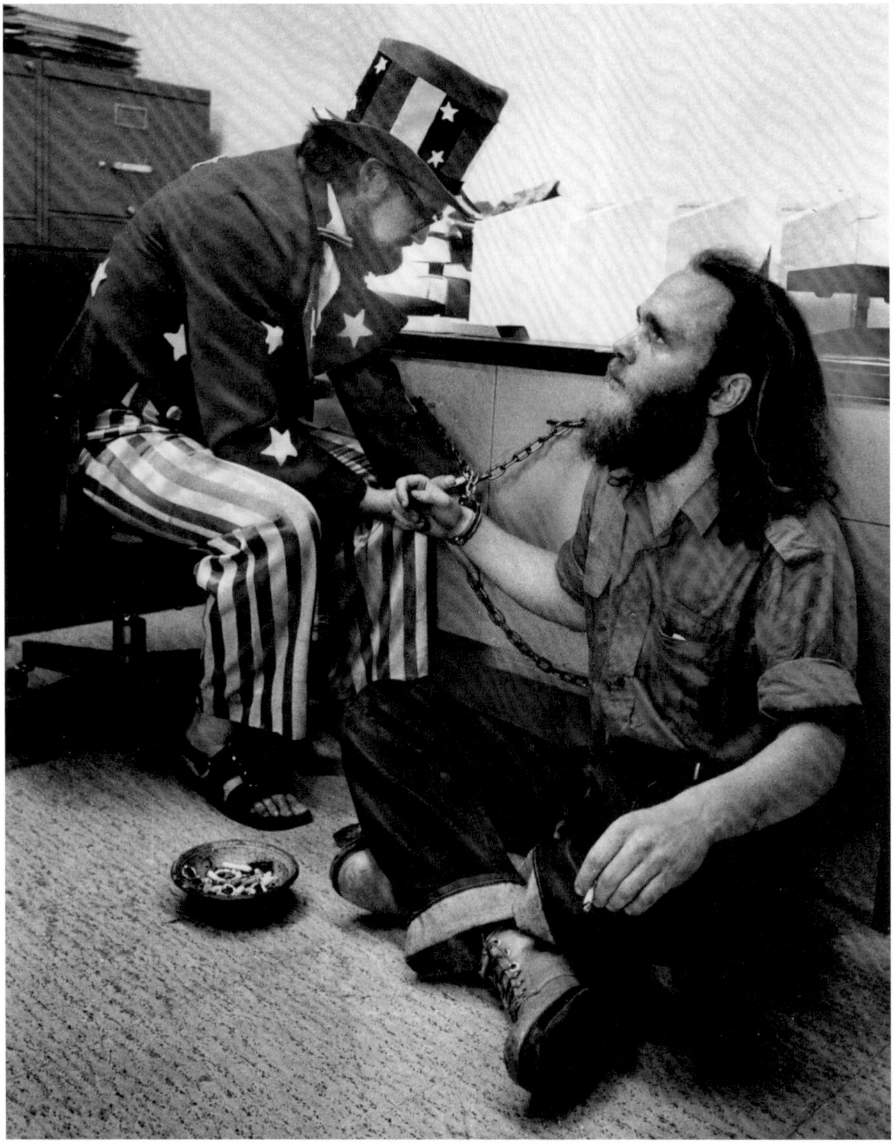

Figure 1.5
Michel Lambeth and Jim Brown chained to furniture in Art Gallery office, 1972.

Wattenmaker's hiring was taken as a betrayal.[3] On 4 July 1972, Wattenmaker, "a husky, cool 31 year-old art historian [who] was already down to his blue shirt-sleeves to take over his appointment,"[4] took on his curatorial duties. Outside, the Committee to Strengthen Canadian Culture marched from Trinity Square in Toronto, past the US consulate, to the AGO where they gathered with a maple leaf flag and a megaphone. After being forbidden from entering the gallery, they moved to the curator's offices (in a nearby building), and several participants chained themselves outside Wattenmaker's office door. They vowed to stage a sit-in until

Wattenmaker agreed to meet with them. They also brought a letter of resignation with them in hopes that Wattenmaker would sign it: "I have come to realize that my appointment as chief curator is detrimental to the people of Canada," it read.[5] Jim Brown, Michel Lambeth, Jerry Malzen, and Milton Acorn were later removed by police, though no charges were laid.[6]

Extensive coverage in local newspapers was mostly sympathetic to Wattenmaker, although also expressing concern with the AGO's comments that there were no Canadian candidates up to the task. Wattenmaker was to replace Mario Amaya (also American), who used his own letter to the editor to distance himself from Wattenmaker ("[he and I] have never met") before noting,

> I am indeed appalled by the attacks that Mr. Wattenmaker has suffered since his arrival in Canada, since during my three years in Toronto I never once heard any objections to my country of origin ... The current fuss over Mr. Wattenmaker's citizenship by certain tiresome and parochial factions in the Toronto art world, I feel, does not speak for the art community at large: for those civilized and intelligent dealers ... for the many Canadian artists with whom I happily work, and for the several collectors and patrons of the Gallery who I had the honor to serve.[7]

Meanwhile, newspapers across the country reported that Wattenmaker "says his wife is wondering 'what sort of country we've come to' because of the scurrilous letters and phone calls he has received since he took the post two months ago ..."[8] In a published interview, Wattenmaker admits he was "'a little shook up' by personal attacks, 'anti-American hate literature' and even a bomb threat. But he doesn't plan 'to let anyone frighten me away from a job I really wanted.'"[9]

Sorting through the AGO's archive of newspaper clippings related to Wattenmaker's hiring, it is clear that mainstream media were unwilling to offer space to the Committee to Strengthen Canadian Culture (which was often mislabelled). Those protesting are rarely named, their concerns are actively dismissed, and Wattenmaker himself refers to at least some of them as "nuts."[10] Included in the archive, however, are several documents from the committee, including one titled "The American Eagle Is Chicken," which includes the following statement: "In 1972, the American 'wave of civilization,' taste, politics, culture, economy, social custom has long washed over us. American 'civilization' and 'culture' is entrenched in nearly every institution we possess, including our schools, universities, art colleges, community colleges, art galleries and museums." The manifesto concludes, "Shout out today that the board of trustees must rescind Wattenmaker's appointment! Demand today that the AGO must have Canadian curators; that the AGO, funded with public moneys, must be administered by Canadians for Canadians."[11]

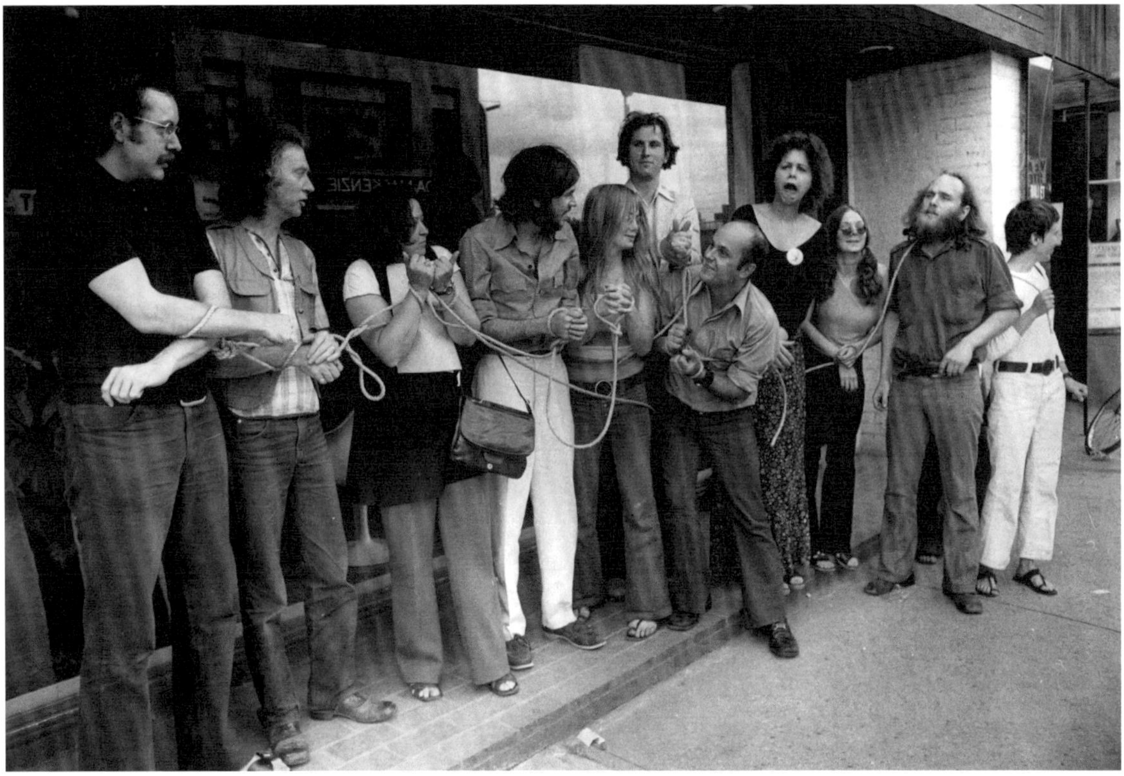

Figure 1.6
Metro artists tie themselves together with rope outside the Isaac Gallery to protest against the appointment of an American, Richard J. Wattenmaker of Philadelphia, as new chief curator at the Art Gallery of Ontario, 1972.

Other demands coming from the committee may have been influenced by the Art Workers' Coalition in the United States (see chapter 1) and include recommendations for a free admission policy, numerous suggestions for responding to local artists, and abolishing the "'men only' luncheons at the gallery."[12] The Committee to Strengthen Canadian Culture was not able to oust Wattenmaker from his position. He remained as chief curator until 1978, when he was replaced by Roald Nasgaard (who had been serving as curator of contemporary art from 1975).[13]

Writing almost fifty years later, the action against Wattenmaker seems indicative of a kind of settler nationalism that has, since the 1990s and much earlier, been vociferously critiqued. This was noted even at the time. In 1976, just before his own exhibition opened at the AGO (chapter 2), Canadian artist Karl Beveridge, writing from New York, argued that the whole premise of CAR depended on a misinterpretation. "The CAR gang are in a bizarrely contradictory position: they expect the establishment to be radical."[14] In an interview conducted in 2015, Beveridge looked back on this time, arguing that the CAR position that members had to be Canadian citizens was exclusionary.[15] For many radical or activist groups today, the nation state upholds many of the inequalities that they are trying to resist, and thus nationalism de facto cannot provide a position from which to launch an oppositional movement. I explore these ideas in a bit more detail in chapter 1 and Interstice 3c and throughout the rest of the book. For now, how was a nation-based radicalism constructed and understood in the 1970s?

Suffice to say here that the Committee to Strengthen Canadian Culture and its supporters believed strongly that Canada was being "colonized" by the United States, primarily through American control of the press, media, arts, and "the prevalence of Americans in key cultural posts in Canada."[16] How were Canadian artists to catch a break, asked artist Greg Curnoe in a CBC documentary from 1975, when those occupying the top gallery and museum positions had no understanding of local culture and brought with them an "attitude that they come from the cultural centre of the world."[17]

In 1974, the province of Ontario gave a grant to the AGO of more than $12 million for two additional wings: one for the Zacks wing (primarily European art) and the other for the Henry Moore Sculpture Centre (which was built to house a donation from the artist of 400 of his own works, valued at $15 million). Those opposed argued that Moore was simply cleaning out his studio, getting rid of models and transferring "warehousing cost ... [to] Ontario taxpayers."[18] Meanwhile the AGO Board of Trustees would not raise the acquisitions budget for contemporary Canadian art beyond $10,000.[19] Representatives from the Committee to Strengthen Canadian Culture and from CAR (many of them the same people) were present at the opening of the new wings, again to draw attention to the lack of funds being allocated to living Canadian artists. Although the gallery had also acquired a donation of Canadian work by artists such as Emily Carr, A.Y. Jackson, Tom Thomson, and Paul-Émile Borduas, the gallery announced the donation by stating that the new collections would make the AGO "unique in its comprehensiveness of art in Canada ... from the Group of Seven to 1969."[20] Living artists need not apply. As Susan Crean put it in her widely read text *Who's Afraid of Canadian Culture*, "Canadian work is good depending on how well it measures up in terms of Art, the art of the grand old imperial centres of Rome, Paris, London, New York and so forth. That, in a nutshell, is the imperialist attitude to culture: '(My)' Art transcends classes and national boundaries; (your) Canadian art is provincial.'"[21]

In November 1973, Lambeth had written directly to artist Henry Moore, asking him to refuse to be "an unwitting agent of cultural imperialism" by allowing his name on the gallery. Instead Lambeth suggested the gallery should be named the Tom Thomson Wing, and if it were not, "CAR will have no alternative but to initiate and present the greatest cultural protest demonstration that has ever been held in Canada."[22] The name of the new gallery was not changed, but a Canadian wing was opened at the AGO in 1977, and in 1975, for the first time, an artist (Joyce Wieland) was admitted to the museum board.[23]

At the 1974 opening of the two new wings, CAR and the committee were not alone. This time, a group of primarily non-white demonstrators also gathered, their placards asking "Canadian Art: Black, Eskimo, Indian? True or False," "Art Is for Which People: White People?" and "AGO ≠ Honesty." The coverage in the AGO's archive file, the mainstream newspapers, and the committee documents contains no information on this counter-protest. Simultaneously, while the Committee to Strengthen Canadian Culture was concerned with what was happening inside the AGO, outside, the gallery's presence in a traditionally ethnically diverse and working-class Chinatown neighbourhood was having a ripple effect that was driving residents and businesses out in a process of gentrification.[24] In an article published at the time, consultant Duncan Cameron, who will show up repeatedly in chapter 2, glibly notes,

> there are some concerns in the community surrounding the gallery that the expansion is changing the character of the neighborhood. It is inevitable. For several decades it has been clear that the area between the art gallery and the University of Toronto campus would change radically as both the university and the gallery grew ... One can sympathize with long-term residents, who may find themselves displaced, but I see no alternative to the inevitable.[25]

The issues involved in the 1972 and 1974 protests at the AGO return repeatedly in this book. Cultural nationalism was and remains both an instigator of and a limiting factor for numerous altercations at galleries and museums. The massive amount of labour that CAR undertook to secure rights for artists remains its legacy and ongoing project.[26] But looking back, it is easy to see that the committee (supported by the nationalism inherent to CAR), though radical in its time, was blind to its own limitations. While the 1972 action sought to open the gallery and Canadian art establishment to new voices, it was certainly not unsettling the central tenets of Eurocentric museum culture but was in fact working to "reinforce and center whiteness" even as they positioned themselves as outsiders to the gallery's vision.[27] The erasure of protests by racialized demonstrators from the mainstream record is indicative of this process. So too are issues of gentrification, which underlie many of the resistances that coalesce around global museum-building projects. Chapter 2 fills in a largely occluded history of contentious politics at the thresholds of museums and galleries in Canada – like the actions described here, the connection of issues across the decades is present.

Part One

Context

2

Protest at the Threshold: A Short History of Contentious Politics at Canadian Museums, 1900–96

This chapter provides an overview of protests in and against Canadian museums from the 1900s through to the 1990s. There are four major waves of action, the first from the 1900s to the 1960s and dedicated largely to debates over what museums and galleries should display and collect, the second in the 1960s and 1970s in support of left-wing efforts to destabilize the elitism of many institutions, the third in the late 1980s and early 1990s around issues of representation, identity, and belonging, and the fourth, covered in the case studies in part 2 of the book, dating from 2002 to the present and focused on issues of sponsorship, settler nationalism, and gentrification. In this chapter, I analyze the contested (and contestable) zone of the museum, looking variously at the ways museums have been targeted for protest and intervention. As noted in the introduction, my goal in filling in this history is to provide the backdrop to the second half of the book but also to argue that when seen together, the number of political actions at the entrances of museums, and occasionally crossing the threshold, is so great that they cannot and should not be considered anomalous. Cultural institutions are, I suggest, one place where culture and politics touch: I see this as a reworking and updating of James Clifford's more ethnographic approach to museums as "contact zones" where different cultures can engage in processes of exchange, contestation, and collaboration.[1] This chapter and the one that follows are organized through a spatial logic. Chapter 2 focuses on the threshold, courtyards, entranceways, and outside spaces where protests tend to unfold at museums. Chapter 3 then turns to the architectural features of new museums or newly renovated institutions, moving into the lobby and past the panels thanking donors and into the exhibition spaces. Finally, we arrive at the archives, where I examine how museums in Canada have tended to resist collecting protest ephemera, though that may be changing.

Australian museum audience analyst Linda Ferguson has helpfully categorized the different kinds of actions against museums. Her classification includes "direct intercession," when an individual or group directly contacts a museum, asking for a change to be made; "indirect intercession," or putting pressure on a museum through a third party (for example, via a letter-writing campaign or lobbying members of Parliament); "publicity," or drawing attention to an issue through statements to the media, through social media, interviews, and so on; "mobilization of other interest groups" as a way to gain strength and visibility (this might also be done in combination with any of the other categories); and "picketing," when, as Ferguson notes, "protesters take their argument and locate it on the borders of the museum's own space, making their 'attack' at the very boundaries of the institution."[2] Ferguson also includes "public demo or rally" in her classification as well as "boycott" and "harnessing other powerful establishments" (such as organized religion, other museums, political systems, and so on). Ferguson's point is that there are numerous ways and means through which museums are targeted, with greater or lesser consequence for the institution. All of these and more show up in Canadian institutions, and I concentrate primarily on those actions with public presence and long-term consequences.

Threshold

Protest in or about museums first shows up in Canadian newspapers in reports on actions that did not take place in Canada. Instead, there is an obvious captivation with suffragists foiled (and not) by police in their attempts to attack exhibitions at the British Museum just before the First World War.[3] According to Suzanne Macleod, in the 1910s numerous museums in London, UK, and elsewhere closed their doors to women following demonstrations outside and attacks by suffragists on art within.[4] Macleod writes:

> At the British Museum, women could gain access if they were accompanied by a man or, if unaccompanied, could only gain access with a letter of recommendation from a gentleman. In addition to the presence of police and plain clothes detectives in the National Gallery from early 1913, identification portraits of "known militant suffragettes" were issued by the police in 1914 and were distributed to warding staff in the National Portrait Gallery.[5]

Newspapers in Canada demonstrate a great deal of fascination with Mary Richardson, a former citizen of Belleville, Ontario, who, in March 1914 slashed Velazquez's *Venus de Rokeby* painting in anger at the imprisonment of suffragist Emmeline Pankhurst.[6] A great deal of column space in Canadian newspapers was devoted to reporting on the destruction of artworks by women trying to secure the vote, and though Richardson was formerly a Canadian citizen, there seems to have been little fear that such actions might take place at Canadian institutions.

In early twentieth-century Canada, especially around 1910, as institutions such as the National Gallery of Canada and the National Museum of Man were expanded and became more stable, grumblings about museums concerned the design and state of a series of new institutions in the capital city.[7] Barbara J. Black has convincingly argued that one of the goals of nineteenth-century museums in Britain was to engage in "educating and elevating people so as to eliminate a crowd mentality."[8] Though not as clearly stated, debates in museums in Canada at the turn of the century had much to do with producing "upstanding" citizens (of the sort who would not slash paintings, one imagines). Ideological debates took place in the gallery and museum in a disguised sense, usually through fights over the place of modernist art in traditional settings. I say disguised but not lacking in ideological conviction. Indeed, from 1910 right up to the present day, squabbles over aesthetics have characterized public debate over the role of museums in Canada. From the 1910s to the 1930s, the debate focused on abstract versus illusionistic art, with conservative commentators dismissing an introduction of modernist art to galleries as tantamount to "a wholly false set of artistic standards and the cluttering of art galleries with rubbish that is either crude or incompetent."[9] This kind of value judgment is found more than sixty years later in vocal critiques of the National Gallery's purchase of Barnett Newman's abstract expressionist *Voice of Fire* in 1990.[10] *Plus ça change*. Nevertheless, from the 1910s to the 1930s, such debates coalesced around the then-nascent Group of Seven, with letters to the editor asking that their works "be relegated to the furnace."[11] In 1932, 118 artists, mostly associated with the Royal Canadian Academy of Arts, signed a petition against modernist trends in painting ("a type of art originating in the grotesque experiments of Cezanne [*sic*], Gauguin and other Frenchmen")[12] and the acquisition of such works by the National Gallery,[13] an action that was met with an answering petition signed by 300 arguing that the Group of Seven and the National Gallery had "forged a new Canadian art."[14]

Divisive arguments over the role of museums in Canada and their purpose in collecting art began in the 1910s, gained steam in the 1930s, and were still present in the 1940s and even 1950s, though by then the bushwhacking art and mythos of the Group of Seven had formed the basis of an anti-modernist narrative of

Canadian nationhood.[15] By the 1930s, the now former members of the Group of Seven, along with their supporters (such as lawyer and diplomat Vincent Massey), were pushing hard for art "naturally reflecting Canadian atmosphere, so that we may be aware of what our country means."[16] Such sentiments would undergird a great deal of cultural policy, from the 1951 Massey Commission to the cultural brokering efforts of the National Gallery of Canada. An important part of that myth is the Group's steadfast refusal to bow to the reaction of the conservative establishment and the often rollicking battles that took place in the newspapers, galleries, and cultural establishments of Toronto and Ottawa.[17]

These stories are well known, and the conflicting sycophantic embrace and unrelenting criticism of the Group have both been vitally important to the study of visual culture in Canada. I'd like to reposition these readings slightly by situating the Group's vicious dismissal by a conservative elite and their championing by the National Gallery of Canada as a foreshadowing of negotiations over belonging in the museum that would, as Ruth Phillips has noted, later characterize the museum sphere in Canada. Importantly, however, while the National Gallery supported the avant-garde in this case, using its clout to privilege modernist styles over traditional ones, as soon as the issues at stake were less about paint on canvas and more about capitalism, race, or cultural oppression, authoritative galleries and museums in Canada tended to be much less willing to lend their support. This is a recognition of Mieke Bal's 1992 comment with regard to the American Museum of Natural History that the "museum is a product of colonialism in a postcolonial era."[18] Thus it was that the radical Group of Seven became staid, while the museum itself became a site of contention. Reporter Kay Kritzwiser criticized the Group in the 1970s, noting, "Out of that decade of depression [the 1930s], relief offices, breadlines and protest, the Canadian painters presumably absorbed very little to give back as historical documentation on canvas."[19] I agree but also find in those early ideological skirmishes over the application of paint to canvas the seeds of battles that were to come: museums and galleries in Canada defended their thresholds, remaining fairly open to mild aesthetic experimentation[20] but closed to the politics that might be behind those experiments.

In the 1930s and 1940s, aesthetic concerns and political action rarely intersected at museums, even though this was a time of massive protests: anti-Depression, anti-war, pro-war, anti-Red and pro-Bolshevik sentiments, massive labour rallies, women's rights and suffrage, and the nascent beginnings of civil rights movements were all found in Canadian cities. Even when unemployed men occupied the Vancouver Art Gallery in 1938 to protest the federal government's lack of action on their behalf,[21] they chose the gallery mostly because it was a convenient location on the march route. The actual targeting of museums, such as was happening in the UK and that is present in Canada from the late 1960s on, was not present in earlier decades or at least was not reported in the mainstream media.[22]

In the 1940s and 1950s, and even through most of the 1960s, while massive social changes took place, museums were largely peaceful places.[23] By the late 1960s, however, everything had changed. "What's this? Barricades around the entrance to the Art Gallery of Ontario? Sandbags blocking the doors of the Royal Ontario Museum? Smelly long-haired students sitting in before our revered Rembrandt? Outraged curators and art historians manning the museum front?"[24] So begins a 1970 article by Kritzwiser titled "Are Museums the New Target for Youth?" The article draws on an interview with Duncan F. Cameron (then national director of the Canadian Conference of the Arts, president of Janus Museum Consultants Ltd, and a Canadian museologist and cultural resources consultant). "We have no real awareness of how volatile an issue this is," Cameron says. "Art schools, galleries, museums are going to be the action centres. We might as well get ready for it before we have the riots."[25] All of a sudden, the ideological debates that pitted the Royal Canadian Academy against the Group of Seven came home to roost as Cameron argued that museums had come to be seen as elite institutions, pointing to left-wing students and artists who "believe that the museum represents the imposition of a bourgeois culture on the masses ... In Europe, there are a lot of leftwing young liberals who believe that museums are establishment fortresses in the class war. They argue that museums have been temples too long."[26] In addition, experimental artists were breaking down the boundaries of the museum, wanting "art to become part of the social-political conflict today."[27] But, Cameron argues, "Sociologically, the temple and the forum have two different functions. We don't sanctify the experiment in history in the art gallery. When the art of the moment is moved into the museum, you're in trouble. A museum is a learning place, a reference library. You can't build action into it."[28] Cameron is referencing an argument that would form the foundation of his 1971 article "The Museum: A Temple or the Forum?," now a mainstay in museum studies. In the influential article, he argues that museums have an identity crisis: are they temples like churches where the worship of unchanging culture could take place? Or are they forums where a variety of public activities and radical aesthetic experimentation could take place? One suspects, looking back on his article, that his point in this interview is that social activism is fine, but the art gallery or museum is not the place for it (his argument, really, is that museums need to improve by becoming better temples rather than becoming forums).[29]

And yet he was not alone in his qualms. Just down the street from the AGO, Peter Swann, then director of the Royal Ontario Museum (ROM), was voicing similar concerns. In an op-ed in the *Globe and Mail* published not long after the Toronto group The Voice of Women held a series of anti-nuclear vigils and protests at the museum entrance,[30] Swann noted that meetings of the American Association of Museums in New York, which he had just attended, "were disrupted and at times broken up by left-wing demonstrations."[31] Swann's piece is lengthy but worth exploring in some depth. He writes:

> [Museums] thought they were secure. Now, in a period of mounting social crisis and hostility, these institutions come under the same attack as the industrial complex – threatened by bombs, riots, demonstrations, pressured to respond to the demands of discontented classes and a revolutionary generation. They are very vulnerable. Their buildings form perfect stages for public protest – far more effective backdrops than the relatively isolated university campuses. Yet the attack is only partly against the institutions. The dissidents feel they belong to the people even if they do not respond quickly to their demands and to their wishes to use them to do their creative things. But the sharpest attack is reserved for what they call the Cultural Establishment which runs them – against the trustees whom they regard as the real enemy and whose wealth or political pull they claim has given them undeserved power and privilege in what should be a democratic society.[32]

He concludes, "The atmosphere is becoming more tense and politically more explosive every month … What is happening in the United State [*sic*] may well come to Canada … We in Canada may have a year or so of grace. Will we do anything to deal with the situation? We have been warned. We could be just in time to avoid this particular danger to our institutions and their treasures."[33]

In his well-known 1971 article, Cameron both agrees and does not. "The Museum" is so often cited for its comparison of temples and forums and so seldom for its description of protests in Europe that I quote it at length here. Cameron writes:

> The argument that there can be no progress in the arts, or in the democratization of the arts, until the Louvre is burned is a cliché in the West European radical art movement. There is protest against the maintenance of great public museums which do nothing more than enshrine the evidence of bourgeois and aristocratic domination of society, protest against arts education in which bourgeois values, exemplified by the Louvre, are imposed on the masses. One may or may not wish to use the vocabulary of radical protest and I doubt that many in the museum world wish to set fire to the Louvre, but I do feel that it must be conceded that the protest against museums and art galleries does have a basis in reality and that museum reform is long overdue.[34]

Cameron concludes that protester demands can be much better addressed by "reform[ing] … the museum as temple … [to make] museums … relevant … there must be concurrent creation of forums for confrontation, experimentation and debate, where the forums are related but discrete institutions."[35] For Cameron, push back could and would happen, and his argument about museums as temples or forums was at least partially concerned with how museums could avoid becoming targets.

Swann and Cameron's fears were not groundless.[36] In the US, massive protests against the Vietnam War defined the moment, as did the Black Power movement, the growing women's rights movement, and the American Indian Movement (AIM). The Artists' Protest Committee (based in Los Angeles) had organized demonstrations against US military action in Vietnam outside the Los Angeles County Art Museum and the RAND Corporation, and also in that city in 1966, 418 artists had come together to build the "Artists' Tower of Protest." Just a year later, artists in New York organized "Angry Arts Week," a series of protests and exhibitions in New York City galleries.[37] From the late 1960s through to 1971, the Art Workers' Coalition in New York made broad demands of museums, insisting that they become more accountable to artists and to their own political role and position (for example, by admitting to the political clout and capital concerns of their board members).[38] The Guerrilla Art Action Group, founded in 1969 in order to reveal the MOMA's relationship with Governor Nelson Rockefeller (who had links to the war in Vietnam) staged a number of actions at the MOMA and other museums in New York City under the banner *Call for the Immediate Resignation of All the Rockefellers from the Board of Trustees of The Museum of Modern Art*, including a performance intervention that involved spilling pig's blood over the floor of the MOMA and a mock gunfight in the gallery's foyer.[39] The group remained active until 1976. Almost 40 artists demonstrated outside of the Metropolitan Museum in 1969 against the exhibition *Harlem on My Mind*. According to Susan J. Cahan's book, which traces a number of actions by Black artists in New York in the late 1960s, "the Black Emergency Cultural Coalition argued that the exhibition profoundly misrepresented African American culture in Harlem."[40] Cahan notes, "The artists jolted the Metropolitan Museum out of the past and brought the civil rights movement to the museum's front door."[41] But despite pickets and demonstrations, museums such as the Met, the MOMA, and the Whitney were willing to include the work of Black artists in exhibitions but not to hire curators of colour.[42]

Protest inspired by actions in New York and elsewhere would come to Canada later than Swann and Cameron expected. But in the late 1960s, performative debates over traditional vs contemporary art in the gallery continued. In 1967, it was

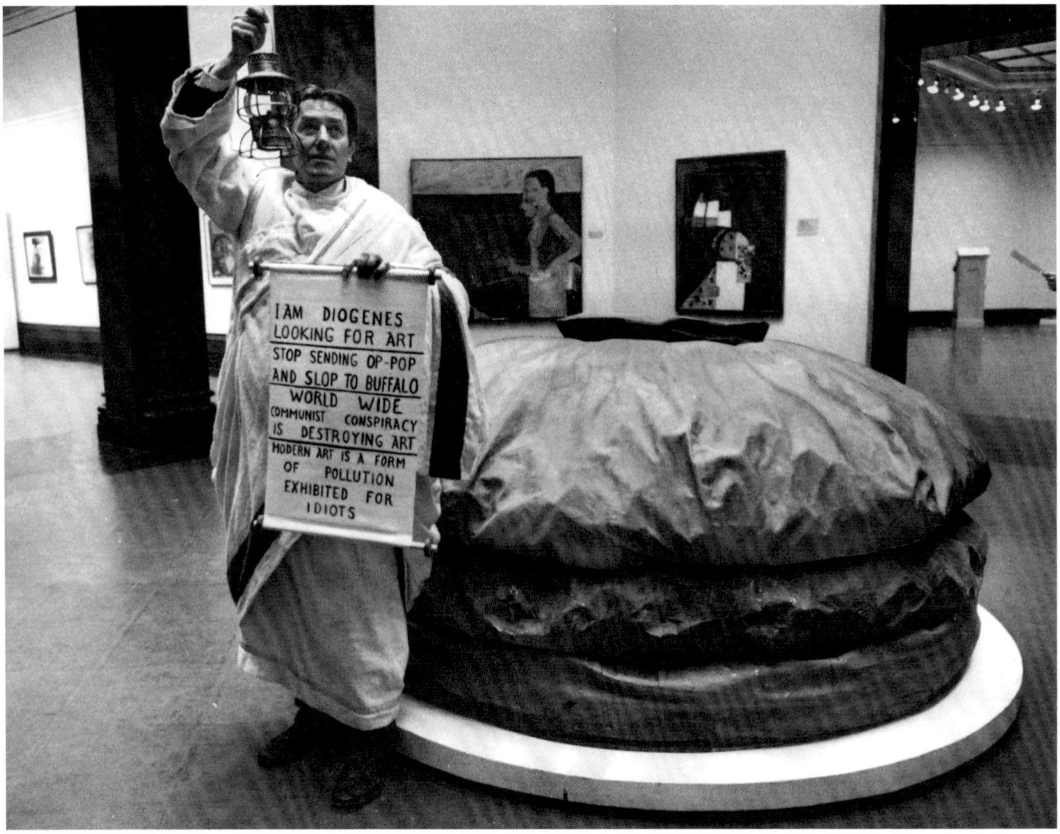

Figure 2.1
Desperate as Diogenes, 18 April 1967.

pop artist Claes Oldenburg's well-known *Floor Burger* (literally, a giant burger installed on the floor, made from painted and stuffed canvas) that drew attention. Art students from Central Technical School marched a giant plywood ketchup bottle to the AGO and "installed" it along with their protest signs "Give Oldenburger the works" and "Don't burger up our gallery." They attempted to donate the bottle to the gallery, which declined the offer.[43] As reporter James Adams notes, a major 1966 controversy over the installation of British artist Henry Moore's abstract sculpture *The Archer* in front of City Hall in Toronto was still recent memory at the time of the ketchup incident.[44] Director of the AGO William Withrow was careful to time a press release that clearly stated tax dollars had not been used for the purchase of Oldenburg's work, attempting to diffuse the situation. When questioned about the protest, Oldenburg responded of the giant ketchup bottle: "They should have made it out of something soft."[45] A write-up on the AGO's current website suggests that the action against *Floor Burger* was indeed the continuation of the ideological debate over modern versus traditional art. Withrow's comments support this interpretation, as does an image, published in the *Toronto Star*, of a lone protester dressed as the ancient Greek philosopher Diogenes, known for criticizing what he saw as the corrupt cultural and social values of Athens. "Modern Art Is a Form of Pollution Exhibited for Idiots," reads his sign. The timing, however, suggests that students may also have been concerned that such a large portion of the gallery's acquisition budget was going to a US-American artist rather than a Canadian one. As shown in Interstices 1a and 3c, the late 1960s and early 1970s was a time when left-wing politics coincided with anti-Americanism and the promotion of Canadian artworks by living artists as deserving of support.[46]

These were tumultuous times. In 1970, Prime Minister Pierre Trudeau invoked the War Measures Act during the October Crisis in Quebec following the kidnapping of a British diplomat and a Quebec politician by the Front de libération du Québec (FLQ).[47] The FLQ, inspired by global liberation movements, had for some years engaged in anti-colonial actions, protests, and interventions aimed at throwing off centuries of Anglo oppression. For a time in the early 1970s, the group achieved a level of organization and targeted violence rarely seen in Canada (although they tended not to target museums, and thus their presence in this book is muted).

Many Canadian artists outside of Quebec had begun to develop a New-Left political stance, one that embraced an anti-war, anti-corporate, and often anti-American politics. Thus it was that in 1972 Swann's fears seemed to come to fruition. A number of artists, among them Joyce Wieland and Michael Snow, stormed the offices of the AGO, protesting the gallery's hiring of an American, Richard Wattenmaker, as chief curator, an action covered in further detail in Interstice 1a. The artists were not successful in their aims, and the protest was dismissed largely as a stunt.

This action, and a number of others that involved crashing AGO board meetings to demand that the museum "stop being a private club of the rich,"[48] were organized by members of Canadian Artists Representation (CAR), an initiative catalyzed by London, Ontario, artist Jack Chambers to form a loosely organized union of artists that worked for copyright reform, compensation of artists for reproductions of their work, exhibition fees, and taxation reform, culminating in attempts to encourage a subsidized guaranteed income for artists.[49] CAR was also deeply involved in nationalist politics, pushing hard for the hiring of Canadians to teach fine arts and for Canadian art history to be taught at universities. CAR actions were indicative of the kind of cultural nationalist position deeply tied to a protectionist, anti-capitalist politics in Canada that lasted well into the 2000s. This politics reached its zenith in the late 1960s and early 1970s in the Canadian art world prior to succumbing on the one hand to global free trade movements and on the other to standpoint politics, which rightly pointed to the active exclusivity of movements that privileged "Canadian-Canadian" viewpoints.

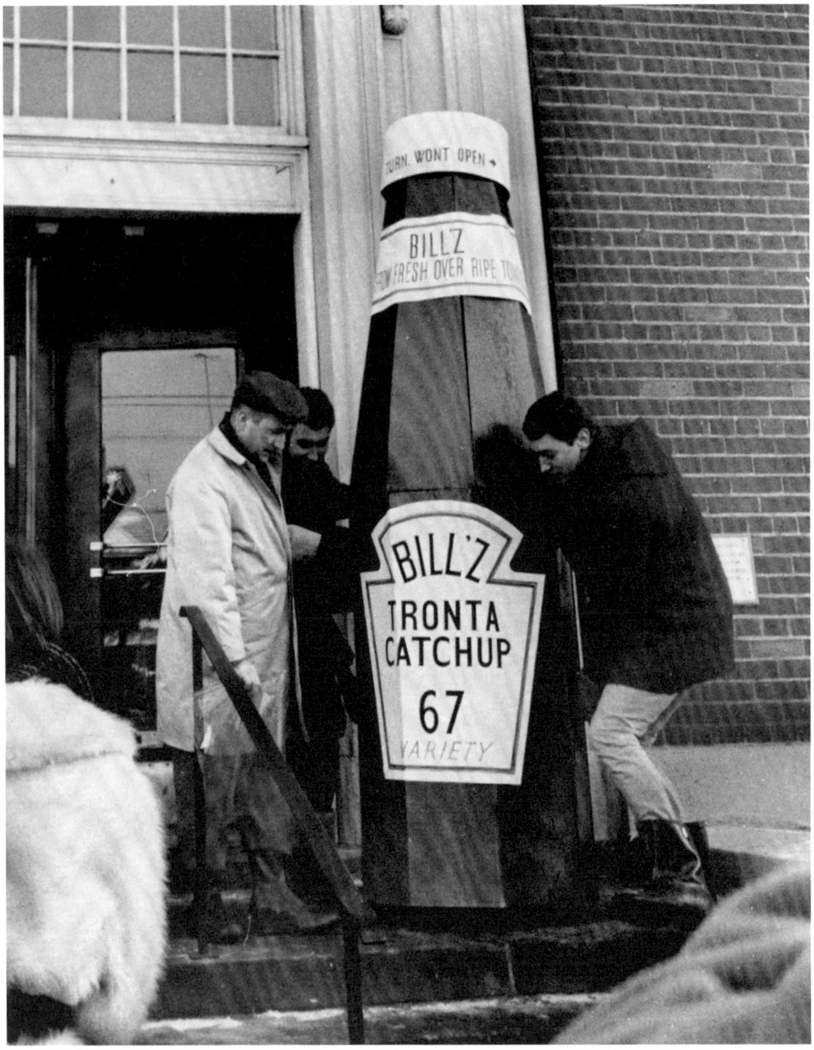

Figures 2.2 above and 2.3 opposite
Students protest AGO purchase of Claes Oldenburg's *Floor Burger* and the *Dine, Oldenburg, Segal: Painting/Sculpture* exhibition (14 January–12 February 1967), 14 January 1967.

Swann was right, however, that activists would target the "Cultural Establishment." "Canada is seventy-two per cent owned by the U.S. industrial complex," reads an inter-title to Wieland's 1968 anti-Vietnam film *Rat Life and Diet*, an epic story of draft-dodging rats (actually gerbils) crossing the US border to Canada and finding an organic farming paradise on the other side. Wieland's use of such statistics was not uncommon: artists were extremely well informed about the interwovenness of Canadian and especially US, but also British, industrial complexes, and a nascent anti-capitalist politics informed many of their protests. Cameron also makes note of the work of cutting-edge artists who might question the status

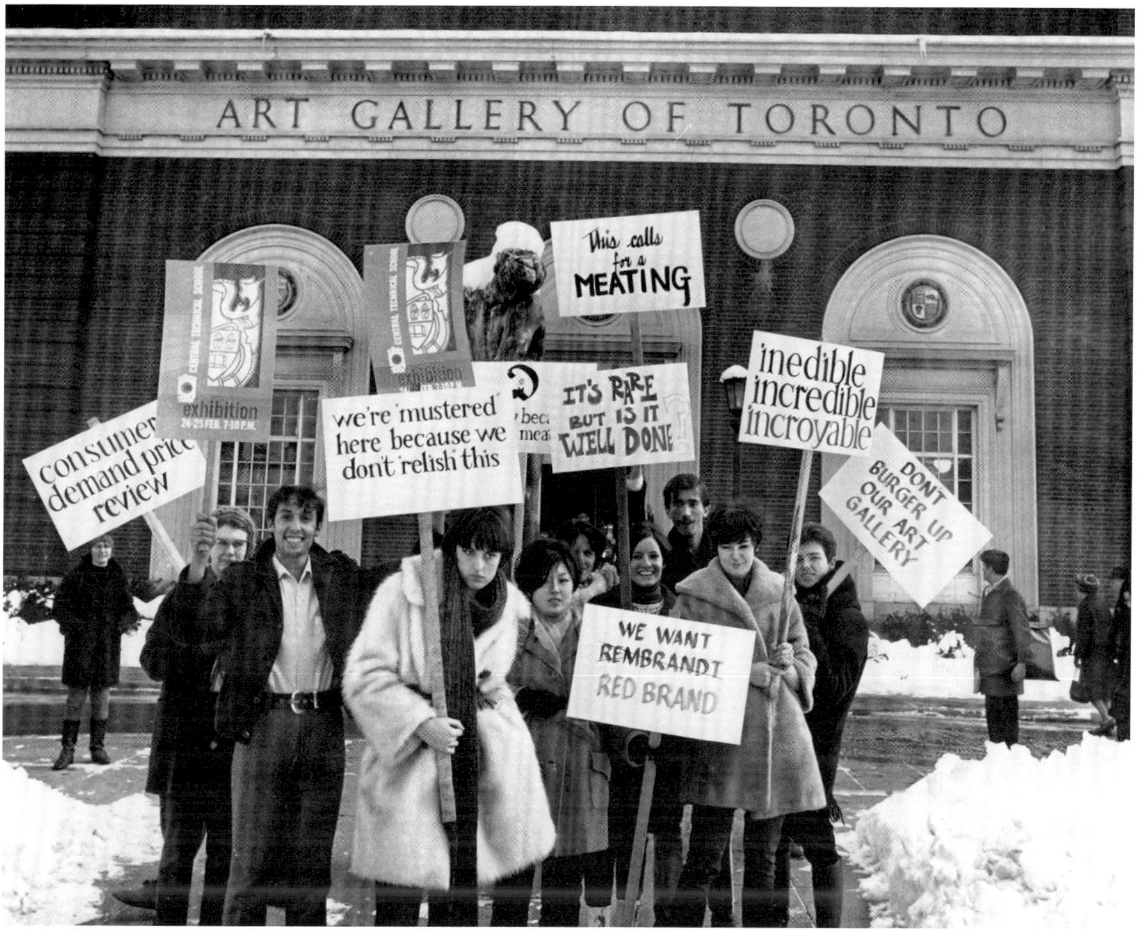

quo. Quoting a York University professor, Cameron asks, "Will the establishment finance the revolution?" a question he answers by stating, "the establishment (and by that is meant the corporations and governments and private individuals) must in effect finance the revolution by creating opportunities for the artists and the critics of society to produce, to be heard, to be seen, and to confront established values and institutions."[50]

In 1976, Carol Condé and Karl Beveridge's exhibition *It's Still Privileged Art* opened at the AGO. The exhibition consisted of a series of posters and a catalogue of cartoons that document the working and living conditions of artists. The exhibition seemed to have more in common with Soviet socialist realism than with the minimalist art that had been expected for the show. As a whole, *It's Still Privileged Art* documented the couple's move from formalist to political artists, their disavowal of the art market, and their questioning of whether institutions such as major museums could be in any way viable locales for the production and dissemination of activist art.[51] ART MUST BECOME RESPONSIBLE FOR ITS POLITICS,

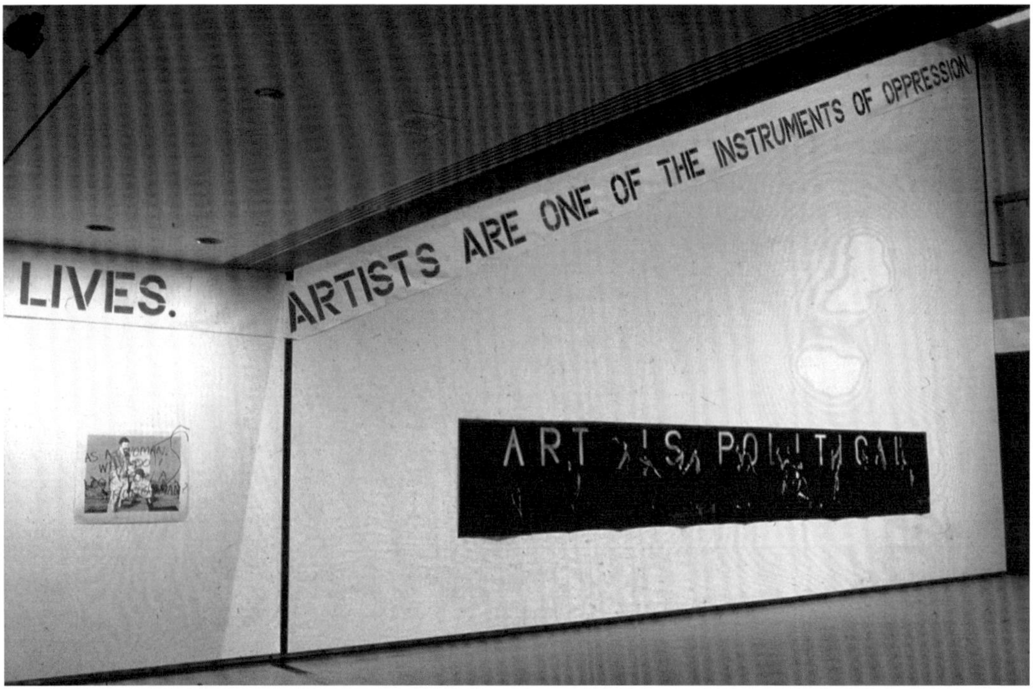

Figure 2.4
Installation view of Carol Condé and Karl Beveridge exhibition, *It's Still Privileged Art* (Art Gallery of Ontario, 24 January–29 February 1976).

declared one of the captions. As Jan Allen writes, "In what amounted to a convulsive rejection of formal aesthetics and the art market of the day, they turned their attention to the mechanics of the art system and the ways in which art and artists might reposition themselves to identify and bring to light ignored and suppressed issues."[52] Not surprisingly *It's Still Privileged Art* was remarkably provocative.[53] The catalogue was removed from the gallery bookstore, the sponsor pulled out, and as Dot Tuer later wrote, "It was one thing to be an artist with politics, it was another matter altogether to incorporate a call to social revolution as the transparent theme of an exhibition."[54] One wonders if this show would have fit with Cameron's idea that "forums" rather than museums were needed for the support of "the most radical innovations in art forms, the most controversial interpretations of history, or our own society ..."[55] In 1971, Cameron was, on the whole, extremely supportive of artists pushing at the status quo but felt that a specially designated exhibition hall, rather than a temple-like museum such as the AGO, was the appropriate venue for exhibitions such as *It's Still Privileged Art*.[56]

Given the prevalence and spread of contemporary art galleries globally, and the growth of the contemporary art market, it is hard to remember that at the time

Cameron was writing, contemporary experimental and conceptual art was often not shown in museums and establishment galleries and that its inclusion was seen as something of a radical gesture. As with his conclusion in the newspaper article quoted above, Cameron felt that the gallery was not the place for *artistic* experimentation, which he collapses into political radicalism. Though temples and forums are both necessary, they are not one and the same. His argument really applies more to aesthetic radicalism than to political, the two in his mind and in several actions outside and at museums in the 1960s and 1970s being closely intertwined. Without irony or judgment, Cameron concludes "the forum is where battles are fought, the temple is where the victors rest."[57]

Also in 1976, 250 people picketed outside the AGO to draw attention to Reed Paper's sponsorship of the exhibition *Changing Visions: The Canadian Landscape*. (This action is covered in detail in Interstice 3c.) Reed Paper was a subsidiary of British-owned Dryden Chemical, and Dryden Chemical had been dumping mercury and untreated wastes into the English-Wabigoon river system of northwestern Ontario through the 1960s.[58] Mercury poisoning destroyed the commercial and sustenance fisheries, deeply affecting the population of the Asubpeeschoseewagong First Nation in Grassy Narrows, many of whom showed symptoms of mercury poisoning. Many of those who demonstrated outside the AGO in 1976 were the same people who had organized against the hiring of Wattenmaker, showing how artists during this period perceived themselves as both a part of and outside of the authoritative museum system. Several members of CAR wrote to the AGO asking to have their work removed from *Changing Visions*.

The prime motivation for the artists protesting the exhibition in 1976 was the poisoning of the environment on the part of a seemingly uncaring corporation. Though settler artists had been involved in fundraising for Cree, Inuit, and Kaskapi displaced by the massive hydroelectric James Bay project in northern Quebec in the mid-1970s,[59] overlap between Indigenous and non-Indigenous artists' concerns tended to be incidental or to adopt a settler framing (for example, by settler artists fighting *for* rather than fighting *with* Indigenous peoples and causes).[60] Indeed, for the most part, "The New Left emphatically asserted that nationalism in a Canadian context could be progressive, emancipatory, countercultural, and ultimately socialist."[61] Indigenous water and land protectors, and those struggling to have land claims acknowledged, would likely have disagreed.[62]

Despite the interventions described above, the actions in Canada in the 1960s and 1970s never reached the level of organization of those in the United States, particularly those undertaken by the Art Workers' Coalition. The so-called "conscience of the Art Establishment," in the late 1960s and early 1970s, the AWC demanded that museums speak out against racism, war, and repression.[63] They actively drew links between the boards of museums such as the MOMA and the war in Vietnam, and they also took museums on in terms of accessibility and opening hours, admission fees, the representation of women, Black, and Puerto Rican artists, and artists' control over their work, calling for an altogether "more open-minded and democratic museum."[64] Where Canadian artists succeeded was through the formation of CAR (later renamed CARFAC) and the institution of pay schedules for artists – a goal that remains well out of reach in the US, despite groups such as W.A.G.E. and the recent Occupy Debt.

On the other hand, despite Swann's warnings and despite the growing number of actions, museums seemed largely unprepared, reacting first by ignoring actions and, if they grew in size, by pushing back. In the US, though there were several attempts (primarily by the Whitney and MOMA) to engage with the AWC, the same was not true for pressures coming from traditionally marginalized groups. In her book on Black protesters working with and against museums in New York City, Cahan demonstrates with great detail and clarity that the establishment present in museums was not, in the 1960s and 1970s, prepared to give up power.[65] A similar pattern was visible in Canada.

As it turns out, aside from a few skirmishes, Swann and Cameron vastly overstated their fears of student and left-wing radicals. Museums would, indeed, be targeted for political action, but that action came most forcefully from a direction that, at least in archival information still available today, Swann, Cameron, and most of the artists mentioned above largely overlooked.

Museums and Indigenous Resistance

For Indigenous peoples living in Canada, 1967 marked a sea change moment in resistance to prevailing salvage paradigm depictions of disappearing Native life in museums. The Indians of Canada Pavilion at Expo 67 signalled a broad shift in Indigenous self-representation that in turn fed a decades-long struggle to advocate for repatriation of objects and rights to self-representation, the culmination of which I analyze in chapter 5. In an essay on Expo 67, Ruth Phillips and Sherry Brydon trace the remarkable emergence of the Indians of Canada Pavilion from

> a traditional suffocating story of aboriginal presence only in Canada's pre-Confederation past overseen by Anglo-Canadians, confined to the forests and insupportable in the present ... to ... a radical intervention in the Expo and Canadian political scene, mounted, overseen and curated by a diverse group of First peoples with varied aims but a common goal.[66]

In this case, the museum itself was a protest, a refusal to kowtow either to stereotypical depictions of First Nations culture or to Expo's emphasis on positive nationalism.[67] Seneca artist and curator Tom Hill (who later became museum director of the Woodland Cultural Centre in Brantford, Ontario) wrote, "The government really wanted a positive image in that pavilion and what they got was the truth. That's what really shocked them the most."[68] The Indians of Canada Pavilion focused on a refusal to assimilate, forward-looking politics, and radical self-empowerment. As Phillips noted years later, "many Indigenous people who worked on the pavilion have identified the experience as a formative moment in the development of an activist Indian cultural politics."[69] The pavilion was a success, attracting 15,000 visitors daily and receiving significant positive feedback, possibly to the surprise of the Department of Indian Affairs and Northern Development.[70]

However, the 1967 pavilion also should not be seen to have emerged in a vacuum. While I stated at the opening that the first visible protests against Canadian museums did not occur until well into the twentieth century, this statement does not reflect long-term and ongoing critique of the *collecting* practices undertaken by many institutions large and small in Canada. Historian Michelle Hamilton documents how as early as 1797 there are instances of Indigenous peoples objecting to the desecration of graves. In some cases, museum and government officials did try to stop the practice. Laws were passed to prevent grave-robbing, but they were rarely enforced.[71] And in many cases, digging in burial sites was legal because they were considered to be property of the Crown.[72] In many if not most instances, the legal digging up of burial sites, often by museum-employed anthropologists, was pervasive and continued through to the 1990s.[73]

When there were protests, the Department of Indian Affairs looked at the intent of the collector. If the digging had been a "scientific endeavour," then typically it was assumed that the action had prevented looting and was for the greater good – the artefacts were safer in museums than they were in the ground. As Hamilton notes, "The presumption was that museums or the members of historical societies – not amateurs, or even Aboriginal communities – were the proper stewards of Aboriginal graves."[74]

Real change in establishment museums would not come until near the end of the twentieth century.[75] In 1976, following the ROM's removal of bones from a seventeenth-century Neutral burial site in Grimsby, Ontario, ten members of the American Indian Movement staged a sit-in at the ROM, demanding the return and reburial of the bones.[76] Though the sit-in was only moderately successful (the bones were eventually returned, but a rift developed between Six Nations leadership and AIM), the AIM protesters were told that "bones will never again be removed from Indian graves in Ontario,"[77] accompanied by an admission from the chief archaeologist at the ROM, Douglas Tushingham, that "We have been quite wrong."[78] Tushingham's statement was at odds with the opinions of numerous other museum personnel, who argued that the bones should not be returned because they held important scientific evidence or because, at thousands of years old, there was no link to contemporary descendants.[79] Obviously, those who called for the return of the remains of their ancestors felt differently.

The 1976 sit-in led to other demands, among them a 1977 request from Michel Gros-Louis of the Wendat of Jeune-Lorette in Quebec asking for the return of the remains of more than 500 people. The bones were held at the ROM and had been excavated in 1947. Hamilton outlines how, "in 1999, the bones were returned, and the ownership of the site transferred to the Lorette band, though the museum considered his request to be a political, rather than a spiritual, bid."[80] A number of requests for the return of ancestral remains were made in the 1970s, but typically it was not until the 1990s and 2000s that ancestral remains were returned from the ROM, the Canadian Museum of Civilization (now the Canadian Museum of History), and elsewhere.[81]

Thus, in 1978, frustrated with slow progress and resistance to their requests, some of those who had taken part in the ROM sit-in organized "The Walk of the Living Dead" with the group Nations of Warriors. The walk began in Windsor at a disputed gravesite and travelled to Queen's Park in Toronto before moving to Kingston, where Nations of Warriors threatened to dig up the remains of Canada's first prime minister, Sir John A. Macdonald. The group additionally pledged to dig up a white cemetery and to display the remains in an "Indian Museum" in a tent pitched on the site.[82] In 1978, and indeed until 1992, settler cemeteries were protected by provincial legislation that made it an offence to disinter remains without permission and supervision by a coroner. First Nations' burial grounds were not accorded the same rights.[83] Said Alec Akiwenzie of the Nations of Warriors, "They were after us alive and now they're after us dead."[84]

Burial grounds remain to this day a source of dispute. It is, in fact, possible to connect the events of 1976–78 in Grimsby and Kingston to the Kanehsatà:ke Resistance[85] in the summer of 1990 and the shooting of Dudley George at Ipperwash, Ontario, in 1995.[86] To disturb a burial ground is not just to disturb the bones of the dead but a crushing reminder of the imposition of a settler nation that took land, tore it up, and turned material histories and human remains over to museums. To assume there would be no reaction to the collection of remains was and is to assume a kind of assimilation and forgetting that never took place. And it is worth remembering that activism to protect burial sites and then to deal with museum collections emerged in the 1970s as the program of mass incarceration and forced assimilation in residential schools was slowly winding down.

Expecting action from the radical student left, the museums sector in Canada seemed totally unprepared for intervention and pressure from the source communities who had contributed the most to their collections (often under duress), First Nations.[87] Even today, the fields of Canadian art history and museum studies almost inevitably place the start of Indigenous action against museums in the very late 1980s and 1990s. But in truth, the groundwork was laid much earlier in protests of the 1960s, 1970s, and 1980s, including, for example, an occupation of the Museum of Anthropology in Vancouver in 1981 by First Nations people protesting a constitutional amendment that appeared designed to encourage the assimilation of all Indigenous peoples into the Canadian mainstream (Interstice 2b).[88] In later chapters, I look for points of contact between settlers and Indigenous peoples in recent interventions into museums. But my research on the 1970s and 1980s shows very little overlap, with the resistance at *Changing Visions* providing one moderate exception.

The Age of "Controversy": Protest at Museums in the 1980s and 1990s

Despite seeming ignorance of the long-standing attempts already underway to unsettle museums, through the 1980s cultural institutions were targeted and provided the backdrop for a number of actions. Occasionally, museums were onside with the actions, and occasionally they were targeted by them. In 1984, after the Vancouver Art Gallery cancelled artist Paul Wong's exhibition *Confused: Sexual Views* because of the sexual content of some of the videos, artists in Vancouver protested and then organized themselves into the Vancouver Artists' League, which attempted (unsuccessfully) to overthrow the gallery's Board of Directors. The league argued that the gallery was disconnected from local artists: "it is quickly becoming a museum, not a contemporary art gallery," they said.[89]

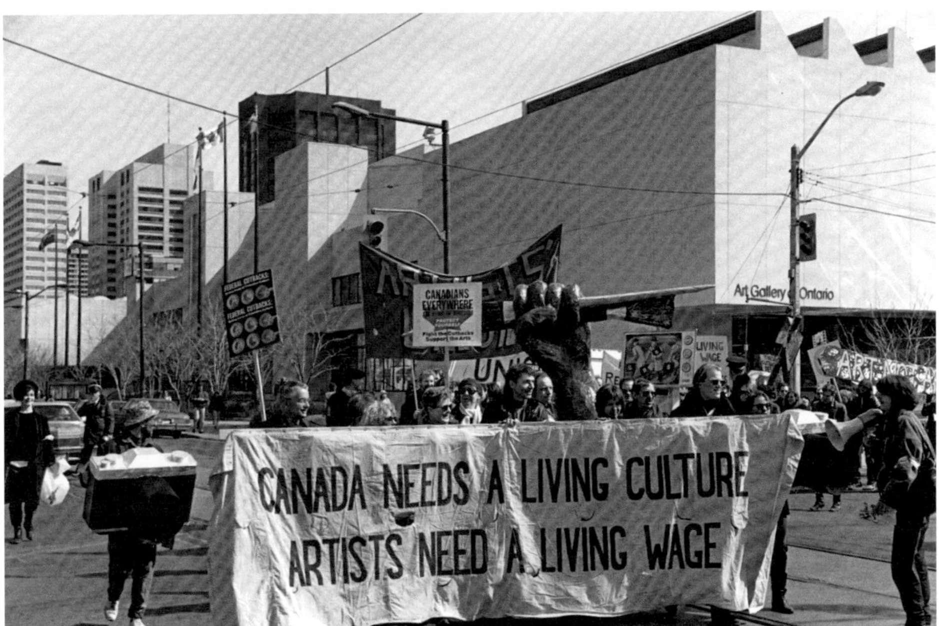

Figure 2.5
Independent Artists' Union Demonstration, "A Living Culture, a Living Wage," 16 March 1985.

"Tell the fat boys at the top, cultural cutbacks have got to stop." In 1985, 350 artists gathered outside the AGO, marching against federal government cuts in financial support to the arts. Seventy-five million dollars had been cut that year from the CBC and $3.5 million from the Canada Council.[90] The 1985 action outside the AGO was just one of many organized by the Independent Artists' Union (IAU), established by artists Condé and Beveridge with a central goal of attaining a living wage for artists.[91] "A Living Culture, a Living Wage" was the IAU's slogan. The IAU and CARFAC coexisted for some time, sometimes overlapping in their work on behalf of artists. Though it only lasted a handful of years, the IAU had a much more internationalist outlook than did CARFAC and resisted many of the nationalist narratives that CARFAC had at its core (Interstice 1a and 3c).[92]

The following year, activists in Toronto organized against the building of the Bata Shoe museum because Bata Ltd manufactured shoes in South Africa under apartheid.[93] In Edmonton, photographers held a demonstration outside the opening of *Contemporary Photography from the Collection of the National Film Board*, offering the public knives with which to slash at a wall of photographs and giving participants a chance to "help the federal Government destroy Canadian photography." The action was in reaction to the 1984 transfer of the still photography

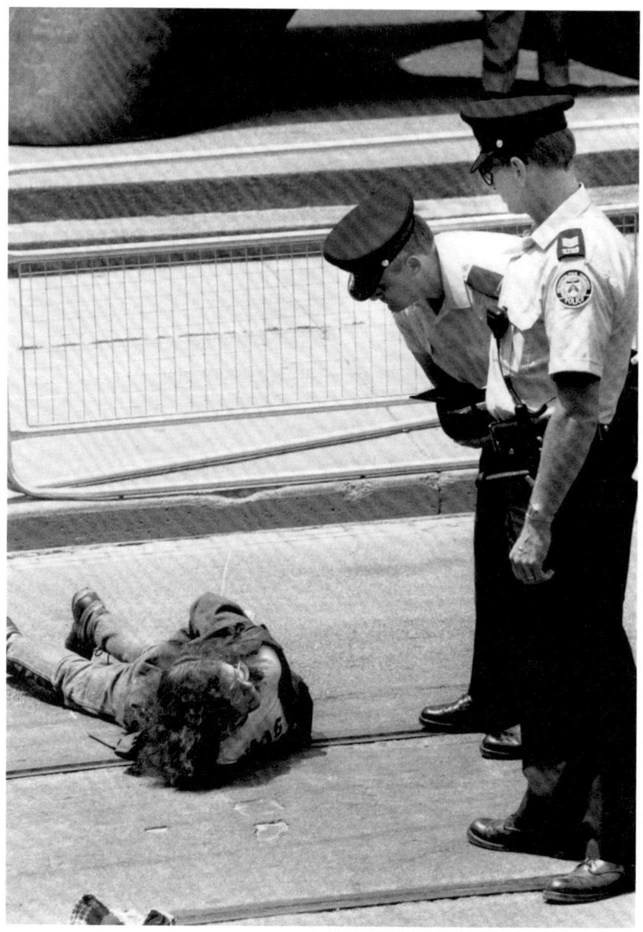

Figure 2.6
Immobilized. Protester lies face down with hands bound behind back during demonstration outside Art Gallery of Ontario where leaders were lunching. Twenty-eight were arrested in clash with police.

division from the National Film Board to the National Museum of Canada, which involved eliminating the budget to purchase new works.[94] In 1985, two Doukhobor women were arrested for burning down community museum buildings near Castlegar, BC. They accused the BC government of trying to destroy Doukhobor culture and targeted the museums for displaying their culture as if it belonged solely to the past.[95]

1988 also saw a protest march against G7 leaders that ended outside the AGO, where the leaders went for lunch. "The gallery, which had been turned into an armed camp for the lunch meeting, was blocked off by a wall of black-suited police backed up by a line of officers on horses."[96] Journalist Michael Valpy describes the arrests that followed: "This sometimes was put informally: 'What's your choice, dear? Up on your own or be carried?' One officer, bending down, knocked my glasses off (because I had my head under his knee trying to hear what he was saying to a protester). 'Very sorry about that,' he said. 'Quite all right, my fault,' I replied."[97] Later, Jack Layton, who became leader of the New Democratic Party but was then a Toronto city councillor, complained that the police were "flexing their muscles" unnecessarily when they arrested the protesters.[98] The dignity with which anti-G7 protesters were treated in 1988 offers a stark contrast with both the way that anti-capitalist protesters were treated in the very same location in 2010 at protests against the G20 and the way that Black protesters and their allies would be treated outside the Royal Ontario Museum only a year later, in 1989.

While most of these actions took place outside or at the threshold, between 1985 and 1988 numerous groups organized *with* museums and other arts organizations to resist the imposition of censorship under pornography and obscenity legislation.[99] For example, "In what has been called one of the largest group civil disobedience actions in Ontario's history, a coalition of over seventy arts organizations joined forces in 1985 to protest the Ontario Film Review Board's prior censorship powers over films and videos. Artists continue to be on the frontlines of anti-censorship marches, protests, and demonstrations."[100] In 1988, museums, artists, and other cultural groups across the country organized against Bill C-54, proposed federal anti-pornography legislation, because it would deeply affect material that could be shown in galleries, particularly contemporary artworks with sexual content.[101] Actions included an all-nude exhibition at the Beaverbrook Art Gallery in Fredericton,[102] the Western Front artist-run centre shut down their film series, and the AGO refused to submit films to the newly formed Ontario Censor Board and instead cancelled a film series.[103] Civil disobedience was widespread, creative, and multi-scalar, taking place in the streets, in artist-run centres, museums and galleries, and the courts.[104] In an article written in 1994, art and policy historian Joyce Zemans compares Canada with the United States, arguing that the legal imposition of censorship through anti-obscenity legislation, and the reaction to it from artists and the wider arts community (including museums),[105] offers an important parallel to the Culture Wars (aimed primarily at cutting public funding to artists and galleries showing "controversial" work) that were happening in the United States.[106] In short, in the late 1980s, culture in North America became a battleground and a place where traditional and progressive values were fought out. Museums were found on all sides of these conflicts.

At the same time, through the 1980s, the discipline of museum studies, emerging both from anthropology and visual culture studies, began to catch up with the criticisms that were coming from the outside. Peter Vergo's 1989 book *The New Museology* is often described as having exposed many of the cultural assumptions of museums, thus launching critical museum studies. But it is important to note that that critique had been occurring performatively long before it was written into the curriculum and canon of the discipline.[107] In Canada, the 1980s was the decade that saw the formation of numerous artist-run centres, the radicalization of artists through CAR and other venues, the emergence of widespread Indigenous activism, the rise of standpoint politics, and the development of the critical project of institutional critique, which turned its attention to the museum as a site that exacerbated and perpetuated inequalities. This constellation of concerns finds its parallel in two major protests at the end of the decade outside the exhibitions *Spirit Sings* and *Into the Heart of Africa* that, as I quote Ruth Phillips in the introduction, profoundly altered museum practice in Canada. These protests were important because they signalled the acknowledgment of BIPOC (Black/Indigenous/People of Colour) activism at museums and because they affected museum policy in Canada, but also because they affected critical museum studies scholarship, particularly in Canada. I look at the reception of these two exhibitions in parallel with the way they have drawn the attention of the academic establishment and suggest that the richness of analysis of these two events should indicate the way that interventions in museums in general can be productive of social change *and* scholarly research. My goal here is to argue that protests at museums must be intersectional and they must acknowledge the multilayered ways in which the museums catalyze and resist intervention. I further suggest that unlike some of the events mentioned in this chapter, protests at *Spirit Sings* and *Into the Heart of Africa* were a part of long-standing and long-term resistance that swelled into two actions in Calgary and Toronto, thus amplifying their impact.

On 29 October 1987, Lubicon Lake First Nation asked 110 museums to boycott the exhibition *Spirit Sings: Artistic Traditions of Canada's First Peoples*, opening at the Glenbow Museum in Calgary in conjunction with the 1988 Winter Olympics.[108] The Lubicon were drawing attention to the fact that Shell Oil Canada Limited, a company that was drilling on land that they claimed, was a major sponsor of the exhibition.[109] As Bernard Ominayak, Chief of the Lubicon Lake First Nation

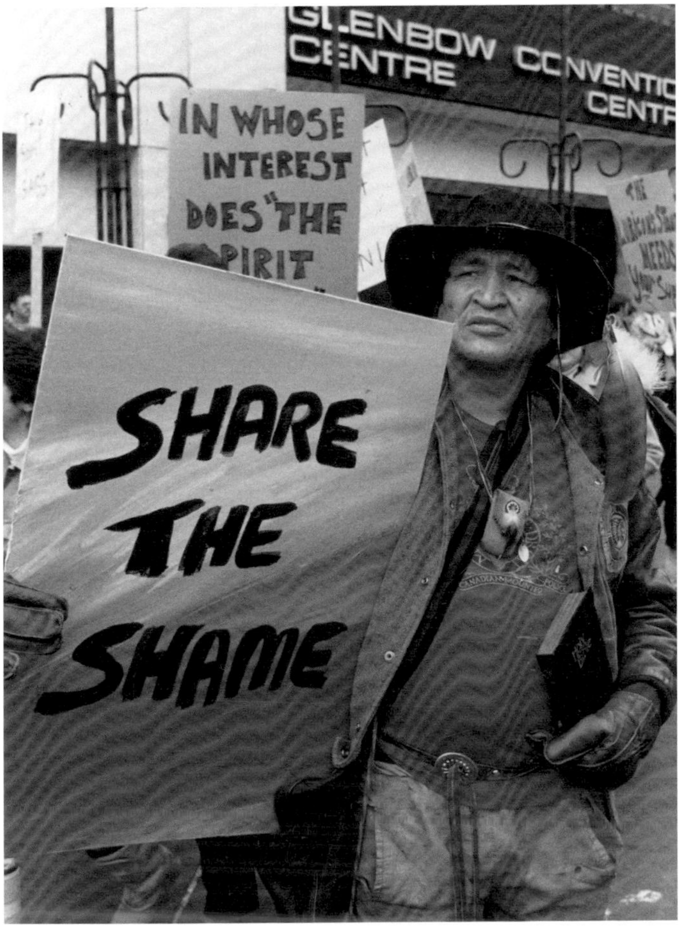

Figure 2.7
Alvin Wanderingspirit protests *The Spirit Sings*, a cultural exhibit outside the Glenbow Museum during the 1988 Winter Games in Calgary.

said, "The irony of using a display of North American Indian artifacts to attract people to the Winter Olympics being organized by interests who are still actively seeking to destroy the Indian people seems painfully obvious."[110] Perhaps convinced by a massive letter-writing campaign that accompanied the Lubicon call, twelve of 110 participating museums agreed to join the boycott, a substantial number given the importance of the exhibition and the fact that organization of the show had been underway for some time.[111] Most museums, however, refused. The McCord Museum in Montreal, for example, stated, "the museum ... has simply decided that it did not wish to get involved in the solution of political issues and and [*sic*] wanted to stick to its cultural mandate."[112] Krista Wrightson quotes Michael Ames, then director of the Museum of Anthropology in Vancouver, who in 1981 had welcomed a First Nations sit-in at his museum (see Interstice 2b). In 1988, by contrast, he argued that "the Lubicon boycott 'was an act of political repression disguised as political advocacy and it displaced the responsibility for the Lubicon situation upon those who were not empowered to change it.'"[113] Duncan Cameron (the same Duncan Cameron quoted above distinguishing between museum as temple and museum as forum but who was at the time of *Spirit Sings* director of the Glenbow) argued strongly in this case for the museum as temple, suggesting that the museum knew more about the artefacts in question than did the demonstrators.[114]

At the same time, the Lubicon were supported by numerous other Indigenous groups (some of whom had formerly supported the exhibition), by some museums, and most vocally by the Canadian Ethnology Society (CESCE), a professional association of about 300 members (most of them university academics). Members of the CESCE called for the Glenbow to release a statement drawing attention to the plight of the Lubicon and claimed that the Glenbow was in violation of a resolution passed at the 1987 International Council of Museums (ICOM) meeting that stated "museums that are engaged in activities relating to living ethnic groups should, wherever possible, consult with the appropriate members of those groups, and such museums should avoid using ethnic materials in any way which might be detrimental and/or offensive to such groups."[115] As Wrightson notes, "The international boycott sponsored by the Cree First Nation was especially effective in garnering international attention. The boycott caused a rift within the museum community, with many colleagues falling on opposite sides of the debate."[116]

The Lubicon's intervention quickly became a catalyst for actions on a number of issues surrounding the display of First Peoples' culture.[117] Phillips writes, "like a magnet set down among iron filings, the contention over corporate sponsorship quickly attracted to itself a host of other issues that have stuck to the exhibition ever since."[118] These included the inappropriate way that ceremonial objects were displayed, the retention of human remains by museums, and the repatriation of cultural objects. In January 1988, a month before the exhibition opened, the Mohawk Council of Kahnawake, Quebec, filed an injunction claiming ownership of eight pieces loaned by museums to the Glenbow.[119] This action was undertaken in support of the Lubicon but also because a false face mask on loan from the ROM was not supposed to be placed on display. The Alberta Court of Queen's Bench did rule that the mask should be withdrawn from the exhibition.[120] But "ten days later, the court order was reversed, citing evidence that the mask had, in fact, been displayed in various museums for years, without objection from Mohawk Indians."[121] When the exhibition moved to Ottawa "at the request of native leaders from the Six Nations Confederacy, a replacement mask made by Chief Jacob Thomas of the Cayuga Band was put on display."[122]

Spirit Sings was a massive undertaking that brought together 650 examples of Indigenous art from institutions around the world, mostly collected during the early years of European contact and largely unknown to most audiences (including the descendants of the makers).[123] Curated by a team of non-Indigenous professionals from well-regarded institutions, with occasional participation from famous

Haida artist Bill Reid, the exhibition had, as one of its overarching goals, the ideal of bringing objects made by First Nations peoples back to Canada.[124] Julia Harrison reports that during meetings in 1986, Lubicon representatives "registered no objection to the content of the exhibition but only to its sponsorship and association with the Calgary Olympics which they were then boycotting."[125] She also argues that "Glenbow staff had, on a number of occasions, declared support for a swift and just settlement of the Lubicon land claim. But they were powerless to do anything which might move along the negotiations between the Lubicon and the government."[126] Ultimately, Harrison, like many others, argued that "museums must remain independent of external political pressures."[127] It is the same argument that one year later would be made at the ROM.[128]

On opening day, 150 protesters marched outside the Glenbow Museum, while 3,500 attendees viewed the exhibition inside. The protest received far-reaching media coverage, while simultaneously the Glenbow and Harrison undertook extensive damage control.[129] After the exhibition opened, Rebecca Belmore, then an emerging artist, performed *Artifact 671B* to protest the way Indigenous culture was presented in Canadian museums. Sitting immobile in a glass case outside the Thunder Bay art gallery, Belmore drew attention both to a specific case – the *Spirit Sings* exhibition – and to the wider issues of land claims, restitution, and repatriation.

Spirit Sings remained open for its full run at the Glenbow and then moved to the Canadian Museum of Civilization in Ottawa. There, however, a symposium was organized to initiate discussion around the exhibition, and from the symposium came the Task Force on Museums and First Peoples, sponsored by the Canadian Museums Association and the Assembly of First Nations and funded by the federal Department of Communications. The task force met at the Woodland Cultural Centre (on Six Nations land) and produced *Turning the Page: Forging New Partnerships between Museums and First Peoples*, a document of unique importance in Canadian museums history.

While the exhibition itself might represent a missed opportunity to connect the concerns of Indigenous peoples with the objects in the exhibition, many of which told stories of disruption and loss, the outcome was an immense reworking of museum approaches in Canada. Phillips concludes that the wide range of issues

> was less a response to the exhibition itself than to a range of problems that had been affecting the Aboriginal population for many years … "The Spirit Sings" controversy marked the beginning of a realization that the museum has *multiple* publics whose needs arise from different cultural formations and that its custodianship of cultural property creates networks of responsibility not only to sponsors and governments but also to the communities from which these collections originated.[130]

Figure 2.8
Orderly protest: A police officer stands guard as one of about seventy-five pickets circles outside the Royal Ontario Museum in protest of an African exhibit within, 1988.

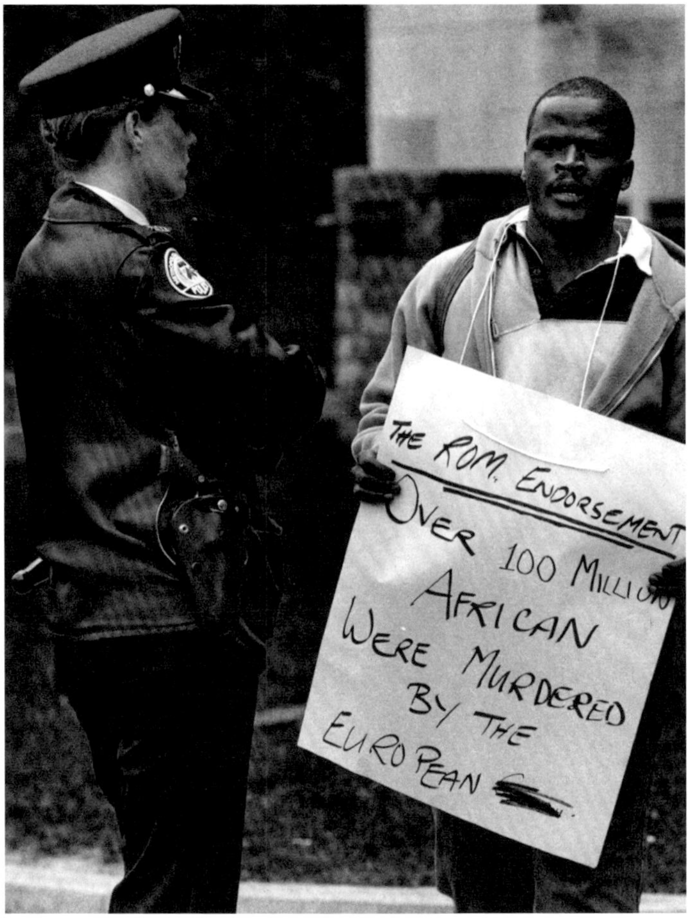

Krista Wrightson is less convinced of the effectiveness of the task force and its *Turning the Page* document in changing museums in Canada. She draws on Glen Coulthard (Yellowknives Dene) to argue that

> the effective inclusion of Indigenous peoples' voices and presences into institutions that substantively undercut the sovereignty of Indigenous peoples does not transform the colonial relations. Rather, it reproduces the structural conditions of settler colonial power ... Thus, given the institutional response to the radical critiques of the Lubicon in the form of cultural accommodation, the task force can be read as an exemplary moment of the move toward what Coulthard identifies as conciliatory forms of colonial accommodation and recognition.[131]

I take up Wrightson's argument in chapter 3 and look again at the demonstrations outside *Spirit Sings* in light of recent performative interventions into a number of museums receiving funding from fossil fuel companies in chapter 6. In chapter 6, I also look at how questions of land that were forefront in the Lubicon Cree's engagement with the exhibition were sidelined to focus on the issues that could be specifically responded to by museums. The broadness of the Lubicon challenge, and their demanding a boycott on the part of more than a hundred loaner museums, moved the issue far beyond the Glenbow Museum. The consequence, however, was a sidelining of the Lubicon's land claim and a quieting of the role played by Shell Canada. Thus, the potential outcomes of protests outside of *Spirit Sings* were simultaneously tempered by unwillingness to address land issues and enhanced by the growing acknowledgment of a number of the loaner museums, including museums in Canada, that the status quo could not stand. The same was not true of another protest that took place a year later outside the Royal Ontario Museum.

"Today, for the third Saturday in a row, a group of very angry black Torontonians will be picketing in front of the Royal Ontario Museum, picketing an exhibit called 'Into the Heart of Africa.'"[132] So begins a newspaper article covering protests outside *Into the Heart of Africa*, an exhibition that opened at the ROM in 1989. The exhibition was curated from a collection of African material history held by the ROM, much of which had been collected in the nineteenth century by Canadian missionaries. According to anthropologist Jeanne Cannizzo, who was hired as a guest curator specifically for this show, the exhibition was meant to acknowledge Canada's colonial past and to deal, at least in part, with the racist assumptions of missionaries and their lack of understanding of the complexities of African cultures.[133] The exhibition used irony, framing racist commentary from missionaries in scare quotes, and tried to illustrate how objects that travelled back to Canada with missionaries lost their context, becoming two-dimensional souvenirs.[134] This is a style of curating that Shelley Butler calls "reflexive curating" in her important book on the organization, display, and response to *Into the Heart of Africa*.[135] The irony, however, didn't work. It was too subtle, too easy to read as fact, and ultimately was overpowered by the images and objects that appeared to celebrate the subjugation of African peoples.[136] Writes Butler, "the effect of these curatorial strategies was to immerse visitors in imperial and missionary ideology."[137] Prior to the exhibition opening, members of the African-Canadian community were consulted (just before opening, when most decisions had already been made), and many expressed deep concern with the exhibition and with an accompanying pamphlet. Though changes were made to the pamphlet, the exhibition remained largely untouched. "How could an exhibition offend so many people from different sides of the political spectrum?" asked Erin Schildkrout shortly after *Into the Heart of Africa* closed.[138] And Butler asks, "Why was productive dialogue between protesters and Cannizzo, and between protesters and the ROM, so impossible?"[139]

Many scholars read the exhibition as overtly racist, an instance of cultural appropriation, and a celebration of the seizure, possession, and removal of African material culture from Africa. The exhibition adopted a Eurocentric perspective, further decontextualizing the objects and silencing the makers. Henry et al. note in their analysis of the exhibition that tour guides referred to Zulus as a "vicious tribe" and told visitors that Africans practised "barbaric rituals." Even the guides misunderstood the exhibition, thus perpetuating the stereotypes that the show ostensibly unpacked.[140]

Henry et al. analyze the numerous newspaper articles and opinion pieces, including the one quoted above, many of which advanced further racist characterization through depictions of Black protesters as "angry," out of line, or unable to understand the exhibition.[141] What *Into the Heart of Africa* did was reveal a deep intolerance at the heart of the Canadian self. In reality, the exhibition presented missionary incursions into Africa with a "nostalgic reverence" and portrayed Africans as passive subjects of colonization; nowhere in the show was there any evidence of resistance.[142] As Butler shows, one of the major problems was that Cannizzo assumed the audience to be white and the exhibition, while an attempt to educate that particular audience, actually perpetuated many racist stereotypes, among them an idea that museums are for white people and that the conveyance of knowledge should be directed toward white audiences.[143] In short, the voices of those whose objects formed the collection at the ROM were silenced and erased.

Protests against the show began slowly but ended tumultuously.[144] The exhibition opened quietly in November 1989, but in March 1990, the Coalition for the Truth about Africa (CFTA) began holding weekly protests outside the ROM. On 14 April 1990, members of the CFTA entered the ROM and blocked entrances to the building. Police were called and protesters removed. The same thing happened a week later. The ROM warned those blocking entrances that "entry was an offense contrary to the *Trespass to Property Act*."[145] On 5 May 1990, thirty-five police officers were called to the museum "where they clashed in a brawl with dozens of protestors. Two people were arrested and charged with assault."[146] The ROM described the altercation as follows: "A number of demonstrators entered the Museum building and, after being informed that their entry was prohibited, assaulted the attending police officers and security staff of the Museum. As a result of this conduct, two individuals were charged with assaulting police officers."[147] But a different description of events also emerged. During the demonstration, two Black men were jumped by eight police officers, one of whom drew a gun.[148] The men had simply been trying to enter the exhibition.[149] Then, in June, nine more people were arrested on counts including obstructing and assaulting police, escaping lawful custody, and assault with the intent to resist arrest, after a riot squad of fifty police officers descended on the protesters.[150] At this point, the ROM applied for (and received) an injunction from the Supreme Court of Ontario (now the Ontario Superior Court) that forbade the CFTA from protesting within 50 feet of the museum's entrance.[151] Cannizzo, who refused to listen to complaints or budge on her stance that the exhibition required no changes, also faced harassment. Her house was spray-painted with the slogans "J. Cannizzo is a racist" and "We will never forget J. Cannizzo. We will smash racist colonialism by any means necessary."[152] The personal targeting of Cannizzo is unfortunate and troubling, but listening to the criticisms, coupled with an apology from the curator, might have gone a long way toward diffusing tensions and opening dialogue between protesters and the museum. Whether the museum would have changed tack remains uncertain.

Throughout, the ROM denied the show was racist and downplayed the "fuss." Gillam claims that the peaceful weekly CFTA protests quickly came to be characterized as the work of "a small group of radicals."[153] In one press release the museum declares, "The ROM denies that the show is racist, and stands by the exhibition as a fair and careful investigation of that period of Canadian/African history."[154] Though he had not worked at the ROM in some time, former director Peter Swann reappeared in the midst of the controversy, penning a letter to the editor of the *Globe and Mail* that echoed the fear of protest that he had expressed some twenty years before. He tears in to the protesters, asking (incorrectly) why Jeanne Cannizzo was not supported by the members, researchers, and Board of Trustees of the ROM.[155] Swann writes,

> A fraction of [members] standing quietly on the museum steps would have chased away a noisy group of activists using the occasion for base and transparent publicity purposes ... Can one imagine that a similar rabble would be allowed to attack the British Museum or the Louvre. But then, of course, the government here is more concerned about minority votes than the integrity of its most important cultural institutions![156]

Swann's comments are xenophobic, but they were in line with the ROM's response to the protesters' demands.[157]

The CFTA, which led the protests, was strongly criticized by the museum and in the mainstream press, both for the purported violence of picketers and for the fact that protests had not begun until a full four months after the show opened. But, as Clement Marshall, who consulted on the exhibition and raised concerns prior to its opening, noted, "If there are now pickets, it is because we have not been listened to when we quietly brought these issues to those who have the power to alter the inaccurate and demeaning portrayal of African peoples."[158] Certainly, the demands of the CFTA to clarify explanatory texts or, failing that, to close the exhibition, were not overtly hostile (or even particularly demanding).[159] As Henry et al. note, "the confrontation between the police and the protesters [was seen by community members as] symptomatic of the everyday forms of oppression and harassment experienced by members of the Black community in their 'encounters with police.'"[160] And as Charles Roach, who was involved in the protests, noted, "The struggles with the ROM and the Metro police are welded together. Inside the ROM is institutional racism and outside is the brutal reality."[161]

As with the reception of *Spirit Sings*, there was resistance on the part of the establishment and its supporters to acknowledging the wider issues underlying the demonstrations outside the museum. But among those at the threshold, this was not the case. On 15 July 1990, the CFTA formed a brief alliance with First Nations peoples, among them members of the Akwesasne Warrior Society who had gathered in Toronto to support Mohawk Warriors resisting the police and military in the Kanehsatà:ke Resistance (colloquially known as the Oka Crisis). Butler quotes Lennox Farrell of the Black Action Defense Committee, who stated, "The black community stands behind the Mohawk people in their demands in Oka and other places."[162] The group marched together from the ROM to the Eaton Centre (a shopping centre that also housed offices of the Quebec government).[163] The brief alliance demonstrated a clear understanding of the intersectionality of issues raised by Warriors at Kanehsatà:ke and by Black residents of Toronto.

Widespread media dismissal of the protests and the brutal suppression of picketers suggests that the actions outside the ROM would have few repercussions for the museum. But the opposite was arguably true. A reporter for the *Toronto Star*, writing some twenty-five years after the events, noted, "The damage, not just to the community but the museum's credibility, was deepening: Amid the controversy, four museums that had signed on to host the show on a North American tour abruptly cancelled, ending its run where it began, inside the ROM's increasingly fortress-like walls."[164]

Did the protests at *Into the Heart of Africa* lead to change? In June 1991, the ROM released a statement noting its regret "for any offence unintentionally caused to members of the African Canadian community and to other groups and individuals."[165] This tepid statement of regret was largely not accepted by former members of the CFTA. Butler points out that the museum tried to move away from the protest, and the exhibition had no presence on the ROM's website until 2015 when it appeared as part of the centennial "ROM Recollects" project in which Yaw Oluwasanjo Akyeaw (a member of the CFTA present at the original protests) was invited to speak.[166] Then in November 2016, the ROM formally apologized for *Into the Heart of Africa* at a reconciliation event with the CFTA. Negotiations for the apology had taken place over two years between the ROM and members of the CFTA. Deputy director Mark Engstrom read a public statement that included the following: "The exhibition displayed images and words that showed the fundamentally racist ideas and attitudes of early collectors, and in doing so unintentionally reproduced a colonial, racist and Euro-centric premise." Doing so "perpetuated an atmosphere of racism."[167] Furthermore, "The museum also apologized for the suffering endured by members of the African-Canadian community as a result of the exhibit."[168] In 2016, the ROM launched *Of Africa*, a large-scale "multiplatform and multiyear project aimed at rethinking historical and contemporary representations of Africa."[169] *Of Africa* consciously avoided many of the mistakes of *Into the Heart of Africa* and included extensive community consultation and collaboration.[170]

Conclusion(s)

As noted above, the late 1980s and early 1990s saw the emergence of critical museology, and an academic apparatus developed through which museums could be understood as compromised even as protests were taking place. As Shelley Butler concludes, "critical museology associated museums with a politics of domination, especially with regard to questions of how the West exhibits non-western cultures. It focuses on museum practices of collecting, classifying, and displaying material culture."[171] All of the demonstrations and interventions described in this section built on actions that had taken place in the preceding decade and expanded the frame for what *could* be protested at the museum. I argue that actions against *Spirit Sings* and *Into the Heart of Africa* are key and deserve their central place in Canadian museum studies. Their importance is linked to the way that each action brought long-term resistance to bear on single exhibitions or institutions, although equally important, it was points of overlap with the growing field of critical museology that resulted in change – issues of race and land remained largely ignored or actively suppressed.

There were numerous other protests outside museums in the late 1980s and early 1990s. In 1988, members of the IAU gathered at the opening of the new building of the National Gallery of Canada to protest the sponsorship of an exhibition of Degas's works by United Technologies, a major US defence contractor.[172] In Montreal in 1990, the Museum of Fine Arts braced itself for protests against the *Passionate Eye: Impressionist and Other Master Paintings*, not because of the exhibition but because it drew on the collection of Emil G. Buehrle, founder of Zurich-based Oerlikon, a weapons company that had sold arms to the Nazis as well as to the Allies during the Second World War.[173] In 1993, Eli Langer's exhibition at Mercer Union Gallery in Toronto resulted in a raid on the gallery for Langer's drawings depicting children engaged in acts that could be construed as sexual. Langer was charged with one count each of making, possessing, and displaying child pornography, and similar charges were laid against Mercer Union's executive director, Sharon Brooks.[174] Artists quickly organized to support Langer and Mercer Union, and the Crown eventually withdrew the charges. This event and the targeting of Langer fall under my definition of a controversy.[175] But I include it here to contrast it with an October 1995 demonstration outside the Vancouver Art Gallery. More than 300 people associated with the Interfaith Coalition against Hate Art gathered in a demonstration against an exhibition that included two Andres Serrano photographs of a crucifix in urine.[176] Serrano's work had also caused significant outcry in the United States. In short, from the mid-1980s to the mid-1990s, many galleries were targeted for their display of sexual work or for work that questioned religion. The outcomes were often a combination of exhaustion on the part of gallery staff and, as Jenny Ellison notes, an unwillingness on the part of many museums and galleries to deal with topics that might prompt outcries.[177]

From Egyptian Coptic Christians protesting an exhibition on Ancient Egypt at the ROM at the turn of the millennium to draw attention to the Canadian government's lack of response to killings in Egypt[178] to fallout from the near success of the Quebec referendum in 1995,[179] from pushback against the removal or censorship of controversial artworks[180] to numerous interventions as a part of the "Days of Action" in Ontario (a series of wide-ranging protests against the Mike Harris provincial neo-conservative government's massive cuts to arts and social services),[181] and from ranchers on horseback gathered outside the Royal Tyrrell Museum in Alberta targeting a meeting of provincial premiers[182] to extensive resistance to normative depictions of Indigenous culture (particularly surrounding the celebrations of Columbus's "discovery" of North America in 1992)[183] and demonstrations against perceived systemic and cultural racism at the AGO demonstrated by the gallery's Barnes Collection exhibition, which included none of the African, Asian, and Native American artworks and artefacts collected by Albert C. Barnes,[184] protests in the 1990s were many, varied, and greeted with relatively light police presence.

In sum, then, the immediate outcome of protests against *Spirit Sings* and *Into the Heart of Africa*, as well as numerous other actions, is a mixed bag. Protesters against *Into the Heart of Africa* were harshly treated, and the aftermath did not lead to significant changes outside the museum – for example, in the policing of Black communities in Toronto. Similarly, very few of the anti-government, single-issue, anti-corporate, or even art protests outlined above had any easily observable or quantifiable effect. Only very occasionally were exhibitions altered, and equally rarely were cuts to the arts or controversial sponsorships reversed.[185]

But change is a funny thing, and, as noted in the preface, the importance of protest comes often not in immediate results but in long-term response. In one instance, following the Task Force on Museums and First Peoples, museum policies changed dramatically, the results of which we will see in the second half of the book. And interestingly, from the 1990s on, museums increasingly became key sites for a growing number of actions.[186] Post-1990s strategies changed to incorporate the museum itself into the protest, particularly by drawing attention to the multi-

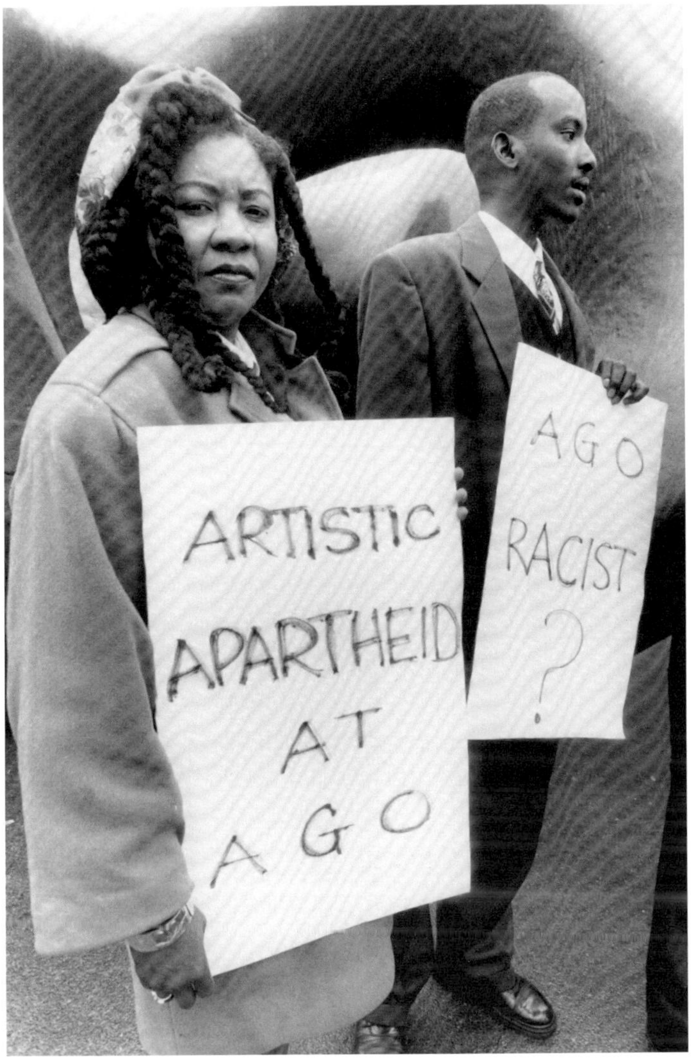

Figure 2.9
Protest at the AGO during October launch of the Barnes Exhibit, 15 December 1994.

faceted role played by museums as public sites for the performance of citizenship, as corporately funded entities, as culture makers, and as authoritative institutions.

All the while, museums scrambled to survive funding cuts. Indeed, it might have seemed that they were under attack from all sides: by former visitors who turned to other forms of entertainment, by marginalized groups under-represented within national and local collections, by Indigenous peoples who exposed museums' roles in projects of colonization, by businesses who perceived the arts as a waste of government money, and by governments that continued to cut and gouge away at cultural budgets. "Some days it must seem as if the dinosaur is a curator's only friend," quipped one reporter.[187]

Serious cuts scaled back museum programming and forced institutions to turn outwards, relying even more on private sponsorship. An important series of demonstrations, letter-writing campaigns, and other actions took place at this time as part of a massive push undertaken at all levels of the arts and culture establishment, from the Canadian Conference of the Arts lobby group to the National Gallery of Canada, to intervene (unsuccessfully) in the 1995 federal budget process, a budget that decimated funding to the arts and social services.[188] It is at this point that this chapter crosses over the timeline with the case studies to follow, with an escalating marketization of culture and, in response, increasingly frantic efforts on the part of activists and citizens groups to protect public funding for culture and social services. Simultaneously, Creative Cities rhetoric, popularized by Richard Florida, was taking hold.[189] Resisting the idea that museums were a thing of the past, the Creative Cities formula highlighted cultural institutions as key elements that make cities liveable, attractive places. Amidst the cuts, scores of cultural building projects began,[190] many of them backdrops to the huge protests taking place in the streets, which aimed to draw attention to, and potentially halt, the spread of neoliberal capitalism as manifested through transnational institutions such as the WTO, G8/G20, IMF, and World Bank.

In the following chapters, as I move across the threshold of the museum and into the galleries and archives, it will become obvious that even when museums consciously attempt to produce exhibitions related to political issues, or even when archives attempt to collect the material culture of activism, they face nearly insurmountable tasks. This is true even of the numerous institutional critique art projects in Canada from the 1960s to the present that attempted to challenge, reimagine, and unravel the museum.[191] Interestingly, at the moment when museums were recast as public forums and as crystalline designs on the city skyline, they were also targeted by movements that stretched far beyond the content and material culture housed within the institution. As shown in the case studies that follow, contemporary actions within and against museums draw on a wide range of platforms and positions, which I argue both reflect and refract the contemporary situation of museums.

Interstice 2b

The UBC Museum of Anthropology as Model

The Museum of Anthropology (MOA) at the University of British Columbia in Vancouver has long been praised for its collaboration with local communities, primarily the Musqueam Nation on whose lands the museum stands.[1] The MOA has been an important innovator and is regularly noted as a key exemplar of what James Clifford calls the museum as "contact zone," a space where different cultures come into contact.[2] The "contact zone" has become something of a catchphrase in museum studies, defined as a positive gesture of reciprocity between museum and source communities. But an important feature of the contact zone, as Clifford borrows the term from Mary Louise Pratt, is that it is often conflictual and often indicative of "radically asymmetrical relations of power."[3] While critical museology tends to see the contact zone metaphor as an indicator of successful reciprocal relationships, I suggest that Pratt's more expansive definition is useful when it comes to acknowledging that contact zones can emerge within agonistic relationships.[4]

The MOA was founded in 1947 and originally housed in the main library at the University of British Columbia. In 1971, the federal government granted money for the construction of a new building, and in 1976 well-known Vancouver-based architect Arthur Erickson was hired to design it. Inspired by the post-and-beam architecture of northwest coast peoples (though communities appear not to have been consulted), Erickson's building has become an icon of Vancouver architecture. At the time of its opening, Michael M. Ames was director. Ames is now well known for his 1992 book *Cannibal Tours and Glass Boxes*, which explores how museums,

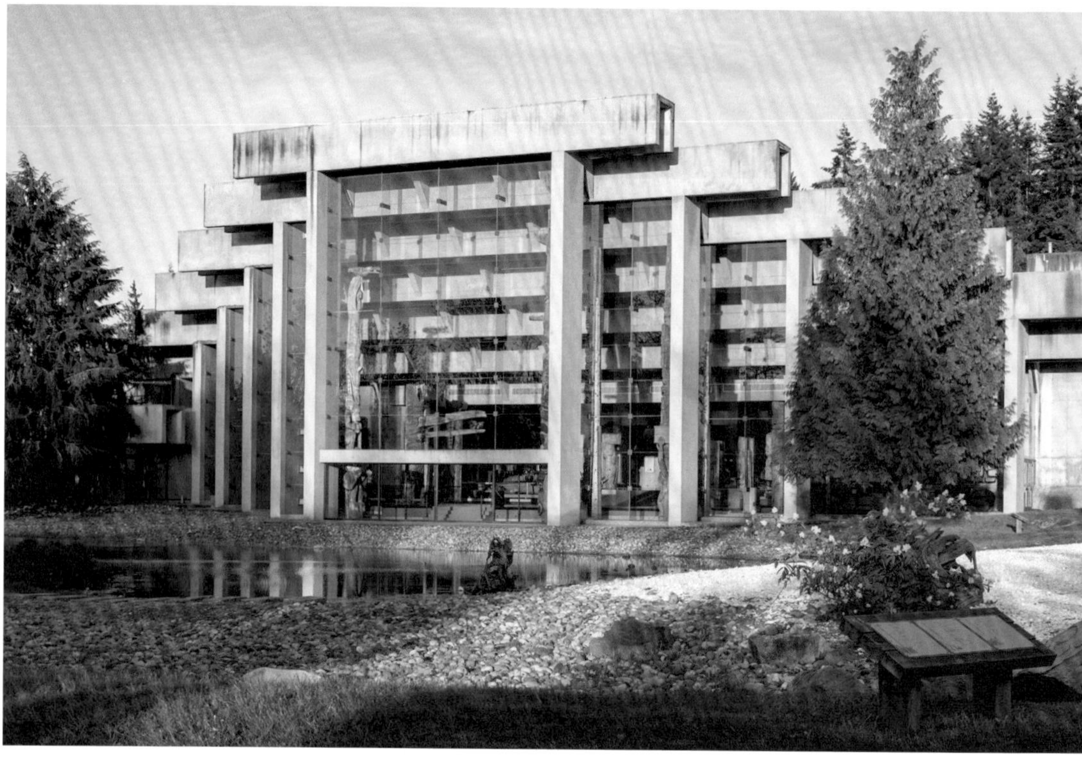

Figure 2.10
Arthur Erickson, Museum of Anthropology, UBC, designed 1976.

and particularly museums of anthropology and ethnography, found themselves at the centre of controversy and division over how best to attract visitors while also being "self-appointed keepers of other people's material and the self-appointed interpreters of other's histories."[5]

Ames knew well what he was talking about. In November 1981, shortly after he took over the directorship of the MOA, a demonstration and occupation took place at the museum. The event was not concerned with the museum's collections or exhibitions but rather with the patriation of Canada's Constitution from Great Britain.[6] At the time, Prime Minister Pierre Trudeau was in the UK, negotiating the Canada Act with the Crown. The act was seen as a nationalistic gesture, and pressure for recognition from First Nations, Métis, and Inuit communities was "not expected."[7]

However, the new Constitution included no codified protections for Aboriginal rights and thereby ignored the Crown's treaty obligations. Demonstrations and occupations were organized across the country. At the MOA, the occupation was the climax of a caravan of four chartered buses that began several days prior and that gathered demonstrators from across the province of British Columbia.[8] Three hundred people initially gathered outside the museum in solidarity, with actions across the country.[9] In Ottawa, more than a thousand gathered in a demonstration on Parliament Hill, while more than 5,000 gathered in Alberta outside the provincial legislature[10] and large crowds met in Winnipeg, Sault Ste Marie, Baffin Island, Halifax, and elsewhere.[11] In Vancouver, demonstrators were joined by a group of First Nations leaders who had been in Europe on the "Constitutional Express," lobbying European politicians to help Indigenous peoples in Canada protect their rights in the new Constitution.[12] Specifically, the argument was that treaties had been signed by the Crown, meaning that responsibility for them resided in the UK. A patriated Constitution that did not specifically recognize treaty rights, in short, was illegitimate, and it was thought that it could be stopped through British (and by proxy European) intervention.[13]

Outside the museum, a man posing as Prime Minister Pierre Trudeau was symbolically stripped of the eagle feathers Trudeau had received from the Bella Coola people in 1970 for his role as a "protector of the Indian people."[14] "With raised arms, fists clenched, and voices chanting in unison," the museum was occupied. Fifty people spent the night in the MOA's great hall surrounded by the cultural production, carvings, and totem poles of generations of northwest coast peoples. George Manuel, Grand Chief of the Union of BC Indian Chiefs, which organized the protest, stated, "We must lay down our lives to defend our identity with our country ... We must be prepared to spill our blood to defend our identity with our land or we will perish."[15]

How would the museum staff respond? The *Ubyssey* student newspaper suggests that the museum was caught by surprise.[16] The *Globe and Mail* reported:

> Michael Ames, museum director, welcomed them [occupiers] and ordered coffee and food for them. A television was secured, and the museum sent telegrams to Trudeau, and to BC Premier Bill Bennett, affirming their support.[17] "I have no objection to this at all," he told them. "I believe that the message you have is important and that it is important that the Canadian people hear what you have to say."[18]

A story in the *Kamloops Daily Sentinel* quotes Steven Point, chairman of the Chilliwack Indian Council, that occupiers were "surprised and gratified" at the museum's response.[19] Looking back on the occupation from 2017, Moya Waters (who was secretary to the director in 1981 and is now associate director of the MOA) remembered the staff's complete surprise at the appearance of hundreds of people at the museum entrance. She recalled a phone call from security asking: "was there a group booked here today?" and the insistent beat of drumming that filtered through the museum. "We went down and there were hundreds of First Nations people drumming themselves straight into the Great Hall. It was amazing. And we all said what do we do now? Once we found out why they were there ... we just said welcome, come on in." Waters describes ordering sandwiches and refreshments, having sleeping bags delivered for staff to spend the night, turning the classrooms into spaces for children's activities, and "[making the museum] as welcoming as possible ... [we wanted to turn] the museum into a forum for discussion." When I ask what might have happened if the museum had turned the occupiers away, Waters says, "It was already happening by the time we got into the lobby ... it was underway, we couldn't stop it. And we didn't want to." She concludes, "It was a remarkable day ... I'll never forget it ... I still have good feelings that we did the right thing."[20]

Twenty-four hours later, the demonstrators left, their point made. By welcoming the occupiers, however, the museum had made its own point – the MOA was an institution connected to current events and to the people whose cultural artefacts it housed. "You have brought meaning to the past by linking us to the present," said Ames as those who had stayed the night got ready to leave, "You are always welcome here. This house of culture is your house of culture."[21] Archie Pootlass, vice-president of the Union of BC Indian Chiefs, agreed, stating in an interview that the museum had been chosen because it was a beautiful site "representing two worlds ... where Indian culture and history have been preserved."[22] But others disagreed. An unnamed source is quoted in the Vancouver Courier stating, "The university represents the wealthy and powerful and at the same time they see fit to take Indian cultural artifacts and use them for display there."[23] The institution did not and could not operate solely in the past.[24] From the MOA, protesters gathered for a rally outside the Union of Chiefs office on Hastings Street and then marched to the Department of Indian Affairs office. Events culminated with a potlatch in downtown Vancouver.[25] In 1982, the Trudeau government enacted the Constitution Act including the Charter of Rights and Freedoms (without Quebec's consent). Both the new Constitution and Charter contained clauses protecting the rights of Indigenous peoples (Indian, Métis, and Inuit) holding Aboriginal and treaty rights.[26]

Only a few years later, in 1988, Michael Ames would vigorously defend the Glenbow Museum during *Spirit Sings*, a position that seems at odds with his brewing coffee during a sit-in at his own institution.[27] But a clue is found in an interview from 1981 in which he states, "It is not appropriate for us to take a political stand as an institution. But [the sit-in] is a legitimate use of space."[28] Ames describes, for example, how, as he was feeling very self-satisfied after a Haida pole-raising, a First Nations artist poked a hole in his confidence, stating, "we don't feel at home in your museums – any of them."[29] Museums were and still are painful reminders of colonial plunder no matter how open the processes of collaboration: the MOA in particular is both a part of and separate from its surroundings. Since Ames's time as director, the museum has dealt with this duality and presents itself as a work in progress. MOA is also part of a university campus, and although it receives federal government funding, it is not a national museum. Its impetus is local, aimed toward the Musqueam nation and often far removed from, or even in opposition to, the nation-building projects of institutions such as the CMHR or CMH.

Nevertheless, while I draw attention to a nearly forgotten sit-in and position the MOA as an important model, Meg Pinto reminds us that an activist framework can itself become calcified. In her analysis of the MOA's cancelled 2011 *Forgotten* exhibition of portraits of missing and murdered women from Vancouver's Downtown Eastside (many of them First Nations) by settler artist Pamela Masik, she describes how the museum listened carefully to Downtown Eastside community groups but also notes the near-cavalier discussions of how much the museum stood to gain or lose if a protest or boycott took place. Was publicity worth the backlash?[30] Nonetheless, in its acceptance that dissent and agonistic engagement are to be encouraged rather than avoided, the MOA stands in clear contrast to the majority of institutions in Canada.

3

Crossing the Threshold: Counter-Histories, Museum Exteriors, Interiors, and Archives

Temporally, this chapter picks up where the last one leaves off, concentrating on the period covered by most of this book, the late 1990s to 2017. While I will return to the actual protests, demonstrations, and interventions outside of museums in Part 2 of the book, this chapter looks at the museum itself, juxtaposing architectural renovations with large-scale re-hangings of permanent collections, archives, and museum holdings. Crossing the threshold of the museum, I look at how major renovation projects, which have largely been understood as illustrations or embodiments of the excesses of neoliberalism, can be contrasted with the slow work of museums, showcased through displays that respond to the political interventions of the previous decade and collecting policies that both hinder and encourage the amassing of political ephemera and material culture. I argue that the contrast that I draw here, illustrative of the wavering on the part of museums between being "temples" and "forums," makes them ideal locations for the actions that I analyze in Part 2 of the book, whether these actions be on the part of veterans hoping to quash critical language in Ottawa or anti-capitalists hoping to draw attention to the museum's links with neoliberal policy in British Columbia. In this chapter, I ask what the contradictory nature of the museum means for the display, collecting, and archiving of activist, political, resistant, and resurgent material culture.

In the previous chapter, I showed how the call for a boycott of, and demonstrations outside of, *Spirit Sings* led to formation of the Task Force on Museums and

First Peoples but did not ultimately result in the settlement of the Lubicon Cree's land claim. Using this and other examples, Kendra Wrightson argues that the response to the actions against *Spirit Sings* was a clear example of settler-colonial politics of recognition whereby decolonizing struggles are recognized and even represented but the power structures enabling the original oppression remain largely intact. In this chapter, I return to her argument to look at how activist curating and attempts to gather certain materials into archives (for example, political and activist material culture, as well as material evidence of Indigenous resistance and resurgence) are complicated by the heritage of museums themselves. There is no present moment in the museum that is not inflected by the past. Essentially, what does it mean for a museum to showcase and collect radical material culture when the same institution has gone through a renovation project that has made it a beacon for the neoliberal creative city and accepts funding from corporations or individuals who might be the targets of activist actions? What does it mean for a museum to collect and display counterculture when its very being is deeply connected to the status quo? Is there any way for these tensions to be productive, or are they always compromising?

My goal here is not to problematically collapse Indigenous resurgence into anticapitalist and other social movements, positing them as a "good" against the museum's "bad." I do, however, argue strongly that now is a good time to ask questions about how museums could and should engage with counter-histories. Looking at the growth in organizing exhibitions about and with activist movements and collecting material from social movements (key among them Occupy and the 2017 Women's March), I argue that museums need to *both* expand their collections of activist material *and* collect in ways that do not then undo solidarity work or privilege mainstream or white-led causes in a "settler move to innocence" of appearing edgy while actually erasing ongoing BIPOC resistance. I also argue that museums should collect in ways that highlight rather than downplay the radicality of activist politics. Taking up such issues, this chapter is organized through a spatial logic that begins with the exterior of the museum, moves to the interior, and culminates behind the scenes in the archives. I use this chapter to provide an overview of the current state of museums, display, and collecting in Canada in order to use this material in Part 2 of the book in the case studies.

Museum Exteriors

Since their introduction to the public sphere in the eighteenth century, museums have been variously understood as elite spaces, as temples for contemplation, as places for rituals of citizenship, and more recently as palaces of entertainment, housed in glittering shells. Arguably, innovative and ostentatious museum renovations and new building projects are together *the* defining feature of museum evolution in the late twentieth and early twenty-first centuries.

Behind each recent renovation project lies the promise of the "Bilbao effect," a by now well-rehearsed story of creative promise, tinged with mythical potency. Although a trend in new museum building began in the 1980s, it was in the late 1990s that the spectacular design of cultural institutions was connected to economic revitalization and development of urban centres. In 1997, the Guggenheim opened a franchise in Bilbao, Spain. Designed by Frank Gehry, the museum was part of a wider plan for the former industrial centre of Bilbao. Suffering the effects of the outsourcing of its ship-building industry, the city decided to use a series of spectacular cultural offerings – a franchise of the Guggenheim (at that time only the third one), an ostentatious bridge designed by Santiago Calatrava, and a public transportation system designed by Norman Foster – to draw tourists to the city. The city would support itself through tourism and cultural consumption, with middle-class consumers drawn to the curved titanium of the Gehry museum like moths to a flame. The plan worked, and the city's financial standing improved quickly and dramatically enough for others to take notice.[1] Cities around the world quickly tried to mirror the Spanish town's success.

The pace of museum building, the global competition for new designs, and the popularity of a very few top-level designers (Daniel Libeskind and Frank Gehry leading the way, along with Zaha Hadid, Santiago Calatrava, Norman Foster, Rem Koolhaas, Renzo Piano, and a handful of others) culminated in a global trend of museum building and renovation.[2] Now, to be "world-class," a city's major museums had to be housed in newly conceived, evocative, original buildings.[3] Though connected with rhetoric of Creative Cities, it should be noted that the building of Guggenheim Bilbao preceded both the influential UK Mapping document on creative industries and the release of Richard Florida's tome on the creative class.

Perhaps the investment in building creative city centres should not be seen as surprising. Already, in 1990, Rosalind Krauss was arguing that museums had become less holders of public patrimony and more corporate entities with extensive assets in the form of cultural works.[4] The new museum, what she called the "synchronic museum," would forego narratives of chronological progress in the name of intensity of experience, thus encouraging the production of large-scale immersive art works. She further argued, referencing the still to-be-built MASS MOCA (Massachusetts Museum of Contemporary Art), that huge spaces would be required in order to view such works. Museums and art galleries would be "not so much temporal as radically spatial."[5] Krauss's prescient comments, and her attempts to understand the marketization of modern and contemporary art (her interest is primarily with minimalism) and the spaces that would be needed to showcase both the art and its commodification, seemed to roll out over the next decade, not just in the creation of massive new spaces for contemporary art but also in the finessing of corporate–museum partnerships that resulted in shiny buildings for even the most ancient and parochial of collections.

Political analyst Thomas Frank turned his attention to the architect, largely left out of Krauss's essay, in his analysis of Seattle's Frank Gehry–designed Experience Music Project (EMP). For Frank, trying to understand the impact of EMP, Gehry was deeply implicated in the "New Economy," not only as a star architect but also because

> there is today no greater champion of "innovation" than management gurus, and for them Gehry has become a living, breathing symbol of creativity. It makes little difference for this school of thought *how* Gehry's work diverges from the boxlike corporate style of the postwar years, just *that* it does, that it incorporates all sorts of wacky building materials and irregular angles. And in those wacky materials and those irregular angles the gurus find an affirmation of the principles of their beloved New Economy: entrepreneurship instead of top-down bureaucracy, frenetic change instead of stability, the chaos of free markets instead of regulation, labor "flexibility" instead of job security. In Gehry's high-profile box-breaking they see a heroic reflection of their own much-celebrated outside-the-box thinking.[6]

As Frank points out in his discussion of the "corporate creativity" manual *New Ideas about New Ideas*, the world of management gurus "repeatedly finds in Gehry's sinuous shapes and his computer-assisted creative process a pattern for the way business must be conducted in the new era we supposedly inhabit."[7] In Gehry's "trademark computer-assisted curves" is represented "the giddy religion of entrepreneurial 'creativity.'"[8] Though the museum has often been criticized as a site for the production and reification of inequality, writers like Frank were now arguing that even the buildings housing artworks and artefacts were participating in the very processes of risk-based venture capitalism that in 2008 would result in a global economic crisis. Though Krauss's argument is by far the more nuanced, together the two illustrate some of the concerns that were emerging as fields such as art production and museum building, previously either actively (in the case of critical art production) or passively (in the case of museum building) removed or placed above economic concerns, now appeared to be right at the centre of a changing economy.

Though cities in Canada did not go through a massive museum building boom in the way that some European cities did (Michaela Giebelhausen describes the city of Frankfurt, with population of 650,000, commissioning thirteen new museum buildings in the 1980s),[9] similar trends can be nonetheless found. While there had certainly been high-profile buildings created for museums prior to the 2000s (to mention just three well-known examples in Canada, Arthur Erickson's light-filled Museum of Anthropology [MOA] at the University of British Columbia in Vancouver [1976]; Moshe Safdie's design for the National Gallery of Canada [NGC] [Ottawa, 1988]; and Douglas Cardinal's sinuous Canadian Museum of Civilization [now the Canadian Museum of History, CMH] [Gatineau, 1989]), by 2010 almost all major cities in Canada had undertaken extensive architectural refurbishment, renewal, or rebuilding of their cultural edifices.[10] Key among these projects were the Daniel Libeskind–designed addition to the Royal Ontario Museum (Toronto, 2007), the Frank Gehry addition to the Art Gallery of Ontario (Toronto, 2008), the Quartier des spectacles in Montreal (2008–), the new Canadian War Museum in Ottawa (2005; see chapter 4), Will Alsop's "tabletop" building at the Ontario College of Art and Design (Toronto, 2004), Randall Stout's new building for the Art Gallery of Alberta (Edmonton, 2010), the Museum for Human Rights in Winnipeg (underway in 2008 and completed in 2014; see chapter 5) in addition to smaller projects elsewhere, among them the building of The Rooms in St John's, a refurbishment of the Art Gallery of Nova Scotia in Halifax, a new addition to the Natural History Museum in Ottawa, a new RCMP Heritage Centre in Regina, and

the new Aga Khan Museum in Toronto. Many renovation and building programs continue to the present day.[11]

As Krauss predicted, contemporary art markets thrived in this milieu, with the result that contemporary art galleries such as MASS MOCA, the Tate Modern, and the Guggenheim(s) enjoyed extraordinary visitorship, particularly from tourists. As Andrew McClellan points out, the same was not true for universal, history, ethnographic, and other non-art museums, some of which struggled during the period despite architectural updating.[12] Given this, perhaps it is also not surprising that this period has also seen a number of establishment museums, among them the British Museum and the ROM, begin collecting and displaying contemporary art.[13] Large-scale public/private festivals, such as Luminato in Toronto or Nuit Blanche in a number of locations, either, depending on one's viewpoint, democratized the arts, bringing them out into the streets and to the people or commoditized and marketized them, creating slick corporate projects that played into the hands of sponsors and organizers.[14]

Interestingly, many of the renovation and building projects listed above, particularly those at the ROM, AGO, and the CMHR, met stiff resistance and occasional picketing. "The gallery is no stranger to protests," noted one representative of the AGO, referring to protests that took place around renovations in the 1990s (which were followed by even louder protests in 2008), "it's just part of our life."[15] Though occurring almost a decade after the building of the Guggenheim Bilbao and

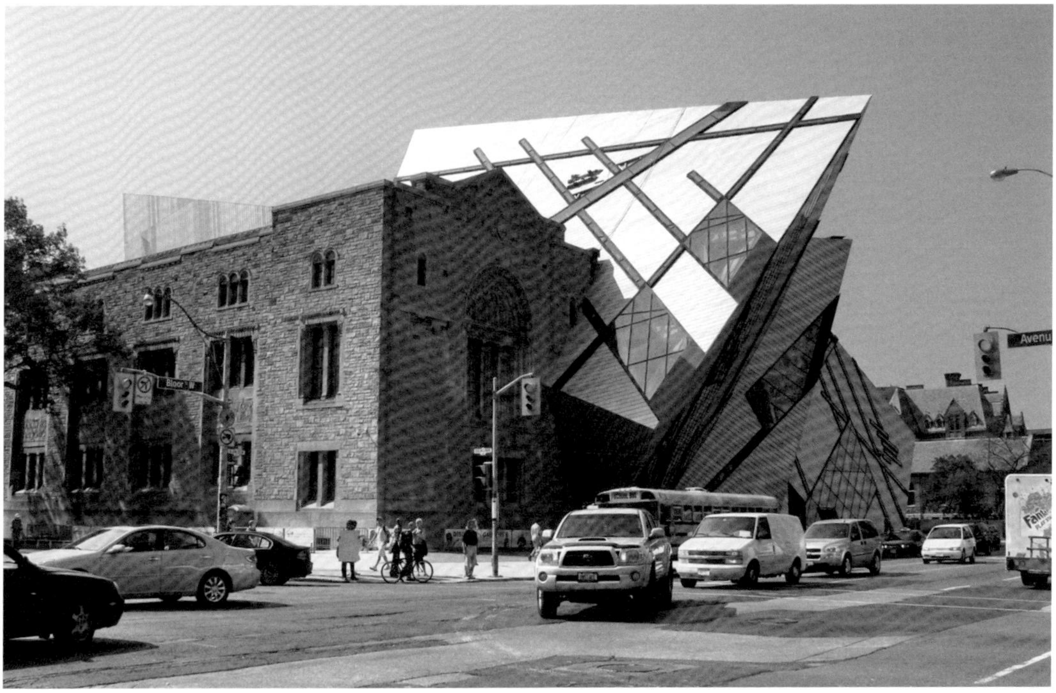

Figure 3.1
Royal Ontario Museum.

its numerous derivatives, the renovations of the ROM and AGO in 2005 and 2008, respectively (which were both quite tame in contrast with museum projects elsewhere) were nonetheless greeted with some discomfort. In Canada, museums remained deeply anchored in imaginings of the nation, province, and even the city. At the AGO and ROM, construction projects were profoundly disruptive for people who actually lived in the area. And at the CMHR, it was felt that adequate archaeological digging of the site had not been allowed because of pressures to build, thus potentially erasing Indigenous presence in the area (chapter 5).[16] In all, renovations dedicated to positioning Canadian institutions as part of a global order of museum building were occasionally at odds with expectations and perceptions of the role of authoritative institutions in Canada. In addition, as noted in Interstice 1a, building projects often conflicted with the lived realities of those who had to coexist with them, as well as with the gentrification that they may or may not bring and the histories that their emergence might erase.[17]

As more and more museum and cultural buildings partook in architectural innovation, a rigorous critique developed. As Joseba Zulaika and Ana Maria Guasch, Robert Hewison, Chin Tao-Wu, and many others cautioned, the sparkling changes to the exterior shells of museums do not necessarily serve the institution or even the public.[18] They might draw tourists, contribute to economic investment in a city, encourage a pleasant viewing experience, or put a city "on the map," but a tension between inside and outside, between the mandate of the museum and its position in other aspects of city, province, and country, could also be the result.[19]

For many, the spree of museum building was deeply connected to the gentrification of city centres, to the neoliberalization of the arts and culture, and to a market-savvy approach to museum maintenance that forced museums into fundraising ever-increasing amounts.[20] As Anne-Marie Broudehoux writes, "Spectacular architecture is now valued for its advertising power and its ability to brand the urban skyline and is considered vital to enhance the prestige and desirability of place ... signature buildings have become essential tools of city marketing."[21] Money for building projects was easy to attract, since the spectacular extensions often came with naming rights. But as projects grew ever larger and more ostentatious, the task of running museums in the aftermath of renovation projects, including such mundane activities as lighting, cleaning, and caring for collections, became ever more financially demanding.[22] Surely museums *couldn't* survive in this new climate without significant private sector funding. Even if that money had to come from questionable sources (chapter 6), without it, it was assumed, museums could no longer function.

Simultaneously, curators and critics, particularly those working in institutions in New York and London, were accused of being "more enmeshed in the market than before," for example, by working for both public and private institutions and thus potentially profiting enormously when the public institutions showed work by artists they represented in their own private commercial galleries. Galleries were also criticized for mounting shows that drew on their trustees' collections (thus raising the value of those collections).[23] As part of her 2012 project for the Whitney Biennale, artist Andrea Fraser drew together some of these critiques by tracing relationships between the art world and the 1%, looking at the ways funds were siphoned from public to private coffers and the resulting widening spread between rich and poor. Ultimately, she argued, artists are de facto supporters of the 1% simply through their relationships with the museums and galleries whose boards are populated by the ultra-rich.[24] She notes that "since public arts funding has mostly declined in Europe and North America since the 1980s, it must be assumed that, directly and indirectly, this increasingly concentrated private wealth has also fueled the enormous expansion in the past few decades of museums, biennial exhibitions, studio art and art related degree programs, art publications, art residencies and awards, etc."[25]

Fraser's points are compelling, but occasionally the problems faced by museums and fundraising projects were/are much more mundane. Naming rights, as Joe Day notes, only go so far, and a number of wealthy individuals left the public sphere and establishment museums, instead creating their own private galleries (chapter 7).[26] In chapters in this book on the CMHR (chapter 5) and the Vancouver Art

Gallery (VAG) (chapter 7), I discuss the difficulty both institutions had (and have) in securing funds for renovation and building projects. The money simply was and is not there, meaning that an evacuation of public funds from the cultural sphere is sometimes met with fundraising efforts that secure monies from suspect or unprincipled sources, but occasionally such campaigns are met with nothing at all, meaning either a return to public funds or a narrowing of possibilities.

In March 2015, a significant investigative report in the *Globe and Mail* showed that despite splashy fundraising receptions and naming rights, many of those involved in the ROM's Daniel Libeskind–led "Crystal" renovation had not come through on their pledges, leaving the museum mired in debt.[27] The ROM had borrowed $72 million from the Canadian Imperial Bank of Commerce to finance the renovation, securing that loan through the promise of funds from wealthy benefactors. When pledges failed to materialize, money to cover a shortfall had to come from the public purse such that Ontario citizens ended up paying the debt even as donors were still receiving credit for pledges they hadn't fulfilled. As the reporters note, the Crystal was financed by "a fundraising campaign that at times placed greater emphasis on the perception that money was being raised than the actual collection of funds."[28] While many of those donors were simply taking their time about paying or had been adversely affected by the 2008 global economic crisis, the ROM's plight is indicative of the negative impact renovations can have. The story also noted that around the time of ground-breaking, the ROM had forty-six curators, but at the time the story was written, only thirty-four remained. It was not clear if the museum's debt led directly to layoffs (as noted in the anecdote at the opening of the introduction, the AGO was also laying off workers around the same time).

Suzanne MacLeod writes, "As museums have come to be consciously recognized as drivers for social and economic regeneration, the architecture of the museum has developed from its traditional forms into spectacular one-off statements and architectural visions."[29] She continues by noting that there is a "tension between iconic architecture and the agendas of access and inclusion that form the central tenets of the modern museum. Often criticized as architectural indulgences, iconic buildings can compound the separation between the building, its contents and its context."[30] She also suggests that signature buildings often overshadow the needs and wants of museum staff: "such buildings may work very well as icons and cultural landmarks without achieving the levels of accessibility, usability and relevance for both visitors and staff, promised during their conception."[31]

Nevertheless, the period that has seen vast museum overhauls is the same period that Ivan Karp and Corinne A. Kratz describe as bringing into being the "interrogative museum," a term that they use to describe a collaborative turn in museum practice, with the following idea at its centre: "exhibit the problem, not the solution," resulting in dialogue-based exhibitions practice. They write, "it means taking museum exhibits as essentially contested, debatable, and respecting the agency and knowledge-ability of audiences when we develop and design exhibits."[32] On the one hand, as museums have channelled funds toward building projects, they have produced an increasing number of blockbuster exhibitions designed specifically to draw in visitors and money, and visitor needs are often positioned ahead of the collection. But on the other hand, the period is also one in which we see museums "open to change … and in touch with contemporary issues and agendas."[33] Perhaps it is a case of museums doing more with less, but it is equally possible that the lessons of the 1990s took hold as museums began to look to the communities of which they were a part. As Richard Sandell and Eithne Nightingale note in the introduction to their book, "the last two decades have seen concerns for equality, diversity, social justice and human rights move from the margins of museum thinking and practice, to the core."[34] These processes have been uneven and have also led to tension (see, for example, the CMHR's refusal to use the word genocide in their exhibition space, chapter 5) but have nonetheless developed into an emergent set of possibilities for museums.

In sum, the reception of major museum building projects tended to be either remarkably celebratory, assuming that the mere presence of unique museum buildings would result in positive change for urban centres, or deeply critical, arguing that such projects were in line with the expansion of neoliberalism into formerly protected spheres.[35] Simultaneously, the calls for change in museums took hold with the development of more open practices of collecting, archiving, and display. For the purposes of my argument, I am interested in how the expansion of museums and focus on their exteriors, in combination with a quite different set of changes taking place on the inside, either worked with or collided with the many instances of political action at the gallery threshold. In the 1990s, as covered in the previous chapter, with the notable exception of *Spirit Sings*, political action and insurgence tended to be halted at the threshold. Has anything changed since the 1990s? The answer to this question is not straightforward. Cathy Ross, in an article on collecting from Occupy London, notes that a move toward contemporary collecting in many large museums, in combination with policies and mandates emphasizing community engagement, education, and promoting active citizenship, has created an environment in which engaging with activists and with groups formerly overlooked by many museums is valued and probable.[36] But reaching out can be interpreted as intrusion, particularly if museums have not engaged in the slow work of repairing and building relationships.

In the next section, I look at the changes to permanent exhibition spaces in Canada in light of the tensions that I outline above. This section is purposely brief and synecdochical. While an entire book or even library could be dedicated to changes in Canadian museum exhibitions since the turn of the millennium, I have narrowed my focus to look solely at how only a few permanent displays have dealt with and/or highlighted activism and Indigenous resurgence. It is often taken as a given that museums display "winner's history" and that they tend to collect primarily from those who hold and maintain power structures. What would it look like for museums to reverse these accepted, and oft-criticized, norms?

Museum Interiors

As I was finishing the writing of this book, museums in the United States and the UK in particular were mounting a huge number of exhibitions dedicated to protest movements, activist ephemera, and "disobedient" design. Gavin Grindon's 2014 *Disobedient Objects* at the V&A undoubtedly led the way (chapter 1).[37] By the summer of 2018, almost every major institution in London, for example, was mounting shows such as *I Object*, the British Museum's 2018 exhibition on objects of dissent,[38] or the Design Museum's *Hope to Nope: Graphics and Politics 2008–2018*, both of which ended in upheaval. The group BP or Not BP staged an intervention in the former, organizing a "protest [exhibition] inside the protest exhibition" that drew attention to the museum's sponsorship by BP, and included:

> [a] photo of the Colombian union leader Gilberto Torres, who sued BP for indirect links to his kidnapping ... the Morning Star flag used by the independence movement in West Papua, where the Indonesian military crushed protests related to foreign resource extraction, [a] tear gas canister from Cairo represent[ing] BP's investments in Egypt, whose government has cracked down on dissent ... [and] a bright blue vest and bowtie reportedly confiscated by British Museum security staff during a previous performance.[39]

The latter action was the more strident of the two, occurring when the Design Museum rented its atrium to Leonardo, one of the world's largest aerospace and defence companies.[40] Many of the artists and designers whose work had been included in *Hope to Nope* demanded that it be removed. Members of BP or Not BP (who had an artefact from one of their performances in the exhibition) organized a march on the museum to remove the works if the institution refused. The museum claimed they were "caught in an argument not of their own making" and resisted being seen as "an easy target and a surrogate for the real target of these campaigners," even as they complained that the artists were "making a fuss" and surmised that such actions would lead to fewer exhibitions of protest art and design.[41] Not surprisingly, the artists, designers, and activists involved in the show wondered at the museum's ability to "criticiz[e] us for being the very thing we were only a minute ago being celebrated for."[42] Ultimately, the Design Museum complied, removed the works, and also announced that it would no longer host private events for defence, fossil fuel, or tobacco companies, at least while it reviewed its policies.[43] In turn, an anti-exhibition called *Nope to Hope* was organized by the Nope to Arms Collective in Brixton, including many of the withdrawn artworks and objects.[44]

While the *I Object* and *Hope to Nope* exhibitions demonstrated the perils of showing activist ephemera without engaging with the politics of the movements, other museums appeared undeterred. The success of the *Disobedient Object* exhibition at the V&A perhaps led to the inclusion of a number of activist elements in the summer blockbuster exhibition *The Future Starts Now*. Meanwhile, in New York, the Whitney Museum opened their large-scale exhibition *An Incomplete History of Protest: Selections from the Whitney's Collection, 1940–2017*.[45] These are just the largest of the many exhibitions that seemed to demonstrate a growing interest on the part of authoritative institutions, particularly in New York and London, in showcasing activism (if not actually participating in it).[46]

In Canada, few exhibitions dedicated specifically to activist material culture took place (I do discuss one, *City on Edge*, in chapter 7). None took place of the size and scope of those in New York and London. But something else quite interesting was occurring. First of all, from the early years of the 2000s and growing massively in the 2010s, a huge number of exhibitions took place that had as their core goal either drawing attention to inequalities, abuses, or other issues or offering possibilities for change and ideations of new worlds. There are far too many to list here, but as examples I nod to *Every.Now.Then* (covered in chapter 1), *Lalakenis/All Directions* (chapter 6), and *It's All Happening So Fast*, a research-heavy exhibition that explored human impact on the world (and resource extraction in Canada) and offered numerous examples of resistance to environmental destruction as well as models for moving forward.[47] And second, a number of large-scale permanent exhibitions at authoritative Canadian institutions were significantly altered, disrupting the status quo of museum culture in Canada. It is to these displays that I now turn.

When I did a survey of permanent exhibition spaces at major museums in Canada in 2012 for this book, I found very few displays acknowledging contentious politics and even fewer showcasing material culture of activism. Some of the few examples included an exhibition on the 1919 Winnipeg general strike at the CMC, which was actually removed in the 2015 reinstallation;[48] an exhibition on 1960s counterculture and resistance in the Strathcona neighbourhood of Vancouver at the Museum of Vancouver; and a tiny (less than a square foot) wall panel describing anti-war activism at the Canadian War Museum. When the CMHR opened in 2014, it included

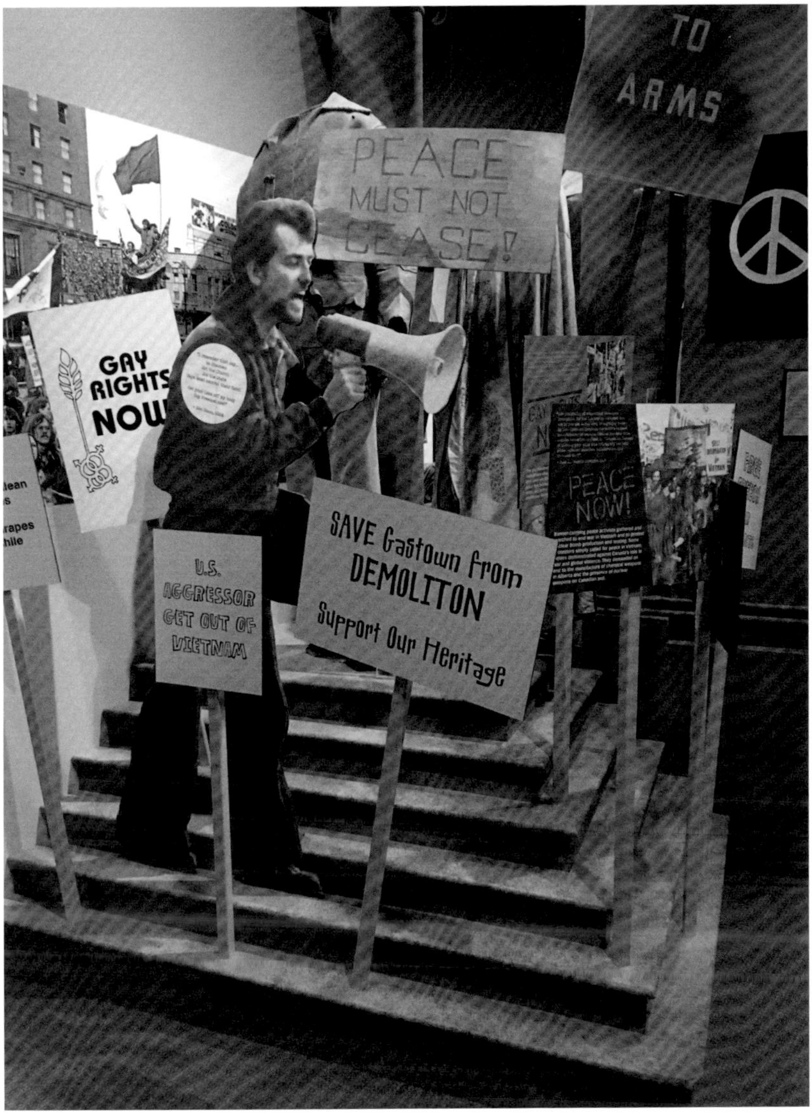

Figure 3.2
Museum of Vancouver, permanent display dedicated to hippie culture.

several images and exhibition cases dedicated to Indigenous resistance and blockades and to the 2012 "casseroles" protests in Montreal against draconian Bill 78.[49] Often these were federally funded, authoritative museums and included extensive exhibitions and displays concerned with narratives of Canadian history and progress. Overwhelmingly, such stories were presented as seamless narratives of progress, tolerance, inclusion, and multiculturalism.[50] What would it mean, instead, for a traditional, authoritative, establishment museum to rework its collection to tell a different story, one with resistance at its centre? When I have presented the idea that permanent collections should be based in counter-histories to students and colleagues, I'm often met with the following: "at the time, everyone supported x [i.e., the residential school system], so is it not the role of museums to show history and to avoid reinterpretations that reflect present values?" Such statements illustrate a belief that museums should showcase settler perspectives, but they also are factually incorrect. The residential school system provides a good example, since its imposition was met with support but also with constant resistance from parents, children, and other family members, Indigenous communities, settler allies, members of the religious orders that had helped to establish the schools in the first place, and even government representatives.[51] Surely such stories also need to be told and such people also need to be acknowledged?

In 2016 and 2017, as the writing of this book came to a close, a deep division emerged in Canadian institutions between celebrations of Canada's 150th "birthday" and resistance to that celebration. At the same time that museums, small and large, were organizing Canada150-themed exhibitions, often drawing on significant funding from various levels of government, they were simultaneously trying to respond to calls from the 2015 Truth and Reconciliation Commission of Canada (TRC) final report and calls to action that specifically called on museums and archives in Canada to fund commemoration projects on the theme of reconciliation, to open access to archives pertaining to residential schools, and to come in line with recommendations from the United Nations Declaration on the Rights of Indigenous Peoples (UNDRIP), which includes sections on repatriation and on the right to culture.[52]

While some museums used Canada150 funds to curate fairly radical exhibitions (see descriptions in the introduction of shows at the AGO and Kitchener Themuseum), most were celebratory and parochial. In response, Inuk curator and scholar Heather Igloliorte writes, "I question how Canada can justify the heavy price tag for these nation-wide activities while telling First Nations, Métis, and Inuit peoples that it does not have the means to honour its responsibility to provide its citizens with urgent, basic needs like clean drinking water and childhood education."[53] How can museums work toward reconciliation while simultaneously celebrating the imposition of a settler nation?

Interestingly, one answer was to participate in Canada150 funding for temporary exhibitions while comprehensively reworking permanent collections to tell more open-ended stories that responded to calls from the TRC and that occasionally used insurgent action to tell the "story of Canada." As Michael Levin states, "the museum, almost by definition, does more than express current social values and tastes; it also makes a cultural statement which goes beyond its own place in history."[54] In short, some museums *did* begin to reconstruct their core narratives of nation-building by taking resistance to that process as a central tenet of the stories the museum was now trying to tell. The success or failure of such permanent exhibitions notwithstanding, I nonetheless point to the effort as a key evolution of museum strategy in Canada.

Two massive reinstallations took place in Ottawa in 2017, coincident with Canada150 celebrations, one at the National Gallery of Canada (NGC), the other at the Canadian Museum of History (CMH). At the NGC, First Nations, Métis, and Inuit cultural materials are now included in each room, building on a reinstallation that took place in 2006 and that addressed the nearly complete lack of Indigenous material in the Canadian history collection.[55] Organized primarily chronologically, the new permanent exhibition uses the continuity and resurgence of Indigenous culture across time to counter the story of a settler Canadian nation built through its art that was the tale of the former historical Canadian galleries. Points of connection and contention are interwoven to tell multiple histories and to contextualize or even (slightly) sideline the story of nation-building via the Group of Seven that has been the gallery's bread and butter since it was established as a formal museum in 1910.[56]

The CMH approach is arguably the more radical of the two. In chapter 6, I look at the background to the reinstallation of the Canadian History Hall. The reworking of the gallery was, to say the least, controversial because it was tied up in the celebratory and parochial nationalism of the Harper Conservative government. Many were the critiques that preceded the reopening of the Canadian History Hall at the CMH, with fears that the exhibition narrative would be focused on "dead white men" and military conflicts in the name of a Warrior Nation (chapter 4).[57] In fact, the Canadian History Hall displays are instead evidence of extensive consultation with communities beyond the museum's walls, and the exhibition is clearly "interrogative." While the Hall does tell the tale of Canadian history and occasionally slips into a celebratory narrative of settler nationality, tolerance, and multiculturalism, for the most part the story told in these galleries is one of ongoing resistance, tied into the continuity and resurgence of Indigenous communities. It is actively reflexive, explaining throughout both the strengths and shortcomings of museums in general. Visitors are told that replicas are used in many exhibits so that artefacts can be repatriated, evidence of collaboration is clearly acknowledged, and technology is used to fill in when objects cannot (for example, in the animated creation stories that welcome visitors to the space or the way that First Nations and Métis storytelling is used to add perspective to a diorama telling the history of Head Smashed in Buffalo Jump).[58] Oral histories are given central space, and wampum is treated as equivalent to written treaties and documents. The Early Canada and Colonial Canada wings tell a much more nuanced story than did the old galleries, and they give precedence to stories of survivance and of overcoming oppression. The Modern Canada wing continues this story, with several exhibits, key among them one dedicated to Idle No More, given over to those who resist rather than contribute to a project of nation-building. In the Idle No More and other displays, progress is equated to resistance, and Canada emerges as a fractured and multiple nation formed through struggle.

In writing this, I am aware of Wrightson's argument with regard to the way that representation alone is compensatory. I also write this aware of arguments coming primarily from art critics that the bringing into the museum of political art leads to its inevitable co-option and the erasure of its politics. Certainly, an exhibition at the CMH does not equate to the end of settler-colonial relations, and it does not imply the return of land or even the halting of colonial relations that have led to boil-water advisories and poor housing conditions on reserves. Nevertheless, I wonder if the changing of the exhibition narrative in two federal institutions can have ripple effects. What does it mean for federal institutions to tell stories that are at odds with much of the legislation coming from government itself? That remains to be seen.

In sum, the combination of changes to permanent installations, alongside numerous temporary exhibitions with transformation at their heart, resulted in an uneven yet significant alteration to the museum sphere in Canada in the first decades of the 2000s. While a surface analysis showing a lack of "disobedient object" exhibitions appears to demonstrate a disavowal or lack of interest in activist politics, I suggest that a more nuanced approach taken in many exhibitions and displays in Canada is worthy of comment. It is incontrovertible that even though Canadian institutions are faced with the same issues as museums elsewhere (for example, the need to seek sponsorships from controversial companies and boards of directors and upper administrations with interests in determining the direction of museums and exhibition practices), over the past decade change has taken place. This is particularly true of exhibitions that engage with Indigenous self-representation. It is also true that such changes are not always consistent and are often reversed, erased, or actively suppressed (see chapter 4, for example).[59] But even so, transformation of the core myths at some authoritative institutions and the active encouragement of numerous interventionist exhibitions should be noted, even as the limits of those changes are actively critiqued.

Having said that, I think it is equally clear that museums in Canada still struggle with the material culture available to them. With the exception of contemporary artworks acquired very recently, the NGC borrowed almost all of the Indigenous artefacts, regalia, and artworks from other institutions, a legacy of divisions between ethnographic and art museums.[60] And the CMH has almost no objects at all in its exhibition halls. First and foremost, this is the result of the visitor-centred approaches typical of recent museum exhibitions (Steven Conn has discussed this issue in depth).[61] Second, as the CMH itself notes, many of the artefacts that the museum holds from source communities should not be on display or should be returned. But, third, one also wonders whether a vastly different narrative undertaken by the museum is one that is not quite supported by materials held in the collections of institutions that have for a long time been collecting in very particular ways and toward very particular ends. While much more could be said about contemporary reinstallations of permanent exhibitions, I leave these descriptions relatively open and move behind the scenes, addressing how museums collect contemporary material culture, with an emphasis on radical, insurgent, and activist artefacts.[62]

Behind the Scenes

The significant gaps in the archive of "disobedient objects" was made clear when I worked with a research assistant to contact all major, and many smaller, museums in Canada to find out what protest ephemera they hold in their archives.[63] Our questions referred both to protests that had taken place at the institutions in question and, more generally, to any kind of political material culture that might be held by major institutions. We additionally asked about material culture pertaining to Indigenous resistance over time.

The answer to the question about protest ephemera is that across the country, very little material can be easily found in collections. When asked why museums don't tend to collect such material, one collections associate wrote, "I can say, anecdotally, that much of what has historically been donated to museums comes from a middle to upper-middle class demographic with European ancestry. This demographic seems to be the most proactive in ensuring their stories are told in a museum setting. They are also a demographic in Canada which, arguably, has had very little to protest."[64] There is one essential caveat to this claim. The curator at the Royal BC Museum, Dr Lorne Hammond, suggested that it was because the Chenhall object classification system used in most Canadian museums is "descriptive of the physical object and does not identify ideas, concepts, actions or cultural events at all."[65] In other words, material objects from protests might be in collections but cannot be easily accessed through a search for "protest."[66] For example, the many documents I found in the AGO archive that had been collected in the 1960s and 1970s and were related to actions that had taken place at the gallery did not show up in my initial search (see Interstices 1a and 3c). Similarly, artefacts related to First Nations blockades and the Kanehsatà:ke Resistance, which I know (having seen or read about them in exhibitions) are held in major collections, did not show up in searches.[67] As noted in the preface, Indigenous peoples tend not to use the word protest, and contemporary collecting from Indigenous communities is not categorized using such terms. Thus, searches through collections were necessarily incomplete.

Nevertheless, almost all of the archivists with whom the research assistant and I spoke noted passionately that their museums' holdings were piecemeal at best and that they themselves wished to improve holdings in material evidence from protests, actions, and interventions of the type discussed in the previous chapter. Gaps in the archive were often visibly present. For example, in the archives dedicated to *Into the Heart of Africa* and *Spirit Sings*, almost no material record of demonstrations or interventions remains aside from press clippings. Although these protests had major effects on museum policy, their legacies are often only visible through mining other materials (newspaper and oral reports, books, and essays written after the fact). If it seems logical that a museum would not collect from a protest that had taken place against it, I'll show later in this section, first, how this creates an incomplete archive and second, how museums are now changing tactics with regard to collecting from such actions. Furthermore, as noted above, for some time in the 1960s and 1970s, the AGO *was* collecting such material, although, interestingly, the push to collect was led by one archivist and documentation in the archive shows that most of the file was lost or misplaced some time in the 1970s.[68]

In terms of protest actions in general, a museum curator wrote to me about a police officer's billy club used on unemployed protesters during the occupation of the Vancouver Post Office in 1938 on permanent display at the Royal BC Museum (this was part of a sit-in that took place across a number of institutional buildings, including the Vancouver Art Gallery).[69] Nothing remains from those engaged in the sit-in. Three red squares worn by the spokespeople of the Maple Spring student-led movement, which took place in Quebec in 2012, were accessioned by the Musée des Civilisations in Quebec City in 2015.[70] Additionally, many museums (including institutions that are not dedicated to art, such as the Canadian War Museum) hold rich collections of visual art that is either didactically activist or that corresponds with, parallels, or illuminates social movements.[71]

Gregory Sholette calls authoritative galleries "the gatekeeper museums," a term that implies an unwillingness to engage with radical thought and performance.[72] He argues that archiving radical art and protest ephemera "could only have been made possible once any actual threat to institutional authority had fully passed."[73] This is a compelling argument, but it is not quite the case with regard to the archives and collections covered here. Perhaps because museums in Canada tend not to be physically threatened by protest movements, collecting or not collecting radical material seems primarily an issue of choice. Most museums responded quickly to requests to detail their protest collections. Some replies were short and to the point: the ROM, for example, responded with an email stating that they had little aside from newspaper clippings from the "*Into the Heart of Africa* protests" and strike posters from a union strike at the ROM.[74] By contrast, the CMH responded with a detailed overview of their collection, noting "we try to keep a certain balance between 'institutional' political history (material related to political parties, the courts, the monarchy, etc.) and anti- or para- or counter-institutional."[75] Even so, while describing the collection, the CMH curator noted that the collections (in environmentalism, feminism, Quebec sovereignty, and anti-racism as well as homophobia and anti-abortion) could use significant expansion.[76] As will be noted in chapter 6, the CMH decided not to keep a section of *T'aaw*, a copper that was broken as part of a shaming ceremony, led by Hereditary Chief Beau Dick (Kwakwaka'wakw), that took place outside the museum in 2014. The copper did end up in the collection of the Haida Gwaii Museum and Heritage Centre in Kay Llinagaay (Skidegate).[77]

Interestingly, in a detail that I will unfold further in chapter 7, the museums that had the most extensive collections of activist/resurgent material culture and ephemera were located in Vancouver. The Museum of Anthropology (MOA) prominently displays Tla-o-qui-hat artist Joe David's welcome figure *Cedar Man*, acquired by the MOA in 1987.[78] The label at MOA reads:

> The figure was first raised at Tin-Wis in Nuu-chah-nulth territory. With the support of the Tribal Council, the carving was raised a second time in front of the Provincial Parliament Buildings during the 1984 Meares Island anti-logging rally in Victoria. The figure stood at the front of the Museum of Anthropology from 1987 to 2008 when it was removed due to construction and a redesign of the museum entrance area. The figure was reinstalled in the Museum's Great Hall in February 2012.[79]

MOA also has a significant collection from the 1997 APEC meetings, which were partially held in the institution's grand hall (see chapter 8, conclusion).[80] This collection was spearheaded by the museum, which wanted to counter the official narrative of APEC with a more nuanced one. Following the APEC meetings, the museum organized Democracy Street, inviting activist groups into the museum.[81] Material from this event was kept by the museum. The Museum of Vancouver (MOV) has an excellent collection of hippie, yippie, and pro-marijuana material from the 1960s and 1970s and extensive anti–2010 Olympics material culture. Jillian Povarchook, the curatorial associate at MOV, notes that "Protest movements figure so prominently in our relatively short history that I think it would be fairly conspicuous if objects related to them didn't make it into the MOV's collection."[82] She further noted of the anti-Olympics collection, "Our collection committee felt strongly that MOV had a responsibility to also represent those who protested the Games being held on unceded traditional Coast Salish territory, as well as the expense of holding the Games while there are so many in Vancouver in desperate need of shelter, safety, and treatment for mental health and addiction issues."[83]

Such policies, which seem to be the status quo at MOV, are certainly not found elsewhere, where protest only occasionally appears in collections. The Vancouver Art Gallery, for example, does not collect anything from the protests that take place right on its doorstep (see chapter 7).[84]

Curator Dr Lorne Hammond of the Royal BC Museum sent a response that was particularly useful and detailed. He took the time to describe some of the difficulties of simply trying to collect contentious material, noting the museum's collecting policy could not overlap with that of other museums, something he encountered when he tried to accession plywood that had been placed over broken windows in Vancouver following the hockey riot in 2011 and then graffitied with messages of support by the Vancouver public. The plywood was accessioned by the MOV. Hammond also notes, "if you look at the recent Burnaby Mountain pipeline protests, they are of provincial significance, however the protest was supported by the Mayor of Burnaby and collecting does fall under the Burnaby municipal museum's mandate."[85] Occasionally too, objects are scattered because of space issues. Talking about the collection of Derrick Mallard, an environmental activist whose papers were accessioned by the University of Victoria, Hammond notes, "I took the larger three dimensional items which they were not able to store, including protest banners and a paper-maché cow used to protest bovine growth hormone, and a 1975 prototype wind turbine blade and some items to teach alternate energy in schools."[86] Hammond continues, "Would I accept placards and protest banners from significant events in British Columbia? Yes. When an individual approaches me with a significant object on protest I assess it for provincial significance and ask the donor's wishes. If I know of another collection where the item should go for preservation I am ethically bound to point that out. If they decide against that option I bring it forward."[87] Hammond also discussed APEC, noting, "In the case of APEC no museum could foresee the events that occurred. In the litigation that followed no one could legally give up 'evidence.'" His comments here are particularly illuminating, and I quote them at length. When he refers to Clayoquot, he is referring to anti-logging protests that took place in Clayoquot Sound (Vancouver Island) in the early 1990s, which grew from the Mears Island demonstration mentioned above.

> The APEC events are a bit Russian doll–like: they involve international, national, provincial, municipal events. They involve events at specific museums and on a university grounds that operates both archives and museums. In the complexity of the commons, who should collect? In my view the pepper spray canister is the most infamous and numinous object from the protest, but there is no donor willing to donate it. How will the event be viewed in 50 years? As significant as the Post Office Occupation [1938]? I don't know. I would say Clayoquot was

significant and one of those people arrested may select to make a donation to the collection, but should a state curator harass them for objects? It is not as simple as it seems if you take your ethics seriously. In my experience people bring to us the items that they value and want preserved. They are usually gifts.[88]

It is this latter point that I find the most interesting. Activists do not tend to trust museums and authoritative galleries and are unwilling or might not think of donating collections. But this often means that those objects are not collected, thus exacerbating museums' ability to show only certain narratives. As Sholette notes, allowing protest material to be accessioned runs the risk of succumbing to "a capacity to exert power 'all the way down,' into the finest of details and historical shadows."[89] There are exceptions (the Glenbow Museum acknowledges that they do not collect protest material on any consistent basis but do have some, including a G8 protest collection gathered by Kyla Tichkowsky when she was an intern at the museum), but I found few examples.[90]

Kylie Message documents a situation both similar and different at the Smithsonian, particularly in the 1960s and 1970s. She quotes Edith Mayo, curator at the Division of Political History at the Smithsonian History and Technology Museum during the years of the Civil Rights movement:

It is often hazardous to collect at such demonstrations, but from such collecting forays have come our most valuable "movement" materials – hats, posters and organizational materials from Resurrection City; posters, literature and banners from anti–Vietnam war demonstrations, American Indian Movement demands and literature from the occupation of the Bureau of Indian Affairs.[91]

Since the protests were taking place right outside the museum on the Washington Mall, it was somewhat easy to collect. Message's research, however, also showed that such collection practices were often unsanctioned and that materials were kept in curators' offices, under desks, or hidden in storage (occasionally to be "added" to the collection when they were "found" later).[92] Collect first, accession later seemed to be the underlying premise at the Smithsonian.

The response of curators at the Smithsonian is illuminating because it demonstrates how involved they were in what was happening around them, as well as the agency that they had in determining collections policy, even if they had to wait many years for accession to take place. Forty years later, by contrast, it became readily apparent that especially at institutions like the CMH, collections policy had to be determined by a number of bodies before items could be accessioned. Archivists and curators could not simply be "secretly" collecting objects to be held for a later time (at least not within the museum).[93] The informal collecting policy used by Smithsonian curators as detailed by Message seems no longer to exist, although institutions in general appear more interested in collecting from political events as they happen.

At this moment, where such collecting practices do exist, for example, the V&A's "Rapid Response" collecting activity, which targets design and manufacturing objects related to major contemporary moments (such as the first 3D-printed gun, a pair of pants made at the collapsed Rana Plaza factory in Bangladesh, and a stuffed animal used at a protest), they are the exception rather than the rule.[94] As Message writes with regard to a series of items not accessioned by the Smithsonian in the 1970s, "The question raised in each of these cases was whether the national museum was simply documenting part of the political culture, or whether it was bestowing historical credibility on something that was either controversial or that potentially undermined the mainstream stories (and values) of American nationalism."[95] She also notes there were other concerns, such as whether images of protesters should be used in exhibition spaces without the consent of those in the images. And if consent is needed, how does one go about obtaining it?[96]

This is a question that remains pertinent.[97] As I was writing this chapter, the Occupy encampments were coming to an end in many cities across North America and the UK. Interestingly, Occupy seems to have provoked a significant number of museums to consider collecting protest ephemera (in Canada, materials from Occupy Vancouver were collected by a university archive at Simon Fraser University).[98] In early 2011, the Smithsonian released an official statement noting that it would collect from Occupy, an action that was followed by numerous other major institutions in New York City (all of which collected specifically from Occupy Wall Street [OWS] and actions in Zucotti Park).[99] The Smithsonian also noted in its press release that its collecting from political events was even-handed and that the American history collection included material from Occupy as well as from the massive Tea Party rally against health care reform in March 2010 and other conservative/right-wing events.[100]

Curator Jim Gledhill's coverage of how the Museum of London (UK) attempted to collect from the Occupy London encampment just outside its doors provides a detailed case study for how such projects might take place.[101] In agreement with Message, quoted above, he writes,

> The curator's a priori decision to collect material from Occupy imbued it with important social historical status that could be interpreted by both participants and critics alike as a source of political legitimacy. From an ethical standpoint, however, the risks inherent in the curatorial decision to engage with the Occupy movement for collecting purposes were offset by the overriding legitimacy of the museum's publicly enshrined mission of preserving London's history.[102]

Gledhill noted that his particular institution, the Museum of London, had a long history of engaging with and collecting from protest movements, including but not limited to the Campaign for Nuclear Disarmament in the 1980s and the anti-road protests of the 1990s. Occupy, however, brought up a particular dilemma because the encampment outside St Paul's Cathedral was in part organized against the Corporation of London, one of the founders of the museum. Gledhill summarizes,

> Both state and financial institutions, and the power relationships they embody, were being questioned by the Occupy movement, within the City of London and nationally, as new camps sprang up elsewhere in the country. For a public institution funded by the state via local government, this represented a challenge to acquire representative material culture which would require active engagement with the movement, while maintaining proper boundaries as a public body.[103]

In Canada, where most museums over a certain size receive both public and corporate funding, these are pressing questions. Though plenty of literature exists discussing how/whether museums are able to keep arm's-length relationships from corporate sponsors when it comes to exhibitions, there are fewer discussions of these problems when it comes to Canadian archives and collections.

A corollary question is what to collect. In an interview about the New York Historical Society's long-term collecting of political material (from across the political spectrum), museum director Margi Hofer noted, "Political buttons or flat objects are easy to store; anything bulky or 'bigger than a toaster' gives … pause … In general, food is a problem."[104] Such considerations, in combination with the comments above noting that events have to be of a certain size and "importance," lead museums to collect in particular ways – protest actions must reach a certain level or strength before they draw the attention of museums. Thus, many institutions have collected, and publicized that they have collected, "pussy hats," the pink hats worn by hundreds of thousands of women marching against the election of Donald Trump.[105] But although museums and archives seem to be collecting material beyond the mainstream, I found far less coverage, with the notable exception of the Smithsonian National Museum of African American History and Culture, showing that authoritative museums other than those specifically dedicated to African American culture were collecting from Black Lives Matter actions.[106]

The potential problems with collecting from protest movements came to a head in 2018 when Donald Trump visited the UK and museums competed to collect "Trump Baby," a "six meter high orange, inflatable baby with a malevolent face and tiny hands"[107] that floated above the demonstrations in London and Edinburgh. An *Artworld* story from July 2018 noted that Trump Baby "is now in high demand among curators. The British Museum, among other institutions, is interested in the diaper-clad, smartphone-carrying, snarling inflatable, which became a mascot for protesters last week."[108] Almost before the protests against Trump had ended, the British Museum announced that it hoped to borrow the balloon for its *I Object* exhibition, while Museum of London proclaimed that it wished to collect it permanently. Before long, the Design Museum, the Science Museum, and the Bishopsgate Institute in East London had all expressed interest. In the meantime, the makers of the blimp released a statement noting, "We haven't discounted the possibility of him ending up in a museum, but our main priority right now is to ensure that he gets as much mileage as possible in a global tour of trolling both Trump and the politics of hate and division that he represents."[109]

Trump Baby highlighted the growing importance of rapid response collecting, but it also raised some important questions. As curator Owen Hopkins (Soane Museum) noted in an editorial, "as this type of collecting becomes ever more prevalent, it seems that press coverage is increasingly becoming an end in itself – a useful shortcut to being relevant, accessible and even contemporary. And at a time when museum budgets have been stripped right back, it's usually far cheaper than most audience-engagement projects."[110] Indeed, the somewhat unseemly competition over collecting Trump Baby did appear to indicate a focus on popular and media-friendly items disconnected from the daily work of resistance. This was especially true as museums sought to collect the object long before its use was complete, thus ostensibly removing it from any contentious situation and quelling its impact.[111] And yet, the media coverage of museums and Trump Baby suffered from a similar elision, focusing on the balloon while ignoring ongoing collection from outside of the mainstream.

For example, in keeping with Hammond's and Sholette's comments above, Gledhill also describes how initial attempts at collecting by the Museum of London were met with suspicion on the part of Occupiers. It is easy to imagine archivists running behind protests, picking up ephemera as it is dropped by those on the front lines, but more formal interventions take time and patience. In Gledhill's case, the museum had to position itself between the Occupiers and the authorities and to do so through "the social value of the museum's core aim of historical preservation."[112] Ultimately, Gledhill notes, the relationship was not always an easy one, and there were tensions present.

Similarly, in August 2016 the Royal BC Museum collected from INTent City, a homeless camp in Victoria (near the museum). A judge had recently ordered the evacuation of the site and the move of residents into social housing purchased by the BC government. In this case, residents played a strong role in determining what would be collected, and in each case relationships were built and permissions sought. Curator Hammond described the experience: "The response was very positive," he said. "It was kind of a whirlwind four hours or so spent visiting and

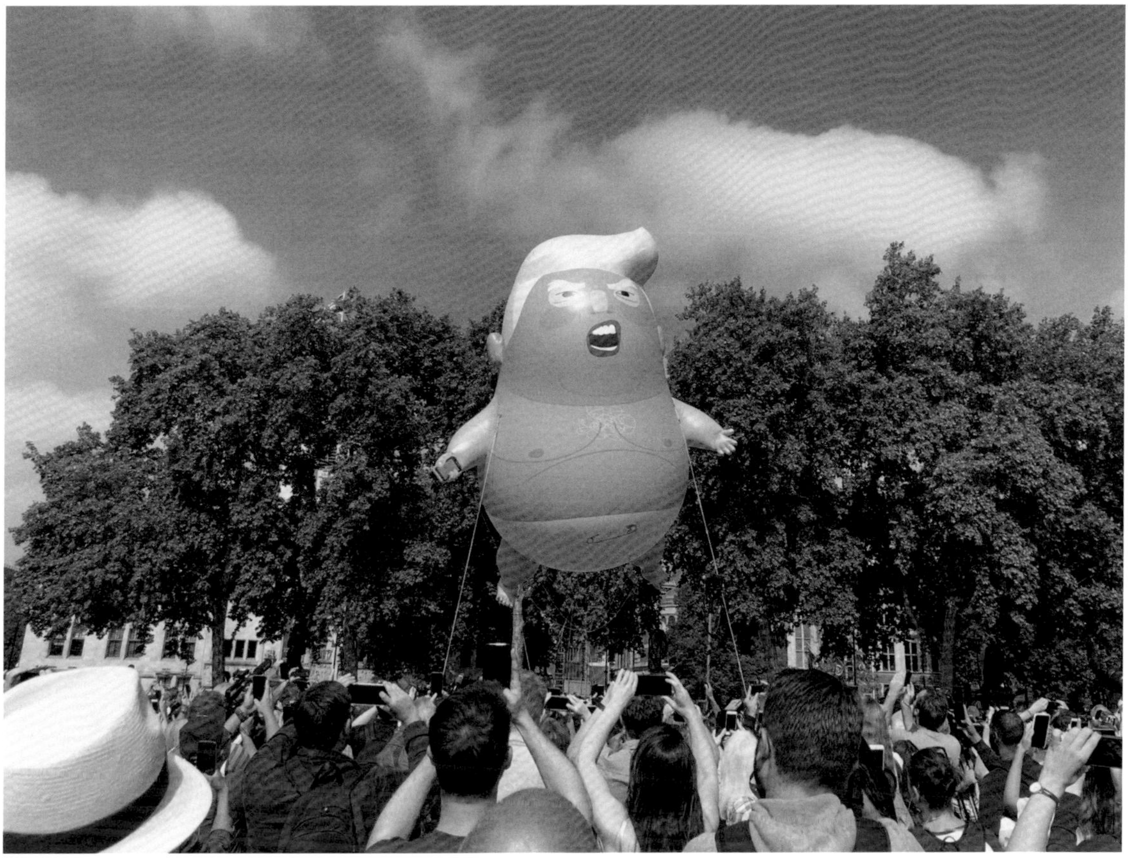

Figure 3.3
Trump Awakens (The Trump Baby Blimp Rises over London's Parliament Square).

listening and talking."[113] Deciding what to acquire, Hammond left the tents behind ("They take up a great deal of space on an exhibit floor") and instead concentrated on personal and handmade items, such as artworks and otherwise ephemeral memorials, including one dedicated to a resident who had recently died of a drug overdose. Hammond reports: "I talked very seriously about whether it would be appropriate to collect that, and they discussed it and thought that would be a good way to remember the person. So that was something that I wasn't expecting to collect which I did collect."[114] Ultimately, in this case, tension arose not from the residents who largely appreciated the museum's role but with members of the general public, some of whom reacted negatively to the collection of such objects. Several angry letters to the museum are also a part of the collection archived by the Royal BC Museum.[115]

There are numerous issues, some of them outlined by the museum professionals above, with collecting taking place from the perspective of the museum rather than from those involved in the actions. Thus, Amy Roberts, a library and information studies graduate student at Queens College (NYC) who helped create and oversaw the archives working group of OWS wrote, "To keep established institutions from shaping the movement's short history, protesters have formed their own archive group, stashing away hundreds of cardboard signs, posters, fliers, buttons, periodicals, documents and banners in temporary storage while they seek a permanent home for the materials."[116]

Writing in parallel to Roberts, Canadian archivist Krista McCracken notes that community-driven archival projects that can then be accessioned by institutions work well, primarily because community-based projects have a much better understanding of the nuance of any situation or action and can thus create more complete versions of the historical records. Such community-based collecting can generate important counter-narratives within institutions, overcoming some of the blocks outlined by Gledhill and the Museum of London.

Community collecting from social movements is not a new phenomenon – women's suffrage collections, for example, tended to be accessioned into large museums and libraries from private collections and long after the fact.[117] In the 1980s, activists and artists in New York gathered to document their own work, resulting in Political Art Documentation/Distribution (an endeavour Sholette refers to as "an archive about unknown artists gathered and organized by other, unknown artists").[118] A more recent example can be found in the Interference Archive, also in New York, an accessible library and research space that grew from the collection of the late activist Dara Greenwald.[119] In Montreal, Dave Widgington has assembled an online archive of posters, cartoons, and other ephemera from the Maple Spring student-led protest movement in Quebec in 2012,[120] and, as noted above, in 2002 Kyla Tichkowsky gathered material related to protests against the G8 meeting in Kananaskis, Alberta, forming a collection that was later accessioned by the Glenbow Museum. I also point to the Canadian Museum of Human Rights Violations at Shoal Lake 40 First Nation (chapter 5) as an example of community archiving that also contributes to SL40's goal of securing federal government funding for a road connecting the reserve to the mainland.

Quoting Yvonne Ng, McCracken suggests that "participatory archive movements are especially valuable in communities that institutional archives have traditionally overlooked or misrepresented, and in communities where archives belonging to the state or other institutions have historically enabled discrimination and abuse."[121] In an important article, Zoe Todd and Crystal Fraser draw attention to the limitations of archival collections in Canada, particularly in terms of the way that they erase or write over Indigenous understandings and knowledges. Todd and Fraser are particularly interested in complicating the notion that "decolonizing" archives is in any way an easy or straightforward task "given ongoing settler-colonial realities that frame and govern archives in Canada."[122] Katie

Shilton and Ramesh Srinivasan agree, writing, "memory institutions have ignored experiences outside of the history of the powerful, creating collecting gaps within archives."[123] The key point is that for museums to create archives *of* actions rather than *about* them (I'm borrowing Shilton and Srinivasan's language here), the museum itself would also need to be a decolonized or at least decolonizing space. Despite legitimate difficulties, I do strongly feel that authoritative museums should work hard to expand their "counter-history" collections, working with communities where possible and collecting widely across a variety of issues, political positions, and standpoints.

Collecting is not a straightforward proposition. For example, the Museum of London collected documents as well as three-dimensional objects from Occupy London,[124] but in a point that would certainly be applicable to Black Lives Matter and Idle no More, Gledhill notes that activist groups and movements increasingly organize and publicize online and digitally. Though OWS was known for its cardboard posters and the Women's March for its woolly hats, hashtags and memes are also the content of activism in the current moment. Gledhill argues that "[b]uilding both the infrastructural capacity and methodological criteria for preserving this material represents a colossal paradigm shift for collecting institutions, whose identity has hitherto been constructed around materiality."[125] How to store digital material, and how to make sure the technological hardware and software needed to access and understand it do not become obsolete, has been a central concern of recent archival scholarship, though to date such studies have not typically been concerned with social movements. Not noted in Gledhill's article but pertinent to my analysis, displaying such material in permanent or temporary exhibition spaces also presents a dilemma. How might the CMH, for example, capture the cross-country support for Idle No More actions as they spread across Twitter? And should they also record the often racist pushback that accompanied many actions?[126] Furthermore, as the Issues and Advocacy research team of the Society of American Archivists notes, how should museums collecting digital material deal with the fact that "lawmakers in several states [and in Canada] have recently introduced legislation that would target and criminalize protests" and "As protest and movement organizing moves to an online and increasingly public sphere, the potential reach of such legislation, in conjunction with increased surveillance and data collection, could expand significantly," potentially even into museum archives.[127] There are currently no clear answers to such questions, though the Issues and Advocacy team suggest a number of strategies for protecting those taking action.

Other questions asked by Gledhill that apply to social movements in general focus on whether or not museums should collect deeply of some movements and events and at a more surface level of others. What moments (squats, parades, blockades, altercations, direct actions) should be archived, and what history will they relate to future researchers? What objects, from the overwhelming number of placards, posters, pamphlets, and other ephemera, should be chosen for museum collections?[128] Taking such questions to heart and also discussing Occupy London, Cathy Ross concludes, speaking specifically to Museum of London and a 2011 anti-cuts march but making a larger point, “maybe the [museum’s] role is less about claiming to ‘represent’ the march to the future through rational and systematic protocols of collecting, and more about trying to ‘join in’ present debates about the meaning of this new wave of dissent by moving some of the materials into a public institution and seeing what happens.”[129]

Ross’s summation is in keeping with my own thinking. As Deborah Gould found when researching ACT UP and AIDS activism in the United States in the 1980s, archives can keep documents and other items of material culture, and they can even record oral histories and keep personal stories, but the emotional impact of the event (what I’ve called the tear gas epiphany) will always escape.[130] My impression is that the lessons being taught about archives – that is, that they are incomplete and compromised – has only been partially learned by those collecting from protest movements. On the one hand, I am happy this is happening, but on the other hand, with these processes it is possible to see the erasure of some actions and the highlighting of others. I also remain curious as to what will happen with the Occupy archives ten or fifteen years down the road.

“There is no political power without control of the archive, of memory,” famously wrote Jacques Derrida.[131] Had Hammond of the Royal BC Museum been able to collect a pepper spray canister from the APEC protest, what would it really tell us? As Hito Steyrl writes about the forensic study of objects, “Things condense power and violence.”[132] A tear gas canister can tell us that a violent interaction occurred. Or can it? It can’t even tell us if it is empty or not, if it has been discharged, if a protester was injured, if someone was arrested, if the police officer was scared or felt powerful, if the protest was effective, if someone had a tear gas epiphany. It is mute. And in this case, it matters not. The canister was not collected.

The period from the turn of the millennium to the present was a time of great change in establishment Canadian museums. Exterior renovations of many museums were paralleled with significant reinstallations of permanent exhibitions. Though Canadian museums appear not, at this moment, to be broadly collecting from protest movements, evidence from the US and UK suggests that this is a current trend in museum collecting that will spread to Canada. As I move toward Part 2 and the case studies, it will become apparent that museums are equally establishment institutions, upholding the status quo, and spaces where change and different futures can be imagined.

Interstice 3c

"She walked in and removed her work from the wall": Artists against Reed Paper at the Art Gallery of Ontario, 1976

In the 1960s, Dryden Chemical Company dumped more than 9,000 litres of mercury into the English-Wabigoon River system, located approximately 120 kilometres east of Winnipeg in northwestern Ontario. The mercury contaminated the water and food supplies of the Asubpeeschoseewagong First Nation, including the Grassy Narrows and White Dog reserves. The effects of mercury poisoning include muscular numbness, hearing and speech defects, paralysis, tremors, choking, difficulty swallowing, loss of strength, insanity, coma, and death, a constellation of symptoms and outcomes often referred to as Minamata disease (after the town of Minamata in Japan where thousands of inhabitants were affected by mercury dumping from the Chisso Chemical Company in the 1950s).[1] Mercury is particularly devastating if ingested by pregnant women, whose babies are often born deformed, with brain damage, and have shortened lifespans.[2] Though in 1970 the federal government advised people living in the English-Wabigoon River area to stop fishing from the river system, the Ontario government concluded that the same fish were, in fact, safe to eat.[3] No cleanup was undertaken, in part because the Ministry of Natural Resources feared that disturbing river sediment would lead to further contamination.[4]

The Dryden Chemical Company was producing chloralkali, a substance that produces other chemicals such as chlorine, sodium hydroxide, and hydrogen, which were used by the neighbouring Dryden Pulp and Paper Company (owned by Reed Paper Limited) for bleaching paper during production. The chloralkali was made using a process called the mercury cell method, and the sewage from the plant was dumped, untreated, into the river. The mercury accumulated, and when fish began dying in the river, affecting the people at Grassy Narrows and sport fishing in the region, it took some time to trace the pollution back to the Dryden Chemical Company. Finally, in 1970, the company was ordered to stop dumping into the river system. Even so, airborne emissions of mercury continued until the plant closed in 1976.[5] As Natalie Ilyniak points out, quoting Judy da Silva (Anishinabek, Grassy Narrows), destroying the river not only poisoned people, it was also a profound instance of environmental injustice that undermined the lifeways that "supplies the community's basic needs for subsistence and is essential to their culture, identity, and 'life as a nation – as Anishinaabe.'"[6] For decades, the people of Asubpeeschoseewagong have resisted "attempts to sever their connection to the land by corporations – previously Reed Paper Limited, Dryden Chemicals, Abitibi, and currently the Weyerhauser logging company – as well as by the provincial and federal governments. The colonial and capitalist attacks included child apprehension, forced relocation, and economic deprivation."[7]

Grassy Narrows seems far removed from Toronto, but in 1976, Reed Paper sponsored the travelling exhibition *Changing Visions: The Canadian Landscape,* organized by the Art Gallery of Ontario and the Edmonton Art Gallery. *Changing*

Visions was a major exhibition, including work from many well-known Canadian artists, among them familiar names such as Iain Baxter, Tom Benner, Jack Bush, Jack Chambers, Alex Colville, Greg Curnoe, Toni Onley, Christopher Pratt, Goodridge Roberts, Michael Snow, Joyce Wieland, and many others. No Indigenous artists were included. The exhibition represented a rethinking of landscape tradition and included performance, photography, and land art – it was meant to be something of a radical intervention into the landscape tradition as it dominated Canadian art history.[8] On the opening night in February, 250 people, led by the Anti-Reed Campaign (ARC), picketed outside the AGO.

Writer Walter Klepac wrote in 1977 that Canadian artists were "increasingly frustrated and angry with … the direction and character of Canadian society."[9] As Klepac noted, "[w]orking together with such organizations as the National Indian Brotherhood, ARC has gathered an impressive body of documentation supporting their claim that a Reed subsidiary continued to discharge mercury waste into the English-Wabigoon River System at a level which endangers the health and economy of Indian reservations in the area."[10] It was ARC that informed artists in the exhibition and Canadian Artists Representation (CAR) about the show's sponsor.

Outside the AGO, visitors to the show were given pieces of frozen fish, jostled, called scabs, and booed as they entered.[11] CAR members Michael Snow, Joyce Wieland, Tony Urquhart, and Greg Curnoe showed up at the protest, working with the demonstration organizers.[12] Painter and CAR founder Jack Chambers wrote to the AGO asking that his work be removed from the show, as did Robin Mackenzie, Reinhard Reitzenstein, Murray Favro, Greg Curnoe, Joyce Wieland, and Michael Snow.[13] Chambers wrote,

> As an artist and a concerned individual I object to the use of my art in this blatant propaganda attempt by the company to present itself as a friend of both the arts and the environment. I am insulted and horrified by the kind of corporate hypocrisy that allows Reed to take credit for an art exhibition glorifying the Canadian Landscape when, in fact, Reed and others like them, are directly responsible for destroying it.[14]

The artists disrupted the opening, but the AGO did not close the show, nor did it remove artists' work when they requested it. According to Iris Nowell, Joyce Wieland, however, marched in and pulled hers right off the wall.[15]

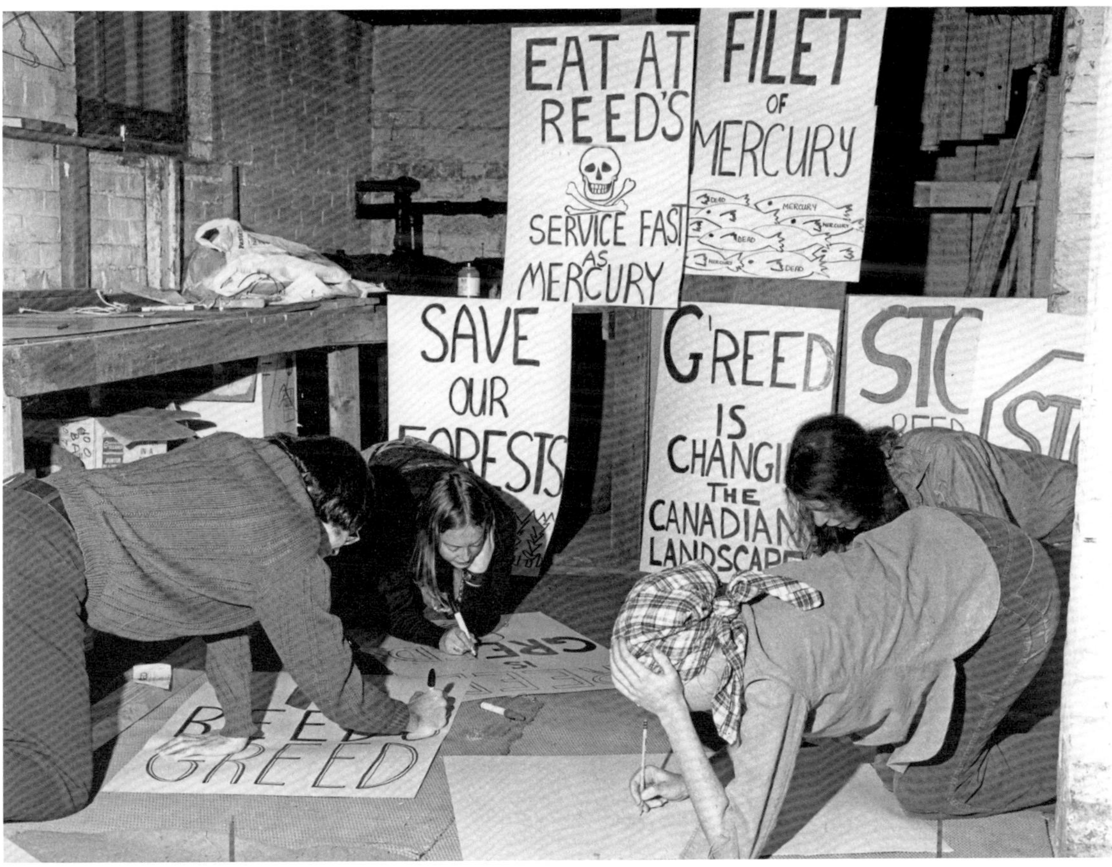

Figure 3.4
Preparations for anti-Reed Protest outside the AGO.

As Klepac recalled, Murray Favro and Robin Mackenzie showed up at the opening reception with their gallerist Carmen Lamanna, who was representing another artist in the show, Reinhardt Reitzenstein. They demanded that either their work be removed or that the exhibition be expanded to include documentation from ARC. The artists met with two curators (unnamed, but one from the AGO and one from the Edmonton Art Gallery). Ultimately, statements were placed next to their works informing visitors about conflicts between the artists and the AGO, but the works remained in the exhibition. Klepac suggests that the gallery promised to respond to Favro and Mackenzie's demands with regard to documentation from ARC but did not, hedging their bets on the artists actually wanting their works to remain in an important exhibition.[16]

The AGO delayed. On 2 March, almost a month after the exhibition had opened, Gary Greenwood, the Ontario representative of CAR, demanded a meeting between CARO (CAR Ontario), the AGO, Reed, and members of ARC. Klepac covers the meeting in some detail, showing the antagonism on all sides. Interestingly, Klepac argues that the AGO representatives saw their role as keeping the exhibition intact, even at the cost of some discomfort to the sponsor. He writes, "It seemed that while there were always some alternative funding sources open to the Gallery, a major exhibition had to maintain the highest aesthetic standards if the Gallery was to preserve its prestige as a leading cultural institution."[17] The meeting concluded with the AGO agreeing that some of ARC's material could be included, though representatives of the AGO would not, ultimately, agree that Reed Paper was guilty of the accusations levelled against them by ARC (particularly those that suggested pollution of the English-Wabigoon River system continued).[18] Just before the show at the AGO closed, and just before it moved to Windsor, an installation was mounted that included letters between the AGO and artists and a brief statement from Reed, which argued that the material from ARC was "not acceptable."[19] Artist Robin Mackenzie included ARC's information in the display, though apparently the gallery had only requested the correspondence. Ultimately, the extra material travelled with the exhibition.[20]

While the protest in 1976 at the AGO was focused on the Asubpeeschoseewagong First Nation in Grassy Narrows, most of the artists involved were familiar with the pro-Canada arguments made just a few years earlier in protests against the hiring of Richard Wattenmaker at the AGO (Interstice 1a). They remained fully committed to the art world in Canada (including the AGO) and supportive of the possibilities of the nation of Canada.[21] The Ojibway Warriors Society, which occupied Anicinabe Park (in Kenora, near Grassy Narrows) in 1974, would likely have disagreed.[22] A response to the local issues of mercury poisoning, resource extraction, and racism, the occupation was inspired by the seventy-one-day occupation and standoff at Wounded Knee, South Dakota. It was the Kenora occupation that really brought mercury poisoning to the public's attention, leading to the formation of ARC and then the protest against Reed Paper's sponsorship of *Changing Visions*.[23]

The protest at *Changing Visions* was one small part of long-term resistance. As Natalia Ilnyak reminds us, "People from Grassy Narrows, and their allies, use a variety of tactics in their attempt to decolonize their land and seek environmental justice." [24] In 2002, a blockade was set up on the road into Grassy Narrows to prevent logging trucks from entering. That blockade was in place until 2009 and remains the longest-running blockade in North American history.[25] It was one of a series of tactics: "members wrote letters of complaints to companies, raised concerns at negotiations about the effects of the industrial projects on their lands, protested in Kenora, and marched all the way to Toronto in protest with limited results."[26] Annual walks also take place at Grassy Narrows, in line with the healing walks in the tar sands described in chapter 6, and in June 2016 a protest held at Queen's Park in Toronto (outside the legislature) saw activists from Free Grassy Narrows pouring a "mysterious substance" (actually corn starch and dye) that looked like mercury down the driveway of the provincial legislature to draw attention to continued inaction on cleaning up the river system.[27] Said da Silva in an interview with Jaggi Singh, "I'd like the people that live in the urban centre, the big cities, to get in touch with the earth. And the earth will give them guidance."[28]

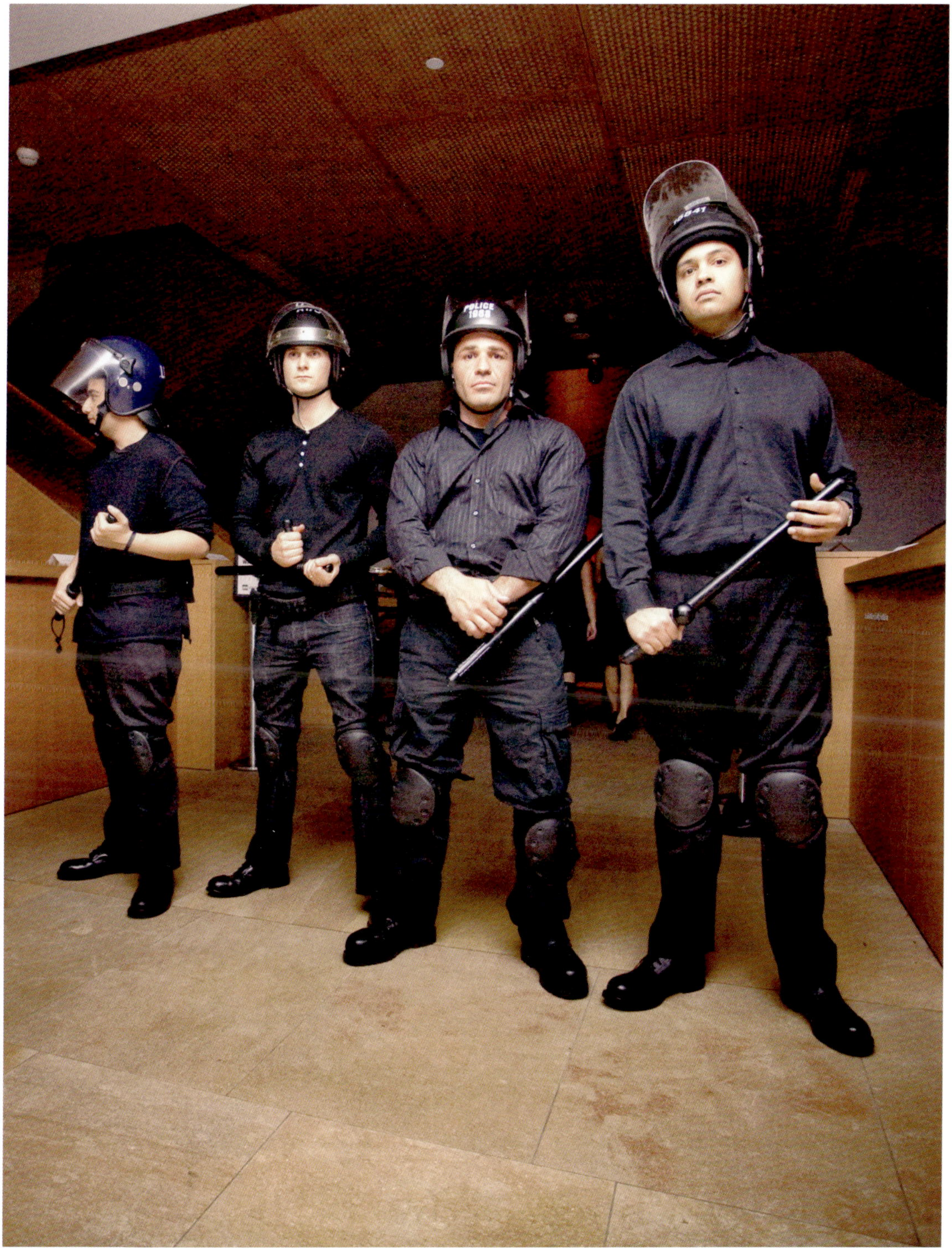

Figure 1.1
Volunteers dressed as riot police greet invitees at "Massive Uprising,"
Art Gallery of Ontario, Toronto, March 2009.

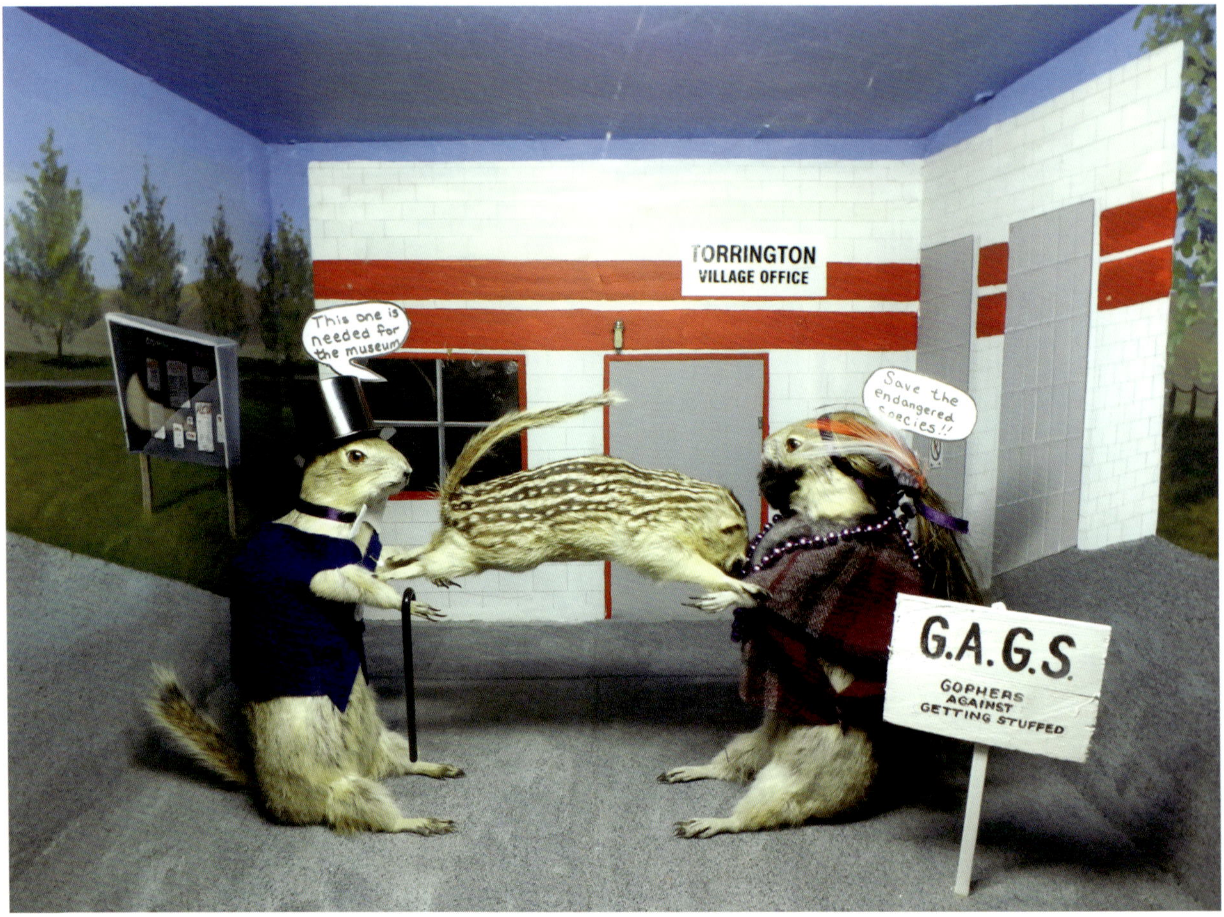

Figure 1.4
Gophers Against Getting Stuffed, a tongue-in-cheek exhibit at the Torrington Gopher Museum in Torrington, Alberta.

Figure 3.2 *Opposite*
Museum of Vancouver, permanent display dedicated to hippie culture.

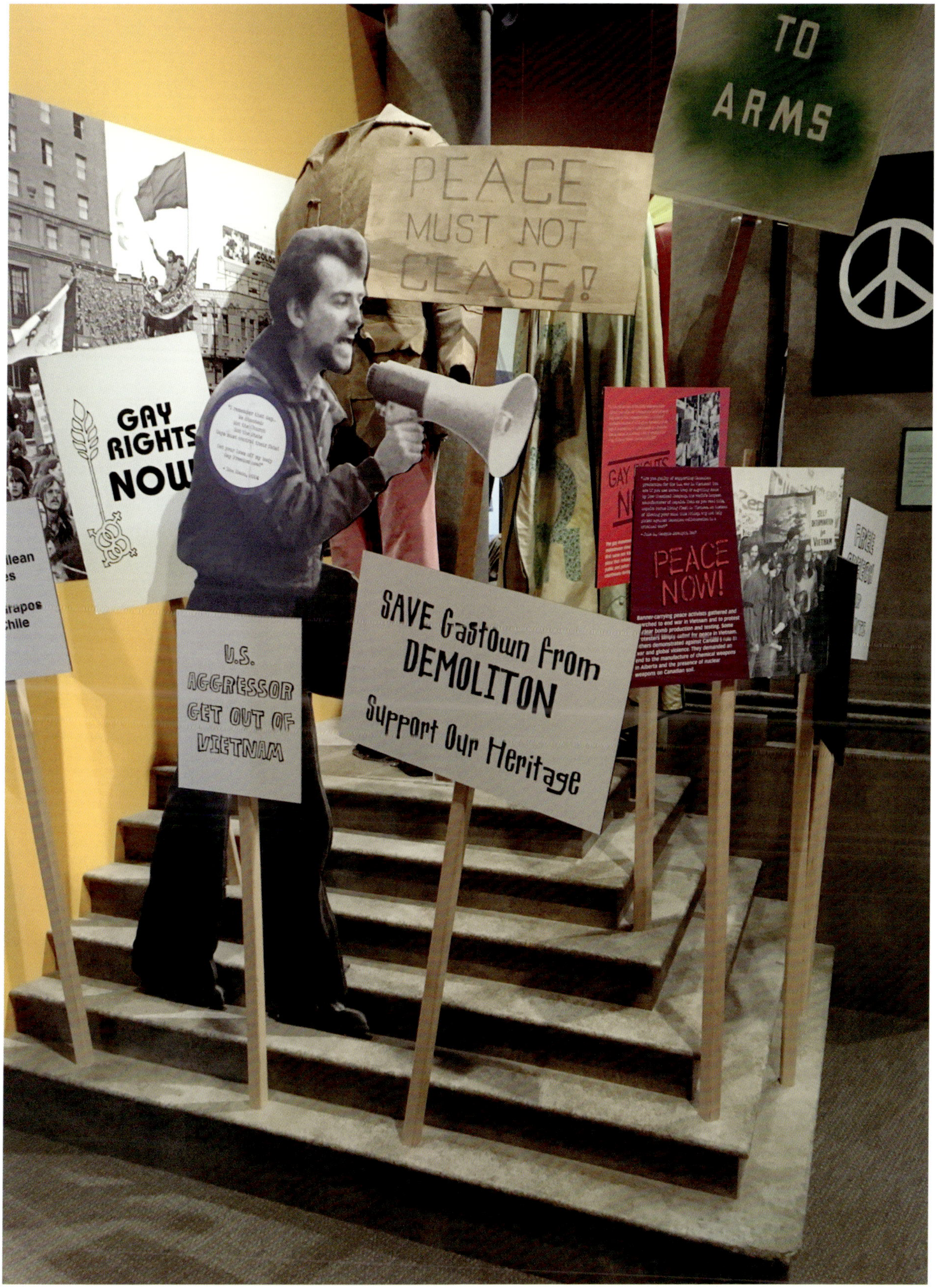
TO
ARMS
PEACE
MUST NOT
CEASE!
GAY
RIGHTS
NOW
U.S.
AGGRESSOR
GET OUT OF
VIETNAM
SAVE Gastown from
DEMOLITON
Support Our Heritage
PEACE
NOW!

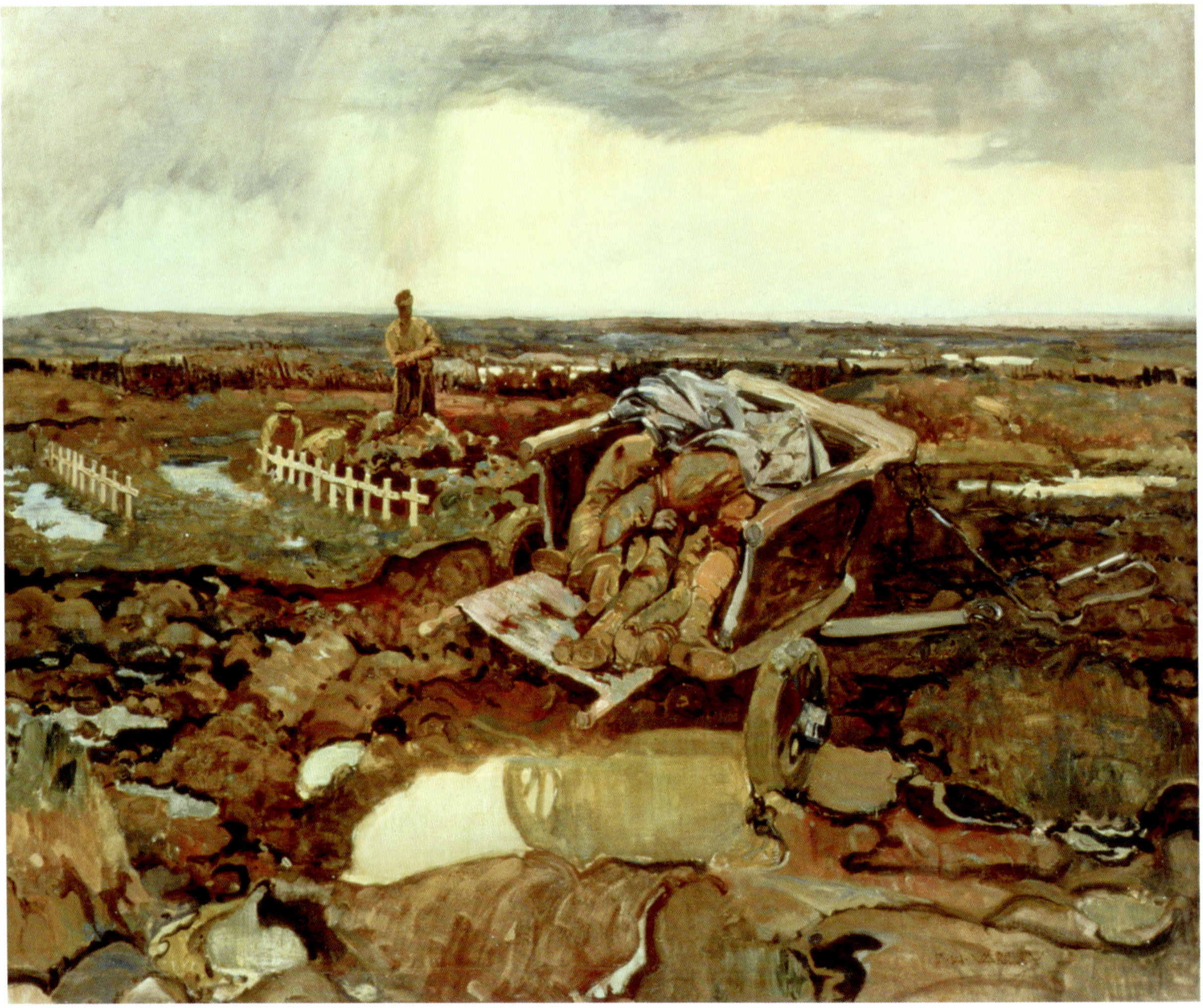

Figure 4.2
Frederick H. Varley, *For What?* 1919, Beaverbrook Collection of War Art, Canadian War Museum.

Figure 4.4 *Opposite*
Regeneration Hall, Canadian War Museum, Ottawa. The window overlooks the Canadian Parliament buildings. The statues are plaster maquettes used by Walter Seymour Allward to design the Canadian National Vimy Memorial at Vimy, France.

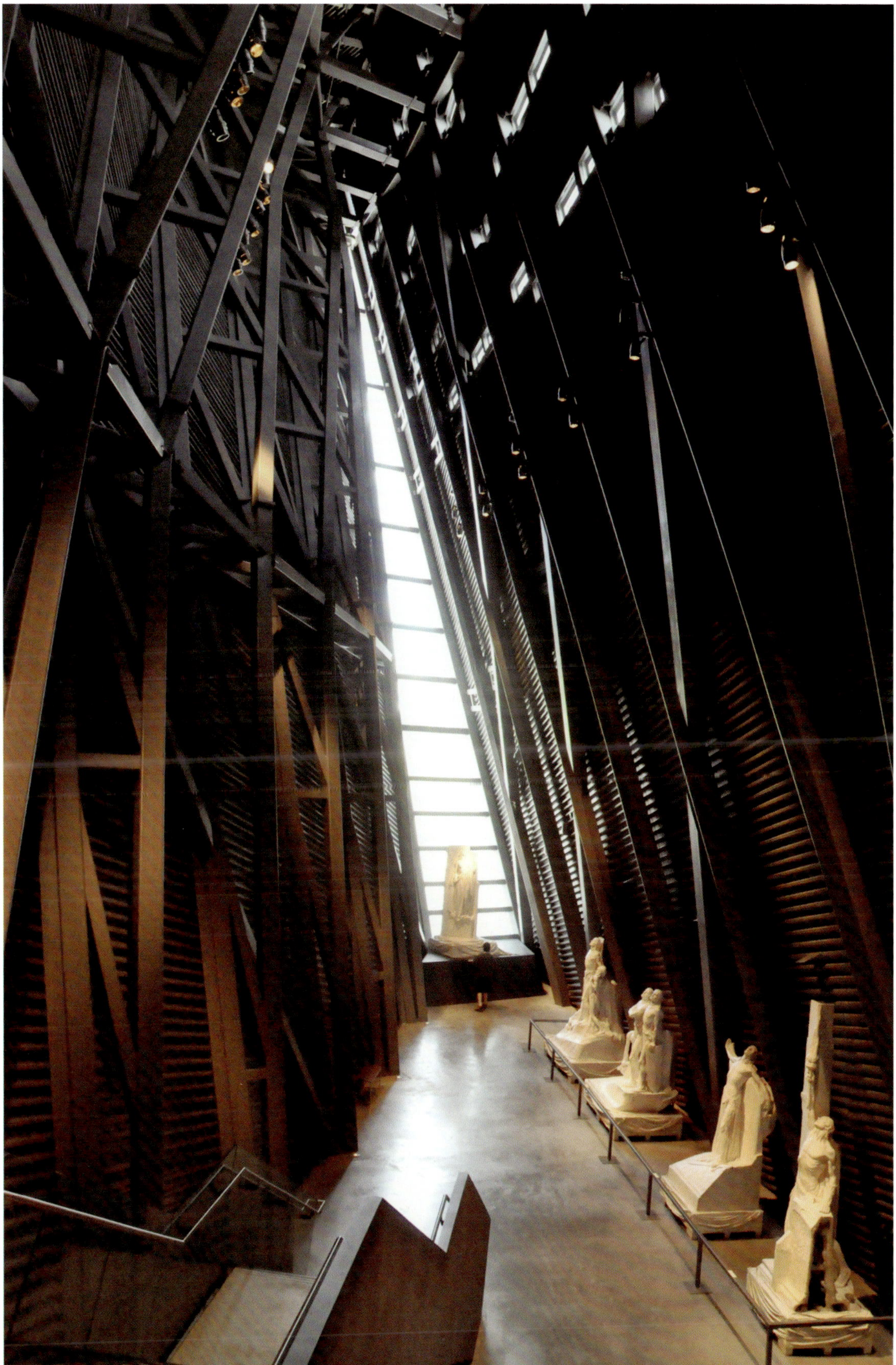

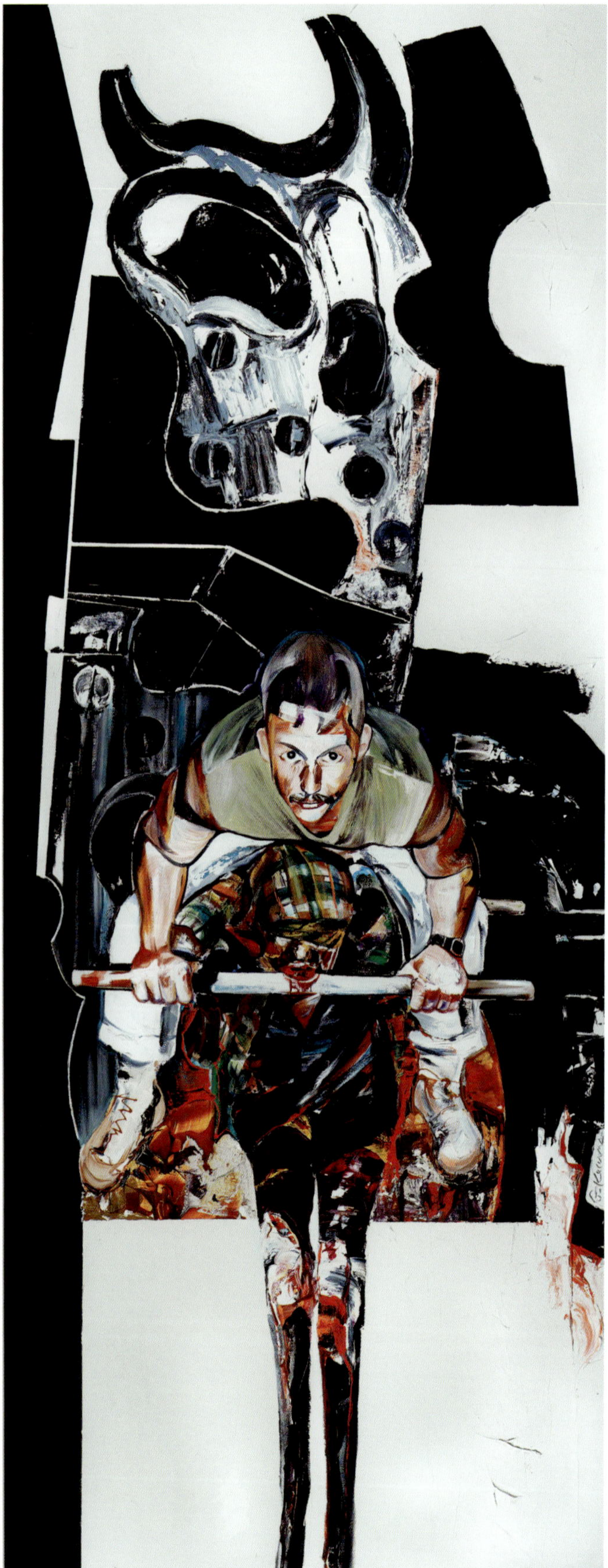

Figure 4.5
Gertrude Kearns, *Somalia #2, Without Conscience*, 1995, Beaverbrook Collection of War Art, Canadian War Museum.

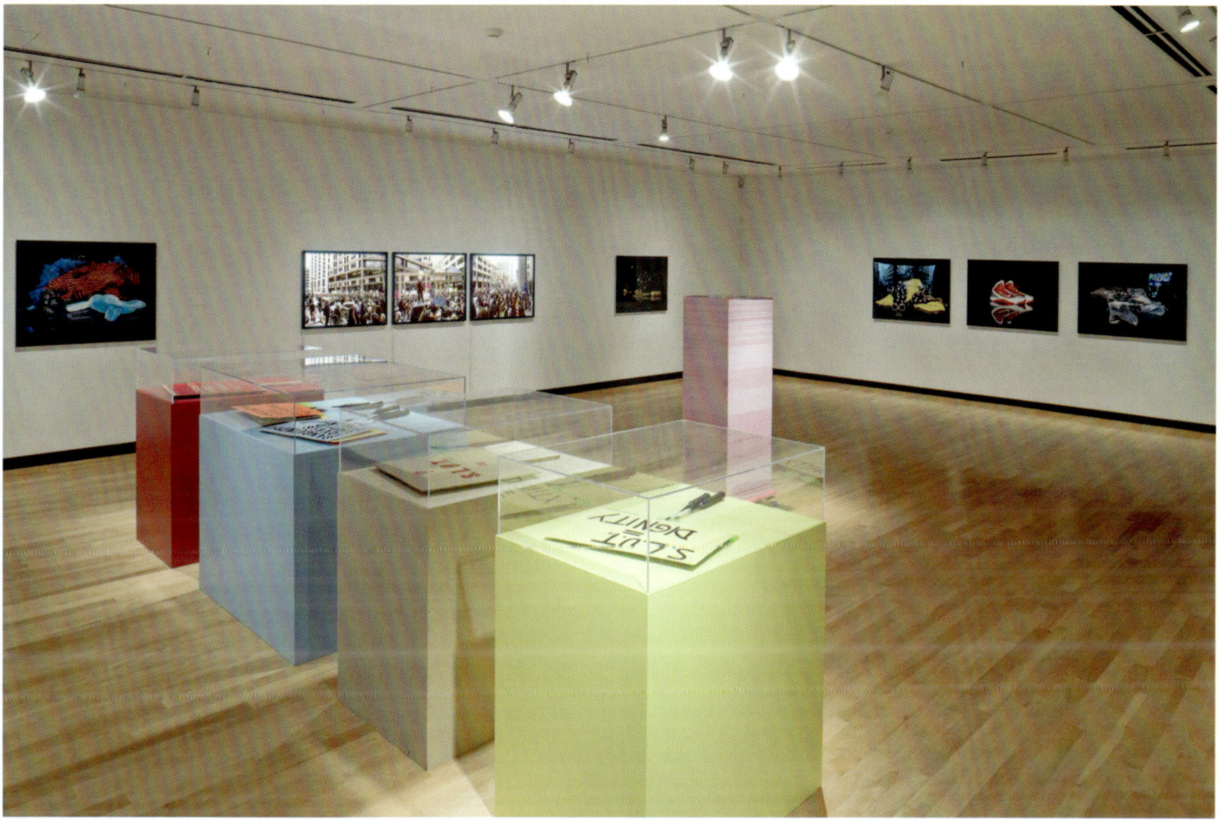

Figure 5.5
Wendy Coburn, *Anatomy of a Protest* installation,
Art Museum at the University of Toronto, 2014.

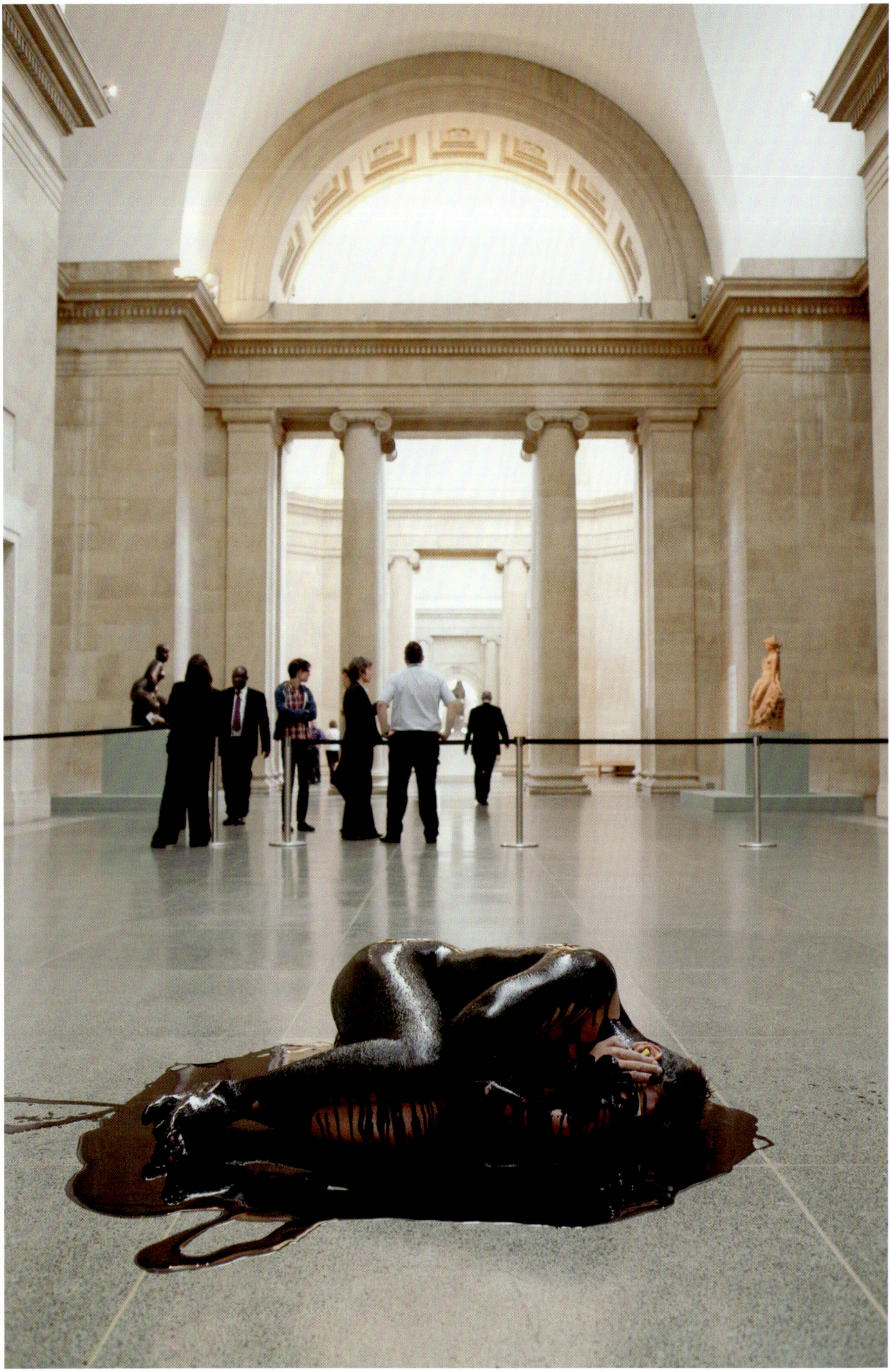

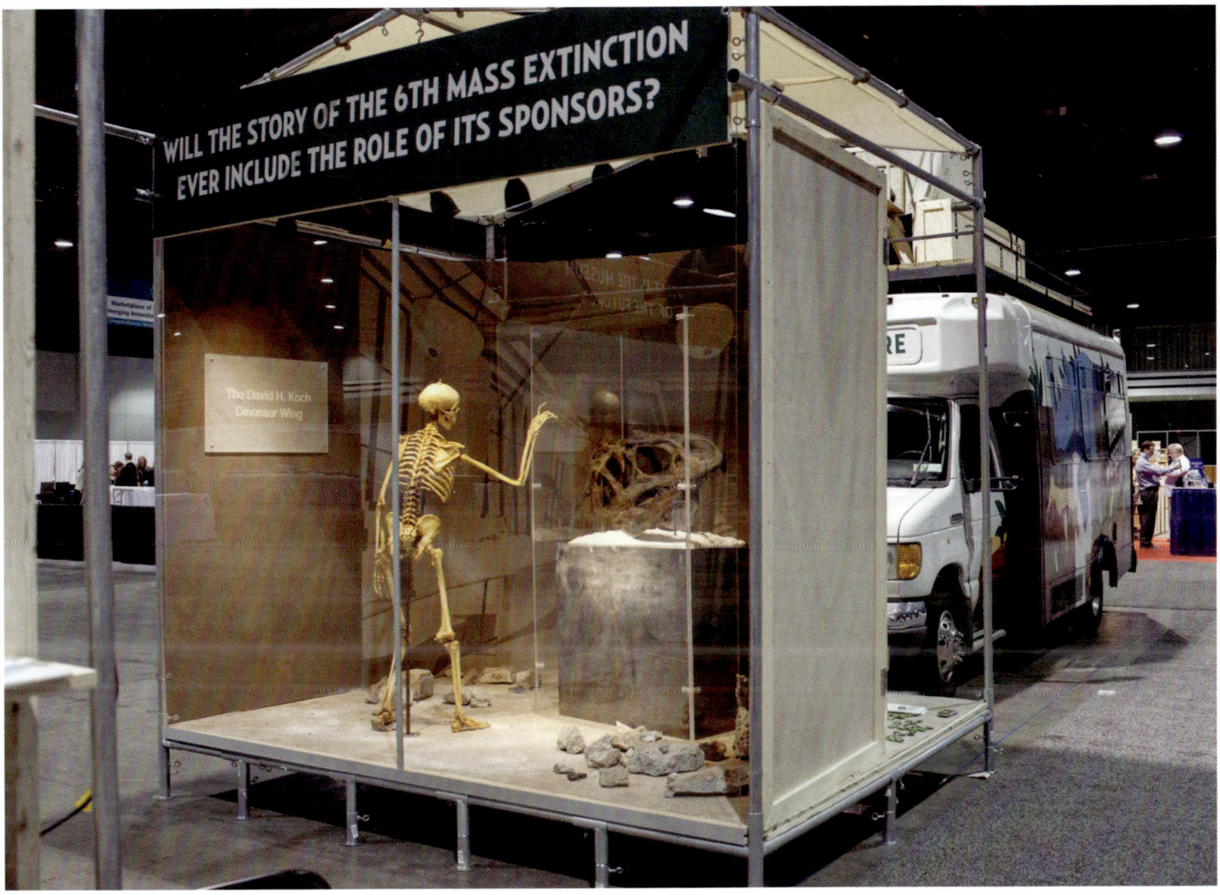

Figure 6.3
Not An Alternative, The Natural History Museum, occupation of American Alliance of Museums, Atlanta, 2015.

Figure 6.1 *Opposite*
Human Cost, Liberate Tate action, Tate Britain Museum, April 2011.

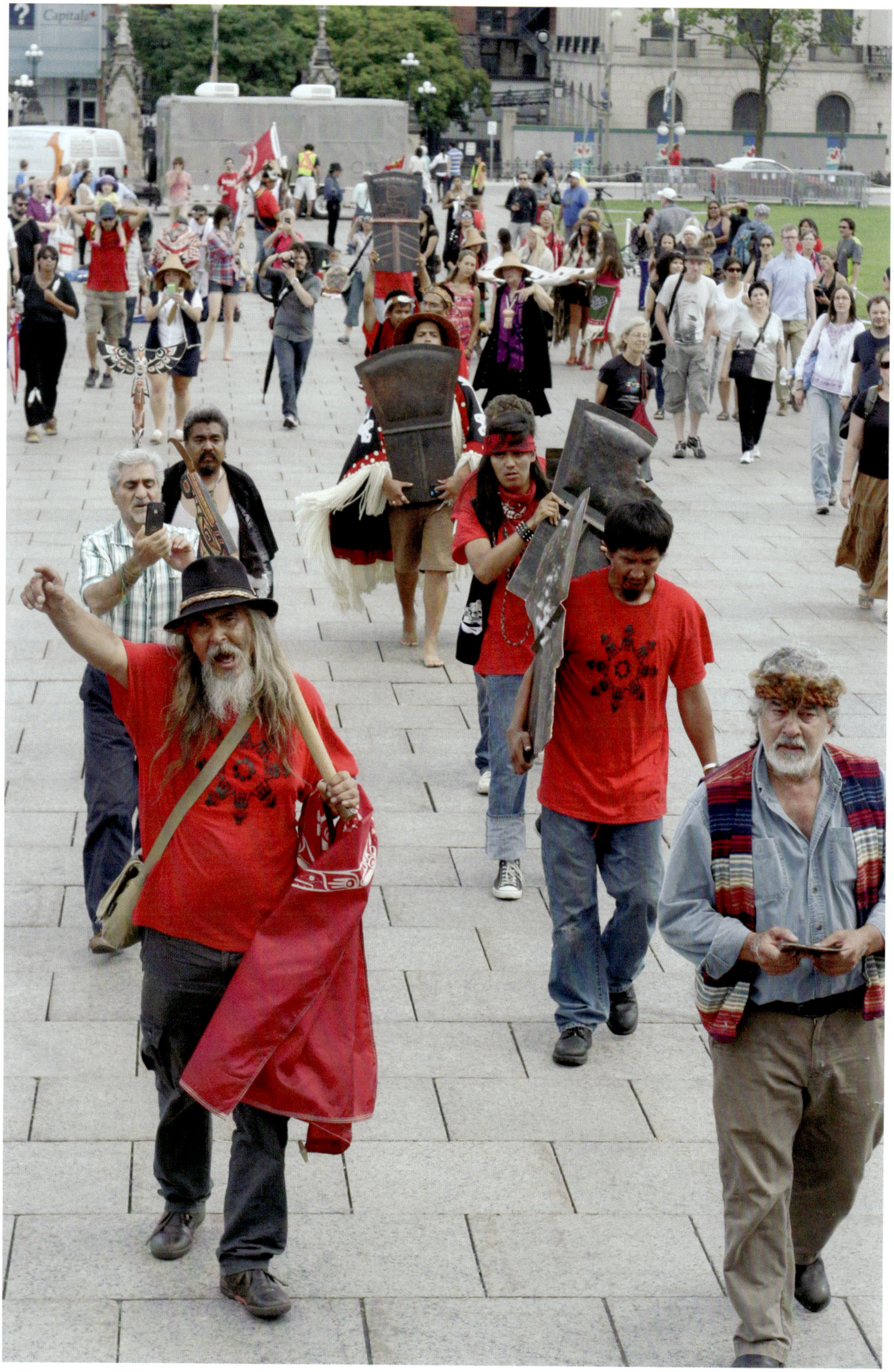

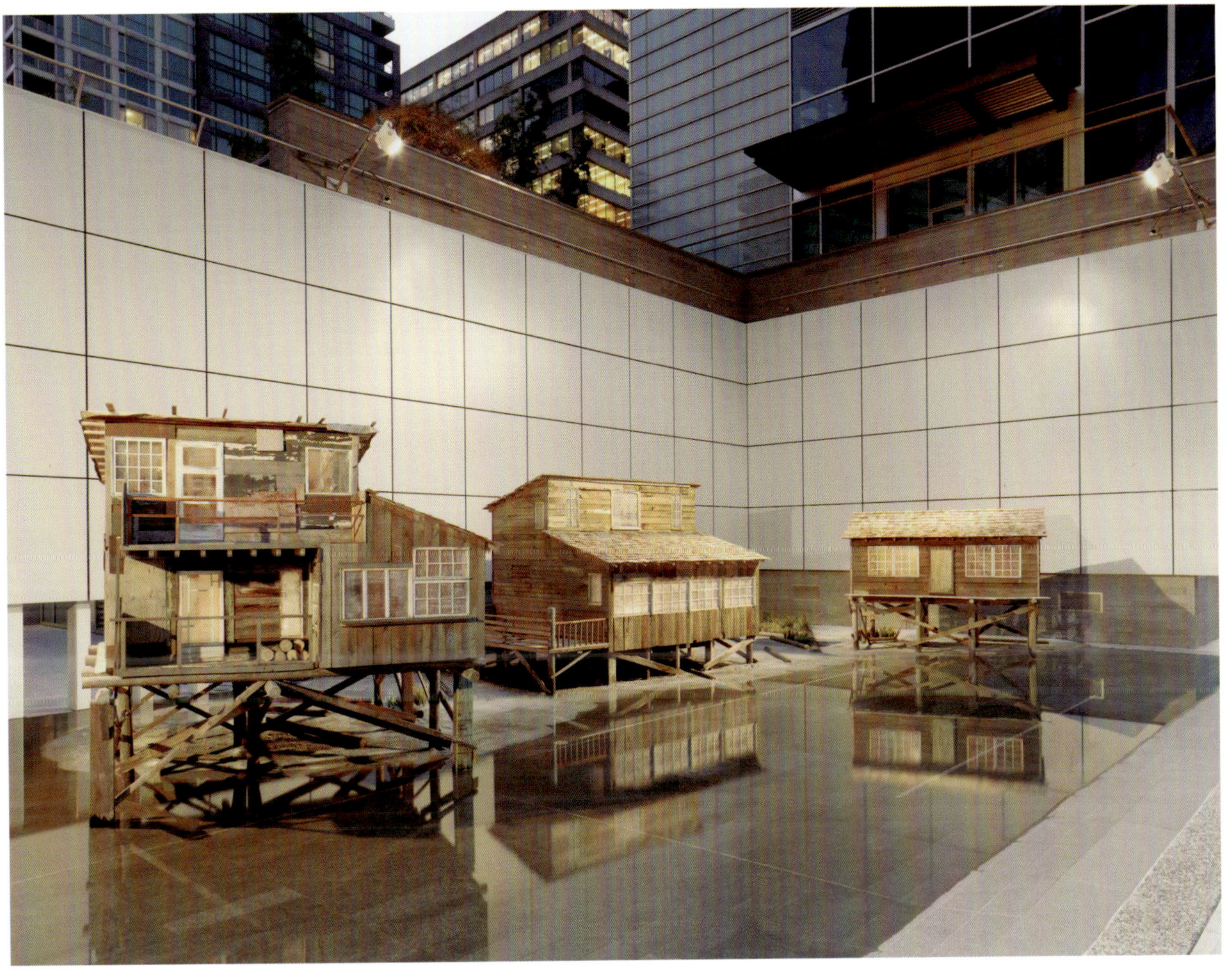

Figure 7.5
Ken Lum, *from shangri-la to shangri-la*, 2010, site-specific installation at Vancouver Art Gallery Offsite, 23 January to 6 September 2010.

Figure 6.6 *Opposite*
During the Copper-Breaking Ceremony on Parliament Hill, Ottawa, 27 June 2014.

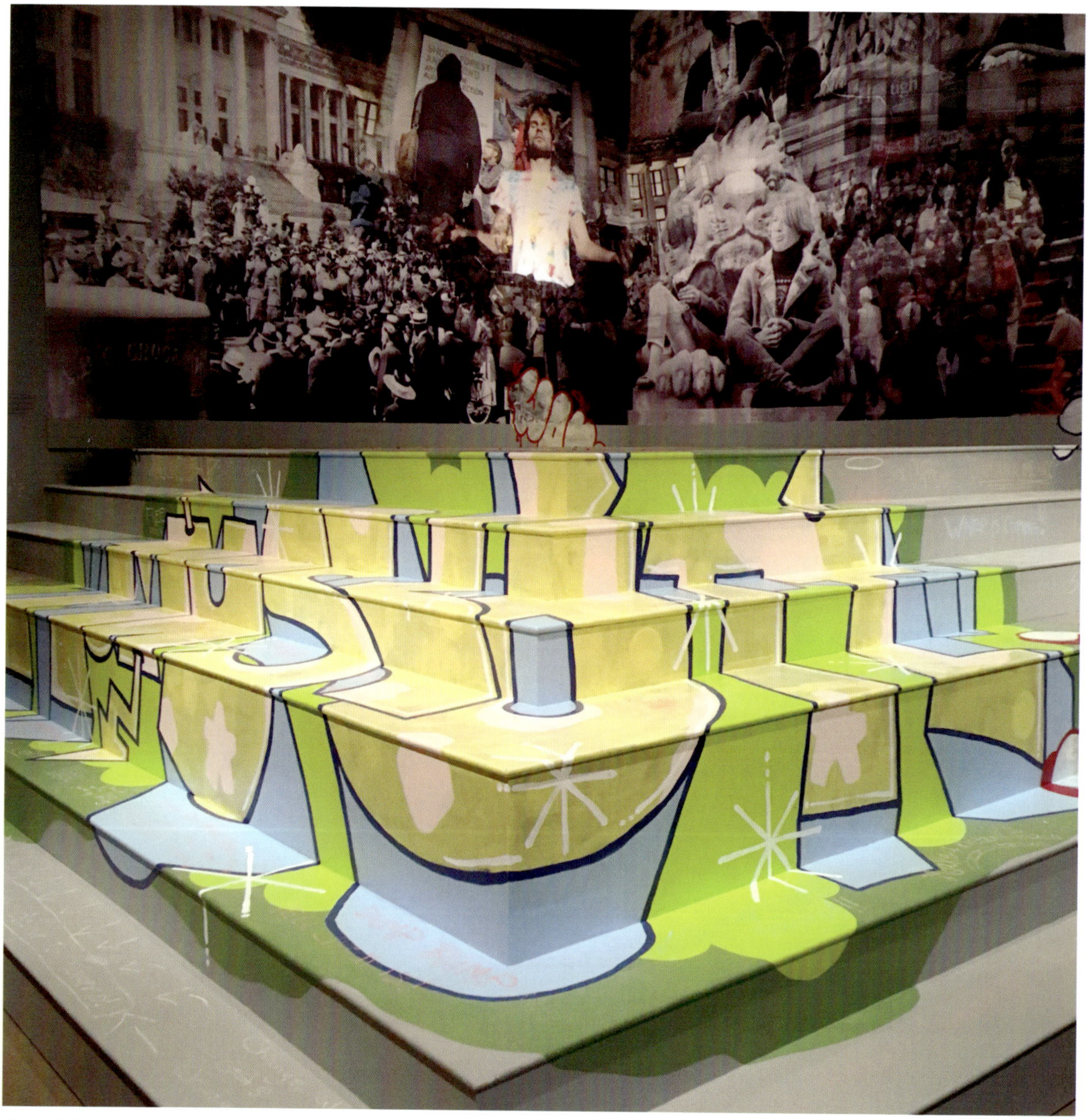

Figure 7.7
City on Edge, installation shot, Museum of Vancouver.

Figure 7.8 *Opposite*
Permanent display, Vancouver History Gallery, Museum of Vancouver.

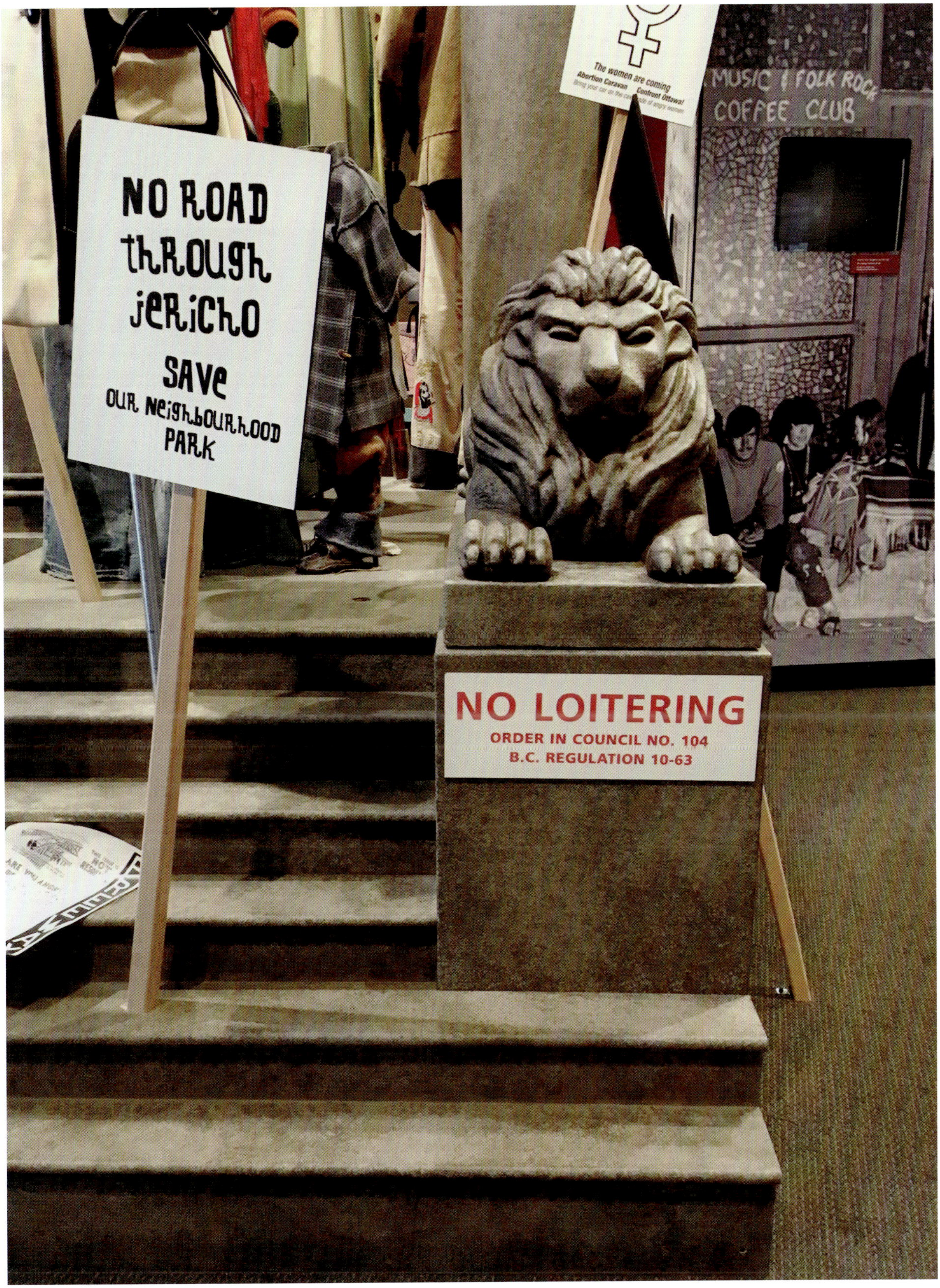

NO ROAD through jeRicho SAVE OUR Neighbourhood PARK
NO LOITERING
ORDER IN COUNCIL NO. 104
B.C. REGULATION 10-63
The women are coming
Abortion Caravan Confront Ottawa!
MUSIC & FOLK ROCK
COFFEE CLUB

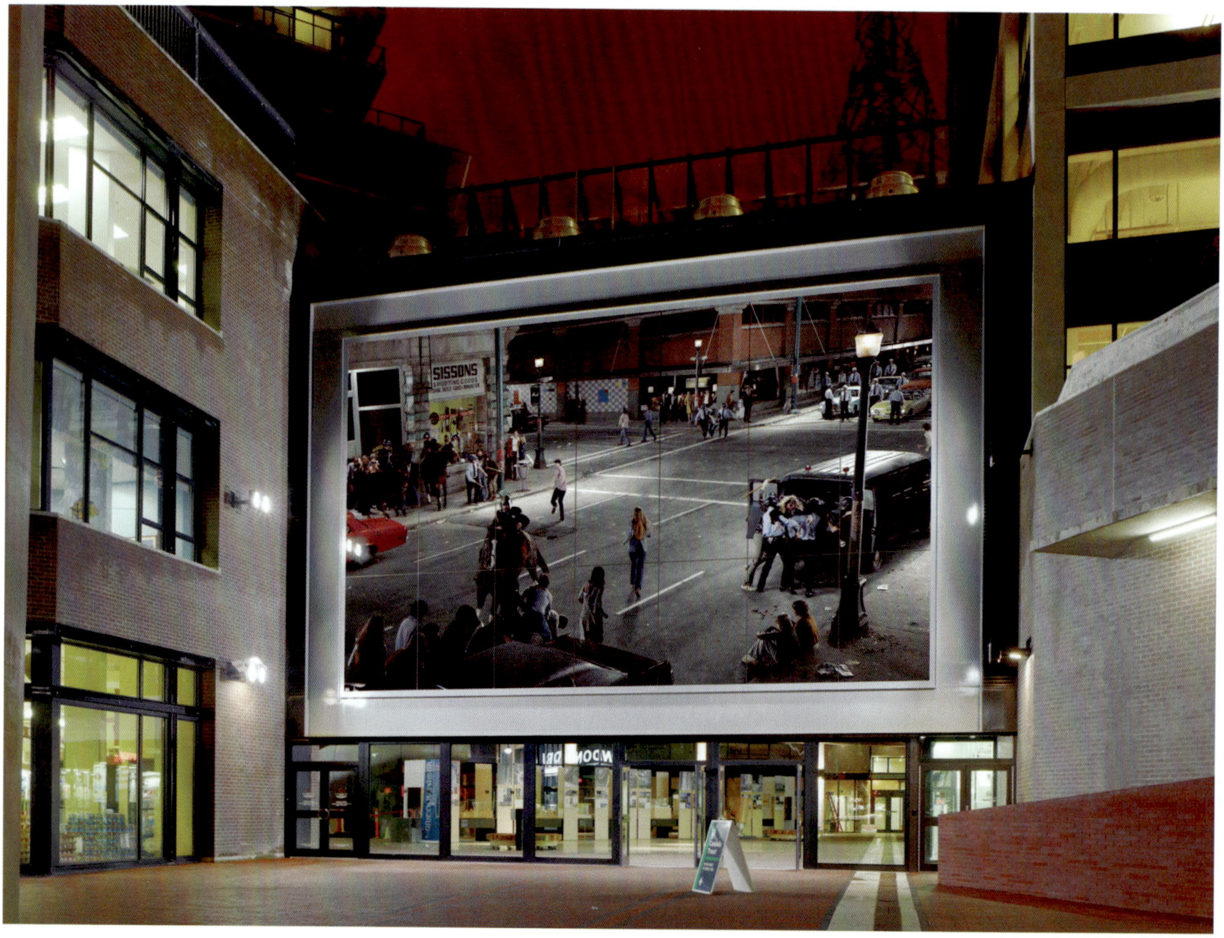

Figure 7.9
Stan Douglas, *Abbott & Cordova*, 7 August 1971 (2008).

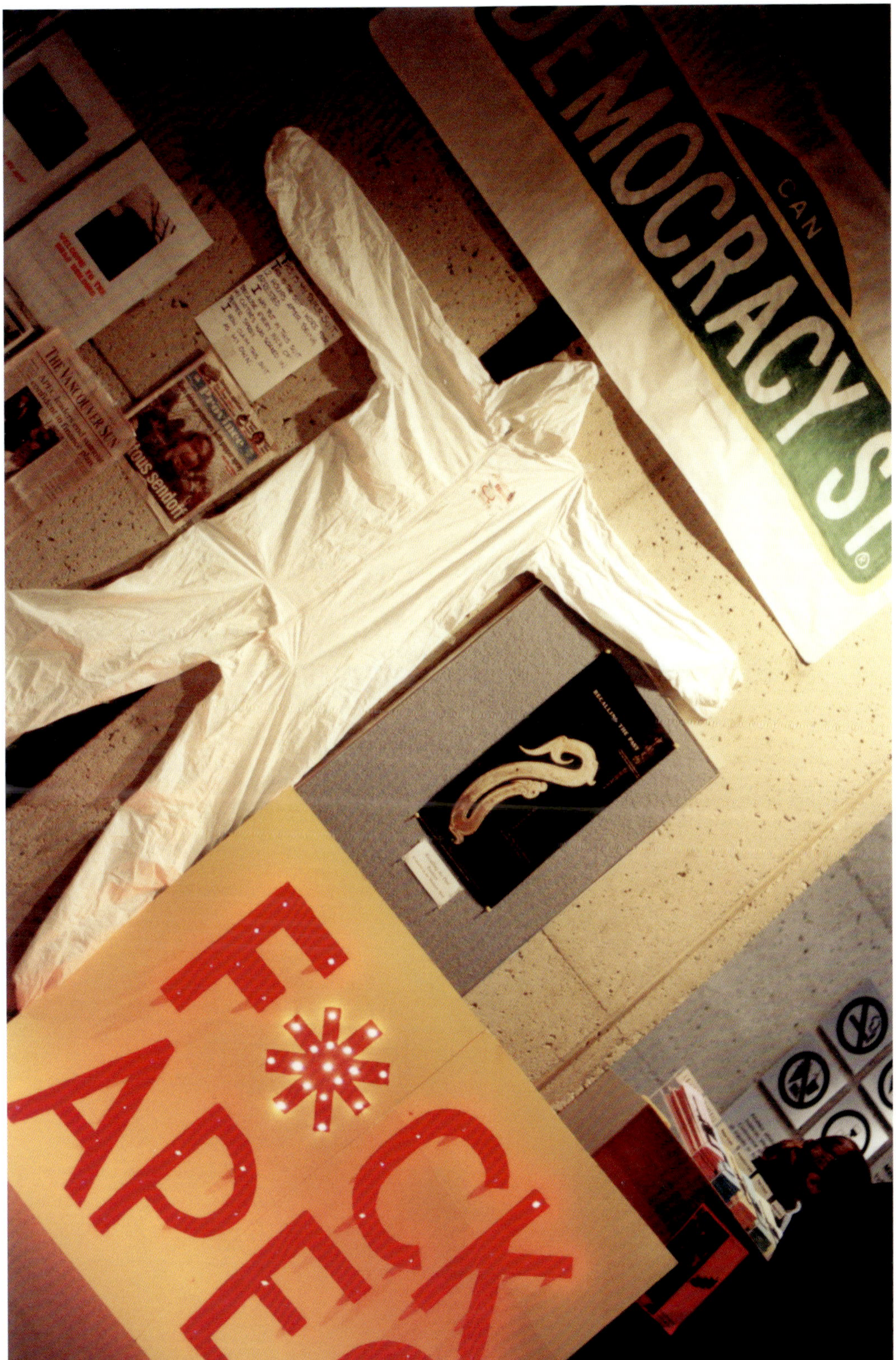

Figure 8.1
Democracy Street Event, 1997, UBC MOA.

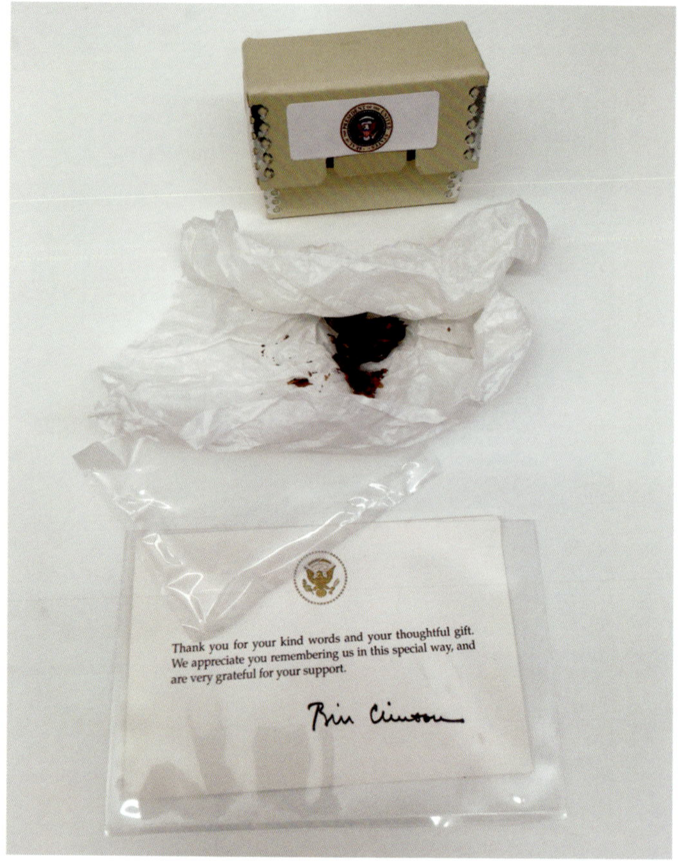

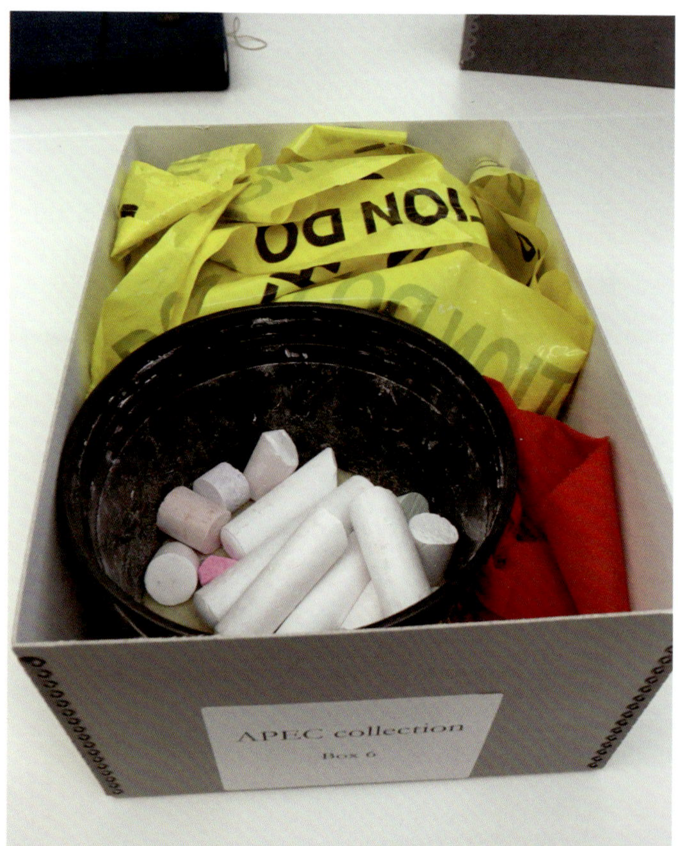

Figure 8.3 *Top*
Image from the APEC Collection, Bill Clinton's cigar and thank you card, UBC MOA, 1997.

Figure 8.4 *Bottom*
Image from the APEC Collection, chalk, police tape, other ephemera, UBC MOA, 1997.

Part Two

Case Studies

4

Reactionary Protest: The Warrior Nation and the Canadian War Museum

In 1980, Carol Duncan and Allan Wallach wrote their ground-breaking article "The Universal Survey Museum." In it, they argued that the architecture of museums tends to recall that of ceremonial spaces and that within universal survey museums, rituals of national citizenship are performed. They wrote, "those who pass through [the museum's] doors enact a ritual that equates state authority with the idea of civilization."[1] In short, "[m]useums embody and make visible the state."[2] Duncan and Wallach's theory applies to museums built during what Ruth Phillips calls the first museum age, the late eighteenth and nineteenth centuries,[3] but their description of how museums were capable of articulating "a distinctive national trajectory ... [with] the nation as final triumphant stage of successive progression"[4] holds true beyond and outside the museums (such as the Louvre and the Metropolitan) to which they apply their theories. "The emergence of the nation-state, the public, and the public museum in the late eighteenth century, were intimately bound together," wrote Sharon Macdonald in 2003.[5] Museums were and are repositories for national culture, for the evidence of international trade (including wealth derived from colonization), and for schools of national painting, which were often positioned in universal survey museums as the apex of human achievement.

Universal survey museums helped to create an exclusive national citizenry by showing visitors the cultural accomplishments of the nation and additionally by creating citizens through small ritual acts of participation in and reverence for that national culture.[6] In 1998, Fiona McLean joined others in addressing the blind spot of Duncan and Wallach's article, writing with regard to museums, "the concept of national identity has become problematic and contentious."[7] The creation of an in-group necessarily involved the expulsion of others from that central definition of belonging (even if, as in the case of Canada, Indigenous peoples had been here long before the core idea of nation was imposed). Though the "museum, the repository of a nation's culture, which connects the past to the present through recounting stories about the artefacts of past cultures, is clearly significant in representing the culture of the nation,"[8] attempts to challenge singular or monolithic stories of nation, coupled with the increasing importance of positioning museums globally (for example, as locales of interest for international tourists) were undermining the ease with which museums could build stories of national competency.

From the 1990s and before, many museums confronted the parochialism of their displays and addressed the culpability of their collections in maintaining systemic injustices. Particularly in the United States, such changes were occasionally greeted with derision and pushback.[9] This case study looks at the Canadian War Museum (CWM), a museum built during the second museum age – the twenty-first century – and dedicated to Canadian participation in conflicts around the globe. The CWM, which began as "a collection of militia artifacts" in the 1880s, is currently part of the Canadian Museum of History Crown corporation and as such has status as a federally funded national museum.[10] The CWM, which moved to a new purpose-built building in 2005, "present[s] the military history of Canada from earliest times to present day, as well as Canada's history of honouring and remembrance."[11] As such, the CWM focuses on conflict, on military heroes, and on Canadian military contributions around the globe. Though self-reflexive about the costs of war, the museum has at its very core a narrative of progressive nation-building of the sort outlined by Duncan and Wallach. Nevertheless, in 2006, shortly after the new building opened, the CWM was targeted by veterans angry about the wording in a text panel related to Allied bombing campaigns during the Second World War. Veterans called for the museum to focus on the bravery and sacrifice of Canadian soldiers rather than highlighting the impacts of the bombing campaign. In short, the goal was not to unsettle the "problematic concept of national identity" but to reaffirm how the legacy of Canadian soldiers would be positively memorialized in a permanent display at a time when the aging Second World War generation was quickly declining.

In this chapter, I look closely at the veterans' campaign to show how veterans developed a proprietary relationship with the museum and because of that felt a right to determine the exhibition's content. When the museum resisted, veterans and others were able to mobilize the mainstream media, government officials, and a Senate subcommittee to advocate on their behalf, eventually forcing the museum to make changes.[12] While on the surface the action and outcome (protest followed by change on the part of the museum) appear to follow those of other influential actions and results (for example, those of demonstrations against the exhibition *Spirit Sings* and the resulting Task Force on Museums and First Peoples), the direction of power in this instance was reversed such that demand for change came from a community outside the museum, but that community was tightly connected with existing systems of power, particularly political power.

Although this incident might fit more comfortably with my definition of a controversy rather than a protest (in that it is not connected to a wider social movement dedicated to change), I include it here in order to understand how the museum itself was portrayed as not fulfilling a duty to its community and was ultimately forced to remove a carefully researched piece of text. I am also cognizant of the fact that veterans did not *need* to protest, picket, or demonstrate outside the museum because they already had strong social and political influence and were able to make use of that in mounting a successful campaign against the institution.

Other confrontations with museums, key among them veterans targeting the 1995 *The Crossroads: The End of World War II, the Atomic Bomb, and the Origins of the Cold War* (colloquially known as the *Enola Gay*) exhibition at the Smithsonian, offer a precedent for the veteran response to wall text at the CWM.[13] I suggest, however, that a key distinction between the targeting of the CWM and the targeting of the *Enola Gay* exhibition was the way that veteran participation in the campaign to secure a new building for the CWM prior to 2005 produced feelings of ownership over the institution that coincided with the outlook of a peculiarly pro-military federal government after 2005. This chapter looks at the campaign to secure funding for a new building for the CWM as part and parcel of the protest that resulted just after its opening.

Campaign for a New War Museum

On 8 May 2005, the sixtieth anniversary of VE Day, the much-anticipated new Canadian War Museum opened in a well-attended ceremony in Ottawa.[14] Reporter Don Butler described the scene on the opening day:

> Propelled by an hour-long standing ovation from thousands of flag-waving spectators, a procession of more than 2,000 Canadian veterans – some in wheelchairs and others aboard vintage military vehicles – inched down Wellington Street to Canada's stunning new $136 million war museum rising from the barren lands of LeBreton Flats "like a ship coming out of a nasty swell at sea," as a *Citizen* editorialist wrote ... It was a day many of the aging veterans thought

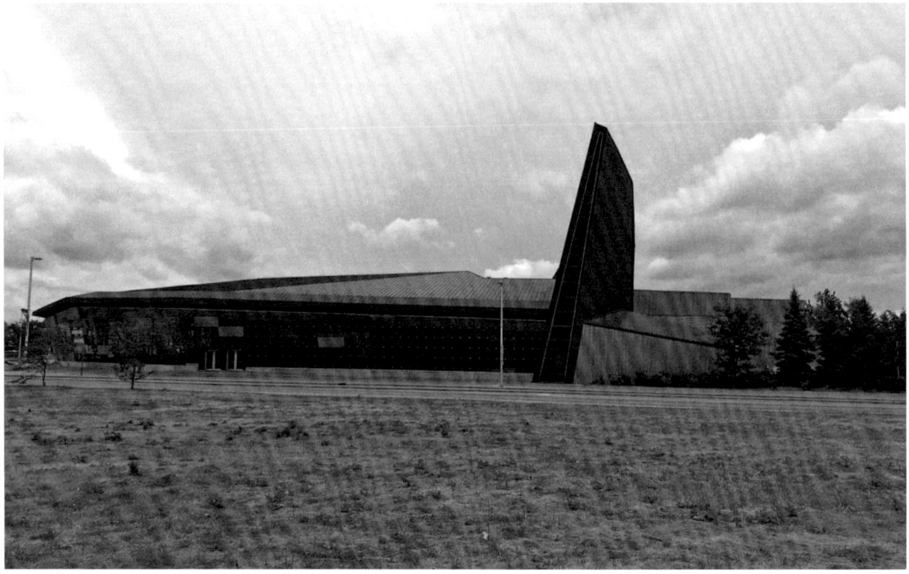

Figure 4.1
The new Canadian War Museum in Ottawa, opened in May 2005.

they'd never see. For nearly four decades, the story of Canada's wartime triumphs and sorrows had been shoe-horned into an antiquated building on Sussex Drive with space to display just two per cent of the museum's 500,000 artifacts and 13,000 pieces of art. It was, most agreed, a national embarrassment.[15]

The new museum, located a few kilometres from its predecessor, hugs the contours of the ground, resembling at once a bunker, a fighter jet, a natural rocky outcrop, and a devastated landscape regenerating in the wake of war. In many ways, the CWM is remarkably understated. Reesa Greenberg describes it as a self-effacing structure and a "landscape of loss."[16] And yet its metal-clad exterior and glass frontage make it also immediately recognizable within the lexicon of new museum building.[17] As noted previously, such museums have become, according to Anna Guasch and Joseba Zulaika, "the new paradigm of contemporary culture."[18] Though the 2007 and 2008 ROM and AGO extensions in Toronto would receive much greater media coverage, the Moriyama & Teshima Architects design of the CWM came first. If the CWM marked Canada's entry into the "second museum age" of spectacular museum building, connected with the neoliberalization of urban centres through Creative City rhetoric, the building's modesty and Ottawa's uneven relationship with culture and creativity make it a fascinating case study.[19]

Hardly a "global city," Ottawa, Canada's capital city, is more often (perhaps unfairly) characterized as a boring, bureacratic town full of government policy analysts and stodgy cultural institutions.[20] And yet in his 2009 book *Who's Your City?*, Richard Florida argued that despite its reputation, Ottawa actually had a higher percentage of creative class workers than any other city in Canada. According to Florida, Ottawa suffers from outdated stereotypes, for in fact, it "has the highest percentage of creative class workers in all of Canada, and one of the highest percentages in the world. Fully 43 per cent of Ottawa's workforce is employed in creative occupations, more than in New York, London, or San Francisco. Ottawa dominates our listings of the best places to live by life-stage."[21] As a centre for research and government, and also the site of the majority of the country's federally funded national museums and galleries, Ottawa scores exceptionally high on an index that measures intellectual labour in terms of potential profit.

Nevertheless, during the period in question, Ottawa also saw extensive de-funding of arts groups.[22] In 2004, reporter Paul Gessell noted that "[f]unding levels in Ottawa tend to be lower on a per-capita basis than in other large Canadian cities."[23] If this is taken to its logical conclusion, then arguably Ottawa is a place where culture is collected, amassed, and consumed but where production, at least in the arts, is discouraged.

Furthermore, a municipal survey of Ottawa employment from 2012 shows that federal administration remains the main employer in the city, followed by health and social services, retail and professional, and scientific research and development. The arts (which includes employment in federal museums) fall well down the list, after manufacturing, construction, and food services.[24] Despite a small decrease in high-tech jobs between 2006 and 2012, the high-tech sector remains strategically important in Ottawa. And the federal government, not surprisingly, dominates all, accounting for nearly 24 per cent of jobs in the city, most of them in administration and defence.[25]

Thus, the framing that Florida gives Ottawa matches the statistics coming from the Ottawa municipal government. But what is entirely missing in Florida's analysis is the role of government and of military and defence research and development in almost all of the key areas of employment in Ottawa. Major institutions for military R&D include the Government of Canada Defence Research and Development Canada Research Centres (which employ close to 1,400 in the city)[26] as well as numerous smaller high-tech military industries, private consultants, lobby groups, think tanks, and two major universities. In Ottawa, military research and development is a key component of the creative industries, ranging from software engineering and design to films, advertisements, military-designed fabrics, weapons invention, and research into non-lethal weaponry, as well as research around oil exploration, mining (both of which were put to use in postwar Iraq) and on and on. And yet, in the popular reception of Florida's work, military research and development does not figure at all. What actually constitutes the high-tech sector on which Florida's theories depend is only ever vaguely defined. And when armies are mentioned, it is more in terms of this glib line from a *National Post* writer, who critiques "smug creatives," as an "army of laptop-wielding theatre directors and Web-commerce consultants."[27] Gay-friendly urbanites are more in keeping with the theory of Creative Cities than are military engineers in lab coats.

Often, those writing about museums and neoliberalism, or museums and Creative Cities, assume a uniformity to the creative class that does not necessarily exist. The idea that creative workers in Ottawa are less game developers than designers of software for tanks and other military vehicles is perhaps unexpected. But a further surprise might be that the CWM, as one of the earliest entries into Canada's second museum age, was not built to partake in the tourism dollars derived from the Bilbao effect but rather was largely lobbied into being by veterans, their fundraising efforts, and a long quest for a space to display a national collection of war art and artefacts.[28]

The Need for a New Canadian War Museum

Prior to 2005, the Canadian War Museum was housed in a nineteenth-century stone building on Sussex Drive in central Ottawa, near the Canadian Mint, the National Gallery of Canada, and Parliament Hill. Despite the good location, the building was too small and in need of extensive repairs.[29] Much of the collection was housed offsite in a leaky and mouldering warehouse complex. An effort to enlarge or move the museum had been underway for some time. Though the project to secure funding for a new museum had been ongoing for decades, never did success look so far-fetched as it did in the 1990s.[30] In the middle of that decade, despite veterans' efforts to record their legacy,[31] interest in the military, in remembrance of past conflicts, and in the relationship of war to the project of Canadian nation-building reached a low.

In 1995, the Canadian Liberal government, faced with a growing debt and following its US and British counterparts, put forward a budget that brutally slashed funding for arts and civil society.[32] Telefilm Canada, the National Film Board, the Canada Council, the National Arts Centre, the Canadian Broadcasting Corporation, and the National Libraries and Museums budgets all faced significant cuts in 1995–96, building on top of cuts that had already been made through the early 1990s.

Reminiscing, Robert Janes refers to the "nasty nineties" when he was director of the Glenbow Museum.[33] He notes,

> [i]n contrast to the nearly unbridled growth of museums in the 1960s and 1970s, the 1990s was an era of budget cuts and financial restraint. Museums

became forcibly aware of their own vulnerability, amidst the strident calls for increased accountability and financial self-sufficiency. Earned revenues were touted as the universal salvation and the dictates of the marketplace arrived with a vengeance.[34]

Shelley Sweeney shows how total federal, provincial, and municipal government spending on museums, libraries, and archives fell by 14 per cent from 1984 to 2004, stemming from a reduction to the budget of the Department of Canadian Heritage of $675 million.[35]

Perhaps surprisingly, it was not just social services and the arts that were cut in the infamous 1995 federal budget but also the military, which suffered devastating financial cuts. The Canadian military had lurched unsteadily through the early 1990s, and anti-military sentiment grew when the torture and death of sixteen-year-old Shidane Arone in Somalia in 1992 at the hands of Canadian soldiers engaged in a UN peacekeeping mission was revealed. The subsequent dismantling of the elite Canadian Airborne Division under what came to be known as the Somalia Affair showed that racism and inequality were rife in the Canadian military. Arone's death, the attempted suicide of one of his torturers, and the resulting inquiry cast a shadow over the military in Canada. *Dishonouring a Legacy* was the title of the report that emerged from the Somalia Inquiry in 1993. This title is important, for despite the behaviour of Canadian peacekeepers in Somalia, despite financial cuts, and despite a widespread lack of interest, an idealized vision of Canadians as tolerant, cosmopolitan, fair keepers of the peace continued to dominate.[36] "We [Canadians] are peacekeepers, not policers," said a famous beer advertisement of the 1990s, reflecting a popular sentiment that unlike Americans, Canadians were not militaristic but were nonetheless important agents of diplomacy and change in the world.[37] To be clear, Canadian peacekeepers were soldiers, and they were and are part of the Canadian Forces, but a tenacious narrative about peacekeeping suggested that Canada's role was to prevent conflict and to help people around the world. The Somalia Affair clearly showed that this vision was more myth than reality.

Interest in the military in general was low. Coverage of Remembrance Day ceremonies was patchy at best. In fact, the *Globe and Mail* received a letter to the editor in 1995 accusing the paper of overlooking the day of memorial entirely.[38] "No matter what people do or say, memories of the two world wars are receding," wrote one reporter that year.[39] This period, from the early 1990s to the early 2000s, came to be known as the "Decade of Darkness" in some military circles. In an atmosphere that privileged a vision of peacekeeping, and with public interest in Remembrance Day and military spending waning, the CWM faced an uphill battle. Further, the museum itself was mired in controversy.

In 1996, a $12 million extension to the existing building was proposed, including the construction of a permanent Holocaust memorial exhibition. Greenberg notes that although there had been a number of similar memorials constructed elsewhere, the proposal for a memorial in Ottawa was leaked to the public before it had government approval or endorsement from Jewish communities and veterans groups, and it quickly became a point of contention.[40] Veterans protested vehemently that the memorial was "unCanadian" in that it did not directly represent Canadian military experience – they felt that Canadians had been neither perpetrators nor victims of the Holocaust. Said Cliff Chadderton, then chairman of the National Council of Veteran Associations in Canada, "The Holocaust gallery has more to do with political correctness than military history."[41] Others obviously felt differently, particularly given Canada's deplorable record in accepting fleeing Jewish refugees, the later immigration of many Holocaust survivors to Canada, and the fact that Canadian soldiers had liberated several concentration camps. Eventually, a Senate subcommittee held hearings in February 1998, and the memorial was quashed in favour of devoting all space in the proposed museum addition to "Canadian" military history.[42] However, the debacle over the memorial delayed the expansion project and contributed to a denial of funding from the federal government. There would be no extension, and the project was put on hold.

Some years later, once the project was back on and funding had been secured for an entirely new building, debate over whether or not to include a Holocaust memorial returned. While there was definitely space in the new museum, it was again decided that a memorial was inappropriate given that it was not "related" to the Canadian military experience. Again, this was not a unanimous decision, and many Jewish groups spoke out strongly against it. Israel (Izzy) Asper, then owner of the media conglomerate Canwest Global, objected so strongly that he began planning a completely separate museum dedicated solely to the Holocaust.[43] This museum would eventually become the Canadian Museum for Human Rights in Winnipeg, a tale covered in chapter 5.[44]

In 1998, then CWM director, historian, and pundit J.L. Granatstein suggested the sale of Hitler's limousine, one of the museum's most famous objects, at a cost of $20 million. Granatstein argued that funds from the sale could be used to partially cover the cost of a new art gallery to house the museum's extensive collection of war art. Again, the public outcry at the sale of the limousine and fear that the limousine might fall into the "wrong hands" prompted the museum to drop its plans.[45]

Thus, when a blockbuster exhibition of war art drawn from the CWM collection opened at its parent institution, the Canadian Museum of Civilization (CMC) in February 2000, a large-scale new facility in downtown Ottawa seemed unlikely ever to be built. But a change in public rhetoric was well underway, and far re-

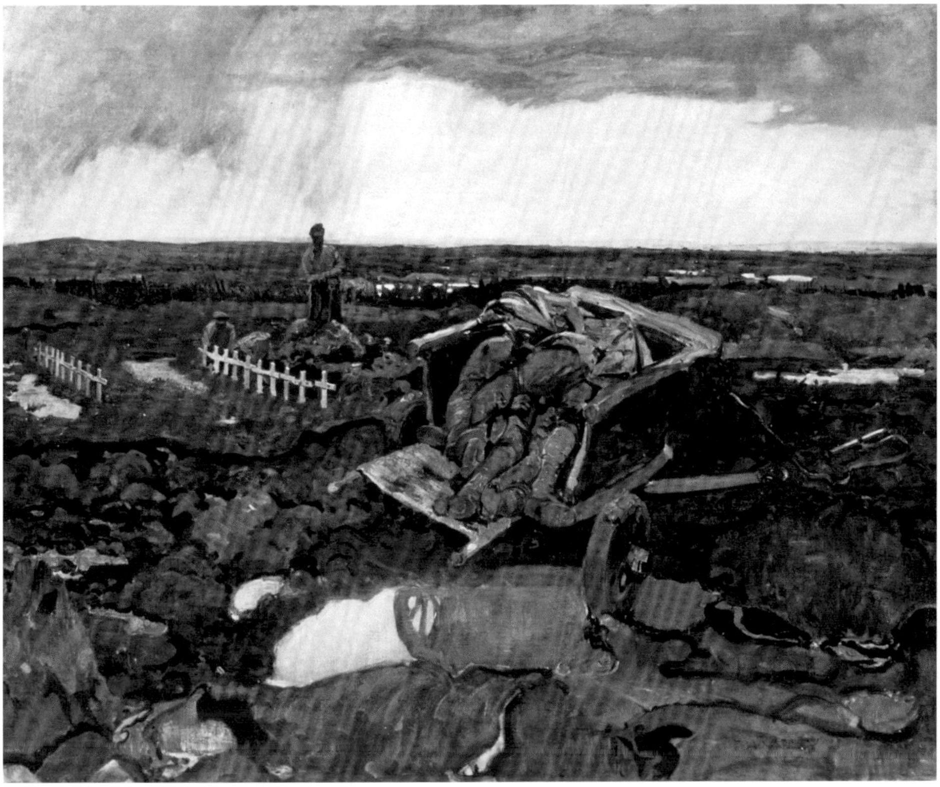

Figure 4.2
Frederick H. Varley, *For What?* 1919, Beaverbrook Collection of War Art, Canadian War Museum.

moved from the sordid photographs of the tortured Arone, the art in the collections of the CWM, inadvertently or not, provided an important visualization of a heroic Canada at war.

Canvas of War included works from the First and Second World Wars, as well as from 1993 peacekeeping missions to Croatia.[46] Although several paintings showcased Victorian-style heroism (particularly from the First World War Canadian War Memorials Fund collection), the exhibition was not celebratory. In fact, *Canvas of War* contained several canvases that could easily be read as anti-war, among them future Group of Seven member F.H. Varley's *For What?*, a painting of dead soldiers in a cart, about to be dumped into a muddy grave, Maurice Cullen's *Dead Horse and Rider in a Trench*, and Jack Nichols's visceral *Drowning Sailor*. And yet, the exhibition certainly was not received as anti-war or pacifist. In fact, quite the opposite.

The exhibition was largely discussed within the framework of heroic nationality. "The timing of *Canvas of War* couldn't be better to help break the growing gap in our knowledge of Canada at war – a result in part of so many misrepresentational contemporary history books and courses that distort national history for politically correct causes," read reporter John D. Habron's review in the *Globe and Mail* shortly after the opening.[47] Habron's reactionary sentiment appeared repeatedly in reviews that lauded the exhibition for its attempt to present a narrative of a nation unified in war, for its heroization of Canada's First and Second World War fighters, and for its attempt to highlight the importance of a narrowly defined Canadian history. Though the exhibition was careful to include representations of women, First Nations soldiers, and racialized members of the Canadian forces, such efforts went largely unnoticed in the coverage in which comments like Habron's were the norm.[48] The exhibition hauled a seemingly forgotten and overlooked collection out of the archives, symbolically pulling it out from beneath the carpet under which it had been swept.[49] The hyperbolic rhetoric about the artworks in the exhibition, which was reflected in media coverage, let visitors know that it was a world-class collection that had been ignored for too long, a collection that showed the "true heart" of the nation. *Canvas of War* provided a powerful visualization of Canada's participation in conflict as an important element of nation-building and also presented a compelling argument for building a new institution to house the collection.

Despite William MacDonnell's painting of sappers in Croatia, *Canvas of War* was very much at odds with the idea, outlined above, that Canada was a nation of peacekeepers. Instead, it foreshadowed what historian Ian McKay and journalist Jamie Swift describe as a transition in the idea of Canada from a peacekeeping to a "Warrior" nation – that is, of Canada as a nation forged in war and bound to support peace through military incursion. Since the mid-1960s, the idea of Canada as a peacekeeper had become a particularly popular way of imagining the "good" nation of Canada in contrast to the military power of its neighbour to the south. Shattering that narrative would have seemed, in the mid-1990s, when the CWM began its campaign for an extension or a new building, inconceivable. Nevertheless, McKay and Swift argue that the concentrated efforts of a number of historians, pundits, policy-makers, journalists, and speech-makers, whom they call the "new warriors," resulted in significant changes in Canada's relationship with its military in the period immediately following the terrorist attacks in New York and Washington in 2001. With historian and former director of the CWM J.L. Granatstein taking a leading role, the new warriors worked hard to foreground a myth of Canada established in blood in the War of 1812, coming together as a nation on the battlefields of the First World War, emerging as a fighting force in the Second World War, and then crushed by the combined effects of "politically correct" histories, immigration, and peacekeeping. The Warrior Nation narrative is a muscular one, reliant on tales of heroism and masculinity. Though McKay and Swift argue that the Warrior Nation narrative emerged post-2001, *Canvas of War* certainly anticipated its arrival.

An underlying premise of *Canvas of War* was that both a national school of art and art patronage emerged from the First World War, and, in keeping with the developmental narrative, it suggested that a government-sponsored national culture emerged in turn from the Second World War. The show included a copy of the 1951 report of the Royal Commission on National Development in the Arts, Letters, and Sciences (more popularly known as the Massey Commission Report) and claimed that the Canada Council emerged directly from Vincent Massey's work for the Second World War art program.[50] By extension, so too did the Museums Act, which led to the formation of the CMC and the CWM as national institutions. In this way, the development of a national culture was presented as an important part of Canada's history and as something that should be mobilized through exhibitions and cultural events such as *Canvas of War* and through federal funding for a new building for the CWM.

The new CWM would not, however, be a solely publically funded venture. During the exhibition at the CMC, pamphlets were handed out asking for donations to a drive for a new building, part of the Passing the Torch campaign that ended up raising millions of dollars. Labelling throughout the exhibition reiterated the deplorable state of the storage facility of the collection. A good number of the reviews
of the exhibition (both in the media and in the comments book for the exhibition) picked up on this sentiment. Wrote one visitor:

> Why are these paintings not on display permanently? As a young country we should certainly be more aware of our glorious beginnings, our past. Once a year on Remembrance Day ... is not enough – Vimy Ridge should be burned into the hearts and minds of every child in this country – we know so little of our heros [*sic*] let alone our distinguished painters.[51]

Canvas of War pulled on the heartstrings, it castigated, it shamed, and then it opened the possibility for redemption via a new museum. How could Canada not house its treasures with dignity?

Though organized at a time when interest in Canada's war history was low and the military was under the cloud of the Somalia Affair, *Canvas of War* opened amid a resurgence of federal government support for culture and growing interest in the First World War. In 1998, only three years after the 1995 budget cuts and perhaps inspired by the UK 1998 *Creative Industries Mapping Document*,[52] the federal Liberal government began to reinvest in culture. The economic crisis of the mid-1990s had not passed. But in 1998, a change in regulations enabled the Canada Council to grant $3.5 million in operating costs to museums and galleries (which had not received significant funds since 1984).[53] This injection of funds came as a result of a $25 million increase in annual funding from the federal government.[54] Culture was back on the state agenda.[55]

Though not directly connected to a resurgence in arts funding, by 1998 Remembrance Day had also taken on a renewed significance, attracting tens of thousands of spectators and a great deal of coverage. In that year, the federal government pledged funding to the National Capital Commission to update Confederation Square, allowing easier pedestrian access to the national War Memorial.[56] Shortly after *Canvas of War*'s opening, the Peacekeeper Monument opposite the National Gallery of Canada was unveiled, and a new ten-dollar bill emblazoned with its image and a stanza of John McRae's famous poem "In Flanders Fields" was released.[57] In 2001, the National Aboriginal Veterans Monument was unveiled in Confederation Park, albeit paid for not by federal funding but through fundraising from First Nations communities.[58]

Interest in Canada's military was growing. The central event was the 1999 Return of the Unknown Soldier – the reinternment of an unidentified soldier's bones brought from the burial ground at Vimy Ridge in France to the War Cenotaph in Ottawa. The ceremony received unprecedented and surprising attention, attracting 20,000 people and becoming a rallying point for the restitution of the reputation of the Canadian military. The narrative forwarded in *Canvas of War* was repeated on a much larger scale, and the coverage was entirely positive, often jingoistic, and aggressively inclusive. Journalist Ron Corbett argued that "the Tomb of the Unknown Soldier would become one of our most important national symbols."[59] As Barney Danson, war veteran and head of the Passing the Torch campaign to secure funding for a new CWM, commented, "Something happened on November 11 [1999] that was different from what I have ever seen since the [Second World] War. It was right across the country – biggest crowd ever on Parliament Hill in living memory, the same at the Cenotaph in Toronto and at Hart House, at places across the country and in schools."[60] Before 11 September 2001 then, the stain left by the Somalia Inquiry was already fading, and the role of sacrifice as a catalyst in the formation of a nation was gaining political and public traction. The so-called "Decade of Darkness" was over.[61]

All of these events and actions played on emotions, fostering a new atmosphere much more welcoming to a militarized redefinition of Canadian nationality. While McKay and Swift point to the work of the new warriors to make the Warrior Nation, naming a series of events, including those mentioned above, alongside speeches, publications, and policy changes, this does not mean that these efforts would be embraced by the general public (even a general public already invested in maintaining settler nationalism). A narrative of nationhood and national belonging is as much affective and embodied as it is a product of persuasive argument. The success of the new warriors owes as much to a mix of pageantry and pedantics as it does to what Lauren Berlant might call the contours of the moment, the "rightness" of a story of a nation coming into being at a particular moment. The feelings generated by seeing the pageantry on display in the Return of the Unknown Soldier or the emotion-tugging paintings in *Canvas of War* are conditioned by social conventions.[62] In her updating of Pierre Bourdieu's writings, Deborah Gould describes an emotional habitus (a knowledge of how to behave in certain situations) that emerges through partially conscious but deeply held affective senses of belonging, patriotism, and so on.[63] McKay and Swift suggest that, "the new warriors effectively mobilized so that, over time, the cry for a new warlike Canada seemed to emanate from the Canadian people themselves."[64] As Gould notes, "By directly affecting what people feel, a collectivity's emotional habitus can decisively influence political action, in part because feelings play an important role in generating and foreclosing political horizons, senses of what is to be done and how to do it."[65]

Gould is writing about AIDS activists and about those reacting against the status quo. The new warriors also saw themselves as activists, working against the narrative of Canada as a peacekeeping nation and resisting what they often referred to as "politically correct" history. But as the Warrior Nation narrative caught on, they moved from the margins to the centre, and suddenly being anti-war or pacifist meant being "anti-troops." Such characterizations were common in the early 2000s, part of what Merje Kuus calls militarization, "a multifaceted social process by which military approaches to social problems gain elite and popular acceptance."[66] Kuus notes that militarization tends to take place most often in peacetime, operating outside of military institutions through civilian structures such as education, entertainment, and the popular media.[67] When an emotional habitus in the public (support for the troops) meets a manipulated affect from government or media, a feedback loop results. Following Judith Butler, support for war is internalized; it is (literally) *incorporated* such that it becomes second nature or, in this case, "the way things are."[68]

While a museum might seem a strange place for a nation's relationship to its military history, to militarization, and to a changing affective landscape of national belonging to play out, as Timothy Luke notes,

> museums are venues where many key cultural realities are first defined; and, in this process of definition, the personal becomes political ... Different social forces – to the left, on the right, and at the center – all are intent on defining what reality is, will be, or has been, and major museums quickly can become embattled bastions of resistance or threatening outposts of invasion in the cultural war that these social forces wage against each other.[69]

On 17 March 2000, at the beginning of the second museum age *and* at a transitional moment when the ideas of the new warriors were catching on, Liberal Heritage Minister Sheila Copps announced a $58.2 million contribution toward the construction of a new facility for the CWM in Ottawa.[70] The Royal Canadian Legion and the Canadian Museum of Civilization added contributions of $500,000 and $7 million, respectively, while the Passing the Torch campaign, led by veterans, raised a massive $16.5 million.[71] Roger Sarty notes, "It was the largest appeal ever for private contributions to a federal agency. Here apparently was a new thread in Canadian nationalism."[72]

With funding secured for the new building, Raymond Moriyama of Moriyama & Teshima Architects, in joint venture with Alex Rankin of Griffiths Rankin Cook Architects, were chosen to design the building. Moriyama, best known for the Bata Shoe Museum in Toronto, was a renowned architect (if not quite a global "starchitect"), and he was also a symbolically rich choice – as a twelve-year-old he was interned in British Columbia, along with his family, as Japanese "enemy aliens." Moriyama's personal history plays through the design of the building, which he says was inspired by a treehouse he built in the British Columbia Slocan internment camp – a place to get away, to meditate, and to be at one with nature amid devastation.[73]

Before construction began, and just a few months after Copps's funding announcement, two planes crashed into the World Trade Center, the Canadian military was deployed to Afghanistan as part of a NATO-led (not UN peacekeeping) force, and Canada joined the so-called "War on Terror."[74] There were very few public rallies against the foray into Afghanistan, which was portrayed in the Canadian media as a just and noble cause (and which many people mistook for a peacekeeping mission).[75] The sod-turning ceremony for the new CWM took place in November 2002, and construction was well underway in February 2003 when hundreds of thousands of Canadians took to the streets to protest the possibility of Canada's participation in the US-led invasion of Iraq. In contrast to Afghanistan, the invasion of Iraq seemed ignoble and possibly illegal (as it would, indeed, turn out to be). McKay and Swift describe the protests as akin to the last attempt to actively resist the imposition of the Warrior Nation, but because Canada did not join the Coalition of the Willing and did not send troops to participate in the invasion of Iraq, resistance quickly faded away.

By the time the new CWM opened in May 2005, Canadian coalition troops were even more encumbered in Afhganistan, and American-led troops were bogged down in Iraq and under the glare of fallout from the Abu Ghraib photos showing guards torturing prisoners. Though the crowds that gathered for a demonstration on the two-year anniversary of the invasion of Iraq still numbered in the thousands,[76] the mass action of 2003 had largely dissipated as the narrative of the

Warrior Nation gained traction. In post-2003 protests elsewhere, particularly in countries where troops were participating in the Coalition of the Willing, museums, among them the Imperial War Museum (UK) and the War Memorial in Australia, emerged as key sites for demonstrations against the ongoing war. The same was not true in Canada.

From 2001, in Canada, I found only two anti-war protests taking place at museums, in both cases because the institutions were being used to host meetings with visiting US president George W. Bush. In Ottawa in December 2004, a highly choreographed visit ended for Bush and the Canadian prime minister with a sniper-protected dinner at the CMC, while protesters were cordonned off a distance away.[77] The following day, Bush visited Halifax, ostensibly to thank Canada for allowing planes to land in Gander, Newfoundland, on 11 September 2001 (a much-discussed oversight in the thank-yous he extended after the attacks). There, 4,000 protesters gathered outside the Pier 21 immigration museum where speeches took place.[78] "That redneck's bullshit offends my Bluenose," said one participant in a moment of levity.[79]

In my research, I did find a smattering of comments calling for the new museum to address anti-war protest. In one letter to the editor of the *Globe and Mail*, peace activist Penny Sanger asked,

> Can we hope that, along with the military dreck [in the new museum], there will be artifacts from Canadians' efforts to oppose war – placards, perhaps, from the huge protest marches against the superpowers' Cold War and baby's teeth showing the toxic effects of the nuclear weapons testing campaigns? Otherwise, the "Canadian War Museum" must be called the Canadian Museum of Military History.[80]

But such opinions were in the minority, or invisible in the mainstream press.

In May 2005, the new museum opened. *National Post* columnist Terrence Corcoran noted shortly after the opening,

> This is no place for bleeding hearts. Not only are visitors surrounded by guns and helmets and other paraphernalia of war – grenades, rifles, bombers, tanks, tomahawks, Cruise missiles, arrows, artillery, pistols, bayonets – they are also enveloped by ideas and history that are so startling and seemingly un-Canadian that they could start a revolution.[81]

Corcoran notes first that the museum is at odds with a familiar idea of Canadian identity: "We are the peacekeepers, the doers of good and the mediators of conflict"[82] before concluding that the Canadian story of peacekeeping is a myth: "the fictional creation of a generation of historians and activists."[83] According to this columnist, Canadians now have "a new vision of the country's history, a fresh perspective." He concludes, "the Canadian War Museum may well be the greatest and most spectacular museum in Canada, and in many ways one of the great museums of the world."[84] His column deeply and profoundly reflects the narrative of the Warrior Nation, brought to life in the new museum irrespective of anti-war protests and even of Canada's refusal to be part of the Coalition of the Willing in Iraq.

While it was a Liberal government that initiated Canada's involvement in Afghanistan and refused to join coalition troops in Iraq, a Conservative minority government elected in 2006 made the military one of its top priorities, immediately pledging $17.1 billion to buy new equipment.[85] Journalist John Geddes, writing in *Macleans* magazine suggests, "After they won power in 2006, the Conservatives embraced the war museum as a model for conveying a compelling national historical narrative."[86] From this point on, the federal government fully supported the Warrior Nation, erasing any haziness over the issue of peacekeeping by reinvesting in the military, pursuing numerous pro-military policy changes, and supporting several programs dedicated to boosting military history (particularly those dedicated to historical conflicts such as the War of 1812).[87] McKay and Swift write, "what truly distinguishes this right-wing current from any we have seen since the Great War of 1914–18 is the extent to which the new warrior campaign is working in tandem with the state's propaganda apparatus to institute a new regime of truth."[88] Further, they suggest, "the mission [to Afghanistan] was not so much about taking democracy to a faraway country as it was about nurturing warriors in Canada, about building a country that was not afraid to go to war."[89] Historians Margaret MacMillan, Robert Bothwell, and Randell Hansen argue that the Harper government was heavily invested in creating unity through the use of a celebratory historical narrative. At a speech on the anniversary of the First World War battle of Vimy Ridge, Harper used the example of Canadian soldiers who died in order "to love our country and defend its freedom forever" (which the historians also note included an unspoken subtext to support Canadian troops in Afghanistan).[90]

Acceptance of the Warrior Nation rhetoric was widespread (though as we shall see in the next chapter, acceptance was far from total), even reaching out to encompass the 2003 anti-war protests. McKay and Swift quote Bob Chamberlain, a Superannuated Colonel addressing a crowd at a Remembrance Day ceremony in Kingston, Ontario, who argued that soldiers brought freedom and democracy and that "it has been soldiers, not campus agitators, who have given us the right to protest."[91] Such opinions were widespread and often presented as a reason to *dismiss* protest in the current moment. "Sensible Canadians believe that support for the military, especially in wartime, is not only commendable, but a requirement of good citizenship," wrote Charles W. Moore, a freelance writer based in Nova

Scotia. "The peaceniks have a right to express their opinions, but their freedom to do so was secured by war and is maintained by willingness and preparedness to go to war."[92] "Canadians," write Swift and McKay, "have witnessed an effort to conscript both the distant past and more recent times into a reshaping of the country's future," and that future was, around the time of the opening of the new War Museum, one in which Canada was a military-dependent Warrior Nation.[93]

Given the ample evidence supporting Swift and McKay's argument, in addition to Corcoran's review of the new museum, one might expect the institution to be a key location for envisaging the Warrior Nation. Certainly a tour of the content and exhibition spaces would at least initially appear to support this claim.

The New Canadian War Museum

The key exhibition space at the CWM is the series of Canadian Experience Galleries (designed by Haley Sharpe of Leicester, UK, and Origin Studios of Ottawa), which are dedicated to "underlining the profound effect that war has had on Canadian development and the significant role Canadians have played in international conflicts."[94] Combining 2,500 artefacts with audio-visual presentations, dioramas, and

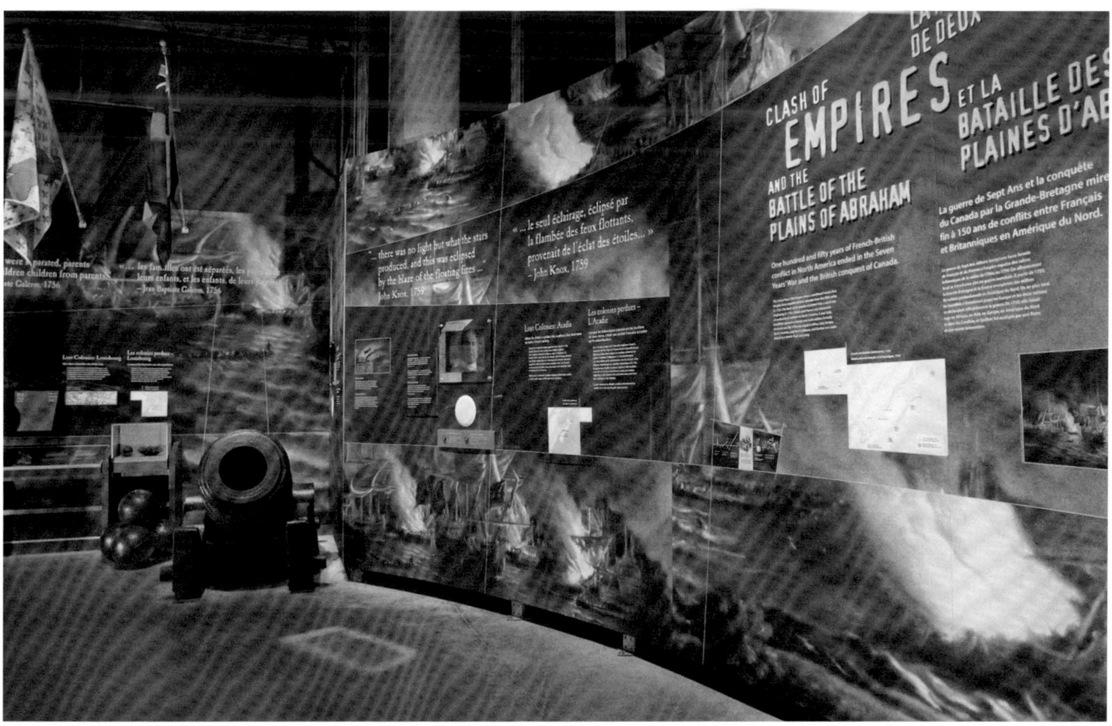

Figure 4.3
Canadian Experience Galleries, The Gallery 1 of the CWM.

hands-on activities, the galleries are busy, loud, and interactive. Here, the Warrior Nation narrative is made obvious through the titles of the display spaces: "Battleground: Wars on Our Soil, from Earliest Times to 1885"; "For Crown and Country: The South African and First World Wars, 1885–1931"; "Forged in Fire: The Second World War, 1939–1945"; "A Violent Peace: The Cold War, Peacekeeping and Recent Conflict, 1945 to Present." A team of designers, curators, and advisors picked themes of geography, politics, brutality, and survival. These themes are explored in each section amid a "rhythm of peace and war," with an "intense level of information" that made it "crucial to adopt a flowing, organic and instinctive hierarchy of messages to avoid overwhelming, confusing or numbing the visitor."[95]

In a document prepared by the design firm in conjunction with the opening of the museum, peacekeeping is not mentioned. As one reviewer noted, "Implicitly, the new museum also downgrades peacekeeping. It was more prominent in the old building, with an entire gallery devoted to the subject."[96] This was on purpose. "The gallery covers 60 years," Granatstein is quoted in a description of the new museum, "and I thought they did about as well as they could. The key is that it doesn't give peacekeeping the pre-eminence it has in Canadians' minds."[97] Museums, Timothy Luke notes, "possess a power to shape collective values and social understandings in a decisively important fashion."[98] Certainly, this seems to be the case in the CWM where display after display articulates the way that the Canadian nation emerged from heroic conflict, overcoming the odds, and exhibiting bravery by standing up to evil.

However, the Warrior Nation narrative is not seamless in the museum. Although permanent exhibits in the gallery "trace the country's war history from Aboriginal conflicts through the World Wars to the post–Cold War era," the stories are not focused solely on "great men," on top military and political leaders, on heroism and bravery, and on major battles; rather, individual stories are scattered throughout, with the goal of extending and in some ways questioning the role of conflict in Canadian history.[99] Said Mark O'Neill (who would become director of the CWM in 2008), the museum is dedicated to showcasing three main stories related to Canada's participation in conflict: "The first was that war is a devastating human experience. 'So there's no glorification of war.' The second was that war has altered the lives of almost everyone in Canada. And the third was remembrance."[100]

Thus, there was some confusion in the reception of the new museum. Most reviews of the CWM exhibitions were largely in line with Corcoran's analysis that the museum shunted peacekeeping aside in favour of a more muscular vision. Not all reviews celebrated this change. One reviewer wrote, "It's not that Canada's war museum celebrates war, although it sometimes comes close. Particularly in the way it seems to suggest the 'sacrifice' of tens of thousands of Canadian men's lives was necessary for the country to become strong and dedicated to making a difference on the international stage."[101] This writer's discomfort resolves into a wish to hold on to the narrative of Canada as peacekeeper. He concludes, "Its weakness is that it makes only a limited attempt to educate visitors about peace."[102] Indeed, although a small section devoted to peacekeeping remains, pacifism and anti-war activism are represented by just one tiny display showing photos of Raging Grannies alongside a brief description of Bruce Cockburn's song "If I Had a Rocket Launcher," which references right-wing death squads in Latin America.[103] The massive protests of 2003 are invisible, as is the ongoing work by citizens groups in Canada such as Project Ploughshares or the Coalition to Oppose the Arms Trade. Anti-conscription riots in Quebec are mentioned in the section on the First World War, but organized opposition, for example, to the war in Vietnam or help given to US draft dodgers, is not.[104]

Nevertheless, the Canadian Experience Galleries, despite their overwhelming adherence to the narrative of the Warrior Nation, end on an ambiguous note. In the final section, visitors are encouraged to speak up and speak back, and although the channels are traditional (writing letters on pre-addressed postcards to the minister of National Defence, Human Rights Watch, the US president, the Royal Canadian Legion, and the Canadian branch of the United Nations), the final room in the museum seems ultimately to suggest action against conflict rather than for it.[105]

Outside the Canadian Experience Galleries, any pro-militaristic stance fades away. The museum created by Moriyama & Teshima Architects is a strange space, clearly divided between the celebratory and busy exhibition spaces and the contemplative, meditative, and dark architecture of the building. If the Experience Canada Galleries are immersive and educational, the rest of the building is potentially more comparable to the ritual space described by Duncan and Wallach as central to the universal survey museum. The outside of the CWM is unpretentious and low to the ground, appearing to merge with its surroundings. Built of concrete with copper sheathing, the building is very much a part of the landscape, which appears mottled as if blown apart by shells. The architecture evokes not only the impact of war on land but also "nature's ability to regenerate and to accommodate the physical devastation wrought by human conflict."[106] The museum also features two sets of windows that spell out "Lest We Forget" in morse code in both official languages and another, larger window through which the sun shines each 11 November, directly illuminating the headstone of an Unknown Soldier inside.[107] Providing a link between exterior and interior, the line the sunbeam casts on 11 November is recorded in dark stone that bisects the entire building. On the inside, "The dramatic angled walls rise from interior floors that are also canted, skewing one's sense of equilibrium."[108] The aim, according to Moriyama, is to provoke a sense of unease within visitors, "sufficient to release some of their physical and emotional inhibitions."[109] Similarly, the foyer creates a sense of compression and confinement, evoking what Moriyama calls "the power of absence" through the bare, austere walls. Outside of the Canadian Experience Galleries, the museum is quiet and contemplative.[110]

While the designers point out the harmony between the building and exhibition spaces, noting a resonance in the angular and trapezoidal shapes used in the exhibition galleries "echoing the Museum's architecture and themes by creating interconnecting spatial volumes that enhance the historical messages," these links are not immediately visible. The architecture, notes the document prepared by Haley Sharpe, is also reflected in the "Spartan palette of materials" used in the Canadian Experience Galleries and the prevalence of concrete, galvanized steel, and wood. But in fact, the distinction between the galleries and the rest of the museum is jarring and obvious. The museum essentially has a series of loud, exuberant galleries that showcase a narrative of national identity steeped in heroism and conflict, housed within a contemplative, dark, memorial structure, emerging from Moriyama's childhood imprisoned in a Japanese internment camp and designed to draw attention to the devastation wrought by conflict.

As Greenberg notes, war museums are "built to glorify victory but must also acknowledge the human cost ... National war museums invariably are conservative and comforting, even though the experiences they present are radical and disruptive."[111] The CWM, while gesturing towards openness and "talking back," ultimately encourages a performative reworking of rituals of belonging toward a romanticized view of conflict. Nevertheless, as evident in the dissimilarity between the architecture and the exhibition space, the CWM has a deep conflict at its core.

An Enduring Controversy

It is not my intention to suggest that the architecture of the museum led to protests by veterans. But I would like to suggest that the museum's annunciation of the Warrior Nation is incomplete and, as such, the institution was open to action from those who had raised the most money and who were most invested in that narrative: veterans and particularly veterans of the Second World War who had watched their legacy be tarnished in the 1990s and were now immersed in a moment of potential as the Warrior Nation myth took hold. In short, a triumphant narrative in the exhibition space, in combination with a building obviously illustrating the costs of war, subdued any "patriotic fete" at the museum.[112] This contrast is exemplified by a small demonstration that took place on the opening day of the new museum.

On that day, veterans of the 1st Canadian Parachute Battalion Association organized a small protest against the display in the foyer of the museum of Gertrude Kearns's paintings of Corporal Clayton Matchee and Private Kyle Brown, two of the soldiers involved in the atrocities in Somalia.[113] Kearns was/is a well-known

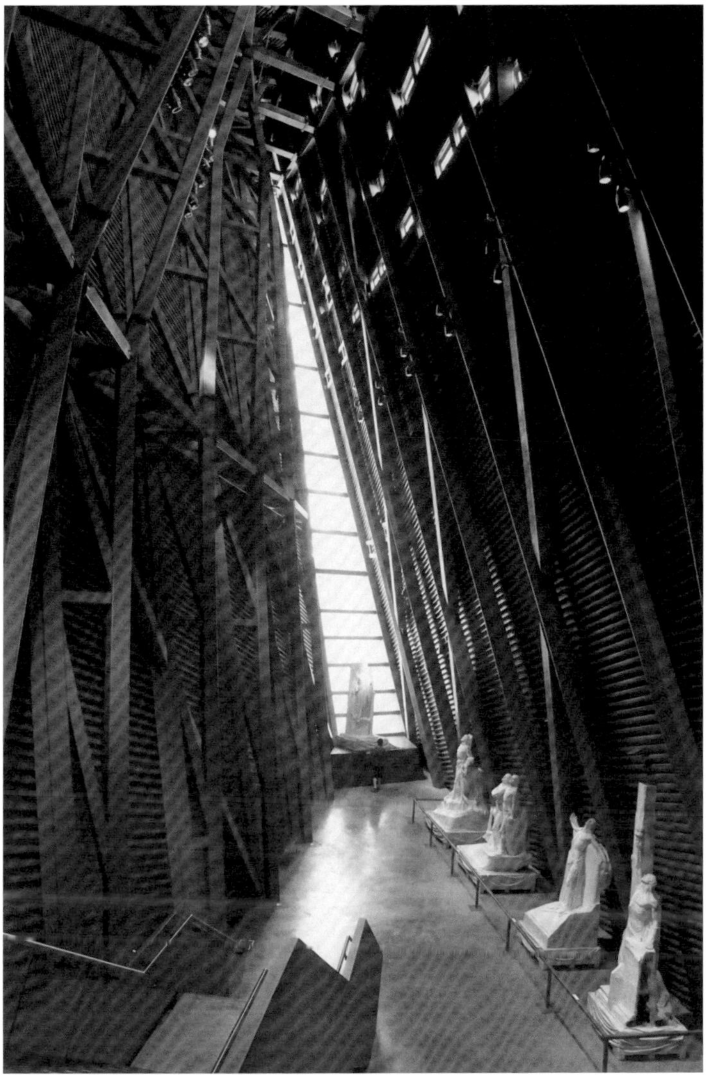

Figure 4.4
Regeneration Hall, Canadian War Museum, Ottawa. The window overlooks the Canadian Parliament buildings. The statues are plaster maquettes used by Walter Seymour Allward to design the Canadian National Vimy Memorial at Vimy, France.

Canadian artist who had long worked both independently and in an official capacity as a Canadian war artist, primarily painting portraits of Canadian soldiers. Her paintings of Matchee and Brown had sparked debate from the time they were made, but the CWM granted them a prominent place at the entrance to the museum, again disrupting or complicating the Warrior Nation narrative present in the galleries.[114] Cliff Chadderton, present again, referred to the paintings a "trashy, insulting tribute" and called for a boycott of the opening ceremonies.[115] The opening went ahead, and Kearns's paintings remained prominently on display.[116]

Just a few months later, the museum found itself mired in a deeper problem. Veterans' groups had organized in an attempt to have the museum change the wording used in a panel in the Second World War gallery (part of the Canadian Experience Galleries) that, under the title "An Enduring Controversy," described the Allied

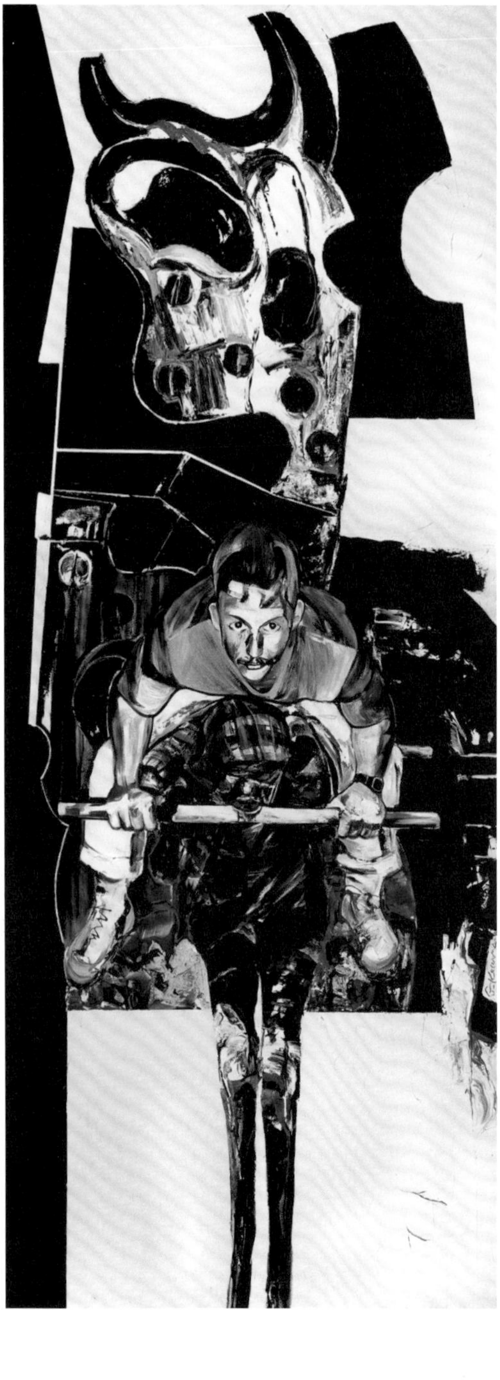

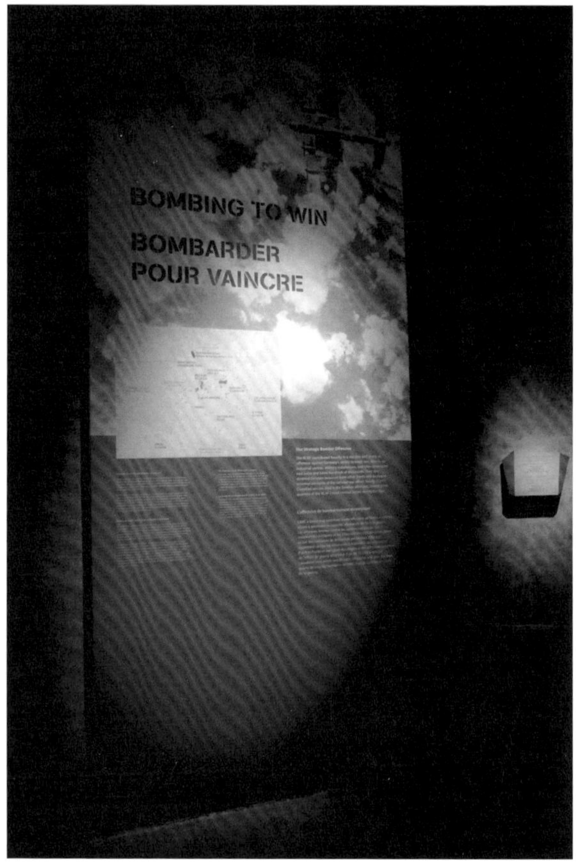

Figure 4.5 *Left*
Gertrude Kearns, *Somalia #2, Without Conscience*, 1995, Beaverbrook Collection of War Art, Canadian War Museum.

Figure 4.6 *Above*
Bombing to Win display, Canadian War Museum.

bomber war, or "Combined Bomber Offensive," in less than celebratory terms.[117] The display referred to the practice of area bombing by British (and thus Canadian) pilots. During the war, rather than using techniques of strategic bombing (for example, trying to hit oil reserves, transportation facilities, or the aircraft industry), most of the offensive was dedicated to bombing cities, often using incendiary devices that resulted in high casualties. The idea was that widespread bombing would batter civilian morale, bringing a quicker end to the war. Over the years, a number of historians have argued that the area bombing campaign had limited results until the very end of the war, though others suggest that it severely damaged the German war economy.[118]

Given previous controversies at the CWM, as well as lingering veteran resentment over a 1992 CBC television series titled *The Valour and the Horror* that had critically questioned the Combined Bomber Offensive,[119] the museum had closely consulted veterans prior to the opening of the gallery. There had been warnings about the "An Enduring Controversy" text panel (particularly a section with the heading "Bombing to Win"), and by the time the museum opened changes *had already been made* in keeping with veterans' requests. Nevertheless, even the updated wording enraged many.[120] Set beside a video showing archival footage of bombing raids, a German anti-aircraft gun, and a display on the airmen who flew the missions, was a label that did not raise ire. It read: "Attacks on industrial centres,
military installations and cities devastated vast areas and killed hundreds of thousands. They also diverted German resources from other fronts and damaged essential elements of the German war effort." And beside this uncontroversial label was the "An Enduring Controversy" panel that included quotations and photos showing destruction (and corpses) in German cities and a central text passage that considered the ethics and morality of the controversial decision to launch the bombing offensive on Germany.[121] This second panel read:

> The value and morality of the strategic bomber offensive against Germany remains bitterly contested. Bomber Command's aim was to crush civilian morale and force Germany to surrender by destroying its cities and industrial installations. Although Bomber Command and American attacks left 600,000 Germans dead, and more than five million homeless, the raids resulted in only small reductions in German war production until late in the war.[122]

In response to veterans' complaints, quotations were added beside the panel. The first was from Sir Arthur "Bomber" Harris, who had overseen the bombing campaign and had always argued strongly that it shortened the war. A second came from economist and diplomat John Kenneth Galbraith, who stated that the bombing campaign helped ground troops. And a third quoted a Canadian airman, who noted, "more than once I wondered 'how many people will those bombs kill'? However, you couldn't dwell on it. That's the way war is."[123] Despite the changes, veterans complained that the wording of the panel made soldiers seem immoral at best and criminal at worst.[124]

A campaign grew across the country led by Paul Manson, a former chief of the defence staff (who incidentally had also chaired the Passing the Torch campaign to raise money for the new museum, headed the CWM board's building committee for the new museum, had also served on the CWM's advisory committee, and had been a member of the CWM Board of Trustees), Cliff Chadderton, chairman of the National Council of Veterans, and Duane Daly, dominion secretary of the Royal Canadian Legion, who assembled the "Mayday committee" to organize lobbying efforts.[125] Letters to the editors of newspapers and magazines, calls to call-in shows, and television interviews were organized. A boycott of the museum was threatened.[126] Prominent media fell onside with the veterans, as did several politicians. Veterans are quoted referring to the museum officials as "judgmental," "grossly unfair," "arrogant," and "morally biased."[127] "The clamour," wrote Margaret MacMillan with Bothwell and Hansen in the aftermath, "proved the accuracy of the War Museum's caption 'an enduring controversy.'"[128]

The museum stood strong (in keeping with the reaction to demonstrations at the *Spirit Sings* and *Into the Heart of Africa* exhibitions elsewhere). Interestingly, veterans called out the museum for not being on their side, revealing an assumption that this national institution should support veterans. An article in *Legion Magazine* argued that "the war museum has proceeded in such an insensitive and hurtful war that many air veterans feel that their fallen comrades are being fingered as immoral – even criminal – by an institution of the very government that sent them on those harrowing missions."[129] The *National Post* further advanced this argument, noting that, "there is the issue of free expression and not caving into the sensitivities of every special interest group. Veterans, though, are not just any special interest group."[130] While Black protesters at *Into the Heart of Africa* or Indigenous protesters at *Spirit Sings* could be dismissed as "special interest groups" whose complaints could (and should) be ignored (or dismissed as "politically correct"), veterans were (at least according to the *National Post* and the veterans themselves) different.

Veterans are, of course, an important constituency of the CWM. As such, it would be wrong to say that they should not be consulted or involved in the exhibitions and displays of the museum. Jennifer Thiverge, for example, argues that "Veterans have the potential to provide rich and unique stories to the curatorial research ... However, as positive as collaboration with veterans may be in practice, in reality, it can become very challenging to implement in a way that is positive for all involved."[131]

The reaction to the panel in the CWM can be compared with that of the response to the installation of the restored *Enola Gay* (the airplane that dropped an atomic bomb on Hiroshima in 1945) in a proposed exhibition at the Smithsonian National Air and Space Museum in Washington in 1995.[132] The display of the *Enola Gay* was to be contextualized with labels and artefacts that referred to the potential damage that could and did ensue from the use of atomic weapons (and included information on the Manhattan project, on the post–Second World War nuclear arms race, and on those who had died in Japan). When the museum asked for feedback from the public prior to the exhibition opening, the mere juxtaposition of the *Enola Gay* with potentially critical materials resulted in what Luke calls "ferocious political combat over America's past."[133] Conservative right-wing Speaker of the House Newt Gingrich, speaking on behalf of the Second World War generation (then in their seventies), stated, "political correctness may be O.K. in some faculty lounge, but the Smithsonian is a treasure that belongs to the American people and it should not become a plaything for left-wing ideologies ... [Americans are] sick and tired of being told by some cultural elite that they ought to be ashamed of their country."[134] US veterans organized quickly and began lobbying the museum and Congress to pressure the Smithsonian into removing its "revisionist" history of the atomic bombings of Hiroshima and Nagasaki.[135] Veterans felt strongly that the museum portrayed "Japan as a victim rather than the aggressor ... implying American servicemen were little more than war criminals."[136] As with the European bombing campaign, American veterans argued strongly that atomic bombs had brought a swift end to the conflict and thus had saved lives. When the museum removed some information to appease the veterans, historians responded by accusing the museum of "historical cleansing."[137] Eventually, under pressure from Congress, the exhibition was cancelled before it was even mounted.[138]

To this point, protests at the CWM unfolded identically. The language mobilized against each museum is also almost identical. But the CWM refused to remove the panel. Under pressure, the museum agreed to consult with four prominent historians. All agreed that the panels were accurate, but two suggested they appeared to "side with one side of the debate" (one commentator focused on wording, and the other took note of the photograph with corpses in it). Serge Bernier, the senior historian at the Department of Defence, who ultimately sided with veterans, asked why it was necessary to emphasize the controversy over the bombing campaign. While he agreed the panel was factually correct, he also argued that it was tendentious and hurtful.[139] Margaret MacMillan, one of the historians who sided firmly with the museum, argued that veterans were incorrect – the panels did not depict the bombing campaign as immoral. She concluded that museums should not respond to criticism, observing, "[I]t cannot allow its programmes and exhibits to be dictated by outside groups ... As we seek to understand ourselves, we must take our own behaviour and past as a whole, not pick out only the pieces which make us feel good about ourselves."[140] Likewise, pro-museum historian Desmond Morton remarked, "if the Museum were to give in to the criticism it would be surrendering to those who wanted to censor history and to re-write the past, a humiliation that would force the Museum's professional historians to resign and a 'gratuitous insult' to 'mature Canadians who visit.'"[141] Later, MacMillan, Bothwell, and Hansen pointed out that the Allied bombing campaign *was* controversial during the war and it has remained so.[142] These were not new interpretations, and to suggest otherwise was to overwrite history with propaganda. Their comments, broadly speaking, echo those supporting the ROM in the wake of *Into the Heart of Africa*. The museum had to stay strong against the intervention of "interest groups."[143]

It is worth pausing here a moment because it will be apparent that members of the Coalition for the Truth About Africa, picketing outside of *Into the Heart of Africa*, and veterans arguing that the CWM should change the wording in a text panel are highly dissimilar groups. The former group argued strongly that the ROM was a racist institution and that its actions in mounting the exhibition and then refusing to close it once its flaws had been pointed out privileged white and missionary viewpoints and actively denied the perspectives of Africans and their descendants living in Canada. By contrast, veterans and their supporters actively resisted the introduction of the kinds of histories demanded by the Coalition for the Truth About Africa, dismissing them as "politically correct" and not "proper" history. They argued rather for a celebratory narrative of military heroism that denied the agency of all but the airmen who had flown missions and wanted to be memorialized in a certain way. And yet, the response that the museum should not bow to pressure from "special interest groups" was the same for both, demonstrating at best an erroneous belief in the neutrality of museums.

The controversy at the CWM, however, had a completely different outcome from that at the ROM in that the latter resisted immediate intervention but participated (eventually) in a long process of reconciliation. Members of the Coalition for the Truth About Africa were harassed and arrested. The same was not true at the CWM. There, veterans' calls for changes did not abate, and by 2006 air veterans were joined by the Royal Canadian Legion (which did not immediately provide public support). CEO and president of the CMC Victor Rabinovitch wrote in recollection, "Throughout 2006, individual air veterans continued to write, phone, and visit – and a real degree of discomfort was now being expressed to me and my staff by our Trustees. The Trustees asked for assurance that CWM staff had really been fair and thorough in their historical assessment."[144]

The Canadian Legion and the Air Force Association of Canada went into overdrive. The issue of the panel was brought up in Parliament, leading to questions in the House of Commons. Then, in a move utterly unlike what had happened at *Into the Heart of Africa*, a Subcommittee on Veterans' Affairs (part of the Standing Senate Committee on National Security and Defence) was convened to study the matter. It should be noted that such a subcommittee hearing was not a given (although one had been convened in 1998 over the issue of a Holocaust memorial at the old CWM). Indeed, the report submitted by the subcommittee opens with the following statement:

> Some questioned the need for a Senate Subcommittee to become involved in this debate at all. While our mandate does not specifically relate to heritage or historical issues, we do have a responsibility to monitor the effective and efficient expenditure of public funds, particularly in relation to issues involving Canadian veterans and so, in line with this duty, we felt it was appropriate for us to examine issues surrounding concern over the Bomber Command display in the Canadian War Museum.[145]

After hearing from a number of veterans, museum personnel, and historians, the subcommittee compiled a report. The report suggested that any slight was "unintentional" but that ultimately the wording could be read "by individual veterans as a criticism of their morality and the value of their contribution to the overall war effort."[146] The museum was not commanded to change the panel, but it was strongly suggested that the CWM try to find a compromise – the display was correct but the insult to veterans should be removed. Finally,

> After due consideration, the Subcommittee respectfully suggests that the Canadian War Museum has both the public responsibility and professional capacity to take the lead in resolving the disagreement. We feel they have the duty to review the detailed presentation of the display panel in question and that they will want to consider alternative ways of presenting an equally historically accurate version of its material, in a manner that eliminates the sense of insult felt by aircrew veterans and removes potential for further misinterpretation by the public.[147]

Throughout the brief report, attention is drawn multiple times to the "significant amount of mail" received by members of the subcommittee from supporters of veterans, something they "[could] not disregard."[148] Equally interesting, the subcommittee turned historical interpretation against itself, noting that the "dispute [over Bomber Command] resides almost exclusively in the academic realm of historians" and "there is indeed more than one way to tell a story accurately. History is, after all, interpretive."[149] Thus, the controversy unfolded along a divide of who knew more – historians and curators or veterans who had actually been there (though many of them, admittedly, had not).[150]

Rabinovitch reports [emphasis in original],

> The Senate Subcommittee hearings and its report received *massive media coverage* – front page banner headlines in some instances. I am still incredulous at this – perhaps it is because some Canadian newspapers are more comfortable reporting on the politics of WWII than on the politics current international policy disputes [*sic*]. In any event, the media coverage was remarkable, prominent and sustained.[151]

Joe Guerts, then director of the museum, resigned (amid unclear circumstances but likely as a result of the controversy). Rabinovitch went on the record in response to the Senate report, stating that telling the museum what to do represented the top of a slippery slope of government intervention into supposedly arm's-length institutions like the national museums and the CBC.[152] Even J.L. Granatstein, who had been so instrumental as a "new warrior," as a supporter of veterans, and as former director of the CWM, argued that the wording should not be changed.[153]

Nevertheless, despite initially refusing to do so, the CWM changed the didactics. After consulting with the Royal Canadian Legion and others (but refusing to give a veto to them), information was added and the panel was extended.[154] The "An Enduring Controversy" panel is now three times as long and focuses on public support for the bombing campaign, the industrial targets of the campaign, and the heavy losses to Allied aircrews. The quotations are gone, but the photos remain. The Royal Canadian Legion and other veterans groups voiced their approval of the changes.

As Margaret MacMillan stated in the aftermath, still angry about the changes that were made: "a museum is not a war memorial. It should allow the public to make up their own minds."[155] In a later article, MacMillan, Bothwell, and Hansen dismissed the calls for changes as demands for "'nursery history' … [simplistic and one-dimensional stories] important perhaps to motivate us and build a sense of community but not good for us in the long run because it is infantile. Historians have an obligation to show the past in its complexity even when it challenges cherished myths."[156] Later in their article, the three authors also note that in their conversations with critics of the museum, they were often told that Canadian schools and museums should teach "proper" history, an ill-defined term that the authors posit means a belief that history should instill pride and patriotism rather than presenting the "darker" side of Canada's past.[157] The same kind of sentiment was visible in reporter John Habron's review of the *Canvas of War* exhibition and in Gingrich's comments about the *Enola Gay* exhibition. MacMillan, Bothwell, and

Hansen argue that there is a place for balance – that pride can be instilled by knowing the past and changing the present.[158] I am less sympathetic to this stance, for as will become clear in later chapters, and in the comparison between the veterans vs the CWM and the Coalition for Truth About Africa, the processes of colonization are ongoing, and systemic inequities built into the telling of Canadian history have very real negative consequences, often for Indigenous and racialized peoples.

In the case of the CWM, protest did not cross the threshold of the museum. There were no placards, no marches, no picketers, no police. Instead, an argument over the semantics of a single panel, eighty-five words out of a total of 315,000 words in the exhibition space,[159] was taken directly to the top to the Senate, a part of the same federal government that oversees, but supposedly has an arm's-length relationship with, national museums. Organization took place in legions and meeting halls, and action took place through letter-writing campaigns, contacting MPs, finding sympathetic journalists, and finally submissions to the Senate subcommittee, which took letters from veterans extremely seriously (ranking them above testimony from historians and museum personnel). Unlike many of the cases mentioned in the introductory chapters, further action was not necessary. Normally, Senate subcommittees are not so readily available.[160]

For example, shortly after veterans reacted to the "An Extended Controversy" panel, the National Association of Japanese Canadians asked the museum to change the way that it depicted the Japanese Canadians during the Second World War.[161] This latter campaign received almost no media attention and certainly did not result in the convening of a Senate subcommittee. Although they had presented themselves as a misjudged minority, veterans achieved the changes they desired through a top-down process – a government committee – and the very channels of power that either blocked, ignored, or criminalized the many other kinds of dissent seen in this book.

Conclusion

With great quickness, by the time the CWM opened in its new building, conflict had become a part of everyday life, the "new normal," as Donald Rumsfeld infamously termed it.[162] The CWM thus stands as a testimony to a quietly contested period of Canadian history – as such, it is a monument not only to Canada's participation in war and peacekeeping but also to Canada itself as it exchanged one narrative of settler nationalism (tolerant peacekeeper) for another (Warrior Nation).

The museum had been initially funded under a Liberal government that prized multiculturalism and a certain vision of culture as a state-protected service rather than a monetized good. As such, the initial funding of the museum fit in with the Creative Cities rhetoric that encouraged investment in urban centres. As noted at the outset of the chapter, however, Ottawa's "creative economy" is one built on government jobs and military research and development – hardly the edgy "creatives" imagined by many creative industry documents and descriptions. While I do not posit a direct link between Ottawa's creative industries and the building of the new museum, I do suggest that the mismatch between the rhetoric and reality of Creative Cities affects the way(s) that city life is understood on the ground and contributes to the manner in which culture in Ottawa is largely something that is consumed, often in large-scale, authoritative institutions that reflect federal standpoints on many (but not all) contentious issues. This latter point did, I suggest, affect the way that the controversy over labelling at the new War Museum played out.

The Conservative government that took over in 2006 and oversaw the opening of the museum and the protests over the signage had very different intents and aims from its predecessor. The new warriors pushed for their cause following the terrorist attacks in New York and Washington in 2001 but came into their own under the Conservative government in the mid-2000s. The planning of the CWM bridged the two, and the script for the exhibitions gallery at the CWM was certainly influenced by the push to show and create a celebratory military history of Canada. Within that narrative, however, contentious moments remained. Writing ten years after the museum opened, then-director Mark O'Neill opined that the museum was the "singular national cultural achievement of a generation. If you were to look at what else has occurred from the late 1990s to 2015 at the national level, you'd be hard pressed to find a more successful national cultural achievement."[163] The museum remains, behind the CMH, the second most popular museum in the national capital region, drawing in some 420,000 visitors per year, far exceeding expectations.[164]

Having raised $16.5 million and having spent years raising awareness of the need for a new museum, veterans obviously felt a certain entitlement to the space of the new museum. For them, the Warrior Nation was one they lived in every day. Distinct from the military R&D that added significantly to Ottawa's economy at this time, their contributions and the memorialization of those contributions to the formation of the Canadian nation were actively and vigorously protected. Such actions were particularly pressing given the age of those involved – the veterans leading this campaign were primarily elderly air force men who had served in the Second World War, not veterans from Afghanistan or peacekeepers from 1990s conflicts in Croatia, Rwanda, or elsewhere.

The CWM remains the only major museum in Canada to have been forced to change its content by a "special interest group." I use this terminology purposefully because during the conflict between the museum and veterans, veterans were repeatedly rendered as distinct from other "politically correct" "special interest groups" whose critiques of museums tend to be dismissed or actively resisted (particularly in the mainstream media), though they are occasionally incorporated over the long term. In this case, typically, veterans were portrayed in mainstream media as a group that had been wronged and the museum as a space that had wronged them. Entitlement and assumptions that veterans would and should be listened to and their demands acted upon were legitimized through the actions of the Senate subcommittee. As Macmillan, Hansen, and Bothwell conclude: "The organized veterans not only see themselves as somehow the guardians of the War Museum, responsible for keeping its management and the government up to scratch, but they are well aware of their own power."[165]

Interstice 4d

The Postponement of *The Lands within Me*: Expressions by Canadian Artists of Arab Origin, 2001

The Lands within Me: Expression by Canadian Artists of Arab Origin was an exhibition set to open at the Canadian Museum of Civilization (CMC)[1] in October 2001.[2] The works included calligraphy, ceramics, and metalwork, as well as videos and installations, many of them concerned with the diasporic experience of migrating from the Middle East to Canada. Following terrorist attacks in New York and Washington in September 2001, however, the museum announced that the exhibition would be "postponed indefinitely." The CMC claimed that it needed time "to add additional information and context on the Arab world" to the exhibition.[3] Although the museum never said as much, journalists quickly assumed that administration at the CMC was worried about two short sections of a video by artist Jayce Salloum, the first showing an Israeli plane bombing Lebanon and the second containing an interview with Soha Bechara, a Lebanese woman, describing her ten years in an Israeli detention centre in southern Lebanon. The video also contained footage and interviews from other world conflict zones, including Palestine and the former Yugoslavia. For the most part, however, the show was "politically benign," most of the artists involved were taken aback by the cancellation, and reaction to the postponement tended toward appalled shock.[4]

The postponement created an immediate furor. Artists included in the show immediately organized and chose a spokesperson (Jayce Salloum). They quickly began a well-coordinated protest and letter-writing campaign. According to one report, "Some 650 emails in 48 hours were received at the Museum on this issue alone."[5] An open letter from artists Jayce Salloum and Rawi Hage and cultural historian Laura U. Marks (known for her work on Arabic and diasporic film) was widely circulated. It stated:

> We believe that the decision [to postpone the exhibition] was a political one. It is unfortunate that in this time of backlashes and a rise of racist attacks against members of our community, a federal government institution (one of the largest public museums in Canada) is assuming such an unproductive and unsupportive position. In the midst of this recent wave of racism and intolerance, governmental agencies and politicians are conducting various campaigns of cultural awareness and tolerance. It is troubling that the Museum of Civilization is taking exactly the opposite stance. It is postponing an important and unique cultural event that has the potential to counteract some of the prejudices that our community has so long endured.[6]

Terms such as "public relations nightmare," "boneheaded move," and "lily-livered" were used in even the most conservative of mainstream newspapers.[7] Then, following a question from NDP MP Alexa McDonough in the House of Commons about the exhibition, "On September 26, 2001, the Prime Minister rose in the House of Commons, to an all-party standing ovation, to denounce what he considered a wrong decision to postpone the exhibit."[8] After extensive pressure from media, artists, the public, and now the federal government, the museum capitulated, and the exhibition opened on time. Salloum, Hage, and Marks's letter nonetheless concluded:

> By postponing or cancelling such an important exhibition, the Museum sends a message with grave implications, for example, 1) that any event involving Arab culture needs to be "spin-controlled" 2) that any present or future event conducted by or for the Arab-Canadian community is liable to be a security risk 3) the assumption that all Canadians hold a position of antagonism towards the Arab-Canadian community, hence the risk of low attendance 4) or simply the assumption could be made that bias, punitive, and racist collective measures have been approved by the Museum of Civilization's board of directors.[9]

Although the exhibition opened on time, scheduled travel did not occur, and Dr Aida Kaouk's position as curator was not renewed (although she was rehired to a different position at the museum).[10]

Paul Gessell reported in the *Ottawa Citizen* that the opening was an uncomfortable affair "in which practically everybody was bad-mouthing practically everybody else in the room."[11] There were other indicators that the museum had not fully embraced the show. Bags were searched in an atmosphere of heightened security, and president and CEO Victor Rabinovitch did not attend. After the opening, complaints came from some members of the Canadian Jewish Congress, who argued that Salloum's video was "propaganda" that "does not deal with the Arab experience in Canada ... It doesn't belong in the museum."[12] Afterwards, one journalist wrote,

> When Canada's new Museum of Civilization opened its door to the public over a decade ago, it did so with the unwavering intention of staying true to its mandate: to foster in Canadians, all Canadians, "a sense of their common identity and their shared past," and "to promote understanding between the various cultural groups that are part of Canadian society." However, recent actions have led some to question, even criticize, whether the museum has been faltering in its mission by neglecting certain groups of Canadian society.[13]

"There is very little, if any, trust with the museum," Salloum said in the aftermath.[14] Nevertheless, the response from other sectors (particularly governmental) is somewhat surprising if taken out of context. But as Keri Cronin and I note in our write-up on the exhibition in the edited volume *Imagining Resistance*, the impetus to stand up for *The Lands within Me* in Parliament and elsewhere represented a celebration of multiculturalism and belonging that covered over or erased the contradictions at the heart of settler nationalism.

5

"It takes a lot of wrongs to make a museum of rights": Indigenous Resistance and the Canadian Museum for Human Rights

It is September 2014, and I am in Winnipeg, Manitoba, for a conference and the opening of the brand new Canadian Museum for Human Rights (CMHR). I am staying for three days in a hotel by the Red River, which runs through the centre of the city. Looking out of my hotel room window to the right, I can see the brand-new glass-encased museum structure, towering over the Winnipeg skyline, and on my left I can see the Alexander Docks, a low wood and cement structure stretching out beside the river. On this September weekend, Alexander Docks is the location of a sacred fire lit by a group keeping vigil over the site where less than a month ago, on 17 August 2014, the body of fifteen-year-old Tina Fontaine of the Sagkeen First Nation was pulled from the river.[1] As Amber Dean describes, on 19 August, just two days after Fontaine's discovery, nearly 2,000 people walked from Alexander Docks to a newly installed memorial for missing and murdered Indigenous women (MMIW) at the Forks of the Red and Assiniboine Rivers, just outside the not-yet-open CMHR, remembering Fontaine and calling for a national inquiry into the more than 1,200 other MMIW.[2] The vigil on the docks is a stark contrast to the slickness of the monumental museum, whose tower casts light down onto the river below.[3] In my hotel room I write these words, watching a small motorboat move slowly back and forth, carrying volunteers who are dredging the river looking for other human remains.[4] When the city of Winnipeg refused such a search, people took it on themselves, certain that the Red River was a moving graveyard.

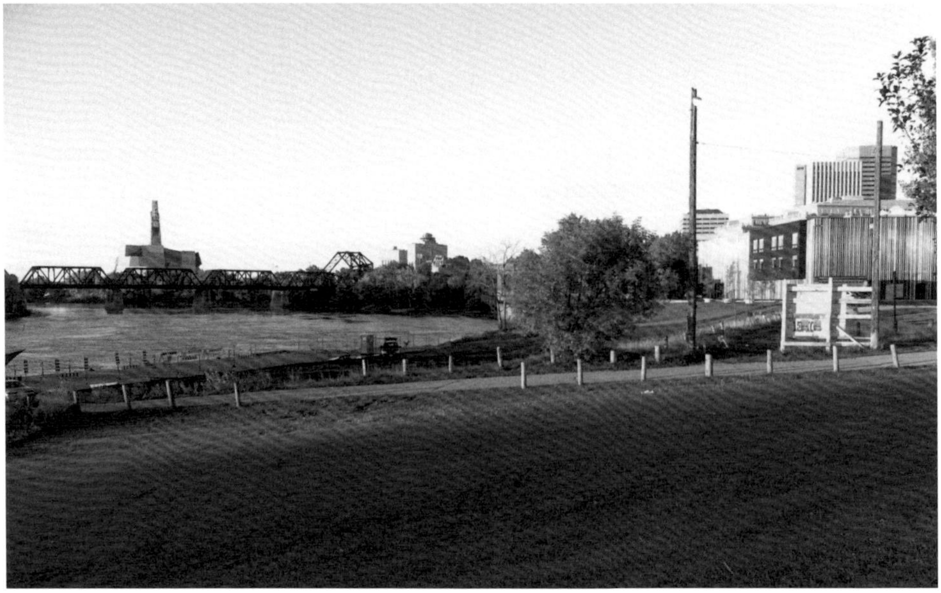

Figure 5.1
Alexander Docks with Museum of Human Rights in the distance.

I, along with a number of others, am in Winnipeg for a "counter-conference," a critical museology meeting on curating difficult knowledge, focused on the CMHR. We cross the muddy ground to the museum, past an Idle No More banner and the Grandmothers' sacred fire, a second memorial and vigil site some 100 feet from the new building. We walk by anti-abortion agitators waving their graphic banners, before joining the lengthy line to enter the building. On the other side of the museum, a third sacred fire is lit on a small hill looking down on the gleaming glass and stone of the museum. This one belongs to Shoal Lake 40 First Nation (hereafter SL40). SL40, nearly 200 kilometres from the provincial capital, is located on an island in the middle of the reservoir lake that supplies Winnipeg with clean drinking water. Yet the Nation had been, at this point, under a boil-water advisory for nineteen years and has no safe access to the mainland.[5] They have brought their struggle to the museum. As we stand in line, rain falls steadily, umbrellas are handed out, and rumours fly that another body had been found in the river.[6] Once we are inside, tour guides with brightly coloured T-shirts imprinted with the slogan "BE INSPIRED" combine campground enthusiasm ("let's have a cheer for human rights," says my guide) with nervousness and a kind of elated exhaustion that the museum is finally open.

This chapter begins with a stark contrast: on one side of the museum a vigil for a murdered First Nations woman and on the other a sacred fire for a First Nation experiencing the fall-out of settler-colonial policies and ongoing systemic racism.

In between, the museum itself emerges as a giant rock and glass outcrop, both part of and apart from the landscape. Focusing on SL40's fight to secure government funding for a road that would connect the reserve to the TransCanada Highway, thus allowing for the import of clean water, this chapter analyzes the role of the CMHR as one player in that struggle. Importantly, SL40 worked with many groups and employed numerous strategies and approaches over several decades to secure funding for the road. I *only* look at the museum. Drawing out both the history of the museum itself and the role of Indigenous (First Nations, Métis, and Inuit) intervention and work in profoundly changing museum cultures in Canada, I argue that SL40's use of the opening of the CMHR was and is a successful element of a long-term strategy for securing funding for the road and attaining clean water *and* part of an ongoing project to question, critique, and change authoritative museums. I argue that over time a reciprocal relationship developed. I suggest that the visibility of SL40's actions stemmed from four intertwined vectors. First, the SL40 action was part of decades of resistance to and negotiations by Indigenous peoples with authoritative museums. Second, the SL40 action appeared to clearly demonstrate a *lack* of human rights that was exacerbated by the museum's refusal to use the term genocide to describe the federal government's relationship with Indigenous peoples in Canada. Third, after a shaky start, the museum, which was trying to appease and work with numerous groups and manage critiques coming from multiple fronts while also creating a compelling narrative of human rights for various publics, demonstrated greatly increased interest in Indigenous issues following the change of the museum from a private to a public institution in combination with the release of the final report of the Truth and Reconciliation Commission on Indian residential schools. And fourth, the museum's complicated relationship with action and activism created a scenario wherein a *real* struggle could find purchase. In the years after the museum's opening, strong allies within the institution helped SL40's cause, but most of this chapter concentrates on the years prior to and just after the opening in 2014. It should be immediately noted that the CMHR's position in Winnipeg, a city with one of the highest urban Indigenous populations in Canada and located in contested Treaty 1 territory and from which numerous Indigenous women and men have gone missing or have been found murdered, suggests a "particular responsibility to document injustices that are occurring locally."[7] Writing shortly after the museum's opening, museums scholar Nadine Blumer concluded, "In many ways, the museum has failed to do this."[8] Looking closely at the case of SL40, I find a relationship that has grown over time, adding complexity to Blumer's statement (with which I fully agreed when I began researching and writing the chapter).

This chapter is purposely and unapologetically broad and follows a trajectory that tracks the path of the CMHR from initial idea to opening day. As a new, large-scale museum, the CMHR has drawn significant attention from scholars of museum studies and other disciplines. Most are interested in the institution as a space for the imagining of a new world (whether successful or not) and amplify its rhetoric of human rights (whether to laud it or criticize it), situating the CMHR in line with other institutions such as the US Holocaust Museum in Washington and the Museum of Memory and Human Rights in Chile.[9] My intention is somewhat different. I am interested in how the CMHR has struggled to manage its many competing goals and stakeholders and in so doing has followed a rocky path to engagement with Indigenous communities on a more equitable basis. Additionally, however, I argue that it was precisely the museum's early stumbles that allowed it to provide so effective a backdrop to SL40's aims.

The Early Days of the CMHR

I begin far from Shoal Lake and Winnipeg, back in Ottawa in the late 1990s as debate erupted over whether or not the Canadian War Museum (CWM) should include a Holocaust memorial (see previous chapter).[10] Sarkis Assadourian, a Liberal MP from the Ontario riding of Brampton Centre, introduced a private member's bill to Parliament calling for a museum that would commemorate crimes against humanity. The issue stayed in the press for several months but never really gained steam.[11] Then, in January 1999, the former director of the Museum of Civilization, George MacDonald, argued that what Canada needed was not a Holocaust memorial but rather a human rights museum. In a letter he published in response to an article describing pushback against a potential Holocaust memorial at the CWM, MacDonald wrote,

> There are numerous Holocaust museums and memorials worldwide, while there is not a single museum of human rights anywhere. Canada's long history of pioneering action in human rights begins with the first legislation in the British Empire to ban slavery, continues with the work of John Humphrey who drafted much of the International Declaration of Human Rights for the United Nations, right up to Canada's action for an international treaty against land mines.[12]

MacDonald went on to argue that such a museum would be of national and international import and should be located in Ottawa adjacent to other federal institutions. MacDonald's idea fell on deaf ears, and instead support grew for the new CWM, which, as shown in the previous chapter, did not include a Holocaust memorial and foregrounded a muscular depiction of Canada's participation in conflict.

But the idea for a human rights museum was not forgotten. Frustrated with the lack of support for a Holocaust memorial, and claiming to build on an idea that he had discussed with former Prime Minister Pierre Trudeau at the time of the writing of the Charter of Rights and Freedoms in 1982, Israel (Izzy) Asper, then director of the Canwest Global Communications and Media Corporation, decided to spearhead the project himself.[13] Asper proposed a large-scale, "starchitect"-designed, comprehensive museum dealing extensively with human rights (in both a positive and negative sense) to the Department of Heritage. The museum would not be in Ottawa; it would be in Asper's hometown of Winnipeg. It would not be a solely public museum but would rely heavily on private funds raised through Asper's philanthropy. Asper hoped that this move would prompt federal government financial support. It did, and on 17 April 2003, the twenty-first anniversary of the signing of the Charter of Rights and Freedoms, the federal Liberal government announced a contribution that would come in at below 50 per cent of the total cost for building a human rights museum in Winnipeg. The partial support created, according to Asper, an "unprecedented partnership of governments, philanthropists and interest groups representing the ethnic and other communities whose stories will be told in the exhibits."[14]

There are three important points to highlight here. First, a private–public museum of this scale had never been attempted in Canada before, and the notion unsettled a Canadian cultural establishment that relied fundamentally on state support. Second, the Asper Foundation's quest to establish the museum resonated with "the model of the US philanthropist as a neoliberal benefactor ... as an alternative to the big state and the unwieldy cultocracy"[15] – a position heightened by Asper's widespread control of numerous media outlets. Third, while the idea for such a museum initially fit well with those who saw Canada as a beacon for human rights and peacekeeping throughout the world (in contrast to the New Warrior vision described in the previous chapter), it became apparent (though not as quickly as might be thought) that there were some homegrown issues to deal with, most notably the historical and ongoing discrimination against Indigenous peoples. Nevertheless, the CMHR project picked up steam, and by 2003 it had become a fundraising engine organized loosely around the idea that Canadians (particularly school-aged Canadians) should be able to learn about human rights in Canada.

Eventually, the CMHR would grant extensive space to Indigenous understandings of human rights, while also acknowledging numerous abuses, key among them a significant display dedicated to residential schools. In 2003, however, the Canadian state and church-led abuse of Indigenous children and consequent cultural genocide[16] was not evident in reportage on the museum. Coverage focused largely on the controversial figure of Izzy Asper, whose unwavering support for Israel and aversion to Palestinian statehood (which extended to oversight and surveillance of the editorial content of the news outlets that Canwest controlled)[17] provided extensive opportunity for critical journalists and scholars to voice their unease with the project. From the beginning, while describing the project as his philanthropic "magnum opus," Asper stressed, "this is not and was not ever an Asper ego trip. This was something that I think has to be done."[18] But many indeed feared that the CMHR *would* be an Asper ego trip. The boundaries of private influence in a public–private partnership were highly unclear. When most large, privately funded museums *are* ego projects, why should it be assumed that this one would be different?[19]

Long before anything was built, the project *immediately* drew squabbles over what would actually be shown inside. Extensive lobbying, particularly from the Ukrainian community, pressured the museum to expand far beyond the Holocaust to recognize, for example, the Holodomor, the man-made famine that killed millions in Soviet Ukraine in 1932–33.[20] An active campaign led by the Ukrainian Canadian Congress and the Ukrainian Canadian Civil Liberties Association grew, consisting primarily of a letter-writing campaign that targeted media and bombarded museum officials and staff. As demonstrated through Karyn Ball and Per Anders Rudling's detailed coverage of the campaign, a sense of belonging within the liberal-order framework of human rights proposed by the museum characterized the increasingly vocal calls from the Ukrainian community to acknowledge the Holodomor not just in terms of visibility but also in terms of physical space equal to that granted to other tragedies such as the Holocaust.[21] Tricia Logan, a former curator at the CMHR, has argued that such lobbying and "competitive suffering" was successful in that, despite the denials of the museum, advocacy did result in the allocation of extensive physical space to the tragedies of the Holocaust and Holodomor.[22] By contrast, she notes, in the early days of the museum, Indigenous groups did not engage the CMHR in the same way. As she reminds us, "The efforts and energies of Indigenous rights lobbyists in Canada are focused on providing safe water, safe homes, food, and better health conditions for Indigenous families. Whether they are lobbying for memory or rights, for many, a museum may not be the logical place to confront rights discourse in Canada for current and ongoing abuses."[23] In short, when the abuses are ongoing rather than safely in the past, a museum is perhaps not the first priority for advocacy.

Indigenous issues also remained strangely absent from early media coverage of the museum. A widely syndicated article from April 2003 describes the future museum in detail, noting highlights including a Causes Gallery "exploring the roots of human conflict and co-operation,"[24] a Holocaust Gallery, a Hall of Fame and Walk of Shame, an exhibit on Canadian history "highlighting such triumphs and tragedies as the nineteenth-century Underground Railway for escaping American slaves and the internment of Japanese Canadians during the Second World War, a gallery highlighting contemporary struggles for human rights; and a seventy-metre-high 'Tower of Hope'" at the centre of the museum.[25] Although it is unlikely that the CMHR was unaware of human rights abuses in Canada, this widely circulated overview made no mention of residential schools or other instances of systemic (and ongoing) abuse of the human rights of Indigenous peoples.

Though a focus on Indigenous issues would grow over the years, what really characterized the museum from the very start was intense lobbying, conflict, and clashing expectations. On the one hand, the museum was involved in a massive fundraising project to raise funds from private sources, including corporations and individuals. Many came forward, among them major banks and other companies, public entities such as the City of Winnipeg and the Province of Manitoba, private citizens, and Ukrainian, Jewish, and Armenian community groups (among others), as well as a significant donation from the Assembly of Manitoba Chiefs. Animosity quickly overflowed, particularly because of the museum's mismanagement of expectations.[26] For example, as Dirk Moses reports, Moe Levy, Izzy Asper's deputy, made the unfortunate remark in 2003 that "We believe the people who pay should have a say in how it is run," which led to an expectation that donations would translate into physical space in the museum.[27]

As shown in the previous chapter, the CWM had had to deal with similar pressures from veterans who had contributed enormously to the fundraising campaign to build a new museum in 2005 and had lost that battle. Here, the stakes were even higher as the CMHR was dealing with multiple communities, often with conflicting expectations and demands, and it appears that the information circulating to those groups was not clear in terms of what fundraising and donations meant. Bogged down in trying to manage expectations, the museum was compelled to address the "competitive victimization" of a number of groups – surely, write scholars Angela Failler and Roger Simon, "a limited dynamic within which to undertake the crucial work of 'remembrance-learning' in Canada."[28] And simultaneously, the museum was trying to craft an educational experience that would result in action on behalf of human rights.

The struggle over space allocation in the museum was matched at the time by attempts to promote Canada as a human rights leader.[29] By accident or design, the narrative of the CMHR contrasted markedly with that of the CWM and the Warrior Nation myth described in the previous chapter. In fact, the CMHR actively celebrated the CWM's bugbear of peacekeeping, as well as justice, the Charter of Rights and Freedom, and John Humphrey, the Canadian diplomat who authored the first draft of the UN Declaration of Human Rights. While Asper referenced "unflinching" coverage of "dirty stories," the CMHR foregrounds a celebratory relationship between human rights and Canada – a different though equally mythic accounting of Canadian history from that of the Warrior Nation. "It's about creating the Canadian brand for human rights leadership," said Charles Coffee, then senior vice-president of the Royal Bank of Canada and advisor to the Aspers.[30]

Managing these competing frames – on the one hand having to balance and placate the many donors to the private project and on the other an attempt to showcase Canada's triumphs as a human rights leader within an "unflinching" account of "missteps" – proved nearly impossible. As I argue here, establishing the museum as a place that would try to please all even as it knew it would likely please none closed avenues for innovative and compelling engagement with difficult histories.

Already bogged down by multiple competing goals and responsibilities, the project briefly faltered when Izzy Asper died in October 2003. Building costs were mounting as a result of a building boom in the west, and the museum was having a hard time attracting a CEO.[31] It looked in November 2004 as if the federal government would refuse the money already promised and would give no monies at all for operating costs (generally given only to national museums – federally funded public museums under arm's-length state control).[32] The federal Liberals were then embroiled in a scandal that would eventually topple the government, and every penny was being closely watched. Furthermore, proponents of the Warrior Nation myth were vocal in their criticism. "It's a can of worms," said J.L. Granatstein, the former head of the CWM, whom readers will remember from the previous chapter. "It's the triumph of hope over reality. It's simply not thinking through the difficulties of this sort of project."[33] Although construction of the museum building was already well underway, the project seemed to be foundering, and a series of questions and concerns that would dog it for years coalesced in these early days: Where would the funding come from? Who would control the content of the museum? Why would/should the government fund a project that might portray it in a bad light? Why should a private project receive public funding?

Before it was even close to opening, the CMHR seemed doomed to fail. But the election of a federal Conservative government was about to change things. While the Harper Conservatives were perceived to be hostile toward the arts and appeared onside with a Warrior Nation narrative at odds with the ethos of the CMHR (one of the first acts of the new government was, in September 2006, to trim $1 billion from programs for human rights, women's issues, museums, youth employment, and other similar initiatives), they also supported the pro-Israel agenda beloved of Izzy Asper, and the private–public partnership of the CMHR fit well with the federal government's vision for trimming government spending.[34] Furthermore, the location of the CMHR was Winnipeg, which, though not a seat of Conservative power, was in the centre-west of the country and outside of the federalist grip of Ottawa.[35] In April 2007, the Harper government announced that the federal government would provide support for the creation and maintenance of the private museum after sufficient funds had been raised through the public and private sectors. That sum was set at $310 million – a huge amount to fundraise in Canada. In addition to government and corporate monies, as well as $20 million from the Asper Foundation, museum fundraisers hoped they could attract large numbers of individual donors.[36] A massive push to secure funds took place. Large donations were secured from corporations, wealthy individuals, NGOs, and others. Small donations were secured from an impressive number of individual donors through events, advertisement, and a widespread campaign that encouraged Canadians to be a part of an important new project. But such a fundraising effort had never before been required for the building of large-scale authoritative museums in Canada, and the task proved insurmountable.[37] With the Asper Foundation unable to take on anything close to the whole amount, and with far less private philanthropic support than needed, the only way forward for the museum was through a return to the public sector. Backtracking on earlier praise for the potential of privately funded museums, the Harper government passed Bill C-42 in early 2008 with very little debate in Parliament. The bill granted the CMHR status as a federal museum by amending the 1990 Museums Act. The project was back on but no longer as a privately led initiative.

The change of heart by the federal government in 2008 signalled a sea change in museum funding in Canada. As reporter Val Ross put it, "What's happening is nothing less than a revolution in federal museum policy."[38] In short, until this date all national museums were in Ottawa. Museums outside the capital region were funded through the Museums Assistance Program as well as by provincial and municipal governments.[39] The granting of "national" status to the CMHR might have seemed a relatively minor policy change, but in fact it opened the door to an entirely new conception of the role of museums in Canada. Public–private partnerships stemming from the visions of wealthy individuals were now possible. So too were institutions of national importance outside Ottawa. At the time, Expo Rail in Montreal and Pier 21 in Halifax were also under consideration for "national" status, while the government was also contemplating moving the much-maligned National Portrait Gallery to the headquarters of EnCana Corporation in Calgary.[40] "Decentralization is a possible scenario. We want national treasures to be enjoyed by as many Canadians as possible," said then minister of Canadian heritage Bev Oda.[41] While the impulse to decentralize might seem democratizing, in the case of the CMHR the combination of national status and Asper's private vision raised some significant questions about who determines national museum policy and for whom. In this instance (and possibly also that of the National Portrait Gallery), decentralization came at the price of private-sector partners, who gained a say in the constitutive focus of the institution. Furthermore, in a controversial move, as a part of cuts to programs such as Prom Arts and Trade Routes, Ottawa had cut $2 million from its roughly $9 million Museums Assistance Program in September 2006.[42] Even as $100 million was granted that year to repair and upgrade museums in Ottawa, institutions were warned that they would be increasingly expected to find private sources to fund exhibition programs and expansions.[43] So too, even as the government pledged its support for the decentralization of museums, the federal government's Exhibition Transport Service was axed, making the transport of art and artefacts across the country much more difficult and expensive.[44] In short, the public–private partnership at the heart of the CMHR offered a neoliberal working model for other institutions, and while it is safe to say that *all* national institutions in Canada have been criticized for parochial representation, the private vision that undergirded the CMHR was something new.

As the CMHR became a federal institution, control was transferred from the Asper Foundation to a government-appointed board. This move seemed to address some of the questions around Asper's lingering legacy and personal focus on the Holocaust. Many journalists, however, switched their target from fear over Asper's interference to fear over federal government interference, particularly given the close role of government officials in appointing and overseeing the CEO and Board of Trustees.[45] James Adams asks, "Would a CEO or curator want to risk [government] funding by backing an exhibition, no matter how even-handed, that might deal with, say, Canadian troops' handling of Afghan detainees?"[46] He quotes an unnamed museum administrator who noted, "If that museum were to do an exhibit on Afghanistan, I can't imagine a scenario under this government where that exhibit might be anything but pro-mission ... How about the Harper government's reluctance to seek the extradition of Canadians facing death sentences in foreign jurisdictions? There's a human-rights dimension to that, I would suggest."[47] Such fears seemed warranted when Conservative Senator Consiglio di Nino expressed hope that the new museum "might consider the situation in Afghanistan, and the important contributions Canadians are making there after the oppressive Taliban rule in which human rights were virtually extinguished."[48]

Despite fears of government intervention, at the forks of the Assiniboine and Red Rivers the "cathedral of freedom" began to grow. Designed by US American award-winning architect Antoine Predock, the building clearly fit within the new lexicon of starchitect museum building, shrouded in specially glazed glass made in Germany and meant to represent two doves' wings caressing and embracing the building.[49] The museum quickly adopted the rhetoric of a meeting place, sited as it was on a traditional meeting place of Anishinaabe, Cree, Dene, and Dakota peoples. But as has been often noted, the Forks in Winnipeg was also a key site for the imposition of a settler-colonial[50] state: the land that had been used by many Indigenous groups was unilaterally given to Thomas Douglas (Lord Selkirk) by the

Hudson's Bay Company to create the Red River Colony in 1811, and that seizure continued through the erasure of Indigenous presence, the construction of the railway, and consequent imposition of capitalism, through the suppression of Métis resistance, and finally through the rebranding of the site of violent colonization as a space of tourism and harmony – a historic "meeting place."[51] Located just beside Winnipeg's downtown, in a core region of the Forks slated for creative redevelopment, the new museum would vastly alter the Winnipeg skyline, but in doing so it would also act as a site of antagonism.[52]

The vast promotion project did catch on, quelling some of the earlier critical coverage of the museum and overshadowing the focus on "competitive victimization." But opinions also split. On the one hand, some felt that the museum would bring visitors to Winnipeg and that its grandiosity would be a boon to the city, but on the other hand, there was a sentiment that the museum would be altogether too much for a city like Winnipeg and altogether too baroque for the catalogue of sins it was to contain.[53] As Larissa Wodtke puts it, "In its conception of the CMHR as an icon, the architectural discourse also appears to conflate the hope of urban regeneration with the hope for progressive human rights, mapping an agenda of transnational capitalism and globalization on to both national identity politics and moral cosmopolitanism."[54]

Thus, a variety of competing interests, narratives, and background stories affected the CMHR long before it opened. Moving from a private vanity project to a full-fledged public–private partnership just in its conceptual phase, the museum faced immense and contradictory pressures around the question of what it could and should be. Stymied by the need to fundraise massive amounts of money, beholden in at least some way to its founder and to the groups donating money or vigorously lobbying, under equal pressure from its transformation into a national museum complete with a government-appointed board, seeing itself as an international location in need of an architectural shell that would be designed long before the content of the museum was settled, and sited at an immensely fraught location, the CMHR's story is, if nothing else, a tale of somehow emerging intact from these battles. But in many ways, struggles were only beginning.

Indigenizing the Museum

As the exterior of the museum was decided upon and interest turned to content, the CMHR faced an important question: how could it cover, in any way, the history of settler–Indigenous relations in Canada? From this point in the chapter, I leave behind the surrounding displays at the CMHR (including those dedicated to the Holocaust and Holodomor) to focus on this question. The lack of any mention of Indigenous issues in the 2003 coverage of the museum speaks volumes about the

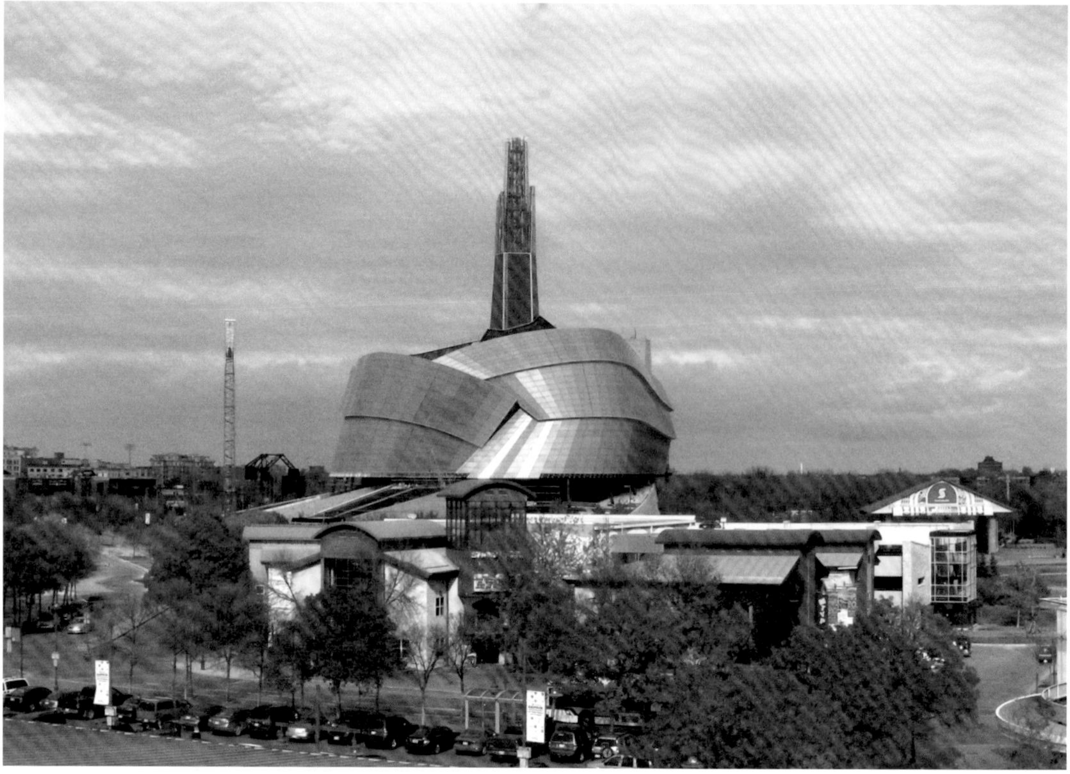

Figure 5.2
The Canadian Museum for Human Rights as seen from the Forks Tower.

general ignorance of human rights abuses in Canada. Land claims and exploitation of Native land and resources, missing and murdered Indigenous women, the Sixties Scoop, iniquitously high rates of incarceration, the paternalism of the Indian Act, and general exploitation and suppression of Indigenous culture could or perhaps should all have been covered in the museum. Faced with what was surely an insurmountable task, the museum made a series of decisions that ultimately resulted in a focus primarily on residential schooling as *the* site of human rights abuses against Indigenous people, although a number of smaller displays on MMIW, water access, and blockades would also appear. In many of the stories told, resilience and survival are key. The CMHR also made an important decision to grant separate space for Indigenous perspectives on human rights, not just as a counter to the abuses perpetuated by mainstream Canada but also as a way of foregrounding Indigenous knowledges and interpretations as equal to those of the UN, the Canadian government, and other bodies.[55] This is even more true in recent years as the museum has strongly foregrounded Indigenous perspectives, moving away from fitting Indigenous stories into larger narratives and instead telling stories that are led by the communities represented and that often have a deeper level of meaning for Indigenous visitors to the museum. I will return to these points when I discuss SL40.

Because others have covered the exhibitions at the CMHR in depth, here I turn my attention instead to the way that long-term Indigenous advocacy in and activism against museums in Canada influenced the CMHR. In chapter 2, I outlined the many actions undertaken by Indigenous peoples from the 1960s through to the present to intervene in museum procedures, displays, and collections. If the debates over content and lobbying from ethnic groups such as the Ukrainian lobby form one thread in the story of the CMHR, the negotiations, debates, and interventions around Indigenous representation in museums form another.

Museums scholar Ruth Phillips writes, "The great period of museums and collection building that began in the mid-nineteenth century coincided almost exactly with the formulation and implementation of official assimilationist policies in the United States and Canada between about 1880 and 1940."[56] Settler-colonial practices at the time created a seemingly self-fulfilling prophecy – as children were forced into residential schools with the goal of assimilation, traditional material culture was collected and taken. In short, cultural objects were deemed worthy of collection and display even as the cultures and practices that made those objects were suppressed or exterminated. Authoritative museums in Canada and abroad benefitted enormously from government programs, among them the suppression of ceremonies such as the potlatch and sun dance and the general disenfranchisement of Indigenous peoples from their lifeways and culture that often went hand-in-hand with poverty and pressure to sell.[57] "We have been experiencing a long process of being continually disinherited and disconnected from our pasts," wrote Mohawk scholar Deborah Doxtator in 1996.[58] Two decades later, Tricia Logan writes, "It can be argued that the 'salvage paradigm' promoted by museums was complicit in the neglect of Indigenous populations, as it supported the prevailing thought that 'they were just going to die anyway.'"[59] Though there have been numerous examples of restitution by museums, key among them the repatriation of objects, community consultation, and hiring of Indigenous curators, settler-colonial practices are still evident in the ongoing exclusion of historical abuses from most mainstream museums.

As covered in chapter 2, demonstrations outside the 1988 *Spirit Sings* exhibition at the Glenbow Museum in Calgary illuminated a link between culture and wider issues of disenfranchisement. Following *Spirit Sings*, the Task Force on Museums and First Peoples was formed, led by the Assembly of First Nations and the Canadian Museums Association. The task force meetings resulted in a series of recommendations designed to begin addressing the inequities built into Canadian collecting and curatorial practice.[60] In 1989, at the introduction to *Preserving Our Heritage: A Working Conference for Museums and First Peoples*, which led to the formation of the task force, then head of the Assembly of First Nations George Erasmus argued that it was time to "get beyond" boycotts and demonstrations.

The museum provided one venue for doing so.[61] Not long afterwards, two important exhibitions of contemporary First Nations art opened, *Land Spirit Power* at the National Gallery of Canada and *INDIGENA* at the Canadian Museum of Civilization, both in 1992, not incidentally the 500th anniversary of Christopher Columbus stumbling upon Turtle Island and starting an ongoing process of genocide (an event that was nonetheless much celebrated in 1992 and which led to concerted resistance and a number of alternative exhibitions such as the two in Ottawa).[62]

There was a central tension in all this revision. At the conclusion of the task force meetings, 'Namgis (Nimpkish) curator Gloria Cranmer-Webster noted, "We don't want museums. The word 'museum' has a negative connotation signifying the place where dead things lie and where native people don't go."[63] In short, authoritative museums are in their very nature institutions through which the colonization of Indigenous peoples took place. Even when open to staging radical interventions into mainstream museum culture, that colonial legacy remains.[64] Nevertheless, the task force report argued strongly for greater Indigenous presence in museums, not only in terms of showing more work by contemporary Indigenous artists or shows curated by Indigenous curators but also in terms of the management of material culture archives.

The task force was supported by the 1996 report of the Royal Commission on Aboriginal Peoples (RCAP), which also held that the relationship between Indigenous peoples and museums in Canada needed to broadly change and become more accessible, that repatriation should be encouraged where possible, that human remains should be returned, and that proactive programming should characterize all Canadian museums.[65] The RCAP report clearly saw museums as places where redress and healing could potentially take place. Further, Canada's initial foot-dragging on, but eventual signing of, the UN Declaration on the Rights of Indigenous Peoples (2007, ratified by Canada in 2016) had a direct impact on museums and heritage sites in Canada that were the repositories of the bulk of Indigenous material and cultural property amassed during the colonial period. The declaration articulated Indigenous rights to "maintain, control and develop their cultural heritage, traditional knowledge and traditional cultural expressions."[66] And finally, the Truth and Reconciliation Commission, established in 2008, released its ninety-four calls to action in 2015 (just after the museum opened), which included the statement: "Through their exhibits, education outreach, and research programs, all museums are well positioned to contribute to education for reconciliation."[67] Arguably, a central tension between museums as key enablers of colonialism and museums as sites where redress can take place continues to characterize almost all interactions between Indigenous peoples and museums, even those that supposedly take place on a level playing field.

Thus, the process of Indigenization in museums should not be seen as in any way easy or inevitable. As Amy Lonetree reminds us, when Indigenous objects reside in museums, "We are not just looking at interesting pieces. In the presence of objects from the past, we are privileged to stand as witnesses to living entities that remain intimately and inextricably tied to their descendant communities."[68] Concerted and ongoing negotiations, interventions, and activism have indeed led to change, but in the years leading up to the opening of the CMHR it seemed that any change at the new institution would take place on the ground of settler understandings of how things should be. Writing about European museums and immigrant communities but making a point that nonetheless applies here, Irit Rogoff analyzes "the ambivalences and disavowals that always seem to surface when museums engage with issues of cultural difference,"[69] arguing that most museums settle on an additive model – bringing in what had been forgotten without addressing the role of the museum within the ethnographic paradigms of exclusion that conditioned the attempted destruction of Indigenous cultures and lifeways from the time of contact through to the present.[70] Rogoff states, "museums' engagement with cultural difference cannot deal exclusively with that which has been lost, marginalized, or vilified. It must actually deal with the effects of those histories and dynamics on the cultures that perpetrated these elisions and remained seemingly inviolate in their wake." She concludes: "the encounter with cultural difference cannot be done by representing a loss or an absence, but needs to come about by the museum acknowledging and enacting a loss of some part of itself."[71]

Ruth Phillips argues that museums in Canada have responded to protests and questioning in sophisticated ways. She looks to the process of Indigenization, which requires "the incorporation into the mainstream museum world of concepts, protocols, and processes that originate in Aboriginal societies."[72] Indigenization demands much more than addition to already existing histories and thus does perhaps illustrate the acknowledgment and enactment of loss suggested by Rogoff.

The efforts and shortcomings illustrated by Rogoff and Phillips are complicated and of particular significance to settler-colonial states such as Canada, Australia, and New Zealand, where, in all three cases, museums have been test sites for modes of reconciliation. But reconciliation, decolonization, and/or Indigenization[73] cannot take place in the museum alone. Museums need to be understood as one among many facets of a problem, which might also include the land on which the museums sit, the various audiences they serve and work with, and the displays they mount. The background of the CMHR sketched out above – including the museum becoming a state entity, the multiple competing viewpoints at stake in designing the museum, and the powerful interests behind fundraising campaigns – always already delineates the limits of the museum's ability to be an innovative space for rethinking established relations. Decolonization cannot be a compromise, and in

2014 it appeared that a museum of the size and complexity of the CMHR would have needed to start from a different place if its goal was to fully unsettle settler–Indigenous relations.[74] To be clear, there were moments of promise at the CMHR from the outset (the Indigenous Perspectives Gallery being a case in point), but at the time of opening, the CMHR largely replicated traditional museum ideology in Canada (though in some but not all ways undertaking the process of Indigenization noted by Phillips). The museum followed the recommendations of the task force, and it anticipated the calls to action of the TRC. Nevertheless, it remained, at heart, exactly what it is: a museum. And although, without a large collection of objects, the CMHR arguably does not carry the colonial material culture baggage of other similar institutions, in its early years it nonetheless stumbled on the same fault lines characteristic of many establishment institutions.

As we move toward the SL40's sacred fire outside of the CMHR site, two questions guide my inquiry: 1. Is there a thread that ties SL40 to previous examples of intervention at museums? and 2. Did the museum respond in a manner typical of institutions facing resistance, or did it develop new strategies beholden to the TRC and other attempts to reimagine how Indigenous peoples and settlers might work toward new futures?

CMHR 2008–14

From 2009 on, the Asper family loosened their grip on the museum. The 2008 decision to make the CMHR a national institution deeply changed its outlook. While some financial pressures were alleviated, the government required the museum to act on a number of recommendations, among them the "desire for the museum to speak for all Canadians, not just for a few 'special interests.'"[75] Stuart Murray (former leader of the Manitoba Conservative Party) was named president and CEO of the museum, and Gail Asper remained as a member of the board and a fundraiser. The 2008 transfer also recommended the creation of a Content Advisory Committee, which, once established, travelled to all of the provinces and territories in 2009–10 asking Canadians what they wanted to see in a human rights museum.

The Content Advisory Committee was hugely important in determining the focus of the museum, and perhaps because of that it was divisive. Freelance reporter Ira Basen argues that the consultations possibly sowed the seeds of future controversy at the museum as "the final report ran to nearly 100 pages of highly empathetic and politically correct rhetoric."[76] Basen quotes Granatstein, who dismissed the report, suggesting, "the scrupulous neutrality required of a national museum will ultimately prove to be incompatible with the CMHR's ambition to be a world leader in the fight for human rights."[77] As shown in the previous chapter, the phrase "politically correct" is often used as shorthand to dismiss perspectives other than those illustrating a typically white, typically male, supposedly "neutral" accounting of history (when in fact, those accounts are anything but neutral).

Although Bill C-42 (which made the institution a national museum) had contained no mention of residential schools but instead described the museum as "the largest museum gallery in Canada devoted to the subject of the Holocaust,"[78] the public feedback gathered into the Advisory Committee Report showed that priority issues included, in descending order: Aboriginal/First Nations (16.1 per cent), genocides (14.8), women (14.7), internments (12.5), war and conflicts (8.7), the Holocaust (7), children (5.9), sexual orientation (3.8), ethnic minorities (3.8), and slavery (2.9). The report concluded by urging the Harper government and the museum to ensure that Indigenous people "have substantive involvement in the planning and implementation of the CMHR, including the recruitment of Aboriginal individuals for both management and non-management positions."[79] The report also acknowledged "the theft of land and resources by settler communities from Indigenous nations" and "the destruction of languages, cultures, spiritualties, and families as generations of Indigenous children were forcibly detained in Indian residential schools."[80]

While Basen and Granatstein argue that the Advisory Committee Report was too unwieldy and "politically correct" to have impact, I argue that the opposite was true. The move of the museum from the private sector to the public pointedly changed its direction, away from some of the projects advocated for by funders and toward a multitude of issues, key among them the treatment of Indigenous children and communities at residential schools. Even though I argue that the museum did not go far enough, the already well-established best practices for working with Indigenous communities employed at other Canadian institutions, influenced by the task force report in particular, were very obviously taken up by the CMHR.

Additionally, the backdrop to the CMHR's move toward a focus on residential schools in particular was a torrent of legal cases from the 1980s onwards that revealed residential school abuse, which coalesced around 2002 in a series of class action lawsuits and culminated in 2005 when the federal Liberal government agreed to a settlement package worth several billion dollars. The package included the creation of a $125 million endowment for the Aboriginal Healing Foundation, as well as $20 million for commemoration projects and the reinvestment of interest paid on the $2 billion compensation fund – approximately $80 million – into benefitting victims, including a $60 million pledge to fund a Truth and Reconciliation Commission (TRC).[81] All of this was decided just before the Liberal government fell in a non-confidence vote in November 2005.

Thus, it was Conservative prime minister Stephen Harper who stood before the Canadian Parliament and representatives of First Peoples in June 2008 and apologized for the treatment of Indigenous children in state and church-run residential schools. The apology not only covered the harsh treatment of children at the schools but also expressed remorse for the concerted attempt to eradicate Indigenous cultural practices that had been a part of government and church policy. As a part of the apology, the government also instituted the promised Truth and Reconciliation Commission that would record for posterity the stories of those survivors who wished to share their suffering and would ostensibly begin to mend the rift between Indigenous peoples living in Canada and non-Indigenous (settler) Canadians.

While there was joy and relief at the apology and the TRC, many also greeted both with trepidation.[82] The apology came only after decades of action and demands, but even so it hived off one element of those demands – recognition of the abuse that took place in residential schools – from other issues, most notably land claims, housing, and access to clean water. As curator cheyanne turions notes,

> The pointed and dispersed traumas by which settler colonialism conditions the lives of Indigenous people is intergenerational and ongoing. The Apology marks a significant moment of critical self-reflection on behalf of the Canadian state, but this alone does not adequately address the scope of harm that settler colonialism has effected upon the self-determination of Indigenous people in Canada.[83]

Run by the state, the TRC would bear witness to what had happened but from a position of complicity. Was it an attempt to alleviate white guilt? Feelings of disquiet seemed warranted when in 2009 in a speech at a G20 meeting in Pittsburgh, Harper told an audience, "We [Canada] also have no history of colonialism. So we have all of the things that many people admire about the great powers but none of the things that threaten or bother them."[84]

The apology and Harper's later statement clearly indicate the hypocrisy inherent in government–Indigenous relations and also can be read as backdrop to the way Indigenous–museum relations initially played out at the CMHR. Even as the TRC began recording statements from survivors of residential schools (6,750 by the end), the museum was turning the apology into a positive event: "We know that the museum plans for its visitors to feel 'proud of Canada's apology' to Indigenous citizens."[85] In short, the museum was certainly willing to follow the Advisory Committee Report's reflections on "The destruction of languages, cultures, spiritualities, and families as generations of Indigenous children were forcibly detained in Indian residential schools"[86] but would do so within a framing that embraced uncomplicated positive outcomes.

By 2012, the museum was again in hot water, this time because of a media report that the museum's Board of Trustees had intervened in the planning of the galleries, asking that the museum reach for a "positive and optimistic tone" and that it contain more "positive Canadian content."[87] Such alleged interventions were met by a critical public (or at least media and scholars) with anger if not surprise. But such incursions speak deeply to the contradiction at the heart of the museum. As Angela Failler notes, "After all, it's hard to contribute to 'civic upswing' if you have a reputation for bringing people down."[88]

The call for a "positive and optimistic tone" was exemplary of what was to come. In July 2013, the CMHR announced that it would not use the word "genocide" in the title of exhibits describing policies over the past century aimed at Indigenous peoples, including residential schools and forced relocations.[89] Former Grand Chief of the Assembly of First Nations Phil Fontaine, along with Michael Dan and Bernie Farber, "called on Ottawa to acknowledge Canada as its sixth officially recognized genocide, alongside the Holocaust and Holodomor, and genocides in Srebrenica, Armenia, and Rwanda."[90] After "extensive internal debate and an ongoing process of revision," the museum's senior staff decided against using the term. It was announced that the museum was neither a court nor a government and that "as a Crown corporation, it's important the museum's terminology align with that of the federal government, which has not recognized Canada's aboriginal policies as a genocide."[91] While the museum denied government and board intervention when it came to including "more positive content," it went straight to government to excuse a difficult situation. It remains unclear whether or not the museum was correct in stating that they "could not" use the term genocide, but what is crystal clear is that the outcry over the missing term was badly mismanaged.

Though to date Indigenous critique of the museum had been muted, the decision not to use the term "genocide" acted as a lightning rod, bringing together a wide array of individuals and groups. In a widely distributed letter to Stuart Murray, the CEO of the museum, Grand Chief Murray Clearsky of the Southern Chiefs Organization (which had donated $1 million to the museum in 2009) wrote, "Your museum's decision not to identify the shameful deceit, marginalization and ongoing attempts to assimilate and eradicate the original peoples of this country is a huge slap in the face for First Nations."[92]Almost simultaneously, in July 2013, historian of food, health, and colonialism Ian Mosby released his research showing that hungry First Nations children and adults were once used as unwitting subjects in nutritional experiments by Canadian government bureaucrats.[93] Revelations coming out of the TRC that Aboriginal children had regularly been exposed to tuberculosis and other diseases and had suffered from malnutrition and other significant health hazards, resulting in widespread deaths and burials in unmarked (still missing) graves,[94] in combination with the active impetus to eradicate culture, made the term genocide hard to avoid. Nevertheless, then-director Stuart Murray replied,

> Public discussion about the use of the term "genocide" in the context of the aboriginal experience in Canada provides an excellent opportunity to raise awareness about the nature of human rights violations in our own backyard … [W]hile a museum does not have the power to make declarations of genocide, we can certainly encourage – through ongoing partnership with the indigenous community itself – an honest examination of Canada's human rights history, in hopes that respect and reconciliation will prevail.[95]

But Métis curator Tricia Logan, who left the museum shortly after the genocide issue erupted, noted,

> As a curator at the CMHR, I was consistently reminded that every mention of state-perpetrated atrocity against Indigenous peoples in Canada must be matched with a "balanced" statement that indicates reconciliation, apology or compensation provided by the government. In cases where those issues are not reconciled or where accusations of abuse against the government continue to this day, the stories are reduced in scope or are removed from the museum. As curator, I have been ordered to limit coverage of stories of Aboriginal children in the child welfare system, missing and murdered women in Canada and climate change. These stories will still appear in the museum, but their treatment has been greatly reduced in each instance. As mentioned above, I was also instructed to remove the terms "genocide" and "settler colonial genocide" from all Indigenous exhibits. The atrocities committed against Indigenous peoples will be labeled in museum text and media productions as "colonialism" … What is entered into public memory and what is essentially erased through the curatorial process and the "cutting-room floor" has meaning.[96]

If I showed above that the 1994 task force and its aftermath resulted in a certain level of Indigenization and outreach to Indigenous communities, the issue of "genocide" revealed the limits of this collaboration. Logan notes that although museums in Canada have dealt with violations against Indigenous peoples, the approach is piecemeal, and "the series of violations against Indigenous peoples are not framed as genocide in a single, explicit exhibit on genocide. Rather, they are portrayed as discrete, discontinuous episodes."[97] Further, and perhaps more importantly, the 1994 task force report suggested that museums could be places for working out difficult problems and new relations. In order to include the word genocide, the CMHR would have had to step into the territory of creating new definitions and new knowledges. As Erika Lehrer writes,

> A fundamental challenge in exhibiting settler colonial genocide is the differently configured nature of its violence – rather than a discrete time period of mass murder, the calculated oppression and dispossession of Indigenous people happened over centuries. And while discrete episodes of human rights violations against Indigenous groups are exhibited (residential schooling, the disproportionately high rate of murder and abduction of Indigenous women), they are not tied together in the context of the larger processes of nation building in which they are implicated.[98]

It turns out that the museum was not willing (or able) to take this step.

Thus, while the museum was careful to include consultation with Indigenous groups at every step, and while the museum listened carefully to the recommendations of the Advisory Committee to include extensive representation of Indigenous stories, to hire Indigenous curators, and to consult with Indigenous groups, it did so within an overarching framework that refused to unsettle museum norms or disrupt mainstream knowledge, that kept a close connection with federal government parameters, and that imagined its audience in fairly parochial terms. Thus, the museum's response to the genocide issue was visibly part of the ongoing process of settler colonialism in its unwillingness to concede the extent of the impact of government and church actions, in keeping with the museum's framing in general. Museum Communications staff member Maureen Fitzhenry said, "We don't want to be seen as advocating or involving ourselves in a debate that is still playing out."[99] As critics pointed out, the museum already used the word "genocide" to describe situations in Guatemala and Cambodia, neither of which had attained parliamentary recognition.[100] Ultimately, a didactic label in the gallery space would invite conversation on whether or not the residential school program in Canada met the definition of the word "genocide" (problematically leaving the decision in the hands of visitors to the museum).[101]

The CMHR prides itself on being an institution at the cutting edge of museum consultation and technology. Without artefacts from which to build stories, the CMHR avoids didacticism and relies on ideas and storytelling. Objects can be sought out, with the participation of communities, to support stories, challenging more typical museum strategies of displaying objects that may have been wrongfully acquired from source communities. In this way, the CMHR is atypical of other authoritative museums in Canada but far from radical in its organization.

In sum, like many other key Canadian institutions (including, but certainly not limited to the National Gallery, the [unrealized] National Portrait Gallery, and the Canadian Museum of Civilization/Canadian Museum of History), from its very inception the CMHR faced criticism from all sides: naysayers, belligerents, pundits, critical scholars, concerned citizens, advocacy groups, and others. Though debate and dismissal seem to be par for the course in the establishment of national institutions in Canada, the early critics of the CMHR seemed better organized, better informed, and more diverse than those groups of naysayers faced by other institutions. Critiques ranged from dismissal of the museum as a whole to attempted interventions into content. Over time, the museum embraced a kind of public consultation that really has not been seen at any other institution to date. Unlike in the cases discussed at the ROM or the CWM, it would be fair to say that the CMHR welcomed lobbying and feedback and occasionally, or even often, responded to it. This was true for groups across the political spectrum. Furthermore, the museum, once it became a public entity, ended up with a different emphasis from what it would have had as a private project, likely with a much greater prominence of Indigenous issues. On the other hand, it would also be fair to say, particularly given the outcry over the unwillingness to use the term "genocide," that public consultation does not necessarily result in much more than a repetition of the status quo with a stamp of approval for its crowd-sourcing. David Garneau writes about exhibitions of Indigenous art in mainstream museums,

> Exhibitions of Aboriginal art shown within a dominant culture space are always informed by the world views of those who manage the resources and the site/sights ... If art galleries and other display spaces are to be potential sites of conciliation, they should not meet the dominant culture viewer halfway in their space in their way; the non-Aboriginal viewer who seeks conciliation ought to enter Aboriginal sovereign display territories as guests.[102]

Such a way of conceptualizing the CMHR would have led to a vastly different articulation of the museum, particularly on the issue of genocide. I briefly consider this train of thought before returning to how the museum's failure to account for its own complicity contributed to its initial effectiveness as a backdrop against which the kinds of actions apparently central to the museum's mandate could be imagined.[103]

As Ruth Phillips notes, a process of decolonization was underway in Canadian museums long before the apology. But she also notes a paradox – that national institutions are, by law, "designed to inscribe in the nation's citizens a distinctive and shared identity."[104] She points out that "these collective constructs of national identity [whether British-imperial, Anglo-Canadian, bicultural, or multicultural] are inherently antithetical to Aboriginal affirmations of sovereignty."[105] And therein lies the real problem. The CMHR saw its mandate as one of catalyzing action and of showing both human rights abuses and victories. These mismatched goals made doing much more than representing a series of events and exhibits impossible. The action remains muted.

Phillips also notes, importantly, that the same period that saw the formation of the CMHR (around 2008) also saw a backtracking on many programs that grew out of the 1994 task force's call to include Indigenous perspectives in museums. She writes,

> Although the financial crisis that began in 2008 is usually cited as the immediate cause of these changes, the Harper government's simultaneous allocations of funding for other projects of public historical commemoration and exhibition make it clear that radical breaks are at work. A renewed focus on settler histories, often at the expense of Aboriginal heritage and demographic diversity, is evident across the heritage system.[106]

Cuts to Library and Archives Canada followed the election of a majority Conservative government in 2011. Cuts to Parks Canada resulted in the closure of numerous heritage sites, many of them dedicated to First Nations and Métis history. Key administrative units were eliminated at the Department of Canadian Heritage, while monies were invested in the commemorative celebration of the British-led War of 1812 (a war that marked the end of many Indigenous sovereignties in what would become Canada, clearing the way for treaties, land grabs, and marginalization). Funds were also designated for a controversial name change of the Canadian Museum of Civilization to the Canadian Museum of History (see chapter 6). The cuts were deep, and they were ideological, tied to cuts to environmental protections and proposed changes to the Indian Act (see chapter 6).[107] If anything, the changes brought about by the task force seemed in retreat.

Because the museum in its final iteration would focus so strongly on action (which was often articulated in the relentless description of the museum following a journey from "darkness to enlightenment"), the ultimate organization of space alternates between traumatic events and progress, a strategy that circumvents the deep impact and ongoing legacy of many of the events covered in the galleries.[108] As Wodtke points out, there is a discrepancy between the museum's apparent wish for openness, collaboration, and community building and its massive size, its solidity and immutability, and its grandiosity.[109] Wodtke notes that some of the problems were built right into the architectural program from the early days of the competition, which tended to align along binaries and absolutes – easily understood metaphors of progress and hope: "this is not a museum building that challenges visitors to encounter difficult knowledge."[110] After all, encouraging tourists to enter the museum is a prime goal of the urban regeneration built into the plan of the CMHR. Thus, the interior of the museum is a space that showcases the impossibility of using narratives and stories of trauma to build what is ostensibly a tourist attraction.[111] And not just any tourist attraction but one with a specific mandate of encouraging action on human rights.

Protest at the Museum

In the Advisory Committee Report presented to the CMHR in 2008, it was suggested that "the individual visitor should come out of the museum motivated with a personal call to action."[112] The "call to action" mode of engagement remains a central tenet of the CMHR and a way of repurposing activism to serve the needs of the institution. The CMHR defines activism as "social responsibility and progressiveness" of approach toward the issues covered in the museum.[113] In the report, there are two definitions of activism, one an apolitical "call to action" belonging to the museum and one deployed by the museum to describe outsiders. Item 50 of the report states, "the CMHR must recognize past historical tragedies (as lessons) and current events in ways that promote critical understanding and social responsibility, not political activism or apathy."[114] Later this wording is unfolded: "Ensure that your board and staff represent a range of views and perspectives so that the exhibit will not cater to one vantage point. Keep people who are 'activists' continuing their work as activists, not serving on the board or staff where they can attempt to hijack a particular agenda."[115] In short, only allow dissent insofar as it builds rather than challenges the museum's message.

Once the museum opened, the *language* and *image* of protest and resistance were everywhere present. In a film shown in one of the main exhibition spaces, a message scrolls across the screen: "This is more than a museum, it's a movement."[116] According to the film's dialogue, the museum as movement brings people from all over the world into the human rights debate, "sparking conversations that are supportive, affirming, challenging, and often controversial." At this moment a famous image from the 1991 Kanien'kehaka Resistance at Kanehsatà:ke and Kahnawà:ke, showing a Mohawk Warrior facing off against a member of the Canadian Armed Forces, comes up on screen. Throughout the exhibition space, there are many images of protesters and land and water protectors, most of them carrying colourful signs and peacefully resisting (rather than, for example, running from tear gas or facing violent arrest). As would become clear, the CMHR respects, indeed encourages, some forms of "activism" but only to a certain extent.[117] This is demonstrated not only by the contested content of the museum but also through the construction of a large outdoor amphitheatre that Basen points out "could easily accommodate hundreds of sign-waving pickets."[118] Basen quotes Gail Asper: "That's where they'll be, and they'll say, 'We don't like your take on this.' We want to encourage good Canadian peaceful, legal, respectful protesting about what goes on in here ... I probably would be disappointed if there weren't protests."[119] Such statements suggest neutralizing or incorporating protests and demonstrations, allowing the museum to stand above any accusations levelled against it. But given the low level of interest in protest demonstrated by other Canadian museums (see chapter 3), the CMHR's embrace of it is certainly a distinctive feature. Does it signify a willingness to engage, or is it more of the same? Is it potentially a radical shift in imagining the role of the museum?

Opening day at the CMHR was met with a series of actions, among them two sacred fires, one organized by SL40, the second by Idle No More. Anti-abortion agitators waved signs at visitors waiting in line, and an Earth Day march against climate change passed by the museum. In the early weeks, a Palestinian action used the museum as backdrop, and trans-rights activists gathered against a talk at the museum by trans-exclusionary feminist Germaine Greer. Idle No More used the CMHR as backdrop for a number of dance circles, and several other demonstrations (for example, against government cuts to refugee health care) have taken place there.

Protests tended to be greeted in one of two ways: first, a very familiar refrain (mostly from the mainstream press) accusing the protesters of futility and second, a much less familiar commentary that perhaps there had not been *enough* protests. In an example of the latter, *Winnipeg Free Press* reporter Mary Agnes Welch wrote, "After opening day, there hasn't even been a big, loud protest outside. There is, more than two months after its pseudo-opening, remarkably little buzz about the $351-million museum that was to be our more current and controversial version of Bilbao."[120] Historian Nadine Blumer notes,

> The hail of indignation everyone expected hasn't materialized, for better or worse. No one has parsed the exhibit on Mexican migrant farm workers and called it out for whitewashing the fundamentally exploitative nature of Canada's program employing temporary farm workers. There's been little public outcry at the near total lack of Palestinian voices or references in the museum.[121]

By contrast, Joseph Brean hyperbolically wrote of the opening day in the *National Post*, "By the time the dignitaries had taken their seats behind the police cordon at the museum entrance, a loud and angry crowd of protesters was already raging against abortion, pipelines, colonialism, pollution, and even the very idea of this unusual museum."[122] Jonathan Kay, in the same paper, began his article on opening day with the evocative subtitle: "Every identity-politics activist known to humanity is attacking Canada's human rights museum,"[123] an exaggerated statement that is not toned down in the article. "Unfortunately ... the museum's 100-metre tall 'Tower of Hope' spire has been transformed into a powerful homing beacon for every single aggrieved identity-politics activist known to humanity," he wrote.[124] Kay's piece is a vicious modest proposal, and it mocks both those critiquing the museum and the museum itself, arguing that Canada already has a Human Rights Tribunal, that the museum is mere fluff, and

> in time, the number of successful human-rights claims against the Canadian Museum For Human Rights might become so enormous that these cases would, themselves, become the subject of an entirely new museum – the Canadian Human Rights Museum-Related Human Rights Museum. And since this, too, would be built on "stolen land," and would necessarily include some cases and exclude others, the cycle of human rights violation, complaint, litigation and resolution would be guaranteed to blossom anew.[125]

A much more measured critique asks, "To date, the CMHR has operated as a stage for 'hearing' dissent, without the use of heavy handed police force. But is the museum really unable to speak out in relation to the human and indigenous rights violations taking place underfoot?"[126]

In answer, long-time social activist David Jacks noted, "I've been an activist in a number of social justice movements for many years, and I feel as if we have exhausted the isolated steps of the Manitoba Legislative Building, the quiet courtyard of City Hall, and the awkward Federal Building at 269 Main Street. Shouting at the Tyndall stone walls of any of these buildings often makes you wonder if anyone is listening. But now we have a place where people are listening. In fact, people assumedly visit the CMHR precisely because they want to listen."[127] But do they want to listen? This question brings us to the case of Shoal Lake 40 First Nation.

Shoal Lake 40 First Nation at the CMHR

The space of the Indigenous Perspectives Gallery in the CMHR includes a circular theatre in the shape of a woven wooden basket that broadcasts a film sharing multi-generational stories of Indigenous rights and responsibilities. "I deserve clean water," says a voice- over, juxtaposed with an image of youth holding up a sign calling for water rights.[128] As visitors make their way through the exhibition space, they can rest in the Garden of Contemplation, a quiet, meditative space

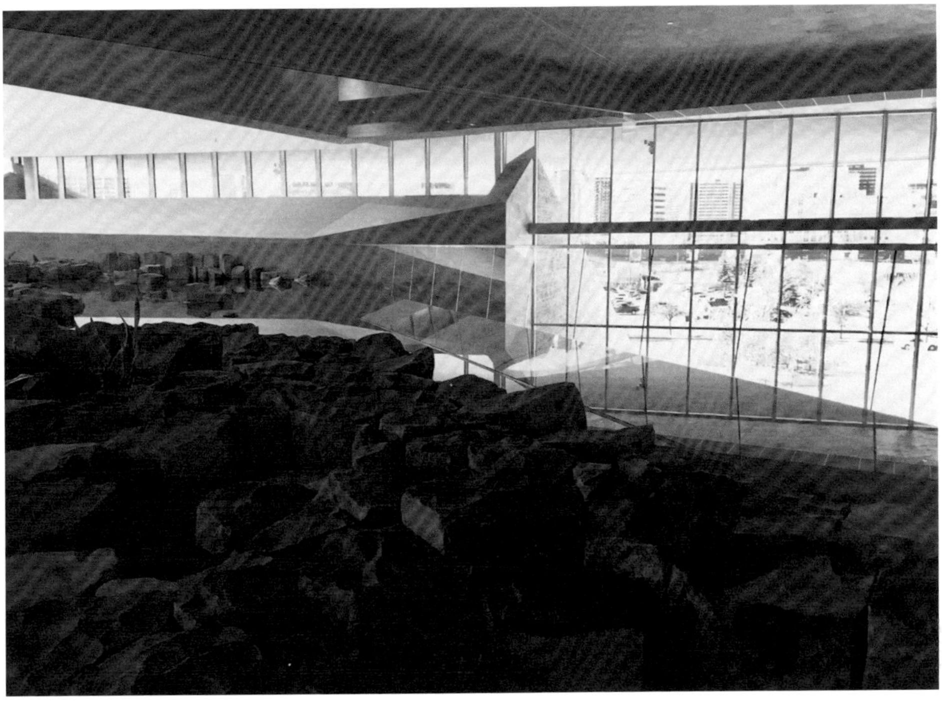

Figure 5.3
Garden of Contemplation at the spot where the plaque acknowledging Shoal Lake Nation 40 will be placed, Canadian Museum for Human Rights.

filled with slowly flowing water, rocks, plants, and benches. The water is Winnipeg municipal water, shipped through a 137 km aqueduct from Shoal Lake to a water processing plant outside the city and then to the homes, businesses, and institutions of Winnipeg.

The aqueduct was built in 1919, not long after a Winnipeg newspaper article reported, "There is practically no habitation, with the exception of a few Indians and an odd mining camp and no possibility of contamination from this source."[129] Those "few Indians" were the SL40 nation, unilaterally forced off their traditional lands (which had been sold to the City of Winnipeg) to make way for the aqueduct.[130] Historian Adele Perry's research of archival and newspaper documents from the early twentieth century shows how the invisibility of Indigenous people was created through settler denial of their presence and that economic motivations were consistently placed ahead of the human rights of Anishinaabe peoples living in the area, including treaty rights that had been skillfully negotiated by ancestors of current SL40 residents.[131] It was the 1876 Indian Act that legally enabled the dispossession of SL40 from their reserve lands, which was appropriated for the intake to the aqueduct.[132]

Some time afterwards, the peninsula to which they had been moved was cut off from the mainland when "engineers cut a channel to divert the tannin-stained waters of Falcon River away from the aqueduct intake," leaving them stranded on an island.[133] Additional impositions from the outside damaged traditional lifeways. First, a commercial and subsistence fishery was shut down to preserve stocks.[134] Then other commercial ventures were blocked, primarily to prevent pollutants from entering what was now the city of Winnipeg's water source. Nevertheless, pollutants in the lake from upriver farming and cottages mean that the water is no longer potable at source and must be treated outside of Winnipeg. In short, SL40, which sits on the reservoir supplying water to Winnipeg, does not itself have access to clean water and has been under a boil-water advisory for more than twenty years (at the time of writing).[135]

As Perry writes,

> At its core the story of the Aqueduct is about the exploitation of Indigenous resources in the interest of settler ones. It is also about the ways in which these difficult histories are elided, put aside, and forgotten, and what happens when settler communities are compelled to acknowledge that their lives, their resources, and their relative prosperity have come at the expense, sometimes the very direct expense, of Indigenous peoples.[136]

In 2007, a group of SL40 residents walked the 140 kilometres to the future site of the CMHR to highlight *decades* of complaints to municipal, provincial, and federal representatives about the state of access and water at Shoal Lake.[137] Several years later, band members also wrote to the architect, Antoine Predock, whose website describes the museum's Garden of Contemplation as "a place of healing and solace" that honours "the First Nations' sacred relationship to water."[138] Chief Erwin Redsky's letter to Predock stressed,

> It is deeply insulting to hear your building promoted as honouring "the First Nation relationship with water" when the water taken from Shoal Lake so clearly represents Canada's continuing violation of human and aboriginal rights … When we look into those pools we will see a century of sorrow. We will see what we lack. Those crystal clear pools hold our tears.[139]

A solution seemed to lie first in drawing attention to the difficulties faced by SL40 and second in leveraging federal funds to build what came to be known as Freedom Road, a 27-kilometre all-weather road running from the Nation to the TransCanada Highway, bringing with it easy access to potable water and much safer passage for inhabitants of the community.[140] Without the road, SL40 was only served by an unreliable ferry in the summer and snowmobiles on the frozen lake in the winter, while at times of freezing and thawing, residents were forced to walk across, risking falling through the thin ice and drowning (something that happens/ed with devastating and shocking regularity).[141]

The building of the CMHR, a *human rights* museum, seemed a particularly apt opportunity to bring attention to ongoing abuses in Canada. At least at first, very little happened. The museum and Predock did not respond to SL40 demands, and the federal government did not budge on funding the road. Media coverage was minimal. From the walk in 2007, SL40 members continued to struggle through seven or eight years of silence while the museum dealt with other issues, notably debates over interior geography, the transition from a private to a national museum, and the apology and TRC. Then two things happened that I suggest completely changed the trajectory of museum and government relations with SL40. The first was the emergence of Idle No More in national media and at a number of sites in Winnipeg, signifying the presence of a widespread and organized Indigenous movement calling for reforms. And second, the controversy over the refusal to use the term "genocide" within the museum bridged the gap between mainstream media and SL40. At first, the plight of SL40 was treated in the media as a *story*, but then it began to be recognized as a real instance of potential human rights violation. The occupation of the grounds outside the museum by members of SL40 seemed a clear illustration of the controversy playing out inside. These events catalyzed attention to SL40's situation, and by 2014 other Indigenous groups, settler allies, and activists, church groups, media, and indeed the museum itself[142] had turned their attention to Shoal Lake.

At that time, SL40 reconfigured itself as a *living museum*,[143] inviting Canadians and the world to visit "a more realistic museum, the Museum of Canadian Human Rights Violations (MCHRV). This is the living museum of our community. Our doors are open."[144] A pamphlet on the MCHRV handed out at the sacred fire outside the CMHR stated,

> We recognize they are harsh stories. We deliver them with an open spirit, inviting Canadians to join us in healing the broken relationship between us. We are glad the museum will raise the profile of values such as respect and equality. We are glad the exhibits will be well-lit and will include healing waters. At the same time we want Canadians to know that for many aboriginal people, the grandiose structure is a bitter reminder of what we do not have. We do not want to have to take our kids to a museum to learn about human rights, we want them to experience it at home.

Shortly afterwards, a CBC news story reported that "the museum is now listening. A half dozen officials from the new facility were on hand. They toured the First Nation and went to the spot on the west side of the reserve where the current Freedom Road abruptly stops and turns into muskeg.[145] They also listened to more than a dozen community members (there were about 100 people in attendance) share powerful stories, many moved to tears, about loved ones lost."[146] But by contrast, CMHR director of communications Angela Cassie was quoted in a museum press release suggesting that "as a Museum, we cannot play the role of advocate and activist, or take a position in disputes, but we can work to build awareness and understanding as part of our educational mandate."[147]

A movement was growing. In June 2015, Conservative federal natural resources minister Greg Rickford visited SL40. He was there to make an announcement, which the community was greatly anticipating. Community members, government officials, a documentary filmmaker, and others joined Chief Erwin Redsky and local and provincial officials to break ground for what would be Freedom Road. After shaking hands and shovelling the dry earth, a *Vice* documentary shows everyone happily returning to the community gym, eagerly awaiting Rickford's announcement. He stands up, his own small child in his arms and announces with a big smile that the government will pledge money to support a design for the road. The announcement is greeted with stunned silence – the federal government had already made the exact same announcement a year earlier, pledging $1 million to a design company far from the reserve itself. The camera turns away from Rickford and focuses on upset residents of SL40, some of them weeping in frustration. Children expecting a celebration look worriedly around. The announcement is devastating.[148] Having already secured municipal and provincial support for the project and needing only federal support,[149] SL40 was no further ahead with the federal government in 2015 than it had been in 2007.

In terms of wider support, the story was different. By 2015, Shoal Lake Nation had amassed a diverse and extensive support network, ranging from other Indigenous individuals and nations, local churches and politicians, and Canadian citizens from all walks of life[150] to the international NGO Human Rights Watch.[151] Shoalidarity and A Road to Freedom campaigns were led by churches in the greater Winnipeg area to draw attention to the situation. An unsuccessful crowd-funding campaign underlined the need for the road, but its lack of success also suggested that the majority of supporters felt strongly that the federal government should fund the road as part of its obligations to First Peoples.[152]

Then came a change in government as the Conservatives fell and the Liberals under Justin Trudeau took over. In December 2015, shortly after the election, the federal government announced it was on-board. In late April 2016, Prime Minister Justin Trudeau visited SL40. He spent time with schoolchildren and helped to haul water jugs to citizens. Chief Erwin Redsky had some strong words for him, pointing out the institutionalized racism that kept SL40 under a boil-water advisory for two decades, stating that he appreciated Trudeau's visit but that the prime minister would only be welcomed back again "If, by your resolve, the young people you met today see real change in their lives and real hope in their future, then you will be most welcome to come back. If you succeed in making those fundamental changes to our relationship, you will deserve the celebration of a feast and an honour song for your accomplishment – and you will have earned it."[153]

At the time of writing, Freedom Road is well underway. The design study was completed in 2017, a timeline was set, and by the summer of 2018, the road was nearing completion (the actual opening is scheduled for summer 2019).[154] Thus, it is possible to say that the SL40 campaign that used the museum to draw attention to their plight was successful. Indeed, Blumer writes, "The Shoal Lake 40 protest and its MCHRV also highlight how a historically marginalized community exercises agency by way of and in reference to a mainstream institution such as the CMHR." She concludes, "It is worth noticing here whether protest outside of the museum does indeed have the potential to influence and change things within the museum and then, in turn (to cite one of the CMHR's mandates) to transform 'human rights into action.'"[155]

When I began writing this chapter in 2014, my argument was that the museum continues to gain from SL40 and the appearance of sympathetic advocacy that actually goes nowhere. Its encouragement of the SL40 sacred fire and visits to the MCHRV made the museum look like a caring institution while it was doing little to ensure a road would be built.[156] It must be recognized, however, that since 2016 the CMHR has learned from earlier missteps and has developed significant community relations with SL40. Curator Karine Duhamel notes that "Reconciliation demands a lot of Indigenous people and communities, and we have to be leery of how much we're asking for."[157] Thus, negotiations take time, and they proceed at a pace led by SL40. A plaque will be installed in the Garden of Contemplation in a location chosen by representatives from SL40 overlooking the calm waters, beside a window looking out over the city of Winnipeg, with a statement, written by SL40 and thus sidelining the museum's voice, acknowledging where the water comes from. Economic relationships have been encouraged, and SL40 sells "Got Water? Thank Shoal Lake" T-shirts in the museum store. Additionally, curators at the museum have worked hard to overcome the museum's initial faux pas, engaging with SL40 on *their* terms and acknowledging that cultivating trust takes time. In short, SL40 has secured the Freedom Road, and in so doing they have also enacted significant change at the CMHR. While at the time of writing it remains unclear how the relationship between SL40 and the CMHR will unfold, it is clear that it will be ongoing and deep.[158]

As Duhamel concludes,

> There are a lot of different levels to this relationship now, which I think is really good. The more complex and interwoven it is, the better chance it has to succeed in the long run. If you're just doing one small thing, it's very easy to walk away from that small thing. But if there are a lot of people involved at a lot of different levels it makes it quite complicated and sometimes really messy, but I think ultimately, it makes for an *actual* relationship, versus an ad hoc, project one off.

Conclusion(s)?

The case of SL40 and the CMHR ultimately brings us to the question of what mainstream establishment museums can or should do when it comes to engaging with communities that are not on board with the content or direction of the museum and have reason to bring their demands to the threshold (or interior) of the institution. Typically, as seen in the case of the ROM and the *Into the Heart of Africa* exhibition and the CWM and veterans angry at the wording in a text panel, museums are encouraged to actively stand their ground and to refuse to budge lest every group taking issue with the museum be allowed to change it. I'd like, for a minute, to give museums a little more credit and to argue that museums can in fact be important allies in struggles that take place far from, but connected to, what happens in their galleries.

Before arguing for this position, I need to line up some caveats. Incontrovertibly, the CMHR engages in what Eve Tuck and Wayne Yang term "settler moves to innocence," actions that appear on the surface to address Indigenous perspectives, or that appear to engage in processes of decolonization, but that are notable for "the emotional relief it can bring the practitioner and the more-or-less unchanged landscape it leaves behind."[159] There is plenty going on at the CMHR that is little more than surface engagement. As Erica Lehrer, for example, writes in reference to the Indigenous Perspectives Gallery at the CMHR, "it is hard not to wonder about the immediate visual appeal of this gallery, which forefronts predictable, palatable tropes of arts and crafts and spirituality rather than historical and ongoing marginalization by and struggle with the Canadian government."[160] Second, I note Métis artist David Garneau's position that there is a need for "irreconcilable spaces of Aboriginality": gatherings, exchanges, communications that take place removed from a settler audience, refusing complete engagement, translation, or explanation, against a settler-colonial mentality that suggests (in line with the CMHR's storytelling) that everything should be knowable, translatable, and, ultimately, exploitable.[161] And finally, I also draw attention to Meg Pinto's argument with regard to the MOA in Vancouver that encouraging dissent can become itself a calcified position whereby action against a museum can simply become part of the institution's modus operandi rather than a way to effect or encourage change.[162]

Even with these cautions, the CMHR has set itself up as a place where dissent can be voiced. The CMHR attempts to present many stories of human rights abuses, from different time periods and geographic regions, under a banner of positive action. They are also trying to balance numerous stakeholders, including groups as diverse as international visiting tourists, the federal government, corporate and private sponsors, residents of Winnipeg (settler and Indigenous), and communities such as SL40. And yet, as a museum encouraging action on human rights it seems essential that the CMHR move beyond the mere *representation* of homegrown abuse, a step the institution has not yet taken.

The question that remains, and which will be taken up in the next chapter, is if a museum that is dedicated to encouraging action and that builds its own protest zone has an uneven relationship to action against it, is there any point at all in using the museum as a vehicle for mobilization? Arguably, in the case of SL40, the museum's lack of real immediate engagement and the previous controversy over the term "genocide" in fact made the museum an impecable target and may ultimately have aided SL40's goal to secure funding for Freedom Road. The museum's missteps and faux pas arguably helped SL40. Controversies and protests at museums in general can and have been shown to lead to significant change. But that seems to be insufficient; not really a position from which to build change.

Garneau writes that successful

> decolonization is about First Nations, Inuit and Métis restoring and strengthening our different ways of knowing and being, and requiring our guests to unlearn and disengage from their colonial habits. Cultural decolonization in the Canadian context is about at once unsettling settlers and, ironically, helping them to adapt, to better settle themselves as noncolonial persons within Indigenous spaces.[163]

What might decolonization look like at the CMHR? How might "unsettling settlers" work with the other kinds of difficult knowledge that form the museum's content? Such questions seem essential to connecting the CMHR to the world of which it is a part and which its tumultuous history has surely demonstrated that it cannot actively avoid.

Interstice 5e

Wendy Coburn: Anatomy of a Protest

In 2011, artist Wendy Coburn began to make a documentary film about the inaugural Slut Walk, a march that had been organized in response to comments from a Toronto police constable who advised women at York University that they should "avoid dressing like sluts" if they did not want to be raped.[1] The Slut Walk mobilized the stance that sexual assault is not about what a woman wore or did: it is about consent, and activists marched both in support of survivors and with pedagogic intent. Coburn had planned to film the march and then use the footage in other projects.

As she viewed the footage, however, Coburn began to notice what appeared to be agents provocateurs at the march – participants who seemed intent on parodying the event of which they were a part. A man and a woman in outrageous costumes (he in cartoon sunglasses, leopard-print leggings, a yellow polka dot shirt, dinner jacket, she, a see-through blouse, black bra, short shorts, and tights that revealed a black thong), carrying ambiguous signs (such as posters stating "slutty is as slutty does," "I was a closet slut," "Will you marry me?" or "I'm with slut"), dancing and cavorting, seemed at once part of the celebratory action of the march but also at odds with its seriousness. In comparison to the popular sign: "Don't tell us how to dress, tell men not to rape," the pair's antics seemed too playful, making a mockery of the other marchers. The two (introduced in the film as Diamond Darryl Kay and Sara Noble) led the protest, and photos of their flamboyant costumes accompanied

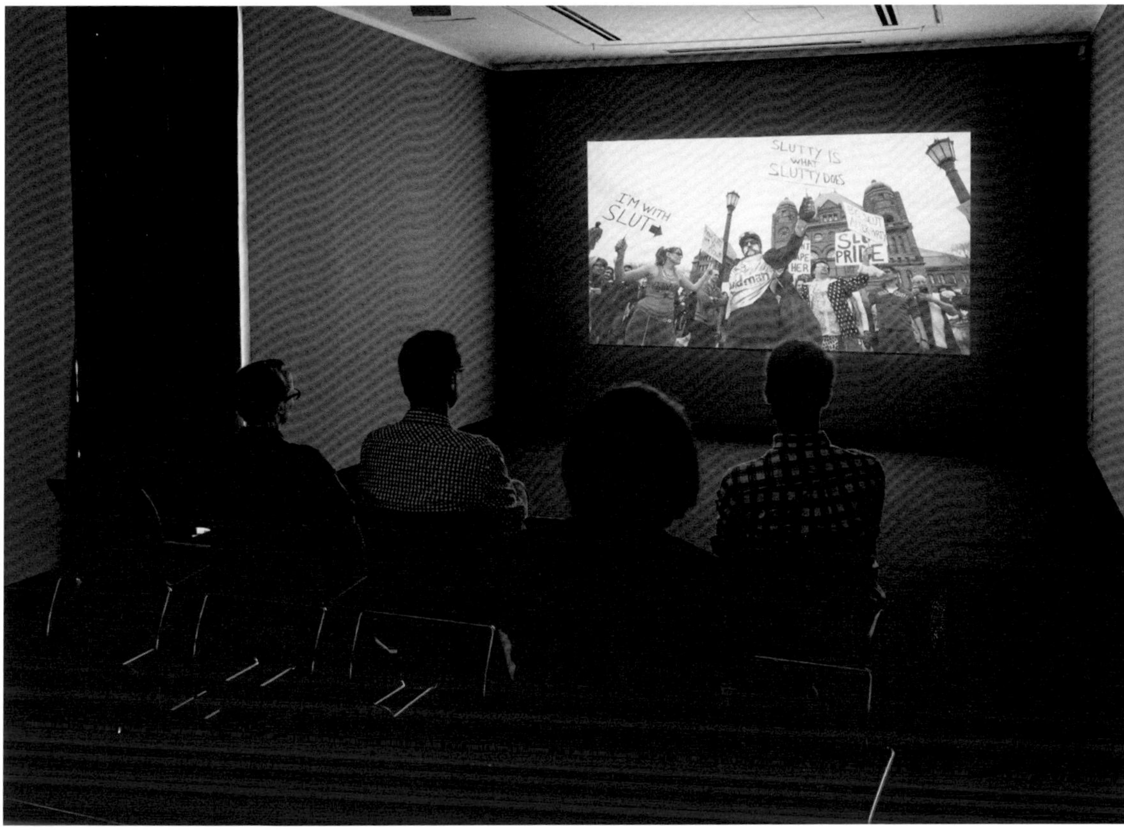

Figure 5.4
Wendy Coburn, *Anatomy of a Protest* film installation, Art Museum at the University of Toronto, 2014.

many reports of the Slut Walk.[2] "They took up a lot of space," said Anna Willats, a member of the Toronto Police Accountability Coalition, which advocates for transparency of local security forces. "They were getting their faces in front of every camera they could find. They seemed different from everybody else: their signs, the way they were acting. They were not in tune with the rest of the crowd."[3]

Who were they? As the film builds to its crux, it hints (though never confirms) that Diamond Darryl Kay and Sara Noble may have been undercover police officers, manipulating an event of which they were themselves the target. Public outrage is turned away from the protested event or issue and back onto those attending the event – just another party. Certainly, there is precedence for such claims, with one of the most well-known examples being from the 2007 North American leaders' summit in Montebello, Quebec, where a video, widely circulated on YouTube, shows police officers (including one carrying a rock) disguised as protesters (yet still wearing their uniform boots).[4] Digging ever deeper, Coburn's film script suggests that the police officers in question have been identified, a claim that is supported through juxtaposing the visual similarities between costumed activists carrying props that are almost, but not quite, on point, and later shots of plainclothes men and women videotaping protesters and leaving in unmarked vehicles. When Coburn, speaking in the film, asks if they are police officers, all mysteriously leave the march.[5]

Coburn never makes an outright accusation in the film. It's possible she's wrong – these could just be flamboyant protesters out for a good time, and later updates seem to suggest that the pair of partyers were not actually police officers.[6] Nevertheless, the film is compelling. The pair are obviously not in complete support of the march's intent, so why are they there? And if they were hired, who hired them? Coburn's work clearly demonstrates the management of protest for different ends, the manipulation of affect, the parodying and hijacking of that fragile, epiphanal moment, and its translation into easily dismissed phenomena. Ultimately, it does not really matter if Diamond Darryl Kay and Sara Noble are police – the artwork created by Coburn clearly shows that even in the midst of tear gas epiphanies and prefigurative politics, the images of protests as they are recorded and sent out on the airwaves are carefully managed, mediated events.

The video concludes with a now well-known image of police cars burning at the 2010 G20 Summit in Toronto. The point is to question again: were the cars actually attacked by a Black Bloc who overcame police presence with an intent to destroy public property? Or were protesters allowed or even encouraged to burn the cars, with an inevitable media-friendly image pitting protesters as hooligans and rioters with little political validity against patient police. Said one reviewer, "Coburn doesn't try to present an open-and-shut case, but I'm convinced by her tie-in of the burning police cars that dominated coverage of the Toronto G20 protests. In 2010, I saw officers under no threat abandoning these vehicles on Queen West to set up this police-generated street theatre."[7]

In the exhibition space, the video was accompanied by a series of props that seemed at once playful and threatening. A pair of red high tops, a toy bubble-blowing set, a pair of jeans, a pair of red basketball shoes – each is a carefully reconstructed prop, identical to those worn by the antagonists of Coburn's video. Finally, a large poster-sized piece that appears to be decorated with yellow polka dots instead reveals the (high) salaries of undercover officers working for the Toronto police.

Anatomy of a Protest is a highly charged artwork. As a work that is viewed in a traditional manner – it does not involve participation – it is at odds with a great deal of successful recent activist art. In fact, non-participatory art is assumed to be

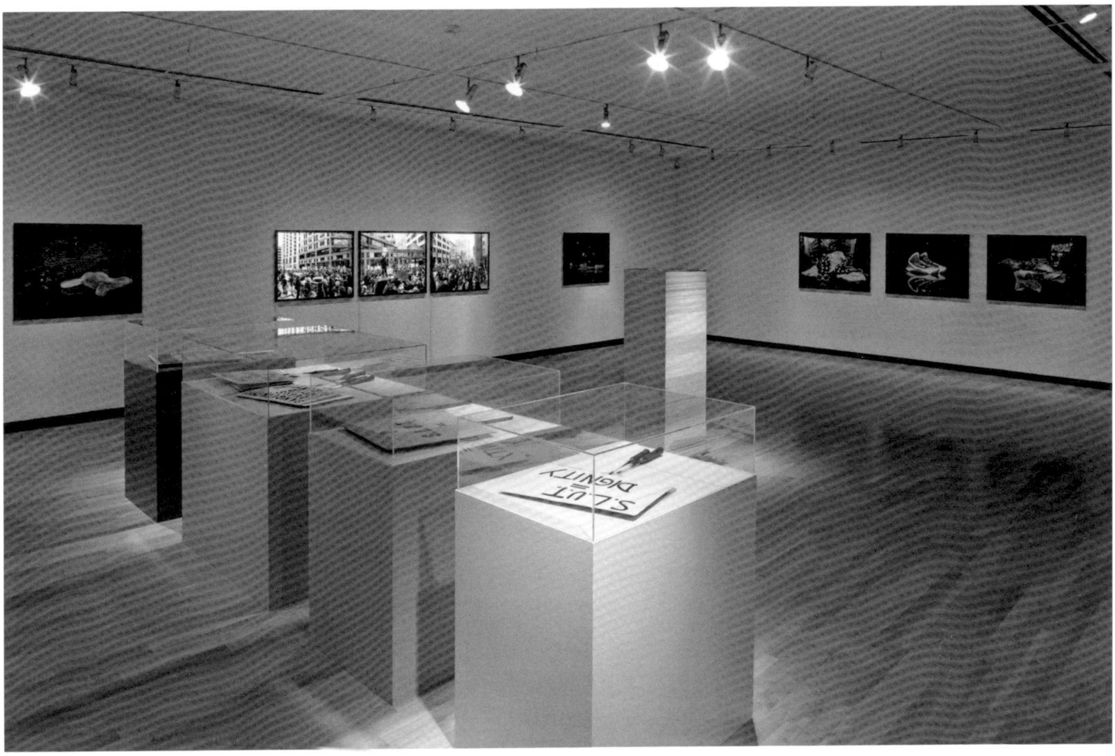

Figure 5.5
Wendy Coburn, *Anatomy of a Protest* installation, Art Museum at the University of Toronto, 2014.

pacifying, a uni-directional stream of narrative from which the viewer can emerge totally unchanged or unscathed by the impact of the work.[8] Coburn's work shows that this is not always the case. It shows how the tear gas epiphany can be undone, but in doing so, it creates a quiet space in the gallery where the contemplation of new potentials, new events, new ways of moving forward, can be imagined.[9]

6

When the Land Comes First: Oil, Museums, and (Missing) Protest

The vampire Alberta stalks across the money market rates
Ducks into a Hummer
The vampire Alberta wears a bowtie and a pin that says
"Support the arts"

John K. Samson, "Vampire Alberta Blues"

On 20 April 2011, the first anniversary of British Petroleum (BP)'s Deepwater Horizon explosion and consequent massive oil spill in the Gulf of Mexico, activists from the group Liberate Tate staged a protest performance in London at the Tate Britain, a museum sponsored by the British petroleum giant.[1] As a crowd gathered around, one of the eight artist-activists removed his clothes and huddled on the floor in a fetal position. Another poured an oil-like substance over him from a BP container. Just one of a number of such actions, the Liberate Tate performance drew attention to the gallery's positive spin on BP's pollution record. Tate responded with a press statement lauding BP as "one of the most important sponsors of the arts in the UK."[2]

When questions about oil sponsorship and the arts arise, two key concerns are always the potential for "greenwashing" the environmental and labour records of the companies doing the sponsoring and the influence that sponsoring corporations may gain over exhibition content (censoring, for example, anti-oil sentiment or

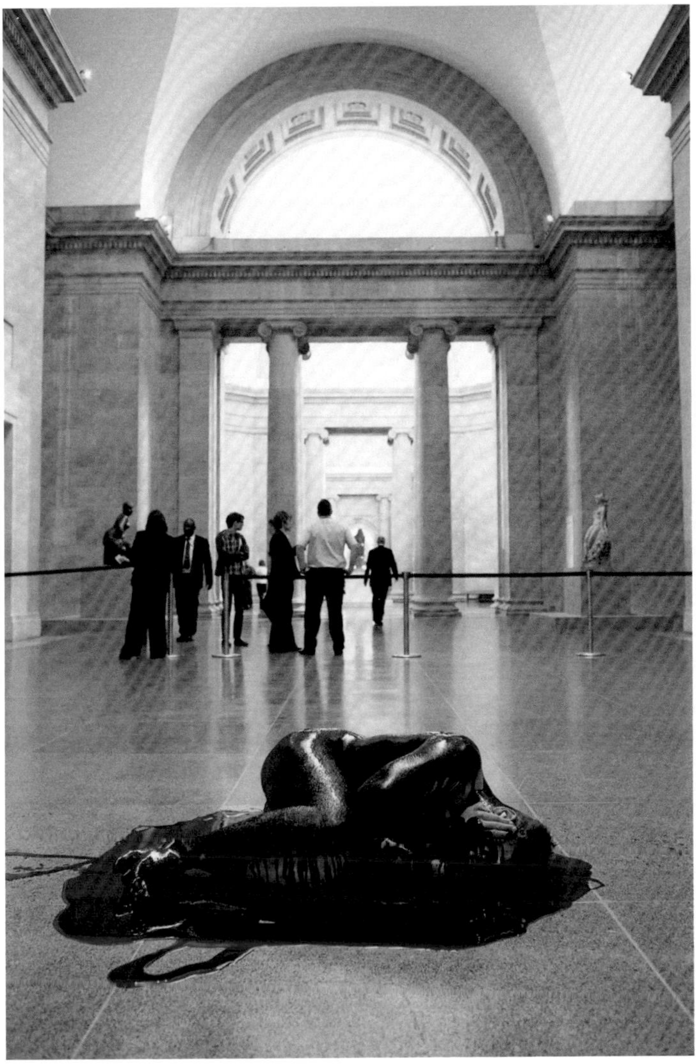

Figure 6.1
Human Cost, Liberate Tate action, Tate Britain Museum, April 2011.

statements about climate change).[3] Such worries have been at the forefront of a large number of recent actions staged by groups such as Liberate Tate, Not An Alternative, Art Not Oil, Platform London, End Oil-Sponsorship of the Arts, Concerned Artists Norway, G.U.L.F. (Global Ultra Luxury Faction), Occupy Museums, Guerrilla Girls, People's Climate Arts, The Yes Lab, Peng Collective, and many others. In recent years, BP's sponsorship of the Tate galleries, Shell's funding of the Southbank Centre, David Koch's sponsorship of the Metropolitan Museum, Shell, BP, and Statoil's sponsorship of the Science Museum (UK), and many others have come under attack.[4] Such interventions into the cultural world, and particularly demonstrations at popular museums, have become an important tool for activist groups in urban centres to draw attention to and work against the unfathomable impact of pollution and climate change.

Oil, gas, mining, and forestry companies are deeply interwoven in the Canadian cultural scene. In fact, a quick overview of large-scale Canadian museums and galleries shows that almost all of them have received operational or exhibition funding from the energy sector.[5] It is a situation seemingly ripe for resistance, particularly given the global growth in protest movements targeting museums since 2010. And yet no such movement has emerged. It was not until 2017 that a series of powerful demonstrations were staged against a museum based on sponsorship and oil/climate change (at the Canadian Museum of History [CMH]). The central question of this chapter is, why not? Why has art activism at museums against oil sponsorships *not* been a common strategy for anti-pipeline and environmental activists in Canada?

To get at why this is the case, I look first to what is happening elsewhere, offering a brief overview of recent interventions into fossil fuel company–sponsored museums, showing how they have become a key site of divestment strategies in the UK and, to a lesser extent, in the United States. I then turn to the few Canadian examples, noting the major historical precedent for large-scale action in 1988–89 against Shell Oil's sponsorship of *Spirit Sings: Artistic Traditions of Canada's First Peoples* at the Glenbow Museum in Calgary but also the lack of more recent events.[6] What has changed?

I argue that, paradoxically, a certain distance from an oil economy is an important component of the creative anti-sponsorship strategies of museum activists. The constant reiteration of an unbreakable connection between extraction and economy in Canada, made by politicians of every stripe and largely accepted by many citizens, makes the organization of protests a weighted undertaking. But more important, the leadership of Indigenous peoples as water and land protectors has developed through other means – blockades, court battles, education, dance circles, and other encounters.[7] Museums, though present, are just one more location among many and often are already perceived as tied up in the colonial apparatus that has led to oil extraction in the first place. This latter point prompts questions that admittedly I struggle with: Given that Indigenous water and land protectors largely take the lead and bear the brunt of violent crackdowns by security forces protecting the energy sector (both physically and symbolically), are calls for museums to refuse energy sector sponsorships simply elitist and largely ineffective? If such actions were to suddenly appear in Canada, how would they acknowledge the links between resource extraction, land, and ongoing settler colonization? Are the dismissals of Liberate Tate and others as "mistargeted, misconceived and massively self-indulgent" valid?[8] Or are activists in Canada missing an important opportunity? After grappling with these questions, I conclude this chapter at the CMH, looking at a series of actions and interventions, among them a protest movement led by academics, a performance by the environmental group 350.org, and a copper shaming ceremony led by artist and Hereditary Chief Beau Dick (Kwakwaka'wakw) that both echo and are utterly distinct from the actions taking place at institutions in the UK and US (and elsewhere). Ultimately, I celebrate the growth and importance of what Paula Serafini calls "art activism," but I suggest that in Canada museums and culture *cannot* be the main focus (although they certainly could be *a* focus) for successful and long-term strategies of anti-oil campaigns.[9]

Museum Protests outside Canada

Since about 2010, museums have become popular targets for anti-oil actions.[10] Most of these protests have a clear message: sponsorship of museums offers key greenwashing opportunities for oil corporations, and those opportunities should be removed. Liberate Tate, one of the central groups in this movement, was established in 2010 with the goal of "free[ing] art from the grips of the oil industry through creativity."[11] They argue that "by entering into a sponsorship agreement with BP and bringing positive attention to its philanthropy, Tate is effectively cleaning up BP's image and diverting attention away from its misdeeds."[12] While their focus is specifically on oil sponsorship, Liberate Tate also draws attention to "the gradual privatization of public cultural institutions and the question of how to reclaim them from corporate power and the private sector in general."[13] Importantly, Liberate Tate's actions are not sanctioned by the museum, they are unauthorized, and while the gallery abides them, it does not commission them (unlike other protest/art hybrids that have taken place in the Tate's galleries).[14] Actions are choreographed, colourful, and often linked to exhibitions taking place at the time or to those specifically sponsored by BP. Mel Evans, writing of Liberate Tate, argues that while activist groups could take on all corporate sponsors of the arts, "the singular impacts of oil make a narrow focus on oil sponsorship both necessary and urgent."[15]

Jodi Dean, in an article about climate change protests, argues convincingly that because it is impossible to see or understand all of the causes and impacts of climate change at once, action against it must proceed from the side, through what she calls "anamorphic politics."[16] Therefore, she argues, it makes sense to target the infrastructure of climate change (pipelines) and to further produce a counter-power through multi-sited actions, including at museums.[17] Such actions, she suggests, break away from "the melancholic catastrophism" of the left and what she labels a consequent "jouissance" or joy in destruction – a kind of power that comes from knowledge of the planet's destruction coupled with an unwillingness to do anything about it.[18] She concludes, "the battle over the political arrangement of a warming planet is in part a cultural battle, a struggle over who and what determines our imagining of our future and the future of our imagining."[19]

Museums in Europe, the US, and elsewhere have seen hundreds of actions.[20] They range from the above mentioned "oil spill" at the Tate to "Birthmark," an ongoing action organized by Liberate Tate in which members of the public are tattooed with the level of atmospheric CO_2 in parts per million corresponding to the day they were born. BP or Not BP's action against BP's sponsorship of the exhibition *Sunken Cities* at the British Museum unfolded when the group "flooded" the space with "a 200-strong splashmob featuring musical mermaids, oily pirates, and a 40-foot BP kraken."[21] A few years later, activists unfurled an oil slick made from fabric that spilled down the steps in front of the Victory of Samothrace, one of the most famous sculptures at the Louvre.[22] Along these lines, one of the most innovative actions was "The Gift." On 7 July 2012, Liberate Tate donated a 1.5-ton, 16.5-metre-long wind turbine blade to the Tate Modern as a gift to the British nation. The gift included documentation of a performance that began in front of St Paul's cathedral and concluded in the Tate's Turbine Hall as well as a letter requesting that the work be considered for inclusion in the Tate's permanent collection. By declaring the intervention a gift, the action instigated Section 7 of

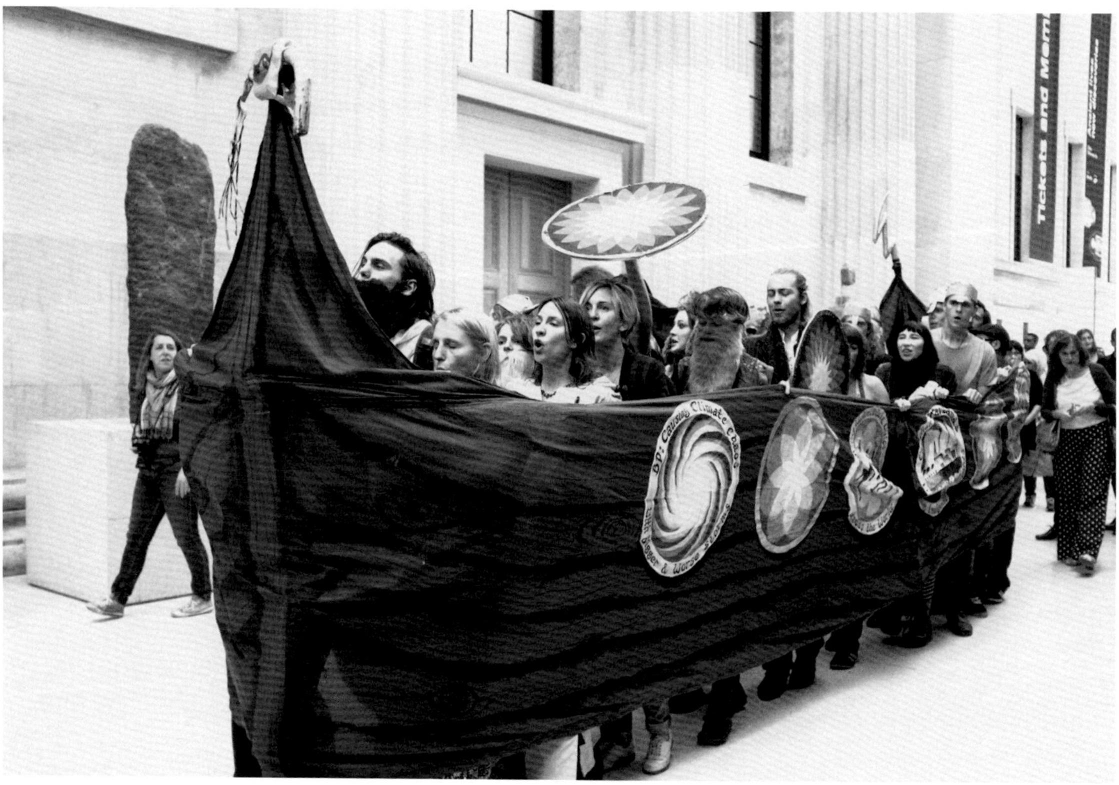

Figure 6.2
BP or Not BP Viking Longship action (Performance 11) at the British Museum, 15 June 2014.

the Museum and Galleries Act of 1992, meaning the Tate Board of Governors was legally obliged to consider and discuss whether to accept the donation.[23] Thus, the action forced board members, at least indirectly, to discuss clean energy and BP's sponsorship. Although Tate did not accession the turbine blade, the museum placed the documentation into their archive, a rare instance of a museum documenting an action against it (see chapter 3).[24]

In the case of "The Gift" and many other actions, Tate and other cultural institutions have responded with a mixture of pushback and acceptance. The interventions are typically allowed to proceed unscathed, but most institutions also vigorously defend their sponsors.[25] For example, Tate worked very hard to keep secret the amount of money that BP donated, and when the relatively small sum was revealed, some interesting questions followed. If the amount was so miniscule, then why was the Tate unwilling to look elsewhere to make up the potential gap that refusal would create? Certainly the museum would not cease operation without BP's meagre contribution.[26]

If such actions started to intensify in the UK around 2010, it was almost five years later that similar events picked up steam in the United States.[27] In April 2015, members of Occupy Museums and Occupy the Pipeline gathered with others to draw attention to the fact that the new location of the Whitney Museum of American Art lies atop the Spectra Energy fracked gas pipeline.[28] The same year, Gulf Labor protested labour conditions at the Guggenheim Museum's expansion in Abu Dhabi.[29] In September 2016, protests broke out over a new plaza at the Metropolitan Museum of Art in New York, which was funded by a $65 million donation from the billionaire David Koch, one of the libertarian family members behind Koch Industries and its massive oil infrastructure holdings (including those in the Alberta tar sands). Members of the activist art group the Illuminator were arrested for projecting the words "Koch = climate chaos" on the side of the museum.[30] Almost simultaneously, the consortium Not An Alternative released an open letter signed by dozens of the world's top scientists, including several Nobel laureates, calling on museums of science and natural history to cut all ties to the fossil fuel industry.[31]

For the most part, actions of this kind are colourful, overtly theatrical, and participatory. They draw in members of the public, asking them to think deeply about what oil company sponsorship of public institutions might mean. Serafini, for example, quotes a member of the BP or Not BP choir stating that singing can ease tension, that members of the choir were seldom arrested, but that their message had more impact than "shouting."[32] There is a clear link between groups like Liberate Tate and the early 2000s anarchic street performances of Ya Basta! The Clandestine Insurgent Rebel Clown Army, the Pink Bloc, and others.[33] As Emma Mahony notes, "Liberate Tate's interventions create temporary counter-public spheres that explode

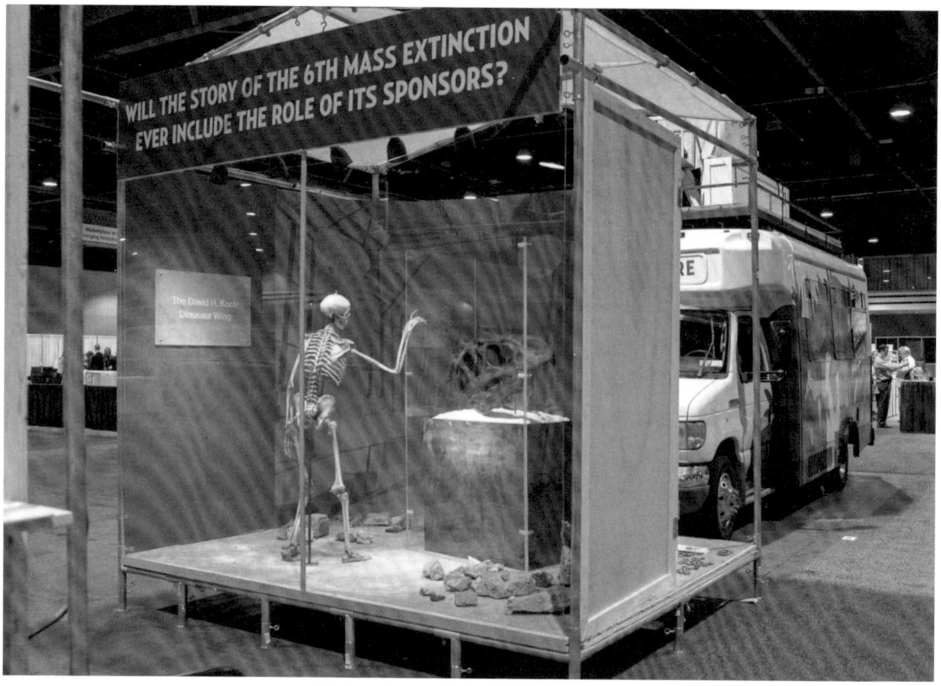

Figure 6.3
Not An Alternative, The Natural History Museum, occupation of American Alliance of Museums, Atlanta, 2015.

the consensus that surrounds the acceptability of corporate sponsorship for cultural institutions," employing language similar to that used to describe the "temporary autonomous zones" created at alterglobalization protests by the groups mentioned above.[34] Influences on theatrical anti-oil performances come from other directions as well. In the UK, many of those participating in the actions are themselves artists who combine activism and art in a manner that owes much to 1960s Happenings, Fluxus, institutional critique, and other avant-garde movements whose works are now housed in the Tate (and elsewhere). The protection of and indeed expectation that culture should be publicly funded is of fundamental importance in UK actions, though this is less so in the United States. In the US, actions followed in the wake of Occupy and have a distinctly less playful feel, a result perhaps of the fact that security and police crackdowns on actions at US museums are much fiercer and often result in arrest (and include the liberal use of pepper spray and intimidation).

Taking a somewhat different approach from the boisterous interventions in the UK, US group Not An Alternative is now well known for its creation of the Natural History Museum, a portable glass display case/museum shown at a number of locations, including the American Alliance of Museums conference, a key gathering place for museum professionals. The portable museum echoes the display tactics of traditional natural history museums but showcases what the world might look like if oil extraction is allowed to continue unfettered.[35] Like the Shoal Lake Nation Museum of Canadian Human Rights Violations (chapter 5), the Natural History Museum uses museum display strategy against itself, staging exhibitions on fossil fuel greenwashing with the goal of encouraging museums to refuse fossil fuel funding, to remove climate change deniers and prevaricators from museum boards, and, ultimately, to revamp museums into places where the dangers of oil extraction and climate change are explored.[36]

Operating as a pop-up people's museum, the Natural History Museum offers exhibits and tours that provide a counter-narrative to the influence of the oil and gas industry on science education. The Natural History Museum, according to Jodi Dean, "also serves as a platform for political organizing, the ostensibly neutral zone of the museum turned into a base camp against the fossil fuel sector. It moves beyond participatory art's creation of experiences and valuation of participation for its own sake to the building of divisive political power."[37] The same group that organized the Natural History Museum, Not An Alternative, also released the letter mentioned above, calling on museums of science and nature to drop energy sponsorships. News of the letter appeared on the front pages of the *New York Times*, *Washington Post*, and *Los Angeles Times* and spread to publications such as the *Guardian*, *Forbes*, *Salon*, and the *Huffington Post*. A petition accompanied the letter; it was signed by more than 400,000 people and delivered to the Smithsonian Institute in Washington, demanding that the museum remove David Koch from its board.[38] Writes Dean: "Just as the museum is a site in the infrastructure of capitalist class power – with its donors and galas and named halls – so can it be a medium in the production of a counterpower infrastructure that challenges, shames, and dismantles the very class and sector that would use what is common for private benefit."[39]

In short, museums, and particularly authoritative museums, are key nodes for action precisely because they are one of the few sites where the public and the oil executives cross paths (however tangentially). Further, the history of museums as sites for questioning, learning, and knowledge-seeking makes them suitable spaces for imagining different worlds and countering the seeming inevitability of climate change and planetary destruction.

In the following section, I turn to Canadian museums, but first I point out that Canadian and Indigenous groups, artists, and causes are intimately tied up in the actions in the UK and US. In 2009, the Indigenous Environmental Network led by Clayton Thomas-Muller (Mathais Colomb Cree Nation) joined members of the Lubicon Cree and Athabasca Chipewyan First Nation to take part in a series of activist events, among them the Camp for Climate Action. There they worked with

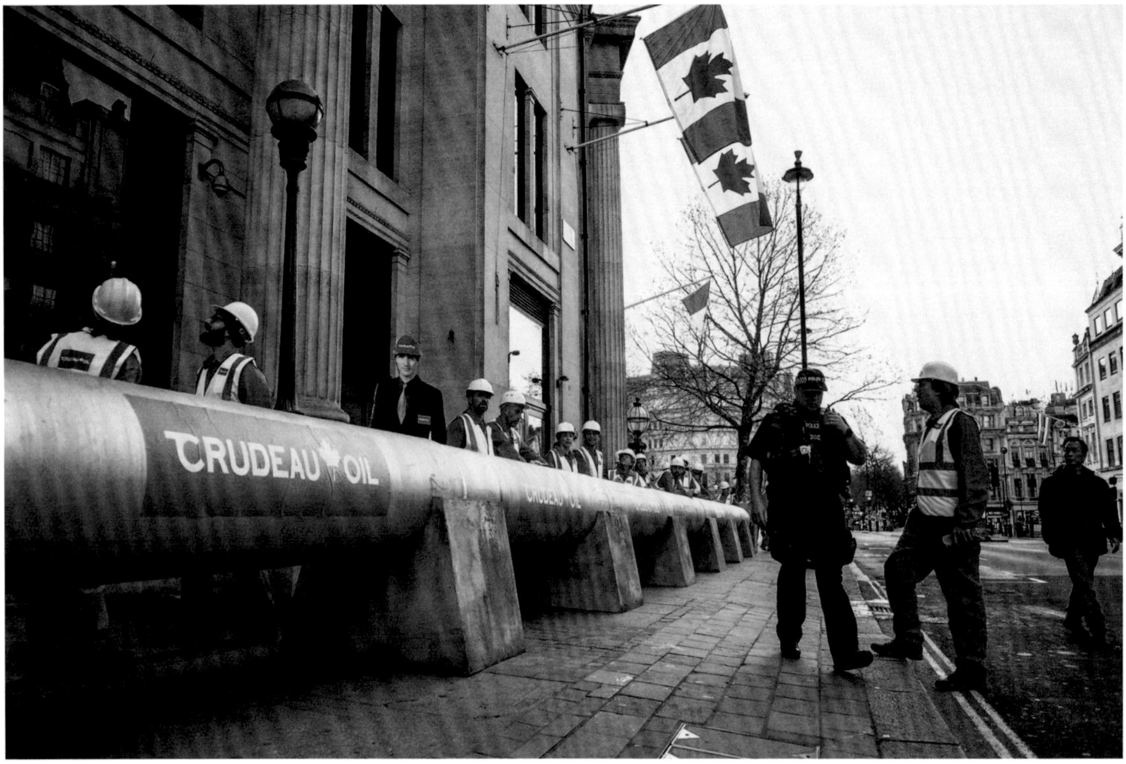

Figure 6.4
Greenpeace, Crudeau Oil Action in London, 18 April 2018.

members of Liberate Tate, Platform, and the UK Tar Sands Network to organize a protest march from Canada House in Trafalgar Square to BP headquarters (where activists glued themselves to the windows).[40] When a year later BP entered the tar sands market by investing in the Sunrise Project, Platform and Liberate Tate organized, and from that point action against the tar sands in Europe and the UK has been common, including the Yes Men intervention discussed in Interstice 6f.[41] In 2018, Canada House was targeted again during a visit to London by Prime Minister Justin Trudeau, this time by Greenpeace, which hung banners and surrounded the building in a handmade "Crudeau pipeline."[42] Further, when Norwegian company Statoil invested in the tar sands, a number of British and Norwegian artists withdrew from the Bergen International Festival in 2013, an event Statoil sponsored.[43] In April of that year, 274 Norwegian authors signed a petition stating that Statoil must withdraw from Canada's tar sands. "It is embarrassing for Norway," they stated in a national Norwegian newspaper.[44]

While acknowledging the importance of such actions, I wish nevertheless to give some space to critiques in order to think through the lack of similar movements and actions at Canadian museums. First, the targeting of museums comes from a specific place and is important to many, but not all, communities. Bluntly stated, does Imperial Oil's sponsorship of an exhibition in Ottawa matter if the more urgent goal is to stop tankers from passing through the ecologically fragile passage at Kitimat, British Columbia? Were an art activism movement to emerge in Canada, would its message be the same, or do different understandings of the role played by culture and by land influence the way that protests might unfold and be interpreted? In Canada, it is always necessary to ask: whose land, air, and water is most in danger from resource extraction?[45] Thus, is the role of artists within these movements overly determined such that the protection of art, and the demise of a sponsorship culture, become goals in and of themselves, outside of or separate from environmental protection? (I think not, but I ask the question regardless).[46] Are museums too "safe" in comparison to shutting down pipelines, activists chaining themselves to equipment, or otherwise engaging in direct action? As Liberate Tate and others have acknowledged, there is privilege that accrues to the fact that the group is primarily made up of white activists (something that is true of the wider environmental movement in the UK).[47] I suspect that museum-based actions tap into the joy of the tear gas epiphany, typically without the threat of actual tear gas or arrest. Therefore, how can we make space for multiple kinds of actions that intersect with one another, all moving toward a similar goal? How can we understand the role of museums as both educators and recipients of funding, and how can we hold both artistic intervention of the kind undertaken by Liberate Tate and other actions together such that multi-sited intervention becomes the norm?

Canadian Museums, Oil, and Activism

It is often forgotten that one of the most significant protests directed against a Canadian museum exhibition was also a protest over oil extraction on unceded territory. Although the 1988 protests against the exhibition *Spirit Sings* at the Glenbow Museum in Calgary have already been analyzed in this book as the catalyst for changing museum policy toward treatment of Indigenous belongings, the inclusion of Indigenous perspectives, and the employment of Indigenous curators, the action specifically targeted Shell Canada Ltd, the principle corporate sponsor of the exhibition (contributing $1.1 million to the $2.6 million budget), which was then drilling on Crown lands that were part of the (traditional) territories of the Lubicon Cree.[48] The Shell sponsorship was at that point the largest sponsorship that had ever been given to an exhibition in Canada.[49] At the time the exhibition opened, the Lubicon Cree had been lobbying for decades to negotiate treaty rights and land claims with provincial and federal governments because they had been left out of the negotiations that led to the signing of Treaty 8 in 1899.[50] Nevertheless, *only* changes to museum policy resulted from *Spirit Sings*. Until 2018, the Lubicon Lake land claim remained unresolved.[51]

Writing in 1987 as the protest was unfolding, Jean Fisher clearly positions the Lubicon land claim first, noting how government intervention from the early 1970s on had opened Lubicon land to oil and gas exploration.[52] In 1973, the Alberta government began construction of a road into Lubicon land. Quoting *Quid Novi*, the McGill University Faculty of Law journal, Fisher notes that

> the Lubicon, clearly alarmed about the influx of outsiders, filed a caveat with the province to give notice to these outsiders that the Cree retained unabrogated aboriginal title to their traditional lands. The province asked the court to postpone hearing the case, while relevant provincial legislation was written, retroactive to before the Indian caveat was filed, which effectively dismissed the Indian action as no longer having any basis in law. Dozens of multi-national oil companies moved in force into the area and deliberately sought to undermine the traditional economy.[53]

Although the language used in 1987 is different from that of today, Fisher clearly shows how the incursion of oil and natural resource exploration and extraction undermined First Nations lifeways and traditional knowledges, leading to massively increased poverty and poor health outcomes.[54] And yet, in the *Report on Business Magazine* in 1987, Shell Canada advertised with regard to *Spirit Sings*, "Just as the discovery and development of Canada's natural resources are at the heart of Shell's business activity, the discovery and development of Canada's cultural richness and diversity are at the heart of our community investment program."[55] Also writing in 1987, Fisher sees no way out and suggests that museums would and will be unable to "face the fact of white perversion of the law and its contempt for human rights."[56] The Glenbow's Julia Harrison, writing in the same year, argued: "If museums allowed themselves to be taken political hostage we would sell ourselves down the river. We would become a political forum. The only thing that's going to ensure our survival is to remain as apolitical as possible."[57] Fisher nicely tackles this comment by saying, "there is a lack of insight here into the distinction between the representation of politics and the politics of representation."[58]

Since *Spirit Sings*, oil sponsorship of culture has not abated. But the attempt by the Lubicon to organize a boycott of the Glenbow exhibition remains the sole major action against a museum accepting funding from a fossil fuel company. The lack of an organized movement against oil sponsorship in Canada suggests a couple of possibilities: first, that action is taking place elsewhere (true); and second, that oil, gas, mining, and other resource corporations are not heavily involved in sponsoring Canadian culture (false). I argue in this section that Canadian-based resource companies benefit from a suturing of Canadian culture and resource extraction, and oil companies, both Canadian-based and international, have proceeded largely unscathed in the cultural sector, easily attaining a "social license to operate" – a term Liberate Tate borrows from the business world to characterize the way oil companies gain and maintain support for what they do.[59]

Led by Enbridge Inc., EnCana Corporation, Syncrude Canada Ltd, and the Canadian Association of Petroleum Producers (CAPP), oil sponsorships cluster in Alberta and Ottawa (although they are present in almost all major and many small institutions). Just a few examples include the Syncrude Gallery of Aboriginal Culture at the Royal Alberta Museum and Enbridge's 2013 partnership with the Montreal Museum of Fine Arts to cover transportation and admission charges to the museum for families facing economic barriers.[60] In Alberta, Enbridge has long partnered with the Art Gallery of Alberta, as well as the Alberta Theatre Projects, Theatre Calgary, Calgary Opera, and Alberta Ballet. Enbridge also gives money to the National Theatre School of Canada in Montreal and contributes to *The Walrus* magazine and the Walrus Talks lecture series. In 2014, Enbridge presented the 2014 Governor General's Performing Arts Awards Gala.[61] A spokesperson for the company noted on that occasion that "our investment in arts and culture has gone a long way to helping establish our organization as a Canadian leader in recognizing the importance of Canadian artists and their art."[62] Suncor, meanwhile, sponsors the Oil Sands Discovery Centre in Fort McMurray (site of the tar sands).
The Suncor Energy Foundation provided $50,000 in matching donations for artists and arts organizations affected by floods in 2013.[63] International companies also participate. Statoil (Norway), a company with a vaunted art collection of its own, has offices in Calgary and has staged a number of exhibitions there while also sponsoring the Calgary Stampede. The Chinese National Offshore Oil Corporation (CNOOC) supports the University of Alberta Museum and the Calgary Central Library and sponsored the *Forbidden City* exhibition at the Vancouver Art Gallery in 2014–15.[64] This is just a tiny sample of the numerous instances of energy sector sponsorship of the arts, which is nearly ubiquitous in Canada. In short, right across Canada, the most cutting-edge and critical culture, as well as the most parochial and nationalistic, is often subtended by oil money. The depth and breadth of sponsorship suggests that many cultural events would collapse were it not for the energy sector.

What, really, is at stake here? As Karen Wall notes, private and public sponsorships have supported culture in Alberta over the long term, "helping to shape a rich community capacity for critical thought and expression. However, the ongoing loss of public funding for cultural production at both federal and provincial levels, coinciding with steady surges of taxpayer-funded oil industry promotional materials, suggests that this potential wealth of voices is becoming increasingly muffled."[65] Wall argues that Alberta is a petro-state wherein the cultural imaginary is actively shaped by state and corporate interests and "the impacts of oil on democratic society are usually sufficiently normalized as to be hidden in plain sight."[66] She concludes by asking, "What political and economic relations rule the distribution of public funds to the creation of culture?"[67] Can resistance be corporately funded? Or is the status quo where it's at?

Judging from the promotional material produced by the largest energy companies in Canada, these corporations are extremely responsible citizens, benignly contributing to a variety of causes, supporting culture with no strings attached, while oil extraction is an environmentally friendly pursuit, providing jobs and stabilizing the Canadian economy as the companies work hard toward reconciliation with Indigenous communities, helping to overcome the difficulties of Canada's divisive past. This messaging is often picked up by politicians, the public, and the mainstream media so that the bonds between "license to operate" and actual contributions to the cultural scene in Canada are difficult to tease apart. Oil companies are among the top collectors of contemporary (settler and Indigenous) art in Canada.[68] In 2000, Petro-Canada gave away most of its private collection, donating almost 1,000 works of art (many of them by First Nations artists) to public collections.[69] Wall points out that one reason oil companies purchase critical art is because it "aligns with narratives of the sponsors' creative innovation and unbiased social responsibility."[70] Oil companies are deeply interested in sponsoring Indigenous cultural and other initiatives, investing in scholarships for universities, youth writing programs, arts projects, exhibitions, and numerous other initiatives aimed rather transparently at gaining the support of First Nations peoples for oil exploration and development. But as S wxwú7mesh community organizer Khelsilem Rivers writes about an oil company–sponsored reconciliation event in Vancouver:

> To accept and use money from these companies is outrageous. It is an obvious contradiction: How can the organizers promote reconciliation while giving Big Oil companies a pass when those same companies are directly involved in damaging Indigenous ways of life? This was the exact purpose of Residential Schools. The Residential School system had sought (among many things) to displace Indigenous peoples from our homelands; yet again, these companies are seeking to displace our peoples from our homelands to reap the benefit at our expense.[71]

Indeed, even outside of the issue of land exploitation, corporate funding is a fickle friend. In 2008, Syncrude abruptly ended its arts funding in Edmonton. Relatedly, after the deaths of hundreds of ducks in one of its tailings ponds received significant media coverage in Canada and abroad, Syncrude abruptly moved its funding from the arts to environmental research and conservation causes. Epcor and Enbridge then stepped in to sponsor Syncrude's abandoned arts groups, and Imperial Oil made an unprecedented donation of $300,000 to the Art Gallery of Alberta. However, Epcor ended its agreement with Calgary's Epcor Centre in 2010. When provincial government funding was withdrawn in 2013, the performing arts facility fell into a critical financial deficit.[72] The presence of energy sector funding is so normalized, but simultaneously its capriciousness so expected, that there is usually little outcry when the flow stops. On the other hand, when there is critique, companies are quick to answer back.

In 2011, artists from Manitoba and Saskatchewan asked the National Arts Centre to reconsider Enbridge's sponsorship of a showcase of music and art from the prairies (Enbridge had already sponsored four previous festivals, none of which had aroused ire).[73] The National Arts Centre refused the request, and Jennifer Varey, an Enbridge spokesperson, said in a written statement that "well-funded and well-organized environmental groups are behind a targeted movement by a small group of artists that seek to undermine the funding that supports hundreds of Canadian artists in communities across Canada." She continued, "Our sponsorships are rooted in our strongly held belief that arts and culture are critical to the health and vitality of communities."[74] Varey's claim that it was not really artists but rather "well-funded and well-organized" environmental groups staging the 2011 complaint speaks both to the way anti-oil activism is repeatedly disavowed in Canada and to the way that artists have not been visibly involved in many anti-oil campaigns.

In contrast to Varey's claims of benign sponsorship, accusations made by Liberate Tate and others that companies may intervene in museum policy (assertions that are vigorously denied by Tate and other institutions) are evident in Canada. In 2011, according to Wall, a newly designed wing of the Art Gallery of Alberta was purposely used "to ameliorate oil industry partnerships," primarily by encouraging wealthy collectors with ties to the global fossil fuel industry to show their collections.[75] A show at Calgary City Hall in March 2013 had its permit revoked when city officials decided that it was "too political."[76] Organized to protest the Northern Gateway pipeline project and titled *Art for an Oil-Free Coast*, the exhibition was shut down, ostensibly because of a bylaw that prevented selling items or demonstrating on City of Calgary property.

Another prime example took place in December 2011. In that month, almost two years after the founding of Liberate Tate, *Le Devoir* and *Maclean's* magazine focused their attention on sponsorship of the exhibition *Energy: Power to Choose* at the Canadian Science and Technology Museum (CSTM) in Ottawa.[77] Environmental groups such as the Sierra Club had written to the museum to draw attention to the energy sector's sponsorship of the exhibition, but the institution claimed that "the final decision about what would be presented was up to the museum."[78] In fact, the CSTM's vice-president replied to the Sierra Club, arguing, "We have the character to stand up for the independence of our editorial content and rest assured that it is and will be fiercely defended."[79] Nevertheless, through an access to information request, reporters for *Maclean's* magazine found documents showing "what appears to have been pervasive influence from the energy sector in shaping the exhibition's content." According to the reporters, during the planning stage an interpreter working on the exhibition wrote to the museum corporation's director of sponsorship sales, telling him that oil industry involvement was necessary. "I think this is a 'good news' oil sand story that we would like to tell, but we really need the assistance of [the Canadian Association of Petroleum Producers], the Govt. of Alberta, or one of the oil companies."[80] An initial invitation from the museum to possible sponsors noted: "Your version of the facts will be part of a balanced approach in order to bring information and perspective to the public that it is not possible to provide through the traditional media filters."[81] Eventually, CAPP donated $50,000 to the museum, and EnCana and Imperial Oil also signed on as sponsors.[82]

While invitation letters might be tailored for specific sponsors, the documents received through access to information do suggest further intervention. The exhibition included information on oil, nuclear energy, wind, and solar power. It also clearly noted environmental concerns, though they were coupled with the following statement: "The oil sands industry takes these challenges very seriously and is working to find solutions."[83] Climate change was briefly mentioned in the exhibition but only in terms of the small contribution made by the oil sands to overall global emissions. When asked about the statistic used in the exhibition (oil sands account for one-tenth of 1 per cent of global emissions), curator Anna Adamek said on CBC Ottawa radio, "This fact comes from research reports that are available at the museum, that were commissioned by the museum." But a CBC News story showed that the commissioned reports came from Imperial Oil and that Imperial Oil Foundation president Susan Swan had sent an email to the museum recommending that the statistic be included, along with information on the oil sands' contribution to the Canadian economy.[84]

When the museum asked sponsors to review and make recommendations for the exhibition, Imperial Oil responded in detail. Though primarily concerned with factual information (e.g., asking that "easy oil" be re-termed "conventional oil" and pointing out sources for the amount of oil held in Venezuela's and Canada's oil reserves), there is editorializing throughout. The writer comments on a "War and Oil" panel that "Producing less oil won't stop wars ... In fact, oil is the most consumed energy source in the world because of the value and benefits it provides."[85] A panel titled "Oil Junkies" is dismissed as "pejorative and not balanced. This has to be removed and rewritten."[86] Throughout its feedback, Imperial Oil accused the museum of "only telling half the story," of, for example, showing strip mining in the tar sands but not showing reclaimed land.[87] Through four pages of criticisms, the company called the museum to task for including information that in its view did not portray the oil sands in the best light. *Le Devoir* reported that CAPP was also not entirely happy with the exhibition and asked that certain images be removed or replaced. *Maclean's* noted that a giant tire from a mining truck was removed from the exhibition at "some oil industry official's" request.[88] The problem, apparently, was that environmental groups often use images of the giant trucks to denounce the industry. The museum complied.[89] In short, it must have been difficult for curators to sort through the recommendations, deciding what was propaganda and what was fact. Not surprisingly, following this process the museum felt that it had done due diligence in resisting influence from sponsors. *Maclean's* and *Le Devoir* disagreed, and although the story gained some traction, there were few ripples.

While the interventions at the CSTM may seem relatively minor (removing some photos of the oil industry and replacing them with others and following some recommendations from Imperial Oil but not others), these actions were undertaken alongside the museum's already apparent willingness to create "a good news story" that encouraged CAPP and other oil companies to sponsor the exhibition. Further, the museum's actions clearly show that sponsors were given the chance to respond to and potentially alter the exhibition.[90]

Intervention was also an issue in a $2 million grant from Talisman Energy Inc. that led to the new Talisman Fossil Gallery in the Canadian Museum of Nature[91] and Barrick Gold Corp.'s contribution of $450,000 toward the new permanent exhibit on mining and minerals that opened in 2012 at the same institution.[92] In both cases, the companies claimed they had not intervened in the exhibition, though neither display addressed the labour, environmental, and human rights abuses associated with international mining. In Barrick's case, the opening was accompanied by a small demonstration during which members of Mining Watch opened *The People's Exhibition of Barrick* anti-museum.[93] The anti-museum included exhibits on Barrick's mining practices around the world and representations from groups such as Mining Watch Canada, Protestbarrick.net, the Diaguita Huascoaltinos Indigenous and Agricultural Community, and the Archuar Indigenous Community.

In 2013, protesters from the Council of Canadians, Ecology Ottawa, and the Polaris Institute briefly targeted CAPP's sponsorship of the CMC/CMH. A snowman holding a sign reading "CAPP pollutes snow" appeared outside the museum, drawing attention to CAPP's $1 million contribution to the museum. The organizations argued that "while CAPP includes tar sands producers that literally pollute snow, air and waterways in Alberta, increased corporate sponsorship threatens to pollute precious cultural institutions like the Canadian Museum of Civilization."[94] Though this intervention only attracted a few people and quickly dissipated, it fed into a larger action that took place at the CMC/CMH in 2017, which I discuss below. Finally, in 2014 Rights Action organized a protest against Hudbay Minerals, a Canadian mining corporation accused of perpetrating or ignoring major human rights abuses, and its sponsorship of the Canadian Museum for Human Rights.[95]

It's safe to say, then, that oil, mining, and other resource extraction companies are heavily involved in sponsoring cultural events, awards, programs, exhibitions, and museums in Canada. Some of these sponsorships meet with small demonstrations, but none of these actions comes close to the efforts of Liberate Tate, Art Not Oil, or Not An Alternative.[96] Typically, they are organized by NGOs who are advocating for alternatives to fossil fuel use in multiple venues and across broad constituencies. In short, the kind of art activism employing theatrical intervention that gained strength in the UK and Europe and to a lesser extent in the US and elsewhere is not present in Canada.

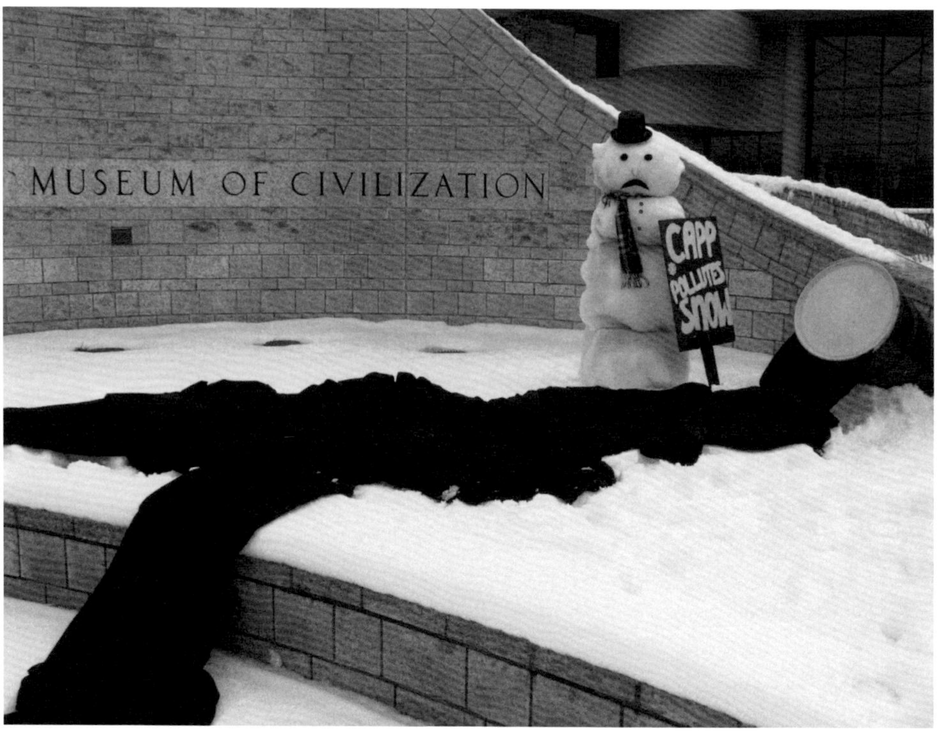

Figure 6.5
Council of Canadians, "CAPP Pollutes Snow," Snowperson protesting Canadian Association of Petroleum Producers (CAPP) sponsoring the Museum of Civilization's snow exhibit.

Though there are many possible reasons for the limited nature of opposition in Canada, a key factor is the extent to which such sponsorships (and sponsors) have been normalized. In Canada, oil *is* culture. By the early 2000s, Canada's economy was imagined as an oil-based one. The emergence of what Sheena Wilson, Adam Carlson, and Imre Szeman term a "petroculture" took place across the social sphere but also in and through museums and cultural events.[97] Furthermore, I suggest below that the equation of oil and culture in Canada actually makes museums a *less* enticing venue for activism. To invoke Jodi Dean again, perhaps an anamorphic politics doesn't quite work in Canada where the links among oil, land, and culture force more straightforward confrontations.

Oil as Culture

In the summer of 2006, during a visit to Washington, DC, to discuss energy policy, then–Alberta Premier Ralph Klein presented an oil truck (the same kind of truck depicted in the images that CAPP asked to have removed from the *Energy: Power to Choose* exhibition) to the Smithsonian as a part of Alberta's contribution to the museum's annual Folklife Festival.[98] For several weeks in the middle of an atypically hot, wet, and humid summer on the US east coast (possibly the result of climate change), Alberta's culture was represented on the Washington Mall by a dump truck with eighteen-foot-high tires. The festival drew thousands of visitors to a pancake breakfast, a display of First Nations dance, storytelling, and a drama troupe, as well as activities that gave visitors a chance to dig for dinosaur bones, wear a Stetson, hear about Alberta beef, join in a line dance, view works donated by the Alberta Crafts Council, and learn about the black gold of the tar sands.[99]

Klein was on an expedition to educate the American government and populace about Alberta oil, and the exhibition at the Smithsonian was an extension of his project.[100] Asked about the $38 million cost of transporting the truck (and the rest of the exhibition) to Washington, Alberta's then minister of intergovernmental affairs Gary Mar completely overlooked the fact that the festival was not about gaining market share but rather about sharing the folkloric culture of the participating regions:[101] "It will be worth the cost if it furthers Alberta's influence in the US capital."[102] Coverage of the festival in Canada repeatedly referenced the statistic that in 2006 only 4 per cent of the American population knew that Canada was their number one supplier of oil.[103] Indeed, it was only in 2006 that Canada made the list of the world's top ten oil producers before moving into the top five in 2014.[104]

Nancy Groce, curator of the Alberta program at the Smithsonian, took a different approach to criticisms of the cost of the exhibition. She noted in contrast to Mar that "the truck is not here as a truck. The truck is to highlight the oil-sands workers who are coming. This is not an ad for the oil industry nor is it an ad for the maker of the truck. It's about the impact that that industry is having on the workers and the people of Alberta."[105] Groce was clear in her statement that the Smithsonian received "no direct money from the oil companies."[106] Oil companies were, however, deeply involved in sponsoring events around the Smithsonian's exhibition. The province arranged for sponsorships from companies including EnCana, Suncor, Conoco Phillips, and Petro-Canada to help defray the cost of forums on technology, energy, and agriculture, a gala with the Edmonton Symphony Orchestra, a reception involving Alberta universities, and a Canada Day pancake breakfast.[107]

The 2006 Smithsonian festival was one gesture in a much wider program to push the relationship between oil and culture in Alberta and more broadly in Canada. As Karen Wall notes, "In Alberta ... the petroleum industry is deeply infused into the social and cultural imaginaries, oil and provincial governments have together shaped discourses of prosperity, identity, and citizenship for generations."[108] If Canada could be a Warrior Nation when the new CWM was built and while soldiers were stationed in Afghanistan and a Peacekeeper Nation promoting human rights when the CMHR was established, it could certainly be an Energy Nation as debate over the tar sands heated up. By the mid-to-late 2000s, a powerful narrative was coalescing around the importance of oil to the Canadian economy, first in Alberta before expanding to the rest of the country with the election of Stephen Harper as prime minister in 2006. Internationally, Canada has since that year billed itself as what might be called an anti-environment environmentalist, coupling its natural resources to economic expansion and positioning its oil as less politically volatile than oil from the Middle East, Africa, or South America (in fact, the Canada as oil narrative maps nicely onto the Canada as Peacekeeper narrative). While this narrative is fraying as I finish this book in 2017, it reached its height in the first decade of the 2000s. When the dump truck decorated the Washington Mall, the tar sands were still a relatively unknown entity. Though there was pushback against the Smithsonian exhibition, a few years would pass before the combination of bitumen from the tar sands and the pipelines that carry it to market became the anamorphic focus of many activist groups.

Tar sands development is relatively new. Suncor opened the first mine on the Athabasca River in northern Alberta in 1967, with other companies following in the 1970s. Investment and exploration grew through the 1990s, reaching full throttle in the early 2000s as global oil prices rose, making the capital-intensive process of separating oil from sand economically viable. Increased extraction from the tar sands maps onto growing concerns about climate change and pollution and a move in environmental activism away from the extremely visible anti-logging protests of the 1980s and 1990s toward the harder-to-quantify and heavily policed climate change protests of the 2000s. Although, as noted in the CSTM's controversial exhibition, the oil sands only contribute a small percentage of global CO_2 emissions, the devastation left in the wake of pit mining and other unconventional oil extraction methods and the vast amounts of energy and water required to convert bitumen to oil and then to refine and ship that oil around the world are, for many, too high a price to pay.[109] More recently, activists have focused their attention on massive pipeline projects proposed to transport tar sands oil to new and expanding markets in Asia and the US as visible and easily targeted manifestations of the oil industry.[110]

The infrastructure of oil in Canada is everywhere though often hidden. Strolling through suburban Burnaby, British Columbia, one feels about as far removed from the tar sands as it is possible to get, except for the signs everywhere announcing the TransMountain pipeline running under foot through carefully groomed backyards and leafy parks. Residents of Windsor, Ontario, can see mountains of pet-coke, a by-product of tar sands oil production, piling up in Detroit and a dark wind blowing across the river.[111] As I write, I sit virtually atop Enbridge's Line 9, which pumps bitumen from Sarnia to Montreal where it is exported to overseas markets. Of course, for the First Nations/Métis peoples living in the area of extraction around Fort McMurray, Alberta – among them the Mikisew Cree First Nation, the Athabasca Chipewyan First Nation, the Fort McKay First Nation, the Fort McMurray No. 468 First Nation, the Chipewyan Prairie Dene First Nation, and Métis locals – the tar sands have always been visible.[112] Protests in the period covered by this chapter have played out around four major pipeline projects: the reversal of Enbridge's Line 9, expanding Kinder Morgan's TransMountain pipeline from Alberta to Vancouver, Enbridge's Northern Gateway project that would run tankers to Kitimat, British Columbia, and especially Keystone XL, a pipeline that would take bitumen from the tar sands to refineries in Texas. But these are just the best-known projects. Even the most remote corners of Canada are connected by a tracery of oil and natural gas pipelines.

The immediate presence of oil marks a key distinction between Canada and other locations, such as New York and London. Liberate Tate activists may rightly note that

> London is one of the global centres of the oil industry. Headquartered here, BP uses the city to extract a combination of financial, political, legal and technological services that enable them to pump, transport, refine and sell oil and gas. They unfold a network of relationships between oil and gas companies and the government departments, regulators, cultural institutions, banks and other institutions that surround them. Museums are porous. This carbon web also runs through Tate.[113]

But this is a primarily immaterial web, distanced from the actual extraction and refinement of bitumen. In Canada, the relationship between production and consumption is an immediate one that affects the ways that intervention takes place.[114]

The tar sands have become a site of ideological battle, not just in Alberta but in the rest of Canada and worldwide. Activists have been immensely successful in labelling the tar sands as dirty oil. And in response, when the tar sands are targeted, an entire operation is mobilized to defend them.[115] Major tropes of the pro-oil lobby include linking oil to the overall health of the Canadian economy as a key provider of stable jobs, suturing oil and nationalism, and contrasting the so-called "ethical" and "environmental" oil being extracted in Canada with "brutal" and "dirty" regimes elsewhere.[116] These strategies, labelled "reactionary environmentalism,"[117] have been remarkably successful. In 2008, the Alberta government launched a $25 million, three-year campaign to boost the province's "brand" – in other words to improve the "idea" of the oil (not tar) sands, if not the tar sands themselves.[118] In 2010, the Alberta government paid for a series of ads to run in Times Square (New York City).[119] Over the next few years, these strategies caught on at the federal level, and eventually this kind of thinking led the government to endorse Legaloil.com, a website led by right-wing gadfly Ezra Levant that seeks to rebrand the tar sands as "ethical oil."[120] Even in the face of major spills and disasters, among them Enbridge's Line 6B, which spilled 1.1 million gallons of diluted tar sands bitumen into Michigan's Kalamazoo River, and the 2013 oil train explosion in Lac Mégantic, Quebec, which killed forty-seven and levelled most of the community's downtown, oil extraction and transport have maintained a largely positive reputation throughout Canada.

Nevertheless, Canadians are also deeply concerned about the environment and about climate change *even as* they worry about the economy and jobs and see the oil patch as providing those jobs. Oil is held in contradiction in Canada – it is both necessity and blight. Glen Coulthard (Yellowknives Dene) sums up this situation: "Canada likes to make claims that its resource base and its extractivist impulses are important because it draws our economic dependency away from more hostile places in the world: dirty oil, blood diamonds, all of these sorts of things. In doing so it tries to present the devouring of our land base here as an ethical response to hostile geopolitics."[121] He continues, "the entrenched association of the oil industry with a certain configuration of social power supports an adversarial rhetoric that posits critical analysis and challenge as being against the common good. The coincidence of government and industry interests raises questions about the limits to public political participation."[122]

I would go even further. For a time, "critical analysis and challenge" of oil extraction was scorned and action was often equated with terrorism with an ease that in retrospect seems more terrifying than perhaps it felt at the time.[123] What would eventually culminate in such extreme accusations emerged from simple logic – being worried about climate change was fine, but because Canadian oil companies were environmentally friendly, positioning oneself against oil was "anti-Canadian." And though in this chapter I associate such rational gymnastics with the Harper Conservative government, they reached their culmination in Liberal prime minister Justin Trudeau's 2016 claim that building pipelines would provide the money necessary to fund climate change solutions and a "green economy."[124]

Anna Tsing argues that the twentieth century brought with it the creation of "resource frontiers" where entrepreneurs were able to disengage "nature from local ecologies and livelihoods."[125] Natural resources were "set free" so that raw materials could be offered up to a greedy world. Often presented as "discovery," the opening up of a frontier nearly always signifies the loss of that zone to local understandings. Though Tsing works on the Indonesian rainforest, parallels are found everywhere in Canada: in the Alberta tar sands, in the Arctic, at Kitimat, in the old growth forests of the west coast, in the gypsum mines of Cape Breton, in the diamond and heavy metals mines of Ontario's "ring of fire," and everywhere on Indigenous land. Tsing argues that resource extraction is often presented as common sense when in fact its impact on the land is often experienced viscerally as tragedy by those who live there and know a place for what it once was. For example, Prime Minister Stephen Harper infamously stated in July 2007: "Canada has a choice when it comes to defending our sovereignty in the Arctic; either we use it or we lose it. And make no mistake, this government intends to use it."[126] "The Arctic is not a frontier. It is our homeland," said Nunavut premier Eva Aariak in response.[127]

On the frontier of oil extraction in Canada, a carefully rehearsed dual narrative is always present. First, extraction does violence to the land, but it is a necessary violence couched in the language of economics and nationalism and occasionally environmental protection and sustainability via remediation. Harper, for example, declared that the development of natural resources is "in the national interest" and profits from the natural resources sector are essential to the economic sustainability of Canada as a nation.[128] But as Tsing concludes, "This assault is no neighborhood storm. It gathers force from afar, entangling multiple local-to-global scales."[129] Oil is portrayed as entangled with identity and with culture, and yet that culture is created through the economic agreements that strongly privilege the global over the local and corporate gain over those (human and more-than-human[130]) living on the ground.

In trying to figure out this complicated posturing, activist journalist Naomi Klein suggests looking back to "the founding narratives of this nation," examining how the ecological limits of Europe were extended by a seemingly "bottomless treasure trove – of fish, fowl, fur, giant trees, and later metals and fossil fuels. And in

Canada, these riches covered a territory so vast, it seemed impossible to fathom its boundaries."[131] Her reworking of the "staples theory" (popular from the 1920s to the 1960s) that claims extraction commodities played a decisive role in the formation of the "institutions that defined the political trends of the nation and its regions"[132] plays up the "inexhaustible" and "infinite" wilderness bounty in Canada, which seemed endless until it wasn't. Klein concludes, "While Indigenous hunting and trapping skills were the backbone of wealth production in the early Canadian economy, Indigenous culture and relationships to the land were always a profound threat to the lust for extraction."[133] In other words, oil-as-nation is settler culture writ large, built on white supremacy, capitalism, and patriotism.[134] As Tuck and Yang note in a slightly different context, a love of the land and belonging to the land are different things, and the former enables a settler innocence that actually perpetuates the destruction of Indigenous land in the quest for profit from and control over territory.[135]

To be clear, I am not arguing that all Indigenous people are anti-oil or that all Nations are standing in the way of resource development – there are conflicts within, across, and outside of communities.[136] The point is that sovereign political status and nationhood as understood in settler terms are not reducible to one another, a point Coulthard makes when he contrasts Indigenous place-based understandings of the world with Western time-oriented (the progression of history) understandings.[137]

> Indigenous struggles against capitalist imperialism are best understood as struggles oriented around the question of land – struggles not only for land, but also deeply *informed* by what the land as a mode of reciprocal relationship … ought to teach us about living our lives in relation to one another and our surroundings in a respectful, nondominating and nonexploitative way.[138]

"Place," Coulthard concludes "is a way of knowing."[139] When writing about the relationship between oil, nation, and land, it is essential to remember these distinctions, brought home to me via Christi Belcourt's (Métis) statement at the 2017 Creative Minds symposium at the Art Gallery of Ontario: "Buffalos are nations. Birds are nations. Our [Indigenous] view of nations is so much bigger and different than to assume that humans are the only ones. Nothing needs us to survive, but we need everything else."[140]

The way nation tangles with oil is key to understanding the quashing of many Indigenous actions. But equally, sovereignty has been a central tenet of many environmental activist groups working to "save" Canada from exploitation by oil companies. Competing understandings of settler nationalism suffuse both the reactionary environmentalism of oil companies and the federal government but also the environmentalism of many mainstream activist groups. Adam Barker suggests that NGOs and left-leaning groups lend support while "reinforce[ing] other (hidden or ignored) structures of colonial power."[141] Reframing such constitutive positions proves difficult, but as Shea Murphy asks with regard to Alutiiq artist and choreographer Tanya Lukin Linklater's water performances, "Rather than talking about the ways that radical performance practices challenge or disrupt the nation state, could we think instead about what kinds of communities and political constituencies they constitute?"[142] Murphy's question unsettles the suturing of land and nation and provides a lens through which to look more closely at the knotty relationship among oil, nation, activism, and culture.[143]

Harper, Science Protests, and Idle No More

By 2012, just at the time Liberate Tate was ascending in the UK, the situation in Canada was dire. In that year, the federal government made cuts to Environment Canada, Fisheries and Oceans Canada, the National Research Council of Canada, and Statistics Canada and abolished the National Round Table on Environment and Economy. A few years earlier, the government had eliminated the office of National Science Adviser and the Law Commission of Canada. These assaults included shutting down the Experimental Lakes area (which was used to study long-term ecological change) and gutting the Navigable Waters Protection Act (which removed protections from building projects such as bridges or dams on the vast majority of Canadian lakes, rivers, and waterways).[144] One of the most visible outcomes was the closure of government-operated libraries and archives belonging to Fisheries and Oceans Canada, many of them holding important research and primary source studies documenting climate change over time.[145]

The evisceration of these entities took place as a part of a series of omnibus bills passed by Parliament, which specifically targeted those who might get in the way of the expansion of the energy sector. Bill C-45, titled the Jobs and Growth Act (2012), seriously weakened environmental protections, as noted above and, among other things, amended the Indian Act through the First Nations Property Ownership Initiative (FNPOI).[146] Reporter Christopher Hume argued that the Harper government was involved in a search-and-destroy effort that targeted the environmental movement and extended to suppressing the work of scientists. At this point, water and land protectors, big green environmentalists, and scientists were all organizing against the omnibus bills. Wrote Hume, "Ottawa has seen countless demonstrations over the decades, none more poignant or disturbing than what unfolded Tuesday when hundreds of scientists took to the street to protest what they call the Death of Evidence."[147] He continues, "Not only was the protest unprecedented, even extraordinary, it struck at the dark heart of the New Canada, a nation more interested in hiding the truth than understanding it, exploiting resources than conserving them."[148]

Though the scientists' protest achieved a great deal of publicity, it was eclipsed by the emergence of Idle No More.[149] That winter, Idle No More began when a teach-in on Bill C-45 organized by Sylvia McAdam (Cree), Jess Gordon (Cree/Anishinaabe), Nina Wilson (Nakota/Cree), and Sheelah McLean grew through social media postings under the hashtag #IdleNoMore[150] and spread into "sharing sessions, protests, blockades, and round dances in public spaces and on the land, in our homelands, and in our sacred spaces."[151] Reaching its height in early 2013, Idle No More brought Indigenous peoples together to push back against C-45 and the First Nations Property Ownership Initiative but also against settler colonialism in general.[152] As Janet Fiskio notes, the word "protest" is not appropriate here because it is not sufficient to cover the fact that many of the actions Idle No More spearheaded were not simply resistance but drew on dancing, singing, drumming, and other practices as "acts of sovereignty, cultural survival, and decolonial struggle" that "create and support Indigenous community, sovereignty, and continuance, and thus exceed the context of settler colonialism."[153] Such actions, Fiskio argues, "are constructive as well as resistance; and while they may respond to environmental racism, they are not acts of environmental activism in the popular sense."[154] The round dances performed in numerous public spaces, among them a shopping centre in Regina, Saskatchewan, the Mall of America in Minneapolis, Minnesota, Dundas Square in Toronto,[155] outside the CMHR, and inside the CMC/CMH, brought "to light the history of Indigenous resistance and resilience in the face of US and Canadian government 'attempts to control, through institutional discipline and punishment of Indian bodies, Indigenous peoples who resisted state authority by continuing to exist.'"[156]

At the same time that the government was dropping environmental protections through Bill C-45, leading inevitably to pushback, others were drawing attention to the "dangers" of blockades. Douglas Bland, then chair of Defence Management Studies at Queen's University, argued that "more than 25 per cent of our GDP comes from exports of raw materials, but especially oil, natural gas and electricity to the United States. It's undefended and undefendable [*sic*] infrastructure … [that] run[s] through aboriginal territories. It would take a very small number of people very little time to bring it down."[157] Tom Flanagan, a former advisor to Stephen Harper, echoed Bland's comments in a report to the Canadian Defence and Foreign Affairs Institute. Flanagan argued,

> A nightmare scenario from the standpoint of resource industries in northern Alberta would be a linkage between warrior societies and eco-terrorists. Members

of warrior societies would brandish firearms and take public possession of geographical sites, while eco-terrorists would operate clandestinely, firebombing targets over a wide range of territory. The two processes could energize each other, leading in the extreme case to loss of life and a shutdown of industry over a wide area.[158]

Hyperbole such as this threatened to make extreme crackdowns on activists possible. A 2013 article in the *Guardian* based on heavily redacted documents secured through access to information reported, "The RCMP, Canada's national police force, and the Canadian Security Intelligence Service (CSIS) view activist activities such as blocking access to roads or buildings as 'forms of attack' and depict those involved as national security threats."[159] The term "climate jihadist" was bandied about in the public sphere, and environmentalists were repeatedly branded as terrorists.[160] Accusations flew that the Canadian government, in concert with oil companies and Canadian spy agencies such as CSIS and the Communications Security Establishment Canada (CSEC), were spying on citizens who might pose a "threat" to energy infrastructure.[161]

The heightened rhetoric is perhaps most evident in an unprecedented letter Natural Resources Minister Joe Oliver wrote and published in the *Financial Times* and elsewhere. In it, he brands environmentalists as people with "radical ideological agendas" funded by "foreign special interest groups" and resistant to "Canada's national economic interest" because they question the economic and environmental impacts of expanding oil markets to Asia-Pacific economies.[162] At the same time, internal documents were revealed showing CSIS and the RCMP referring to Greenpeace, a civil organization originally started by Canadian journalists, as a "multi-issue extremist group," a pejorative term that along with "climate jihadist" enjoyed popularity at the time.[163] Oliver's letter stated,

> These [environmental] groups threaten to hijack our regulatory system to achieve their radical ideological agenda. They seek to exploit any loophole they can find, stacking public hearings with bodies to ensure that delays kill good projects. They use funding from foreign special interest groups to undermine Canada's national economic interest. They attract jet-setting celebrities with some of the largest personal carbon footprints in the world to lecture Canadians not to develop our natural resources. Finally, if all other avenues have failed, they will take a quintessential American approach: sue everyone and anyone to delay the project even further. They do this because they know it can work. It works because it helps them to achieve their ultimate objective: delay a project to the point it becomes economically unviable.[164]

The solution, Oliver suggested, was to dismantle the regulatory system, which is exactly what the government's omnibus bills did.[165]

At the same time, the Conservative government upped the fight against Canadian green groups on another front, arguing that they were exploiting their charitable status. "There is political manipulation. There is influence peddling. There are millions of dollars crossing borders masquerading as charitable donations," stated Senator Nicole Eaton upon the launch of a Senate inquiry into the "interference of foreign foundations in Canada's domestic affairs" and their "abuse" of the Canada Revenue Agency's (CRA) tax exemption for charities.[166] In the 2012 budget, funding for the Canadian Revenue Agency was topped up to allow the agency to conduct sixty political activity audits of charities.[167] Though the CRA audits were meant to be confidential, many groups publicly self-identified, and it did appear that community benefit groups (including environmental and social justice causes) were overrepresented in the pool.[168] According to those targeted by the CRA, the Conservative tactics were all about suppressing resistance, making it harder to use tax-free charitable status to fundraise and therefore to effectively oppose projects such as the development of Alberta's tar sands.[169]

Cross-border cooperation among green groups is a fact. Activist groups do collaborate on cross-border issues such as pollution in the Great Lakes or the Keystone pipeline, and Canadian and First Nations activists have participated in many of the events organized by Liberate Tate and Platform. Later, as seven major environmental groups (among them the David Suzuki Foundation, Tides Canada, West Coast Environmental Law, and the Pembina Foundation) were audited, Finance Minister Jim Flaherty said, "There are some terrorist organizations, there are some organized crime organizations, that launder money through charities and that make donations to charities and that's not the purpose of charitable donations in Canada."[170]

All this conflating of oil and nation in government and stakeholder policy and rhetoric had unsettling consequences for those hoping to protect land and water. In effect they were ejected from systems of national belonging. For settler protesters, the ouster often involved accusations of anti-Canadianism, terrorism, or the specter of "foreign influence." For Indigenous water and land protectors, it often culminated in even more hostility that extended the long-practised violence of colonialism. For both, "subversive and simply suspicious conduct became lumped together under categories of terrorism and extremism, leading to the criminalization of dissent."[171]

These trends came to a head in October 2013[172] when a demonstration by Mi'kmaq land protectors against seismic testing (exploration for shale gas reserves/fracking) on unceded territory in Elsipogtog (New Brunswick) "turned into what resembled a war zone after the RCMP showed up with guns, Tasers, and dogs."[173]

In 2009, the New Brunswick government provided a licence to Texas-based company Southwestern Energy, allowing them to search more than a million hectares of land for natural gas reserves. A letter-writing campaign supported by settler and First Nations residents of New Brunswick received little government attention, which, in 2013, led to a blockade at Elsipogtog and other forms of direct action.[174] In October 2013, a peaceful demonstration became violent: five police cars were set on fire, and forty people were arrested on charges of intimidation, uttering threats, and mischief.[175] "We had no idea this was going to be happening. They showed up with guns in our faces this morning. It was terrifying. They even brought dogs with them today, it was so scary and unbelievable," said Susan Levi-Perf, a member of the Mi'kmaq.[176] Security forces blamed blockaders, claiming that they were armed with IEDs. Local newspapers claimed the violence "demonstrated by several of these environmental radicals is no less zealous than radical Islam or other sources of international terrorism – for example, burning RCMP vehicles and threatening violence against others who dare to dissent."[177] Levi-Perf, however, argued that the Mi'kmaq were awaiting the outcome of consultations. "As far as we knew there were still talks on the table and were going to appear in court tomorrow. We were getting ready for that."[178] And as Pam Palmater (Eel River Bar First Nation) noted, the lack of mandated consultation was a treaty violation and thus illegal.[179]

What happened at Elsipogtog had the look of a rehearsal for violent crackdown. It differed from actions against mainstream environmental groups in that the altercation took place on contested land, it made extensive use of security forces, courts, and bail, and blockaders could not be associated with "foreign influence." Rather than an audit, blockaders at Elsipogtog faced extreme suppression. But in fact, Mi'kmaq blockaders at Elsipogtog were invoking treaty rights and established legal precedent that "interested parties [should] engage in consultation with Indigenous Nations prior to undertaking any industrial or settlement projects that could have an adverse impact on treaty land."[180] Though Prime Minister Justin Trudeau recently argued that this right did not mean First Nations had a "veto" to development on land,[181] and though this right is regularly overlooked and ignored,[182] self-determination and sovereignty, as well as decolonization and reconciliation, are important components of current conflicts over oil. *R v. Sparrow* (1990), for example, legally requires the Crown to consult with and accommodate Indigenous peoples "when the Crown contemplates conduct that might adversely impact potential of established indigenous or Treaty rights."[183] In combination with the United Nations Declaration on the Rights of Indigenous Peoples (UNDRIP), to which Canada eventually became a signatory, protections for lands and resources are guaranteed (though not legally binding).[184] At Elsipogtog, such rights were trampled, and First Nations land protectors were treated as having less right to unceded territory than the company doing the testing.[185] According to Anishinaabe scholar, musician, and poet Leanne Betasamosake Simpson (Mississauga Nishnaabeg),

> Extraction and assimilation go together. Colonialism and capitalism are based on extracting and assimilating. My land is seen as a resource. My relatives in the plant and animal worlds are seen as resources. My culture and knowledge is a resource. My body is a resource and my children are a resource because they are the potential to grow, maintain, and uphold the extraction-assimilation system. The act of extraction removes all of the relationships that give whatever is being extracted meaning.[186]

In short, then, in Canada during the early 2000s a harsh disciplinary state attempted to crush resistance to environmental exploitation by drawing on narratives of normalized belonging, "common sense," fear of economic disaster, love of profit, and fear of Indigenous resistance. Resistance was, nevertheless, widespread, and it was risky, particularly for Indigenous land and water protectors. It resulted in violent crackdowns, even on unceded and disputed land. Thus, as Preston notes, "While ... oil and gas companies engage in greenwashing campaigns, presenting their 'equity offers' to individual Indigenous band councils, and promoting their 'Aboriginal and Native American Policies' of corporate social responsibility, the police, military, intelligence and border control agencies combine forces to criminalise and surveil any resistance to the development of the tar sands."[187] Within such a context of suspicion, disenfranchisement, and violence, museum sponsorships could not but have strings attached, and those strings created a web knotting together the exploitation of natural resources with the suppression of Indigenous ways of being and claims to land, the suppression and surveillance of mainstream green groups through various methods, and a federal government that encouraged a settler nationalism built on oil.

Museums, Oil, Resistance

While the federal government was painting activists and Indigenous land protectors as the enemy, energy companies were using museums to consolidate their social licence to operate. Museums remain effective greenwashing laundromats. As Carol Duncan and Allan Wallach famously argued, museums are ritual spaces wherein citizenship is performed and maintained. In Canada, this performance often attempts to reconcile the paradox between a fear of environmental disaster and oil as national culture. Despite major conservation projects and green initiatives at many museums in Canada, on balance the cultural sphere remains pro-oil because there is not much choice in the matter. As one anonymous museum worker noted in 2010, "The current government is very pro-business, right-wing. It is now possible in Ontario to clear thousands of hectares of forests but there's no way that this museum could talk about that because we get so much money from the province. In the environmental community this is a very serious issue."[188] When public sector funding comes from pro-energy municipal/provincial/federal sources and some of the most available and generous sponsors are oil companies, museums find turning away a difficult proposition.

In October 2012, James Moore, the minister of Canadian Heritage, announced that the Canadian Museum of Civilization would change its name to the Canadian Museum of History (CMH). Not long afterwards, the CMH announced a partnership with the Canadian Association of Petroleum Producers (CAPP). According to reporter Bruce Cheadle, CAPP would provide $200,000 annually for five years, and in return, the CMH would link a number of exhibits to the oil industry.[189] Officially, the CAPP funding would go toward *1867* (a show organized for 2014–15 in the lead-up to the 150th anniversary of Confederation in 2017) and would also sponsor the brand new (and controversial) Canadian History Hall. This kind of direct intervention and quid pro quo in museums is rare. Much more typical are the "no strings attached" sponsorships whereby greenwashing takes place via proxy and good feeling. Such an overt intervention into museum planning and display is rare. As the CMHR in Winnipeg became more public over time, eventually securing national museum status, the CMC/CMH seemingly became much more private.

As I show in the introduction to the book, when the CMH finally reopened the Canadian History Hall, the displays were, in fact, roundly praised, and aside from the sponsorship wall, CAPP's presence was not obvious, but in 2012 the change in name fell in line with other projects undertaken by the Harper government to highlight Canada's historical links to Britain, monarchy, patriotism, and the military. The name change proved immensely controversial.[190] "There is a kind of a narrowing of a sense of the Canadian past with this emphasis on the military and on deeds of State," said Allan Greer, a professor of history at McGill University. "The discomfort comes from the sense that so much else is being erased and getting less attention."[191] Changing the name and mandate required a change to the 1990 Museums Act (which had also been altered to establish the CMHR), a process that was completed in December 2013. Whereas formerly "the museum's purpose was the increase of critical understanding, knowledge and appreciation for 'human cultural achievements and human behaviour,'" the revised act refers only to the "events, experiences, people and objects that reflect and have shaped Canada's history and identity."[192] The CMH seemed set to turn away from critical research and toward a presentation of heroic myths of nationality.[193] The Canadian Association of University Teachers, the Canadian Anthropology Society, the Canadian Historical

Association, and the Canadian Archaeological Association, among others, all expressed alarm at the museum's new mandate, which seemed to place "a disproportionate emphasis on Canadian history after confederation"[194] – that is, on settler histories. Lord Cultural Resources was hired to organize a cross-Canada public consultation process to collect feedback from interested citizens and groups and develop a permanent exhibition slated to open in 2017 as a part of Canada150 celebrations (themselves immensely controversial for overshadowing violent process of colonization that established the settler nation).[195]

In opposition, the Liberal Party decried the changes made to the CMC, calling the name change an attempt to "turn the museum into a subsidiary of the Conservative Party spin machine."[196] New Democrat MP Marjolaine Boutin-Sweet warned in the House of Commons that the museum could "become a propaganda machine" and demanded to know, "Is it now the mission of our museums to promote the oil lobby?" In response, Rick Dykstra, the Conservative junior heritage minister, responded that New Democrats should "stand up and support the museum of history – stand up and support Canadian history."[197] Once in power, Liberal Government House Leader Dominic Leblanc sent a letter in December 2015 to Harper appointee and president of the federal Crown corporation that operates the Canadian Museum of History and the Canadian War Museum, Mark O'Neill, asking that he resign.[198] Change was short-lived, however. Just a few weeks later, the new Liberal minister of Heritage backed O'Neill's reappointment. Both Conservative and Liberal governments explicitly or implicitly supported the CAPP sponsorship.

Opposition appeared elsewhere too. Sociology and anthropology professor Frances M. Slaney notes that the source communities for many of the artefacts held by the museum and "whose cultural heritage still forms the heart of the CMH's collections" are often "vehemently oppose[d to] CAPP's extraction industries and pipeline projects on their lands."[199] The collections held at the CMH "have figured strongly in legal procedures between First Nations communities and Canadian governments."[200] Slaney also argues that "[e]xperienced curators know that big oil can spell trouble in Canada's museum world, ever since the 1988 Calgary Olympics when Lubicon Cree boycotted the Glenbow museum's *The Spirit Sings* exhibition because of its Shell Oil sponsorship" and suggests that CAPP sponsorship was at odds with the Task Force on Museums and First Peoples that had emerged, in part, from that protest.[201]

Nevertheless, the name change went through, and the CMH proceeded with its renovations apace. It was soon announced that "Canada's 150th birthday is being brought to you by the Canadian Association of Petroleum Producers."[202] As the deal between CMH and CAPP was announced, the president of CAPP opined that a "$1-million sponsorship of the Canadian Museum of Civilization is a great opportunity to get the oil and gas industry's message out to Canadians." He continued, "The advantage of partnering with an institution like this museum is it has national presence, it's obviously got significant profile in Ottawa but it also has national reach in terms of travelling exhibits and so on ... It's a way for us to get the industry's presence more broadly identified and visible across the country."[203] O'Neill argued on behalf of the museum that "[CAPP] represents industries that create 90 per cent of the energy in the country. They directly and indirectly employ some half a million Canadians. This is an extremely important institutional sector for Canada."[204]

To date, three notable protests have taken place against the new CMH, each of which complicates strategies of performance art activism while also speaking to the difficulties of intersectional environmental activism in Canada, particularly at museums. First, the above-mentioned outcry from the academic establishment drew public attention to the way that the newly minted CMH would turn away from research into and portrayal of Indigenous lifeways prior to Confederation (the previous mandate of the CMC) and toward an Anglo-centric, parochial, and uncritical view of Canadian history that highlighted "great men" and (assumedly a few) "great women."

Second, in 2014, shortly after the initial sponsorship deal with CAPP was announced, the well-known artist, activist, and hereditary chief Beau Dick (Kwakwaka'-wakw) began *Awalaskenis II: Journey of Truth and Unity*, a 5,000-kilometre journey from UBC/Vancouver to Ottawa and Parliament Hill, with many stops en route to meet with various First Nations communities.[205] With them, the group carried a copper shield named *T'aaw*, made by Giindajin Haawasti Guujaaw, Raven of the Haida Nation, carver, Hereditary leader, and former president of the Haida Nation. *T'aaw*, the name bestowed upon the copper, means oolichan (fish) oil and refers to "respect for the great life-giving oolichan oil/in stark contrast to the poison from the Tar Sands."[206] As the website dedicated to the project describes it,

> Along the way, the travellers visited First Nations communities across the country to gather support and to increase the value of the copper through ceremony. Through social media, they drew attention to the journey. Many artists and communities contributed sacred objects collected from up and down the continent – some of them considered to be sentient beings – to be carried to the copper-breaking event.[207]

In July 2014 on Parliament Hill, on top of a banner (made by artist Cathy Busby) displaying the text of Harper's apology for residential schools, Dick, along with twenty others who had joined the walk, broke the shield in a shaming ceremony "as a means of calling out the Conservative federal government's broken

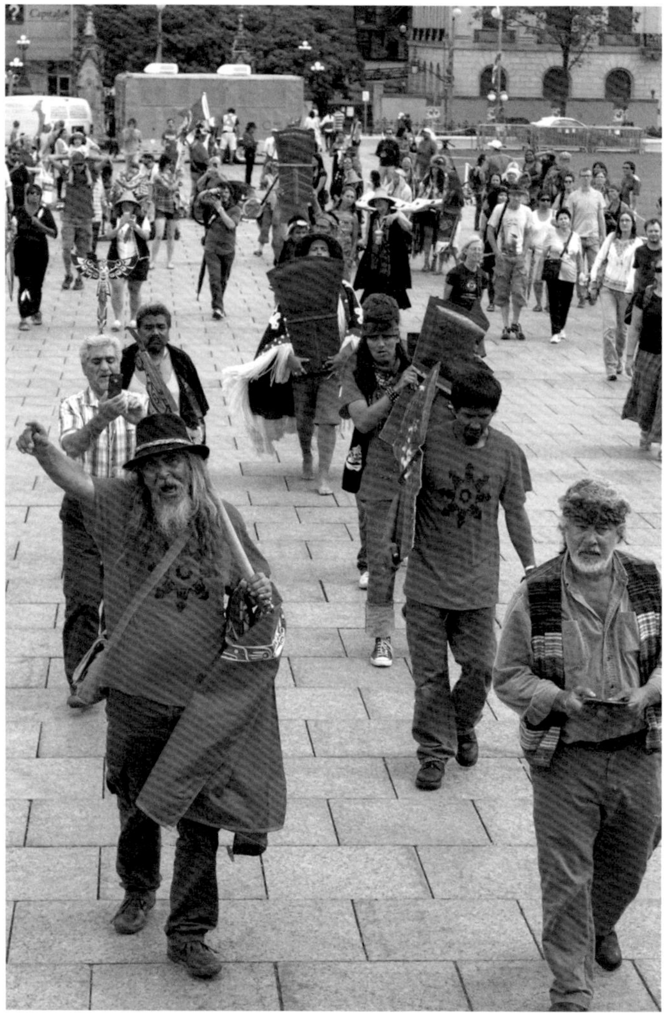

Figure 6.6
During the Copper-Breaking Ceremony on Parliament Hill, Ottawa, 27 June 2014.

treaties, assimilationist policies, and the ongoing degradation of rights for Indigenous peoples."[208] The ceremony marked "a ruptured relationship in need of repair, and pass[ed] the burden of wrongs done to First Nations people from them to the Government of Canada."[209]

As curator Candice Hopkins describes, "The pieces of copper were then rolled up and left on the steps of Parliament as evidence of the act (a copper breaking can be undertaken to bring great shame upon another person, as well as an offer of peace and a gift)."[210] Dick and other collaborators then moved on to Gatineau where they performed a second shaming ceremony outside the CMH. Earlier, Dick had contacted the CMH, asking if it would be possible to see the coppers the museum had in storage. The answer was no.[211] Media coverage of the action recorded Dick saying, "The museum plays an important role and we understand that. But when it's hiding stuff in the archives and nobody gets a chance to see it, it isn't handling our things responsibly."[212] He later wrote, "As an artist, bringing the broken copper to go visit the old ones was a gesture that I felt strongly about. Our group was shut out and it was embarrassing – but not for us."[213]

After the ceremony, the piece of copper was sent to a museum in British Columbia.[214] While at first this act seems an ironic commentary on Dick's words, fitting the sentient copper into an already established paradigm and taxonomy of collecting and archiving that could potentially place it and its shaming action out of sight and out of use, in fact the copper was given to the Haida Gwaii Museum and Heritage Centre at Kay Llinagaay (Skidegate), an Indigenous-run and -oriented institution that knows well how to care for *T'aaw*.[215] The ceremony showed "how deeply traditional practices can be deployed to address and engage urgent and contemporary politics," and the cut piece of *T'aaw* has since been shown at the MOA at UBC as part of a collaboration between six Indigenous communities showcasing five cultural centres and museums in their communities: the Musqueam Cultural Education and Resource Centre, the Squamish-Lil'wat Cultural Centre, the Heiltsuk Cultural Education Centre, the Nisga'a Museum, and the Haida Gwaii Museum and Haida Heritage Centre at Kay Llnagaay.[216] Thus, in 2014, as part of calling the federal government to account, Dick voiced a strong critique of Canadian museums. For Dick and his collaborators at the shaming ceremony, the very collecting paradigms lauded by academic societies critiquing the name and mandate change were implicated in the continued processes of settler colonization and environmental crisis. In the years since, *T'aaw* has participated in a number of exhibitions that have addressed the shaming ceremonies at Parliament Hill and the CMH, continuing to play a role that began with *Awalaskenis II*. Simultaneously, as curator Scott Watson said of Dick's action: "Indigenous culture is something we can all learn from as a way of being with, dealing with, and dialoging with nature that would lead us away from resource extraction and domination model."[217] The shaming ceremony and *T'aaw* continue to have ripple effects.[218] Importantly, the CAPP sponsorship was not mentioned at either ceremony.

Finally, building on the Council of Canadians' 2013 action, on Thursday, 6 April 2017, a number of organizations led by 350.org organized a protest event outside the CMH that directly targeted the CAPP sponsorship. "The Museum of History has a dark secret," read an article in the *Ottawa Citizen* prior to the action. "Big Oil is using it to sell environmental destruction and rejection of climate change ... This sponsorship is anything but a gift."[219] Now, years after the sponsorship was announced, a movement against it was finally gathering steam.[220] Though attendance was small, the initial 2017 protest gained publicity when the American activist Bill McKibben, co-founder of 350.org, published a much-circulated opinion piece in the *Guardian* that, among other things, referred to CAPP as "sleazy oil lobbyists" and called for the CMH to cut ties with the organization.[221] The first action grew into a second on 24 April 2017 when members of 350.org and their supporters attended the CMH's annual general meeting, holding "a land recognition, a grounding ceremony, and a short rally" before moving inside where the group called on Mark O'Neill to cut ties with CAPP. They delivered a petition with 6,000 signatures asking for an end to the sponsorship.[222] In July 2017, just after the new wing of the museum opened, 350.org activists were there again, this time staging an unsanctioned exhibition in the foyer of the museum, putting "big oil on display."[223] Several members of 350.org stood holding framed posters showing the impact of the oil industry on the Canadian environment.

Liberate Tate, BP or Not BP, Decolonize This Place, Not An Alternative, and many of the other groups mentioned in this chapter are heavily invested in the museums they critique. They visit them, read about them, and are immensely knowledgeable in their interpretations of them.[224] Liberate Tate and others trace their heritage to institutional critique, to Michael Asher, Hans Haacke, Fred Wilson, and Andrea Fraser.[225] Though differentiating themselves from those artists through their affinity with social movements, they nonetheless put their defence of culture front and centre in the fight for museums to drop fossil-fuel sponsorships.[226] The museum or gallery is central here; as Serafini puts it, Art Not Oil and others are part of an "international museum liberation movement," and their actions (in the UK specifically) draw on an emotional connection and sense of ownership of the London public to cultural institutions in the city.[227] 350.org, meanwhile, is one of the "foreign-funded" climate activism groups singled out by the Harper government. Its projects focus almost exclusively on "effort[s] to raise awareness of the need to decrease carbon dioxide concentration in the atmosphere to *350* parts per million."[228] Although divestment is one of their key goals, the CMH is not a focal institution in the way that the Tate is for Liberate Tate. And indeed, though involving Clayton Thomas-Muller, who worked with Platform and Liberate Tate in the UK, the action at the CMH lacked the panache of many of the UK actions. The CMH is not a contemporary art institution as the Tate is. It does not have a history of artistic institutional critique.

If museums are central institutions for the performance of ritual citizenship (something that is written right into the CMH's mandate) and if that citizenship is elsewhere tightly reticulated with resource extraction and the active disavowal of Indigenous sovereignty, then a performance to protect the institution from the very nation it depicts, even if it is via an action against oil sponsorship, seems fractured at best. On the other hand, protesting the CAPP sponsorship also protests the idea of citizenship that pitches oil and culture as inseparable.[229] At this juncture, I refer back to my discussion of Not An Alternative to draw attention to the fact that when pipelines cross Indigenous land and resistance is about protecting land and water and acknowledging treaties, then actions at museums against fossil-fuel

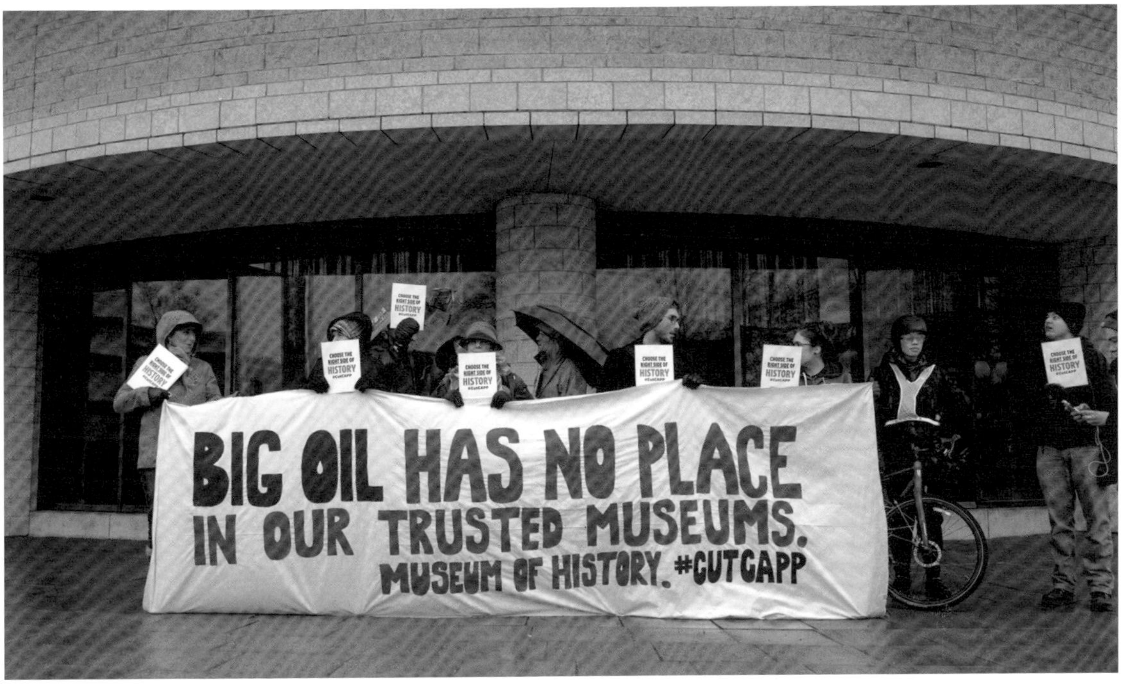

Figure 6.7
350.org, Big Oil Has No Place in Our Trusted Museums, #CutCAPP Demonstration at the Canadian Museum Association Conference, 7 April 2017.

sponsorships can only be the support rather than the central actions. I draw again on Jodi Dean's idea of anamorphic politics to suggest that actions at museums are the (important) periphery to action on the land. The copper breaking ceremonies undertaken by Dick and others, for example, foregrounded much of what is often (though not always) left out of art activism performances that focus solely on the museum and the sponsorship as the site of the action rather than the multiple and uneven impacts of resource extraction. In this instance, sponsorship was not mentioned, and instead, the lifeways that had been affected by government intervention and control, residential schooling, environmental destruction (in large part led by resource extraction), *and* the colonial impact of museum collecting formed the basis of a ceremony designed to alter a broken relationship and draw attention to environmental crisis. My goal here is not to say that art activism against sponsorship has no import but rather to show that the *absence* of such large-scale actions in Canada has reasons beyond a lack of organization.

In this sense, Canadian groups, as well as Liberate Tate and others, could look back to the 1988 protests against *Spirit Sings* to find a model for intersectional action.[230] I argued above that the actions against that exhibition resulted in changes in museum policy at the expense of the Lubicon Cree's land claim and at the expense of halting Shell Oil's drilling on Lubicon land. What would it mean to revisit that action now? Would it be possible to develop a broad coalition that simultaneously draws attention to oil sponsorships and to Indigenous land claims? And would defending the museum on the grounds of protecting culture allow for a way to discuss how far museums have to go on the path to decolonization?

What would it mean to involve museums in the debate? Currently, many establishment museums in Canada are accepting sponsorships from fossil fuel companies, resulting in a greenwashing relationship. But arguably, oil companies, which have much to gain from appearing to be onside with Indigenous communities, are benefitting from the hard work that has taken place at museums. From the perspective of 350.org and other groups, the problem should not just be that fossil fuel companies are having their own environmental records greenwashed but additionally that oil companies benefit from the work done by museum personnel and communities who have forged relationships at the CMH and elsewhere and from the intense reworking of the CMH Canadian History Hall, with its much greater emphasis on Indigenous histories. As cheyanne turions writes in a slightly different context and specifically of the NGC, while authoritative museums "cannot grant many of the political demands necessary for Indigenous self-determination,

such as the repatriation of lands and resources, [they] can recognize [their] own complicity in the settler-colonial project and work to materially recognize the distribution of aesthetic/cultural power and privilege that it traffics in."[231]

At the same time, as Nika Collison, curator at the Haida Gwaii Museum (which staged its own exhibition, *Thanks But No Tanks*, on the theme of opposition to the proposed Enbridge oil pipeline and increased numbers of oil tankers on the Pacific coast of British Columbia) noted at the Museum Futures conference in Montreal, "Objects have to be used to address broken treaties, unceded territories, killing of land and water."[232] As trusted venues, museums can and do have a role to play in resisting climate change, in countering fossil fuel extraction, in supporting land claims, and in imagining new futures. They also have a responsibility to repair the broken relationships pointed out in the shaming ceremony outside of the CMH. Such goals should not be "neutered by PR concerns and the maintenance of funder relationships,"[233] and it is my hope that this chapter has shown that the one cannot take place without the other. The difficulty of bringing these different approaches together may offer a suggestion for why a movement such as Liberate Tate has not emerged in Canada. But working through those difficulties might in turn offer a more complex challenge both to sponsors and to museums.

Interstice 6f

Reversing the Flow: Yes Men Tackle the Canadian Government

The 2009 United Nations Climate Change Conference (COP15) held in Copenhagen gave a clear indication of the position Canadian officials were going to take internationally on oil, other natural resources, and climate change and the way that activists intended to respond to their plans. COP15 was held at the height of the Harper government's promotion of Canada's anti-environment agenda,[1] and Canada was painted by activists as a global pariah.[2] COP15's aim was to replace the Kyoto Protocol, a UN framework that committed signatory states to reduce greenhouse emissions and that was set to expire in 2012. To give a sense of the Harper government's position, the Kyoto Protocol had been accused by some (including Stephen Harper prior to becoming prime minister) of being a covert wealth-transfer plot, since it required rich nations, unable to reach difficult targets, to buy carbon indulgences from poorer ones. The protocol was, in Harper's mind, a "socialist scheme to suck money out of wealth-producing nations."[3]

In December 2002, the Kyoto treaty had been ratified by the Canadian House of Commons. There was, however, no plan for its implementation. Fear over job losses, intra-government arguing over departmental control, and provincial complaints over a lack of consultation and over division of funds undermined attempts to implement the protocol. Calls for a "made-in-Canada" plan came from Alberta, where the demands of Kyoto were seen as particularly onerous.[4] In answer, Greenpeace climbers hung a massive banner from the CN Tower in Toronto protesting inaction on climate change, while others set up solar panels on Alberta premier Ralph Klein's home (much to his chagrin).[5] As negotiators landed in Copenhagen, the stakes were high.

Art played a significant role at the Copenhagen talks, and so did museums. Many exhibitions and artworks were organized to provoke and inform audiences, to draw attention to climate change and environmental issues, and to remind negotiators of why they were in Copenhagen and what was at stake.[6] While many of the exhibitions were highly praised, the cultural programming appeared to have no effect whatsoever on the Canadian contingent. "We won't be swayed by the Copenhagen hype," said Canadian environment minister Jim Prentice as Canada received the "colossal fossil" award for its "reckless arrogance."[7]

But one group was able to get through. In the wake of COP15, Prentice wrote a letter to the editor of the *Toronto Star*, arguing that "pranksters" had received too much attention in Copenhagen.[8] Prentice was referring to the political performance art group the Yes Men, who (together with Canadian, Danish, and Ugandan youth making up the Climate Debt Agents group) had put together a hoax involving fake Environment Canada websites. During COP15, an email was circulated, apparently from Environment Canada, stating that Canada had reversed its stance on climate change. A Twitter message ostensibly from Environment Minister Jim Prentice detailed Canada's ambitious plan to cut greenhouse gases. Canada's "Agenda 2020" set a goal of a 40 per cent reduction in emissions from 1990 levels by 2020 – a dramatic change from the actual goal of 3 per cent. It also created a new fund, to which Canada pledged an enormous $13 billion, to help developing nations deal with climate change. "We believe all people will benefit from an equitable climate deal that truly energizes the world economy," read a quote attributed to Prentice. The news lit up the Bella Centre, the vast Copenhagen convention hall where the climate change negotiations were taking place. A story popped up on an apparent European affiliate of the *Wall Street Journal*. In a video on what looked to be a UN site, a Ugandan official congratulated Canada for its change of direction after "holding a loaded gun to our heads."[9] "For a brief, shining moment, the world loved Canada's new commitment to the environment," wrote one reporter.[10]

The hoax received a great deal of coverage that paralleled the critical coverage that Canada had been receiving in the international media.[11] Now the Canadian delegation had to awkwardly deal with the fallout of this hoax.[12] Government spokesperson Dimitri Soudas publicly attacked Quebec-based NGO Equiterre leader Steven Guilbeault, mistaking him for one of the perpetrators of the hoax: "You think it's a game but it's not a game. It's a serious issue," Soudas shouted, while waving a hand dismissively, in an exchange captured by the CBC. "You can criticize from the bleachers, Steven," he finishes.[13] Equiterre later released a statement: "We also deeply regret Canada's position on climate change is nowhere near the one presented on [the fake] Environment Canada's website."[14] Prentice refused to comment.

The Yes Men, actually Andy Bichibaum and Mike Bonanno (not their real names), "infiltrate conferences, produce fake newspapers, and do various other weirdness in order to expose the wrongdoings of miscellaneous, mostly corporate evildoers."[15] They call their approach "laughtivism," and their primary tactic, as seen in the COP15 action, is to pretend to be experts speaking on behalf of organizations or corporations and then to call those corporations out by saying the opposite of what is expected, employing satirical language or simply speaking the truth (against the obfuscating language of much corporate- and government-speak). According to Bonnano, quoted in the Guardian, "It's always rewarding to announce the future you want to see ... You can see on people's faces the realization that this could actually be happening."[16]

Arguably, the Yes Men action had little to no measurable impact, at least on the position of Canadian negotiators. But perhaps that is not the correct way of measuring impact, for the hoax achieved a great deal of publicity and galvanized the environmental movement as a whole. A different question might be how the Yes Men prank fit in with other actions, including those at museums in Copenhagen.

In Ottawa, Greenpeace activists scaled the outside of the Parliament buildings (which turned into a fiasco over security), a flash mob stripped on the Vancouver Skytrain, walking around in the cold in their underpants,[17] and 124 climate scientists in Canada circulated an open letter arguing that climate change should be dealt with immediately regardless of economic consequences, the alternative being catastrophe (economic, environmental, and otherwise).[18] In October 2009, protesters had been ejected from Parliament for chanting "sign it, sign it, sign it" when Bill C-311, an NDP bill that would have set deep greenhouse-gas emission targets for Canada in advance of COP15, was introduced in the House of Commons (it was not successful).[19] Six people were arrested. In the same month, sixteen Greenpeace activists scaled a crane and smokestack at a Shell upgrader, hoping to draw attention to Canada's and Alberta's stance on climate change. They were arrested and charged with mischief and breaking and entering. A small controversy erupted around the fact that two of the activists were not Canadian. Premier Ed Stelmach called them "tourists" who threatened the province's livelihood.[20]

Meanwhile, in Copenhagen, a huge number of cultural events were taking place. Among the most visible were artists Mark Coreth and Duncan Hamilton's World Wildlife Fund–sponsored *Ice Bear*, a sculpture of a polar bear that melted in the warm climate of Copenhagen to reveal a bronze skeleton, and *RETHINK: Contemporary Art and Climate Change*, an exhibition featuring well-known artists such as Bright Ugochukwu Eke and Tomás Saraceno, whose large-scale conceptually oriented projects tackled climate change, pollution, and future worlds at the Copenhagen Centre for Contemporary Art.[21]

The most obvious difference between these artworks and the Yes Men action is that the latter was able to enter the space of negotiators and force them to respond to activist demands. In this, the intervention was unarguably successful and impactful. In combination with the joyful reception of the Canadian "announcement," the Yes Men were able to expose the Canadian delegation to a critique that did receive widespread coverage. But as I showed in the previous chapter, action against the fossil fuel industry and against climate change requires constant vigilance on the part of many environmental groups as well as Indigenous land and water protectors. It is the constancy of action that is fundamentally important to sustaining action and encouraging change.

Thus, in the end, a very weak deal emerged from COP15, which later became the Paris Accord. The final "agreement" was more of a framework; it failed to set significant milestones – and it was non-binding. Thus, while it talked of reducing global emissions by "50 per cent from 1990 levels by 2050, with the developed world slashing emissions by 80 per cent, and … that global temperatures should not be allowed to rise more than two degrees Celsius," no legislation was put in place to make these measures happen, and no agreement to replace Kyoto was achieved. Instead, the timing for these changes was left until COP21, held in Paris in 2015.

At COP21, a massive action, possibly inspired by the Yes Men but more likely by groups such as Art Not Oil, took place at the Louvre as a huge fabric "oil slick" spilled down the stairs from the famous Victory of Samothrace statue.[22] By 2015, such performances were widespread, and theorists such as Paula Serafini were expressing some concern that museums might become comfortable with these kinds of interventions. She suggests that if there is no tension with the institution, art activism loses its strength as direct action and is potentially absorbed as inconsequential critique.[23] She argues that actions need to be "transgressive" rather than "reformist," that they need to move beyond merely halting oil sponsorship of the arts to examining institutional structures that uphold an oil economy.[24] Both she and I value the ongoing role of interventionist art activism at museums, but nonetheless it is worth noting the slightly different and highly effective tack taken by the Yes Men at COP15 – surely a transgressive action if there ever was one.

7

"Intellectual Properties": Real Estate, Occupy Vancouver, and the Vancouver Art Gallery

In June 2002, *Carr, O'Keefe, Kahlo: Places of Their Own* opened at the Vancouver Art Gallery (VAG). An exhibition of work by artists Emily Carr, Georgia O'Keefe, and Frida Kahlo, organized by the McMichael Canadian Art Collection in Kleinburg, Ontario, as a companion to the release of Sharyn Rohlfsen Udall's book of the same name, *Places of Their Own*, travelled from Kleinburg to Santa Fe, to Washington, DC, and then to Vancouver. What had been planned as a fairly minor exhibition quickly grew in size and scope, benefitting significantly from the growing popularity of the three artists and record attendance in Kleinburg.[1] Interest in Canadian Emily Carr and Mexican Frida Kahlo in particular was on the upswing – Canadian rock singer Bryan Adams had recently publicized his interest in Emily Carr (although admittedly in part because he was auctioning off his collection), and there was a great deal of attention on Madonna, then perhaps Kahlo's most famous fan, who refused to lend her paintings to the exhibition.[2] Deirdre Hannah in *Now Magazine* noted, "The hype has been huge. It doesn't hurt that Kahlo is the art world's woman of the moment, with a movie biopic coming out this year and her paintings going for more than $5 million US on the auction block."[3]

By the time the exhibition opened in Vancouver, the popularity of the three artists had been folded into a celebration of their gender: not only were these three famous artists gathered together for the first time, each had overcome obstacles and difficult lives in order to succeed.[4] This gender focus, however, did not necessarily mean a feminist approach. "The Drama. The Passion. The Estrogen" was one of

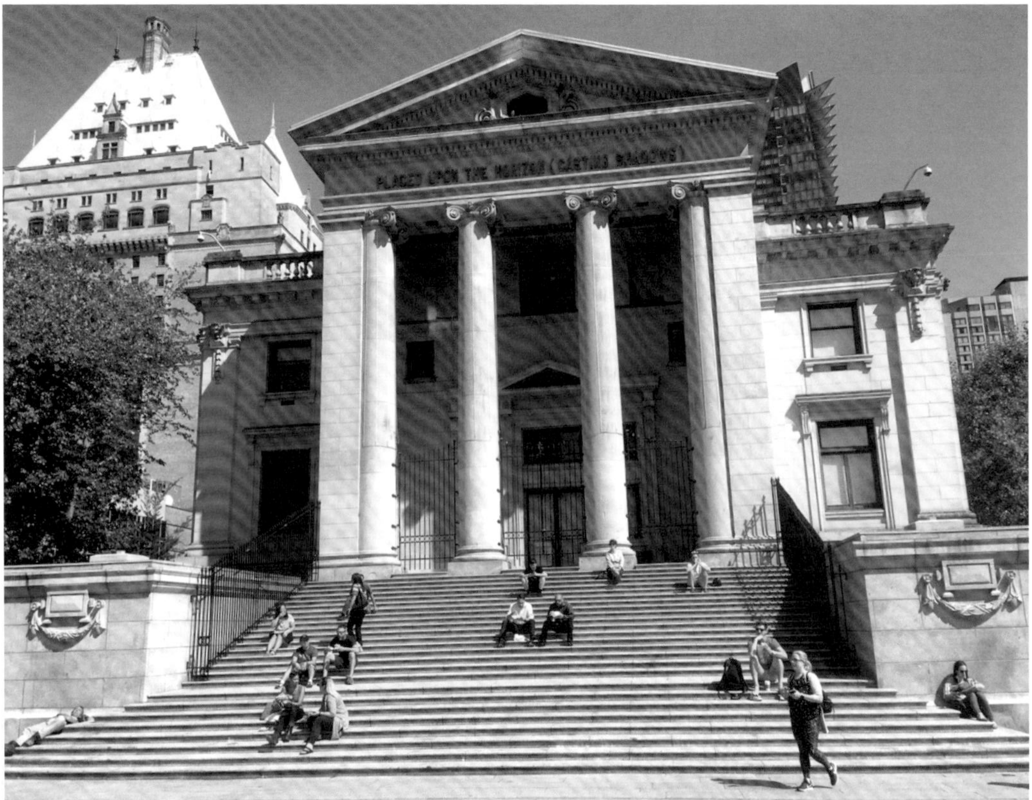

Figure 7.1
Robson Street south façade of the Vancouver Art Gallery.

the taglines used to advertise the show.[5] So, too, the economic integration of North America as evidenced by NAFTA and the then recent failure to sign the Free Trade Area of the Americas Agreement in 2001 were used to add contemporary relevance to the exhibition.[6] When it showed in Vancouver, *Places of Their Own* was dubbed "the NAFTA show,"[7] and the artists were called the "NAFTA Feminist 3"[8] and "the best-known women artists this century from the three NAFTA countries."[9] Nevertheless, both of these interpretive framings were quickly pushed into the background. By the time *Places of Their Own* opened, the gallery had other issues on its hands.

On 14 June 2002, just before the exhibition opened, an email was sent to staff of the VAG, noting that the premier would be attending the members' opening of the exhibition and a protest should be expected. Although it was noted that a contingency plan was in place, Kathleen Bartels, director of the VAG, nonetheless stated: "Our position is that the Gallery is an apolitical institution that acknowledges and respects different points of view. The Gallery supports freedom of expression and has always encouraged open dialogue about art, culture and ideas."[10] It was further noted that Public Programs would distribute flyers to the protestors, inviting them to see the exhibition and reminding them of the radicalism of the three artists.[11]

The following day, former Vancouver mayor and, at the time, British Columbia premier Gordon Campbell arrived at the VAG. Myriad groups showed up, using the exhibition opening as a chance to address severe cuts to social programs that had been made by the Campbell provincial Liberal government. Interestingly, although the gender of the artists came up (particularly via cuts to women's programs), the link to NAFTA did not, except indirectly – it was Gordon Campbell's presence that drew protesters rather than the cultural politics of the exhibition itself.[12] In an article written in the aftermath, *Vancouver Sun* reporter Michael Scott described the event:

> As art openings go, this one was a definite typhoon. Two people were arrested, platform guests ... were roughed up, and mild-mannered art patrons had to fight their way past the commotion in order to look at the paintings ... [VAG director] Kathleen Bartels was experiencing a hostess's nightmare last Friday – her big summertime party ruined by uninvited guests, armed police threatening to use pepper spray, the guest of honour too frightened to show his face – when she turned to a bystander, smiled unexpectedly and said: "This is what art is about."[13]

Turning the situation into a happening, Scott took Bartels's comment as a reminder that "good art is always a variety of protest."[14] Bartels quipped that she was happy so many Vancouverites had come to the gallery to express their opinions but noted, "It's just unfortunate that people have chosen to disrupt what was supposed to be a celebration for the whole community."[15]

While the mainstream press largely ignored the *reasons* protesters had for showing up, the Insurrectionary Anarchists of the Coast Salish Territories (IAofCST) and the Anti-Poverty Committee, who organized the event, defined it by noting that the choice of venue, "an opening [of an exhibition] of feminist and revolutionary artists, was an insult to everyone living under his [Campbell's] policies."[16] Bringing together a number of groups including the Vancouver Anti-Poverty Committee, the BC branch of the Guerrilla Girls, and the newly formed "Andy Warhol Gang,"[17] the action was intended to draw attention to Campbell's cuts to women's centres and slashing of funds for many social programs directly affecting women, artists, and the underprivileged, leading to further precarity and contributing to the homeless problem in Vancouver.[18]

On the night in question, a number of anti-Campbell, anti-poverty activists came to the opening, many of them dressed in costume. A group of five artists dressed identically as Andy Warhol and, wearing pictures of soup cans on their backs with signs reading "Campbell's Cuts," circulated through the crowd passing out leaflets entitled "Five reasons BC artists don't like Gordon Campbell."[19] Others dressed in gorilla masks in honour of the New York–based Guerilla Girls feminist collective (one of whom uses the pseudonym Frida Kahlo). Many protesters were members of the VAG and thus had legitimate invitations, blurring the conventional line between who is allowed in and who is kept out. In one of the few occasions that protest crossed the threshold of the museum, numerous protesters were able to enter the gallery even as police set up barricades outside, ostensibly to keep the protest "out," particularly of the reception and speeches taking place on the gallery steps.[20]

Uniformed and mounted police, plainclothes undercover officers, private security guards, Canadian Security and Intelligence Service (CSIS) agents, and the premier's security detail were all on hand when a "well-dressed young man in his 20s" (Anti-Poverty Committee activist Ivan Drury) climbed on stage, pushed news anchor and emcee Gloria Macarenko out of the way, and called for demonstrators to pull down the barricades. With several hundred protesters chanting, singing, and carrying banners, the largest of which read "Campbell's cutbacks equal class war," Michael Scott observed, "in the seconds it took for police and security guards to wrestle the man to the ground, it felt like it."[21] The heavy podium overturned and the "young man" was tackled, handcuffed, and taken away.[22]

Security shut the doors to the reception, whisked the premier away, and refused to allow anyone wearing a mask over the threshold. Scott described the strange scene of VAG volunteers walking down one side of the line of people waiting to enter the gallery, telling them they would have to take off their masks, while protesters walked down the other side handing out leaflets, encouraging people to keep their masks on and chanting "Shame!" at the police, volunteers, and security detail.[23] As protesters began to shake the barriers, police threatened to use pepper spray.[24]

Though widely reported in the press the next day, the incident quickly died down, leaving in its wake Scott's observation that "the three artists in the exhibition were no strangers to protest in their own lives" and that although confrontation had erupted between the "colourful and outspoken" museum patrons and the neoliberal premier, he concluded that the gallery must continue building its relationship with government.[25] Taking the opposite view, Reed Eurchuk noted, "For the first time since his coronation as emperor of BC, Gordon Campbell has been stopped. Stopped from desecrating the memory of three great artists, and stopped from reciting some clichéd statement celebrating the marriage of art and capital in the form of art tourism."[26]

The anger aimed at Premier Gordon Campbell during the opening of *Places of Their Own* was just one of a number of actions against the imposition of neoliberal

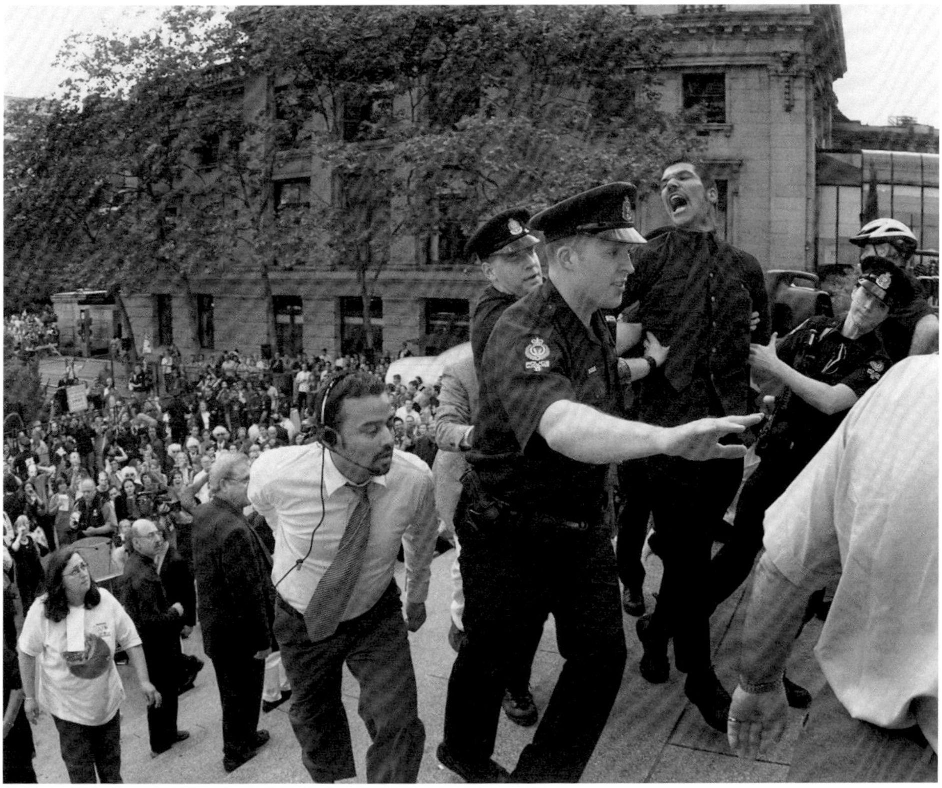

Figure 7.2
A man is arrested by Vancouver Police at the Vancouver Art Gallery at the opening of the big summertime show *Places of Their Own.*

policies in British Columbia and Vancouver during and after the election of the Campbell Liberal government in a landslide victory in May 2001.[27] But it is the location of the 2002 action that is of importance here. The two courtyard plazas, north and south, of the VAG, owned and overseen by the City of Vancouver, are two of the few public spaces in the downtown core of Vancouver, and not coincidentally both are gathering spaces that host many political actions, often (but not always) distinct from the gallery itself.[28] The south plaza tends to host smaller events and the north plaza large-scale demonstrations. Unlike the CMHR (chapter 5), which includes in its architecture an outdoor space reserved for free speech and protest, the VAG's attachment to the events outside is coincidental, and often gallery-goers must pick their way through political actions, moving to the back or sides of the building in order to enter.[29]

The plaza outside the VAG is intimately tied up with the particularities of Vancouver as an urban centre and with the ways that the city imagines itself as a counter-narrative to many other urban locales. If this is a book in large part focused on how museums must be interpreted as part and parcel of the events and situations that surround and run through them, the VAG provides a near-perfect case

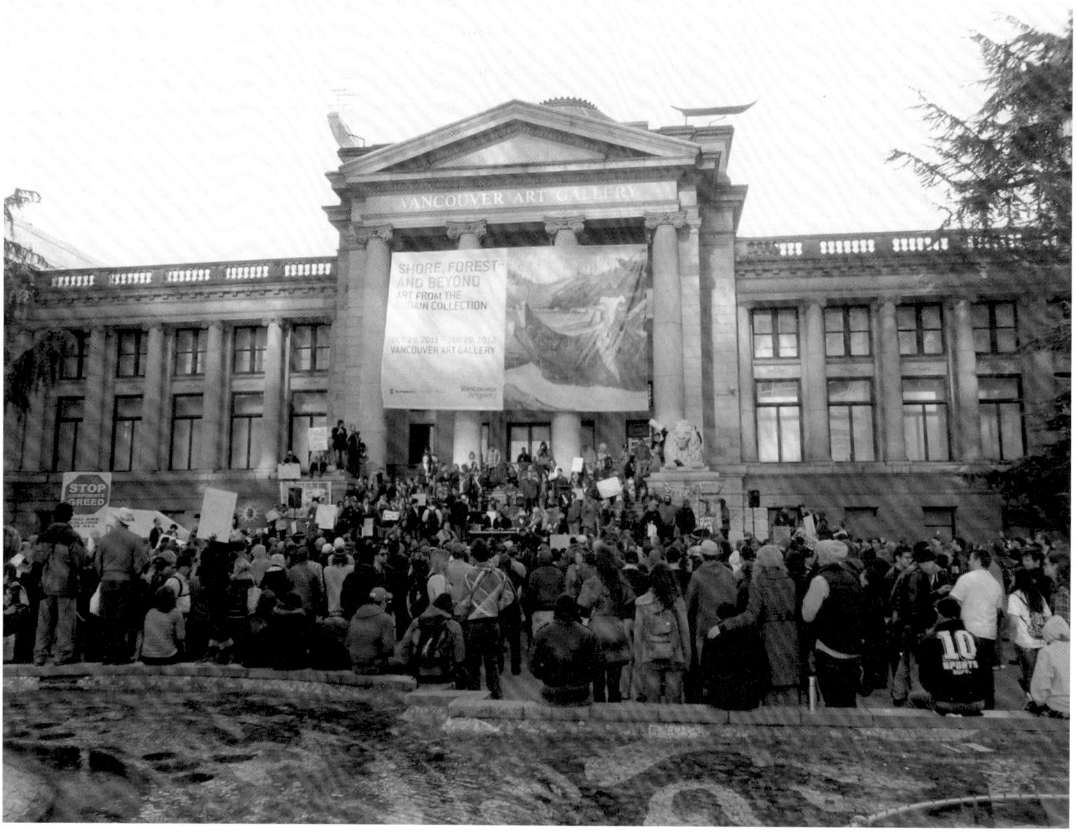

Figure 7.3
Occupy Vancouver protest in front of the Art Gallery, 15 October 2011.

study for showing how the gallery and its location and uses are co-productive. Thus, in this chapter I use the north plaza of the VAG to work outward into the city space and to examine how both the gallery's place in the city and many of the political actions in Vancouver coalesce around an art-land-economy triumvirate or around the production of contemporary art, gentrification, real estate, and "Creative Cities" narratives.[30]

The Vancouver Art Gallery Courtyards

The building that currently houses the VAG was originally built in 1906 and until 1983 was the provincial courthouse. As such, the location has had an intimate relationship with protest and riots in the city.[31] It was in the 1960s, during rallies against the Vietnam War, that "politics began to encroach on the space. There was concern over long-haired hippies hanging out on the lawn and bathing in the courthouse fountain."[32] Joan Seidl of the Museum of Vancouver notes of the north plaza: "From the mid-1960s, it [has] been identified as the place you go to voice your alternative opinions. It … represented the powers that be and the establishment."[33] In the late 1960s, the city passed an anti-loitering bylaw, and several people who were lingering outside the courthouse were arrested.[34] Pushback against the arrests helped to solidify the spot as "the default place for dissidents in Vancouver, even after it was converted into the art gallery in 1983."[35]

On most days, the two flights of stairs at the northern and southern ends of the gallery are gathering spots for workers on lunch break, street-affiliated youth, skateboarders, loiterers, and postmodern flaneurs, for artists selling their works, chess players, hotdog vendors, and gallery visitors.[36] Though the steps and courtyards are non-partisan (the north plaza has been host to rallies by skinheads, anti-abortionists, pro- and anti-government activists, anti-racist actions, Take Back the Night, unions, anti-capitalist and global justice demonstrators, Hari Krishnas, Falun Gong, teachers, nurses, students, and government officials, among others), as a meeting place they add a visible political dimension to what is often considered simply the "cultural" space of the urban gallery or museum. By 2010, approximately fifty protests per year were taking place outside the VAG, "from massive demonstrations that attract thousands to small gatherings of a handful of people waving placards about all manner of topics."[37] As the VAG's 2003–06 strategic plan notes, "Robson Street area is highly-trafficked, well known among locals and a significant tourist destination … the courthouse buildings have long been a scene of protest and demonstration, and as a result are frequently shown on TV newscasts (although some sorts of activities can also deter prospective visitors)."[38] This quotation suggests some ambivalence toward the political actions that take place outside the gallery, as well as the way that the gallery is implicated in and affected by the protests. For the most part, the VAG downplays any significant connection to the actions taking place outside its doors. One archivist noted of collecting from the actions outside the gallery: "It would be a very interesting collection, but I fear that our resources are stretched thin already, and we can barely keep up with archiving what happens inside the Gallery."[39]

Nevertheless, I suggest that the VAG is not insulated from the political gatherings at its threshold. The plaza outside the VAG is what Hannah Arendt called a "space of appearance"; a space where being-in-public and speaking and acting together as equals is synonymous with the emergence of the political.[40] The plaza could also be read as a Habermasian bourgeois public sphere, where people exchange opinions and form a public capable of creating (theoretically) state policy. It is also a space closely in keeping with Nancy Fraser's concept of a subaltern counterpublic (a reworking of Habermas's bourgeois public sphere) that welcomes those left out of the primarily European male imagining of the public sphere or a place wherein Michael Hardt and Antonio Negri posit that the multitude could emerge or the commons could come into formation. The relatively small courtyard is a place that fits with many existing philosophical theories of the public, the commons, and the public sphere from the twentieth and twenty-first centuries.[41] In this sense, it is comparable with other museum/public square relationships, such as that between the National Gallery of Britain and Trafalgar Square in London or between the Smithsonian and the National Mall.[42] But importantly, it is also so much a part of the city of Vancouver and the particularities of that site that theory applies only insofar as it can account for the specific nature of the often contradictory setting and politics of Vancouver.

Though many protests have occurred on the north plaza since the gallery opened at the old courthouse site, I use two actions to bookend my analysis – the 2002 intervention into Campbell's speech at *Places of Their Own* (discussed above) and the Occupy Vancouver tent city erected outside the VAG in late 2011. On a Saturday in mid-October of that year, at least 4,000 people gathered on the north plaza of the VAG to inaugurate Occupy Vancouver. Though numbers declined through the following week, those who remained dug in for the long haul, setting up a tent city outside the gallery.[43] Occupiers quickly pitched close to 150 tents and instituted food, health, and safety services, following on similar occupations across the United States and in Montreal, Toronto, and a number of other cities in Canada. Unlike the protest against Campbell, this event was static and unmoving, though many of the issues, particularly wealth distribution, poverty, and government inaction on housing/homelessness, were largely the same.

While I could have chosen any one of many other protests to focus on, such as the widespread pushback against the 2010 Vancouver Winter Olympics or two hockey riots that took place in the immediate vicinity of the gallery, I settled on these two interventions for the multiple ways they intersected with the gallery and brought a local lens to international uprisings (particularly in the case of Occupy). The protest against *Places of Their Own* used an exhibition opening to target the province's neoliberal policies and the city's gentrification, particularly as they affected women.[44] Occupy Vancouver settled in the north plaza to draw attention to government inaction on housing, uneven wealth distribution, and issues of poverty and precarious living. Though ostensibly separate from the gallery itself, I argue that in fact, Occupy Vancouver, like the *Places of their Own* event, highlighted the economic backdrop of the city that has plagued the VAG in its attempts to secure funding for the kind of architect-driven renovation project seen in cultural institutions in many cities in Canada and, indeed, in wealthy cities around the world. Since the early 2000s, the VAG has been trying to secure a new site and funding for a new building, a project that is still underway. In this chapter, I analyze the gallery itself as well as the actions taking place outside, bringing them together through the emergence of Vancouver as an important node of contemporary art production

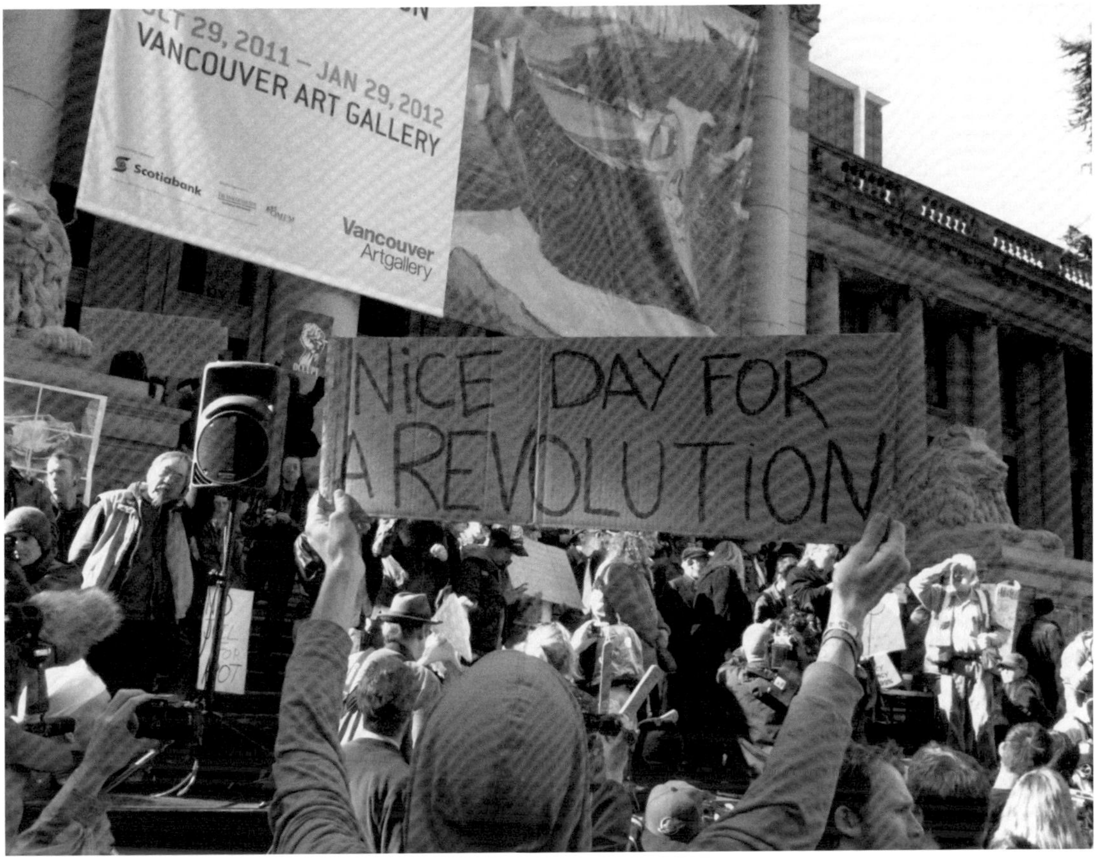

Figure 7.4
Occupy Vancouver, Nice Day for a Revolution, October 2011.

and as a "Creative City" in Richard Florida's sense – an appellation that Occupy profoundly resisted.

In the time between *Places of Their Own* and Occupy Vancouver, Vancouver was frequently described in some circles as an "impressive urban renaissance" and in others as a site of intense gentrification and displacement aimed at creating comfortable spaces for affluent consumers and residents.[45] Indeed, an ongoing battle over gentrification has played out block by block in Vancouver, often bringing together art, activism, and real estate development in surprising ways. In this chapter, I analyze the role of the VAG in these protests, borrowing a question that Bik Van der Pol asked of the Vancouver-based art collective Urban Subjects: "What effect do urban planning and the imagination of developers have on constructing public space and a public imagery?"[46]

The tangle of art, land, and economy is often noted in Vancouver and undergirds both critique and celebration of the spectacular city. I analyze the role of real estate within this relationship and focus my study on the less-than-one-kilometre-square area separating the current location of the VAG and the place it is scheduled to move to by 2021. More than in any of the other chapters, art is central here, and the VAG is the only major art gallery closely analyzed in the book. Questions raised in the chapter deal with a central concern: what will it mean for the gallery to move away from the courtyard to which it is physically linked though symbolically separate? What does it mean when a major art institution also provides the best political platform in the city but remains disconnected from that platform? This is a chapter about thresholds, about the point at which the gallery separates itself from the street and where the "real" in real estate makes material the separation between action, which is kept firmly outside, and the image of that action, which is spectacularly welcomed within. As Terminal City, the end of the rail lines, Vancouver is also the culminating point of the project of this book, a place where protest and creative industries rhetoric both intersect and repel one another, making it nearly impossible to consider one without the other.

Real Estate, Creative Cities, and the Arts

Not long after the 2002 opening of *Carr, O'Keefe, Kahlo: Places of Their Own*, VAG director Kathleen Bartels wrote in the gallery's annual report:

> Each year as we look back on the Gallery's accomplishments and our work in the community, I'm struck with the amazing – and continually expanding – confluence of international art influences in Vancouver. It is remarkable to realize that perhaps no other city our size *in the world* is more cosmopolitan in its creative energies and support for the visual arts.[47]

The figure of the contemporary artist was, at this time, playing an important role in debates over the creative industries. Just prior to the publication of Richard Florida's book on Creative Cities and his argument for innovative urban centres built for (and on the backs of) "creative workers" (a category that includes artists, tech workers, and others), branding of the creative industries came to the foreground in the UK, which began positioning artists as agents of economic growth. Anthony Davies and Simon Ford called this initiative the "surge to merge" artists, institutions (such as the Institute of Contemporary Art in London and the then new Tate Modern in London), advertising/media/PR firms (such as Saatchi and Saatchi advertising), and government agencies (such as the British Council and the government's millennial Cool Britannia campaign).[48] The surge to merge coupled the production of contemporary "edgy" artists with the entrepreneurial spirit of the new economy, folding the branding of nation (the Cool Britannia campaign) into the re-creation of London as a financial centre and tourist destination. As Young British Artists (YBAs) such as Tracey Emin and Damien Hirst became "art stars," any separation between art and its market, symbolic or otherwise, collapsed, and any expression of resistance was immediately rendered ironic.[49] As noted in chapter 1, now the positioning of artists as creative workers in the new economy is taken largely as a given (and actively resisted), but in 2002 it was a key premise of a great deal of critical theory focused on links between contemporary art and cities.

I've shown in the rest of this book how Florida's theory of Creative Cities was taken up unevenly in Canada, but Vancouver offers a special case. While the VAG tried to position itself as the leading gallery in an important contemporary art node (potentially following the UK model), municipal government–oriented creative industries rhetoric in Vancouver tended toward theorizing creativity as a buzzword à la Richard Florida, closely linked with tourism, film production, and software development, with the arts as added value.[50] In 2008, the City of Vancouver Creative Cities Task Force released a report titled *Culture Plan 2008–2018* that echoed Florida's theories almost word for word, noting that "Vancouver is alive with creativity ... Culture is inextricable from Vancouver's livability. It helps our citizens to develop, learn, and participate in the life of our city. It helps our city attract business, workers and tourists."[51]

Though culture is central, it is only vaguely defined – artists did not really register in the government plan. Just a year earlier, in 2007, professor/consultant Pier Luigi Sacco had noted the less-than-ideal circumstances for artists in a report for VanCity (a credit union that invests heavily in culture in the city) titled *The Power of the Arts in Vancouver: Creating a Great City*. According to Sacco, the city had no idea of its own cultural wealth. Artists such as Jeff Wall, Stan Douglas, and Rodney Graham were well known on the international stage, but "an outstanding majority of Vancouverites haven't the faintest idea of who they might be."[52] Vancouver, he continued, had made itself a centre for film production, but the skyline and buildings stood in for any city but itself.[53] The city would stagger on, he suggested, until it found a way out of its "identitarian conundrum,"[54] a process that would only be possible with adequate funding and support at all levels. Sacco's report received a small amount of publicity but then largely disappeared. Nevertheless, Vancouver emerged as a "Creative City" but one that followed neither the logic of the UK model nor of Florida's writings, instead developing rather a somewhat strange concatenation of simultaneous celebration of and resistance to creative industry rhetoric and form.

If the YBAs rendered political commentary inevitably ironic, the same is not true of Vancouver artists and their earnestly political art production that characterized (and characterizes) the Vancouver contemporary art scene. Much of this art, primarily photo-conceptualism and installation, has showcased the "economic

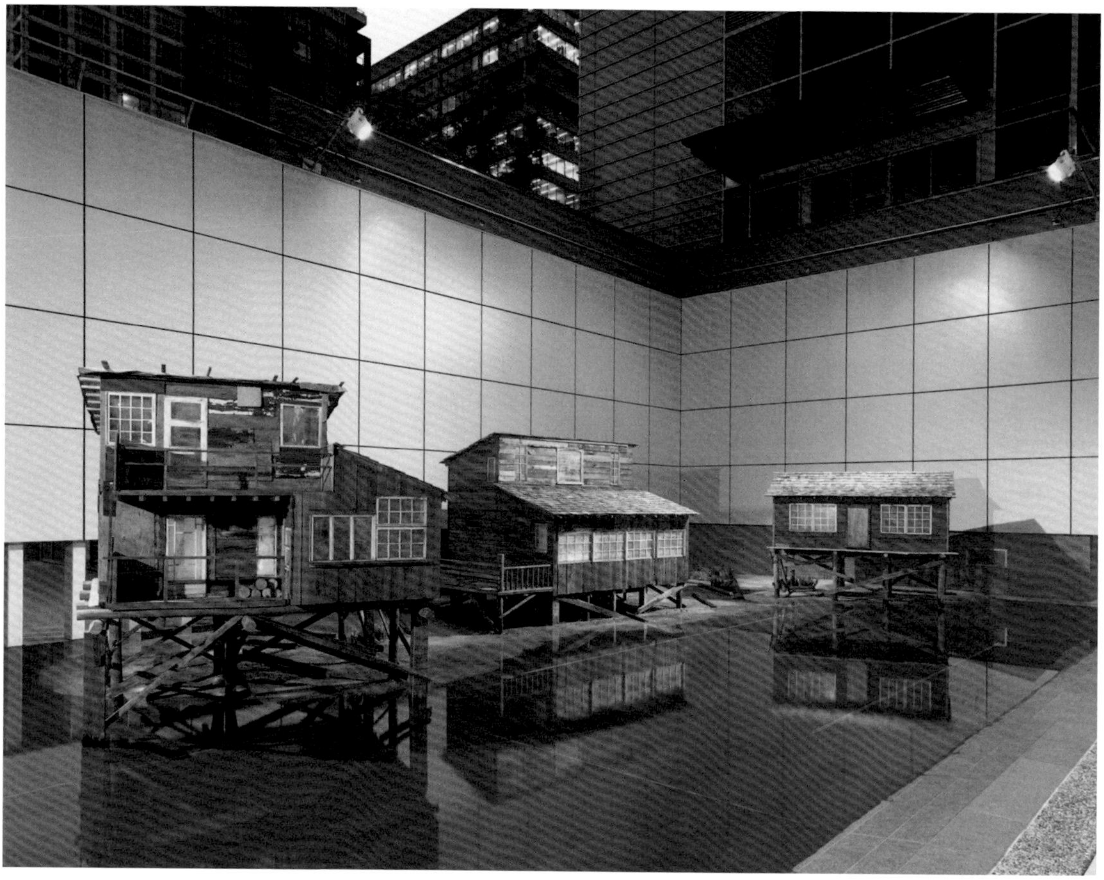

Figure 7.5
Ken Lum, *from shangri-la to shangri-la*, 2010, site-specific installation at Vancouver Art Gallery Offsite, 23 January to 6 September 2010.

landscape" of Vancouver, from the destruction of forests to the building of monster homes and condominiums and the ejection of the poor and marginal from the city space.[55] To take just one example among many, Ken Lum's site-specific installation titled *from shangri-la to shangri-la* (2010), comprising three wooden shacks snuggled at the base of the controversial luxury condominium complex and hotel, Living Shangri-La (the tallest building in Vancouver),[56] is a clear contestation of condo development and gentrification. But it is also a reference to the richly political squatting culture in Vancouver, alluding directly to the wooden shacks that occupied the intertidal zone of Vancouver's North Shore mud flats from the early 1900s to 1971 when they were burned and razed to the ground by the police.[57] Subtly critical yet aesthetically intriguing, Lum's installation illustrates the way that a notable percentage of Vancouver art references the city itself, often through a critical lens and often by drawing on a particular historical moment or event (see Interstice

79). Dieter Roelstraete and Bart De Baere, for example, describe Vancouver's recent art history as revolving around two poles: intellectual and physical retreat from the rest of the world on the one hand and political and social engagement or activism on the other.[58]

The political efficacy of works such as Lum's are much debated. On the one hand, *from shangri-la to shangri-la* and other artworks like it intervene directly into local battles over the changing city, bringing memory into physical form in a way that directly questions the changing living quarters from a community squat outside of capitalist private property to an expensive condo accessible to only a few. Writes curator Melanie O'Brian of art production in Vancouver: "Art is important for its response to the world around us, to rethink or reassess economies."[59]

But on the other hand, the impact of such gestures remains questionable. For example, a number of reviews of the 2004 *Baja to Vancouver* exhibition at the VAG, which brimmed with works commenting critically on Vancouver, noted that "even when artists in this exhibition address disturbing matters, their work remains deceptively casual in appearance."[60] One of the curators even noted, "Also addressed is the fallen notion of social protest and revolt that flourished in the 1960s but is now adrift in consumerism and the creeping age if [*sic*] its original participants."[61]

Despite contestation over its efficacy, the Vancouver art world's critical self-referentiality seems of a particular order, a specific and unique case rather than a generality that can be applied to the global or even North American art world. The political economy of Vancouver itself provides the fodder both for some of the anti-gentrification protests taking place at the threshold of the VAG and elsewhere in the downtown core and for a significant portion of the art produced in the city. This is not to say that artists necessarily participate in the insurgent actions documented in this chapter (although some certainly do) but that there is a thread of political commentary in a great deal of contemporary art production in Vancouver that weaves in and out of the debates taking place in the city. As I pointed out in chapter 3, although the VAG does not collect the ephemera from the events at its threshold, other museums and archives do, most particularly the Museum of Vancouver.[62] Vancouver's political action can thus be traced through a series of reverential/referential artworks, which may or may not function as appendages to wider activist movements, and in turn those artworks often end up being shown or collected at the VAG or in the collections of several philanthropists/collectors (many of whom are developers responsible for the city's wild gentrification). Meanwhile, the detritus of protests against that gentrification (and other issues) ends up in the museum. Is it possible then, that the works of Vancouver artists enter a scenario defined by Greg Sholette, Susan Buck-Morss, and Julian Stallabrass, among others, who argue that museums co-opt resistant standpoints or allow the freedom to make activist statements that have no real impact because the museum space turns action into

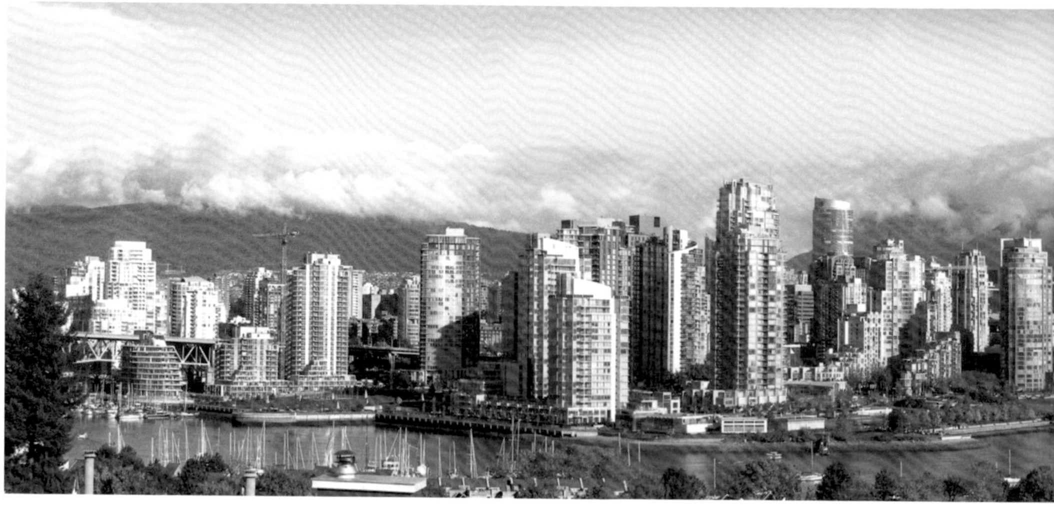

art and art allows the performance of critique without consequence?[63] The answer to this question is not straightforward.

Art production in Vancouver is just one of the ways the city imagines itself as post-national, belonging to differently mapped and understood locales – the Asian perimeter, the west coast. Vancouver is the Terminal City, the Port City, the City of Glass.[64] Poet and critic Jeff Derksen, writing of Vancouver, points out that "where once culture was imagined ... at the national scale, it is now imagined at the urban scale."[65] Vancouver clearly illustrates his point as a city of multiple imaginings: outdoor paradise, drug heaven (haven/hell), real estate dream/nightmare. Thus, more than the other institutions covered in this book, most of which operate under federal legislation for national museums, the VAG, though it too receives funding from multiple levels of government, operates within a city that strives for world city or global city status.

Saskia Sassen's renowned book *Global Cities*, published around the time of the protest against Campbell at the VAG, offers a much bleaker analysis than does Florida's Creative Cities panegyric, released around the same time. In Sassen's book, the global city is one marked by the economic passages of globalization and caught up in the flows of international finance. While Vancouver doesn't produce the "hypermobility of capital" that is central to her argument, it has become a place where that capital briefly stops, in the luxurious condos and real estate market that have sprung up since the late 1980s.[66] Vancouver has become a place to enjoy wealth made elsewhere, a point made repeatedly by the tourism and government officials geographer Jamie Peck interviewed for his study of Vancouver as a Creative City negatively impacted by the effects of neoliberalism.[67] It is, in fact, impossible to understand the protest at the opening of *Places of Their Own*, or Occupy Vancouver, or even the VAG's attempt to move to a new site without first understanding the role of developers in Vancouver.

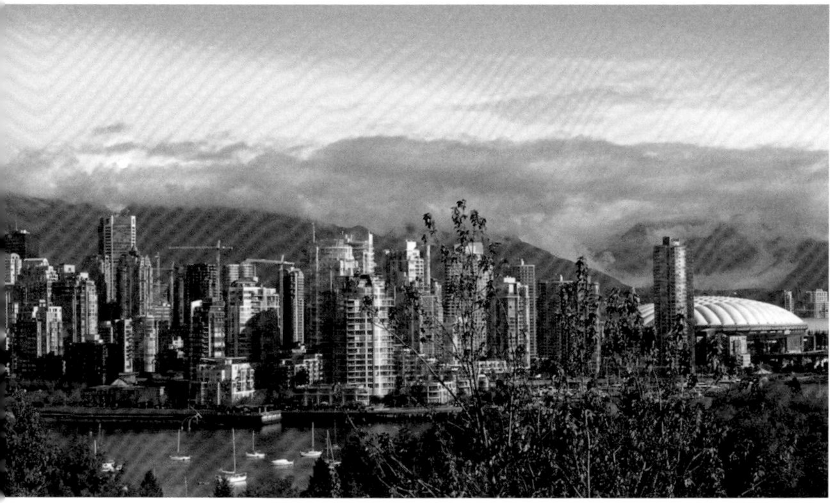

Figure 7.6
Vancouver skyline.

Condos and Neoliberalism in the City of Glass

Neoliberalism, Peck notes, doesn't take the same form in any two cities. Vancouver, he suggests, has made its own neoliberal journey from a resource economy coordination hub to a "real estate growth machine."[68] Geographer Nick Blomley, also writing about Vancouver, agrees, noting: "neoliberalism is, in part, a language of property – a return to central axioms of eighteenth-century liberalism, which places private property as the foundation for the individual self-interest, which when exercised through the free market, is to lead to optimal social good."[69] Central to this conceptualization is the fact that although Vancouver regularly attains high scores as a "livable" city, housing and labour markets are "dramatically decoupled" because the cost of living and the capacity to earn are almost entirely disconnected.[70] Vancouver has developed rapidly, almost giddily, into one of the most expensive cities in the world.[71] It is a city where median income and real estate prices are vastly at odds, in large part because housing in Vancouver is part of a global real estate market where non-local buyers account for significant purchases and use properties solely as investments, unlived in and unrented. It is only in small pockets of resistance, particularly in the Downtown Eastside (DTES), that affordable housing and single-room-occupancy spaces have been preserved.

The first condominium was built in the Greater Vancouver region in 1968, and almost immediately evictions resulting from the conversion of rental units into condos began. It is the legal structure of the condominium, Douglas C. Harris notes, that provides the most visible evidence of gentrification in Vancouver, in part because of the way it "subdivides land in three dimensions."[72] Ownership of land switched from the horizontal to the vertical, detached from the soil and layered into units, packaging private and common ownership, which could be determined only by the height and depth of the building.[73] The building of new condominiums was already controversial in the early 1970s, and pickets and pushback followed the move of condo developments into areas both affluent and poor.

Condos, soaring rents, bidding wars, absentee owners, and skyrocketing house prices have become the name of the game in Vancouver, a city where geography has particular significance – the spectacular landscape attracts buyers, but the mountains and ocean also limit sprawl. Vancouver is what Lorna Brown of the Other Sights art collective calls a FIRE city: "an acronym for finance, insurance, and real estate – now the world's principal source of wealth creation. It has transformed our political, economic, and social landscapes with a complex web of global finance, light regulation, debt, risk tolerance, and property bubbles."[74] Vancouver, Peck notes, has an affordability crisis in which condos act as units of speculation, inflating house prices to a level where the "City of Glass" becomes an urban spectacle, a glittering skyline, made up of units that as living spaces are out of reach for most residents of the city. According to Alissa Firth-Eagland, Vancouver is a city built on "image exportation,"[75] while Peck notes that the city "lives and feeds off its young,"[76] who struggle to enter the real estate market and become the service providers for a wealthy elite that has re-created Vancouver as something of a resort economy – a place for "permanent tourists" to invest, rest, and play in. And yet, notes Peck, echoing my comments above about self-referentiality, Vancouver is profoundly narcissistic and "extraordinarily impressed with itself," even exporting its model of urban development under the title "Vancouverism" for other cities to emulate.[77]

As Graeme Fisher and Andrew Witt noted in a much-circulated article from the radical online journal the *Mainlander*, the speculative housing market in Vancouver emerged hand-in-hand with Creative Cities rhetoric. They point out that the new industry targets culture as a future source of revenue.[78] However, this equation is much more complicated than that outlined in the "surge to merge" theory or in the figure of the culturepreneur. On the one hand, it is now well known that self-entrepreneurship is essential to neoliberalism, as is a burgeoning service sector. As "old" jobs disappear, the "flexible personality," outlined by Brian Holmes in a 2001 article on creative industries and ability to adapt to economic change, becomes less of a choice and more of a necessity.[79] Artists, who are often self-employed as creators but support their artmaking through service sector jobs, occupy both realms and are thus important figures in maintaining the illusion of the Creative City as a fun place to live and work in. Artists are winners and losers in Creative Cities; they benefit from increased interest in the arts but suffer from continued low incomes – only a few reach the heights of the Vancouver School and enter the international art market. And in Vancouver, the emergence of the condominiums and the development of formerly low-rent areas are in fact tightly connected to the patronage of at least certain forms of art.

"Willingly or grudgingly, developers in Vancouver and Toronto have become some of the greatest patrons of public art in Canada," writes Albert Watson, who notes that Vancouver has policies requiring that developers purchase works of art in exchange for rezoning density bonuses (the right to build bigger or taller edifices than zoning on a site allows).[80] But simultaneously, developers have become enthusiastic collectors, arguably deeply influencing the direction of art production and display. Bob Rennie, founder of Rennie Marketing Systems and the so-called "Condo King," who has marketed such developments as Living Shangri-la and the Woodward's department store redevelopment, with mottos like "Intellectual Property" and "Be Bold or Move to Suburbia" (see Interstice 7g), now owns a gallery in Chinatown at the edge of the DTES where the Rennie Collection (one of the largest contemporary art collections in Canada) is shown.[81] He is also chair of the Tate's North America Acquisitions Committee and a member of the Art Institute of Chicago's Board of Trustees, and he recently made a large donation of works to the National Gallery of Canada.[82] Rennie is often discussed alongside Michael Audain, the CEO of Polygon Homes and a long-time supporter of the arts in Vancouver. The Michael Audain Foundation funds the cutting-edge Audain Gallery at Simon Fraser University (one part of which is housed in the aforementioned Woodward's building, now the SFU Goldcorp Centre for the Arts) as well as North Vancouver's well-known Presentation House Gallery, renamed the Polygon Gallery when it moved to a purpose-built new building on the North Shore waterfront in 2017.[83] Both Rennie and Audain have been deeply involved (often antagonistically) in the VAG's quest to secure a new space.

As Fisher and Witt remind us, even as developers have invested heavily in the arts and in arts infrastructure (for example, Reliance Properties recently made a large donation to art school Emily Carr University's new building),[84] the city has become an increasingly difficult place for artists to live in. Artists are often found in the first wave of gentrifiers.[85] They move in to central, low-income neighbourhoods, displace the residents, and make the area appear safer and more appealing to wealthier property owners, who in turn displace the artists.[86] At the opening of *Places of Their Own*, activists gathered in part to take on Gordon Campbell's cuts to women's programs, but a corollary to this was the way that government initiatives, particularly at the municipal level, had broadly accepted and even celebrated the "renoviction" of working-class, single-room-occupancy hotels and studio apartments in more affordable parts of Vancouver in favour of a vision of the city as a "creative class paradise disconnected from the working class history of the area."[87] In the years preceding that protest, provincial funding for social programs had been cut drastically, and "as the level of state funding withered, some artist-run centres in Vancouver uncritically turned toward private/public funding structures that led them to enter into arrangements with real-estate developers. These types of public sector–private sector arrangements now typify neo-liberal urban regeneration programs."[88] Thus, even as some artists benefit from public works programs included in condo building, others are displaced from the city, and still others have their work collected by those most involved in changing the city.[89]

Vancouver Art Gallery

Given the previous description of a City of Glass, renowned for the near-constancy of its pace of change, the Vancouver Art Gallery itself has remained on the outside looking in. The City of Vancouver has largely avoided attempts to encourage a "Bilbao effect" and has not enthusiastically supported the starchitect-redesign of its cultural buildings.[90] Unlike that of the majority of slick new cultural institutions gracing other Canadian cities, the architecture of the VAG, for example, retains the idea of the museum as "temple."[91] With pillars at both front and rear entrances, marble lions gracing the front gates, and a rotunda capped in oxidized copper, the stone building echoes the architecture of traditional museums, banks, temples, and other establishments associated with power and wealth. Not only is the VAG out of step with the spread of the Bilbao effect, it is also at odds with architectural innovation in Vancouver, the exportable "Vancouverism" mentioned above. Alissa Firth Eagland writes, "Vancouver's buildings possess a supreme self-awareness of the tourist gaze/documentation/media/lens/camera."[92] And yet, Vancouver remains one of the few major municipalities in Canada that has not overhauled its major cultural institution.[93] Why not? Reasons include the particularly evocative site on which the gallery is currently located, the extreme lack of space in Vancouver, the fact that the building housing the VAG is one of the few early twentieth-century buildings left in the city, and the cost of real estate.

Artist Stan Douglas, writing in 1991, noted that the VAG opened in the former courthouse in 1983 just as the British Columbia Social Credit party was elected to government. As Douglas notes, the goals of the Social Credit party foreshadowed the neoliberal adjustments that were to come to fruition in the 1990s.[94] In 1983, the party's policies of "restraint" were met with reaction and solidarity in a series of province-wide demonstrations culminating in an alliance known as the Solidarity Coalition and a 30,000-strong demonstration outside BC Place Stadium (a large downtown sports stadium) on 11 July 1983. Dissent against the budget grew, but despite opposition and stalling tactics, the proposed legislation was pushed through and became law. On 15 October 1983, a Solidarity demonstration drew 60,000 people to a march that passed the Social Credit convention then taking place at the Hotel Vancouver (which fronts the north plaza of the VAG). Talk grew of a general strike, and through late October, teachers and members of the public service union walked off the job. However, the coalition fractured, separate labour agreements were negotiated, and the government's restraint program emerged largely intact.[95] Douglas calls the demonstration "aborted sedition" and uses it as a parable to introduce the "frequently bizarre politics that are the perpetual backdrop of cultural activity in this province."[96] He notes:

> As they passed Hornby Street, a few thousand of the Solidarity demonstrators who marched down Robson in October 1983 may have noticed a considerably smaller gathering outside the old provincial courthouse – where at 10:00 AM, Governor General Edward Schreyer was delivering one of the speeches that would constitute the official opening of the VAG. For the previous four years, VAG director Luke Rombout had mounted an extremely successful campaign to "take the gallery to court," and move his institution from its old quarters at 1145 Georgia to the 1906 courthouse building three blocks away.[97]

Writing in the reissued *Vancouver Anthology* in 2011, Douglas mused that the demonstrations of 1983 now "seem hardly possible because the policies of privatization and deregulation seen by many as unthinkable in 1983 are, for the time being, the natural order of things."[98]

The strategic plans put forward by the VAG over the years document a fast-changing scenario following the 1983 collapse of Solidarity. In the early 1980s, following protests against the cancellation of artist Paul Wong's exhibition *Confused: Sexual Views*, antagonism grew between the gallery and local artists, a rift that would take some years to heal.[99] In 1985, 75 per cent of the gallery's budget came from government sources, a percentage that fell to less than 50 by 2002. By 2008, the gallery was hoping to generate one-third of its income from government funding, one-third from earned income, and one-third from contributed income.[100] The need to collect funds required the tactical repositioning of the VAG as an important and cutting-edge cultural institution, both locally and globally. Thus, the 2007–10 strategic plan included a series of "New Institutional Core Values" in keeping with the presentation of Vancouver as a global participant in the international art scene. The VAG thus came to be both an important player in the Vancouver art world and a promotional vehicle, demonstrating the vitality of the local art scene for export (a drastic change from the early 1980s). This dual mandate is a clear change from the 2002–04 (much thinner) strategic plan, which was concerned largely with getting the gallery on an even financial keel. The period also saw the controversial end of Alf Bogusky's time as director and his replacement by Kathleen Bartels and a consequent emphasis on encouraging donations, building memberships, innovative programming and curating, and making the most of the location.[101] The goals of this early plan were modest: try to develop a recognizable brand identity and increase government support.[102] There was no mention of a new building.

By 2003, however, a new gallery space was clearly a concern. The annual report of that year notes that following a national advertisement, twenty-three architectural firms expressed interest in potentially designing a new building and a master planning committee had been established.[103] A summary in the 2004–06 *Strategic Plan* states, "By October, 2006, we expect to have finalized plans for a vastly improved facility that will double our existing space, dramatically increase our impact on the lives of hundreds of thousands of British Columbians, and further elevate Vancouver's status in the international art world."[104] Along with a lack of earthquake protection and infrastructure at the existing site, the report notes that one of the prime motivations for moving or renovating is "an unwelcoming exterior" (although it is not explained whether that means the architecture or those gathering outside).[105] So, too, an inability to showcase the permanent collection or emerging artists (both local and international) is cited as a reason for a new space.[106] The 2004 annual report notes that Michael Maltzan Architecture of Los Angeles had been selected to work with Henriquez Partners of Vancouver to explore options for expanding the current site of the VAG.[107] This was approximately at the same time that the ROM and AGO were undergoing renovations in Toronto. By 2005, the Board of Trustees had abandoned that plan and was looking for other sites in the city.[108]

By 2009, according to *Vancouver Magazine*, "the VAG ha[d] seen non-government funds (i.e., gifts and income) grow fivefold, from $1.9 million to $9.8 million. The gallery's foundation, meanwhile, ha[d] skyrocketed from $200,000 to nearly $10 million. Numbers like that allow institutions to begin functioning independent of the whims of government."[109] Nevertheless, it was also noted that government support in Vancouver and British Columbia fell far behind provincial and federal funds in Ontario and Quebec (other provinces are not mentioned) for similar institutions and that the VAG was largely supported by the Vancouver public. In fact, memberships, admittance, the museum store, and rentals accounted for a whopping 48 per cent of the VAG's budget, a far higher percentage than at most comparable institutions.[110]

The various plans and reports on the possibility of a new site are peppered with Creative City rhetoric. For example: "an expansion of the Vancouver Art Gallery would provide the City of Vancouver with a visual arts institution that matches the ambitions and growing international stature of our community … while further elevating Vancouver's international status as a key cultural centre with connections to the Asia Pacific arena and the rest of the world."[111] Further, "it is our hope that [the VAG's] new home … [will be] significant and powerful in design and scope, giving the City of Vancouver an instantly recognizable visual landmark not unlike those found in other major cities around the world."[112] This sentiment is repeated in the 2007–10 strategic plan, which recognizes the economic importance of tourism and states, "it is the Gallery's hope that a new facility could ultimately become to Vancouver what the Opera House is to Sydney, the Guggenheim Museum to Bilbao, and the Eiffel Tower to Paris – a recognizable symbol of the city, and an attraction for tourists from around the world."[113]

Despite the VAG's promise to finalize its plans by 2006, it was only in 2008 that an initial budget appeared. The developer Michael Audain helmed the board's Real Estate Committee for Facility Expansion. In that year, the gallery decided on a site just a few blocks from the current one, known as Larwill Park, but a request came from the provincial government to consider moving to False Creek (southeast of downtown) to land that had been used for Expo 86.[114] The False Creek recommendation did not last long, and by 2009 the VAG had again set its sights on the Larwill Park site.[115] This was the state of things in 2011 when Occupy began.

Eviction, Occupy, and the VAG

Encouraged in large-part by a call in the Vancouver-based *Adbusters* magazine, the Occupy movement began as Occupy Wall Street in September 2011.[116] Emerging from the Arab Spring and uprisings in Tunisia, at Tahrir Square in Egypt, and elsewhere, Occupy coalesced around the idea of an international global uprising against the 1% (and those who benefit from the concentration of wealth among the top-earning 1%).[117] "We are the 99%" was a popular unifying slogan of Occupy, which attempted to show that the vast majority of people in the world were getting poorer and paying for the risk-taking strategies and wealth accumulation of the ultra-rich. Beginning with Occupy Wall Street at Zuccotti Park in New York City, Occupy spread to other US cities and then across the globe, largely taking the form of occupations of streets and public spaces. In response to the alterglobalization movement (which was one of its immediate predecessors), it answered the critique that protest was little more than carnival by staying put and creating a commons for and by the people. Occupy was characterized by encampments, squatting, and small, horizontally organized, anarchist-inspired communities. "Occupation is … an art of duration and endurance, manifesting the paradoxical synthesis of social *movement* and *mobilization* with *immobility*, the refusal to move."[118] It was defined by the slogan "This is not a protest. This is a movement."[119] Occupy was specifically leaderless, and it refused to issue a set of demands.

In searching through the Occupy Archives, held by the SFU Special Collections and gathered from a number of participants, what becomes immediately obvious is that Occupy Vancouver may have been leaderless but it was highly and effectively organized.[120] Volunteer Coordination Committee meetings show Occupiers recruiting, communicating, volunteering, arranging subcommittees, organizing outreach, figuring out what needed to be done at the encampment, and how to do it.[121] Work groups, activities, and seminars emerge on topics such as animal liberation, housing and homelessness, art and activism, electoral reform, racism faced by international students, poster-making, and "organic astronaut training" (no explanation).[122] The General Assembly, held 8 October to kick off Occupy Vancouver, noted that "no one group, person, or website could ever speak for this diverse gathering of individuals," but broad principles, among them an overarching premise that this was a "non-violent movement for social, economic and political change," resulted. Pamphlets handed out encouraged passersby to participate to "oppose systemic inequality, militarization, environmental destruction, and the erosion of civil liberties and human rights."[123] The minutiae of running the relatively small Occupy encampment as an open and inclusive space is immediately apparent in the archive, along with attempts to teach Occupiers how to work with consensus models, efforts to peacekeep and deal with confrontation, overdoses, and competing visions for the camp and for the future of the world.[124]

Following the General Assembly, Occupy Vancouver set up an encampment outside the VAG on 15 October 2011. In his analysis of the early days of the encampment, poet and activist Stephen Collis notes, "The enthusiasm was hard to resist." Quoting Arendt, he argues, "people wanted, above all else, to learn from each other, to teach each other, to share their thoughts and ideas, to listen and to be heard. They wanted a place for this free exchange. They wanted an agora. And they still do."[125] The tent city included a first aid tent, a library, portable toilets, a stage, a food tent, and almost 150 tents, and it lasted more than a month before the Occupiers were evicted. Though it had many goals, for the purposes of this chapter I look at Occupy Vancouver's link to the courtyard outside the VAG, and at the way it dealt with land, gentrification, and real estate. I'm interested in how this particular encampment outside the gallery brought together many of the issues circulating at the time so that the protest itself took on a certain self-referentiality. Furthermore, squabbles over the direction of Occupy Vancouver clearly indicated and highlighted some of the gaps and erasures in activist culture in Vancouver and elsewhere.

While Occupy was setting up camp outside the VAG, visitors to the gallery would have seen banners for *Shore, Forest and Beyond: Art from the Audain Collection*, an exhibition that opened on 29 October of that year. The show consisted of 170 objects from Michael Audain and Yoshiko Karasawa's collection.[126] As noted above, Audain is a well-known philanthropist for the arts, and he is also a prolific housing developer as director of Polygon Homes Ltd. His support of cutting-edge projects clearly demonstrates some of the contradictions at the heart of Vancouver (in his earlier years, Audain was also an anti-nuclear activist). Audain and Karasawa have made numerous gifts to the VAG over the years and more to the Vancouver art world, primarily via the Audain Foundation, which underpins many politically astute exhibitions (including many discussed in this book). Nevertheless, the personal exhibition of a developer's collection, on display during a protest focused largely on gentrification and homelessness, created an ironic backdrop to the encampment.

Housing has lurked in the background throughout this chapter, and yet it has also been central to the issues under consideration, contributing to a lost generation of young workers in Vancouver who cannot afford to live in the city, fraying the edges of the perfect Floridian Creative City, padding the coffers of the city's developers, and eventually contributing to the VAG's uncomfortable situation of needing a new building but finding little space on which to build one. And of course, all of these matters circle around the central quandary of Vancouver's success as a livable city – collateral homelessness and the plight of those who are simply unable to keep up with the accelerating cost of rent and the push downward on social housing and SROs (single-room occupancies) that used to characterize the DTES. The VAG's potential move to the *last* undeveloped block in the downtown core ripples through the whole city as development forces out precarious communities.

What Occupy Vancouver had in its favour was the success of previous protest encampments in Vancouver. These include (among others) the squats of the 1970s, Woodsquat (2002) (see Interstice 7g), and the tent city organized on an East Hastings (DTES) site owned by developer Concord Pacific during Vancouver's 2010 Winter Olympic Games.[127] Woodsquat and the 2010 tent city placed the housing crisis in the spotlight and resulted in the building of social housing units (even though they were granted reluctantly or scaled back from post-encampment promises).[128] Further, previous occupations and encampments had led to a BC Supreme Court decision in 2009 reversing a long-standing Vancouver bylaw that stated that camping in public parks was not allowed because it blocked other uses of the park. The Supreme Court decision allowed camping if no alternative shelters were available.[129]

There was, however, one significant different between Occupy and the previous tent encampments in Vancouver. Many of those organizing Occupy Vancouver were not, in fact, homeless. Emerging from the Occupy Wall Street encampment at Zuccotti Park in New York City, Occupy tended to be "driven by the frustration of the young educated middle classes ... confronting societies controlled by hugely rich ruling elites but having little hope of a secure future for themselves, despite their university educations."[130] Occupy was not about homelessness, but rather, as renowned feminist artist and activist Martha Rosler argued of Occupy Wall Street,

"Many of the protesting students and young postgraduates, for their part, were preparing for jobs in what we have come to call the knowledge industries, or, more recently, the creative industries, a branch of the former."[131]

In Rosler's write-up, Occupy equalled resistance to the Creative City and to its underpinning in a neoliberal framework that ruined prospects for the future, creating a precarious workforce with few opportunities. Rosler writes specifically of Occupy Wall Street:

> The popular reception of art and its greatly expanded audience have allowed, in the present moment, a mutual visibility between artists and other underemployed groups, both educated and undereducated ... How else to explain the peculiar position of artists at or near the vanguard of capitalist organization? ... The artists and artist-run groups, and others belonging to the creative-class demographic – which often overlaps with the group of those who identify as grassroots activists, whether or not they have been to art school – have been at the center of instituting, strategizing, and energizing the Occupy Wall Street movement at New York's Zuccotti Park – renamed Liberty Park.[132]

Trying to understand the professionalization of arts, the rise in the art market, cultural industries, post-Fordist labour, and Richard Florida, Rosler argues that artists have been highly complicit in "the renegotiation of urban meaning for elites" and yet also hold the key to resisting their own precarity.[133] Rosler draws this relationship out in detail, but the gist of it is that artists and their corollary needs (small art galleries, studios, coffee shops, etc.) lead inevitably to the gentrification of neighbourhoods even as economic opportunity is chipped away. The Creative City is a clear articulation of Lauren Berlant's "cruel optimism," "when something you desire is an obstacle to your flourishing."[134] "Artists," Rosler writes, "are hardly unaware of their positioning by urban elites, from the municipal and real estate interests to the high-end collectors and museum trustees. Ironically, perhaps, this is also the moment in which social engagement on the part of artists is an increasingly viable modality within the art world."[135] In other words, artists are exploiters, but they are also exploited, and this dual position can be used as a stage from which to launch resistance. Here, Rosler could be talking directly about Vancouver, with its self-referentiality, its extreme gentrification, its critical art scene, and its developers. She concludes, "Florida says gentrify, we say Occupy."[136] In Vancouver, though artists were not taking the lead in Occupy, similar rhetoric was pervasive, possibly because artists have been profoundly involved in and also resistant to gentrification in the city.

At the start of Occupy Vancouver, Mayor Gregor Robertson inadvertently echoed some of Rosler's sentiments when he offered his support for the protest. "In these turbulent economic times, I recognize and appreciate the concerns and angst that people, especially young people, feel about the economy, rising inequality, the environment, and state of the world right now," he noted. "I fully support the right of people to demonstrate those concerns publicly and peacefully."[137] Support, in short, was offered for creative workers.[138] The tent city would not be permanent; it would not echo the tent cities that had been previously installed elsewhere in the city. Even as Robertson expressed his support, signs were installed by city workers stating that tents could not be pegged to the ground. It quickly became clear that the city supported Occupy Vancouver only insofar as tents at Occupy were being used by those who had somewhere else to go when the winds picked up or the weather turned fierce. In this manner, Robertson avoided homelessness in his statement, offering support only for youth struggling in the conditions of neoliberalism (who might otherwise have entered the market if they were able to find jobs). Occupy was "made safe" in the mayor's message and also in the mainstream media and in later interpretation of events by rendering it as a space for creative workers to announce their angst at the Creative City.

Of course, this was not really what was taking place outside the VAG. Within the camp itself, a steep learning curve was required. As Mohawk organizer with the Native Youth Sexual Health Network in Toronto Jessica Yee put it just after the formation of Occupy Wall Street: "There's just one problem: THE UNITED STATES IS ALREADY BEING OCCUPIED. THIS IS INDIGENOUS LAND."[139] The appellation of the 99% vs. the 1% was thus intensely problematic because it collapsed difference to a single factor under the umbrella of an occupation. Konstantin Kilibarda argues that Occupy's organization against austerity measures, global inequity, and labour precarity elided "settler-colonial dispossession, genocide, slavery, imperial adventurism, indentured and precarious labour, as well as patriarchal, xenophobic and anti-immigrant nationalisms."[140] As Kilibarda notes, in Canada the use of the term Occupy was particularly problematic given the way that blockades and "occupation" have often been used as strategies of Indigenous resistance to state appropriation of their lands.[141] Occupation was also, of course, an important tactic used by the civil rights movement and in sit-ins by any number of marginalized groups.[142] Occupy tended to overlook and sometimes actively erase many previous efforts and ongoing resistances.[143]

In Vancouver, as Indigenous peoples, homeless peoples, long-time community activists from the DTES and elsewhere, drug users and educators, street nurses, anti-capitalist activists, creative workers, students, and others moved into the north plaza, the encampment changed and evolved.[144] What becomes clear in Kilibarda's analysis is that in 2011, "there was very little crossover" between anti-capitalism critiques and Indigenous solidarity.[145] From the first mass protest outside the VAG, Occupy Vancouver acknowledged that it was "taking place on un-ceded Coast

Salish territories" but nevertheless tripped on the question "how can we reclaim/ liberate space without recolonizing/reoccupying it?"[146] In answer, an Indigenous Solidarity committee was formed. Ongoing education in the camp attempted to show that "all the economic and political injustices [we are protesting] are built on the history of colonialism and that colonialism and indigenous struggles are foundational."[147] As the camp changed, possibilities for education and exchange grew, but simultaneously, the City changed its tune.

In early November 2011, following the tragic death of Ashlie Gough from a drug overdose at the camp, Premier Christy Clark sought a province-wide injunction against Occupy Vancouver (citing health and safety concerns).[148] On 4 November 2011, the Office of the City Manager of Vancouver posted laminated notices on the Occupy site, noting a city bylaw that "a person must not erect or place a structure or tent on City Lands without the prior written consent of the City Manager."[149] It was pointed out that the VAG plaza was City lands and no written consent had been provided and thus the tents "are in contravention of the City Land Regulation By-law."[150] On 7 November, a second notice from the City Manager appeared, this one more conversational, beginning, "The City has long supported the right to gather and carry out peaceful protest. The Occupy movement is a global project addressing a number of important issues of concern to our citizens."[151] After noting an "escalation of safety concerns in the area of fire safety, injection drug use, the presence of pests and other hazards," it declared that "Staff have been directed to end the encampment in a way that can be done safely and peacefully while respecting the right to protest."[152] Finally, it concluded: "The Vancouver Art Gallery site will remain a site where protest is welcome – the city commits to retain the stage and electric power for the sound system to support the ongoing Occupy Vancouver protest. However, *by this notice, we ask you to take your tents, belongings and any other items or structures off the site immediately so that the safety concerns can be addressed*" (emphasis in original).[153] Occupiers fought back in court and received a court order stating that with a few changes (for example, removing tarpaulins from the top of tents and allowing fire access routes), Occupy Vancouver would no longer be in violation of fire regulations, which was interpreted as a legal right to stay put.[154] On 10 November, the Office of the City Manager released another notice stating that the tents were still in contravention of the City Land Regulation By-Law.[155] Simultaneously, a sacred fire that had been lit by the Coast Salish Elders Committee became a site of altercation. The fire was lit to provide "warmth, connection, [and] morale … fire is one of the four sacred elements of life." It was also lit in memory of Ashlie Gough.[156] According to Collis, "the VPD and fire department chose to force their way in and douse what was little more than a source of some smoke around which people peacefully prayed."[157] There was a scuffle, and allegedly a police officer was bitten and kicked.[158] At the

General Assembly, Occupy Vancouver decided to accept most of VFD's safety regulations and to reaffirm the encampment's non-violent stance.[159]

Throughout Occupy Vancouver, the VAG did not intervene. Nevertheless, it provided the backdrop to the encampment and was used (symbolically or otherwise) by Occupiers and their evictors. On 7 November 2011, during hearings regarding the injunction for Occupy Vancouver, the acting manager, Film and Special Events Office, Streets Administration Branch of the Engineering Department of the City of Vancouver, entered the following in an affidavit that supported the City Manager's call for the eviction of the Occupy encampment. After explaining why permits for public events are necessary and explaining how permissions are assigned, he stated,

> The north plaza is a very sensitive area. There is a very large underground vault comprising a number of rooms which lies beneath roughly on [*sic*] third of the north plaza. That vault holds the permanent art collection of the Vancouver Art Gallery when it is not on display, as well as offices. The vault is protected by a waterproof membrane which is roughly a foot below the surface of the plaza. Any damage to the membrane could result in damage to the permanent art collection. My office always directs applicants who use the north plaza that there is to be no staking of tents or structures, only sandbags or cement blocks and digging is not permitted.[160]

He also noted that other events that typically take place were threatened with cancellation (including, potentially, the annual erection of a Christmas tree) and that the Santa Claus parade would have to be moved.[161] Similar comments about the fragile protection of the VAG's collection were included in other affidavits, among them that of the director of Facilities Design and Management of the City of Vancouver. He additionally notes that he observed Occupiers digging trenches to divert water away from the tents and that residents were smoking near the air intakes to the VAG: "On November 1, 2011, I accompanied staff into the Art Gallery and noted a very strong smell of marijuana throughout the exhibition area."[162] On 18 November 2011, this story was picked up in the media, and *Metro News Vancouver* reported that city lawyer Ben Parkin had used the issue of ditch-digging and tent pegs to argue for an injunction against Occupy Vancouver.[163] The story also reported that Parkin argued for other protests, suggesting that Occupy was taking up the space normally used by "many groups, hundreds of groups over the years."[164]

The VAG itself remained totally silent on the topic of Occupy Vancouver – the encampment was something that was taking place on City land and was thus disconnected from the gallery. On the other hand, Occupier Lee Bacchus writes,

> The Occupy … tents enlightened. They claimed space and provided shelter, but more than that they arrested attention and demanded to be included in the inventory of the visible city. They also made their inhabitants feel validated and *seen*. In this sense, the Occupy tent city was an inadvertent art installation, and its settlement on the Art Gallery grounds entirely appropriate. The tent city's fragile, cubist forms mirrored and revealed by its very nature the flimsy nature of late capitalism, the widening cracks in its foundation and its increasing inability to protect the vulnerable from socio-economic storms.[165]

An idea that Occupy Vancouver could be activism and art was picked up again in the *Mainlander* when Andrew Witt argued,

> [Lawyer Ben] Parkin's argument, and many others made in a similar vein during the occupation, demonstrated how the VAG's grounds were not only occupied, but mentally perforated. This is the power of critique as occupation, critique keyed to the promise and threat of occupation … However diminutive, the occupation perforated the psychic life and power of the VAG's professional edifice.[166]

Meanwhile, as poet and activist Steven Collis explained:

> The question of art and revolution has hovered around Occupy Vancouver, perhaps to an extent not seen in other urban occupations, in part simply because *this* occupation was on the lawn of its city's art gallery, and because *this* city's space most clearly identified with political demonstration is, in fact, an art gallery lawn … The idea was in fact proposed, several times, by different individuals, to declare the occupation a "site-specific" or "performance" work, or an "installation." Essentially, this would have been done to "get the city off the occupation's back," rather than to say anything specific about art or revolution or the relationship between art and revolution.[167]

Whether sculpture, revolutionary artwork, or emcampment, Occupy Vancouver was evicted peacefully on 21 November 2011. As Kilibarda notes, following the eviction it kept going, and "a major focus of local Occupy activism has in fact shifted to long-standing anti-gentrification actions represented by the newly formed #occupycondos campaign – thus creatively bringing together the energy of Occupy with longer-standing campaigns in Vancouver."[168] Thus, in mid-November, more than 100 Occupiers left the VAG and gathered several blocks away outside of Bob Rennie's art gallery. They released an open letter stating:

> You sir, are not an artist. But that won't stop you for masquerading as one. To re-use a phrase popularized by #OccupyVancouver, your *oeuvre* is real estate speculation and your *medium* is displacement ... You have declared war on the poor across Vancouver – in Chinatown, on the DTES, Mount Pleasant, there is a war everywhere but in your own back yard. You have profited off our backs, and now you use the arts to resuscitate your tainted name.[169]

While the presence of art, art workers, Creative Cities, and gentrification is everywhere, a chasm remains between Rosler's argument with regard to Occupy Wall Street and what happened at Occupy Vancouver. The "creative class" was certainly present in Vancouver, but the concerns of young precarious creative workers butted up against ongoing and long-standing inequalities that were present both within and outside the encampment. One of the key results of Occupy was, as W.J.T. Mitchell notes, to change the mainstream media discussion from deficit reduction to income inequality.[170] But as many have noted, that was but one part of the problem.

A New Building for the Vancouver Art Gallery?

As the Occupy encampment drew to a close, efforts to secure a site for a new gallery building ramped up. In the meantime, Bob Rennie and economic forecaster David Baxter circulated a report that suggested distributing the VAG's collection across several different venues. Their idea (which was rapidly associated solely with Rennie) quickly became divisive, with Audain at the VAG leading the push for a new single site in a city with very little space available and Rennie arguing strongly for a different solution. Said Rennie, a single site "is an artifact of a time long past, a museum piece itself, reflecting the old debt-fuelled economy of unconscious spending that is long, and forever, gone."[171] Rennie's idea to divide the gallery across seven different sites, each catering to a different kind of art (First Nations, Emily Carr, contemporary, etc.) met with a chilly response from the gallery, but Rennie nonetheless declared: "My job is to city-build."[172] Bartels argued that the plan would stretch resources, undermine the education component of the gallery's mandate, and prevent broad exhibitions. Rennie retorted by drawing attention to the huge amount of fundraising that would be required for a single building and hinted that the VAG would not be up to the task: "Once you've given away naming rights to the building, it does get difficult to raise large sums of money ... This way we have eight to 10 different naming rights." He concluded by offering a potential example: "the Vancouver Art Gallery's Michael Audain Museum of Contemporary First Nations Art."[173] Soon, according to local reporters, Rennie and Bartels were no longer speaking, and more than 200 artists in Vancouver had signed a petition advocating for a single site.[174] Eventually, the VAG asked Lord Cultural Resources to comment on and evaluate the Rennie and Baxter idea. Its memo runs to seven pages and summarily dismisses the multi-site proposal, arguing that capital expenditures and operating costs would be high, that attendance and memberships would drop, and that in turn these would affect the gallery's ability to attract government funding and philanthropic donations.[175] Rennie responded by stating, "The Response reads not as a thoughtful response to a plausible option, but rather that the assignment was to attack, not to inform about how our proposal compares and contrasts to the big box alternative."[176]

While such rancour arguably made the VAG's quest for a new space even more difficult (particularly in an intensively competitive real estate market that Rennie had contributed significantly to creating), what also resulted was a narrowing of the spectrum of possibility into a choice between the contrasting visions of two developers. Then Audain, in a move that surprised everyone, left the board of the VAG (though he publicly maintained his support for the institution and remained honorary chairman of the Board of Trustees), and his collection is now the base of a newly established private gallery in Whistler, a move that was widely perceived as a slight to the VAG.[177] The show of his collection that had taken place during Occupy Vancouver marked the apex of his relationship with the gallery.

This was the situation in early 2013 when Bartels made a presentation to City Council advocating for a place for the VAG at Larwill Park.[178] Wrote one reporter, "the block, worth a conservative $150 million or so, is also expensive in other ways. Rennie, in his own presentation to the panel, calculates it would cost the city $202 million once it factored in lost taxes and potential contributions from developers who might buy the site."[179] At that point, Rennie suggested that the city sell the block (to developers) and use the funds to help the VAG expand its current site.[180] But Rennie's proposal was overruled, and council granted the VAG a long-term lease for two-thirds of the land, although with conditions attached: the block had to be shared with an office tower, and the gallery would have to raise $100 million from the federal government and $50 million from the provincial government by 30 April 2015. Any other costs would have to be covered by private sources. In making the announcement, the mayor of Vancouver again repeated Creative Cities rhetoric, positioning the gallery's move as a financial boon to the city: "In every respect on the arts scene," the mayor stated, "we are well-deserving of elevating to a purpose-built art gallery that brings all of this together and enables us to celebrate and to benefit from the significant economic impact that a new gallery will have."[181]

In 2013, having received approval from the city for the lease of two-thirds of Larwill Park, the VAG announced an open process for proposals for the new site and shortlisted five architectural firms.[182] In April 2014, the VAG settled on architects Herzog & de Meuron (known for the Tate Modern in London and the Bird's Nest in Beijing) to design their new building.[183] But by April 2015, the gallery had met none of the City's conditions.[184] Nevertheless, the firm released their proposed design in 2016, and eventually the memorandum of understanding between the City and the gallery for raising funds for the site was extended to December 2018.[185]

Heavy on natural materials, including a wood cladding very much at odds with the titanium swirls of Frank Gehry's buildings or the strict metal and glass lines of Libeskind museums yet in keeping with the spectacular offerings of contemporary galleries, the building designed by Herzog & de Meuron evokes both Asian and Indigenous influences (though to my knowledge extensive consultation of members of either of those communities in Vancouver was not part of the plan). The VAG's website announced: "The rich design offers appealing public spaces, thoughtfully integrated with a unique and compelling building."[186] The new site will be about 28,800 square metres (310,000 square feet), approximately twice the size of the current building, and is scheduled to open in 2021. The design clearly links the new gallery to the former north plaza, noting, "The Larwill Park site holds a unique place in the history of Vancouver – as a parade ground, a sports field and a fairground, as a site *for celebration and for protest*" (emphasis added).[187] The design, however, equally clearly suggests that while the site may have a history of protest, the new gallery will not include a gathering space of the stature of the current location.

The question remains, then, what will happen to that history when the physical link is broken and the gallery moves to the Larwill Park site? One commentator noted, "I imagine the stewards of the VAG cant [*sic*] wait to break ground at the proposed new gallery location at Larwill Park so they can merely be the city's art gallery and not have to worry about whos [*sic*] outside on any given day with picket signs and djembes."[188] What will it mean for the gallery to no longer be the location of the vast majority of political interventions in the city? How close was the link? What did the gallery gain from the political action that regularly took/takes place on its doorstep? And alternately, what do actions, interventions, and occupations gain from the presence of the VAG? The gallery's continued silence on actions taking place outside suggests that breaking the link with the site may be one of their goals. Notably, there is also a consideration of what will move into the VAG's former building if/when it moves. In contention is the Museum of Vancouver (MOV), which, as noted earlier in the chapter, currently collects and archives ephemera from many of Vancouver's protest movements. In many ways, the MOV is more connected to the north plaza than is the VAG.[189] Other proposals for the site include a major concert hall and a national Aboriginal art gallery.[190]

Though the above suggestions all make sense, the power of developers in Vancouver is such that in September 2015 a group of artists released a prank website for Canvas Georgia, a thirty-two-storey mixed-use residential and commercial tower that would emerge from the current temple building of the VAG and scatter the works from the existing gallery across the public and private spaces of the building (including a private six-floor penthouse that would house upwards of 630 existing artworks found at the gallery). The space of the gallery would "increase tenfold!" noted the website. A one-bedroom, 700-square-foot condo in the building was priced at $799,999. So accustomed are Vancouverites to extravagant developments that Canvas Georgia was not immediately dismissed as a joke and even inspired a Change.org petition to stop it in its tracks.[191]

Though Canvas Georgia is not likely to come to fruition, as I write in 2017 the future of the gallery's move seems equally fraught. Currently, the budget for the new building is $350 million, a sum in keeping with the build cost of the CMHR but significantly more than large-scale projects such as the ROM and AGO renovations in Toronto.[192] In addition to $50 million from the province (promised in 2008), $100 million from the federal government (not secured at the time of writing), and an additional $50 million from the province, the gallery will be tasked with raising $150 million from the private sector ($100 million for capital and $50 million for the endowment).[193] By 2017, newspapers in Vancouver were citing a lower total sum of $100 million that needed to be raised from the private sector, and the gallery publicized the fact that it had raised $43 million, with $57 million to go.[194] To be clear, the CMHR, which had a much higher national profile even before it became a national museum, was unequal to a similar task. Further, while the Harper Conservative government was in power, it was made clear to the VAG that $100 million would not be provided, while the BC government remained uncommitted as well.[195] In April 2017, the VAG made a request for $100 million to the Trudeau Liberal government, hoping for a more sympathetic audience, but at the time of writing no funds have been granted.[196]

Though in 2017 a spokesperson for the VAG publicly stated, "We're on target, on budget, on time,"[197] an earlier report in *BC Business* noted, "The VAG's fundraising challenge is something of a perfect storm. Both levels of government have nothing to be gained politically from dishing out hundreds of millions of dollars for what's perceived, in the hinterland, as an elite big-city institution; it's not the power base of either the provincial Liberals or the federal Conservatives. And the VAG is one of several cultural projects planned or underway that draws on a similar, small pool of benefactors."[198] "This project is simply too expensive," a spokesperson for then Conservative Canadian heritage minister Shelly Glover is quoted as saying in the article, an opinion also shared by a spokesperson for the then–Liberal

BC minister for community, sport, and cultural development, who noted that there would be no new capital funding.[199] Additionally, the gallery was still smarting from the loss of Audain. As the same report in *BC Business* put it:

> It's difficult to overestimate Audain's role in building support for the VAG's Larwill Park plan. At the peak of his involvement, Audain had drawn $40 million in commitments from the private sector for the capital campaign and became the public face of the fundraising effort. With Audain out, there is no prominent voice in the business community rallying for the move to Larwill Park – only carping from the sidelines from oft-quoted VAG critic, realtor Bob Rennie.[200]

Perhaps not surprisingly, the VAG will have to reach beyond the small pool of traditional philanthropists in Vancouver.

> Part of the VAG's evolving pitch has been intersecting its programming with areas of interest to donors; last year's blockbuster *Forbidden City* exhibit, which received $1 million in funding from the China National Offshore Oil Corporation, a major investor in Canada's oil sands, and $500,000 from Vancouver donor Robert Ho ... Indeed, the VAG has promised a permanent space for Asian art in its new building, with Bartels promising "significant funding from donors who live part of the year in China and part in Vancouver."[201]

Even here there is competition. In 2017, in keeping with architectural historian Joe Day's theory that the uber-wealthy prefer establishing their own private collections over making large-scale contributions to public institutions, Vancouver-based Singaporean billionaire Oei Hong Leong publicly discussed a potential private gallery showcasing his collection of Asian and Buddhist art at the very False Creek site that had been dismissed by the VAG in 2008.[202]

Additionally, it seems to me that some avenues are cut off to the VAG, precisely because of the city's history, its location, and also, perhaps indirectly, because of the kinds of political debates taking place on the north plaza. For example, prior to Kinder Morgan withdrawing its bid to build the TransMountain pipeline, there may have been a moment when the greenwashing opportunities provided by museums and galleries for oil companies in the UK (see chapter 6) might have been a possibility in order to make the pipeline seem more palatable to Vancouverites. After all, the Kinder Morgan Foundation is a major arts philanthropist in its home base of Texas. It is my view, however, that such a sponsorship would have created a fundamental rift between the art producers in the city and the gallery, not to mention many of the patrons who make up the VAG's remarkably high rate of member sponsorship.[203] The VAG has accepted money from natural resource companies in the past – the sponsorship of the China National Offshore Oil Corporation is not anomalous. However, the kinds of funds the gallery is searching for are of an order of magnitude far greater than $1 million for a single exhibition. The ambient relationship created between the north plaza, critical art production, and the gallery would be destroyed or would come home to roost, depending on one's viewpoint. Certainly, the threshold would be crossed. Additionally, with several developers either opening their own galleries or refusing to speak to/work with the gallery, the VAG faces challenges that will continue even if or after a new building is secured.

Elsewhere, it is not clear who is lobbying for the VAG in Ottawa. While the CMHR had Izzy Asper and his legacy to do some of the work of fighting for Winnipeg, the VAG is less a public–private partnership than a provincial institution hoping for funding akin to that granted to federal institutions. For example, the Royal Alberta Museum was granted $122.5 million from the federal government for a rebuild.[204] In comparison, the Art Gallery of Alberta, a provincial institution, received $20 million from the federal government for a major renovation that totaled $48 million, designed by Randall Stout Architects.[205] The federal government also recently granted $15 million to the Winnipeg Art Gallery for an Inuit Centre.[206] These sums are in keeping with a number of rebuild and renovation programs throughout Canada, including projects in St John's, Montreal, Quebec City, Ottawa, Toronto, Banff, and Saskatoon.[207] My research did not turn up any provincial or municipal project receiving anything near the amount requested by the VAG. Though a donation from the Chan family was announced in 2019, whether the VAG will be able to overcome these hurdles remains, at the time of writing, to be seen.

It is here that the VAG appears as a prescient cautionary tale. The gallery is simultaneously onside with neoliberal gentrification but directly opposed to the austerity politics that emerged in the wake of the 2008 economic crisis and the chastening of Creative Cities rhetoric. Has the VAG missed the boat, so to speak? Unable to get its own project going in the early 2000s when the ROM and AGO were renovated in Toronto, the VAG seems to have been left behind in a new era when even Florida admits that Creative Cities rhetoric was a little off, a bit over-enthusiastic.[208] There are two ways of reading this unfolding failure: on the one hand, the gallery remaining in or unable to move from its current site can be read as an act of resistance to the giddy gentrification of Vancouver, particularly when a developer's plan to split the institution up and scatter it about the city was rejected. On the other hand, the resistance staged by artists against gentrification, hand-in-hand with the skyrocketing prices of land and real estate in Vancouver, has in fact desperately affected the arts – the lack of a new, larger space for display will only hurt Vancouver artists. This latter scenario is another clear example of the demise of the welfare state and of a publicly funded arts model unable to stand against the encroachment of private interests in the arts and private monies ramping up the market for land and art.

When Occupy Vancouver encamped in the courtyard outside the gallery, such contradictions and questions were brought to the foreground, both in terms of the myriad goals of Occupy and in terms of the way that the movement was reconfigured as an activist artwork by its supporters and a danger to art by its detractors. Occupy Vancouver began with an outpouring of joy and solidarity, which was maintained for some time, even as many of those organizing were asked to confront their own privilege. Any idea that Occupy Vancouver was for creative workers struggling in a system that both espoused and despised them was nipped in the bud. To be in any way legitimate, Occupy Vancouver also had to tackle issues of homelessness that are arguably exacerbated by the presence of creative workers in formerly affordable neighbourhoods and had to not just acknowledge but also enact the fact that this was an occupation taking place on already occupied land: unceded Musqueam, Squamish, and Tsleil-Waututh First Nations territory.

Conclusion

In November 2015, the City of Vancouver announced that the north plaza of the VAG would be redesigned. Prior to the Olympics, the space had been covered by grassy lawns, which were pulled up and replaced by bark mulch in 2010.[209] Among other things,

> The design will gut the entire plaza, removing the bark mulch, existing pavement, and the broken fountain. The area will be flattened and covered with a new pattern of custom precast pavers, made of three custom colours, and accent granite to give the new surface an appearance of a web of trapezoids … A single row of trees will also be planted on the north side along West Georgia Street, seemingly closing off the plaza – preventing the crowds of large events from spilling over onto the road. [210]

In 2017, the plaza was closed to allow for the first phase of the renewal project – the replacement of the membrane that had been leaking water into the Vancouver Art Gallery's underground vaults (the same membrane apparently compro- mised by Occupy Vancouver). Finally, in 2018 the north courtyard was renamed as part of a City of Vancouver reconciliation project. Recognizing "the colonial legacy of naming in Vancouver the plaza naming process sought to

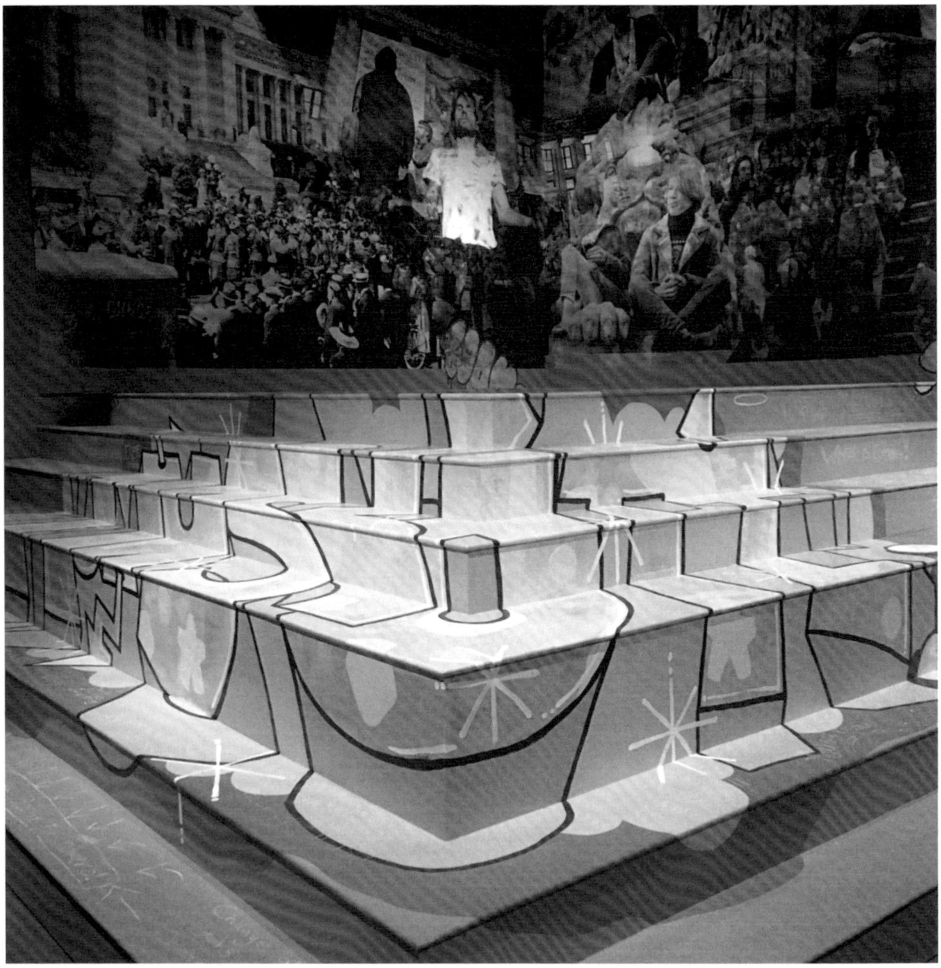

Figure 7.7
City on Edge, installation shot, Museum of Vancouver.

return decision-making to the original inhabitants of this land and bring more visibility to the local Indigenous languages and cultures."[211] The plaza is now known as səlílwətaʔɬ (Tsleil-Waututh) in an act of reclamation undertaken by the City rather than the Occupiers.

In October 2017, I visited Vancouver and walked around the fenced-off courtyard. The plaza was deserted except for three construction workers and piles of material, its usual role quietened. Not far away, however, the Museum of Vancouver (MOV) had just opened the exhibition *City on Edge: A Century of Vancouver Activism*, a photo-based exhibition drawn from one of the local newspaper's archives, dedicated to "exploring how protest demonstrations have shaped Vancouver's identity."[212] In it, the VAG's north plaza shows up repeatedly as images

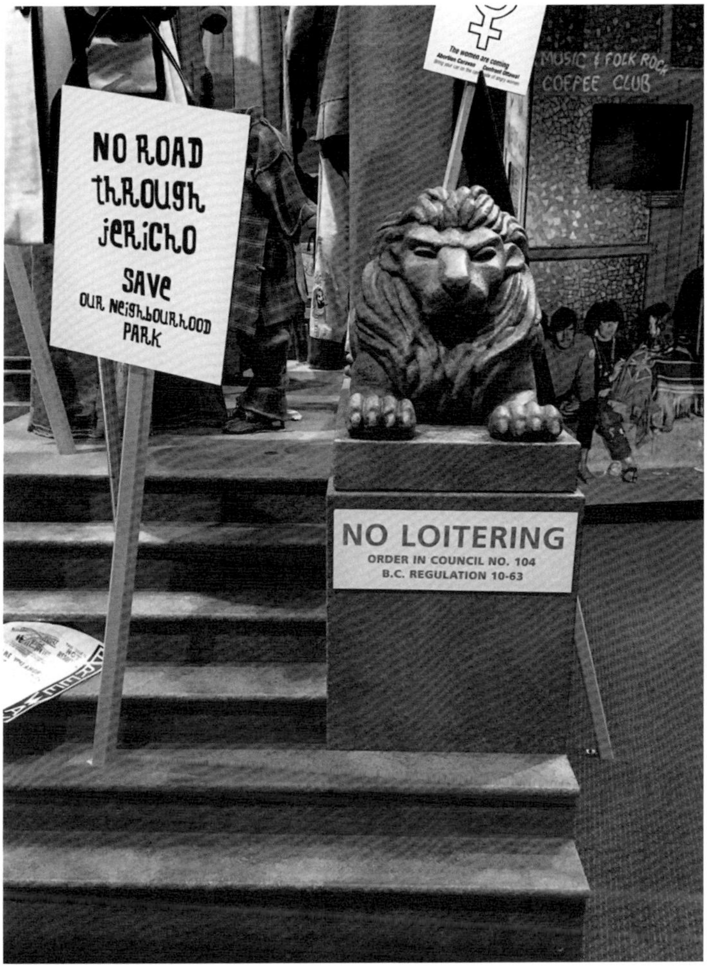

Figure 7.8
Permanent display, Vancouver History Gallery, Museum of Vancouver.

of protest after protest circulate on the museum's screens. In fact, a three-dimensional replica of the VAG's front stairs shows up twice at the MOV, first in a display from *City on Edge* showing an activist from Occupy Vancouver and second in the museum's permanent display in an exhibition on hippie protests at the courthouse in the 1960s and 1970s. In *City on Edge*, the sounds of protest were piped into the gallery space, accompanying the huge number of images showing interventionist culture in Vancouver, ranging from hippie demonstrations to First Nations protecting Indigenous rights. Forgoing the power of contemporary art to interpret the issues or backgrounds to political engagement in the city, the two MOV curators, Viviane Gosselin and Kate Bird, instead went straight to the source such that despite its repeated presence in the exhibition, the VAG itself fades to the background, becoming solely the backdrop, while the MOV becomes an active participant in recalling and foregrounding the city's contentious past and present. As the VAG attempts to cleave itself from its site, the quelling of protest outside one museum and its reappearance as image and sound at another seems prescient and timely, a symbolic renunciation of the VAG's site and role in the city as it turns its attention, belatedly and finally, to its move to a new building where it will nestle beneath a tower of glass.

Interstice 7g

Stan Douglas and the Woodward's Redevelopment

In an article on Vancouver-based artist Stan Douglas, curator Reid Shier opens with a discussion of Woodward's Department Store, a large complex in the centre of the DTES that had long served as the heart of the community. "When it was open," Shier notes, "Woodward's catered – popularly – to Vancouverites from every stripe."[1] In 1968, Woodward's had been a part of the city's *Project 200*, a plan to revitalize Vancouver's downtown core by knocking down buildings in Chinatown and Gastown (now both heritage destinations) and replacing them with cement towers and freeways. Only the Woodward's parking lot was ever built as a part of this plan because residents in Chinatown and the DTES teamed up to resist the development.[2] Less than twenty years later, "[Councilman] Jim Green first started working on the purchase of the Woodward's building in 1985, when he made a proposal to the Canadian International Development Agency to treat the Downtown Eastside 'like a Third World country' and spend federal government money rejuvenating the area."[3] This also would not happen. Instead, like so many other downtown institutions, Woodward's suffered heavily in the 1970s and 1980s from the establishment of suburban shopping malls, and its closure in 1993 "ripped a hole in Hastings Street."[4] As the major shopping institution in the area, the repercussions of its closure were deeply felt, and numerous other shops, restaurants, and businesses also closed as the drug trade moved in in force.[5] The DTES's reputation as an open drug market and scene of vice grew from this time. Nevertheless, the profound citizen-led organizing, visible in groups like Vancouver Area Network of Drug Users (VANDU), Carnegie Community Action Project (CCAP), Downtown

Eastside Residents Association (DERA), and the Portland Hotel Society suggest a very different picture of the DTES, particularly because the area has been able to resist some forms of gentrification in ways that other parts of Vancouver have not (chapter 7).

When Woodward's closed, there was a great deal of hope that it would be turned into social housing. Both the developer who owned the store and the city dragged their feet, squabbling over how many units would be available for low-income residents. The developer dropped out, and the building sat empty.[6] When it looked as if the building would be turned into luxury condominiums, residents took matters into their own hands. Woodward's was occupied by squatters trying to raise attention to the homelessness problem in Vancouver. Once occupied, Woodward's became Woodsquat, a tent city that lasted for ninety-two days in the fall of 2002.

Woodsquat began on 14 September 2002, just three months after the protests at the opening of *Places of Their Own* and while that exhibition continued just a few blocks away (chapter 7). The Anti-Poverty Committee (whose member Ivan Drury had been at the centre of the protests at the VAG) had formed in the spring of 2002 to address increasing poverty under the neoliberal Gordon Campbell provincial government. Woodsquat lasted far longer than the protest at the VAG, but nonetheless participants were forcibly evicted in November 2002.[7]

Though they were kicked out of Woodward's, community activists won a contempt application – and Woodsquat moved to the sidewalk outside Woodward's.[8] Instead of ending Woodsquat, the eviction brought it to the street, into the outdoor space of Vancouver.[9] However, as the protests were brought into the public space, sympathy for the homeless that had characterized coverage of the squat quickly descended into a strict separation between homeless squatters and ill-defined "activists," the latter almost inevitably positioned as troublemakers. Activists were accused of having "no regard for the niceties of civilized people and little or no respect for any person who is not like them."[10] In the *Province* newspaper, moonlighting policeman Mark Tonner grumbled about "latté leftists."[11] In essence, there was anger at organization. So long as the homeless were chaotic, they were worthy of help and aid. Once organization began, it brought with it great suspicion. "Ever since the Woodward's squat began, controversy has raged over whether the squatters are homeless activists in search of low-cost housing or more anarchists looking for a little rabble-rousing. As the squat enters its seventh week, it looks more and more like the latter."[12] And another, "They're the only ones here by choice, after all. The homeless have nowhere else to go, while the police are bound to maintain order and obey the courts – not to mention facilitate legitimate protest. There is a chance, here and now, for the Woodward's building to stand as an icon of compassion and accountability. It would be a shame if it were knocked off the rails by people whose only loyalty is to rebellion."[13]

Eventually, the city and province did appear ready to move forward with a development plan that promised social housing, even though it seemed as much geared toward gentrifying the neighbourhood as helping the homeless.[14] As an Anti-Poverty Committee newsletter noted, "After 92 days of struggle to defend the Woodward's squat against the threat of police, engineers, social workers, the legal system and poverty pimps, the tent city ended quietly."[15] Tired, demoralized, and hungry, squatters were rehoused by the Portland Hotel Society.

Then in March 2003, the City of Vancouver purchased the building from the province. Members of the community were actively involved in the redevelopment process – a unique undertaking in the city's history. In early 2005, the Portland Hotel Society and Affordable Housing were selected by City Council to operate the 200 units of non-market housing. Shortly thereafter, Woodward's was redeveloped into a mixed-use residential building that includes social housing units, luxury apartments, a café, London Drugs Pharmacy, a grocery store, the SFU Goldcorp[16] Centre for the Arts, and other units.[17]

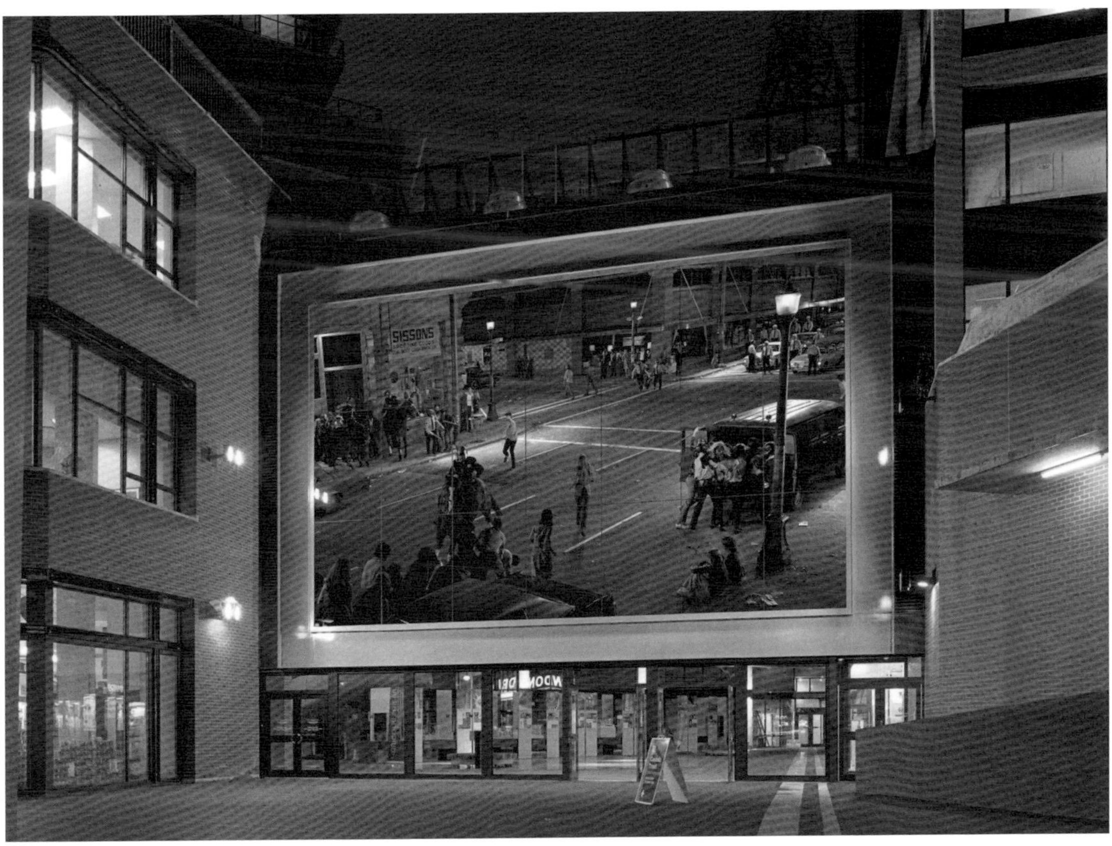

Figure 7.9
Stan Douglas, *Abbott & Cordova, 7 August 1971* (2008).

At the threshold of the redeveloped Woodward's foyer, visible both from the interior and exterior, is a light-filled photographic mural showing police gathering up a young man resisting arrest while others either observe or run away. This is Stan Douglas's striking photo mural *Abbott & Cordova*, a re-enactment of the 1971 "Gastown Riot," which happened less than a block away from where the installation can now be found.[18] At the time, in the late 1960s and early 1970s, the neighbourhood around Woodward's was changing. Most of the inhabitants were retired resource workers. When younger people, many of them the hippies described in chapter 7 as hanging around the courthouse fountain, moved into the area, police harassment quickly followed. In response, a group of youth organized a peaceful "be in" and smoke-up at Maple Tree Square, near the intersection of Abbott and Cordova Streets. Though the celebration was allowed to proceed for some time, as dusk fell the crowd was ordered to disperse, and when it did not, riot police charged, causing panic.[19] Attendees at the "be in" were dragged by the hair, pushed into windows, chased by police on horseback, and beaten with nightsticks and batons.[20] According to Douglas, *Abbott & Cordova* shows the periphery of the riot at the moment everyone was starting to disperse.[21] Douglas has said of the image that although in some ways the protest was "frivolous," it "was about ... the curtailment of civil liberties."[22] It was an important moment in Vancouver's history and in the history of resistance in Canada. Douglas also recollects that in discussions with architect Gregory Henriquez and developer Ian Gillespie, who were overseeing the Woodward's redevelopment, "to my surprise they were very enthusiastic about the idea of making a picture of a riot." [23]

Abbott & Cordova is one of a series of four photographs by Douglas, each recreating political events in the city's history. These include a free speech demonstration that took place in 1912 (gatherings of more than three people had been banned because the Communist-leaning Wobblies were trying to organize workers),[24] an image of the Battle of Ballentyne Pier (when city and provincial police clashed with union workers trying to attack scabs working at Ballantyne Pier), and an image of Hastings Racetrack in 1955. This last photograph is not an image of political action, but instead shows a crowd (apparently) watching a horse race. Like the other photographs, however, it "represent[s] the organization of people into a group or a body by either internal or external forces."[25]

Abbott & Cordova is a surprising image in the foyer of the Woodward's redevelopment. Douglas himself expected a negative reaction, and when none came he notes, "I was very surprised ... I was actually waiting for someone to – I was kind of disappointed that nobody was upset about this project, about this idea. I thought I was being very subversive, and no one's complaining." He adds, "What the hell's going on?"[26] Though the work is of the neighbourhood, it appears at odds with its surroundings, a situation that prompted Jesse Proudfoot to ask, "what function does it perform here in the historically overdetermined space of the Woodward's building?"[27] He asks whether, on the one hand, we can read in the image an indictment of police brutality and whether it "offers an important corrective to sanitized histories of the neighbourhood that efface the traces of conflict from the palimpsest of the Downtown Eastside."[28] But on the other hand, Proudfoot also asks whose community is represented in this image and notes that hippies are not the first or the only community suppressed in the area – first it was the working class (an important corrective to the primarily middle-class hippies arrested and beaten in 1971), and via connection to the present moment "we find the depiction of a riot concerned not with the politics of redistribution but the politics of (marijuana) consumption."[29] For Proudfoot, it is questionable whether or not the image actually provokes or paves the way for gentrification, reclaiming the spot as one of middle-class presence. Notably, Proudfoot steps back from this analysis, acknowledging that Douglas's intent was to provoke conversation and concluding that the photomural certainly does that.[30] Nevertheless, he surmises, these kinds of conversations are necessary "especially when real estate developers are actively engaged in writing their own histories of the neighbourhood with the goal of making it safe for property speculation rather than political discussion."[31]

In the years since the Woodward's building reopened post-renovation, gentrification has continued in the DTES, primarily around "zones of exclusion," such as cafes and restaurants with prices out of reach to residents in the area who may have benefitted from activism to save SROs and create social housing but could no longer afford commodities in the area (see chapter 7).[32] In the meantime, SFU has thrived. Interestingly, Woodsquat was memorialized in the SFU building in the W2 Community Media Arts, which was a legacy project demanded by activists involved in Woodsquat. As part of its mandate, W2 had the role of teaching media skills to residents of the area. W2 quickly became a hub for many of Vancouver's radical activists. Occupy Vancouver held its initial planning meetings at W2, along with a host of other grassroots organizations. Unfortunately, in 2011 W2 was evicted, in part because it could not meet the terms of its rental agreement, which essentially asked for it to be a profit-generating entity.[33] With W2 gone, the history of Woodsquat has largely been erased, though Douglas's photomural remains, a testament to at least some of the political actions in the neighbourhood.

8

Conclusion

I finished writing this book in the fall of 2017 in a very different world from the one in which I began researching almost ten years earlier. In 2017, President Donald Trump was in power in the United States, and his leadership was having profound effects both on the public emergence of and the constant resistance to white supremacist groups in the United States and in Canada. The bugbear of "free speech" had unleashed a torrent of intolerance in the public sphere, and it became obvious that many of the favoured tactics of left-wing activists were being repurposed and used by the far right and white nationalists to secure a foothold for their views. Marches and demonstrations, cries of intolerance toward minorities (in this case a perceived but not actual persecuted white minority), and class warfare were all adopted and skewed to advocate for anti-immigrant, racist, anti-women, homophobic, and Islamophobic perspectives that even in Canada, under a supposedly benign Liberal government led by Justin Trudeau, were coupled with often vicious continued anti-Indigenous racism that formed a backlash against reconciliation efforts in the mainstream.

But people resisted. Everywhere, they resisted. Indigenous resurgence, refugee welcoming committees and sponsorship rallies, education workshops and teach-ins, negotiations, rallies, petitions, marches, demonstrations, opinion pieces and op-eds, social media blitzes and Twitter campaigns; resistance ran the gamut from armchair clicktivism to antifa violent counteractions at white supremacist rallies.

Throughout, people organized, and they stood strong. Some of these actions took place outside museums, with many of those altercations documented in this book. But museums responded as well – by rehanging their collections, closing their doors, removing offending artworks, organizing exhibitions that took on specific political positions, or reinstalling permanent collections toward more critical aims. If there is one thing that has happened over the time in which this book has been written, it is a distinct shift away from insularity as many if not most major establishment museums (in the locales considered in this book) have begun to at least acknowledge the political conditions of the day. Museums, including major institutions such as the MOMA, the National Holocaust Museum, the CMHR, and many other institutions in Canada are tackling profoundly political topics in a way that simply has not been seen in the past. Many museums have also started to collect political ephemera, and it is with that in mind that I would like to conclude *Tear Gas Epiphanies*, a book that traces political engagement with museums in Canada from the 1900s through to the present, by advocating for deep collection by establishment museums from political movements. Notably, I argue strongly for activist-led collecting, even if this means that certain objects cannot be acquired by museums.

In 2017, in order to complete my research, I travelled to Vancouver to check the Museum of Anthropology (MOA) archives for their press clippings file on the First Nations occupation that took place in 1981 (see Interstice 2b). While there, I asked to see the APEC file.[1] In 2000, art historian and anthropologist Ruth Phillips wrote about her experience as director of the MOA during 1997 meetings of the Asia Pacific Economic Cooperation (APEC).[2] APEC was immensely controversial and was greeted by extensive protests at UBC, which in turn were greeted with police suppression and the widespread use of pepper spray. In the aftermath, the policing of APEC was controversial enough to warrant a national inquiry.[3] In her article, Phillips describes her discomfort as the director of the MOA with several incidents at APEC, among them a number of government-led actions (such as cancelling a welcome from an Elder or removing much of the content of Chief Gail Sparrow's welcoming speech) that damaged the museum's relationship with the Musqueam Nation on whose land the museum sits. Following the APEC meetings, in order to address what had happened at the museum, the MOA invited the activists in, organizing an exhibition titled *This Is Not an Exhibition* (which included artefacts and photos from APEC) and a one-day event in the MOA's Great Hall, organized by the Democracy Street group. What occurred was a "public reclamation" of the museum.[4] Two graduate students, Maria Roth and Todd Tubutis, were commissioned to create an archive for the museum "that would document the event as it unfolded in all its complexity."[5] Phillips describes the event as follows:

> The Democracy Street theatre group performed a parody of the APEC leaders' meeting in front of the museum using characters modelled on those of the children's program *Sesame Street*. Inside the lobby the Raging Grannies sang protest songs, and groups such as Students for a Free Tibet, Amnesty International, the Women Opposed to Political Intimidation Group, and the East Timor Alert Network set up booths ... [Participants] restaged the official "family photo" taken on the berm behind the museums. When they turned around, large letters attached to their backs spelled out "PEOPLE ARE THE BOTTOM LINE!" Chief Gail Sparrow's message was finally proclaimed on the grounds of the Museum of Anthropology.[6]

The APEC Archive is not very large. It occupies only 25 cm of shelf space, with an additional large box that contains an APEC uniform worn by an employee and posters hung around UBC by various activist groups. The majority of the archive is documents collected from the official meetings, from activist organizations, and from members of the Musqueam Nation. Chief Gail Sparrow's heavily edited speech can be found, as can faxes back and forth between the Musqueam Nation and the Government of Canada in a dispute over whether a helicopter transporting leaders could land on a helipad in Musqueam territory. The official economic narrative of APEC is clearly evident in the files, which include material about each country in APEC, tourism information, pamphlets on Canada and Vancouver, and information about an arts and crafts exhibition organized for APEC attendees. But this narrative is not seamless, and it is punctured repeatedly by activist material showcasing the other side of APEC's economic policy. Posters and pamphlets documenting human rights abuses, labour and environmental shortcomings, and the lack of transparency of APEC form the bulk of the archive, along with ephemera from teach-ins and notes taken by participants in some of the meetings that took place, as well as numerous press clippings showing both mainstream and marginal coverage of the events.

Digging deeper into the archive turns up material artefacts: chalk used to draw slogans on the sidewalks and buildings, police tape used to fence off parts of the campus, even a coffee cup used by then president Bill Clinton and a mostly smoked cigar, allegedly confiscated from Clinton when he entered the museum building. Numerous photographs of the Democracy Street event are granted the same archival space as official photographs of the leaders of each of the APEC countries. Cassette recordings of the Democracy Street speakers are also included in the archive, as is an audio recording of Chief Gail Sparrow's speech.

The APEC Archive at the MOA does something extremely important. It documents an official event that took place at the museum and that should be archived.

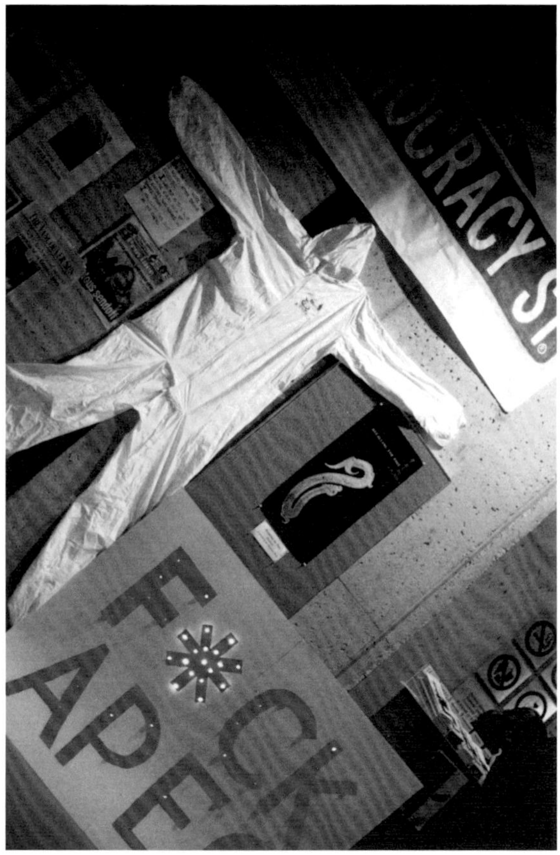

Figure 8.1 *Right*
Democracy Street Event, 1997, UBC MOA.

Figure 8.2 *Below*
Democracy Street Event, 1997, UBC MOA.

Figure 8.3 *Opposite left*
Image from the APEC Collection, Bill Clinton's cigar and thank you card, UBC MOA, 1997.

Figure 8.4 *Opposite right*
Image from the APEC Collection,
chalk, police tape, other ephemera, UBC MOA, 1997.

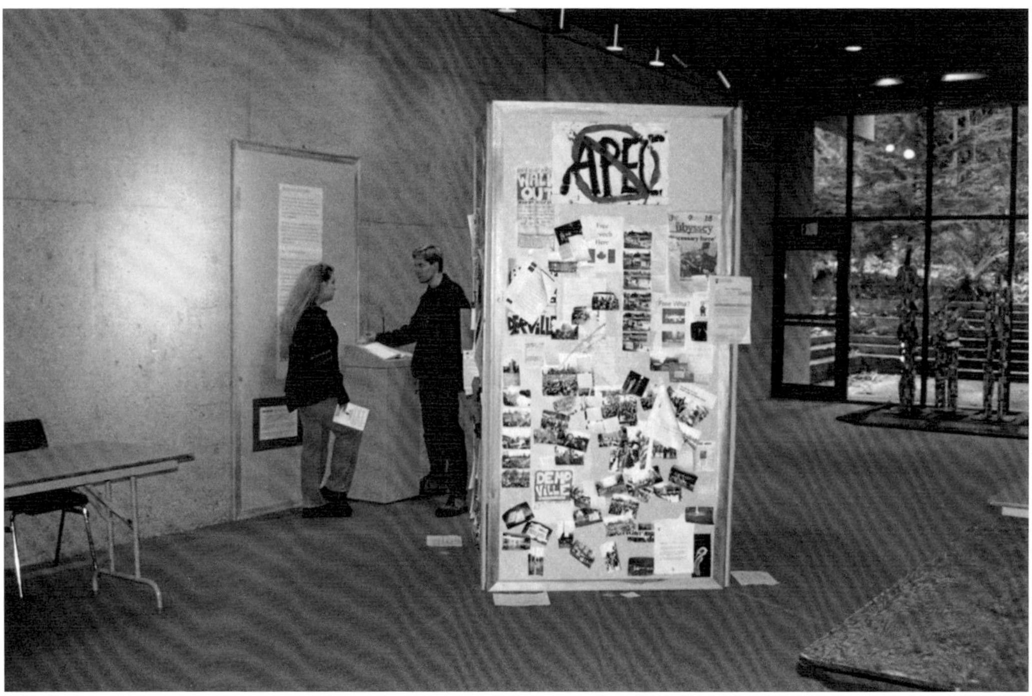

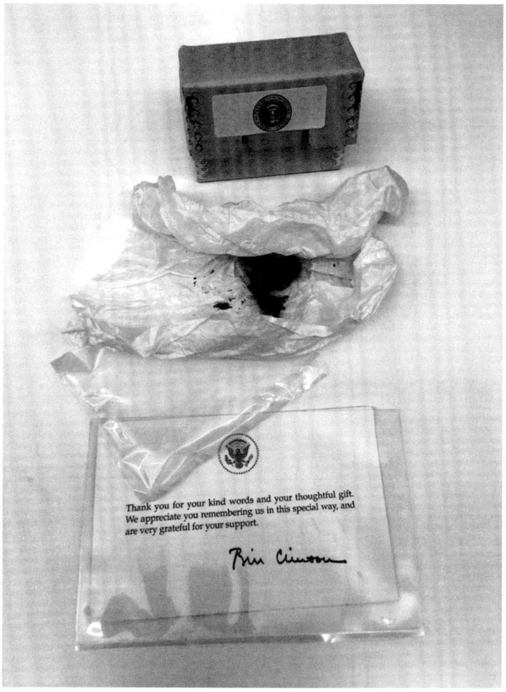

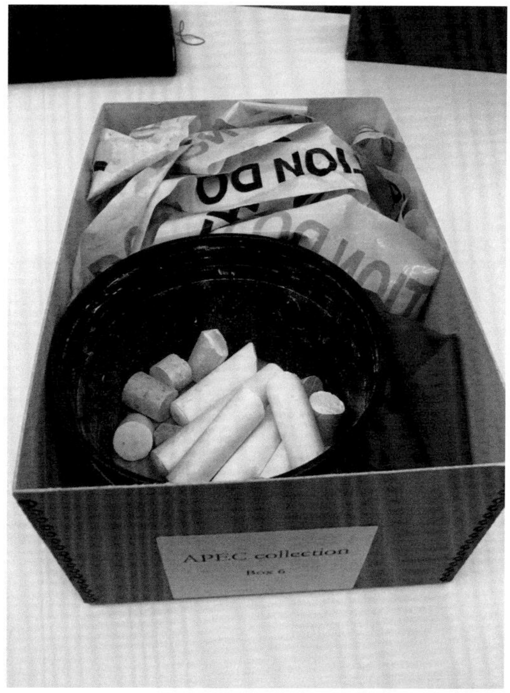

But it also documents the resistance to those events and the kinds of responses that are often lost to history. Because the APEC meetings happened at a particular museum and because the director of the museum was not entirely comfortable with the unfolding of the events, the museum itself sought to archive what had happened and played an active role in deciding how to acknowledge the history and what to keep.

I suggest that, as with Occupy Wall Street, activists need to start thinking about archiving as a way to materially halt the process of erasure of resistance and that museums need to help by creating the time and space for these acquisitions. Furthermore, when galleries and museums organize exhibitions *about* protest or celebrating activist art, the context in which those artworks were made could and should be foregrounded. I began in a place highly critical of museums and ended up somewhere more ambiguous. Over the time during which I was writing this book, many museums did engage with contentious politics in significant ways, such as by organizing exhibitions and programming, by funding rapid response collecting, or by working with curators deeply connected with activist communities. I argue throughout the book that often these processes were experienced somewhat differently in Canadian museums such that, for example, a movement such as Art Not Oil has not emerged and there have been few exhibitions of protest ephemera. On the other hand, one finds numerous examples of groups using museums in incredibly sophisticated ways to achieve goals as diverse as changing the language in an exhibition panel and securing federal funding for necessary infrastructure. One also finds numerous thought-provoking and evocative exhibitions that take political action not as a design element or an object but rather as an underlying premise of curation. And finally, although my initial queries to museums in Canada seemed to reveal that major institutions had collected almost nothing related to activist movements, over the course of writing the book, I found that the issue proved to be a little more complicated than I initially had assumed – first, because I kept finding collections that did not come up as a result of keyword searches and second, because several museums that had not been collecting had, by 2017, pledged to do so. Thus, I end on a note of optimism as I turn to Beka Economopolous's (of Not An Alternative) claim that museums have power and authority that we are given to critique but that power and authority can be used to help mobilize, educate, and open up new stories and new framings.

London, 2018

Figures

1.1 Volunteers dressed as riot police greet invitees at "Massive Uprising," Art Gallery of Ontario, Toronto, March 2009, photo by Andrew Hyfen, printed with permission. | 2
1.2 Bartenders serve "Capitalist Cocktails" and "Moscow Mules" at "Massive Uprising," Art Gallery of Ontario, Toronto, March 2009, photo by Andrew Hyfen, printed with permission. | 5
1.3 Exterior of the closed AGO during the G20 meetings, photo by Kirsty Robertson, 26 June 2010. | 6
1.4 *Gophers Against Getting Stuffed*, a tongue-in-cheek exhibit at the Torrington Gopher Museum in Torrington, Alberta, photo by Kirsty Robertson, 2014. | 7
1.5 Michel Lambeth and Jim Brown chained to furniture in Art Gallery office, 1972, photo by Reg Innell, Toronto Public Library, Toronto Star Photo Archive, accession number tspa_0011702f. | 32
1.6 Metro artists tie themselves together with rope outside the Isaac Gallery to protest against the appointment of an American, Richard J. Wattenmaker of Philadelphia, as new chief curator at the Art Gallery of Ontario, 1972, photo by Fred Ross, Toronto Public Library, Toronto Star Photo Archive, accession number, tspa_0011697f. | 34
2.1 Desperate as Diogenes, 18 April 1967, photo by Boris Spremo, Toronto Public Library, Toronto Star Photo Archive, Group 2 129 GT 299. | 46
2.2 Students protest AGO purchase of Claes Oldenburg's *Floor Burger* and the *Dine, Oldenburg, Segal: Painting/Sculpture* exhibition (14 January–12 February 1967), 14 January 1967. Photo credit: Toronto Telegram. Image courtesy of the Edward P. Taylor Library and Archives, Art Gallery of Ontario, [A-193901]. | 48
2.3 Students protest AGO purchase of Claes Oldenburg's *Floor Burger* and the *Dine, Oldenburg, Segal: Painting/Sculpture* exhibition (14 January–12 February 1967), 14 January 1967. Photo credit: Toronto Telegram. Image courtesy of the Edward P. Taylor Library and Archives, Art Gallery of Ontario, [A-193899]. | 49

2.4 Installation view of Carol Condé and Karl Beveridge exhibition, *It's Still Privileged Art* (Art Gallery of Ontario, 24 January–29 February 1976). Image courtesy of the Edward P. Taylor Library & Archives, Art Gallery of Ontario, [E-18160]. | 50
2.5 Independent Artists' Union Demonstration, "A Living Culture, a Living Wage," 16 March 1985. Photo credit: Ric Amis. Image courtesy of Queen's University Archives 2319.7-3-16. | 55
2.6 Immobilized. Protester lies face down with hands bound behind back during demonstration outside Art Gallery of Ontario where leaders were lunching, photo by Andrew Stawicki, Toronto Public Library, *Toronto Star* Photo Archive, accession number tspa_0011990f. | 56
2.7 Alvin Wanderingspirit protests *The Spirit Sings*, a cultural exhibit outside the Glenbow Museum during the 1988 Winter Games in Calgary, *Montreal Gazette*, 13 February 2013, photo by Dean Bicknell, material republished with the express permission of: *Montreal Gazette*, a division of Postmedia Network Inc. | 59
2.8 Orderly protest: A police officer stands guard as one of about seventy-five pickets circles outside the Royal Ontario Museum in protest of an African exhibit within, 1988, photo by Andrew Stawicki, Toronto Public Library, *Toronto Star* Photo Archive, accession number tspa_0012054f. | 62
2.9 Protest at the AGO during October launch of the Barnes Exhibit, 15 December 1994, photo by Moira Welsh, Toronto Public Library, *Toronto Star* Photo Archive, accession number tspa_010935f. | 69
2.10 Arthur Erickson, Museum of Anthropology, UBC, designed 1976, photographed by Xicotencatl, 19 April 2015, licensed under Creative Commons Attribution-Share Alike 4.0 International License/section 32.2(1)(b) Copyright Act (Canada). | 72

3.1 Royal Ontario Museum, photographed by "Gisling," 2007, licensed under Creative Commons Share and Share Alike 3.0 Unported. | 81
3.2 Museum of Vancouver, permanent display dedicated to hippie culture, photo by Kirsty Robertson, October 2017. | 87
3.3 Trump Awakens (The Trump Baby Blimp Rises over London's Parliament Square), photo by Michael Reeve, 13 July 2018, licensed under Creative Commons Attribution ShareAlike 2.0 Generic. | 99
3.4 Photo of preparations for anti-Reed Protest outside the AGO, *Globe and Mail*, 10 February 1976, photo by Derek DeBono, printed with permission. | 105
4.1 The new Canadian War Museum in Ottawa, opened in May 2005, photo by Sarah E.K. Smith, July 2018, printed with permission. | 114
4.2 Frederick H. Varley, *For What?* 1919, Beaverbrook Collection of War Art Canadian War Museum, CWM 19710261-0770. | 119
4.3 Canadian Experience Galleries, The Gallery 1 of the CWM, photo by Frank Defalco, 15 July 2010, printed with permission. | 127
4.4 Regeneration Hall, Canadian War Museum, Ottawa, photo by Guinness323, 20 June 2010, Creative Commons 3.0 Unported license. | 131
4.5 Gertrude Kearns, *Somalia #2, Without Conscience*, 1995, Beaverbrook Collection of War Art, Canadian War Museum, CWM 19990022-001. | 132
4.6 "Bombing to Win" display, Canadian War Museum, photo by Sarah E.K. Smith, July 2018, printed with permission. | 132
5.1 Alexander Docks with Museum of Human Rights in the distance, photo by Kirsty Robertson, September 2014. | 146
5.2 The Canadian Museum for Human Rights as seen from the Forks Tower, photo by CCyyrree, 7 October 2012, licensed under Creative Commons CC0 1.0 Universal Public Domain Dedication. | 156

5.3 Garden of Contemplation at the spot where the plaque acknowledging Shoal Lake Nation 40 will be placed, Canadian Museum for Human Rights, photo by Kirsty Robertson, October 2017. | 171
5.4 Wendy Coburn, *Anatomy of a Protest* film installation, Art Museum at the University of Toronto, 2014, photo by Tony Hafkenscheid, printed with permission. | 179
5.5 Wendy Coburn, *Anatomy of a Protest* installation, Art Museum at the University of Toronto, 2014, photo by Tony Hafkenscheid, printed with permission. | 181
6.1 Human Cost, Liberate Tate action, Tate Britain Museum, April 2011, photo by Amy Scaife, printed with permission. | 183
6.2 BP or Not BP, Viking Longship action (Performance 11) at the British Museum, 15 June 2014, photo by Hugh Warwick, printed with permission. | 186
6.3 Not An Alternative, The Natural History Museum, occupation of American Alliance of Museums, Atlanta, 2015, printed with permission. | 188
6.4 Greenpeace, Crudeau Oil Action in London, 18 April 2018, photo by Chris J. Ratcliffe, printed with permission. | 190
6.5 Council of Canadians, "CAPP Pollutes Snow," Snowperson protesting Canadian Association of Petroleum Producers (CAPP) sponsoring the Museum of Civilization's snow exhibit, 6 December 2013, licensed under Creative Commons Attribution Non Commercial ShareAlike 2.0 Generic. | 198
6.6 During the Copper-Breaking Ceremony on Parliament Hill, Ottawa, 27 June 2014, photo by Sue Heal, printed with permission. | 214
6.7 350.org, Big Oil Has No Place in Our Trusted Museums, #CutCAPP Demonstration at the Canadian Museum Association Conference, 7 April 2017, licensed under Creative Commons Attribution Non Commercial ShareAlike 2.0 Generic. | 217
7.1 Robson Street south façade of the Vancouver Art Gallery, photo by Timothy Pearson, August 2018, printed with permission. | 224
7.2 A man is arrested by Vancouver Police at the Vancouver Art Gallery at the opening of the big summertime show *Places of Their Own*, Vancouver Sun, 15 June 2002, B2, photo by Stuart Davis, material republished with the express permission of *Vancouver Sun*, a division of Postmedia Network Inc. | 227
7.3 Occupy Vancouver protest in front of the Art Gallery, 15 October 2011, photo by Eviatar Bach, licensed under Creative Commons CCO 1.0 Universal Public Domain Dedication. | 228
7.4 Occupy Vancouver, Nice Day for a Revolution, October 2011, photo by Stephen Collis, printed with permission. | 231
7.5 Ken Lum, *from shangri-la to shangri-la*, 2010, site-specific installation at Vancouver Art Gallery Offsite, 23 January to 6 September 2010, photo by Rachel Topham, Vancouver Art Gallery, printed with permission. | 234
7.6 Thom Quine, Vancouver Skyline, October 2005, Creative Commons Attribution 2.0 Generic Licence. | 236
7.7 *City on Edge*, installation shot, Museum of Vancouver, photo by Kirsty Robertson, October 2017. | 258
7.8 Permanent display, Vancouver History Gallery, Museum of Vancouver, photo by Kirsty Robertson, October 2017. | 259
7.9 Stan Douglas, *Abbott & Cordova, 7 August 1971* (2008), © Stan Douglas. Courtesy of the artist, David Zwirner, New York/London/Hong Kong and Victoria Miro, London/Venice. | 263
8.1 Democracy Street Event, 1997, UBC MOA, image appears courtesy of UBC Museum of Anthropology, Vancouver, APEC Collection, B-48 Maria Roth photographs 6-1, photo by Maria Roth, printed with permission. | 270

8.2 Democracy Street Event, 1997, UBC MOA, image appears courtesy of UBC Museum of Anthropology, Vancouver, APEC Collection, B-48 Todd Tubutis photographs 6–9, photo by Todd J. Tubutis, printed with permission. | 270
8.3 Image from the APEC Collection, Bill Clinton's cigar and thank you card, UBC MOA, 1997, photo by Kirsty Robertson, October 2017, printed with permission. | 271
8.4 Image from the APEC Collection, chalk, police tape, other ephemera, UBC MOA, 1997, photo by Kirsty Robertson, October 2017, printed with permission. | 272

Notes

Preface

1 These terms are complex and are defined in depth in chapters 1 and 2.
2 See, for example, many of the essays in McKay, DIY *Culture*; as well as Boje, "Carnivalesque Resistance to Global Spectacle"; McNally, *Another World Is Possible*, 276; Dworkin and Young, *Another World Is Possible*; Graeber, *The New Anarchists*; Graeber, *Direct Action*, 568; Neale, *You Are the G8, We Are the 6 Billion*; Yuen, Burton-Rose, and Katsiaficas, *Confronting Capitalism*, 410.
3 Whitaker, Kealey, and Parnaby, *Secret Service*.
4 Teitel, "Anti-Mask Legislation Defies Logic."
5 See chapters 1, 5, and 6 for more on why the term protest in not always appropriate, particularly when it comes to actions led by Indigenous peoples.
6 This was the time of the alterglobalization movement, when tear gas was used liberally on mostly peaceful activists. I considered changing the term to "protest epiphany" because most of the actions discussed in this book were not met with tear gas (although pepper spray was used on several occasions) but decided against it.
7 Lewis, *Walking with the Wind*.
8 Koutsoukis, "The Night When Tahrir Square Exploded in Joy."
9 DePape, "Idle No More Is a Christmas Gift to Us All."
10 Notes from Nowhere, "Carnival: Resistance Is the Secret of Joy," 173.
11 Drury and Novelli, "Collective Joy and the Power of the Crowd."
12 Emirbayer and Goldberg, "Pragmatism, Bourdieu, and Collective Emotions in Contentious Politics," 474. See also Pignare and Stengers, *Capitalist Sorcery*. Their discussion of what they inherited from protests in Seattle in 1999 and how we can become "children of the event" is particularly fitting here.
13 Canadian Security Intelligence Service, "Anti-globalization."

14 Durkheim, *The Elementary Forms of the Religious Life*, 240–1.
15 Turner, *The Ritual Process*.
16 Le Bon, *The Crowd*, 219. It is only very recently that emotion, much less affect, has been studied in relation to protest movements. Though early studies of protest and mass movements did focus on emotion, the approach was often accusatory and linked to perceptions of mob mentality. From the mid-1960s to the mid-1980s, many social movement theorists were concerned with deconstructing Gustav Le Bon's (1895) fear of the emotion of the crowd. The literature here is immense. Sources I relied on most include Goodwin et al., *Passionate Politics*; Goodwin and Jasper, *Rethinking Social Movements*; Gould, *Moving Politics*; Jasper and Poulsen, "Recruiting Strangers and Friends"; Jasper, *The Art of Moral Protest*; Reed, *The Art of Protest*; Yang, "Achieving Emotion in Collective Action"; Schechner, *The Future of Ritual*, 85; and Graeber, "On the Phenomenology of Giant Puppets," 28.
17 Klein, "The Bonding Properties of Tear Gas."
18 In Helms, Vishmidt, and Berlant, "Affect and the Politics of Austerity." See also Schechner, *The Future of Ritual*, 283; Jordan, "The Art of Necessity"; Jordan and Whitney, "Resistance Is the Secret of Joy," 24–5.
19 Butler, "Bodies in Alliance and the Politics of the Street."
20 Bakhtin, *Rabelais and His World*, 48; Klein, *This Changes Everything*; Neitzsche, *The Genealogy of Morals*. See also Anker, *Orgies of Feeling*.
21 Polletta, *It Was Like a Fever*.
22 Emirbayer and Goldberg, "Pragmatism, Bourdieu, and Collective Emotions in Contentious Politics," 473.

23 See Ehrenreich, *Dancing*, for a historical account of the suppression of what she calls "collective joy." See Protevi, *Political Affect*, for a detailed overview of the philosophical and sociological roots of current theories of affect and politics and what he calls bodies politic. One might also look to anarchist Emma Goldman's political philosophy. See, for example, Gornick, "Love and Anarchy."
24 Bookchin, *Post-scarcity Anarchism*, 12.
25 Crossley and Eyerman, "How Social Movements Move," 43.
26 da Silva, "Grassy Narrows."
27 Taylor, "The Politics of Passion."
28 Ibid.
29 Ibid.
30 Butler, "Bodily Vulnerability, Coalitions, and Street Politics," 100.
31 Bendik-Keymer, "Reconsidering the Aesthetics of Protest."
32 White, *The End of Protest*.
33 For a detailed analysis, see Drimonis, "The Unbearable Whiteness of Being (Oblivious to Privilege)."
34 Williams, "The Politics of Denunciation."
35 Hedva, "Sick Woman Theory."
36 Ahmed, "Pentagon Preparing for Mass Civil Breakdown"; Baiko, *Rise of the Warrior Cop*; Graham, *Cities under Siege*; Tam, "Dear White Protesters."
37 X, "Give Up Activism." See also the introduction to Graeber, *Revolutions in Reverse*.
38 One major exception to this is Gould, *Moving Politics*. For a few other exceptions, see Dowling, "Introduction"; Linsley, "How to Write Protest"; and Nanopolitics Group, "Nanopolitics."

Chapter One

1 See also Robertson, "Capitalist Cocktails and Moscow Mules."
2 For more on the AGO renovation, see Robertson, *Policy Matters*, 288; and Orpana, "Transformation AGO."
3 See Graeber, "The New Anarchists," on different terminology, such as "anti-capitalist," "anti-globalization," and "alterglobalization."
4 Forkert, "Tactical Media and Art Institutions," 592; Grindon, "Art and Activism," 11.
5 Golding and Modest, *Museums and Communities*.
6 White, "AGO: Massive Downer."
7 All monetary figures are in Canadian dollars unless otherwise noted.
8 Jenkins, "Toronto's Cultural Renaissance."
9 See Florida, *The Rise of the Creative Class*. For a critique, see Peck, "Struggling with the Creative Class."
10 The AGO closed its doors to the public during the G20 meetings.
11 Modest, "Keynote."
12 So much so that perhaps it should come as no surprise that what is arguably *the* central text of critical museum studies, Krauss's "The Cultural Logic of the Late Capitalist Museum" begins with a description of a protest in the streets of Paris, which is then starkly contrasted with an exhibition of minimalist art in the same city.
13 Macleod, "Civil Disobedience and Political Agitation."
14 Editorial Staff, "This Day in History: June 19, 1938."
15 The Art Worker's Coalition pressured galleries and museums into taking a stance against the Vietnam War and to include more women artists and artists of colour. Bryan-Wilson, *Art Workers*; Frascina, *Art, Politics, and Dissent*.
16 Community activists pressured for the transfer of funds to those who had experienced apartheid and continued to live in poverty in the area around the museum. Editorial Staff, "PE Residents Force Anti-apartheid Museum to Close."
17 A few key texts from the 1990s that illustrate museum shortcomings and occasionally new museum strategies include Ames, *Cannibal Tours*; Karp and Lavine, *Exhibiting Cultures*; MacDonald and Fyfe, *Theorizing Museums*; and Rogoff and Sherman, *Museum Culture*.
18 Rectanus, *Culture Incorporated*; Wallis, "The Art of Big Business"; Wallis, "Selling Nations."
19 McTavish, "The Torrington Gopher Hole Museum."
20 Evans, *Artwash*.
21 Lippard, "Biting the Hand," 79.
22 See Message, *Museums and Social Activism*, especially 22.
23 See, for example, Laghi and Freeman, "Bush Gets Along Nicely with Martin and the Protests …"
24 See Message, *The Disobedient Museum*, 36.
25 See especially Kennedy, "Two Groups Scuffle," and Steinhauer "Anti-Fascists Clash," which describe a 2017 altercation at the Minneapolis Institute of Art where a group that referred to itself as part of the "alt-right movement" showed up at the museum ostensibly to protect the European art from the left-wing International Workers of the World who were holding a demonstration against white supremacism on the steps of the gallery. The bizarre targeting of Shia Laboeuf's exhibition *He Will*

Not Divide Us at the Museum of Film in New York City is another case in point. See Associated Press, "Shia LaBoeuf"; Mumford, "Shia LaBoeuf"; Lamoureux, "How 4Chan's Worst Trolls."

26 Janes and Sandell, "Call for Chapters." See also Carter and Orange, "It's Time," for a similar argument with regard to what they call human rights museology.

27 Janes, *Museums without Borders*, 8.

28 Message, *The Disobedient Museum*, 4, takes up some of these lines of thought in her theorization of the "disobedient museum" as a concept and approach for how to think and write about museums, or "a project space that identifies institutional edges as potential sites of affective action."

29 Phillips, *Museum Pieces*, 3.

30 Ibid., 4.

31 Ibid., 5. A word on terminology is necessary. Like Phillips, I used the terms "settler" and "settler colonialism" in the same manner as Patrick Wolfe, who defines the term as a logic coterminous with the extermination of Indigenous peoples. "Settler colonialism," he writes, "is inherently eliminatory," and its primary motivation for the elimination of Indigenous peoples (either through death or assimilation) is access to territory and occupancy by settlers. Though having genocidal qualities, settler colonialism is "a structure not an event." It is perpetuated across time and space and is naturalized through the structural and systemic implementation of settler/European society atop and in place of Indigenous possession and ways of self-governing. I discuss these terms in further detail in the chapters that follow. See Wolfe, "Settler Colonialism and the Elimination of the Native," 388.

32 Livingstone, "Controversy as Catalyst."

33 See, for example, the successful boycott by artists of the Sydney Biennale in 2014, asking the Biennale to cut its ties with Transfield, a sponsor and company owned by Biennale chairman Luca Belgiorno-Nettis that had ties to offshore detention centres built by the Australian government. Begg and Ögüt, "In and out of the Biennale," and Warsza, *I Can't Work Like This*, especially 52–5.

34 Walia, "Decolonizing Together."

35 Ibid.

36 See, for example, Derrida, *Archive Fever*; Fraser and Todd, "Decolonial Sensibilities."

37 Jameson, *The Cultural Turn*; Jameson, *Archaeologies of the Future*, 480.

38 Guasch, *Global Museums*; McClellan, *The Art Museum*, especially 1–40.

39 Caves, *Creative Industries*, 454; Hartley, *Creative Industries*; Koenig, "Creative Industries"; UK Department for Culture, Media, and Sport, *Creative Industries Mapping Document* (1998); Evans, *Artwash*, 44.

40 See Bishop, *Radical Museology*, 10–11 in particular. Bishop notes that Rosalind Krauss saw this coming in her famous article, "The Cultural Logic of the Late Capitalist Museum."

41 Yúdice, *The Expediency of Culture*.

42 See Frieling, "Introduction"; Hein, *Public Art*.

43 Florida, *The Rise of the Creative Class*. Also, Florida, *Cities and the Creative Class*.

44 Szeman, "Out with the New." See also Boltanski and Chiapello, *The New Spirit of Capitalism*, for a historical look at how an artistic critique (which they consider insufficient) may have emerged from May 1968, obscuring what they call the "social critique," which they associate with the working class (601). Maurizio Lazzarato takes issue with their stance, arguing that the precarity movement, which brought

together artists, cultural workers, service workers, and the former working class, proved them wrong. Lazzarato, "The Misfortunes of the 'Artistic Critique' and of Cultural Employment." See also Ross, *Nice Work If You Can Get It*, especially 32.

45 Gill and Pratt, "Precarity and Cultural Work in the Social Factory," 3.

46 Szeman, "Out with the New."

47 Crary, 24/7.

48 McRobbie, drawing on Foucault in "Re-Thinking Creative Economy as Radical Social Enterprise."

49 Gill and Pratt, "Precarity and Cultural Work in the Social Factory," 2. See also Vishmidt, "Precarious Straits"; Raunig, "The Monster Precariat"; Ross, *Nice Work If You Can Get It*, 264.

50 Jackson, "Counter-Carnival in a Performance-Friendly World," 53.

51 Ibid.

52 For a slightly earlier analysis, see Jay, *Downcast Eyes*. See also Retort and Boal, *Afflicted Powers*, 211.

53 McRobbie, "Everyone Is Creative."

54 Ibid.

55 For one example, see Conn, *Do Museums Still Need Objects?*

56 Yúdice, *The Expediency of Culture*.

57 See Stallabrass, *Art Incorporated*, 4–9; Groys, *Art Power*.

58 See, for example, Bishop, *Artificial Hells*; Bishop, "The Social Turn"; Enwezor, "The Production of Space as Artwork"; Felshin, *But Is It Art?*; Finkelpearl, *What We Made*; Jackson, *Social Works*; Kester, *Conversation Pieces*; Kester, *The One and the Many*; Lacy, *New Genre Public Art*; Raunig and Derieg, *Art and Revolution*; Stimson and Sholette, *Collectivism after Modernism*; Thompson, *Living as Form*.

59 Bourriaud, *Relational Aesthetics*.

60 Agamben, *Homo Sacer*; Badiou, *Being and Event*; Deleuze and Guattari, *Thousand Plateaus*; Nancy, *The Inoperative Community*; and most especially Rancière, *The Emancipated Spectator*; Rancière and Corcoran, *Dissensus*.

61 See, for example, Biddle, "Re-Animating Joseph Beuys' 'Social Sculpture'"; Bishop, "Introduction"; Buck-Morss, "What Is Political Art?"; McKee, *Strike Art*; Moore, "A Brief Geneaology of Social Sculpture"; Rosenfeld, "This Is Not an Essay on Political Art"; Thompson, *Seeing Power*.

62 Yuen and Burton Rose, *The Battle of Seattle*.

63 They are referring specifically to the autonomous Marxist volume *Empire*, which became an important text for the alterglobalization movement. Interestingly, *Empire* and a number of other works in the same genre do criticize the impact of immaterial labour, though the critique of the creative industries in particular was only picked up much later by a large social movement, possibly only in 2011. See Hardt, "Immaterial Labor and Artistic Production"; Hardt and Negri, *Empire*, 478; Hardt and Negri, *Multitude*, 427; Lazzarato, "Immaterial Labour"; Lazzarato, *The Misfortunes of the "Artistic Critique"*; Murphy and Mustapha, *Resistance in Practice*, 265; Virno, *Grammar of the Multitude*; Virno and Hardt, *Radical Thought in Italy*, 270.

64 Dowling, Nunes, and Trott, "Immaterial and Affective Labour," 5.

65 Bauman, *Globalization*; Harvey, *The New Imperialism*, 253; Lash and Lury, *Global Culture Industry*, 240; Miller and Yúdice, *Cultural Policy*. Neoliberalism is often associated with the "Washington Consensus," a set of policies that advocated for the dismantling of the welfare state and a move toward free-market policies oriented toward the liberalization of trade regulations and tariffs, the deregulation of industry,

privatization, and deep cuts to social programs, combined with tax cuts to private and corporate interests.

66 Somewhat confusingly, the G7 became the G8, and then the G20 emerged in 2010. At the time of writing, the G8 has returned to the G7 with Russia's suspension in 2014, and the G20 continues as a separate body.

67 McRobbie, "Re-Thinking Creative Economy."

68 Editorial Staff (*Time*), "*Time* Person of the Year: The Protester."

69 Ibid.

70 Yates, "The Arts of Occupation." The UK's implementation of austerity measures in lieu of celebrating the creative industries actually contributed to the US cause, showing how fickle such initiatives were and how, at heart, they did not really care about artists.

71 Fischer, "Agency in a Zoo." See also Demos, "The Great Transition." And see Loewe, "Basically Ignore the Exhibition," for a critique of Fisher's article from a different activist position. See also Grindon, "Protest Camps and White Cubes."

72 Fischer, "Agency in a Zoo." See also Sholette, "Merciless Aesthetic," and Sholette, *Delirium and Resistance.*

73 Ibid.

74 Global Ultra Luxury Faction (GULF), "On Direct Action."

75 Wu, *Privatising Culture*; Ross, *The Gulf: High Culture/Hard Labor.*

76 See also Andrea Fraser, *L'1% c'est moi.*

77 Searle, "Schlock and Awe." I contextualize Searle's comment in Robertson, "'This Is What Democracy Looks Like?'"

78 One exception to this (and there are others) was the flourishing of Indigenous contemporary art in Canada and the concerted activism aimed at re-hanging historical collections in Canadian galleries, at producing new forms of art and new art spaces, and at undoing a legacy of colonial rule.

79 Fischer, "Agency in a Zoo."

80 Cotter, "Making Museums Moral Again"; Gardenswartz, "How Museums Are Quietly Resisting President Trump." See also Karp and Kratz, "The Interrogative Museum," for a scholarly take on how museums have turned toward a more active framing of exhibitions and programming.

81 Cotter, "Making Museums Moral Again."

82 Britzmann and Pitt, "Speculations on Qualities of Difficult Knowledge in Teaching and Learning." See also Failler and Simon, "Curatorial Practice and Learning from Difficult Knowledge"; Lehrer and Milton, "Introduction: Witnesses to Witnessing."

83 Cotter, "Making Museums Moral Again."

84 Ibid.

85 Fischer, "Agency in a Zoo." See also Williams, "The Transformation of the Museum," 32.

86 Bowley, "Museums Chart a Response to Political Upheaval."

87 For example, the Smithsonian National Museum of African American History and Culture has a significant section on Black Lives Matter, including a Black Lives Matter T-shirt, a Justice 4 Trayvon placard, and artefacts related to the death of Frederick Gray in Baltimore police custody. Bowley, "How Do You Tell the Story of Black America in One Museum?"

88 Message, *Museums and Social Activism.*

89 Grindon and Flood, *Disobedient Objects*; Tancons and Thompson, "EN MAS.'"

90 Grindon and Flood, *Disobedient Objects*, 19. In 2016, the Tate acquired a "replica"

of Brian Haw's protest camp, which he had set up outside Parliament in London, UK, in 2001. It remained until 2011 when he died of cancer. Mark Wallinger's State Britain replicated his camp. Associated Press, "UK's Tate Gallery Acquires Replica." W.J.T. Mitchell, *Occupy*, Loc. 1665 of 2013. The Museum of London acquired the actual posters and ephemera from Haw's protest camp in 2012. See Ross, "Occupy Collecting," 239.

91 Tancons, "Keynote."

92 See Claire Bishop's review of "Revolutions in Public Space" for her account of the successes and failures of socially engaged art practices ("Art & Education: Public Opinion"). In this, I distance myself somewhat from affect theory, suggesting that the affective impact of art cannot always encourage further action. See Julian Stallabrass, who writes scathingly of an art world "return" to the political that comes not with a politics but with fashion. "The Politics of the Political Catalogue Essay." See also Rogoff, "What Is a Theorist"; Rancière and Corcoran, *Dissensus*, 230.

93 Szeman, "Out with the New."

94 Cauter, Roo, and Vanhaesebrouck, *Art and Activism*, 334; Klanten, Hubner, and Bieber, *Art and Agenda*; Platt and Selz, *Art and Politics Now*; Raunig and Derieg, *Art and Revolution*, 319; Firat and Kuryel, *Cultural Activism*, 261.

95 See Bennett, *Empathic Vision*, 188; Meskimmon, *Contemporary Art and the Cosmopolitan Imagination*, 119.

96 Sholette, "Merciless Aesthetic." For a specifically Canadian case study that parallels Greenwald and MacPhee's definition of social movement culture, see Léger, "Afterthoughts on Engaged Art Practice." See also Sholette, *Dark Matter* and *Delirium and Resistance*, and Sholette and Thompson, *The Interventionists*.

97 Bishop, "The Social Turn," 178.

98 Bishop, "Participation and the Spectacle," 140.

99 See Forkert, "Tactical Media and Art Institutions"; Grindon, "Art and Activism," 9–12; Robertson, "Capitalist Cocktails and Moscow Mules."

100 Jackson, "Counter-Carnival in a Performance-Friendly World," 16.

101 See also Tosone, "Get to Know."

102 Bowles, "The 1970 New York Artists' Strike."

103 Ibid.; Hobbs, "Galleries to Close on Inauguration Day."

104 Scott, "New York Museums Signal Their Resistance to Trump."

105 Bowley, "Museums Chart a Response to Political Upheaval."

106 Janes and Sandell, "Call for Chapters"; See also Janes, *Museums in a Troubled World*; Janes, *Museums without Borders*; Sandell, Dodd, and Garland-Thomson, *Re-Presenting Disability*, 2010.

107 Cameron. "Introduction," 1. The essays in this volume are extremely helpful for filling in the history of museums covering contentious topics. The essays are cited throughout *Tear Gas Epiphanies*, but I draw attention to the book here as one of a few not focused solely on the "big" controversies of the 1990s.

108 Museums Association, "Do Sponsorship Protests Damage Relations?"

106 Ibid.

110 Jones, "Slick Art Sponsorship."

111 MuseumNext, "Should Museums Be Activist?" Those who voted "no" tended to correlate with those who did not regularly visit museums. Again we see a spike in interest from people aged under 30, with 51 per cent of this age group saying that they would be more likely to visit a museum that took a stand and a further 20 per cent saying it might make them more likely to visit.

112 Ibid.
113 Ryan, "As Protesters Take on the Tate."
114 Ellison, "Controversies in Context," 180.
115 Ibid.
116 Ibid.
117 Butler, "The Politics of Exhibiting Cultures," 77. See also Aruna D'Souza's 2018 book *Whitewalling*.
118 D'Souza, *Whitewalling*.
119 For many Indigenous people, celebrating Canada's 150th anniversary was tantamount to celebrating 150 years of colonization, genocide, and ongoing systemic racism. Palmater, "Canada 150 Is a Celebration of Indigenous Genocide."
120 Whyte, "Canada Revisited at the Art Gallery of Ontario."
121 Canadian Press, "Kitchener Museum's Giant Canadian Flag Vandalized."
122 Not An Alternative, "Institutional Liberation."
123 Sassen, *Cities in a World Economy*, 1.
124 Sloan, "Urban Art Histories," 272.
125 Good, "Introduction," 5.
126 I'd like to thank Kelsey R. Wrightson for reminding me of this article, one of my favourites. Wrightson quotes the same passage in her article "The Limits of Recognition."
127 Ibid., 37. She is drawing on Coulthard's argument about the politics of recognition and Indigeneity in his book *Red Skin, White Masks*.
128 For important exceptions, see Cahan, *Mounting Frustration*; Butler, *Contested Representations*.

129 Lehrer, "Thinking through the Canadian Museum for Human Rights," 1198. I also found Shelton, "Critical Museology: A Manifesto," useful for thinking through a critical approach to museums.
130 Kreps, "Museum Anthropology in the Age of Engagement."
131 Message, *The Disobedient Museum*, 2–4.
132 Cahan, *Mounting Frustration*; Message, *Museums and Social Activism*; Sholette, *Dark Matter*.
133 The Art Gallery at Guelph University collected numerous posters following the 2017 Women's March.
134 Lippard, *Undermining*, 9.
135 Graeber, *Direct Action*.
136 For coverage and analysis of just some of these incidents, see Dubin, *Displays of Power*; Howells, Ritivoi, and Schachter, *Outrage*; Luke, *Museum Politics*; Macdonald, *The Politics of Display*; Nochlin, "Issues and Commentary"; Rothfield, *Unsettling Sensation*.
137 I remain a fan of the work of other authors, such as D'Souza, *Whitewalling*, 5–7, who do use the term controversy *even as* they draw attention to different kinds of controversy. D'Souza writes (contrasting the conservative-led Culture Wars of the 1980s and 1990s with more recent outcries over appropriative work by white artists): "The crucial difference is that the first type of culture war is a war on culture by those who exploit the financial and legislative power of the state to demonize art, attack artists, and defund institutions for political gain. The second type is a war to expand the terms of culture by those who are largely artists, and who want to participate fully in the art world even as they challenge its terms."
138 Barber, Guilbaut, and O'Brian, *Voices of Fire*.

139 McKee, *Strike Art*, 3.
140 See cheyanne turions for an excellent background on the oppositional stance of artist-run culture in Canada, as well as an evaluation of its current political role. "Thinking Again about Artist-Run Culture." See also Gregory and Robertson, "No Small Matter?"

Interstice One

1 Interestingly, the exhibition *Changing Visions*, discussed in Interstice 2b, was in part a response to artist concerns.
2 William Withrow, director of AGO, quoted in Charles A. Mills, "What Place Canadian Identity," *Art Magazine*, Toronto (winter 1973), n.p., AGO Archives, Staff, 1972/72 Season, C3-7-5.
3 These observations are gleaned from research in the CARFAC fonds, the Jack Chambers fonds, the Greg Curnoe fonds, and the Joyce Wieland fonds.
4 Kritzwiser, "Wattenmaker Cool for D-Day at AGO." *Globe and Mail* (5 July 1972), AGO Archives, Staff, 1972/72 Season, C3-7-5.
5 Ibid.; "Protesters at Art Gallery Put Themselves in Chains," *Toronto Star*, n.d., n.p., AGO Archives, Staff, 1972/72 Season, C3-7-5.
6 "Protesters at Art Gallery Put Themselves in Chains," *Toronto Star*, n.d., n.p., AGO Archives, Staff, 1972/72 Season, C3-7-5.
7 Amaya, "Curator Corrects Successor," *Art Magazine* (winter 1973), n.p., AGO Archives, Staff, 1972/72 Season, C3-7-5.
8 "Imported Gallery Curator Threatened," *Sault Ste Marie Star* (27 September 1972), AGO Archives, Staff, 1972/72 Season, C3-7-5.
9 Ibid.
10 Ibid.
11 Committee to Strengthen Canadian Culture, "The American Eagle Is Chicken," (1972), AGO Archives, Staff, 1972/72 Season, C3-7-5. At this point, many members of the committee were involved with the Waffle wing of the New Democratic Party, which had written a "Manifesto for an Independent Socialist Canada" that called attention to American influence over and ownership of Canadian industry. Nowell, *Joyce Wieland*, 89. Greg Curnoe was developing a politics of personal anarchism in London, Ontario, establishing (but not leading) the Nihilist Party, which had no leaders and was a true "anti-organization." Curnoe also vocally argued to "close the 49th parallel," and his mural, which contained anti-Vietnam War references, was removed from Dorval airport in 1968. Cholette, "Memory and Mythmaking," 232.
12 Committee to Strengthen Canadian Culture, "Build Canadian Culture," AGO Archives, Staff, 1972/72 Season, C3-7-5.
13 In 2017, it might have seemed that history was repeating itself when Andrew Hunter quit his position as AGO curator of Canadian art. In part, his decision was motivated by the fact that "it is highly unlikely that the currently vacant position of chief curator – a critical role, from which many content decisions flow – will be filled by a Canadian." What had changed by 2017 was, first, that the call for a Canadian chief curator was coming from someone with a senior position within the institution and, second, that this call was wrapped up in a critique of the systemic barriers in art institutions such as the AGO to people of colour and Indigenous peoples. Hunter ostensibly quit to "give space" to voices that had been kept out of the AGO. Hunter, "Why I Quit the Art Gallery of Ontario."

14 Karl Beveridge, letter to Ann B., Carole Condé and Karl Beveridge fonds, 13 May 1976, Queen's University Archives, 5131, Box 10, Correspondence 1969–80.
15 Quoted in de Peuter, "Interview." Beveridge did return to CARFAC in the late 1980s, taking the lead on many of the negotiations that characterized the 1990s.
16 CBC, *Painter Greg Curnoe Champions Canadian Artists.*
17 Ibid.
18 Crean, *Who's Afraid of Canadian Culture?* 153.
19 Ibid.
20 Lee, "The Year of the Miracles at AGO."
21 Crean, *Who's Afraid of Canadian Culture?* 12.
22 Stanners, "Adopting Moore and Modernity in Toronto," 83. See Stanners on the 1955 controversy over the acquisition of Moore's *Warrior with Shield* by the AGO and the even more controversial 1966 installation of Moore's *Three Way Piece No. 2* outside the new Toronto City Hall.
23 Withrow, "To Herald the Opening"; Crean, *Who's Afraid of Canadian Culture?* 175. The process through which Wieland became a board member was itself a staged intervention into gallery procedures. For a description, see Crean, "Up Front with the Artists."
24 Toronto Ward Museum, "Our Living History"; Martin, "Will Downtown Progress Kill Toronto's Chinatown?" The gentrification of Chinatown is a process that continues to this day. Bright Pearl, "To 'The Invitational.'"
25 Cameron, "The Coming of Age of the Art Gallery of Ontario."
26 This work is evident in the CARFAC fonds held by the Archives of Ontario as well as in the Jack Chambers fonds held by the Art Gallery of Ontario.
27 This phrase is from D'Souza, *Whitewalling*, 9.

Chapter Two

1 Clifford, *Routes*. See also Cameron, "Introduction," 1.
2 Ferguson, "Strategy and Tactic," 40–1.
3 *The Globe*, "Suffragettes Foiled by London Police."
4 Macleod, "Civil Disobedience and Political Agitation," 46; Nead, *The Female Nude*, 35–7.
5 Macleod, "Civil Disobedience and Political Agitation," 46. See also Anon., "The Damaged Venus"; Anon., "National Gallery Outrage"; Nead, *The Female Nude*, 37.
6 Lauder, "Slasher Mary."
7 *The Globe*, "An Architect's Protest."
8 I'd like to thank Katie Oates for pointing me to this quotation in Black's text. Quoted in Paul, *Poetry in the Museums of Modernism*, 20.
9 McAree, "Modernist Art Regarded as Racket."
10 Barber, Guilbaut, and O'Brian, *Voices of Fire.*
11 *The Globe*, "Marred by Pink and Green Hair"; *The Globe*, "'Group of Seven Art' to Be Hung Again."
12 *The Globe*, "Canadian Artists Protest Actions, National Gallery"; *The Globe*, "Old Style Art Is Exemplified at Exhibit"; *The Globe*, "Art Cross-Section of Canadian Life Is Fresh and Vital"; *The Globe*, "Exhibition of Canadian Art at National Gallery, Ottawa."
13 *The Globe*, "Canadian Artists Protest Actions."
14 McCarthy, "Art Criticism Vigor Defended by Massey."

15 Jessup, "Bushwhackers in the Gallery." See also the furor over a potential renovation and two-year closure of the McMichael Gallery in Kleinburg, Ontario. Hill, "Graveyard and Giftshop"; Littman, "Controversy at the McMichael Gallery."
16 McCarthy, "Art Criticism Vigorously Defended"; McCarthy, "Art and Artists."
17 See Dawn, *National Visions, National Blindness*.
18 Bal, "Telling, Showing, Showing Off," 561. I first came across this quotation in Butler, "The Politics of Exhibiting Culture," 74.
19 Kritzwiser, "Another Age of Revolution."
20 This is not to suggest that there weren't numerous disputes. Abstract groups such as Les Automatistes and the Painters Eleven often faced commotion and protest if their works were shown in such traditional settings. See Nowell, *Joyce Wieland*, 89–90.
21 "When the protesters eventually left, the gallery had to pay $402.31 to clean the premises, including applying disinfectant, cleaning and reconditioning of paintings and statuary, and repairs to plumbing and ventilation. City Council refused to pay." *Globe and Mail*, "Splendid Setting Enhances VAG's Membership Drive."
22 MacLeod, "Civil Disobedience and Political Agitation," 44.
23 Museums tended not to be targeted even when artists were attempting to overthrow the social order – for example, in the case of the publication of the anti-establishment *Refus Global* by a group of artists in Quebec in 1948.
24 Kritzwiser, "Are Museums the Next Target for Youth?"
25 Ibid.
26 Ibid.
27 Ibid.
28 Ibid.
29 Cameron, "The Museum: A Temple or the Forum?" 197. Incidentally, in the article Cameron offers his own commentary on the disruption of the American Association of Museums in New York City in 1970, mentioned also by Swann. Cameron argues that while many attendees at the conference were surprised by the interruption, he was not, having just come from Europe where he saw first-hand an "alliance of artists with the intellectuals and with the radical student movements of protest in Europe ... I had heard much discussion of the anti-museum protest movement."
30 *Globe and Mail*, "VOW Keeps Silent Protest."
31 Swann, "Stage for Protest."
32 Ibid.
33 Ibid.
34 Cameron, "The Museum: A Temple or the Forum?" 197.
35 Ibid.
36 In fact, the research for this chapter showed a number of altercations not covered here because they were not precisely about the museum. Just one example of many included university students storming a talk by at the ROM given by Dr Clark Kerr, who was fired by Governor Ronald Reagan but found the ire of students aimed his way because he had overseen the suppression of protests at Berkeley in the late 1950s and early 1960s (described in a newspaper article that quite amazingly quotes Herbert Marcuse). See Burns, "Bissell, Student Scuffle."
37 Frascina, *Art, Politics, and Dissent*. See also Bryan-Wilson, *Art Workers*; and especially Lippard, "Biting the Hand."
38 Lippard, "Biting the Hand," 92–5; Shlegel, "My Lai."
39 Evans, *Artwash*, 142; Sholette, "Merciless Aesthetic."
40 Cahan, *Mounting Frustration*, 31. See also Zorach, "Art and Soul."

41 Cahan, *Mounting Frustration*, 33. See also D'Souza, *Whitewalling*, 113–29.
42 Ibid.
43 Art Gallery of Ontario, "AGO History."
44 Vyhnak, "Once upon a City."
45 Adams, "It's a Whopper All Right."
46 Kenneally and Sloan, *Expo 67*; Holmes, "Negotiating Citizenship."
47 Though the FLQ targeted cultural objects such as statues, museums seem not to have been of interest to them.
48 Nowell, *Joyce Wieland*, 313. Though not discussed here, many of these artists showcased their politics through their work. Joyce Wieland and Greg Curnoe in particular developed irreverent but politically astute art practices. Joyce Wieland's memorable 1971 *True Patriot Love/Veritable Amour Patriotique* exhibition at the NGC brought live ducks into the foyer of the gallery in an exhibition that addressed Canada's economic and political sovereignty, the Vietnam War, ecological damage in Canada's north, and feminism. See Sloan, "Joyce Wieland at the Border," 81.
49 Cholette, "Memory and Mythmaking," 247.
50 Cameron, "The Museum: A Temple or the Forum?" 197.
51 Bonin, "Here, Bad News Always Arrives Too Late."
52 Allen, "Working Culture," 19. Because quite a lot has been written about *It's Still Privileged Art*, I haven't covered it in great detail in this book. However, I will say that the Carole Condé and Karl Beveridge archive at Queen's University is a trove of information, showing how the two artists successfully navigated the institutional politics of the AGO to mount the show, even as the AGO both supported and pushed back against their vision.

53 In an interesting side note, in an interview with Clive Robertson, Condé and Beveridge make note of a formative moment, a demonstration in 1976 outside the Whitney Museum, which was then showing the Rockefeller Collection of American Art. The protest focused both on the Rockefellers as landlords and the lack of diversity in the exhibition. See Robertson, *Policy Matters*, 41. Incidentally, the now almost completely lost *anti-catalogue* produced as a part of this protest is held in the PAD/D (Political Art Documentation/Distribution) archive at the MOMA. Sholette, *Dark Matter*, 56.
54 Tuer, "Is It Still Privileged Art?" 195.
55 Cameron, "The Museum: A Temple or the Forum?" 197.
56 Ibid., 198.
57 Ibid., 199.
58 *Globe and Mail*, "Gallery-Goers Harassed."
59 Nowell, *Joyce Wieland*, 317.
60 See Holmes, "Imagining and Visualizing 'Indianness' in Trudeauvian Canada."
61 Sloan, "Joyce Wieland at the Border," 89–90.
62 See Coulthard, *Red Skin, White Masks*, especially 51–78.
63 Schlegel, "My Lai," 58.
64 Ibid., 58.
65 Cahan, *Mounting Frustration*.
66 Phillips, *Museum Pieces*, 44.
67 Bryan Palmer reports that the "mildly critical" tone of the exhibition came as such a surprise to Minister of Indian Affairs Arthur Laing that he "just about shit" (Palmer, *Canada's 1960s*, 391).
68 Quoted in Phillips, *Museum Pieces*, 27.

69 Ibid., 29.
70 Ibid., 46.
71 Hamilton, *Collections and Objections*, 81–2.
72 Ibid., 81.
73 Ibid., 4–5. Such practices may continue to take place today, but they are illegal.
74 Ibid., 83.
75 This is not to say that Indigenous people were not organizing elsewhere. See Palmer, *Canada's 1960s*, 378–90, on Aboriginal activism in the 1960s, especially around the Trudeau government's 1969 White Paper (with its goal of assimilating Indigenous populations into the mainstream). Actions in Canada were closely linked to actions in the United States undertaken by the American Indian Movement. See Message, *Museums and Social Activism*, for a fascinating history of the relationship between AIM and the Smithsonian Museum, particularly around the repatriation of cultural artefacts.
76 Another protest, not covered here, took place in 1977 when 200 Mohawk gathered to protest the gathering of artefacts and bones from a burial site near Williamsburg, Ontario (*Globe and Mail*, "Indians to Protest Archaeological Dig"). Richard Isaac, the elected Chief of Six Nations had allowed the ROM field archaeologist to remove the bones in Grimsby. AIM, at the time, did not recognize elected band councils, instead following Hereditary Chiefs. Thus, there was also conflict within Indigenous societies about what to do with remains disturbed by construction. Grant, "Indians End ROM Sit-in."
77 Grant, "Museum Pressed to Return Remains to Grimsby Site." The bones were removed by Dr Walter Kenyon, a man described as "a character" but one who was totally unrepentant in his approach to grave excavation. An archaeologist "lusts after bones like a Christian lusts after righteousness," he is quoted as saying.
78 Grant, "Indians End ROM Sit-in," 5.
79 Ibid.
80 Hamilton, *Collections and Objections*, 191.
81 See ibid., 191 for other cases.
82 *Globe and Mail*, "Indians Plan Their Own 'Museum.'"
83 *Globe and Mail*, "Indian Leader Threatens to Dig Sir John A.'s Grave."
84 Ibid.
85 Rather than using the more popular Oka Crisis to refer to the events in 1991, I am following Kiera L. Ladner and Leanne Simpson, *This Is an Honour Song: Twenty Years Since the Blockades*, in using Kanehsatà:ke Resistance or, even better, Kanien'kehaka resistance at Kanehsatà:ke and Kahnawà:ke to acknowledge that "Oka Crisis" was the appellation determined in sympathy with the white population of the nearby towns of Oka and Chateauguay.
86 Harries, "Ministry Allows Ruin of Sacred Sites."
87 Swann was forced out of the directorship of the ROM in 1972 by a conservative board of governors that did not like the ROM's move toward more populist and community-based shows. Artists (notably including some of the same artists who would stage numerous actions against the AGO between 1972 and 1976) swiftly organized into A Citizen's Committee to Save the Museum and rallied to his defense. Crean, *Who's Afraid of Canadian Culture?* 139–41.
88 *UPI Archives*, "Indians Left the Museum of Anthropology at the University."
89 Johnston. "V.A.L. at V.A.G."
90 *Globe and Mail*, "Artists Stage Rally."

91 de Peuter, "Interview." See also de Peuter and Smith, *"A Living Culture, A Living Wage."* The Condé Beveridge archive at Queen's University also contains a wealth of material on Condé and Beveridge's political organizing, from their early days in New York where they demonstrated outside a number of museums (that were known for not displaying the art of women and artists of colour), as well as their work with the Art & Language group, their establishment of *The Fox* (a publication criticizing the art world), their meetings with the Art Workers' Coalition, and their later work with unions and artist organization in Canada. Some of this material was included in my previous co-edited book *Imagining Resistance*, and some will be included in de Peuter and Smith's forthcoming book.

92 de Peuter, "Interview."

93 York, "Shoe Museum Not Apartheid Issue."

94 *Globe and Mail*, "Gala Draws Protesters."

95 *Globe and Mail*, "Elderly Doukhobor Gets 10 Years."

96 *Globe and Mail*, "Economic Summit '88."

97 Valpy, "Police Do Better at Second Protest."

98 Also, unlike later protests, leaders were greeted by cheering crowds. Ibid.

99 For an overview, see Margolis, *Free Expression, Public Support, and Censorship*; and especially Sirove, *Ruling out Art*, and Zemans, "How Far Will the Rust Spread."

100 Johnson, "Introduction," 5.

101 Ibid.

102 *Globe and Mail*, "Gallery Bares All to Protest Bill C-54."

103 Mays, "Anti-Censorship Protest Grows"; Mays, "Anti-Porn Bill C-54 'Must Be Amended.'" For the backstory, see Robertson, *Policy Matters*, 44–9.

104 Taryn Sirove's forthcoming book, *Ruling Out Art*, covers these actions in detail.

105 Though not always. See the Vancouver Art Gallery's censorship of Paul Wong in February 1984 when his exhibition *Confused: Sexual Views* was cancelled. See Ditta, "Please Don't Touch the Art." For a timeline of other controversies, see Johnson, *Suggestive Poses*.

106 Dubin, *Displays of Power*.

107 There were several other protests at museums during this period not covered in this chapter but noted here for posterity. In 1973, the re-hanging at UBC of a 1939 painting by Charles Comfort showing Captain George Vancouver standing above three northwest coast Native individuals prostrate on the ground before him attracted significant attention. The demonstrators won, the painting was removed and was eventually transferred to the Confederation Centre in PEI. In 1997, Kwakwaka'wakw artist David Neel and Cree artist Jane Ash Poitras both created works criticizing the ongoing display of Comfort's painting. *Globe and Mail*, "Criticized by BC Indians, Mural Gets Home in PEI"; MacAndrew, "Native Art Honoured at Festival." See also the controversial shutting down of CORRIDART in Montreal by then Mayor Jean Drapeau; Gauvin, "CORRIDART Revisited."

108 See Gillam, *Hall of Mirrors*, 108–14, on the organization of the boycott. See Janes, *Museums without Borders*, 40–7, for a contextualization of the Glenbow Museum's policies with regard to the collection, care, and repatriation of Indigenous artefacts. This boycott had begun as a more general boycott of the Winter Olympics before focusing on *Spirit Sings* as an appropriate venue.

109 *Globe and Mail*, "Natives Urge Boycott of Artifact Exhibition." The Lubicon band, 457 members strong, was then involved in a nearly 50-year-long struggle with the federal and Alberta governments over land claims. Specifically, the Lubicon were

viewed as squatters on land that they had occupied for years. The Lubicon had never signed a treaty with a reservation but had been promised a reserve in 1940. However, the governments argued that a reserve would not come with mineral rights. See Gillam, *Hall of Mirrors*, 103, for an in-depth overview of the political and economic machinations behind the destruction of Lubicon land and lifeways. See also Vogel, "The Glenbow Controversy." For the perspective of one of the curators, who concludes by cautioning the Lubicon over the potential failure of the boycott, see Feest, "The Glenbow Incident."

110 Quoted in Phillips, *Museum Pieces*, 48.

111 Harrison and Trigger, "'The Spirit Sings' and the Future of Anthropology," 6. See also Gillam, *Hall of Mirrors*, on the high-level diplomatic assistance given to the museum to secure loans from European museums, 121.

112 Poirier, "Museum Says No to Band." The McCord's actions led to the public resignation of the honorary curator of ethnology at the McCord, Bruce Trigger (see Wrightson, "The Limits of Recognition," 40; McLoughlin, "Museums and Representation," 11). For the most part, museums maintained distance from the protest. The same was not true elsewhere. The Canadian Press reported that "former chief of security for the Los Angeles Olympics has compared the goals of a Canadian native group to those of Palestinian terrorists who killed 17 at Munich in 1972." Canadian Press, "Natives' Protest Likened to Killings at 1972 Olympics."

113 Ames, "Boycott the Politics of Suppression."

114 Ferguson, "Lawsuit by Indian Band Sours Olympic Art Launch." In this instance, Cameron was speaking specifically to the issue of the false face masks.

115 Quoted in Harrison and Trigger, "'The Spirit Sings' and the Future of Anthropology," 7.

116 Wrightson, "The Limits of Recognition," 39.

117 Other museums, among them the Museum of the American Indian in New York and the Peabody Museum of Archeology and Ethnology (Harvard), did support the boycott. Eventually, the Lubicon persuaded 26 museums not to participate, and there was support in Europe for their land claim. See Cox, "Protest at Games Still On, Indians Say"; and Coody Cooper, *Spirited Encounters*, 22.

118 Phillips, *Museum Pieces*, 49. Phillips argues that it is reductive to see the exhibition only in terms of its aftermath. She suggests that the exhibition itself can be seen as hybrid and transitional but was wrapped in an ill-conceived marketing campaign and made many mistakes common to the era.

119 Ferguson, "Lawsuit by Indian Band Sours Olympic Art Launch."

120 Baele, "The Spirit Sings: A Discordant Voice."

121 *Calgary Herald*, "Spirit Sings and Soars with Cultural Exhibition." See also Phillips on false face masks and the ways that museum displays have changed in response to requests from specific communities. *Museum Pieces*, 111–31.

122 Baele, "The Spirit Sings"

123 Phillips, *Museum Pieces*, 48.

124 Coody Cooper, *Spirited Encounters*, 21–2. I have not really dealt with Julia Harrison's defense of *Spirit Sings*, but in its aftermath she was very vocal in arguing against many of the exhibition's critics. See Harrison and Trigger, "'The Spirit Sings' and the Future of Anthropology," 6–7.

125 Ibid., 7.

126 Ibid.

127 Ibid.

128 A more complicated response, however, occurred at the Canadian Museum for Human Rights when it faced a similar action in 2014 (see chapter 5).
129 Coody Cooper, *Spirited Encounters*, 24–5.
130 Phillips, "The Museum of Art-Thropology," 16.
131 Ibid., 42
132 Drainies, "Black Groups Protest African Show."
133 See Gillam, *Hall of Mirrors*, 183–4, on the control that Cannizzo had over the exhibition.
134 See Hutcheon, *Irony's Edge*, 169–95.
135 See Butler, *Contested Representations*. See also Butler, "The Politics of Exhibiting Culture," 82. For example, Butler, who is largely critical of Cannizzo's approach also points out that the (failed) critical museology employed by curator Jeanne Cannizzo was not welcomed. Some members of the Coalition for Truth About Africa wanted a traditional exhibition about Africa that employed its own generalizations and stereotypes in the construction of a celebratory narrative (84). Schildkrout picks this up as well, noting that protesters were asking the museum to "tell the truth," but critical museum studies had shown this was impossible ("Ambiguous Messages and Ironic Twists," 22). Both nevertheless conclude that Cannizzo's approach was not the way to go about testing the framing of museum exhibitions, particularly because African Canadians were completely absent from the dialogue.
136 Hutcheon, *Irony's Edge*, 172.
137 Butler, "The Politics of Exhibiting Culture," 78.
138 Schildkrout, "Ambiguous Messages and Ironic Twists," 16. Scott, "New York Museums Signal Their Resistance to Trump."

139 Butler, *Contested Representations*, 16.
140 Tator, Henry, and Mattis, *Challenging Racism in the Arts*, 44. Tator, Henry, and Mattis's analysis of *Into the Heart of Africa* could be productively read alongside Phillips's analysis of *The Spirit Sings*. In both cases, it appears that marketing departments played a strong role in steamrolling the nuance of the exhibitions and catalyzing community pushback (something that might be unfair to the curators but might overall result in positive change within the museums).
141 Butler, *Contested Representations*; Tator, Henry, and Mattis, *Challenging Racism in the Arts*. For an example of such prose see Drainies, "Black Groups Protest African Show.'"
142 Butler, *Contested Representations*, 47.
143 Ibid., 86.
144 Ibid., 63–4. In addition to organizing pickets, the CFTA also produced a pamphlet, which intervened in and extended the exhibition material. As Butler notes, quoting Stephen Inglis, the pamphlet potentially represented "a new genre in 'museum' publication." The pamphlet was called "The Truth about Africa" and included a six-page list of "Africa's contributions to humanities," including contributions to medicine, art, science, astronomy, architecture, mathematics, religion, and so on (72). See also Gillam, *Hall of Mirrors*, 186–7.
145 The unfolding of the protest is described in ibid., 63–4.
146 Whyte, "'Of Africa' at the ROM Aims to Repair Old Wounds."
147 Quoted in Butler, *Contested Representations*, 63.
148 Not all protesters were Black. Ibid., 57.
149 Tator, Henry, and Mattis, *Challenging Racism in the Arts*, 58.

150 There is some discrepancy between newspaper reports as to whether eight or nine people were arrested. Butler, *Contested Representations*, 81.
151 Tator, Henry, and Mattis, *Challenging Racism in the Arts*, 42.
152 Butler, *Contested Representations*, 10.
153 Gillam, *Hall of Mirrors*, 184.
154 Quoted in ibid., 87.
155 In fact, the museum director did make a public announcement stating that the ROM would stand by the show and the curator (Tator, Henry, and Mattis, *Challenging Racism in the Arts*, 41).
156 Swann, "Where Were They?"
157 See, for example, Tator, Henry, and Mattis's account of newspaper coverage of *Into the Heart of Africa*, which almost without fail accused the protesters of being "radicals," of wanting to censor the exhibition, of being self-righteous, etc. There were even accusations that the protesters were engaging in "reverse racism" or of wanting only one version of the truth (their own) (56).
158 Marshall, "Paternalism Promotes Racism at ROM."
159 Tator, Henry, and Mattis, *Challenging Racism in the Arts*, 41.
160 Ibid., 58.
161 Butler, *Contested Representations*, 81. In her book, Butler outlines a series of events around the exhibition including the death of Marlon Neal, shot by Metro Toronto police, and the death in custody of Hazel Alonzo.
162 Ibid., 82.
163 Ibid.
164 Whyte, "'Of Africa' at the ROM Aims to Repair Old Wounds." It should be noted that support for the picketers can also be found in newspapers of the time, although typically in letters to the editor responding to stories written as "news." See also Cayley, "Trouble Out of Africa." See also protests against the Metropolitan Museum's controversial 1969 exhibition *Harlem on My Mind*, a photo-documentation exhibition of Harlem organized by a white curator that "either ignored or, even worse, unsubstantially represented the advisory resources of the Black artistic and intellectual community" (quoted in Lippard, "Biting the Hand," 84). Although the protests at the Met resulted in the development of the Black Emergency Cultural Coalition and a great deal of critical scholarship in subsequent years, the museum world itself offered very little response. See Cooks, "Black Artists and Activism"; D'Souza, *Whitewalling*.
165 Quoted in Butler, *Contested Representations*, 102.
166 Whyte, "'Of Africa' at the ROM Aims to Repair Old Wounds."
167 Crawley, "Royal Ontario Museum Apologizes"; Crean, "The ROM's Apology for Its Racist 1989 Exhibit Is a Start."
168 Crawley, "Royal Ontario Museum Apologizes." The full text of the apology read as follows: "The Royal Ontario Museum produced the exhibition *Into the Heart of Africa*, which opened at the Museum in November 1989. This exhibition was intended to critically examine the colonial relationships and premises through which collections from African societies had entered museums. The exhibition displayed images and words that showed the fundamentally racist ideas and attitudes of early collectors and, in doing so, unintentionally reproduced the colonial, racist, and Eurocentric premises through which these collections had been acquired. Thus, *Into the Heart of Africa* perpetuated an atmosphere of racism and the effect of the exhibition

itself was racist. The ROM expresses its deep regret for having contributed to anti-African racism. The ROM also officially apologizes for the suffering endured by members of the African-Canadian community as a result of *Into the Heart of Africa.*"

169 Royal Ontario Museum, "Of Africa."

170 Ibid.

171 Butler, *Contested Representations*, 74.

172 This action was brought to my attention by Clive Robertson, who posted photographs and recollections on his Facebook page in August 2012.

173 One of the better-known paintings in the collection was Renoir's *Portrait of Mademoiselle Irene Cahen d'Anvers*, which had been in the collection of Hermann Goering. The family, of course, had a different stance, pointing out that the painting had been repatriated from Germany after the war and bought from an Italian collection. They also argued that the Oerlikon factory had provided far more weapons to the Allies than to the Nazis. Godfrey, "An Overwhelming Eyeful."

174 Metcalfe, "The Wardens of Memory," 32. See also Watson, "'Pornography Disguised as Art.'"

175 Metcalfe, "The Wardens of Memory."

176 Johnson, *Suggestive Poses*, 151.

177 Ellison, "Controversies in Context"; Ditta, "Please Don't Touch the Art," 72.

178 Gill, "ROM Egyptian Art Gala Opens with Protest."

179 *Globe and Mail*, "Our Beleaguered Museums and Galleries."

180 Allemang, "Sniffy's Ordeal"; Kelly, "Banned Work Takes to the Street."

181 Renzetti, "Artists Will Act up in Days of Action."

182 Mahoney, "Angry Ranchers Protest Oil Law."

183 Phillips, *Museum Pieces*, 162. Two exhibitions, *INDIGENA* at the CMC and *Land Spirit Power* at the National Gallery of Canada, were particularly important examples. As Phillips writes of the difference between the two exhibitions: "*INDIGENA* mounts a powerful lesson about history and cultural survival. *Land, Spirit, Power*, while not eschewing the political, is first of all about art." *Globe and Mail*, "Cross Current: Museums."

184 Tator, Henry, and Mattis. *Challenging Racism in the Arts*, 63.

185 In Canada, massive change in exhibition and collections approaches took place through ethnographic collections and spread into the art world primarily through Indigenous contemporary art and exhibitions such as *INDIGENA*, shown at the CMC in 1992. In the United States, the 1980s saw the opening of authoritative museums and galleries to displays of political art from the 1920s–1960s and the creation of a new canon of political art, which was paralleled in the invitation of current activist art groups such as Group Material into major galleries. See Sholette, *Dark Matter*, 51–2.

186 This chapter has not considered in any depth the many protests on the part of artists, community members, and galleries themselves against the various appointments of members to boards or the firings of directors. Such struggles are endemic to the arts scene in Canada at museums large and small, but because they are disconnected (typically) from wider social questions, they are not considered here. The same is true of union grievances, strikes, and picketing of museums – again things that happen regularly at Canadian museums. Except in passing, I have also not considered controversies over the accession of specific artworks (for example, Barnett Newman's *Voice of Fire* by the National Gallery of Canada in 1991 or Jana Sterbak's 1987

Meat Dress). For a thorough analysis of these controversies, see Barber, Guilbaut, and O'Brian, *Voices of Fire*. See also Walcott, "Lament for a Nation."

187 *Globe and Mail*, "Cross Current: Museums."

188 Conlogue, "Arts Groups Rally against Rumoured Budget Cuts."

189 Rosler, "The Artistic Mode of Revolution: From Gentrification to Occupation."

190 This moment is the transition between what Ruth Phillips calls the first museum age and the second museum age. The first museum age, dating from the 1880s through to the 1920s, saw the building of many if not most of the authoritative institutions in North America – temple-like institutions steeped in prestige, elitism, and intellectualism that had as their mandate reaching broad audiences through public exhibitions, encouraging democratic engagement and nation-building, often through encyclopedic collections. (Phillips, "Re-placing Objects," 84). The second museum age, suggests Phillips, began in the 1980s, the offspring of post-structuralist and post-colonialist research and pressures to decolonize and open institutions. Nevertheless, as Phillips cautions, the potential of the second museum age, particularly in terms of continued opening of the collections, has been undone as "the public is being invited to consider the grand new museum projects primarily as spectacles of architectural virtuosity, whose realization will bring major economic benefits to Canadian cities" (85).

191 There is, of course, an important history of radical artist-run centres in Canada that has gone largely unrelated in this book, in part because that history is well covered elsewhere but also because I am particularly interested in authoritative museums. See Bonin, "Here, Bad News Always Arrives Too Late"; Gale and Bronson, *Museums by Artists*; Robertson, *Policy Matters*.

Interstice Two

1 See Clifford, *Routes*; Phillips, *Museum Pieces*.

2 Clifford, "Museums as Contact Zones," in Clifford, *Routes*.

3 Pratt, quoted in Clifford, *Routes*, 192.

4 Two articles in particular, Ruth Phillips's overview of APEC protests outside the MOA in 1997 and Meg Pinto's analysis of a protest that did not take place around a cancelled exhibition of portraits of missing and murdered Indigenous women, inform this interstice. Phillips, "APEC at the Museum of Anthropology"; Pinto, "Pamela Masik and the *Forgotten* Exhibition."

5 Ames, *Cannibal Tours and Glass Boxes*, 140.

6 UPI Archives, "Indians Left the Museum of Anthropology."

7 Sanders, "The Indian Lobby and the Canadian Constitution," 151. Sanders's article gives the context of the patriation debates, tracing Indigenous resistance to it back to responses to the 1969 White Paper, "which proposed the end of special status ... dismissed aboriginal title claims and trivialized treaty rights," 153. Both the White Paper and the proposed Constitution were aimed at assimilating Indigenous peoples into settler Canada rather than acting on treaty obligations.

8 "Natives Occupy Museum," *Kamloops Daily Sentinel*, 20 November 1981. MOA at UBC Archives, Press Clipping File, 1981.

9 The number is reported as 400 elsewhere. "Indians Make Protest," *Terrace Daily Herald*, 20 November, 1981, n.p. MOA at UBC Archives, Press Clipping File, 1981.

10 Originally, a parliamentary committee had proposed a clause in the Constitution that "recognizes and affirms" Aboriginal and treaty rights, but a later version was

released without the clause, and then, after much pressure, a final version was accepted by government (but not by most Indigenous groups) stating only that the Constitution would affirm existing rights. In 1983, when few land and other claims had been legally upheld, the clause would have effectively extinguished most Aboriginal rights. Sanders, "The Indian Lobby," 176–7.

11 Canadian Press, "Native Protest for Their Rights," *Brantford Expositor*, 20 November 1981, MOA at UBC Archives, Press Clipping File, 1981; *Globe and Mail*, "Protesters Urge Indians to Fight for Their Rights"; *Globe and Mail*, "NS Indians Protest"; *Globe and Mail*, "Inuit Children Kept out of Schools." See also Mulgrew, "Unfriendly Crowds Mar BC Visit," which includes an in-depth description of Prime Minister Pierre Trudeau's argument with Chief Wayne Christian, vice-president of the Union of BC Indian Chiefs, including Trudeau's claim, at a protest in Kelowna, that he did not understand the term "aboriginal rights" during which placards read, "Fuddle duddle the Constitution" and "The Rolling Stones Support Us. Maggie, Too."

12 UPI Archives, "Indians Left the Museum of Anthropology."

13 Sanders, "The Indian Lobby," 176–7.

14 Ibid. See also Sanford, "Indians Make Stand in UBC Museum," *The Ubyssey*, 20 November 1981. MOA at UBC Archives, Press Clipping File, 1981.

15 Sanford, "Indians Make Stand in UBC Museum," *The Ubyssey*, 20 November 1981. MOA at UBC Archives, Press Clipping File, 1981.

16 Ibid.

17 "Natives Occupy Museum," *Kamloops Daily Sentinel*, 20 November 1981. MOA at UBC Archives, Press Clipping File, 1981. Another article, however, reports that UBC officials organized a strong security presence to ensure no "infiltrators" would turn violent. "Indians Make Protest," *Terrace Daily Herald*, 20 November 1981. MOA at UBC Archives, Press Clipping File, 1981.

18 *Globe and Mail*, "Protesters Urge Indians to Fight for Their Rights."

19 "Natives Occupy Museum," *Kamloops Daily Sentinel*, 20 November 1981. MOA at UBC Archives, Press Clipping File, 1981.

20 All quotes from an interview conducted 3 October 2017 at the UBC Museum of Anthropology, printed with permission.

21 "Trudeau Repudiated by BC Indians," *Vancouver Sun*, 20 November 1981, A15. MOA at UBC Archives, Press Clipping File, 1981.

22 "Natives Occupy Museum," *Kamloops Daily Sentinel*, 20 November, 1981. MOA at UBC Archives, Press Clipping File, 1981.

23 "Native Fight," *Vancouver Courier*, 25 November 1981. MOA at UBC Archives, Press Clipping File, 1981.

24 I am not suggesting that the MOA has been faultless in its relations with Indigenous people. Many of the relationships built by the MOA have taken time and work – being open to collaboration is not the same thing as working with communities that may have very different feelings about collections and display. See Clapperton, "Contested Spaces, Shared Places"; Phillips, "APEC at the Museum of Anthropology."

25 "Trudeau Repudiated by BC Indians," *Vancouver Sun*, 20 November, 1981, A15. MOA at UBC Archives, Press Clipping File, 1981.

26 Montpetit, "Rights Set in Constitution."

27 Ames, "Boycott the Politics of Suppression."

28 "Trudeau Repudiated by BC Indians," *Vancouver Sun*, 20 November 1981, A15. MOA at UBC Archives, Press Clipping File, 1981.

29 Ames, *Cannibal Tours and Glass Boxes*, 54.
30 Pinto, "Pamela Masik and the *Forgotten* Exhibition."

Chapter Three

1 See, for example, a critical perspective and a celebratory perspective in Lord, "The 'Bilbao Effect.'"
2 There are of course other examples around the world that pre-date the building spree of the late 1990s.
3 See Foster, *The Art-Architecture Complex*.
4 Krauss, "The Cultural Logic of the Late Capitalist Museum," 5.
5 Ibid.
6 Frank, "Rocking for the Clampdown," 63–5.
7 Ibid., 63. Although it might be noted that after 9/11, funding to culture was immediately devastated in the US and in New York in particular. The New York Guggenheim, to be redesigned by Gehry, was a fatality of these cuts. See Guasch, "Global Museums versus Local Artists," 197.
8 Frank, "Rocking for the Clampdown," 64.
9 Giebelhausen, "Symbolic Capital," 75.
10 Canadian buildings tended toward renovation rather than rebuilding. Notably, the biggest building campaigns in the UK were funded almost entirely through the advent of the National Lottery, a funding vector that did not exist in Canada at that point. Hewison, *Cultural Capital*, ch. 1.
11 Jenkins, "Toronto's Cultural Renaissance," 179.
12 McClellan, *The Art Museum from Boullée to Bilbao*, 2.
13 Spring, "Art, Resistance and Remembrance." There are other reasons for these collections. As I show elsewhere in the book, contemporary art can offer ways to critique and unsettle historical collections of artefacts in ways that didactic labelling cannot. See, for example, Failler's "Hope without Consolation," 242–6, discussion of the way that Rebecca Belmore's work *Traces* intervenes in the CMHR displays.
14 Levin and Solga, "Building Utopia," 41.
15 Adams, "Protesters to Greet Gehry Unveiling."
16 Wiebe, "Digging Up Dirt on the Museum."
17 See Jenkins, "Toronto's Cultural Renaissance," for a detailed account of funding of cultural projects in Toronto.
18 Frank, "Rocking for the Clampdown"; Guasch and Zulaika, *Learning from the Bilbao Guggenheim*; Hewison, *Cultural Capital*; Wu, *Privatising Culture*.
19 Macleod, "Introduction," 2.
20 Levin and Solga, "Building Utopia," 37.
21 Broudehoux, "Images of Power," 54.
22 Jenkins, "Toronto's Cultural Renaissance."
23 Day, "Hubrispace"; Wu, *Privatising Culture*.
24 Fraser, "L'1%, c'est moi," 1–2.
25 Ibid., 4.
26 Day, "Hubrispace"; Kino, "Welcome to the Museum of My Stuff." For a Canadian example, see Pullen, "The Plutocrats' Playground."
27 McArthur, Taylor, and McNish, "Crystal Myths."
28 Ibid.

29 MacLeod, "Introduction," 2.
30 Ibid.
31 MacLeod, "Rethinking Museum Architecture," 10.
32 Karp and Kratz, "The Interrogative Museum," 281.
33 MacLeod, "Introduction," 3.
34 Sandell and Nightingale, "Introduction," 1. This book in particular provides a useful overview and case studies of what particular museums have done and how they have addressed the inclusion of socially activist material into their collections and displays as well as into their programming.
35 For a celebratory take, see Browne, *Bold Visions*. For a more nuanced overview, see Newhouse, *Towards a New Museum*.
36 Ross, "Occupy Collecting," 238.
37 There were certainly other exhibitions prior to this one, such as *The Interventionists* (2004), curated by Nato Thompson at MASS MOCA, but there did seem to be a huge number of exhibitions in 2016–18, demonstrating widespread interest in the ephemera of protest and activism.
38 British Museum, "New Special Exhibition on Dissent Announced."
39 Ro, "A BP Oil Protest Spills through the British Museum's Protest Exhibition."
40 Marshal, "A Museum Held a Show of Protest Art." See also Steve Lyons's discussion of *Agitprop!* at the Elizabeth A. Sackler Center for Feminist Art at the Brooklyn Museum, an exhibition that also ended in protest when the museum hosted the Brooklyn Real Estate Summit. Lyons, "*Disobedient Objects*," 10.
41 Ibid.

42 Ibid.
43 Ibid.; Dawood, "From Nope to Hope."
44 Dawood, "From Nope to Hope"; Nope to Arms, *From Nope to Hope.*
45 This exhibition did not mention the recent outcry over Dana Schutz's painting *Open Casket*, shown at the Whitney Biennial the previous year. See D'Souza, *Whitewalling*, for an in-depth analysis.
46 This period also saw the firing of Helen Molesworth from Los Angeles MOCA and Laura Raicovich from New York's Queen's Museum, both of whom had tried to bring more activist agendas to their institutions. In short, while exhibitions might have engaged with activist material on the surface, behind the scenes many museums remained committed to the opposite. Carrigan, "Art World Heavyweights 'Stupefied.'"
47 Zardini, *It's All Happening So Fast.*
48 Smith, "Museum of History to Exclude Winnipeg General Strike Exhibit."
49 "Les casseroles" were connected to the 2012 Maple Spring student strike in Montreal. Bill 78 attempted to control the protests through emergency legislation that was perceived to strip civil liberties, thus leading to nightly "noise" protests undertaken by a wide swath of the Montreal population. Canadian Press, "Emergency Bill Would See Quebec Student Leaders Fined"; Ha and Perreaux, "Anti-Protest Legislation Passes"; Bherer and Dufour, "Our Not-So-Friendly Northern Neighbor." Jeremie Battaglia's video of the casseroles went viral in May 2012. Battaglia, *Casseroles.*
50 See Mackey, *The House of Difference.*
51 See Mosby, "Administering Colonial Science"; Dupuis, "An Untold History of Resistance."
52 In chapter 6, I more fully outline some of the critiques from Indigenous communities of the process of the Truth and Reconciliation Commission. Truth and Reconcilia-

tion Commission of Canada, *Calls to Action*, 8 (calls to action numbers 67–70). Further, in November 2018, Ian Mosby showed that the vast majority of TRC calls to action had not been met, including #68, which called for the federal government and the Canadian Museums Association to establish a fund for commemoration projects on the theme of reconciliation.

53 McTavish et al., "Critical Museum Theory/Museum Studies."

54 Michael Levin, quoted in Giebelhausen, "Introduction," 2.

55 Whitelaw, "Placing Aboriginal Art at the National Gallery of Canada."

56 These observations are based on a visit to the gallery in August 2017.

57 See Slaney, "Harper's History Museum Betrays First Nations," for an excellent summary of some of the critiques aimed at the museum.

58 See also Government of Canada, "Caring for Sacred and Cultural Sensitive Objects."

59 For example, see cheyanne turion's critique of the National Gallery of Canada for distancing itself from a work made by artist Nadia Myre (*For Those Who Cannot Speak: The Land, the Water, the Animals and the Future Generations*, 2013), who wanted to include a label quoting from a speech given in support of Chief Theresa Spence's hunger strike, "an action taken to draw attention to the degradation of treaty rights by the Canadian government." The gallery hung a label alongside, proclaiming: "The views expressed in this work are those of the artist and do not reflect the views of the National Gallery of Canada." turions, "How Not to Install Indigenous Art as a Feminist," 243–5.

60 Whitelaw, "Placing Aboriginal Art."

61 Conn, *Do Museums Still Need Objects?*

62 For an early look at collecting activist material, see Cooper, "The Politics of Protest Collections."

63 Stephanie Grace Anderson was the research assistant.

64 Museum of Vancouver archivist, email message to the author, March 2015.

65 Dr Lorne Hammond, curator, Royal BC Museum, email message to the author, 10 March 2015. The current reference work is Bourcier, Rogers, and Nomenclature Committee, eds., *Nomenclature 3.0 for Museum Cataloging*. Robert Chenhall left his work in the insurance industry to devise the first object classification system for archaeological Indigenous artefacts in the American southwest in the 1970s, a system now widely adapted by museums. Dr Hammond's title has been used at the request of the Royal BC Museum.

66 Ibid.

67 Phillips, *Museum Pieces*, 218.

68 AGO Archives, Staff, 1972/72 Season, C3-7-5.

69 Hammond email to author, 10 March 2015, published with permission.

70 Houde, "Les carrés rouges entrent au Musée de la Civilisation." The red square comes from a French saying, "carrément dans le rouge," which means "squarely in the red" or completely in debt.

71 For example, as a part of the reinstallation, the National Gallery of Canada now prominently displays Paraskeva Clark's 1937 painting *Petroushka* with a label that notes that the painting is Clark's response to the Chicago police killing of ten striking steel workers in 1937. Clark is quoted as "challeng[ing] her contemporaries to 'come out from behind the Pre-Cambrian shield and dirty [their] gown[s] in the mud and sweat of conflict.'" National Gallery of Canada, label 295.

72 Sholette, *Dark Matter*, 26.

73 Ibid., 69.

74 Royal Ontario Museum, email message to the author, 11 March 2015.
75 Xavier Gélinas, Canadian Museum of History, email message to the author, 9 March 2015.
76 Ibid. In a follow-up email in 2018, Gélinas let me know that the CMH is taking steps toward addressing the gaps in its collection. Xavier Gélinas, Canadian Museum of History, email message to the author, 1 August 2018.
77 Hopkins, "In Memoriam: Beau Dick."
78 For an in-depth overview, see Mills, "The Meares Island Controversy and Joe David," 64.
79 MOA, "Cedar Man." See also Mulgrew, "A Long Battle to Avoid Scars"; *Globe and Mail*, "Community Fights Plans for Logging on BC Island"; *Globe and Mail*, "Indians Take Stand on Logging in Park"; Morrow, "Two Major Artworks Continue to Inspire." On 20 October, a demonstration took place outside the legislature in Victoria, attended by more than 1,200 people. The protest drew attention to the cause, but preliminary logging was actually halted by a land claims court case. The court ruled that because the Nuu-chah-nulth had claimed the whole of Meares Island as part of their traditional territory, no logging could take place until the claim was resolved. For the first time in British Columbia history, a resource development on Crown land was halted because of an Aboriginal title claim. Mills, "The Meares Island Controversy and Joe David," 60.
80 Ann Stevenson, archivist, Museum of Anthropology, Vancouver, email message to the author, 20 April 2015. Stephenson writes that the museum also has a T-shirt made by the artist Jim Hart with the logo "Haida Bucks Coffeehouse." In 2003, Starbucks sued the coffee house on Haida Gwaii for infringement but after negative publicity withdrew the case.

81 See Ruth Phillips's excellent essay, "APEC at the Museum of Anthropology."
82 Jillian Povarchook, collections associate, Museum of Vancouver, email message to the author, 25 March 2015.
83 Ibid.
84 Cheryl Siegel, Vancouver Art Gallery, email message to the author, 21 April 2015.
85 Hammond, Royal BC Museum, email message to the author, 10 March 2015.
86 Ibid.
87 Ibid.
88 Ibid.
89 Sholette, *Dark Matter*, 69. Sholette himself remains ambivalent on whether or not "rebel archives" belong in gatekeeper museums.
90 Glenbow Museum, Calgary, email message to the author, 9 March 2015.
91 Quoted in Message, *Museums and Social Activism*, 81.
92 Ibid.
93 See Message, *Museums and Social Activism*, 92–4, for an extremely interesting discussion of the tensions between curatorial staff and museum administration, who often work at cross purposes.
94 Victoria and Albert Museum, *Rapid Response Collecting*. For more on this and other international collections, see Flood, "Museums and Protest."
95 Message, *Museums and Social Activism*, 83.
96 Ibid., 87.
97 Davenport, "Data from the Dark Side."
98 And it should be noted that there are a number of university-held document archives pertaining to radical action, among them the Anarchist Archive at UVic, the Occupy

Archive at SFU, and UBC. Museums often don't collect such artefacts, but universities sometimes do. McCracken, "Archives as Activism," covers a number of Canadian archives that have documented social movements in Canada, among them the archival records of land claims, Indigenous rights, and resistance to colonialism held by the Union of British Columbia Indian Chiefs, the SFU Special Collections and Rare Books Occupy Vancouver Collection, the Canadian Women's Movement Collection held by the University of Ottawa Archives, the Canadian Lesbian and Gay Archives, and a few others.

99 Ross, "Occupy Collecting," 238.

100 Matthews, "Occupy Wall Street Becomes Highly Collectible." For a detailed story on the OWS archives, see Dean, "The Struggle for the Occupy Wall Street Archive."

101 Gledhill, "Collecting Institutions and Social Protest Movements."

102 Ibid., 344.

103 Ibid., 343.

104 Hester, "Curating Symbols of a Country in Turmoil."

105 Miller, "Signs of the Times"; Ryan, "Museums across the World."

106 Newberry Library, "Building a Living Archive of Modern Protest"; Toler, "Missouri History Museum Collects Ferguson Protest Artifacts; PBS News Hour, "Museums Are Curating an Era of Social Movements." My wording in this sentence is carefully chosen. I did not contact museums about their collections from BLM, and my evidence is based on media coverage. It is entirely possible that museums are collecting from BLM but that the mainstream media does not consider such collecting worthy of comment.

107 https://www.crowdfunder.co.uk/trump-baby.

108 Rea, "The British Museum Wants to Borrow That 'Baby Trump' Balloon."

109 Ibid. In fact, a GoFundMe campaign to send Trump Baby on a world tour was wildly successful, raising much more than anticipated.

110 Hopkins, "Museums Need to Focus Less on Collecting Headlines." Hopkins also argues that the quest to collect mostly from left-leaning political groups represents a "politicization of collecting." I strongly disagree with this and note, first, that many institutions also collect from right wing groups (see Message, *Disobedient Museum*) and, second, that collecting only from the mainstream gives a false image of contemporary life.

111 See also coverage of the V&A's collection and display of part of the Robin Hood Gardens housing estate following its demolition. The museum was heavily critiqued for playing a role in the displacement of low-income residents by celebrating the gentrification of the former council estate neighbourhood. Singh, "V&A Director Fights Back"; Bennes, "What Installing a Demolished London Estate in Venice Says."

112 Gledhill, "Collecting Institutions," 344.

113 Kines, "Royal BC Museum Aims to Preserve a Montage of Tent-City Life."

114 Ibid.

115 Lorne Hammond, email to the author, 1 August 2018.

116 Matthews, "Occupy Wall Street Becomes Highly Collectable." For a detailed overview of the ins and outs of community archiving at OWS, see Samtani, "The Anarchivists"; and Evans, Perricci, and Roberts, "Why Archive?"

117 LSE Library Services, "The Women's Library Suffrage Collection."

118 Sholette, *Dark Matter*, 25–6, 48–70. Interestingly, the PAD/D archive was incorporated into the Library of the Museum of Modern Art (New York).

119 See the Interference Archive at http://interferencearchive.org.

120 "Artéfacts d'un printemps québécois," https://quebec2012archives.wordpress.com.
121 McCracken, "Archives as Activism."
122 Fraser and Todd, "Decolonial Sensibilities." For an annotated bibliography on the pitfalls and promises involved in decolonizing archives, see McCracken, "Ten Books to Contextualize Reconciliation."
123 Shilton and Srinivasan, "Counterpoint." The authors also note that such questions have been brought up since the mid-1970s, but change is slow and piecemeal.
124 Ross, "Occupy Collecting," 241.
125 Gledhill, "Collecting Institutions," 345.
126 My own answer to this question is no. The fact that racist responses happened can be recorded in archival form without granting further space or authority to those words.
127 General News Media Research Team, "Research Post."
128 Ross, "Occupy Collecting," 243, describes the Museum of London's grappling with the issue of choice.
129 Ibid., 243–4.
130 Gould, *Moving Politics*.
131 Derrida, *Archive Fever*, 4.
132 Steyerl, "A Thing like You and Me."

Interstice Three

1 Ilyniak, "Mercury Poisoning in Grassy Narrows." I am currently in the process of writing a longer article on *Changing Visions* and the mercury poisoning of Grassy Narrows that explores some of the issues raised here in more depth (forthcoming 2020).
2 Farber, "Decades Later, Mercury Still Poisons These Native Reserves."
3 Ilyniak, "Mercury Poisoning in Grassy Narrows"; Vecsey, "Grassy Narrows Reserve."
4 Hanlon, "Mercury and Trees," 227.
5 Farber, "Decades Later, Mercury Still Poisons These Native Reserves."
6 Ilyniak, "Mercury Poisoning in Grassy Narrows"; see also Vecsey, "Grassy Narrows Reserve"; da Silva, *Defenders of the Land*.
7 Ilyniak, "Mercury Poisoning in Grassy Narrows."
8 Wilkin and Nasgaard, *Changing Visions*.
9 Klepac, "The Art of Dissent," 5.
10 Ibid.
11 *Globe and Mail*, "Gallery-Goers."
12 Purdie, "Artists Protest Firm's Sponsorship of Exhibit."
13 *Globe and Mail*, "Gallery-Goers."
14 Klepac, "The Art of Dissent," 5.
15 Nowell, *Joyce Wieland*, 347. I have found no other confirmation for Nowell's statement and remain unsure that it happened, although it is in keeping with Wieland's political outlook.
16 Ibid., 7.
17 Ibid., 8.
18 Some months after this conversation took place at the AGO, the *Globe and Mail* published a report showing that mercury levels were, in fact, not decreasing in the river system. *Globe and Mail*, "Little Reduction in Mercury Levels."

19 Klepac, "The Art of Dissent," 8.
20 Ibid.
21 Sloan, "Joyce Wieland at the Border," 89–90.
22 For a much more in-depth contextualizing of the events in Kenora and AIM, see Lannon, "From the Red Power Movement to Idle No More."
23 Rutherford, "Canada's Other Red Scare," 151.
24 Ilyniak, "Mercury Poisoning in Grassy Narrows."
25 Ibid.
26 Ibid.
27 Vendeville, "Protesters March on Queen's Park."
28 da Silva, "Grassy Narrows." As I was finishing this book, the CMHR announced an exhibition that would include a display on Grassy Narrows, anti-logging actions, and the blockade. As I did not have a chance to see the exhibition, I have not included it in this section.

Chapter Four

1 Duncan and Wallach, "The Universal Survey Museum," 450.
2 Ibid.
3 Phillips, "Re-placing Objects."
4 Macdonald, "Museums, National, Postnational and Transcultural Identities," 3.
5 Ibid., 1.
6 See also Anderson, *Imagined Communities*; and Duncan, *Civilizing Rituals.*
7 McLean, "Museums and the Construction of National Identity," 244.
8 Ibid.
9 See Luke, *Museum Politics*; and Dubin, *Displays of Power.*
10 Canadian War Museum, "About."
11 Ibid.
12 The Senate subcommittee was not organized specifically to advocate on veterans' behalf but rather to advise on a solution to the quandary.
13 Interestingly, a very similar battle took place over the brand new Museum of the Second World War in Gdansk, Poland, which opened in 2017 and faced immediate pressure to change the international focus of its permanent exhibition to one "focus[ed] on the history and accomplishments of the Polish Army of the Second Republic of Poland." For more, see Steel, "Polish Supreme Court to Rule on Future of Museum."
14 Though there are certainly other war museums (the Imperial War Museum in England being a key case in point), most museums dedicated to conflict are actually organized around memorials and peace. This is true of famous examples such as the National Cambodian Heritage Museum and Killing Fields, the Hiroshima Peace Memorial Museum, the Jewish Museum (Berlin), the Holocaust Memorial Museum (Washington), the Australian War Memorial, the Kigali Genocide Memorial (Rwanda), the Museum of Memory (Chile), and many others.
15 Butler, "10 Years on."
16 Greenberg, "Constructing the Canadian War Museum," 192.
17 There are examples – Moishe Safdie's 1989 post-USFTA National Gallery of Canada and Douglas Cardinal's 1991 design of the Canadian Museum of Civilization were both architecturally innovative in their time.
18 Guasch and Zulaika, "Introduction," 8.

19 Another example here is the Jewish Museum in Berlin, which was one of Libeskind's initial forays into museum architecture.
20 *Huffington Post*, "Most Boring City in Canada Award Goes to Ottawa."
21 Gray, "Florida Gives Ottawa Its Cool." See also Florida, *Who's Your City?*
22 Gessell, "City Budget Woes Threaten Funding."
23 Ibid.
24 City of Ottawa, *Ottawa Employment Survey 2013*.
25 Ibid., iii.
26 There are eight centres altogether, four of which are in and around Ottawa.
27 Kay, "The Problem with Richard Florida."
28 Duncan, "From the Princely Gallery to the Public Art Museum."
29 The CWM also suffered from the building of the National Gallery of Canada next door, which used up its parking lot and destroyed one of its buildings. Visits to the old museum dropped to 125,000 per year in the 1990s, less than half what they had been in the 1970s and early 1980s. Sarty, "The Nationalization of Military History," 123.
30 The CWM was established as Canada's first national museum in 1942. In 1991, a report by the Taskforce on Military History Museum Collections in Canada referred to the War Museum as "an embarrassment" and called for renewal. Chatterley, "Canada's Struggle with Holocaust Memorialization," 191.
31 Sarty, "The Nationalization of Military History," 123.
32 "In 1995, the government also identified cultural affairs as a pillar of Canadian foreign policy. The same year, however, the government instituted spending reductions across the government. Heritage and culture programs were reduced from $2.9 billion in fiscal year 1994–95 to $2.2 billion in 1997–98. This represented a 23.3% reduction, compared to an 18.9% reduction in overall government spending. The CBC's budget (which stood at $1.2 billion in 1990) was reduced by about $414 million, or 34.5%." Dewing, *Federal Government Policy on Arts and Culture*, 6.
33 Janes, *Museums without Borders*, 6.
34 Ibid., 76–7, 187, also 226–7.
35 Sweeney, "Lady Sings the Blues," 17.
36 Sherene Razack's research on the connections between "racism, peacekeeping, and the violent events we now know to be an aspect of most if not all peacekeeping ventures" (6) provides an exceptional and detailed overview of the links between Canadian nationalism, peacekeeping, and underlying racism. Razack, *Dark Threats and White Nights*.
37 See McCready, "Tie a Yellow Ribbon"; Whitworth, "Militarized Masculinities and the Politics of Peacekeeping." J.L. Granatstein has been tireless in his crusade against the peacekeeping "myth," which he dismisses as untrue and anti-American. See, for example, Granatstein, "The Peacekeeping Myth."
38 Booth, "Remembrance Day: What We Do When We Remember Why."
39 Gold, "War Is Now Car Bombs, Landmines."
40 Greenberg, "Constructing the Canadian War Museum," 186.
41 Quoted in Chatterley, "Canada's Struggle with Holocaust Memorialization," 191.
42 The Senate established a Veterans Affairs subcommittee on the Holocaust gallery, and more than fifty witnesses testified in 1998. The CMC (part of the same corporation as the CWM) announced in February 1998, "The Canadian War Museum will not include a controversial Holocaust gallery. The Holocaust story can best be told

in a separate venue fully dedicated to it. The Museum will look for an alternative site for a stand-alone Holocaust gallery, the preferred choice of both veterans and Jewish groups" (quoted in Chatterley, "Canada's Struggle," 98).

43 In 2014, it was announced that Ottawa would get its own Holocaust memorial. Funded by the federal government, the winning project bid came from Lord Cultural Resources. The memorial opened in 2017. Knelman, "Holocaust Memorial in Ottawa Corrects 70-Year Mistake."

44 David Dean also notes that after the controversy over the Holocaust memorial, the CWM decided that future decisions regarding content of the museum should be undertaken through a much more extensive and formally structured consultative process. This had repercussions when the controversy over Bomber Command emerged. Dean, "Museums as Conflict Zones," 3.

45 For a further account of the changing display of the limousine over the years, see Greenberg, "Constructing the Canadian War Museum."

46 Among all of the canvases showing peacekeeping missions that could have been chosen, the Canadian mission to Croatia under the auspices of UNPROFOR is an interesting choice because it is the sole peacekeeping mission in which Canada faced a battle, the so-called "secret battle" of Medak Pocket. The gun battle was initially denied by the Canadian government, but the inclusion of the work would certainly have struck a chord with the "new warriors," who later cited Medak Pocket as an example of Canadian bravery. Off, *The Ghosts of Medak Pocket.*

47 Habron, "War Paint." Habron was a long-time journalist and had also been a former lieutenant commander in the Royal Canadian Navy.

48 While the curators were careful to represent non-white and female participants in the Canadian military, some of the works were themselves questionable, with racist titles or showing stereotypical depictions of "women's work."

49 Before 1971, the National Gallery of Canada held the entire collection of war canvases. When the collection was transferred to the CWM that year, the NGC kept what were then considered the most artistically important canvases, among them those by British artists Paul Nash, Wyndham Lewis, and Christopher Nevinson. The NGC decided not to keep the Group of Seven canvases, transferring them to the CWM. It appears that, at the time, Canada's vehement anti-conflict position towards the US's Vietnam War made these particular Group works unpalatable. Brandon, "A Unique and Important Asset."

50 This is a significantly different interpretation of how the Massey Commission emerged from that mobilized by most cultural nationalists. These latter interpretations tend to see the Massey Commission as encouraging nation-building through culture in the face of the influx of US mass culture.

51 Canadian War Museum; Canvas of War exhibit – Visitor Comments; 2006-002, Box 3.

52 UK Department for Culture, Media and Sport, *Creative Industries Mapping Document*. See also Miller and Yúdice, *Cultural Policy*, 91.

53 Everett-Green, "Canada Council Dispenses Riches to Museums."

54 Ibid.

55 For a more in-depth analysis of these changes, see Maloney, "The Canadian Commitment to Culture."

56 Greenberg, "Constructing the Canadian War Museum," 187.

57 In 2018, the Flanders Field ten-dollar bill was replaced by a bill featuring Viola

Desmond. Desmond was a Black woman who refused to move from the whites-only section of a segregated New Glasgow, NS, cinema in 1946. She has often been seen as a pioneer of a Canadian version of the US civil rights movement.

58 *Veterans Affairs Canada*, "National Aboriginal Veterans Monument."

59 The next time it made the news was in November 2006 when two university students were photographed while urinating on it. Proudfoot, "War Vets Want Action after Revelers Urinate on National War Memorial."

60 Quoted in Fraser, "Danson Lived Dream."

61 Greenberg, "Constructing the Canadian War Museum," 188.

62 Gould, *Moving Politics*, 21.

63 Ibid., 32.

64 McKay and Swift, *Warrior Nation*, 213

65 Gould, *Moving Politics*, 32.

66 Kuus, "Cosmopolitan Militarism?" 547.

67 Ibid.

68 Butler, *Excitable Speech*, 154; Gould, *Moving Politics*, 33.

69 Luke, *Museum Politics*, xiii.

70 In the introduction to *In Search of a Soul*, Moriyama notes the vigorous interest of Heritage Minister Sheila Copps and Prime Minister Jean Chrétien in the project from beginning to end.

71 Dean, "Museums as Conflict Zones," 3.

72 Sarty, "The Nationalization of Military History," 111. Sarty makes a strong argument for the role played by military conflict in the development of Canadian nationality and sees the CWM as a logical outcome of this. His back history of the relationship between the CWM, the CMC, the government, and the military is extremely useful though outside of the scope of this chapter.

73 Moriyama, *In Search of a Soul.*

74 Weeks later, the CMC postponed an exhibition of Arab-Canadian art, *The Lands within Me*, ostensibly worried about public response to the exhibition (see Interstice 4d).

75 McQuaig, "Canadian 'Peacekeeping' Troops in Afghanistan."

76 Quinn, "Marchers Slam War in Iraq."

77 Galloway and Richer, "Ottawa, Halifax on Lockdown."

78 Richer, "Opponents, Supporters Greet Bush in Halifax."

79 Ibid. The *Bluenose* is a famous schooner, built in Lunenburg, Nova Scotia, and reproduced on the Canadian ten-cent coin. Nova Scotians are nicknamed "bluenosers."

80 Sanger, "Marching to the Museum."

81 Corcoran, "No Place for Bleeding Hearts."

82 Ibid.

83 Ibid.

84 Ibid. Corcoran defines the "bleeding hearts" history as follows: "It would not, above all, look at history through themes or special interests without regard to chronology. Thus there are no galleries dedicated to women in war or regimental histories or other generalized themes."

85 Granatstein, "Paper Promises or Real Defence Purchases?"

86 Geddes, "How Stephen Harper Is Rewriting History."

87 Smith, "Reinventing Canada."

88 Mckay and Swift, *Warrior Nation*, 9.

89 Ibid., 235.

90 Bothwell, Hansen, and MacMillan, "Controversy, Commemoration, and Capitulation," 372.
91 McKay and Swift, *Warrior Nation*, 10.
92 Moore, "Air Show Censorship Soars over the Top."
93 McKay and Swift, *Warrior Nation*, 11.
94 Canadian War Museum, Canadian Experience introductory panel.
95 Bill Haley, *The Canadian War Museum: Design Approach.*
96 Todd, "War and Peace."
97 Abley, "Of War and Regeneration."
98 Luke, *Museum Politics*, xiii.
99 Geddes, "How Stephen Harper Is Rewriting History."
100 Butler, "10 Years On."
101 Todd, "War and Peace," A15.
102 Ibid.
103 A search through the digital collections with terms such as anti-war activism, peace activism, draft dodgers, protest, and activism does reveal a small number of other artefacts, key among them pacifism and anti-conscription posters from the First World War.
104 These observations are garnered from visits to the War Museum in 2005, 2006, and 2010. By contrast, the Imperial War Museum in London, UK, has engaged extensively with anti-war protesters and pacifists, although these invitations are not always welcomed by protesters, who often prefer to stage their actions outside government-sponsored institutions. See Imperial War Museum, *Anti-War Protest Discussional Forum.* Further, unlike many of the Canadian museums analyzed in this book, the Imperial War Museum is a key holder of anti-war ephemera, including the sound archives of the twentieth-century anti-war movement. See Smith, *Voices against War.*
105 Although the intention could equally be to provide a place for the rehearsal and broadcast of the emotional habitus created by the Warrior Nation myth – to speak back to or echo the refrain of the previous galleries.
106 Canadian War Museum brochure.
107 This headstone refers to all unknown soldiers and is different from the Tomb of the Unknown Soldier at the cenotaph, the ceremony for which I described earlier in the chapter.
108 Moriyama, *In Search of a Soul*, 69.
109 Ibid.
110 Notably, in the catalogue published by Moriyama, there is not a single photo of the crowded exhibition spaces. This may simply have been because they were not open yet, but the messaging of the catalogue is in keeping entirely with the architecture rather than with the displays.
111 Greenberg, "Constructing the Canadian War Museum," 185.
112 Luke, "Nuclear Reactions," 197, uses the term "patriotic fete" to describe the narrow and celebratory exhibition that resulted in 1995 after the cancellation of the initial *Enola Gay* exhibition at the Smithsonian.
113 In 2009, the museum placed a moratorium on collecting contemporary art. As reporter Paul Gessell noted, "The art debate comes as military-themed artists are increasingly deviating from traditional, documentary depictions of heroic battlefield scenes to create works far more critical and questioning of military activities." "A Different Battle Brews."

114 In researching this section, I came across a Canadian Forces discussion site dedicated to the paintings, the War Art program, and the opening day. Although the initial post is from someone calling for a boycott of the museum, responses are much more nuanced, highlighting the importance of the paintings and of the War Art program. Army.ca, "War Museum Controversy."

115 CBC News, "War Museum's Paintings Anger Veterans Groups."

116 The Canadian Forces Artist Program (which formed following the successful First and Second World Wars' government-sponsored war records production programs) was cancelled in 1995 and reinstated in 2001. Support for the production of art about war by embedded artists thus followed the general trajectory of disavowal in the mid-1990s, followed by reinstatement just years later, shortly after the showing of *Canvas of War*.

117 See also MacMillan, *The Uses and Abuses of History*.

118 Bercuson, "Canadian War Museum and Bomber Command." Bercuson notes that before the debacle, when he first saw the label he was troubled by its wording but felt that the museum should not be forced to change it.

119 I have chosen not to mention the controversy over the television program *The Valour and the Horror* here, but readers might wish to consult Bercuson, *The Valour and the Horror Revisited*, to read about how two television episodes characterized the killing of German civilians by Canadian bombs.

120 In contrast to the vast majority of coverage around the *Into the Heart of Africa* demonstrations, veterans were also supported by members of the public, journalists, politicians, and academics. See, for example, Bashow, "Bomber Command Deserves the Credit It Gets."

121 Dean, "Museums as Conflict Zones," 3.

122 Canadian War Museum panel, 2005.

123 Quoted in Dean, "Museums as Conflict Zones," 4.

124 These terms are from a quote in MacMillan, *The Uses and Abuses*, n.p.

125 Ward, "War Museum, Vets Reach Compromise."

126 Ross, "Fighting Words Rile Historians."

127 Ward, "War Museum, Vets Reach Compromise."

128 Bothwell, Hansen, and MacMillan. "Controversy, Commemoration, and Capitulation," 368.

129 Quoted in MacMillan, *The Uses and Abuses*, n.p. See also MacMillan, "Memory Fails."

130 Quoted in MacMillan, *The Uses and Abuses*, n.p.

131 Thiverge, "Exhibiting Dark Heritage," 157.

132 For more information, see Linenthal and Englehardt, *History Wars*; Wallace, "The Battle of the *Enola Gay*"; Zolberg, "Museums as Contested Sites of Remembrance."

133 Luke, *Museum Politics*, 22.

134 Quoted in ibid., 21.

135 Ibid., 24.

136 Quoted in ibid., 26.

137 Ibid., 24.

138 Ibid., 30.

139 Quoted in Bothwell, Hansen, and MacMillan, "Controversy, Commemoration, and Capitulation," 369. In his own article, Bercuson, "Canadian War Museum and Bomber Command," 61, argues that Bothwell, Hansen, and MacMillan misinterpret his comments over the controversy.

140 Margaret MacMillan, quoted in Dean, "Museums as Conflict Zones," 5
141 Dean, "Museums as Conflict Zones," 5.
142 Bothwell, Hansen, and MacMillan, "Controversy, Commemoration, and Capitulation," 372.
143 See Tator, Henry, and Mattis, *Challenging Racism in the Arts*.
144 Rabinovitch, *Public History and the Bomber Command Controversy*, 1.
145 Subcommittee on Veterans Affairs of the Standing Senate Committee on National Security and Defence, *An Enduring Controversy*.
146 Ibid.
147 Ibid.
148 Ibid.
149 Ibid.
150 Dean, "Museums as Conflict Zones," 1.
151 Rabinovitch, *Public History and the Bomber Command Controversy*, 3.
152 Gessell, "Mind Your Own Affairs."
153 CBC Arts, "Canadian War Museum Changes Controversial Wording."
154 CTV News Staff. "War Museum to Reword Controversial WWII Display."
155 Ross, "Fighting Words Rile Historians."
156 The term "nursery history" was coined by British historian Michael Howard. Bothwell, Hansen, and MacMillan, "Controversy, Commemoration, and Capitulation," 371.
157 Ibid., 372.
158 Bothwell, Hansen, and MacMillan "Controversy, Commemoration, and Capitulation."
159 Rabinovitch, *Public History and the Bomber Command Controversy*, 2.
160 Notably, the Senate had also called for subcommittee reports on the controversial television series *The Valour and the Horror* (which also focused on Bomber Command) and the potential Holocaust memorial proposed for the former location of the War Museum.
161 Specifically, the association wanted the CWM to mark the fact that despite most Japanese Canadians being interned for the duration of the war post–Pearl Harbor, a significant number volunteered to serve in the Canadian Army. Further, the association pressured the museum to show internment as part of a much wider and long-term campaign of racism. The museum did not make the changes requested. Ross, "Museum Faces a Second Offensive."
162 Cheney, "Vice President Cheney Delivers Remarks."
163 Butler, "10 Years on."
164 Ibid.
165 Bothwell, Hansen, and MacMillan, "Controversy, Commemoration, and Capitulation," 374.

Interstice Four

1 The Canadian Museum of Civilization is now the Canadian Museum of History. Because it was the CMC in 2001, I have used the name CMC in this interstice.
2 See also Cronin and Robertson, *Imagining Resistance*, which contextualizes the closure and reopening of this exhibition within competing notions of national identity, 141–6.
3 Lawlor, "Museum Backpedals."

4 Gessell, "Museum Pulls Plug on Arab-Canadian Art Exhibit." In a later interview with CMC president and CEO Victor Rabinovitch, conducted as part of the research for her MA thesis, Elayne Oliphant notes that Rabinovitch was also uncomfortable with the exhibition's focus on art and particularly on commissioned artworks, which he felt were not in keeping with the CMC's mandate to focus on historical and material culture. Oliphant, "Il n'y a pas de 'Potentially Hot Issues,'" 20.

5 Professional Institute of the Public Service of Canada, "Two Wrongs Don't Make It Right." I have not found corroborating evidence for the number of emails sent, although many of the emails and letters are archived at the CMC/CMH. Oliphant, "Il n'y a pas de 'Potentially Hot Issues,'" 42.

6 Hage, Marks, and Salloum, *Open Letter on "The Lands within Me."*

7 *Vancouver Sun*, "The Show Should Go On." It is also noted in this article that the MOA's scheduled show of Islamic Art was not cancelled.

8 Professional Institute of the Public Service of Canada, "Two Wrongs Don't Make It Right."

9 Hage, Marks, and Salloum, *Open Letter on "The Lands within Me."*

10 In Hage, Salloum, and Marks's letter, it is pointed out that Dr Aida Kaouk was the only female of non-European background employed by the museum in 2001. Professional Institute of the Public Service of Canada, "Two Wrongs Don't Make It Right." Dr Kaouk did remain employed by the museum, although her position changed to head of research on Canadian women from northeast Africa. The program devoted to the Middle East and Southwest Asia was permanently discontinued. Oliphant, "Il n'y a pas de 'Potentially Hot Issues,'" 46. Kaouk died in 2006 in a car accident.

11 Gessell, "Arab Art Show Gets Off to Rough Start."

12 Ibid.

13 Farah, "Arab-Canadians Cry Foul."

14 Lawlor, "Museum Backpedals."

Chapter Five

1 Police came upon Fontaine's body as they were searching for the body of a man named Faron Hall, a Winnipegger and member of Dakota Tipi First Nation whom witnesses had earlier observed struggling in the river's strong currents. Hall's body was, in the end, recovered from the river on the same day as Fontaine's. CBC News, "Tina Fontaine, Faron Hall Deaths." See also Razack, "Gendered Racial Violence and Spatialized Justice," for a deeper analysis of space and place and a lack of justice that accompanies the murder of Indigenous women.

2 Dean, "The CMHR and the Ongoing Crisis," 147–8. Since then, it has been suggested that the number of MMIW might actually be much higher.

3 See also Ade, "Spectacle over Substance."

4 *Vice* Staff, "Drag the Red."

5 SL40 also cannot access emergency services, cannot remove garbage effectively, and cannot adequately treat sewage on site. Perry, *Aqueduct*, 17.

6 It turned out that this set of remains were not human. I debated whether or not to start this chapter in this manner. I reasoned that the juxtaposition of the murder of Tina Fontaine and the museum might seem insignificant because it has been often used in the spate of new literature analyzing the museum (Dean, "The CMHR and the Ongoing Crisis," 147, for example, begins in a manner similar to mine). However, I made a decision to include this scene because the glamour of the opening of the

museum was strongly affected by the vigil fires. To *not* have included it when I was indeed there would also have been a disservice. Dean's excellent article covers the relationship between Fontaine, MMIW, and the CMHR, drawing out that analysis to also encompass other museums such as the MOA in Vancouver.

7 Blumer, "Expanding Museum Spaces," 137.

8 Ibid.

9 See, for example, Carter and Orange, "'It's Time to Pause and Reflect.'" Kelsey Perrault has also drawn attention to the relationship between the CMHR and the US Holocaust Museum in her graduate work at Western University.

10 See also many of the essays in Busby, Muller, and Woolford, *The Idea of a Human Rights Museum*.

11 The museum would have been called the Museum of Reconciliation (it did not refer to Indigenous/settler reconciliation but rather to healing following genocide). Ukemonde, "Press Release."

12 MacDonald, "Museum of Human Rights." Today there are numerous human rights museums, so many, in fact, that in 2010 they formed the Federation of International Human Rights Museums. There are now human rights museums in Chile, Paraguay, Belgium, Japan, Taiwan, South Korea, Pakistan, and Indonesia.

13 In 2000, Canwest purchased most of Conrad Black's Hollinger Inc. for $3.2 billion. It was the height of the company's success: Canwest would not survive to see the opening of the CMHR. In February 2010, Gail and David Asper resigned from the Board of Directors of Canwest Global Communications, relinquishing control of the media company that had been founded by their father. Their younger brother, Leonard Asper, remained CEO of Canwest. Debt holders took over ownership of the company, which had been placed in court protection in October 2009. Canwest had not been able to keep up with the debt servicing costs on the $4 billion that it owed. Cash, "Aspers Quit Canwest Board."

14 Quoted in Boswell, "Asper Museum to Rise as Shrine to Tolerance." Though not on the same scale, veterans, as a part of the Passing the Torch campaign, had just raised huge amounts of money for the CWM, showing that such fundraising projects were at least theoretically possible. Even in the case of the CWM, however, private fundraising accounted for far less than 50 per cent of the total needed.

15 Miller and Yúdice, *Cultural Policy*, 186.

16 Here I purposely use the term cultural genocide to echo the term used by the CMHR at this point in time. By 2017, the CMHR had included the word "genocide" in displays related to the treatment of Indigenous peoples in Canada.

17 See Edge, "The Asper Slam on News Media"; and Fisk, "Journalists Are under Fire for Telling the Truth."

18 Boswell, "Asper Museum to Rise as Shrine to Tolerance."

19 See Day, "Hubrispace."

20 See Ball and Rudling, "The Underbelly of Canadian Multiculturalism," for full coverage of this lobbying.

21 Ibid.

22 This did not stop further complaints.

23 Logan, "National Memory and Museums."

24 Boswell, "Winnipeg to Get Human Rights Museum."

25 Ibid.

26 Moses, "Protecting Human Rights and Preventing Genocide," 47.

27 Ibid.

28 Failler and Simon, "Curatorial Practice and Learning from Difficult Knowledge," 168.
29 Perreault, "Remembrance as Presence."
30 Coffey, "Reaching for the Stars."
31 Ross, "Museums in Waiting." The museum also wanted a green building, which added to costs. Rollason, "Rights Museum Needs $45M." And additionally, the budget did not include municipal taxes, which had to be factored into the final cost. Rabson, "Human Rights Museum Budget Already Short."
32 Samyn, "Ottawa Not Likely to Fund Winnipeg Human Rights Museum."
33 Basen, "Memory Becomes a Minefield." See a critique of this article at Lett, "Measured Museum Debate Welcome."
34 Clark, "Backing Israel a 'Moral Imperative.'"
35 Basen, "Memory Becomes a Minefield." Winnipeg at this time had MPs from all major federal parties.
36 Ibid.
37 Oosterom, "Harper Vows Winnipeg Showpiece Will Be a National Institution."
38 Ross, "Coming to a Town near You."
39 Ibid.
40 Ibid. Decentralization did not, ultimately, help the cause of the National Portrait Gallery. In 2001, the then-Liberal federal government planned to convert the former US embassy in Ottawa (across the street from Parliament Hill) into a permanent home for the collection. Renovations were already underway in 2006 when the newly elected Conservative government stopped progress and suggested a new plan to move the collection to Calgary, where it would be shown in a space funded by EnCana in their Norman Foster–designed new headquarters (which was, at the time of discussion, under construction). In 2007, EnCana announced that their building would not, in fact, be used. At that point, the government announced a competition, inviting nine cities to submit bids for the gallery. Although plans were submitted from Edmonton, Calgary, and Ottawa, the competition was cancelled in November 2008 and the whole project shelved. Cohen, "Welcome to the Quiet Devolution"; Taylor, "Portrait Gallery a Capital Idea"; McGuinty, "Portrait Gallery Move Paints a Grim Picture"; Gessell, "Gallery Plan a Potential 'Disaster'"; Tayler, "EnCana in Talks for National Gallery." See also Janes, *Museums without Borders*, 331–2, for an account of a near-collaboration between Foster, EnCana, and the Glenbow Museum.
41 Ross, "Coming to a Town near You."
42 Ibid.
43 This process had been ongoing since the 1980s. When the National Gallery attempted to fundraise for its new building in the 1980s, other museums and galleries cried foul, arguing that as a federal museum the National Gallery should not be fundraising, taking from the already small pool of funds available to all cultural institutions. *Globe and Mail*, "Funding Campaign for Gallery Draws Fire."
44 Ross, "Museums Decry Funding Pullout."
45 Caplan, "Human Rights Museum Is Indifferent to Some Human Rights."
46 Adams, "Now Comes the Hard Part."
47 Ibid. See also Knelman, "Museum Caught in Backlash."
48 Adams, "Now Comes the Hard Part."
49 Rochon, "Asper's Dream Will Be a Sci-Fi Castle."
50 See chapter 1, note 31. Wolfe, "Settler Colonialism and the Elimination of the Native," 388.

51 Gray and Gardner, "(In)Visible Histories." For further background, see Perry, *Aqueduct*.
52 Wodtke, "A Lovely Building for Difficult Knowledge," 210. Wodtke gives a detailed overview of the various groups, committees, and planners in charge of redeveloping the area of the Forks.
53 Fallding, "Toward Radical Transparency."
54 Wodtke, "A Lovely Building for Difficult Knowledge," 208.
55 See Amy Freier on this gallery, "Exhibiting Human Rights."
56 Phillips, *Museum Pieces*, 113.
57 Clapperton, "Contested Spaces, Shared Places," 13.
58 Doxtator, "The Implications of Canadian Nationalism," 59.
59 Logan, "National Memory and Museums," 115.
60 Martin, "The Politics of Inclusion and Exclusion."
61 Assembly of First Nations and Canadian Museums Association, *Turning the Page*, 4.
62 See also the Aboriginal Curatorial Collective, established in 2005.
63 Quoted in Doxtator, "The Implications of Canadian Nationalism," 64. Cranmer-Webster was then curator of the U'Mista Centre.
64 This is also true outside of Canada. A recent action by Decolonize This Place at the Natural History Museum in New York City raises similar issues. Pinto, "In Dishonor of Columbus"; Chen, "Some of the Exhibits."
65 Phillips, "Beyond Difficult Histories," 301.
66 Quoted in ibid., 302.
67 The CMHR and the TRC are intimately connected. See Canadian Museum for Human Rights, "Truth and Reconciliation."
68 Lonetree, *Decolonizing Museums*, xv. See also Janes, *Museums without Borders*, 23. In this essay, Janes describes a very different approach to collaboratively establishing a museum, this one the Prince of Wales Northern Heritage Centre (PWNHC) in Yellowknife, Northwest Territories, in the late 1970s.
69 Rogoff, "Hit and Run," 64
70 Ibid.
71 Ibid.
72 Phillips, *Museum Pieces*, 10.
73 Reconciliation refers to a two-way process of forgiveness and healing; Indigenization is a way of reconfiguring the museum from one or more Aboriginal perspectives; and decolonization is a more difficult term that is often used metaphorically in museums to equate with Indigenization but that is tied to land and undoing colonial relations. These terms are further explored in the rest of the chapter. See also Tuck and Yang, "Decolonization Is Not a Metaphor."
74 See Wrightson, "The Limits of Recognition."
75 Busby et al., "Introduction," 10.
76 Basen, "Memory Becomes a Minefield." The irony of the CWM (of which Granatstein had been director) being forced into a far from neutral position by veterans should not go unnoted here.
77 Ibid.
78 Parliament of Canada, "Bill C-42."
79 Adams, "Report Urges Autonomy for Rights Museum."
80 Content Advisory Committee, *Final Report*.
81 Woods, "Liberals Add New $9 Billion."
82 turions, "Decolonization, Reconciliation." For more on why some could not accept

the apology, see Chrisjohn et al., "A Historic Non-apology" for a collective answer, which also links the apology to the government's unwillingness to admit it committed a crime, i.e., genocide.

83 turions, "Decolonization, Reconciliation."

84 Quoted in Wherry, "What He Was Talking About."

85 Moses, "Protecting Human Rights and Preventing Genocide," 57.

86 Content Advisory Committee, *Final Report*, 70.

87 Milne, "Human Rights and/or Market Logic," 119.

88 Failler, "Hope without Consolation," 232.

89 Welch, "CMHR Rejects 'Genocide' for Native Policies." For an in depth analysis, see Wysote, "Risk Your Life Accessing the Museum."

90 Busby et al., "Introduction," 12. A copy of Fontaine, Dan, and Farber's article is now included in an exhibit at the CMHR.

91 Welch, "CMHR Rejects 'Genocide' for Native Policies."

92 APTN National News, "Manitoba First Nation Organization Slams Human Rights Museum."

93 *Globe and Mail*, "Canadian Government Withheld Food from Hungry Aboriginal Kids."

94 Paul, "Where Are the Children Buried?"

95 Quoted in Sharma, "Governing Difficult Knowledge," 191–2.

96 Logan, "National Memory and Museums," 120.

97 Ibid., 118.

98 Lehrer, "Thinking through the Canadian Museum for Human Rights," 1202.

99 Quoted in Sharma, "Governing Difficult Knowledge," 191–2.

100 Moses, "Protecting Human Rights and Preventing Genocide," 56.

101 Busby, "Change of Plans," 116. Similarly, in a press release issued at the time of the controversy, CMHR president and CEO Stuart Murray noted, "The Museum believes this discussion provides an excellent opportunity to raise awareness about the nature of human rights violations in our own backyard. The Canadian Museum for Human Rights, as a venue for education, reflection and dialogue, strongly supports and encourages this conversation." Dhamoon, "Re-presenting Genocide," 11. See also Freier, "Exhibiting Human Rights"; Perrault, "Remembrance as Presence"; Wysote, "Risk Your Life Accessing the Museum."

102 Garneau, "Imaginary Spaces of Conciliation and Reconciliation," 37. David Garneau notes the vast semantic chasm between conciliation and reconciliation, which presupposes a (fictional) moment of harmony in the past that must be brought back into being (35).

103 Had I had more space I would have considered Rebecca Belmore's work *Traces*, which is installed in the Indigenous Perspectives Gallery of the CMHR. For an analysis of this important work, see Failler, "Hope without Consolation."

104 Phillips, "Beyond Difficult Histories," 297.

105 Ibid.

106 Ibid., 298.

107 Ibid., 310.

108 Wodtke, "A Lovely Building for Difficult Knowledge," 212. During an interview, curator Karine Duhamel told me that the description of the museum as a path from darkness to light is a mischaracterization of the goals and set-up of the CMHR.

109 Ibid., 215.

110 Ibid., 209.

111 Arguably, the Holocaust Museum in Washington has been able to address this tension. See Perrault, "Remembrance as Presence."
112 Content Advisory Committee, *Report to the Minister of Canadian Heritage*, 26.
113 Ibid., 5.
114 Ibid., 8.
115 Ibid., 13. The report never defines who these activists are, and the language could be referring to members of the Ukrainian community who had lobbied for more space for coverage of the Holodomor, to the many groups who were upset over the lack of use of the term "genocide," or to others.
116 Plum Creative, *Canadian Museum for Human Rights.*
117 Edmonds, "Asper Foundation's Human-Rights Museum Given Federal Kickstart"; Khan, "We Sell the Charter to Muslim Countries."
118 Basen, "Memory Becomes a Minefield."
119 Ibid.
120 Welch, "CMHR No Conversation Starter."
121 Blumer, "Expanding Museum Spaces," 140–1.
122 Brean, "Canadian Museum for Human Rights Opens."
123 Kay, "Every Identity Politics Activist."
124 Ibid.
125 Ibid.
126 Butler, "On Mixed Metaphors, Herding, and Burning Issues."
127 Jacks, "Picking and Choosing."
128 Lehrer, "Thinking through the Canadian Museum for Human Rights," 1200.
129 Neufeld, "Sucked Dry." On the background of the Winnipeg Aqueduct, I strongly suggest Adele Perry's short volume *Aqueduct.*
130 Failler and Sharma, "Shoal Lake 40's Living Museum."
131 See Perry, *Aqueduct*, 48–56, for coverage of the abuse that took place and the ignoring of treaty rights.
132 The devious processes by which this took place are explained in Perry, *Aqueduct*, 59–70.
133 Neufeld, "Sucked Dry."
134 Ibid. According to the *Tyee*, "In 1989, Winnipeg and Manitoba offered a $6-million fund in exchange for both Shoal Lake reserves agreeing not to endanger the drinking water with economic initiatives." Ball, "Will Canada Unblock This People's 'Road to Freedom?'"
135 At the time of writing, 119 other First Nations communities in Canada still lacked clean drinking water.
136 Perry, *Aqueduct*, 14–15.
137 In this chapter, I have concentrated on SL40, but the lights illuminating the museum's galleries also are linked directly to a decades-old development that benefits Manitoba at the expense of Indigenous peoples. "Starting in the 1950s, Manitoba Hydro constructed a northern hydroelectric system that has profoundly affected roughly 35,000 aboriginal people, including Pimicikamak, a nation of 8,000 Cree people and their lands, some 500 kilometres north of Winnipeg. Like the people of Shoal Lake, we as Pimicikamak people live with loss. The dams permanently flood 65 square kilometres of land and destabilize hundreds of kilometres of critical shoreline habitat. This undermines land-based industries and traditional practices. The dams also create unpredictable ice conditions in winter and submerged wood debris (from shoreline erosion) in summer, which have caused fatal snowmobile and boating

accidents, respectively. We have received some compensation and Manitoba Hydro has taken some measures to mitigate the damage, but still, our once-beautiful and bountiful homeland is a mess. The dams are a wound on the land and in our hearts. Each light in the museum will plug directly into this wound." *Globe and Mail*, "For Our First Nations, New Museum a Monument to Hypocrisy."

138 Neufeld, "Sucked Dry."

139 *Globe and Mail*, "For Our First Nations, New Museum a Monument to Hypocrisy."

140 Perry, *Aqueduct*, 16.

141 Leaving Shoal Lake is not an option. See Taylor, "Why First Nations People Can't Just Move," on the connection to land, family ties, and environment. Additionally, treaty obligations and the continued battle to secure traditional lands make moving solely a settler solution to a settler problem.

142 *Globe and Mail*, "For Our First Nations, New Museum a Monument to Hypocrisy."

143 Neufeld, "Sucked Dry."

144 Museum of Canadian Human Rights Violations, pamphlet, handed out in Winnipeg at the opening of the CMHR.

145 At the time of writing, the Manitoba government was resisting the name "Freedom Road," preferring instead the generic Shoal Lake Road. Ward, "What's in a Name?"

146 Kinew, "Human Rights Museum Needs to Act."

147 Quoted in ibid.

148 *Vice* Staff, "Canada's Waterless Communities."

149 Ward, "Shoal Lake Residents Weep."

150 Bell, "Open Letter to Prime Minister Stephen Harper."

151 CBC News, "International Watchdog Human Rights Watch to Look at Shoal Lake 40."

152 Harp, "Shoal Lake 40."

153 Redsky, "Statement by Chief Erwin Redsky."

154 Brandson, "Shoal Lake 40 Inching Closer." This interview is also notable for how it introduces community worries about the new road, which might also bring with it increased access to drugs and other forms of exploitation.

155 Blumer, "Expanding Museum Spaces," 139.

156 See Pierre Eliadis, whose commentary after the museum opening clearly articulates this point. Eliadis, "CMHR a Symbol for Dissent and Protest."

157 All quotes from an interview conducted 10 October 2017 at the CMHR, printed with permission.

158 Pinto, "Pamela Masik and the *Forgotten* Exhibition," 4–17.

159 turions, "Decolonization, Reconciliation."

160 Lehrer, "Thinking through the Canadian Museum for Human Rights," 1,200.

161 Garneau, "Imaginary Spaces of Conciliation and Reconciliation," 265.

162 Pinto, "Pamela Masik and the *Forgotten* Exhibition," 4–17.

163 Garneau, "Extra-Rational Aesthetic Action and Cultural Decolonization."

Interstice Five

1 Grief, "Why Toronto's Slut Walk Is as Important as Ever."

2 Whyte, "Anatomy of a Protest."

3 Ibid.

4 CBC News, "Quebec Police Admit They Went Undercover." Protesters claimed that the three officers were attempting to agitate the crowd and encourage violence, an allegation police denied.

5 Schechter, "Slut Nation."
6 The *Toronto Star* later printed a retraction of some of their coverage of Coburn's project. "The 'young woman in the brown coat' Coburn portrays in her first piece of video art is not an undercover agent of the police. She came forward to the *Star* this week to identify herself as Mandy Pipher, 30, a Toronto political activist and 'staunch feminist' who attended Slut Walk because she believes sexual assault is an important issue." English, "Slutwalk and the Fact of the Art."
7 Schechter, "Slut Nation."
8 An excellent comparison could be made with Lara Schnitger's *Suffragette City* installation, a piece that asks viewers to participate in a miniature, sex-positive protest, carrying her installation around town. See: *Frieze*, "Lick My Legs: *Suffragette City*."
9 Coburn died tragically, not long after the showing of *Anatomy of a Protest* in Toronto.

Chapter Six

1 Nayeri, "Anti-BP Activists Stage Nude Lie-In." BP also sponsors the British Museum, the Royal Opera House, and the National Portrait Gallery (UK), giving approximately 1 million pounds per year to the arts. See also Art Not Oil, *Culture beyond Oil.*
2 Brown, "Tate's BP Sponsorship was 150,000 to 330,000 a Year," *Guardian*, 26 January 2015.
3 Spence, "Who Funds the Arts and Why We Should Care."
4 Garrard, "With Entry Changes and Oil Sponsorship." For a take on these actions from a (relatively sympathetic) business/management perspective, see Chong, "Institutions Trust Institutions."
5 I looked at sponsorships of major exhibitions at authoritative galleries in each province (excluding the territories) from 2012 to 2017. Energy companies are leading sponsors of exhibitions across the country. Banks, construction companies, engineering firms (most of them involved in the resource industry), restaurants, department stores, and individual donors are also major funders of exhibitions in Canada.
6 Although there were few protests at museums, there were important artistic responses to resource extraction. The anti-logging protests of the 1980s and 1990s, as well as many other precedent-setting events (such as Hans Haacke's work on Alcan and Alcan's response to the National Gallery of Canada's acquisition of Haacke's work) are present only as backdrop in this chapter. See also Hodgins and Thompson, "Taking the Romance out of Extraction," 396.
7 Toledano, "How Activists Shut Down."
8 Jones, "Slick Art Sponsorship."
9 Serafini, *Performance Activism.* I am also very aware that museums are not monolithic and that many of them have been leaders in sharing knowledge about climate change and in developing plans to "green" themselves. For another take, see Stephanie LeMenager's analysis of several oil museums, including the Oil Sands Discovery Centre in Fort McMurray. LeMenager, *Living Oil*, 142–82. See also Cameron and Neilson, *Climate Change and Museum Futures*; Newell, Robin, and Wehner, *Curating the Future*; and Janes, *Museums without Borders*, 168 and 188–392.
10 There are examples prior to 2010. Art Not Oil, for example, grew out of Rising Tide UK in 2004. Nevertheless, the number of actions has increased tremendously since 2010.

11 Mahony, "Locating Simon Critchley's," 13. For some wonderfully in-depth descriptions of the Liberate Tate actions, see Evans, *Art Wash*.
12 Ibid.
13 Ibid.
14 Ibid., 14.
15 Evans, *Art Wash*, 8. See also Clarke, Evans, Newman, Smith, and Tarman, eds., *Not If but When*; see also Not An Alternative, "Institutional Liberation."
16 Dean, "The Anamorphic Politics of Climate Change."
17 Ibid.
18 For a description of this action, see Cotter, "Making Museums Moral Again."
19 Dean, "The Anamorphic Politics of Climate Change."
20 For precedent, see the Neo-Naturists, who had a less political platform but employed the same kinds of interventionist tactics as Liberate Tate and other groups, combining performance, cabaret, and theatre. Studio Voltaire, *The Neo Naturists*.
21 BP or Not BP, "Performances and Films."
22 Mathiesen, "Anti-Fossil Fuel Activists Stage Louvre Oil Slick."
23 Mahony, "Locating Simon Critchley's."
24 Ibid., 17.
25 Serafini, *Performance Action*. In this book, Serafini describes numerous actions organized by BP or Not BP and shows how museums both contain protests (for example, by not allowing props through security) while simultaneously allowing the actions to take place in their spaces.
26 Rustin, "Tate and Oil." Tate refused to disclose the sum donated to the museum by BP, despite freedom of information requests, and when documents were released, they were heavily redacted. Tate had to appear at an information tribunal called by the UK information commissioner. Following the tribunal, Platform and Request Initiative brought a legal case against Tate to receive further details of the sponsorship agreement. See Platform London, "Infographic"; Liberate Tate, "Confronting the Institution in Performance," 78–80. This article also contains a detailed description of the Liberate Tate performance "Hidden Figures," which dealt with the redacted documents.
27 Such actions can also be found outside the US and UK, for example in the work of Stopp Oljesponsing av Norsk Kulturliv, a group of artists and musicians who challenge Statoil sponsorships in Nordic countries. Further, in 2011 the Brazilian Museu de Arte Moderna in Rio de Janeiro was protested by artists who wanted the museum to drop sponsorship deals with Vale, Petrobras, and Chevron. Evans, *Artwash*, 153–4. To see how Canada has used diplomatic exhibitions of art to forward its mining and oil interests in Brazil, see Robertson et al., "More a Diplomatic Than an Aesthetic Event."
28 Vartanian, "Art Protest Groups Join Forces."
29 Sutton, "May Day Occupation." These protests were primarily about labour conditions in Abu Dhabi but touched on oil through the connection to Middle East oil exports to the United States and the oil money behind the building of new cultural institutions. See also Ross, *The Gulf*.
30 Three members of Illuminator were charged with illegal advertising, but a judge dismissed the case.
31 Natural History Museum, "Our Letter Has Gone Viral." Importantly, Not An Alternative has staged actions with Occupy Homes and Occupy Faith (among others). They are not solely concerned with museums and sponsorships but with a host of

connected issues ranging from housing rights to climate change (see McKee, *Strike Art*, 128–34). Decolonize This Place is another important New York-based example but not included in the list because their actions tend not to focus on oil.

32 Serafini, *Performance Action*, Loc. 907 of 4717.

33 Mahony, "Locating Simon Critchley's," 23. See also McKay, *DIY Culture*, for this description of Reclaim the Streets and the anti-road protests of the 1980s and 1990s.

34 Mahony, "Locating Simon Critchley's," 24.

35 Not An Alternative, "Interview with the Natural History Museum."

36 Natural History Museum, "Exhibition of Fossil Fuel Industry Greenwashing."

37 Dean, "The Anamorphic Politics of Climate Change."

38 Ibid.

39 Ibid. Greenpeace also created an online museum called the Museum of Oil, which imagines the future if oil is left in the ground. Andrew and Pippa, *The Museum of Oil*.

40 Worth, "Getting Europe out of the Tar Sands."

41 Platform London, "An Open Letter in Support of the Tar Sands Blockade"; Platform London, "Social License."

42 Berthiaume, "Pipeline Protest Greets PM Trudeau in London."

43 Centre for Climate Safety, "Uprise among Artists against 'Dirty Oil Money.'"

44 Ibid. The full statement reads: "Norway's international reputation as a good climate campaigner can only persist if Statoil withdraws from the tar sands project in Canada. We sharply distance ourselves from Statoil's current project in Canada, because this causes major carbon emissions that contribute to climate degradation, and because strong economic interests put free speech principle at risk. Extraction of tar sands is incompatible with the international goal that global temperatures must not rise more than two degrees. Statoil must withdraw."

45 It has been argued that colonial power is furthered in Canada through infrastructure – pipelines, mines, and resource extraction that often takes place on Indigenous land. Spills often take place in remote areas nearest to or on Indigenous land. For example, Lou and Sharp, "Canada Oil Pipeline Spills 200,000 Liters."

46 Liberate Tate has worked with cleaners, mostly to tell them what the substances are and how to clean up. Art Not Oil has worked with the Public and Commercial Services Union (museum workers) to support their campaigns. BP or Not BP has recently expanded its framework to "include the repatriation of objects, workers rights, social and environmental justice, exposure of the [British] museum's colonial legacy" (Serafini, *Performance Activism*, Loc. 3559 of 4717).

47 Serafini, *Performance Action*, Loc. 1498 of 4717. Rarely are activists arrested, although they are frequently removed from the galleries. The "safety" of such actions contrasts with actions at the Smithsonian where anti-drone protesters were pepper-sprayed or in actions against the Coalition for the Truth About Africa in 1989 at the ROM. There, protesters were violently arrested, a situation that was likely driven by racism.

48 Wrightson, "The Limits of Recognition," 39.

49 Janes, "Crediting the First Blockbuster."

50 Devine, "After the Spirit Sang," 218.

51 See Laboucan-Massimo, "Awaiting Justice." Laboucan-Massimo (92) writes, "Currently, there are more than twenty-six hundred oil and gas wells in our traditional territories. Over fourteen hundred square kilometres of leases have been granted for tar sands and fracking development in Lubicon territory, and almost 70 per cent of

the remaining land has been leased for future development." It was only as I was doing the final edits on this book, in October 2018, that the Lubicon Lake Band and the government of Alberta reached an agreement that included the return of land for the creation of a reserve. Graney, "'It's Been a Long Time Coming.'"

52 I'd like to thank Steve Lyons for bringing this article to my attention. Fisher, "The Health of the People Is the Highest Law."

53 Ibid., 64.

54 Ibid.

55 Quoted in ibid., 64. Fisher's article is also concerned with *Re-Visions*, an exhibition that was organized at the Banff Centre for the Arts in order to respond to *Spirit Sings*. While I do not discuss the exhibition here, it is important that it not be forgotten.

56 Ibid., 72.

57 Quoted in ibid.

58 Ibid.

59 Liberate Tate, "Confronting the Institution in Performance," 81. Also Marriott, "A Social Licence to Operate." There is also precedent in Canada (as elsewhere) for government intervention into sponsorship. In 1997, a Canadian policy came into effect prohibiting the display of tobacco sponsors' branding at sporting and arts events. Evans, *Art Wash*, 19.

60 Enbridge, "Enbridge to Sponsor Coup de Pouce aux Familles Program." Enbridge's contribution focused on families in the east end of the city, incidentally where the Enbridge terminal (the endpoint of the controversial Line 9 pipeline) is located.

61 National Arts Centre, "2014 Governor General's Performing Arts Awards Gala."

62 Lederman, "D'Arcy Levesque."

63 Calgary Arts Development, "Alberta Arts Flood Rebuilding Fund."

64 Evans, *Artwash*, 29.

65 Wall, "Sharpest Knives in the Drawer," 334–6.

66 Ibid., 336.

67 Ibid.

68 Ibid., 342. Further, important fossils are occasionally revealed during digging and strip mining of the tar sands. In 2011, Syncrude found a twenty-metre-long plesiosaur fossil at its site. The fossil was carefully moved and transferred to the Royal Tyrrell Museum of Paleontology (a public museum that also receives support from the oil industry and that contains a number of exhibits pertinent to the energy sector). CBC News, "Fossil Treasure Trove Found at Oilsands." See also Staff Writer, "Imperial Donation Inspires New Art Gallery Exhibit."

69 CBC News, "Petro-Canada Gives Away Its Art Collection."

70 Wall, "Sharpest Knives in the Drawer," 343.

71 Rivers, "Why Is Big Oil Funding Reconciliation Week Events?"

72 Wall, "Sharpest Knives in the Drawer," 342. Another example is the fate of the National Portrait Gallery of Canada. See chapter 5, note 40.

73 Pearson, "Artists' Group Wants NAC to Drop Enbridge."

74 Ibid. One could also point to a brief spat over hotdogs that took place in 2016. De Souza, "Trudeau Liberals to Reimburse Enbridge."

75 Wall, "Sharpest Knives in the Drawer," 340.

76 *Huffington Post*, "Pipeline Art Show Permit Pulled."

77 There was another controversy at the Canadian Science and Technology Museum over a video called "Sex: A Tell-All Exhibition." See Kay, "Ottawa Sex Exhibition."

I did try to consult the museum's archives for *Energy: Power to Choose* but was informed that nothing had been kept in the archives from the exhibition.

78 CBC News, "Imperial Oil's Role in Museum's Energy Exhibit Questioned."

79 Ibid.

80 Geddes, "The Museum Is the Message." The quote is very slightly different in French, and it is unclear whether the original was in French or English. For the French version, see Buzzetti, "Sables bitumineux."

81 Geddes, "The Museum Is the Message"; Buzzetti, "Sables bitumineux."

82 Geddes, "The Museum Is the Message," also notes: "The Calgary-based industry group also served on an advisory committee created by the museum, made up largely of industry representatives, along with some government officials, academics and consultants. Sponsors and advisory committee members were invited to review and comment on the show's content."

83 Ibid.

84 CBC News, "Imperial Oil's Role in Museum's Energy Exhibit Questioned." Not all of Imperial Oil's recommendations were accepted, including one that advocated for "an illustration for Polar Oil and Gas Reserves be changed from red to blue," arguing that red "has a negative connotation" bringing to mind "blood oil." The change was not made.

85 Ibid. The Imperial Oil documents were published on Scribd but have since been removed. They are cached on the CBC News article. Note the clear parallel between the language used by Imperial Oil in the document and the language used to explain extraction of bitumen from the tar sands as related by Stephanie LeMenager in her tour of the Oil Sands Discovery Centre. In her text, *Living Oil*, 162–4, LeMenager carefully analyzes how the language used by the tour guide covers over the polluting aspects of strip mining while also providing visitors with key phrases that can be used elsewhere to promote oil sands development.

86 It is unclear, in retrospect, whether this panel was included in the exhibition or not.

87 Imperial Oil advocated for signage to be changed to read: "Oil sands mining dramatically change [*sic*] the landscape while in production but will be returned to nature once mining is complete." Interestingly, 2016 documents from archived internal corporate records of Imperial Oil held by the Glenbow Museum show the company had conducted extensive research on the environmental impacts of its oil and gas extraction and that as early as 1970 admitted that "A problem of such size, complexity and importance cannot be dealt with on a voluntary basis. The protection of the interests of society as a whole requires the establishment of legal controls on pollution and on other anti-social acts." De Souza, "Imperial Oil Described Its Climate-Warming Business as 'Anti-Social.'" The Glenbow's archive was used by activists to show that companies such as Exxon were long aware of the contributions of carbon dioxide pollution to climate change. The archive had been given to the Glenbow in 2006 as part of a $4 million gift from Imperial Oil to the museum. Glenbow Museum, "Media Release."

88 Geddes, "The Museum Is the Message."

89 Buzzetti, "Sables bitumineux."

90 See Rectanus, *Culture Incorporated*; Wallis, "The Art of Big Business"; and Wu, *Privatising Culture*, on the problems of such sponsorships and the issues with allowing sponsors to dictate museum content.

91 Ross, "Coming to a Town near You."

92 Reily, "Opinion: Why Are Our Museums So Bland?" The museum insisted that

Barrick did not drive the exhibit, which was mostly a straightforward account of how gold is mined and the importance of various minerals to the Canadian economy. Senior museum officials did travel to Toronto to show a final concept plan to the mining company, and Barrick requested less emphasis on history and more on contemporary mining practice.

93 Indigenous Peoples Solidarity Movement Ottawa, "The People's Exhibition of Barrick at the Museum of Nature!"

94 Evans, *Artwash*, 154; Powless, "Museums Tar Sands Funding Pollutes Snow."

95 Rights Action, "Petition the Canadian Museum for Human Rights."

96 One of the few exhibitions was *Thanks but No Tanks* at the Haida Gwaii Museum. *The Beat*, "Thanks but No Tanks."

97 Wilson, Carlson, and Szeman, *Petrocultures*.

98 Alberts, "Monster Truck in DC Showcases Alberta's Strengths"; Alberta Community Development, "Final Report." See also Robertson, "Crude Culture"; Wall, "Sharpest Knives in the Drawer."

99 Robertson, "Crude Culture"; Wall, "Sharpest Knives in the Drawer," 344–5.

100 Freeman, "Mr. Klein Goes to Washington with Oil Message."

101 CBC Arts, "All Things Albertan Focus of Smithsonian Festival."

102 Hunt, "Alberta Takes Over US Capital."

103 *Gazette*, "Americans Unaware That Canada Is Their Largest Oil Supplier"; Markusoff, "Energy Exports Generated Revenues."

104 Shrivastava and Stefanick, "Framing the Debate on Democracy and Governance," 4.

105 Freeman, "Alberta's Gift to Culture."

106 Groce notes that oil companies paid the salaries of workers to attend the festivities with the truck. She also admits that Caterpillar lent the truck and that it came from Illinois (rather than Alberta) and after the festival would be sent to a quarry in Virginia. Quoted in ibid.

107 Ibid.

108 Wall, "Sharpest Knives in the Drawer," 333.

109 Kunzig, "The Canadian Oil Boom."

110 I wrote the bulk of this chapter in 2016–17 prior to the rise in action against the proposed route of the TransMountain pipeline in Burnaby. I decided not to update the chapter in large part because those protests took place at the site of the proposed pipeline (rather than at a museum) and because Kinder Morgan is not (as I note in chapter 8) a large-scale sponsor of arts and culture in Canada.

111 Goldenberg, "Detroit's Mountains of Petroleum Coke."

112 See also Preston, "Neoliberal Settler Colonialism," 47–9, on how Treaty 8 extinguished Aboriginal and Métis title to the Athabasca resources that are now the tar sands.

113 Liberate Tate, "Confronting the Institution in Performance," 79.

114 A comparison could be made, for example, to anti-road, anti-runway, or anti-nuclear campaigns in the UK where activism tends to be at the site of the proposed building site, often employing tactics of lockdown and encampment. Feigenbaum et al., *Protest Camps*.

115 Green, "Tarmageddon."

116 *Globe and Mail*, "Engage the Activists."

117 This term was coined by Katz-Rosene, "The Rise of Reactionary Environmentalism," 25.

118 Cryderman, "Oilsands the Poster Child of Bad Oil."

119 CBC News, "Oilsands Campaign Hits Times Square."
120 Platform London, "Legal Oil, Ethical Oil." Ethical Oil was promoted as a "grassroots" group of Canadians supporting the oil industry and the Alberta tar sands. A controversy erupted over whether it was in fact grassroots or received funding from Enbridge. Enbridge denied the claims. Yaffe, "Does Enbridge Donate to Ethical Oil?"
121 Coulthard, "The Colonialism of the Present."
122 Wall, "Sharpest Knives in the Drawer," 333.
123 Klein, "Canada's Founding Myths Hold Us Back."
124 McSheffrey, "Trudeau Says Pipelines Will Pay."
125 Tsing, *Friction*, 28.
126 Den Tandt, "'Use It or Lose it.'"
127 CBC News, "Nunavut Irked by Arctic Sovereignty Talk."
128 Proulx, "Colonizing Surveillance," 85.
129 Tsing, *Friction*, 50.
130 This term was introduced to me by Métis anthropologist Zoe Todd, "Fish, Kin and Hope."
131 Klein, "Canada's Founding Myths."
132 See the work of Harold Innis in particular, and see Shrivastava and Stefanick, "Framing the Debate on Democracy and Governance," 12–15, for an overview and updating of neostaples theory.
133 Klein, "Canada's Founding Myths."
134 See also Preston, "Neoliberal Settler Colonialism," 42–3 and 49.
135 Tuck and Yang, "Decolonization Is Not a Metaphor," 15.
136 I'm referring here particularly to the learning that I've been doing reading work by Tuck and Yang, Betasamosake Simpson, Todd, and many others. See also Murphy, "Gathering from Within," 167–8.
137 Coulthard, *Red Skins White Masks*, 60–1.
138 Ibid., 60.
139 Ibid., 61.
140 These words were recorded and tweeted by Rina Espirity @rinabang on 21 April 2017. See also Justice, *Our Fire Survives the Storm*, 46.
141 Barker, "A Direct Act of Resurgence," 57.
142 Murphy, "Gathering from Within," 169.
143 Ibid. LeMenager's *Living Oil* writing on the Oil Sands Discovery Centre is remarkably interesting in light of the way that nation and oil are collapsed in many rhetorical descriptions of the tar sands. By contrast, LeMenager reads Fort MacMurray from the US perspective, travelling there and visiting the museum to see where the US was and (at the time of her writing) would be getting much of its petroleum. She reads the tar sands development as an answer to a US problem – not an issue of Canadian nation-building at all. See Proulx, "Colonizing Surveillance," 84–5, for a lucid discussion of the role of corporate influence in Canadian policy.
144 Rowland, "Protecting Canada's Lakes, Rivers." For example, the NWPA had protected 32,000 lakes, but its gutting left only 97 lakes protected. At the time of writing, the Trudeau government had left most of this legislation in place, and environmental protections remain gutted and ineffectual. Council of Canadians, "Why the Trudeau Government Must Restore."
145 Nikiforuk, "Secret Memo Casts Doubt."
146 The Indian Act is typically seen as a racist and patronizing document. However,

repealing it would threaten Indigenous treaty rights. For example, the FNPOI opened up reserve lands for private ownership, which had the corollary effect of opening them to non-Indigenous buyers and developers (Preston, "Neoliberal Settler Colonialism," 49). Bill C-45 did not actually make this legislation law but opened the door to FNPOI. See Coulthard, *Red Skin White Masks*, 160–70.

147 Hume, "Stephen Harper Is Blind to Science."

148 Ibid.

149 One of the best sources for firsthand accounts of Idle No More actions is Kino-nda-niimi Collective, *The Winter We Danced.*

150 For the important role social media played in the movement, both in public and behind the scenes, see Barker, "A Direct Act of Resurgence," 51.

151 Kino-nda-niimi Collective, *The Winter We Danced*, 22.

152 For a more in-depth description, including an overview of Chief Theresa Spence's hunger strike to draw attention to conditions in her community of Attawapiskat, see Barker, "A Direct Act of Resurgence."

153 Fiskio, "Dancing at the End of the World." See also Ostaman, "We're Protecting, Not Protesting," 226. See also Simpson, "Aambe! Maajaadaa!"; and Klein and Simpson, "Dancing the World into Being."

154 Fiskio, "Dancing at the End of the World."

155 See Recollet, "Glyphing Decolonial Love."

156 Murphy, "Gathering from Within," 30. Fiskio, "Dancing at the End of the World," who uses Murphy's interpretation in much the same way that I do, drew this book to my attention. More than 1,000 people participated in the round dance at the Mall of America.

157 Quoted in Belanger and Lackenbauer, "Introduction," 5.

158 Thank you to Preston, "Neoliberal Settler Colonialism," 52, for bringing this document to my attention. Flanagan, *Resource Industries and Security Issues.*

159 Leahy, "Canada's Environmental Activists Seen as 'Threat to National Security'"; Groves and Lukacs, "Mounties Spied on Native Protest Groups"; Diabo and Pasternak, "First Nations under Surveillance"; Tait, "Ottawa Launches Alberta Counterterrorism Unit." See also Preston, "Neoliberal Settler Colonialism," 43. See also Monaghan and Walby, "Making up 'Terror Identities,'" 133–51, for more detail on the background of these new policing structures and the introduction of the term "multi-issue extremism." Proulx, "Colonizing Surveillance," particularly 88–90.

160 For precedent, see the FBI classification of the Environmental Liberation Front (ELF) as a domestic terrorist group. Kershaw, "Ecoactivist Performance."

161 Lukacs and Groves, "Canadian Spies Met with Energy Firms"; Lukacs and Groves, "Mounties Spied on Native Protest Groups."

162 Natural Resources Canada, "Media Room."

163 Nikiforuk, "Opinion: Understanding Harper's Evangelical Mission."

164 Natural Resources Canada, "Media Room." See also Proulx, "Colonizing Surveillance," 88.

165 Ibbitson, "'Radical Groups' Spur Tories." See also Proulx, "Colonizing Surveillance," 88, on how such strategies resulted in surveillance and police crackdowns on Indigenous peoples and environmentalists. He draws attention to the "'blurring' of the categories of terrorism, extremism, and activism [even peaceful activism] into 'an aggregate threat matrix.'"

166 Raj, "Nicole Eaton Green Charities Using Foreign Cash."

167 McRae, "CRA Audits of Charities Look Fair but Feel Foul."

168 Ibid.
169 Raj, "Nicole Eaton Green Charities Using Foreign Cash."
170 Dobbin, "Has Big Oil Hijacked Democracy?"
171 Proulx, "Colonizing Surveillance," 88.
172 Although the two are not connected, the crackdown at Elsipogtog took place at almost precisely the same time that the Canadian Museum of History announced its partnership with CAPP.
173 Hennessy, "The RCMP Ambushed"; Schmidt, "Indigenous Canadian Fracking Protesters." This section was influenced by my reading of L. Hudson McLellan's thesis, "Contemporary Settler Colonialism," which focuses on media framing of the conflict at Elsipogtog.
174 Howe, *Debriefing Elsipogtog*.
175 Hennessy, "The RCMP Ambushed."
176 Ibid.
177 Quoted in McLellan, "Contemporary Settler Colonialism," 22.
178 Hennessy, "The RCMP Ambushed."
179 Palmater, "Feathers versus Guns."
180 Preston, "Neoliberal Settler Colonialism," 47. As Wilkes et al. remind us, land is central here. "Nationalism and Media Coverage," 49–50.
181 Postmedia News, "Trudeau Says First Nations 'Don't Have a Veto.'" In Fall 2018, Trudeau's interpretation appeared to have been upheld in court in *Mikisew Cree First Nation v. Canada*, a case that concerned the 2012 omnibus bill discussed elsewhere in this chapter. Bergner et al., "Supreme Court of Canada Confirms."
182 Preston, "Neoliberal Settler Colonialism," 47.
183 Quoted in Proulx, "Colonizing Surveillance," 87.
184 See Moreton-Robinson, *The White Possessive*, 173–89, esp. 183–4.
185 Proulx, "Colonizing Surveillance," 83. See also Wilkes et al., "Nationalism and Media Coverage," 42 and 47. A review of the existing literature shows that media framing of Indigenous collective action is predominantly negative and that protest tends to be more predominantly framed as criminal and unlawful.
186 Quoted in Barker, "A Direct Act of Resurgence," 45.
187 Preston, "Neoliberal Settler Colonialism," 53.
188 Quoted in Cameron, "Risk Society," 63. The study was published in 2010; the museum worker's comment may have been made earlier.
189 Cheadle, "Museum of Civilization Taps Big Oil."
190 These projects included, among many others, high levels of funding for events commemorating the War of 1812 and the display of a portrait of the Queen at all missions and embassies abroad. Taber and Galloway, "War of 1812 Fund."
191 CBC News, "Civilization Museum's $25M Rebranding." Arguably, the focus on the War of 1812 echoed and played up the Warrior Nation status found in the CWM, which is part of the same corporation as the CMH.
192 Turk, "Whose History on Display?" This letter was written by James L. Turk, executive director of the Canadian Association of University Teachers.
193 The announcement that a room dedicated to the Winnipeg General Strike would not be included in the new display seemed to confirm this fear. Smith, "Museum of History to Exclude Winnipeg General Strike."
194 Canadian Archeological Association, "Change in Name and Purpose of the Canadian Museum of Civilization"; and Canadian Historical Association, "The CHA President Writes to the President." The museum argued the opposite, suggesting

that there would be greater representation of First Nations history. CBC News, "Canadian Museum of History Plans Revealed."

195 Craig, "What's Gone On behind Closed Doors." Craig also outlines another controversy over the acquisition of artefacts from the *Empress of Ireland*.

196 Ibid. See also CBC News, "Civilization Museum's $25M Rebranding." The *Buzzfeed* article suggests that there was at the very least indirect pressure from government representatives on the museum while the changes were taking place.

197 Cheadle, "Museum of Civilization Taps Big Oil."

198 Canadian Press, "Liberals Accuse Tories."

199 Slaney, "Harper's History Museum Betrays First Nations."

200 Ibid.

201 Ibid.

202 Cheadle, "Museum of Civilization Taps Big Oil."

203 Ibid.

204 Ibid.

205 Troian, "Copper Broken on Parliament Hill." *Awalaskenis I* had taken place in 2013 and involved a journey from Quatsino on the northern tip of Vancouver Island to Victoria and a copper shaming ceremony on the steps of the BC legislature to draw attention to environmental crisis and Idle No More. The complexity of the *Awalaskenis II* journey and the *Lalakenis/All Directions* exhibition cannot be conveyed in this short segment, and I recommend the catalogue for the exhibition.

206 Guujaw, "The Copper," 27.

207 See *Lalakenis/All Directions: A Journey of Truth and Unity*.

208 Hopkins, "In Memoriam: Beau Dick."

209 Watson and Brown, "Introduction," 13.

210 Hopkins, "In Memoriam: Beau Dick."

211 Dick, "The Coppers," 23.

212 CBC News, "Showcasing Heritage."

213 Dick, "The Coppers," 23.

214 Hopkins, "In Memoriam: Beau Dick."

215 Ibid.

216 Marsha Lederman, "Three History-Making Exhibitions."

217 Scott Watson, quoted in Kevin Griffin, "*Lalakenis* Recounts Indigenous Journey."

218 APTN National News, "'Idle No More' at the Canadian Museum of Civilization." The CMH had, almost simultaneously, been the site of an Idle No More drum circle on the 250th anniversary of the Royal Proclamation. CBC News, "Idle No More Protests."

219 Perfitt, "Museum of History Needs to Cut Ties."

220 Canadian Museum of History, "Canadian Museum of Civilization Welcomes CAPP."

221 Ivison, "Radical US Environmentalist Calls Trudeau 'Stunning Hypocrite.'"

222 Right Side of History, "Canadian Museum of History AGM Flooded."

223 Coalition of Museums for Climate Justice, "CAPP & the Canadian Museum of History."

224 Not An Alternative, "Institutional Liberation."

225 See Liberate Tate, "Confronting the Institution in Performance," to see an example of how the activist group positions itself within, outside of, and against contemporary performance art and contemporary art criticism/scholarship paradigms and as an extension of institutional critique.

226 Demos, "The Great Transition."

227 Serafini, *Performance Action*, Loc. 3348 and 3484 of 4717.
228 350.org, "Get Involved."
229 See also events such as the ROM's theatrical mock trial of famous environmentalist David Suzuki. Royal Ontario Museum, "Museums and Climate Change."
230 As I was finishing the final edits of this book, a number of actions in the UK, the US, and elsewhere showed that performance activism groups were moving toward intersectional action. BP or Not BP's 2018 unofficial "Stolen Goods" tour of the British Museum provides a case in point, as do many actions organized in New York City and elsewhere by Decolonize This Place. The Natural History Museum's collaboration with the Lummi Nation, resulting in a number of pop-up exhibitions at authoritative museums (all of which questioned fossil fuel dependency), provides a second important caveat to my statements in the text.
231 turions, "How Not to Install Indigenous Art," 249.
232 *The Beat*, "Thanks but No Tanks."
233 turions, "How Not to Install Indigenous Art," 247.

Interstice Six

1 In December 2008, Canada was ranked fifty-fifth out of fifty-seven industrialized countries and emerging economies for having inadequate policies to prevent average global temperatures from rising by two degrees Celsius. *Gazette*, "Canada Ranked 2nd Worst." As a part of the Kyoto Accord, Canada had pledged to reduce emissions by 6 per cent from 1990 levels. Instead, they had increased by 26 per cent by the time of COP15. Simpson, "When It Comes to Climate Change."
2 This description calmed with the election of Justin Trudeau, although arguably his environmental policies are equally destructive.
3 Libin, "Climate 'Debt' Comes Due." In December 2011, Canada withdrew from the Kyoto Accord.
4 Glenn and Otero, "Canada and the Kyoto Protocol," 490.
5 Mahoney, "Kyoto Protest Angers Klein."
6 Grindon, "Art and Activism"; Robertson, "Capitalist Cocktails and Moscow Mules."
7 *Toronto Star*, "Canada the Ant." Simultaneously, the well-known environmentalist and thinker George Monbiot published an excoriating article in the *Guardian*, which was republished in the *Globe and Mail*. It added significantly to the bad feeling against Canada in Copenhagen. "Please Canada, Clean up Your Act," cried the headline in the *Globe and Mail*.
8 *Toronto Star*, "Canada's Role Constructive."
9 Reguly and Taber, "How US Pranksters Hoaxed the World."
10 Ibid.
11 Cryderman, "Toronto Mayor Hangs Head in Shame."
12 Yaffe, "Tories May Be Close to Mood of Populace." The Yes Men accused the Canadian government of asking a German Internet service provider, Serverloft, to shut down the fake websites, a move that also temporarily shut down thousands of other websites in an effort to get rid of the fake ones. Serverloft said that it would only restore the other websites if the Yes Men took theirs down. *Windsor Star*, "Pranksters Say Canada Wiping Out Websites."
13 Reguly and Taber, "How US Pranksters Hoaxed the World."
14 Equiterre, "Statement."

15 Yes Men, "About."
16 Taylor, "Who Are the Yes Men?"
17 Yaffe, "Tories May Be Close to Mood of Populace."
18 Weaver, "Consider Environment When Voting."
19 Curry, "Protesters Disrupt Question Period."
20 Mclean, "Protesting 'Tourists' Want Albertans to Care."
21 Robertson, "Capitalist Cocktails and Moscow Mules."
22 Yedlin, "Weak Climate Deal."
23 Serafini, *Performance Action*, Loc. 1760 of 4717.
24 Ibid., Loc. 2027 of 4717. She is borrowing the terms "transgressive" and "reformist" from Jordan, *Activism!*

Chapter Seven

1 Varga, "Sightings," 22.
2 Hauser, "The Year of Emily," W12.
3 Hannah, "Estrogen Art."
4 I am using the term female here rather than women because it was used regularly in coverage of the exhibition. In the years since 2002, use of the term female has been criticized, in part because it has been taken up on Twitter and other forms of social media as a pejorative term and also because it is not human-specific but refers to all female species that can reproduce and thus does not include female-identified people who do not have typically female primary sex characteristics.
5 Hannah, "Estrogen Art."

6 Smith, *Art and the Invention of North America.*
7 Hauser, "The Year of Emily," W12; Haggo, "Women Whose Brilliance Knows No Boundaries"; Smith, *Art and the Invention of North America.*
8 Ditmars, "In a Notable Constellation"; Laurence, "Iconic Artists Together at Last," 65. The term was picked up by Ditmars and Laurence from curator Dr Sharyn Rohlfsen, who used the label "NAFTA Feminist 3."
9 Gessell, "Kahlo Gets Star Billing."
10 Email from Kathleen Bartels to VAG staff, sent 14 June 2002. Vancouver Art Gallery, Exhibition Files, Accession number 04.20 Carr Kahlo O'Keefe, quoted with permission.
11 Ibid.
12 For example, no connections were made between the unceded territory of Vancouver (acknowledged in the organizer's name) and the Zapatista call for an international uprising against NAFTA that had begun in 1994 and was still ongoing at the moment of the opening. The Zapatista uprising had inspired the global justice movement that had blossomed into a major protest against the FTAA in Quebec City in April 2001 and reached its height (and potentially its downfall) in Genoa, Italy, only months before the *Places of Their Own* opening. Although there certainly are exceptions (among them major protests against the APEC meetings in 1997), many protests in Vancouver focus closely on Vancouver and British Columbia issues.
13 Scott, "Art of Protest," H6.
14 Ibid.
15 Ibid.
16 Insurrectionary Anarchists of the Coast Salish Territories, "Premier's Speech Shut Down."

17 Laurence, "Iconic Artists Together at Last," 76.
18 Insurrectionary Anarchists of the Coast Salish Territories, "Premier's Speech Shut Down."
19 Scott, "Campbell Protesters Disrupt VAG Exhibition Opening."
20 See Su Ditta's description of the controversy over the cancellation of artist Paul Wong's exhibition in 1984 for at least one other example of protest crossing the threshold of the VAG. "Please Don't Touch the Art," 65–9.
21 Scott, "Campbell Protesters Disrupt VAG Exhibition Opening." Scott writes in the *Vancouver Sun* that CSIS agents were present at the protest. I have found no further evidence to confirm or deny that this was the case.
22 Ibid.
23 Ibid.
24 Ibid.
25 Ibid.
26 Eurchuk, "Campbell Prevented from Speaking."
27 See Barnholden, *Reading the Riot Act*, for further examples of actions against the Campbell government.
28 Much of the action against *Places of Their Own* took place on the south plaza because Campbell's speech was to take place there, outside one of the gallery's main entrances (at the side of the building). In part due to the number of political actions, as well as the layout of the gallery, both "formal" entrances are merely ornamental. The north plaza is typically where large protests take place, and entrances are on the east and west sides of the building.
29 This was certainly the case during the annual 420 sit-ins that have grown in size and scale over the past decade.
30 In 1997, a Supreme Court of Canada decision in the *Delgamuukw v. British Columbia* case stated that Aboriginal title had never been extinguished in British Columbia.
31 So too does the VAG itself. In 1938, prior to moving to its current site, the VAG was the location of part of a large sit-in and protest by unemployed male workers at 1145 Georgia St – then the location of the Vancouver Art Gallery (and currently next door to the controversial Trump Tower and across the street from Living Shangri-la, mentioned later in the chapter). However, the action mainly took place at the Vancouver Post Office some blocks away. The month-long sit-in culminated in Bloody Sunday when Communist-sympathetic workers and police clashed, resulting in numerous arrests, injuries, and charges of brutality against the police. Vancouver Anarchist Online Archive, "Great Depression Radical History of Vancouver."
32 Keller, "Art Gallery Expected to Continue Protest Tradition."
33 Ibid.; Boddy, "Squaring off with Protesters," B4.
34 Keller, "Art Gallery Expected to Continue Protest Tradition."
35 Ibid.
36 When I visited the gallery in 2018, it appeared that significant gentrification of these spaces had taken place.
37 Ibid.
38 Vancouver Art Gallery, *Strategic Plan 2003–2006*, 10.
39 Email correspondence between Stephanie Anderson and Library and Archives at the Vancouver Art Gallery, 21 April 2015, printed with permission.
40 See also Butler, "Bodily Vulnerability, Coalitions, and Street Politics," on Arendt and protest in the street.

41 Some of the comparisons among Arendt, Habermas, and Fraser in this paragraph are drawn from Martin, "Public and Common(s)." See also McKee's critique of such ideas in terms of Occupy. *Strike Art*, 102.

42 See Message, *Museums and Social Activism*, on the relationship between the Washington Mall and the Smithsonian.

43 Kane, "Occupy Vancouver Camps Out at Art Gallery."

44 See Christopher Shaw as well on the relationship between art, the Olympic Winter Games in Vancouver in 2010, and real estate development. Shaw argues that the Olympics, in Vancouver and elsewhere, were little more than a real estate and developer deal, wrapped up in the history of the games. Shaw, *Five Ring Circus*, 4–14.

45 Harris, "Condominium and the City," 695. For most of the period in question in this chapter, the political coalition Vision Vancouver ran the municipal government. Though apparently left-leaning and interested in social justice and housing, anti-poverty advocates often accused Vision Vancouver of being something like the equivalent of New Labour in Britain – neoliberal capitalists in socialist trappings. Drury, "The Rise of Philanthrocapitalism."

46 Van der Pol, "In Dialogue," 32.

47 Bartels, "Director's Report," 4.

48 Davies and Ford, "Culture Clubs"; Forkert, "Transgression, Branding and National Identity," 18.

49 See McRobbie, *Be Creative*, on this point and how those on the left in the 1970s who called for a collapse of high and low culture could not have foreseen the result of the creative industries (which do exactly that).

50 I'd like to draw attention to the work of graduate student Ahlia Moussa, whose MA thesis looked at Vancouver art, the Vancouver Art Gallery, and the positioning of Vancouver as a contemporary art node. Moussa, "Point of Origin."

51 City of Vancouver, Cultural Services, *Culture Plan for Vancouver 2008–2018*.

52 De Baere and Roelstraete, "Introducing Intertidal," 11. Douglas, *Vancouver Anthology*, originally published in 1989, and later O'Brian, *Vancouver Art and Economies*, were important contributors in declaring Vancouver's regional importance and also its insularity.

53 Sacco, *The Power of the Arts in Vancouver*, 28.

54 Ibid.

55 Modigliani, *Engendering an Avant-Garde*.

56 When it was built, Living Shangri-la was the tallest building in Vancouver and was designed for mixed use, including retail, condominiums, and a luxury hotel. Both the height, which threatened the views from buildings around it, and its exorbitant cost were seen as reasons to criticize it. Burns, "More Highrises Set to Mar Vancouver's Skyline." Living Shangri-la is near the equally controversial Trump Tower in Vancouver, site of a number of recent protests and incidentally built on the site that housed the VAG's original art deco building.

57 Watson, "Urban Renewal," 35. Watson (41) writes, "Squatting became symbolic of everything that was slated for demolition and for the possibility of protest. This was authentic uncommodifiable human habitation; the polar opposite of the condo." Though it will not be discussed here, it is notable that Greenpeace was in part originally organized by people who had squatted in the mudflats.

58 De Baere and Roelstrate, "Introducing Intertidal." See also Witt, "Splendour without Diminishment," for a description of the role of photography in Vancouver and in

particular for an analysis of Roy Arden's work. See also Turner and O'Brian, "Melanie O'Brian's View on Vancouver."

59 Turner and O'Brian, "Melanie O'Brian's View on Vancouver."

60 Rugoff, "Baja to Vancouver," 18.

61 Vargas, "Baja to Vancouver Exhibits."

62 The Museum of Vancouver blog, MOVments, remains an excellent source for information on social movements in Vancouver.

63 Buck-Morss, *Thinking Past Terror*, 66; Sholette, *Delirium and Resistance*; Stallabrass, *Art Incorporated.*

64 See Coupland, *City of Glass*, for a celebratory and aestheticized take on the condo-building in Vancouver. See Harris, "Condominium and the City," 695, for a much more nuanced take on the way that condominiums provided "the legal architecture for the remaking of Vancouver."

65 Derksen, "How High Is the City."

66 Sassen, "The Global City."

67 Peck, *Neoliberal Urbanism.*

68 Ibid.

69 Blomley, *Unsettling the City*, 30.

70 According to Statistics Canada, *Median Total Income*, the median salary in Vancouver in 2016 was $67,090, but many different real estate sites price the average house at well over $1,000,000 (the Royal LePage House Price Survey for 2016 gives the sum of $1,179,482). CTV News, "In Charts."

71 Siemiatycki, Hutton, and Barnes, "Trouble in Paradise," 183, also argue that Vancouver's creative economy is not sustainable, in large part because it can be easily replicated elsewhere. See also Dean, *Remembering Vancouver's Disappeared Women*, xvii, who notes that in 2002, a year in which the *Economist* ranked Vancouver as tied for most livable city in the world, Robert Pickton was arrested under suspicion of having murdered dozens of women missing from the DTES, prompting Dean to ask: "livable for whom?" Of course, 2002 was also the year of the protest at *Places of Their Own* and of Woodsquat (see Interstice 7g).

72 Harris, "Condominium and the City," 696.

73 Ibid.

74 Many of the projects organized by Others Sights respond to this crisis. Brown, "Hosts and Guests," 14. See also Urban Subjects, *Works on Housing.*

75 Firth-Eagland, "Invisible Becoming," 6. See the short book Min, *Vancouver Matters*, for a more in-depth exploration of the "material conditions," the architecture, facades, flora, and fauna of Vancouver.

76 Peck, *Neoliberal Urbanism.*

77 Ibid.

78 Fisher and Witt, "Fabricating the Creative City."

79 Holmes, "The Flexible Personality"; McRobbie, *Be Creative*, 11.

80 Watson, "Developers Build up Public Art."

81 The full marketing text for the Woodward's condos read: "This is an authentic area, not a sanitized environment. Neighbourhoods like this are rare and offer a creative mix of cutting-edge culture, heritage and character. That's why the intelligent buyer will get in early. This is the future. This is your neighbourhood. Be bold or move to suburbia." McMartin, "Woodward's Opens Door."

82 See also Rennie, "Bob Rennie Reflects." One exception to this is Bob Rennie's

donation of 197 works of art to the National Gallery of Canada as a "gift to the nation" in 2017 in exchange for the naming rights of the Galerie Rennie Gallery. The works are by Vancouver as well as Canadian and international artists. This represented the largest donation of contemporary art to the NGC. Griffin, "Bob Rennie Donates Art." Said Rennie of the donation: "It's great to sell condos, but it's not what we want to be known for [referring to his family]. We'd like to be known for changing the arts and culture landscape in Canada." Kearney, "Vancouver Real Estate Magnate Donates."

83 The Polygon has been successful in asking for funding from all levels of government. In July 2015, "the Government of Canada announced it was investing $2.5M in the project, matching funds provided by the Province of British Columbia and the City of North Vancouver, for a total of $7.5M in public funding." A further $6.5 million in private donations was collected, leading to the naming of the building. The name comes from Polygon Homes Ltd, of which Michael Audain is the CEO. Lederman, "Building a Mystery"; The Polygon, *Funding from All Levels of Government*.

84 Sherlock, "Vancouver Developer Donates $7 Million."

85 Witt, "The Vancouver Art Gallery and the Eviction of a Political Idea, Parts 1 and 2"; Rosler, "Culture Class Part 1"; Rosler, "Culture Class Part 2"; Ley, "Artists, Aestheticisation and the Field of Gentrification."

86 Wood, "The Vancouver Carts," 10–11.

87 Stewart, "No Fun? No Point."

88 Smith and Derksen, "Urban Regeneration," 75.

89 I'd like to thank Robin Simpson for bringing this essay to my attention. Fraser, "L'1%, c'est moi."

90 Guasch and Zulaika, *Learning from the Bilbao Guggenheim*.

91 Cameron, "The Museum, a Temple or the Forum?" In Cameron's definition of the museum as forum, museums are sites of contestation and exploration. In this sense, the VAG is a forum despite its exterior.

92 Firth-Eagland, "Invisible Becoming," 7.

93 I am not the first to notice this. The palimpsest history of Vancouver shows up frequently. Notions of haunting, erasure, and invisibility come up again and again. See, for example, Culhane, "Their Spirits Live within Us"; Oleksijczuk, "Haunted Spaces"; Dean, *Remembering Vancouver's Disappeared Women*; Baloy, "Spectacles and Spectres." See also Williams, "A Working Chronology of Feminist Cultural Activities," 183. Already in 1990, members of the arts community were asking why there were not more people of colour being asked to present on Vancouver art and in turn were told to provide a list, as if such people couldn't possibly exist. Williams writes of this exchange, noting it "reveal[ed] an unfortunate lack of familiarity on the part of the organizer with regard to the ideological factors that determine visibility for some and maintain invisibility for others." A statement that surely still holds true.

94 Douglas, "Introduction," 11.

95 Ibid., 14–15. See also Derksen, "Approaching the Long Moment."

96 Douglas, "Introduction," 15.

97 Ibid., 15–16.

98 Douglas, "Afterword," 303.

99 The tension between gallery and artists is laid out in Harris, "All Yours?" In this article, Harris also traces the corporate funding behind the VAG's 1984 "Take the Gallery to Court" campaign.

100 Vancouver Art Gallery, *Strategic Plan 2003–2006*, 80.
101 Dafoe, "Arts Community Rallies"; Gill, "Bartels Facing a House Divided."
102 Vancouver Art Gallery, *Strategic Plan 2002–2004*, 15.
103 Killy, "Message from the Chair 2003," 4.
104 Vancouver Art Gallery, *Master Planning Summary*.
105 Ibid.
106 McDowell, "New Spot to Park the Carrs."
107 Killy, "Message from the Chair 2004."
108 Ibid.
109 *Vancouver Magazine*, "The Philanthropist."
110 Bula, "The Fight for the Vancouver Art Gallery."
111 Killy, "Message from the Chair 2005."
112 Ibid.
113 Vancouver Art Gallery, *Strategic Plan 2007–2010*, 29.
114 McDowell, "New Spot to Park the Carrs." There was, in fact, some evidence that the announcement that the gallery would move to Plaza of Nations came as a surprise both to the gallery and to City Council, which may explain why it did not come to fruition. Bula, "Vancouver Art Gallery Might Have to Bail."
115 Mackie, "It's Vancouver, but Not as We Know It." By 2009, the gallery board had decided that the Larwill Park site was better suited, although it was not until 2013 that they were given the go-ahead by City Council.
116 Elliott, "The Origins of Occupy Wall Street Explained." Occupy Museums is an action group that grew out of Occupy Wall Street. I have not discussed it in the chapter, but it does show up in the introduction to the book. See also Occupy Museums. See also Milne, "Human Rights and/or Market Logic," 114–15 on the CMHR, Occupy, and Winnipeg.
117 The term originally derived from economist Joseph Stiglitz's article titled "On the 1%, by the 1%, for the 1%" in *Vanity Fair* in May 2011, focused on criticizing wealth inequality in the US.
118 Mitchell, "Image, Space, Revolution," Loc. 1388 of 2013.
119 Christopher, Langille, and Smith, "Why They Joined Occupy Vancouver."
120 Interestingly, the archivist at SFU told me that cataloguing the collection was complicated by the fact that many of the donors to the Occupy Archive did not want to be recognized by name, perhaps fearing repercussion for their participation in Occupy Vancouver (synopsis of our conversation printed with permission).
121 SFU Occupy Archive MSC146 1.1 Occupy Vancouver Volunteer Coordinating Committee.
122 SFU Occupy Archive MSC146 1.2 Info Tent, Workgroups, Activities, Seminars.
123 SFU Occupy Archive MSC146 1.3 City Orders, Bylaws, Official Documents.
124 SFU Occupy Archive MSC146 1.4 Occupy Vancouver Safeguard Unit.
125 Collis, *Dispatches from the Occupation*, xiii.
126 Thom and Arnold, *Shore, Forest and Beyond*. The exhibition was on view from 29 October 2011 to 29 January 2012.
127 Concord Pacific was a sponsor of the Vancouver Olympics and owner of the False Creek location that was proposed as a potential site for the gallery.
128 Mogel, "Model Cities," 75. Three years after Occupy ended, Oppenheimer Park Occupation began. When the city issued eviction notices to homeless people sleeping in the park on 15 July, protesters moved in and claimed the land as unceded First Nations territory.

129 Chan, "Do Tent Cities Work?"
130 Rosler, "The Artistic Mode of Revolution."
131 Ibid. See also Sholette, *Delirium and Resistance*, 48–50.
132 Ibid.
133 Ibid.
134 Berlant, *Cruel Optimism*.
135 Rosler, "The Artistic Mode of Revolution."
136 Ibid.
137 *Vancouver Courier*, "Occupiers Vow to Stay."
138 Ibid.
139 Kilibarda, "Lessons from #Occupy in Canada," 26–7. See also Tuck and Yang, "Decolonization Is Not a Metaphor," 23–8.
140 Ibid., 24. See also Gill, "An Interview with Cornell West"; Maharawal, "Occupy Wall Street"; Walia, "Decolonizing Together." Harsha Walia's article gives a detailed overview of the Indigenous and settler activism and concludes by noting that "any serious attempt by non-natives at allying with Indigenous struggles must entail solidarity in the fight against colonization." Although it is only cited here once, I found this article extremely helpful in thinking through this section.
141 Kilibarda, "Lessons from #Occupy in Canada," 27.
142 Ibid., 32. So, too, a number of interventions took place at Wall Street in an attempt to draw attention to the whiteness of Occupy and its eclipsing of issues of race and power.
143 See in particular Occupy Oakland, which received a great deal of coverage for its radicality but which refused to acknowledge that it was occupying Indigenous lands, thus creating a rift in the camp. Tuck and Yang, "Decolonization Is Not a Metaphor," 23–8.

144 Similar splits were noted elsewhere, including Occupy Wall Street where divisions emerged among "radical hipsters from Brooklyn" and the homeless, and Michael Taussig notes that there were quips about an "Upper East side" of tents in the park and rumblings about gentrification "as if this utopic space is reproducing what it is against." Taussig, "I'm So Angry I Made a Sign," Loc. 224 of 2013. Nevertheless, no real discussion of race or land takes place in Taussig's book.
145 Kilibarda, "Lessons from #Occupy in Canada," 27.
146 Jasmine Rezaee, quoted in ibid., 29.
147 Ibid., 30.
148 Ibid., 33–4.
149 SFU Occupy Archive MSC146 1.3 City Orders, Bylaws, Official Documents.
150 Ibid.
151 Ibid.
152 Ibid.
153 Ibid.
154 Ibid.
155 Ibid.
156 Ibid.
157 Collis, *Dispatches from the Occupation*, 79.
158 Ibid., 80.
159 Ibid., 81.
160 SFU Occupy Archive MSC146 3.1 Affidavits.
161 Ibid.

162 Ibid.
163 Torrevillas, "Tent City Poses Danger," 6.
164 Ibid.
165 Bacchus, "Gary Mason and the Inclement Weather." Similar language was used at OWS. McKee, *Strike Art*, 100–1, notes several instances when the encampment was compared to a public artwork._
166 Witt, "The Vancouver Art Gallery and the Eviction of a Political Idea – Part II."
167 Collis, *Dispatches from the Occupation*, 139. See a parallel description of events at the MOMA as part of OWS, McKee, *Strike Art*, 146–9.
168 Kilibarda, "Lessons from #Occupy in Canada," 33–4. The police response to most Occupy encampments was significantly more violent. See Mitchell, Harcourt, and Taussig, *Occupy*, Loc. 1105 of 2013.
169 No Author, "An Open Letter to Bob Rennie."
170 Mitchell, Harcourt, and Taussig, *Occupy*, Loc. 143 of 2013.
171 Bula, "The Fight for the Vancouver Art Gallery"; Smith, "Bob Rennie Condemns."
172 Vinnick and Gerszak, "The Collector vs the Director"; Labossiere, "Guest Post." See Brown, "Hosts and Guests," especially 14–15.
173 Vinnick and Gerszak, "The Collector vs the Director."
174 Lederman, "Artists to Have Say in Gallery's New Home."
175 Lord and Silberberg, "Memo."
176 Smith, "Bob Rennie Condemns." See also Lederman, "Big Name Artists Square Off."
177 Lederman, "Big Name Artists Square Off."
178 City of Vancouver, "Administrative Report RR1."
179 Bula, "The Fight for the Vancouver Art Gallery."
180 Lederman, "Building a Mystery."
181 Witt, "The Vancouver Art Gallery and the Eviction of a Political Idea, Part I."
182 *Canadian Architect*, "High-Profile Shortlist Announced."
183 Cole, "Vancouver Art Gallery."
184 Lederman, "Building a Mystery."
185 Lederman, "Is No News Good News."
186 Vancouver Art Gallery, "The New Conceptual Design."
187 Ibid.
188 Chapman, "The Revolution Won't Be Occupied."
189 Thomson, "MOV of Vancouver Mulls Moving."
190 Werb, "Vancouver Concert Hall and Theatre Society"; Lord Cultural Resources, *National Aboriginal Art Gallery*.
191 Chan, "Fake Condo Tower Proposal."
192 The final cost of the CMHR was $351 million, the ROM renovation cost approximately $270 million, and the AGO renovation cost just over $200 million. The CMHR is the most like the VAG in that it is a new, purpose-built edifice rather than a renovation of an existing structure. As noted in the introduction, the ROM continues to struggle with the debt it incurred in financing the addition to its building. McArthur, Taylor, and McNish, "Crystal Myths."
193 Lederman, "Is No News Good News."
194 I have not been able to find any material accounting for the two different totals, although perhaps by 2017 the gallery was publicly concentrating on capital and leaving endowment for later. The later totals come from Kevin Griffin, "Provincial Government Waits."
195 Lederman, "Is No News Good News."

196 Griffin, "Vancouver Art Gallery Seeks $100m."
197 Lederman, "Is No News Good News."
198 BC *Business*, "Got $300 Million?"
199 Ibid.
200 Ibid. Elsewhere the sum is quoted as $23 million raised from private funds.
201 Ibid.
202 Chiang, "Singaporean Billionaire Plans to Build."
203 For example, when Kinder Morgan made a donation to Kwantlen Polytechnic University to fund scholarships for apprenticeships and trades programs, the Student Council retorted that students would refuse the money and released a statement arguing that acceptance of the money amounted to a "tacit endorsement" of the TransMountain pipeline. Mendoza, "Kinder Morgan Donation Scholarships Refused." Kinder Morgan has donated to arts programs elsewhere in Canada and has donated millions to the arts in the United States.
204 Alberta Infrastructure, "Royal Alberta Museum."
205 Withey, "Art Gallery of Alberta Timeline."
206 Brait, "Ottawa Adds $15 Million in Funding."
207 Bradshaw, "Tories Say Building Money 'Is Flowing'"; CBC Arts, "Rem Koolhaas to Design"; Boles, "Federal Government Pledges $1.9 Billion"; Giles and Wilson, "More Federal Funding for Remai"; Nova Scotia, "Gallery Expands into Southwest."
208 Florida, *The New Urban Crisis*.
209 Chan, "New Vancouver Art Gallery Plaza Design Revealed."
210 Ibid.
211 "City of Reconciliation."
212 MOV, "City on Edge."

Interstice Seven

1 Shier, "Introduction," 14.
2 Mackie, "Life and Times of Woodward's"; Mitchell, "Global Diasporas and Traditional Towns."
3 Mackie, "Old Lady of Hastings."
4 Shier, "Introduction," 14.
5 Ibid.
6 Mackie, "Life and Times of Woodward's"; Steffenhagen, "Injunction Sought to Evict Activists"; Colebourne and Ivens, "'Safety' behind Move to Shift Squatters"; Bula, "700 Social Housing Units Given Belated Go-Ahead."
7 Wulwik, "Squatting as an Organizing Tool," 19; Hogben and Hall, "Protesters Abuse Police."
8 Ivens and Middleton, "Judge Sets Protesters Free."
9 Zacharias, "Protesters Camp at Woodward's Door."
10 Yoshida, "Protesters Pose Threat"; Hume, "Hijacking the Homeless"; Sullivan, "Home at the Woodward's Squat"; Editorial, "Just Say No to Anarchy."
11 Sullivan, "Home at the Woodward's Squat."
12 Editorial, "Just Say No to Anarchy."
13 Tonner, "Latte Leftists Not Helping Homeless."
14 Bula, "Council Backs Developer's Plan for Woodward's."
15 Woodward's Anti-Poverty Coalition, *Community News*, np.

16 From the beginning, SFU students were very active in trying to prevent Goldcorp's sponsorship of the building. No Goldcorp at SFU, "Demands."

17 See Tucker-Abramson, "Spectacle Capitalism," on the way that SFU and UBC have reconfigured themselves as property developers and landlords alongside their ongoing corporatization as universities.

18 Griffin, "Gastown Riot Recreated."

19 Guilbaut, "Lightning from the Past," 29. For an in-depth discussion of the Gastown Riot, see Boudreau, "'The Struggle for a Different World.'"

20 Guilbaut, "Lightning from the Past," 29.

21 Griffin, "Gastown Riot Recreated."

22 Alberro, "An Interview with Stan Douglas," 14.

23 Ibid., 17–18. In this interview, Douglas directly connects the Gastown Riot to legislation that was passed in the neighbourhood disallowing residential occupancy. Woodward's failed in 1993 in part because the neighbourhood could not sustain it, particularly when malls began to be built outside the downtown core. In turn, that legislation eventually paved the way for the gentrification of the late 1990s onwards.

24 Stan Douglas, quoted in Alberro, "An Interview with Stan Douglas," 18. Douglas notes that at the time, only the Salvation Army was allowed to make speeches and the Industrial Workers of the World (IWW) organized a barge in English Bay from which they made speeches using a megaphone.

25 Ibid. Douglas has also recently created a series of photos dedicated to the 2011 riots in London, UK. See Yates, "Artist Stan Douglas."

26 Stan Douglas, quoted in Kamping-Carder, "At the Gastown Riot."

27 Proudfoot, "The Derelict, the Deserving Poor, and the *Lumpen*," 90.

28 Ibid.

29 Ibid., 90–1.

30 Ibid.

31 Ibid., 91.

32 Baker, "Gentrification Report Calls Out Dozens"; *Maclean's*, "The Gentrification War."

33 MacLeod, "W2 Arts Hub Locked Out of Woodward's."

Conclusion

1 Asia-Pacific Economic Cooperation (APEC) Collection, Museum of Anthropology, Vancouver, Ref: 98, 1996–2000.

2 Phillips, "APEC at the Museum of Anthropology," 171–92.

3 Pue, *Pepper in Our Eyes*.

4 Phillips, "APEC at the Museum of Anthropology," 87.

5 Ibid., 85.

6 Ibid., 87.

Bibliography

Archives

Asia-Pacific Economic Cooperation (APEC) Collection. UBC Museum of Anthropology, Vancouver, Ref: 98, 1996–2000.
Canadian War Museum. Canvas of War exhibit – Visitor Comments; 2006-002 Box 3.
CARFAC Ontario Fonds. Archives of Ontario. F4403-1-F4403-11.
Carole Condé and Karl Beveridge Fonds. Queen's University Archives. Archive no. 2391_7 and 5131.
Carr Kahlo O'Keefe. Vancouver Art Gallery, Exhibition Files, Accession no. 04.20. Assembled 2002.
Exhibitions: Curatorial, 1975–76 1. Art Gallery of Ontario Archives and Special Collections.
Greg Curnoe Fonds. Art Gallery of Ontario Archives and Special Collections. 14-11; 23-4; 14-15; 14-16.
Jack Chambers Fonds. Series 7 Canadian Artists Representation Files. Art Gallery of Ontario Archives and Special Collections.
Joyce Wieland Fonds. Clara Thomas Archives and Special Collections. York University. F0445.
Occupy Archive. Simon Fraser University Archives and Special Collections. Archive: MSC146.
MOA at UBC Archives. Press Clipping File, 1981.
Press Clippings, 1967–1976. Art Gallery of Ontario Archives and Special Collections.
Registration – External Correspondence 1952–76. Art Gallery of Ontario Archives and Special Collections: A5.9.9/B3-6-6.
Staff 1972/1973 Season. Art Gallery of Ontario Archives and Special Collections. Archive: C3-7-5.

Toronto Star Photograph Archive. Toronto Reference Library.
Toronto Telegram Fonds. Clara Thomas Archives and Special Collections. York University. F0433.

Books and Articles

350.org. "Get Involved." https://350.org/campaigns.
Abley, Mark. "Of War and Regeneration." *Canadian Geographic* 125, no. 6 (November/December 2005): 58–65.
Adams, James. "It's a Whopper All Right: Floor Burger Returns to the AGO." *Globe and Mail*, 15 January 2016: https://www.theglobeandmail.com/arts/art-and-architecture/its-a-whopper-all-right-floor-burger-returns-to-the-ago/article28230063.
– "Now Comes the Hard Part." *Globe and Mail*, 12 April 2008, R7.
– "Protesters to Greet Gehry Unveiling." *Globe and Mail*, 27 January 2004, R3.
– "Report Urges Autonomy for Rights Museum." *Globe and Mail*, 6 May 2008, R1.
Ade, Kris. "Spectacle over Substance: CEO Sleep-out and the Canadian Museum for Human Rights." *Spectator Tribune*, 20 July 2015: https://spectatortribune.com/spectacle-over-substance-ceo-sleep-out-and-the-canadian-museum-for-human-rights.
Agamben, Giorgio. *Homo Sacer: Sovereign Power and Bare Life*. Stanford University Press 1998.
Ahmed, Nafeez. "Pentagon Preparing for Mass Civil Breakdown." *Guardian*, 12 June 2014: http://www.theguardian.com/environment/earth-insight/2014/jun/12/pentagon-mass-civil-breakdown.
Ahooja, Sarita. *Defenders of the Land: A Network of Indigenous Communities and Activists in Land Struggle across Canada*. Video recording. Isuma TV, 2008: http://www.isuma.tv/en/defenders-land/judy-dasilva.
Alberro, Alexander. "An Interview with Stan Douglas." In *Stan Douglas*: Abbott & Cordova, *7 August 1971*, 12–26. Vancouver: Arsenal Pulp Press 2011.
Alberta Community Development. "Final Report: Mission to Washington DC." (2006): http://www.culture.alberta.ca/international_travel/Alberta_Week_in_Washington_and_the_Smithsonian_Folklife_Festival_Final_Report.pdf.
Alberta Infrastructure. "Royal Alberta Museum." (2016): http://www.infrastructure.alberta.ca/3654.htm.
Alberts, Sheldon. "Monster Truck in DC Showcases Alberta's Strengths." *Edmonton Journal*, 27 June 2006, A4.
Allemang, John. "Sniffy's Ordeal, or a Portrait of the Artist as a Rat Fink." *Globe and Mail*, 30 January 1990.
Allen, Jan. "Working Culture." In *Condé and Beveridge: Class Works*, edited by Bruce Barber. Halifax: The Press of the Nova Scotia College of Art and Design in collaboration with the Agnes Etherington Arts Centre 2008.
Ames, Michael. "Boycott the Politics of Suppression." *International Council of Museums of Ethnography* 12 (December 1988): 12–13.
– *Cannibal Tours and Glass Boxes: The Anthropology of Museums*. Vancouver: University of British Columbia Press 1992.
"An Open Letter to Bob Rennie." *We Don't Back the Juiceman* (15 November 2011): https://wedontbackthejuiceman.tumblr.com/post/12850727845/an-open-letter-to-bob-rennie.
Anderson, Benedict. *Imagined Communities: Reflections on the Origin and Spread of Nationalism*. London: Verso 1991.

Andrew & Pippa. *The Museum of Oil (in Conjunction with Greenpeace and the Territorial Agency).* (2016): http://www.andrewandpippa.com/greenpeace-museum-of-oil.
Anker, Elizabeth. *Orgies of Feeling: Melodrama and the Politics of Freedom.* Durham: Duke University Press 2014.
Anon. "National Gallery Outrage." *The Times (London)*, 11 March 1914, 9.
Anon. "The Damaged Venus." *The Times (London)*, 12 March 1914, 6.
APTN National News. "'Idle No More' at the Canadian Museum of Civilization." (27 January 2013): https://www.youtube.com/watch?v=m7d5l3gxq20.
– "Manitoba First Nation Organization Slams Human Rights Museum for 'Genocide' Exclusion." (31 July 2013): http://aptn.ca/news/2013/07/31/manitoba-first-nation-organization-slams-human-rights-museum-over-genocide-exclusion.
Army.ca. "War Museum Controversy." *Forums* (28 October 2006): https://army.ca/forums/index.php?topic=3110.450.
Art Gallery of Ontario. "AGO History: The Controversial Arrival of Claes Oldenburg's *Floor Burger*." AGO *Art Matters Blog* (22 October 2012): http://artmatters.ca/wp/2012/10/ago-history-the-controversial-arrival-of-claes-oldenburgs-floor-burger.
Art Not Oil. *Culture beyond Oil.* (2011): http://www.artnotoil.org.uk/blog/culture-beyond-oil-full-publication.
Assembly of First Nations and Canadian Museums Association. *Turning the Page: Forging New Partnerships between Museums and First Peoples.* Task Force Report on Museums and First Peoples, Ottawa 1994.
Associated Press. "Shia LaBoeuf's Trump Art Project Closes after Becoming 'Flashpoint for Violence.'" *Guardian*, 10 February 2017.
– "UK's Tate Gallery Acquires Replica of Anti-War Protest Camp." *Washington Times*, 21 September 2016.
Badiou, Alain. *Being and Event*. Los Altos: Mansell Publishing 2006.
Bacchus, Lee. "Gary Mason and the Inclement Weather at Occupy Vancouver." *The Mainlander*, 22 November 2011: http://themainlander.com/2011/11/22/column-gary-mason-and-the-inclement-weather-at-occupy-vancouver
Baele, Nancy. "*The Spirit Sings*: A Discordant Voice." *Ottawa Citizen*, 16 January 1988, C1.
– "*The Spirit Sings*: Three Centuries of Native Culture." *Ottawa Citizen* (final edition), 2 July 1988.
Baiko, Radley. *Rise of the Warrior Cop: The Militarization of America's Police Forces.* New York: Public Affairs 2013.
Baker, Rafferty. "Gentrification Report Calls Out Dozens of DTES Businesses." CBC News, 23 February 2017.
Bakhtin, Mikhail. *Rabelais and His World*. Bloomington: Indiana University Press [1968] 1984.
Bal, Mieke. "Telling, Showing, Showing Off." *Critical Inquiry* 18, no. 3 (spring 1992): 556–94.
Ball, David. "Will Canada Unblock This People's 'Road to Freedom?'" *The Tyee*, 24 June 2015: https://thetyee.ca/News/2015/06/24/Peoples-Road-to-Freedom.
Ball, Karen, and Per Anders Rudling. "The Underbelly of Canadian Multiculturalism: Holocaust Obfuscation in the Debate about the Canadian Museum for Human Rights." *Holocaust Studies: A Journal of Culture and History* 20, no. 1 (2014): 33–80.
Baloy, Natalie J.K. "Spectacles and Spectres: Settler Colonial Spaces in Vancouver." *Settler Colonial Studies* 6, no. 3 (2016): 209–34.

Barber, Bruce, Serge Guilbaut, and John O'Brian. *Voices of Fire: Art, Rage, Power, and the State*. Toronto: University of Toronto Press 1995.

Barker, Adam J. "Already Occupied: Indigenous Peoples, Settler Colonialism and the Occupy Movements in North America." *Social Movement Studies* 11, nos 34 (2012): 327–34.

– "'A Direct Act of Resurgence, a Direct Act of Sovereignty': Reflections on Idle No More, Indigenous Activism, and Canadian Settler Colonialism." *Globalizations* 12, no. 1 (2015): 43–65.

Barnholden, Michael. *Reading the Riot Act: A Brief History of Riots in Vancouver*. Vancouver: Anvil Press 2005.

Bartels, Kathleen. "Director's Foreword." In *How Soon Is Now*, Kathleen Ritter, curator, 5. Vancouver: Vancouver Art Gallery 2009.

– "Director's Report." In *Annual Report 2004*. Vancouver: Vancouver Art Gallery 2004: 4.

Basen, Ira. "Memory Becomes a Minefield at Canada's Museum for Human Rights." *Globe and Mail*, 20 August 2011.

Bashow, David L. "Bomber Command Deserves the Credit It Gets," *Ottawa Citizen*, 12 November 2008, A15.

Battaglia, Jeremie. *Casseroles*. 24 May 2012: http://vimeo.com/42848523.

Bauman, Zygmunt. *Globalization: The Human Consequences*. Cambridge: Polity Press, 1998.

BC Business. "Got $300 Million? The Vancouver Art Gallery Would Like to Talk." 5 March 2015: https://www.bcbusiness.ca/got-300-million-the-vancouver-art-gallery-would-like-to-talk.

Begg, Zanny, and Ahmet Ögüt. "In and out of the Biennale: Transfield, Mandatory Detention, and the Biennale of Sydney." *Afterimage* 42, no. 2 (September/October 2014): 4–7.

Belanger, Yale D., and P. Whitney Lackenbauer, eds. *Blockades or Breakthroughs: Aboriginal Peoples Confront the Canadian State*. Kingston and Montreal: McGill-Queen's University Press 2014.

Bell, Steve. "Open Letter to Prime Minister Stephen Harper Regarding Shoal Lake 40 First Nation." *Steve Bell Blog* (28 July 2015): http://stevebell.com/2015/07/open-letter-to-prime-minister-stephen-harper-regarding-shoal-lake-40-first-nation.

Bendik-Keymer, Jeremy. "Reconsidering the Aesthetics of Protest." *Hyperallergic* (7 December 2016): https://hyperallergic.com/343410/reconsidering-the-aesthetics-of-protest.

Bennes, Crystal. "What Installing a Demolished London Estate in Venice Says about Our Housing Crisis." *Frieze* (14 May 2018): https://frieze.com/article/what-installing-demolished-london-estate-venice-says-about-our-housing-crisis.

Bennett, Jill. *Empathic Vision: Affect, Trauma, and Contemporary Art*. Stanford: Stanford University Press 2005.

Bennett, Tony. *Birth of the Museum: History, Theory, Politics*. London and New York: Routledge 1995.

Bercuson, David J. "Canadian War Museum and Bomber Command: My Perspective." *Canadian Military History* 20, no. 3 (summer 2011): 55–62.

– *The Valour and the Horror Revisited*. Kingston and Montreal: McGill-Queen's University Press 1994.

Bergner, Keith B., John Olynyk, Toby Kruger. "Supreme Court of Canada Confirms There Is No Duty to Consult Indigenous Groups in the Development of Legislation." *Project Law Blog* (11 October 2018): https://www.lawsonlundell.com/project-law-blog/supreme-court-of-canada-confirms-there-is-no-duty-to-consult-indigenous-groups-in-the-development-of-legislation.

Berlant, Lauren. *Cruel Optimism*. Durham: Duke University Press 2011.
Berthiaume, Lee. "Pipeline Protest Greets PM Trudeau in London." *CTVnews.ca* (18 April 2018): https://www.ctvnews.ca/politics/pipeline-protest-greets-pm-trudeau-in-london-1.3889769.
Bherer, Laurence, and Pascale Dufour. "Our Not-So-Friendly Northern Neighbor." *New York Times* (23 May 2012): http://www.nytimes.com/2012/05/24/opinion/our-not-so-friendly-northern-neighbor.html.
Biddle, Erika. "Re-animating Joseph Beuys' 'Social Sculpture': Artistic Interventions and the Occupy Movement." *Communication and Critical/Cultural Studies* 11, no. 1 (2014): 25–33.
Bishop, Claire. "Art & Education: Public Opinion." *Art Forum* (29 October 2009): http://artforum.com/diary/id=24062.
– *Artificial Hells: Participatory Art and the Politics of Spectatorship*. London and New York: Verso 2012.
– "Introduction: Viewers as Producers." In *Participation*, edited by Claire Bishop, 10–17. Cambridge, MA: MIT Press 2006.
– "Participation and the Spectacle: Where Are We Now?" In *Living as Form: Socially Engaged Art from 1991–2011*, edited by Nato Thompson. Cambridge, MA: MIT Press 2012.
– *Radical Museology: Or What's Contemporary in Museums of Contemporary Art?* Köln: Walther König 2013.
– "The Social Turn: Collaboration and Its Discontents." *Artforum* 44, no. 6 (2006): 178–83.
Blomley, Nick. *Unsettling the City: Urban Land and the Politics of Property*. London and New York: Routledge 2004.

Blumer, Nadine. "Expanding Museum Spaces: Networks of Difficult Knowledge at and beyond the Canadian Museum for Human Rights." *Review of Education, Pedagogy, and Cultural Studies* 37, nos 2–3 (2015): 125–46.
Boddy, Trevor. "Squaring Off with Protesters." *Vancouver Sun*, 28 March 2003, B4.
Boje, David M. "Carnivalesque Resistance to Global Spectacle: A Critical Postmodern Theory of Public Administration." *Administrative Theory and Praxis* 23, no. 3 (2001): 431–58.
Boles, "Federal Government Pledges $1.9 Billion to Canadian Arts and Culture." *Thump* (23 March 2016): https://thump.vice.com/en_ca/article/nzm8jb/trudeau-federal-government-pledges-19-billion-canadian-arts-culture.
Boltanski, Luc, and Eve Chiapello. *The New Spirit of Capitalism*, translated by Gregory Elliott. London: Verso 2007.
Bonin, Vincent. "Here, Bad News Always Arrives Too Late." *Filip* 16 (spring 2002): http://fillip.ca/content/here-bad-news-always-arrives-too-late#notes.
Bookchin, Murray. *Post-Scarcity Anarchism*. London: AK Press [1971] 2004.
Booth, William James. "Remembrance Day: What We Do When We Remember Why." *Globe and Mail*, 10 November 1995, A21.
Boswell, Randy. "Asper Museum to Rise as Shrine to Tolerance." *Edmonton Journal*, 17 April 2003, A8.
– "Winnipeg to Get Human Rights Museum." *Vancouver Sun*, 17 April 2003, A3.
Bothwell, Robert, Randall Hansen, and Margaret MacMillan. "Controversy, Commemoration, and Capitulation: The Canadian War Museum and Bomber Command." *Queen's Quarterly* 115, no. 3 (fall 2008): 367–87.
Boudreau, Michael. "'The Struggle for a Different World': The 1971 Gastown Riot in

Vancouver." In *Debating Dissent: Canada and the Sixties*, edited by Gregory Kealey, Dominique Clément, and Lara Campbell, 117–34. Toronto: University of Toronto Press 2012.

Bourcier, Paul, Ruby Rogers, and Nomenclature Committee, eds. *Nomenclature 3.0 for Museum Cataloging: Third Edition of Robert G. Chenhall's System for Classifying Man-Made Objects*. New York: Alta Mira Press/American Association for State and Local History 2010.

Bourriaud, Nicolas. *Relational Aesthetics*. Paris: Presses du Reel 2002.

Bowles, John. "The 1970 New York Artists' Strike That Prefigures #J20." *Hyperallergic.com* (18 January 2017): goo.gl/zwzjAP.

Bowley, Graham. "How Do You Tell the Story of Black America in One Museum?" *New York Times*, 26 March 2017: http://www.nytimes.com/2016/03/27/arts/design/how-do-you-tell-the-story-of-black-america-in-one-museum.html.

– "Museums Chart a Response to Political Upheaval." *New York Times*, 13 March 2017: https://www.nytimes.com/2017/03/13/arts/design/museums-politics-protest-j20-art-strike.html.

BP or Not BP. "Performances and Films." https://bp-or-not-bp.org/performances-and-films.

Bradshaw, James. "Tories Say Building Money 'Is Flowing.'" *Globe and Mail*, 5 January 2009.

Brait, Ellen. "Ottawa Adds $15 Million in Funding for Winnipeg Art Gallery's Inuit Art Centre." *Globe and Mail*, 2 August 2016.

Brandon, Laura. "A Unique and Important Asset? The Transfer of the War Art Collections from the National Gallery of Canada to the Canadian War Museum." *Material Culture Review* 42 (fall 1995): https://journals.lib.unb.ca/index.php/MCR/article/view/17664/22309.

Brandson, Ashley. "Shoal Lake 40 Inching Closer to 'Freedom Road' Completion." *APTN National News*, 3 July 2018: http://aptnnews.ca/2018/07/03/shoal-lake-40-inching-closer-to-freedom-road-completion.

Brean, Joseph. "Canadian Museum for Human Rights Opens Amidst Controversy and Protests." *National Post*, 19 September 2014.

Bright, Pearl. "To 'The Invitational,' Arts Patrons and Workers, and Visitors to Chinatown." *Medium*, 27 October 2018: https://medium.com/@brightpearlto/to-the-invitational-arts-patrons-workers-visitors-to-chinatown-3b8e2048db2.

British Museum. "New Special Exhibition on Dissent Announced." *Britishmuseum.org* (blog): https://blog.britishmuseum.org/new-special-exhibition-on-dissent-announced.

Britzman, Deborah, and Alice Pitt. "Speculations on Qualities of Difficult Knowledge in Teaching and Learning: An Experiment in Psychoanalytic Research." *International Journal of Qualitative Studies in Education* 16, no. 6 (2003): 755–76.

Broudehoux, Anne-Marie. "Images of Power: Architectures of the Integrated Spectacle at the Beijing Olympics." *Journal of Architectural Education* 63.2 (March 2010): 52–62.

Brown, Lorna. "Hosts and Guests." *Public (Mega-Event Cities)*, edited by Peter Dickinson, Kirsty Johnston, and Keren Zaiontz. 53 (2015): 13–21.

Brown, Mark. "Tate's BP Sponsorship Was 150,000 to 330,000 a Year." *Guardian*, 26 January 2015.

Browne, Kelvin. *Bold Visions: The Architecture of the Royal Ontario Museum*. Toronto: ROM 2007.

Bryan-Wilson, Julia. *Art Workers: Radical Practice in the Vietnam War Era*. Oakland: University of California Press 2011.

Buck-Morss, Susan. *Thinking Past Terror: Islamism and Critical Theory on the Left*. London and New York: Verso 2003.
– "What Is Political Art?" In *inSITE 97: Private Time in Public Space*, edited by Sally Yard, 14–27. San Diego and Tijuana: inSITE 1997.
Bula, Frances. "700 Social Housing Units Given Belated Go-Ahead," *Vancouver Sun*, 15 March 2002, B5.
– "Council Backs Developer's Plan for Woodward's." *Vancouver Sun*, 23 October 2002, A1.
– "The Fight for the Vancouver Art Gallery." *Vancouver Magazine*, 13 March 2013: http://vanmag.com/city/arts-culture/the-fight-for-the-vancouver-art-gallery.
– "Vancouver Art Gallery Might Have to Bail on False Creek." *State of Vancouver*, 3 June 2009: http://www.francesbula.com/uncategorized/vancouver-art-gallery-might-have-to-bail-on-false-creek.
Burns, Grant. "More Highrises Set to Mar Vancouver's Skyline." *The Thunderbird*, 5 November 2009: https://thethunderbird.ca/2009/11/05/vancouver-plans-more-controversial-high-rises-downtown.
Burns, John. "Bissell, Student Scuffle: Radicals Storm Kerr Lecture at Museum." *Globe and Mail*, 6 February 1969.
Busby, Karen, Adam Muller, and Andrew Woolford. "Change of Plans: Conceptualizing the Inaugural Exhibits at the Canadian Museum for Human Rights." In *The Idea of a Human Rights Museum*, edited by Karen Busby, Adam Muller, and Andrew Woolford, 111–27. Winnipeg: University of Manitoba Press 2015.
– "Introduction." In *The Idea of a Human Rights Museum*, edited by Karen Busby, Adam Muller, and Andrew Woolford, 1–26. Winnipeg: University of Manitoba Press 2015.
Butler, Don. "10 Years On, War Museum Established as One of the World's Best." *Ottawa Citizen*, 7 May 2015.
Butler, Judith. "Bodies in Alliance and the Politics of the Street." *cipcp.net*, September 2011: http://www.eipcp.net/transversal/1011/butler/en.
– "Bodily Vulnerability, Coalitions, and Street Politics." *Critical Studies* 37 (2014): 99–119 and 247.
– *Excitable Speech: A Politics of the Performative*. New York and London: Routledge 1997.
Butler, Shelley. *Contested Representations: Revisiting* Into the Heart of Africa. Peterborough: Broadview Press 2008.
– "On Mixed Metaphors, Herding, and Burning Issues at the CMHR." *CEREV blog*, 8 October 2014: http://cerev.org/cerev/blog/shelley-ruth-butler-on-mixed-metaphors-herding-and-burning-issues-at-the-cmhr.
– "The Politics of Exhibiting Culture: Legacies and Possibilities." *Museum Anthropology* 23, no. 3 (2000): 74–92.
Buzzetti, Hélène. "Sable bitumineux." *Le Devoir*, 20 December 2011.
Cahan, Susan E. *Mounting Frustration: The Art Museum in the Age of Black Power*. Durham: Duke University Press 2016.
Calgary Arts Development. "Alberta Arts Flood Rebuilding Fund Is Doubling Donors' Dollars." 5 July 2013: https://calgaryartsdevelopment.com/news_releases/alberta-arts-flood-rebuild-fund-is-doubling-donors-dollars.
Calgary Herald. "Spirit Sings and Soars with Cultural Exhibition." [Final Edition] 14 January 1998, D2.
Cameron, Duncan. "The Coming of Age of the Art Gallery of Ontario." *Globe and Mail*, 19 October 1974, 27.
– "The Museum: A Temple or the Forum?" *Journal of World History* 14, no. 1 (1972): 189–202.

Cameron, Fiona. "Introduction." In *Hot Topics, Public Culture, Museums*, edited by Fiona Cameron and Lynda Kelly, 1–16. Newcastle, UK: Cambridge Scholars Publishing 2010.

– "Risk Society, Controversial Topics and Museum Interventions: (Re)reading Controversy and the Museum through a Risk Optic." In *Hot Topics, Public Culture, Museums*, edited by Fiona Cameron and Lynda Kelly, 53–75. Newcastle, UK: Cambridge Scholars Publishing 2010.

Cameron, Fiona, and Brett Neilson, eds. *Climate Change and Museum Futures*. London and New York: Routledge 2015.

Canadian Archeological Association. "Change in Name and Purpose of the Canadian Museum of Civilization." 11 December 2012: https://canadianarchaeology.com/caa/about/public-advocacy-committee/change-name-and-purpose-canadian-museum-civilization.

Canadian Architect. "High-Profile Shortlist Announced for the Vancouver Art Gallery's New Home." 59, no. 2 (February 2014): 9.

Canadian Historical Association. "The CHA President Writes to the President of the Canadian Museum of Civilization." 3 December 2012: http://www.cha-shc.ca/english/advocacy/the-cha-president-writes-to-the-president-of-the-canadian-museum-of-civilization.html#sthash.U5rfHlcF.8rmE2IUW.dpbs.

Canadian Museum for Human Rights, "Truth and Reconciliation." https://humanrights.ca/exhibit/truth-and-reconciliation.

Canadian Museum of History. "Canadian Museum of Civilization Welcomes CAPP as National Sponsor and Official Partner." 25 November 2013: http://www.historymuseum.ca/media/canadian-museum-of-civilization-welcomes-capp-as-national-sponsor-and-official-partner.

Canadian Press. "Emergency Bill Would See Quebec Student Leaders Fined up to $35K for Blocking Classes." *National Post*, 18 May 2012: http://news.nationalpost.com/2012/05/18/bill-78-quebec.

– "Kitchener Museum's Giant Canadian Flag Vandalized on Canada Day." *Toronto Star*, 4 July 2017: https://www.thestar.com/news/canada/2017/07/04/kitchener-museums-giant-canadian-flag-vandalized-on-canada-day.html.

– "Liberals Accuse Tories of 'Abuse of Process.'" *National Post*, 9 December 2015.

– "Natives' Protest Likened to Killings at 1972 Olympics." [FIN Edition] *Toronto Star*, 28 September 1987.

Canadian Security Intelligence Service. "Anti-Globalization – A Spreading Phenomenon." Ottawa: Government of Canada 2000: http://www.csis-scrs.gc.ca/pblctns/prspctvs/200008-eng.asp.

Canadian War Museum, "About." http://www.warmuseum.ca/about.

"Canvas of War Comments Book," Canvas of War archive, Canadian War Museum, consulted in 2000.

Caplan, Gerald. "Human Rights Museum Is Indifferent to Some Human Rights." *Globe and Mail*, 3 October 2014.

Carrigan, Margaret. "Art World Heavyweights 'Stupefied' by Sexist Museum Firings." *Observer*, 20 March 2018: https://observer.com/2018/03/museum-firings-of-helen-molesworth-laura-raicovich-create-outrage.

Carter, Jennifer J., and Jennifer A. Orange. "'It's Time to Pause and Reflect': Museums and Human Rights." *Curator: The Museum Journal* 55, no. 3 (July 2012): 259–66.

Cash, Martin. "Aspers Quit Canwest Board." *Winnipeg Free Press*, 11 February 2010, B5.

Cauter, Lieven de, Ruben De Roo, and Karel Vanhaesebrouck. *Art and Activism in the Age of Globalization*, vol. 8. Rotterdam, New York: NAI 2011.

Caves, Richard E. *Creative Industries: Contracts between Art and Commerce*. Cambridge, MA: Harvard University Press 2000.
Cayley, David. "Trouble out of Africa." *Globe and Mail*, 10 August 1990.
CBC Arts. "All Things Albertan Focus of Smithsonian Festival." 27 June 2006: http://www.cbc.ca/story/arts/national/2006/06/27/alberta-smithsonian.html.
– "Canadian War Museum Changes Controversial Wording on WWII Bombing." 11 October 2007: http://www.cbc.ca/news/entertainment/canadian-war-museum-changes-controversial-wording-on-wwii-bombing-1.635963.
– "Rem Koolhaas to Design Quebec City Museum." *CBC News*, 1 April 2010: http://www.cbc.ca/news/entertainment/rem-koolhaas-to-design-quebec-city-museum-1.919757.
CBC Digital Archives. "Painter Greg Curnoe Forms Artists' Union." *CBC Digital Archives*, 10 March 1975: https://www.cbc.ca/archives/entry/painter-greg-curnoe-forms-artists-union.
CBC News. "Canadian Museum of History Plans Revealed." 30 July 2013: http://www.cbc.ca/news/canada/ottawa/canadian-museum-of-history-plans-revealed-1.1389617.
– "Civilization Museum's $25M Rebranding to Focus on History." 16 October 2012: http://www.cbc.ca/news/canada/ottawa/civilization-museum-s-25m-rebranding-to-focus-on-history-1.1225802.
– "Fossil Treasure Trove Found at Oilsands." 24 November 2011: http://www.cbc.ca/news/canada/edmonton/fossil-treasure-trove-found-at-oilsands-1.1076896.
– "Idle No More Protests Mark Proclamation's 250th Anniversary." 7 October 2013: http://www.cbc.ca/news/politics/idle-no-more-protests-mark-proclamation-s-250th-anniversary-1.1928276.
– "Imperial Oil's Role in Museum's Energy Exhibit Questioned." 23 January 2012: http://www.cbc.ca/news/canada/ottawa/imperial-oil-s-role-in-museum-s-energy-exhibit-questioned-1.1165219.
– "International Watchdog Human Rights Watch to Look at Shoal Lake 40." 11 August 2015: http://www.cbc.ca/news/canada/manitoba/international-watchdog-human-rights-watch-to-look-at-shoal-lake-40-1.3187026.
– "Nunavut Irked by Arctic Sovereignty Talk." 9 April 2010: http://www.cbc.ca/news/canada/north/nunavut-irked-by-arctic-sovereignty-talk-1.881954.
– "Oilsands Campaign Hits Times Square." 11 September 2010: http://www.cbc.ca/news/canada/edmonton/oilsands-campaign-hits-times-square-1.958781.
– "Petro-Canada Gives Away Its Art Collection." 3 November 2000: http://www.cbc.ca/news/canada/petro-canada-gives-away-its-art-collection-1.232776.
– "Quebec Police Admit They Went Undercover at Montebello Protest." 23 August 2007: http://www.cbc.ca/news/canada/quebec-police-admit-they-went-undercover-at-monte bello-protest-1.656171.
– "Showcasing Heritage." 29 July 2014: http://www.cbc.ca/beta/news/canada/ottawa/showcasing-heritage-1.2721110.
– "Tina Fontaine, Faron Hall Deaths: Candles Still Burning after Winnipeg Vigil." 19 August 2014: http://www.cbc.ca/news/canada/manitoba/tina-fontaine-faron-hall-deaths-candles-still-burning-after-winnipeg-vigil-1.2740432.
– "War Museum's Paintings Anger Veterans Groups." 3 May, 2005: http://www.cbc.ca/m/touch/canada/story/1.552891.
Centre for Climate Safety. "Uprise among Artists against 'Dirty Oil Money.'" 30 August 2013: http://climatesafety.info/uprise-among-artists-against-dirty-oil-money.
Chan, Cheryl. "Do Tent Cities Work? A Look at Winners and Losers in Vancouver's History of Park Protests." *Province*, 29 July 2014 (updated 31 July 2014).

Chan, Kenneth. "Fake Condo Tower Proposal at Vancouver Art Gallery Trolls Internet." *VanCity Buzz*, 17 September 2015: http://www.vancitybuzz.com/2015/09/fake-condo-tower-vancouver-art-gallery.
– "New Vancouver Art Gallery Plaza Design Revealed." *VanCity Buzz*. 19 November 2015: http://www.vancitybuzz.com/2015/11/new-vancouver-art-gallery-plaza-design.
Chapman, Aaron. "The Revolution Won't Be Occupied: Vancouver Art Gallery May Not Be Best Place for Civic Showdown." *Vancouver Courier*, 26 October 2011.
Chatterley, Catherine D. "Canada's Struggle with Holocaust Memorialization: The War Museum Controversy, Ethnic Identity Politics, and the Canadian Museum for Human Rights." *Holocaust and Genocide Studies* 29, no. 2 (2015): 189–211.
Cheadle, Bruce. "Museum of Civilization Taps Big Oil to Help Fund Canada's 150th Birthday." *Huffington Post*, 25 November 2013: http://www.huffingtonpost.ca/2013/11/25/museum-of-civilization-oil-producers_n_4338159.html.
Chen, Michelle. "Some of the Exhibits at the Museum of Natural History Are … Not … Good … " *The Nation*, 19 October 2016: https://www.thenation.com/article/some-of-the-exhibits-at-the-museum-of-natural-history-are-not-good.
Cheney, Dick. "Vice President Cheney Delivers Remarks to the Republican Governors Association." *The White House* (recovered website) 25 October 2001: http://georgewbush-whitehouse.archives.gov/vicepresident/news-speeches/speeches/vp20011025.html.
Chiang, Chuck. "Singaporean Billionaire Plans to Build Asian Art Museum in Vancouver." *Vancouver Sun*, 19 April 2017.
Cholette, Katie. "Memory and Mythmaking: The Role of Autobiography in the Works of Jack Chambers and Greg Curnoe." PhD dissertation, Carleton University, 2007.

Chong, Derrick. "Institutions Trust Institutions: Critiques by Artists of the BP/Tate Partnership." *Journal of Macromarketing* 33, no. 2 (2012): 104–16.
Chrisjohn, Roland, Andrea Bear Nicholas, Karen Stote, James Craven (Omahkohkiaayo i'poyi), Tanya Wasacase, Pierre Loiselle, and Andrea O. Smith. "An Historic Non-apology, Completely and Utterly Not Accepted." June 2008: http://marxmail.org/ApologyNotAccepted.htm.
Christopher, Ben, Justin Langille, and Robyn Smith. "Why They Joined Occupy Vancouver." *The Tyee*, 15 October 2011: https://thetyee.ca/News/2011/10/15/OccupyVancouver.
City of Ottawa. *Ottawa Employment Survey 2013*. http://documents.ottawa.ca/sites/documents.ottawa.ca/files/documents/employment_survey.pdf.
City of Vancouver. "Administrative Report RR1: A New Vancouver Art Gallery at 688 Cambie Street – 10010." 15 April 2013: http://council.vancouver.ca/20130423/documents/rr1.pdf.
City of Vancouver, Cultural Services. *Culture Plan for Vancouver 2008–2018*. 2008: vancouver.ca/creativecity.
"City of Reconciliation." *City of Vancouver*. June 2018: https://vancouver.ca/people-programs/city-of-reconciliation.aspx.
Clapperton, Jonathan Alex. "Contested Spaces, Shared Places: The Museum of Anthropology at UBC, Aboriginal Peoples, and Postcolonial Criticism." *BC Studies* 165 (spring 2010): 7–30.
Clark, Campbell. "Backing Israel a 'Moral Imperative' for Global Democracy, Harper Says." *Globe and Mail*, 20 January 2014.
Clarke, Jo, Mel Evans, Hayley Newman, Kevin Smith, and Glen Tarman, eds. *Not If but When: Culture beyond Oil*. London: Platform/Liberate Tate 2011.

Clifford, James. *Routes: Travel and Translation in the Late Twentieth Century*. Cambridge, MA, and London: Harvard University Press 1997.
Coalition of Museums for Climate Justice. "CAPP & the Canadian Museum of History." 12 July 2017: https://coalitionofmuseumsforclimatejustice.wordpress.com/2017/07/12/capp-the-canadian-museum-of-history-pt-2.
Coffey, Charles. "Reaching for the Stars: Creating the Canadian Brand for Human Rights Leadership," speech, Windsor Arms, Toronto, 19 October 2005: http://www.rbc.com/newsroom/speeches/20051019coffey.html.
Cohen, Andrew. "Welcome to the Quiet Devolution." *Ottawa Citizen*, 17 November 2007, B7.
Cole, Yolande. "Vancouver Art Gallery Selects Herzog & de Meuron as Architect for New Facility." *Georgia Straight*, 29 April 2014: https://www.straight.com/arts/634801/vancouver-art-gallery-selects-herzog-de-meuron-architect-new-facility.
Colebourne, John, and Andy Ivens. "'Safety' behind Move to Shift Squatters." *Province*, 20 November 2002, A12.
Collis, Stephen. *Dispatches from the Occupation: A History of Change* (Advance Reading Copy). Vancouver: Talon Books 2012.
Conlogue, Ray. "Arts Groups Rally against Rumoured Budget Cuts." *Globe and Mail*, 15 February 1992.
Conn, Steven. *Do Museums Still Need Objects?* Philadelphia: University of Pennsylvania Press 2010.
Content Advisory Committee. *Final Report to the Canadian Museum for Human Rights*. 25 May 2010: http://publications.gc.ca/collections/collection_2011/mcdp-cmhr/NM104-1-2010-eng.pdf.
– *Report to the Minister of Canadian Heritage on the Canadian Museum for Human Rights*. 2008: http://publications.gc.ca/collections/collection_2008/ch-pc/CH4-133 2008E.pdf.
Coody Cooper, Karen. *Spirited Encounters: American Indians Protest Museum Policies and Practices*. Lanham: Alta Mira Press 2008.
Cooks, Bridget R. "Black Artists and Activism. Harlem on my Mind, 1969." *Journal of American Studies* 48, no. 1 (2007): 5–40.
Cooper, Sarah. "The Politics of Protest Collections: Developing Social Action Archives." *Provenance: Journal of the Society of Georgia Archivists* 5.1 (January 1987): 8–16.
Corcoran, Terrance. "No Place for Bleeding Hearts." *National Post*, 11 November 2006, A12.
Cotter, Holland. "Making Museums Moral Again." *New York Times*, 17 March 2016: https://mobile.nytimes.com/2016/03/17/arts/design/making-museums-moral-again.html.
Coulthard, Glen. "The Colonialism of the Present." *Jacobin*, 13 January 2015: https://www.jacobinmag.com/2015/01/indigenous-left-glen-coulthard-interview.
– *Red Skin, White Masks: Rejecting the Colonial Politics of Recognition*. Minneapolis: University of Minnesota Press 2014.
Council of Canadians. "Why the Trudeau Government Must Restore the Navigable Waters Protection Act." 8 December 2016: https://canadians.org/blog/why-trudeau-government-must-restore-navigable-waters-protection-act.
Coupland, Douglas. *City of Glass: Douglas Coupland's Vancouver* (Revised). Toronto: Douglas and McIntyre 2009.
Cox, Kevin. "Protest at Games Still on, Indians Say." *Globe and Mail*, 6 October 1987.
Craig, Sean. "What's Gone on Behind Closed Doors at Canada's Most-Visited Museum."

Buzzfeed, 14 January 2016: https://www.buzzfeed.com/seancraig/a-history-of-turbulence.
Crary, Jonathan. *24/7: Late Capitalism and the Ends of Sleep*. London: Verso 2014.
Crawley, Mike. "Royal Ontario Museum Apologizes over Racist Exhibit ... 27 Years Later." *cbc.ca*, 9 November 2016: http://www.cbc.ca/news/canada/toronto/rom-apology-into-heart-africa-royal-ontario-museum-1.3840645.
Crean, Susan. "The ROM's Apology for Its Racist 1989 Exhibit Is a Start – Now Diversify the Board." *Now magazine*, 7 December 2016: https://nowtoronto.com/art-and-books/art/rom-recovers-credibility-apology-racist-1989-start.
– *Who's Afraid of Canadian Culture?* Don Mills: General Publishing 1976.
– "Up Front with the Artists: The AGO Affair." *Canadian Forum* (November-December 1973): 63-67.
Crossley, Nick, and Ron Eyerman. "How Social Movements Move: Emotions and Social Movements." In *Emotions and Social Movements*, edited by Helena Flam and Debra King, 42–56. New York and London: Routledge 2005.
Cryderman, Kelly. "Oilsands the Poster Child of Bad Oil." *Calgary Herald*, 2 November 2008, B1.
– "Toronto Mayor Hangs Head in Shame." *Calgary Herald*, 12 December 2009, A4.
CTV News. "In Charts: Tracking House Prices in Canada's Hottest Housing Markets." 18 April 2017: http://www.ctvnews.ca/canada/in-charts-tracking-house-prices-in-canada-s-hottest-housing-markets-1.3373632.
CTV News Staff. "War Museum to Reword Controversial WWII Display." 28 August 2007: http://www.ctvnews.ca/war-museum-to-reword-controversial-wwii-display-1.254276.

Culhane, Dara. "Their Spirits Live within Us: Aboriginal Women in Downtown Eastside Vancouver Emerging into Visibility." *American Indian Quarterly* 27, nos. 3–4 (summer-autumn 2003): 593–606.
Curry, Bill. "Protesters Disrupt Question Period over Climate Bill." *Globe and Mail*, 27 October 2009, A5.
Dafoe, Chris. "Arts Community Rallies in Support of VAG Director." *Globe and Mail*, 5 April 2000: https://www.theglobeandmail.com/news/national/arts-community-rallies-in-support-of-vag-director/article25459345.
da Silva, Judy. *Defenders of the Land: A Network of Indigenous Communities and Activists in Land Struggle across Canada*. Retrieved from Isuma TV: http://www.isuma.tv/en/defenders-land/judy-dasilva.
– "Grassy Narrows." (16 September 2009): http://www.isuma.tv/defenders-land/judy-dasilva.
Davenport, Christian. "Data from the Dark Side: Notes on Archiving Political Conflict and Violence." *Political Science and Politics* 43, no. 1 (January 2010): 37–41.
Davies, Anthony, and Simon Ford. "Culture Clubs." *Mute* (2000): http://www.metamute.org/editorial/articles/culture-clubs.
Dawood, Sarah. "From Nope to Hope: The Exhibition Protesting the Design Museum." *Design Week*, 27 September 2018: https://www.designweek.co.uk/issues/24-30-september-2018/from-nope-to-hope-anti-arms-exhibition-protesting-design-museum.
Dawn, Leslie. *National Visions, National Blindness: Canadian Art and Identities in the 1920s*. Vancouver: University of British Columbia Press, 2007.
Day, Joe. "Hubrispace: Personal Museums and the Architectures of Self-Deification." In *Evil Paradises: Dreamworlds of Neoliberalism*, edited by Mike Davis and Daniel Bertrand Monk, 219–40. New York: New Press 2007.

Dean, Amber. "The CMHR and the Ongoing Crisis of Murdered or Missing Indigenous Women: Do Museums Have a Responsibility to Care?" *The Review of Education, Pedagogy, and Cultural Studies* 37 (2015): 147–65.
– *Remembering Vancouver's Disappeared Women: Settler Colonialism and the Difficulty of Inheritance*. Toronto: University of Toronto Press 2015.
Dean, David. "Museums as Conflict Zones: The Canadian War Museum and Bomber Command." *Museum and Society* 7, no. 1 (2009): 1–15.
Dean, Jodi. "The Anamorphic Politics of Climate Change." *e-flux* 69 (January 2016): http://www.e-flux.com/journal/69/60586/the-anamorphic-politics-of-climate-change.
Dean, Michelle. "The Struggle for the Occupy Wall Street Archive." *The Awl*, 21 December 2011: https://theawl.com/the-struggle-for-the-occupy-wall-street-archives-c8dc59 32b4d3#.85doxb9q9.
De Baere, Bart, and Dieter Roelstraete, "Introducing Intertidal." In *Intertidal: Vancouver Art and Artists*, 7–16. Vancouver: The Morris and Helen Belkin Art Gallery 2005.
Deleuze, Gilles, and Felix Guattari. *Thousand Plateaus: Capitalism and Schizophrenia*. Minneapolis: University of Minnesota Press 1987.
Den Tandt, Michael. "'Use It or Lose It': Harper's Arctic Strategy More Than Just a Political Gambit." *National Post*, 24 August 2014.
DePape, Brigitte. "Idle No More Is a Christmas Gift to Us All." *Maclean's*, 25 December 2012: http://www.macleans.ca/news/canada/idle-no-more-is-a-christmas-gift-to-us-all.
De Peuter, Greig. "Interview. The Art of Collective Bargaining: An Interview with Carole Condé and Karl Beveridge." *Canadian Journal of Communication* 40 (2015): https://www.cjc-online.ca/index.php/journal/article/view/2994/2549.
De Peuter, Greig, and Sarah E.K. Smith. *"A Living Culture, A Living Wage": A Case Study of the Independent Artists' Union*, forthcoming.
Derksen, Jeff. "Approaching the Long Moment." In *Momentarily: Learning from Mega-Events*, edited by Bik Van der Pol, Alissa Firth-Eagland, and Urban Subjects, 14–19. Vancouver: Western Front 2010: http://www.urbansubjects.org/images/learning_from_vancouver/Momentarily%20Learning%20from%20Mega-Events.pdf.
– "How High Is the City, How Deep Is Our Love." *Filip* 12 (fall 2010): https://fillip.ca/content/how-high-is-the-city-how-deep-is-our-love.
Derrida, Jacques. *Archive Fever: A Freudian Impression*. Chicago: University of Chicago Press 1996.
De Souza, Mike. "Imperial Oil Described Its Climate-Warming Business as 'Anti-Social.'" *National Observer*, 26 April 2016: https://www.nationalobserver.com/2016/04/26/news/exxon-canadian-affiliate-slammed-anti-social-actions-causing-climate-change-1970.
– "Trudeau Liberals to Reimburse Enbridge for Hot Dogs over Pipeline Concerns." *National Observer*, 15 August 2016: http://www.nationalobserver.com/2016/08/15/news/trudeau-liberals-reimburse-enbridge-hot-dogs-over-pipeline-concerns.
Devine, Heather. "After the Spirit Sang: Aboriginal Canadians and Museum Policy in the New Millennium." In *How Canadians Communicate III: Contexts of Canadian Popular Culture*, edited by Bart Beaty, Derek Briton, Gloria Filax, and Rebecca Sullivan, 217–39. Athabaska: Athabaska Press 2010.
Dewing, Michael. *Federal Government Policy on Arts and Culture*. Ottawa: Parliament of Canada 2010: https://lop.parl.ca/Content/LOP/ResearchPublications/2008-41-e.pdf.
Dhamoon, Rita Kaur. "Re-presenting Genocide: The Canadian Museum of Human Rights and Settler Colonial Power." *Journal of Race, Ethnicity, and Politics* 1, no. 1 (2016): 5–30.
Diabo, Russell, and Shiri Pasternak. "First Nations under Surveillance." *The Media Co-Op*, 7 June 2011: http://www.mediacoop.ca/story/first-nations-under-surveillance/7434.

Dick, Beau. "The Coppers." In *Lalakenis/All Directions: A Journey of Truth and Unity*, edited by Scott Watson and Lorna Brown, 20–3. Vancouver: Morris and Helen Belkin Art Gallery, UBC 2014.
Ditmars, Hadani. "In a Notable Constellation, Canada Embraces Its Star." *New York Times*, 16 July 2002.
Ditta, Su. "Please Don't Touch the Art: Sex, Art and Controversy in Canada's Public Museums." In *Suggestive Poses: Artists and Critics Respond to Censorship*, edited by Lorraine Johnson, 61–80. Toronto: Photographers Workshop and the Riverbank Press 1997.
Dobbin, Murray. "Has Big Oil Hijacked Democracy?" *The Tyee*, 10 February 2014: https://thetyee.ca/Opinion/2014/02/10/Big-Oil-Democracy-Hijacked.
Douglas, Stan. "Afterword." In *Vancouver Anthology*, 2nd edition, edited by Stan Douglas, 303–6. Vancouver: Talon Books 2009.
– "Introduction." In *Vancouver Anthology*, 1st edition, edited by Stan Douglas, 11–22. Vancouver: Talon Books 1991.
– ed. *Vancouver Anthology*. 2nd edition. Vancouver: Talon Books 2009.
Dowling, Emma. "Introduction: Mobilisations, Interventions, and Cultural Policy." *Lateral* 1, no. 1 (2012): http://lateral.culturalstudiesassociation.org/issue1/content/dowling.html.
– Rodrigo Nunes, and Ben Trott. "Immaterial and Affective Labour: Explored." *Ephemera* 7, no. 1 (2007): 1–7.
Doxtator, Deborah. "The Implications of Canadian Nationalism for Aboriginal Cultural Autonomy." In *Curatorship: Indigenous Perspectives in Post-colonial Societies, Proceedings*, 56–69. Hull: Canadian Museum of Civilization with the Commonwealth Association of Museums 1996.
Drainies, Bronwyn. "Black Groups Protest African Show at 'Racist Ontario Museum.'" *Globe and Mail*, 24 March 1990.
Drimonis, Toula, "The Unbearable Whiteness of Being (Oblivious to Privilege)." *Ricochet. media*, 15 May 2017: https://ricochet.media/en/1820/the-unbearable-whiteness-of-being-oblivious-to-privilege.
Drury, Ivan. "The Rise of Philanthrocapitalism: What Passes for Progressive City Politics Today." *Briarpatch*, 1 September 2014: https://briarpatchmagazine.com/articles/view/the-rise-of-philanthrocapitalism.
Drury, John, and David Novelli. "Collective Joy and the Power of the Crowd." *Fabrica Blog*. Brighton: Fabrica Gallery 2011: http://www.sussex.ac.uk/profiles/92858.
D'Souza, Aruna. *Whitewalling: Art, Race and Protest in Three Acts*. New York: Badlands Unlimited 2018.
Dubin, Steven. *Displays of Power: Controversy in the American Museum from the Enola Gay to Sensation!* New York: NYU Press 2001.
Duncan, Carol, and Alan Wallach. *Civilizing Rituals: Inside Public Art Museums*. London and New York: Routledge 1995.
– "From the Princely Gallery to the Public Art Museum: The Louvre Museum and the National Gallery, London." In *Representing the Nation: A Reader*, edited by David Boswell and Jessica Evans, 304–31. New York and London: Routledge 1999.
– "The Universal Survey Museum." *Art History* 3, no. 4 (1980): 447–69.
Dupuis, Josée. "An Untold History of Resistance to Residential Schools." CBC *News*, 27 October 2016: http://www.cbc.ca/news/canada/montreal/resisting-residential-schools-1.3823181.

Durkheim, Emile. *The Elementary Forms of the Religious Life*. Translated by Joseph Ward Swain. New York: The Free Press [1912] 1965.
Dworkin, Mark, and Melissa Young, dirs, *Another World Is Possible*. Oley, PA: Bullfrog Films 2002.
Edge, Marc. "The Asper Slam on News Media." *The Tyee*, 23 November 2007: https://thetyee.ca/Mediacheck/2007/11/23/AsperSlamsMedia.
Editorial. "Just Say No to Anarchy." *Ottawa Citizen*, 2 November 2002, B7.
Editorial Staff (*News24*). "PE Residents Force Anti-Apartheid Museum to Close." *News24*, 5 May 2015: http://www.news24.com/SouthAfrica/News/PE-residents-force-anti-apartheid-museum-to-close-20140731.
Editorial Staff (*Time Magazine*). "*Time* Person of the Year: The Protester." *Time Magazine*, 14 December 2011: http://www.time.com/time/specials/packages/article/0,28804,2101745_2102132_2102373,00.html.
Editorial Staff (*Vancouver Sun*). "This Day in History: June 19, 1938." *Vancouver Sun*, 19 June 2012: http://www.vancouversun.com/news/This+history+June+1938/6806416/story.html.
Edmonds, Scott. "Asper Foundation's Human-Rights Museum Given Federal Kickstart." *Globe and Mail*, 18 April 2003, A5.
Ehrenreich, Barbara. *Dancing in the Streets*. New York: Picador 2006.
Eliadis, Pierre. "CMHR a Symbol for Dissent and Protest." *Winnipeg Free Press*, 24 September 2014.
Elliott, Justin. "The Origins of Occupy Wall Street Explained." *Salon Magazine*, 4 October 2011: https://www.salon.com/2011/10/04/adbusters_occupy_wall_st.
Ellison, Jenny. "Controversies in Context: Communication, Hot Topics and Museums in Canada." In *Hot Topics, Public Culture, Museums*, edited by Fiona Cameron and Lynda Kelly, 176–93. Newcastle upon Tyne: Cambridge Scholars Press 2010.
Emirbayer, Mustafa, and Chad Goldberg. "Pragmatism, Bourdieu, and Collective Emotions in Contentious Politics." *Theory and Society* 24 (December 2005): 469–518.
Enbridge. "Enbridge to Sponsor Coup de Pouce aux Familles Program at the Montreal Museum of Fine Arts." *Cision*, 27 June 2013: http://www.newswire.ca/news-releases/enbridge-to-sponsor-coup-de-pouce-aux-familles-program-at-the-montreal-museum-of-fine-arts-512664671.html.
English, Kathy. "Slutwalk and the Fact of the Art." *Toronto Star*, 12 December 2014.
Enwezor, Okwui. "The Production of Space as Artwork: Protocols of Community in the Work of *Le Group Amos* and *Huit Facettes*." In *Collectivism after Modernism: The Art of Social Imagination after 1945*, edited by Blake Stimson and Gregory Sholette, 223–51. Minneapolis: University of Minnesota Press 2007.
Equiterre. "Statement." (14 December 2009): http://www.stephentaylor.ca/2009/12/jumping-into-todays-climate-hoax.
Eurchuk, Reed. "Campbell Prevented from Speaking at Art Gallery." *The Republic of East Vancouver*, 27 June 2002, 4.
Evans, Mel. *Artwash: Big Oil and the Arts*. London: Pluto Press 2015.
Evans, Siân, Anna Perricci, and Amy Roberts. "'Why Archive?' and Other Important Questions Asked by Occupiers." In *Informed Agitation: Library and Information Skills in Social Justice Movements and Beyond*, edited by Melissa Morrone. Sacramento: Library Juice Press 2014.
Everett-Green, Robert. "Canada Council Dispenses Riches to Museums, Galleries Get $3.5-Million." *Globe and Mail*, 16 April 1998, D1.

Failler, Angela. "Hope without Consolation: Prospects for Critical Learning at the Canadian Museum for Human Rights." *Review of Education, Pedagogy and Cultural Studies* 37, nos 2/3 (2015): 227–50.
Failler, Angela, and Karen Sharma, "Shoal Lake 40's Living Museum, a Photo Essay." University of Winnipeg (23 July 2015): https://www.uwinnipeg.ca/csrg/projects/shoal-lake-photo-essay%20.html.
Failler, Angela, and Roger Simon. "Curatorial Practice and Learning from Difficult Knowledge." In *The Idea of a Human Rights Museum*, edited by Kathy Busby, Adam Muller, and Andrew Woodford, 165–79. Winnipeg: University of Manitoba Press 2015.
Fallding, Helen. "Toward Radical Transparency at the Canadian Museum for Human Rights: Lessons from Media Coverage during Construction." In *The Idea of a Human Rights Museum*, edited by Karen Busby, Adam Muller, and Andrew Woolford, 70–86. Winnipeg: University of Manitoba Press 2015.
Farah, May. "Arab-Canadians Cry Foul of Early Closure of Ottawa Exhibit," *The Daily Star*, 21 September 2003: http://www.16beavergroup.org/mtarchive/archives/000490.php.
Farber, Bernie. "Decades Later, Mercury Still Poisons These Native Reserves." *Huffpost*, 10 December 2012: http://www.huffingtonpost.ca/bernie-farber/mercury-poisoning-canada_b_2268748.html.
Feest, Christian. "The Glenbow Incident: The Spirit Sinks." *European Review of Native American Studies* 2, no. 1 (1987): 61–3.
Feigenbaum, Anna, Fabrian Frenzel, and Patrick McCurdy. *Protest Camps*. London: Zed Books 2013.
354 Felshin, Nina. *But Is It Art? The Spirit of Art as Activism*. Seattle: Bay Press 1994.
Ferguson, Derek. "Lawsuit by Indian Band Sours Olympic Art Launch." *Toronto Star*, 15 January 1988, A10.
Ferguson, Linda. "Strategy and Tactic: A Post-modern Response to the Modernist Museum." In *Hot Topics, Public Culture, Museums*, edited by Fiona Cameron and Lynda Kelly, 35–52. Newcastle upon Tyne: Cambridge Scholars Press 2010.
Finkelpearl, Tom. *What We Made: Conversations on Art and Social Cooperation*. Durham: Duke University Press 2013.
Firat, Begüm Özden, and Aylin Kuryel. *Cultural Activism*, vol. 21. Amsterdam: Rodopi 2011.
Firth-Eagland, Alissa. "Invisible Becoming." In *Momentarily: Learning from Mega-Events*, edited by Bik Van der Pol, Alissa Firth-Eagland, and Urban Subjects, 5–13. Vancouver: Western Front 2010: http://www.urbansubjects.org/images/learning_from_vancouver/Momentarily%20Learning%20from%20Mega-Events.pdf.
Fischer, Noah. "Agency in a Zoo: The Occupy Movement's Strategic Expansion to Art Institutions." *Field* 2 (winter 2015): 15–40: http://field-journal.com/issue-2/fischer.
Fisher, Graeme, and Andrew Witt. "Fabricating the Creative City: Public Art's New Terrain, Parts 1–3." *The Mainlander*, 3 January 2012: http://themainlander.com/2012/01/03/fabricating-the-creative-city-public-arts-new-terrain-part-13.
Fisher, Jean. "The Health of the People Is the Highest Law." *Third Text* 1, no. 2 (1987): 63–75.
Fisk, Robert. "Journalists Are under Fire for Telling the Truth." *The Independent*, 18 December 2002.
Fiskio, Janet. "Dancing at the End of the World: The Poetics of the Body in Indigenous Protest." In *Ecocriticism and Indigenous Studies: Conversations from Earth to Cosmos*,

ebook, edited by Salma Monani and Joni Adamson. np. New York and London: Routledge.
Flanagan, Tom. *Resource Industries and Security Issues in Northern Alberta*. Ottawa: Report Prepared for the Canadian Defence and Foreign Affairs Institute (2009): http://www.cdfai.org/PDF/Resource%20Industries%20and%20Security%20Issues%20in%20Northern%20Alberta.pdf.
Flood, Catherine. "Museums and Protest." *Victoria and Albert Museum* (blog), 1 July 2014: http://www.vam.ac.uk/blog/disobedient-objects/museums-and-protest.
Florida, Richard. *Cities and the Creative Class*. New York: Routledge 2005.
– *The New Urban Crisis: How Our Cities Are Increasing Inequality, Deepening Segregation, and Failing the Middle Class and What We Can Do about It*. New York: Basic Books 2017.
– *The Rise of the Creative Class: And How It's Transforming Work, Leisure, Community and Everyday Life*. New York: Basic Books 2002.
– *Who's Your City? How the Creative Economy Is Making Where to Live the Most Important Decision of Your Life*. Toronto: Vintage Canada 2009.
Forkert, Kirsten. "Tactical Media and Art Institutions: Some Questions." *Third Text* 22, no. 5 (September 2008): 589–98.
– "Transgression, Branding and National Identity." *Fuse* 29.1 (January 2006): 16–27.
Foster, Hal. *The Art-Architecture Complex*. London: Verso 2013.
Frank, Thomas. "Rocking for the Clampdown: Creativity, Corporations, and the Crazy Cacophony of the Experience Music Project." In *Commodification and Spectacle in Architecture*, edited by Williams S. Saunders, 60–77. Minneapolis: University of Minnesota Press 2005.
Frascina, Francis. *Art, Politics, and Dissent: Aspects of the Art Left in Sixties America*. Manchester: Manchester University Press 2000.
Fraser, Andrea. "L'1%, c'est moi." New York: Whitney Museum 2012: http://whitney.org/file_columns/0002/9848/andreafraser_1_2012whitneybiennial.pdf.
Fraser, Crystal, and Zoe Todd. "Decolonial Sensibilities: Indigenous Research and Engaging with Archives in Contemporary Colonial Canada." *L'Internationale*: http://www.internationaleonline.org/research/decolonising_practices/54_decolonial_sensibilities_indigenous_research_and_engaging_with_archives_in_contemporary_colonial_canada.
Fraser, Graham. "Danson Lived Dream," *Toronto Star*, 17 March 2000, A8.
Freeman, Alan. "Alberta's Gift to Culture." *Globe and Mail*, 7 June 2006.
– "Mr. Klein Goes to Washington with Oil Message." *Globe and Mail*, 28 June 2006, B9.
Freier, Amy. "Exhibiting Human Rights: Making the Means of Dignity Visible." PhD dissertation, Western University, 2018.
Frieling, Rudolph. "Introduction." In *The Art of Participation: 1950 to Now*, edited by Rudolph Frieling et al. New York: Thames and Hudson 2008.
Frieze. "Lick My Legs: Suffragette City." (17 June 2015): http://exploregram.com/lick-my-legs-suffragette-city-2015-by-lara-schnitger-is-an-installation.
Gale, Peggy, and A.A. Bronson, eds. *Museums by Artists*. Toronto: Art Metropole 1983.
Galloway, Gloria, and Shawna Richer. "Ottawa, Halifax on Lockdown in Preparation for Bush Visit." *Globe and Mail*, 30 November 2004, A4.
Gardenswartz, Jacob. "How Museums Are Quietly Resisting President Trump." *Vox*, 21 April 2017: https://www.vox.com/policy-and-politics/2017/4/21/15331340/museums-resistance-president-trump.
Garneau, David. "Extra-Rational Aesthetic Action and Cultural Decolonization." *Fuse Magazine*, September 2013.

– "Imaginary Spaces of Conciliation and Reconciliation." *West Coast Line: Reconcile This!* 74 (summer 2012): 28–38.
Garrard, Chris. "With Entry Changes and Oil Sponsorship, the Science Museum Has Lost Its Way." *Guardian*, 17 October 2016.
Gauvin, Kim. "CORRIDART Revisited: Excavating the Remains." *Journal of Canadian Art History* 18, no. 2 (1997): 6–67.
Gazette. "Americans Unaware That Canada Is Their Largest Oil Supplier." 28 June 2006, A19.
– "Canada Ranked 2nd Worst: Only Saudi Arabia Has Weaker Climate-Change Plan." 11 December 2008, A19.
Geddes, John. "How Stephen Harper Is Rewriting History." *Maclean's*, 29 July 2013: http://www.macleans.ca/news/canada/written-by-the-victors.
– "The Museum Is the Message: Federal Science Museum Offers a Polished Image of the Oil Sands." *Maclean's*, 19 December 2011: http://www.macleans.ca/news/canada/the-museum-is-the-message.
General News Media Research Team. "Research Post: The Evolving Landscape of Collecting Protest Material, Part I." *Issues and Advocacy*, 6 April 2017: https://issuesandadvocacy.wordpress.com/2017/04/06/research-post-the-evolving-landscape-of-collecting-protest-material-part-1.
Gessell, Paul. "Arab Art Show Gets Off to Rough Start." *Ottawa Citizen*, 19 October 2001.
– "City Budget Woes Threaten Funding." *Ottawa Citizen*, 6 February 2004, F10.
– "A Different Battle Brews; Contemporary Art Acquisitions Halted at War Museum." *Saskatoon Star-Phoenix*, 3 February 2009, C2.
356
– "Gallery Plan a Potential 'Disaster.'" *Ottawa Citizen*, 9 December 2006, F1.
– "Kahlo Gets Star Billing at Mexican Art show." *Ottawa Citizen*, 5 November 1999.
– "Mind Your Own Affairs, War Museum Boss Tells Senators." *Ottawa Citizen*, 14 June 2007, A1.
– "Museum Pulls Plug on Arab-Canadian Art Exhibit," *Ottawa Citizen*, 26 September 2001, A1.
Giebelhausen, Michaela. "Introduction." In *The Architecture of the Museum: Symbolic Structures, Urban Contexts*, edited by Michaela Giebelhausen, 1–14. Manchester: Manchester University Press 2003.
– "Symbolic Capital: The Frankfurt Museum Boom of the 1980s." In *The Architecture of the Museum: Symbolic Structures, Urban Contexts*, edited by Michaela Giebelhausen, 75–107. Manchester: Manchester University Press 2003.
Giles, David, and Jacqueline Wilson. "More Federal Funding for Remai Modern Art Gallery." *Global News*, 1 March 2017: https://globalnews.ca/news/3280887/more-federal-funding-for-remai-modern-art-gallery.
Gill, Alexandra. "Bartels: Facing a House Divided." *Globe and Mail*, 20 December 2000.
– "ROM Egyptian Art Gala Opens with Protest." *Globe and Mail*, 11 February 2000.
Gill, Parmbir, and Shozab Raza. "An Interview with Cornel West on Occupy, Obama and Marx." *Counterpunch*, 30 November 2012: https://www.counterpunch.org/2012/11/30/an-interview-with-cornel-west-on-occupy-obama-and-marx.
Gill, Rosalind, and Andy Pratt. "In the Social Factory? Immaterial Labour, Precariousness and Cultural Work." *Theory Culture & Society* 25, no. 7–8 (December 2008): 1–30.
Gillam, Robyn. *Hall of Mirrors: Museums and the Canadian Public*. Banff: Walter Phillips Gallery 2001.
Gledhill, Jim. "Collecting Institutions and Social Protest Movements in the 21st Century." *Social Movement Studies* 11, nos 3–4 (August–November 2012): 342–8.

Glenbow Museum. "Media Release: Imperial Oil Announces $4.0 Million Gift to Glenbow Museum." (9 February 2006): https://www.glenbow.org/media/GlenbowNews releaseFINALFeb9_000.pdf.
Glenn, Jane Matthews, and José Otero. "Canada and the Kyoto Protocol: An Aesop Fable." In *Climate Change and the Law*, edited by Erkki J. Hollo, Kati Kulovesi, and Michael Mehling. 489–508. New York: Springer 2013.
Global Ultra Luxury Faction (G.U.L.F.). "On Direct Action: An Address to Cultural Workers." *e-flux*, 25 June 2015: http://supercommunity.e-flux.com/texts/on-direct-action-an-address-to-cultural-workers.
Globe and Mail. "Artists Stage Rally to Protest Cutbacks in Cultural Budget." 18 March 1985.
– "Canadian Government Withheld Food from Hungry Aboriginal Kids in 1940s Nutritional Experiments." 16 July 2013.
– "Community Fights Plans for Logging on BC Island." 21 November 1984, N4.
– "Criticized by BC Indians, Mural Gets Home in PEI." 4 April 1973.
– "Cross Current: Museums." 7 September 1992.
– "Economic Summit '88: 29 Arrested in Demonstration before AGO Summit Luncheon." 22 June 1988.
– "Elderly Doukhobor Gets 10 Years in Castlegar Museum Arson Case." 4 October 1985.
– "Engage the Activists." 16 September 2009, A16.
– "For Our First Nations, New Museum a Monument to Hypocrisy." 24 September 2014.
– "Funding Campaign for Gallery Draws Fire." 12 April 1984, E1.
– "Gala Draws Protesters." 15 September 1984.
– "Gallery Bares All to Protest Bill C-54." 22 March 1988.
– "Gallery-Goers Harassed: 250 Picket on Mercury Pollution." 14 February 1976, 4.
– "Indian Leader Threatens to Dig Sir John A.'s Grave." 11 December 1978.
– "Indians Plan Their Own 'Museum' by Digging Up White Pioneers." 19 December 1978.
– "Indians Take Stand on Logging in Park." 22 October 1984.
– "Indians to Protest Archaeological Dig." 30 August 1977.
"Inuit Children Kept out of Schools to Protest Dropping Native Rights Thursday." 19 November 1981.
– "Little Reduction in Mercury Levels." 2 October 1976.
– "Natives Urge Boycott of Artifact Exhibition to Press Land Claims." 26 December 1986.
– "NS Indians Protest." 25 November 1981.
– "Our Beleaguered Museums and Galleries." 7 August 1995.
– "Protesters Urge Indians to Fight for Their Rights." 20 November 1981.
– "Splendid Setting Enhances VAG's Membership Drive." 26 October 1985.
– "VOW Keeps Silent Protest." 13 May 1963.
Godfrey, Stephen. "An Overwhelming Eyeful." *Globe and Mail*, 14 August 1990, C11.
Gold, William. "War Is Now Car Bombs, Landmines." *Calgary Herald*, 13 November 1995, A10.
Goldenberg, Suzanne. "Detroit's Mountains of Petroleum Coke Are 'Dirtier Than the Dirtiest Fuel.'" *Guardian*, 7 June 2013.
Golding, Viv, and Wayne Modest, eds. *Museums and Communities: Curators, Collection, and Collaboration*. London: Bloomsbury 2013.
Good, Carl. "Introduction: Ungoverned Specificities." In *The Effects of the Nation: Mexican Art in an Age of Globalization*, edited by Carl Good and John V. Waldron. Philadelphia: Temple University Press 2001.
Goodwin, Jeff, and James Jasper, eds. *Rethinking Social Movements: Structure, Meaning and Emotion*. Lanham, MD: Rowman & Littlefield 2004.

Goodwin, Jeff, James Jasper, and Francesca Polletta. *Passionate Politics: Emotions and Social Movements*. Chicago: University of Chicago Press 2001.
Gornick, Vivian. "Love and Anarchy: Emma Goldman's Passion for Free Expression Burns On." *The Chronicle of Higher Education*, 23 October 2011: http://chronicle.com/article/LoveAnarchy/129467.
Gould, Deborah. *Moving Politics: Emotion and* ACT UP*'s Fight against* AIDS. Chicago: University of Chicago Press 2009.
Government of Canada. "Caring for Sacred and Cultural Sensitive Objects." Canadian Conservation Institute 2015: http://canada.pch.gc.ca/eng/1448995219999.
Graeber, David. *Direct Action: An Ethnography*. Edinburgh and Oakland: AK Press 2009.
– "The New Anarchists." *The New Left Review* 13 (January–February 2002): 61–73.
– "On the Phenomenology of Giant Puppets: Broken Windows, Imaginary Jars of Urine, and the Cosmological Role of the Police in American Culture." An address to the Anthropology, Art, and Activism Seminar Series at Brown University's Watson Institute, 6 December 2005. Accessed 6 September 2017: https://libcom.org/files/puppets.pdf.
– *Revolutions in Reverse: Essays on Politics, Violence, Art, and Imagination*. London: Minor Compositions, 2012.
Graham, Stephen. *Cities under Siege: The New Military Urbanism*. London: Verso 2011.
Granatstein, J.L. "Paper Promises or Real Defence Purchases?" *Globe and Mail*, 4 July 2006.
– "The Peacekeeping Myth." *National Post*, 31 January 2007, A19.
Grant, Donald. "Indians End ROM Sit-In." *Globe and Mail*, 4 December 1976.
– "Museum Pressed to Return Remains to Grimsby Site: Ontario Promises End to Removal of Indian Bones." *Globe and Mail*, 2 December 1976.

Graney, Juris. "'It's Been a Long Time Coming': $121 Million Land Claim Settlement Struck with Lubicon Lake Band." *Edmonton Journal*, 24 October 2018.
Gray, Ken. "Florida Gives Ottawa Its Cool." *Ottawa Citizen*, 19 March 2009.
Gray, Mandi, and Karl Gardner. "(In)Visible Histories: Colonialism, Space and the Canadian Museum for Human Rights." *The Annual Review of Interdisciplinary Justice Research* (2016): 312–32.
Green, Jonathan. "Tarmageddon." *Daily Mail*, 9 June 2012.
Greenberg, Reesa. "Constructing the Canadian War Museum/Constructing the Landscape of a Canadian Identity." In *(Re)Visualizing National History: Museums and National Identities in Europe in the New Millennium*, edited by Robin Ostow, 183–99. Toronto: University of Toronto Press 2008.
Gregory, Helen, and Kirsty Robertson. "No Small Matter? Micromuseums as Critical Institutions." RACAR 43, no. 2 (2018): 89–101.
Grief, Amy. "Why Toronto's Slut Walk Is as Important as Ever." *blogTO*, 5 August 2016: http://www.blogto.com/city/2016/08/why_slutwalk_toronto_is_as_important_as_ever.
Griffin, Kevin. "Bob Rennie Donates Art Worth $12 Million to National Gallery in Ottawa." *Vancouver Sun*, 5 November 2017.
– "Gastown Riot Recreated in Contemporary Woodward's Photograph." *Vancouver Sun*, 5 January 2010.
– "Lalakenis Recounts Indigenous Journey That Shamed the Federal Government." *Vancouver Sun*, 14 January 2016: https://vancouversun.com/news/staff-blogs/lalakenis-recounts-indigenous-journey-that-shamed-the-federal-government.
– "Provincial Government Waits on Giving Another $50m to New Vancouver Art Gallery." *Vancouver Sun*, 6 July 2018: https://vancouversun.com/news/local-news/provincial-government-waits-on-giving-another-50m-to-new-vancouver-art-gallery.

– "Vancouver Art Gallery Seeks $100m from Feds for New $350m Home." *Vancouver Sun*, 3 April 2017.
Grindon, Gavin. "Art and Activism." *Art Monthly* 333 (February 2010): 9–12.
Grindon, Gavin and Catherine Flood. *Disobedient Objects*. London: V&A 2014.
Groves, Tim, and Martin Lukacs. "Canadian Spies Met with Energy Firms." *Guardian*, 9 October 2013.
– "Mounties Spied on Native Protest Groups." *Toronto Star*, 4 December 2011.
Groys, Boris. *Art Power*. Cambridge, MA: MIT Press, 2008.
Guasch, Anna Maria. "Global Museums versus Local Artists: Paradoxes of Identity between Local and Global Understandings." In *Learning from the Bilbao Guggenheim*, edited by Anna Maria Guasch and Joseph Zulaika, 120–32. Reno: Centre for Basque Studies, University of Nevada 2005.
Guasch, Anna Maria, and Joseph Zulaika, eds. *Learning from the Bilbao Guggenheim*. Reno: Centre for Basque Studies, University of Nevada 2005.
Guilbaut, Serge. "Lightning from the Past: Police, Pot, Public, and Stan Douglas." In *Stan Douglas:* Abbot & Cordova *7 August 1971*, 26–46. Vancouver: Arsenal Pulp Press 2011.
Guujaaw. "The Copper." In *Lalakenis/All Directions: A Journey of Truth and Unity*, edited by Scott Watson and Lorna Brown, 26–7. Vancouver: Morris and Helen Belkin Art Gallery 2014.
Ha, Tu Thanh, and Les Perreaux. "Anti-Protest Legislation Passes in Quebec." *Globe and Mail*, 18 May 2012: http://www.theglobeandmail.com/news/politics/quebecs-anti-protest-legislation-tramples-basic-rights-legal-experts/article2436933.
Habron, John D. "War Paint." *Globe and Mail*, 11 November 2000, D16. 359
Hage, Rawi, Laura Marks, and Jayce Salloum. *Open Letter on "The Lands within Me."* (1 October 2001): http://www.nettime.org/Lists-Archives/nettime-bold-0110/msg00004.html.
Haggo, Regina. "Women Whose Brilliance Knows No Boundaries" *The Spectator*, 21 July 2001, M15.
Haley, Bill. *The Canadian War Museum: Design Approach*. (8 May 2005): http://www.warmuseum.ca/app/DocRepository/12/About_the_Museum/haleye.pdf.
Hamilton, Michelle. *Collections and Objections: Aboriginal Material Culture in Southern Ontario*. Kingston and Montreal: McGill-Queen's University Press 2010.
Hanlon, Joseph. "Mercury and Tress." *New Scientist* 28 (October 1976): 226–9.
Hannah, Deirdre. "Estrogen Art." *Now Magazine*, 26 July–1 Aug 2001: https://nowtoronto.com/art-and-books/art/estrogen-art.
Hardt, Michael. "Immaterial Labor and Artistic Production." *Rethinking Marxism: A Journal of Economics, Culture & Society* 17, no. 2 (2005): 175–7.
– and Antonio Negri. *Empire*. Cambridge, MA: Harvard University Press 2000.
– *Multitude: War and Democracy in the Age of Empire*. New York: The Penguin Press 2004.
Harp, Rick. "Shoal Lake 40: Road to Reconciliation." *FundRazr*: https://fundrazr.com/810jw4?ref=ab_2YE09Pf6ZTc2YE09Pf6ZTc.
Harries, Kate. "Ministry Allows Ruin of Sacred Sites, Ipperwash Forum Told." *Globe and Mail*, 9 December 2005, A20.
Harris, Douglas C. "Condominium and the City: The Rise of Property in Vancouver." *Law & Social Inquiry* 36, no. 3 (2011): 694–726.
Harris, Steve. "All Yours? Buy an Inch, Buy an Admission, Buy a Membership, Buy Stock in 'Your' New Vancouver Art Gallery." *Fuse Magazine* (spring 1984): 276–80.

Harrison, Julia, and Bruce Trigger. "'The Spirit Sings' and the Future of Anthropology." *Anthropology Today* 4, no. 6 (December 1988): 6–10.
Hartley, John, ed. *Creative Industries*. Oxford: Blackwell Publishing 2005.
Harvey, David. *The New Imperialism*. Oxford: Oxford University Press 2003.
Hauser, Susan. "The Year of Emily." *Wall Street Journal*, 9 June 2001, W12.
Hedva, Johanna. "Sick Woman Theory." *maskmagazine.com*, January 2016: http://www.maskmagazine.com/not-again/struggle/sick-woman-theory.
Hein, Hilde. *Public Art: Thinking Museums Differently*. Oxford: AltaMira Press 2006.
Helms, Gesa, Marina Vishmidt, and Lauren Berlant. "Affect and the Politics of Austerity: An Interview with Lauren Berlant." *Variant* (2010) 39–40: http://www.variant.org.uk/39_49texts/berlant39_40.html.
Hennessy, Angela. "The RCMP Ambushed a Peaceful Mi-kmaq Anti-Fracking Protest." *Vice*, 18 October 2013: https://www.vice.com/en_ca/article/4w7ymm/did-the-rcmp-just-ambush-a-peaceful-native-anti-fracking-protest.
Hester, Jessica Leigh. "Curating Symbols of a Country in Turmoil." *citylab.com*, 19 January 2017: https://www.citylab.com/life/2017/01/museums-collecting-election-ephemera/513452.
Hewison, Robert. *Cultural Capital: The Rise and Fall of Creative Britain*. London: Verso 2014.
Hill, Richard William. "Graveyard and Giftshop: Fighting over the McMichael Canadian Art Collection." In *Beyond Wilderness: The Group of Seven, Canadian Identity and Contemporary Art*, edited by John O'Brian and Peter White, 211–16. Kingston and Montreal: McGill-Queen's University Press 2007.
Hobbs, Alegra. "Galleries to Close on Inauguration Day to Protest 'Normalization' of Trump." *Dnainfo.com*, 18 January 2017: https://www.dnainfo.com/new-york/20170118/lower-east-side/art-strike-gallery-closures-inauguration-protest-march-rally.
Hodgins, Peter, and Peter Thompson. "Taking the Romance out of Extraction: Contemporary Canadian Artists and the Subversion of the Romantic/Extractive Gaze." *Environmental Communication* 5, no. 4 (fall 2011): 393–410.
Hogben, David, and Neal Hall. "Protesters Abuse Police: Woodward's Squatters Confront Officers after Possessions Thrown in Garbage." *Vancouver Sun*, 24 September 2002, B4.
Holmes, Brian. "The Flexible Personality: For a New Cultural Critique." *Eipcp*, January 2002: http://eipcp.net/transversal/1106/holmes/en.
Holmes, Kristy A. "Imagining and Visualizing 'Indianness' in Trudeauvian Canada: Joyce Wieland's 'The Far Shore' and 'True Patriot Love.'" RACAR 35, no. 2 (2010): 47–64.
– "Negotiating Citizenship: Joyce Wieland's *Reason over Passion*." In *The Sixties: Passion, Politics, and Style*, edited by Dimitry Anastakis, 42–70. Kingston and Montreal: McGill-Queen's University Press 2008.
Hopkins, Candice. "In Memoriam: Beau Dick (1955–2017)." *Documenta 14* (2017): http://www.documenta14.de/en/notes-and-works/17052/in-memoriam-beau-dick-1955-2017-.
Hopkins, Owen. "Museums Need to Focus Less on Collecting Headlines." *Dezeen.com*, 20 July 2018: https://www.dezeen.com/2018/07/20/museums-rapid-response-collecting-trump-baby-blimp-opinion-owen-hopkins.
Houde, Isabelle. "Les carrés rouges entrent au Musée de la civilisation." *Le Soleil*, 7 January 2015: http://www.lapresse.ca/le-soleil/arts-et-spectacles/expositions/201501/06/01-4833037-les-carres-rouges-entrent-au-musee-de-la-civilisation.php.
Howe, Miles. *Debriefing Elsipogtog: The Anatomy of a Struggle*. Toronto: Fernwood Publishing 2015.

Howells, Richard, Andreea Deciu Ritivoi, and Judith Modell, eds. *Outrage: Art, Controversy, and Society*. New York: Palgrave 2012.
Huffington Post. "Most Boring City in Canada Award Goes to Ottawa," *Huffington Post Canada*, 24 May 2013: http://www.huffingtonpost.ca/2013/05/24/most-boring-city-canada-ottawa_n_3333161.html.
– "Pipeline Art Show Permit Pulled." (17 April 2013): http://www.huffingtonpost.ca/2013/04/17/anti-pipeline-art-show-calgary-city-hall_n_3101092.html.
Hume, Christopher. "Stephen Harper Is Blind to Science." *Toronto Star*, 13 July 2012.
Hume, Mark. "Hijacking the Homeless: True Street People Would Not Know How to Organize Strategic Strikes or Issue Press Releases." *National Post*, 29 October 2002, B1.
Hunt, Stephen. "Alberta Takes over US Capital: Special Events to Sell Province's Virtues." *Calgary Herald*, 26 June 2006, A1.
Hunter, Andrew. "Why I Quit the Art Gallery of Ontario: Former Canadian-Art Curator Andrew Hunter Explains." *Toronto Star*, 3 October 2017: https://www.thestar.com/entertainment/visualarts/2017/10/03/andrew-hunter-why-i-quit-the-art-gallery-of-ontario.html.
Hutcheon, Linda. *Irony's Edge: The Theory and Politics of Irony*. London and New York: Routledge 1994.
Ibbitson, John. "'Radical Groups' Spur Tories to Speed Pipeline Review Process." *Globe and Mail*, 9 January 2012.
Ilyniak, Natalia. "Mercury Poisoning in Grassy Narrows: Environment Injustice, Colonialism, and Capitalist Expansion in Canada." *McGill Sociological Review* 4 (February 2014): 43–66.
Imperial War Museum, *Anti-War Protest Discussional Forum*. (2013): http://www.hangingout.org.uk/anti_war_forum.htm.
Indigenous Peoples Solidarity Movement Ottawa. "The People's Exhibition of Barrick at the Museum of Nature!" (17 April 2012): https://ipsmo.wordpress.com/tag/mining-watch-canada.
Insurrectionary Anarchists of the Coast Salish Territories. "Premier's Speech Shut Down at the Vancouver Art Gallery." [website no longer available; last accessed 2005].
Ivens, Andy, and Greg Middleton. "Judge Sets Protesters Free and Gives Them Each $100." *Province*, 8 November 2002, A13.
Ivison, John. "Radical US Environmentalist Calls Trudeau 'Stunning Hypocrite.'" *National Post*, 20 April 2017.
Jacks, David. "Picking and Choosing: The Unintentional Side Effects of the Canadian Museum for Human Rights." *The Uniter*, 24 September 2014: http://uniter.ca/view/picking-and-choosing.
Jackson, Shannon. "Counter-Carnival in a Performance-Friendly World." In EN MAS': *Carnival and Performance Art of the Caribbean*, edited by Claire Tancons and Krista Thompson. ICI Press 2016.
– *Social Works: Performing Art, Supporting Publics*. London and New York: Routledge 2011.
Jameson, Fredric. *Archaeologies of the Future: The Desire Called Utopia and Other Science Fictions*. London: Verso 2005.
– *The Cultural Turn: Selected Writings on the Postmodern, 1983–1998*. London: Verso 1998.
Janes, Robert R. "Crediting the First Blockbuster." *National Post*, 1 November 1998, 8.
– *Museums in a Troubled World: Renewal, Irrelevance or Collapse?* London and New York: Routledge 2009.

– *Museums without Borders: Selected Writings of Robert R. Janes.* Abingdon and New York: Routledge 2016.

Janes, Robert R., and Richard Sandell. "Call for Chapters: A New Book on Museums and Activism." Accessed 6 September 2017: https://www2.le.ac.uk/departments/museumstudies/AboutUs/people/Prof%20Richard%20Sandell/CFPMuseumsandActivismfinal.pdf.

Jasper, James. *The Art of Moral Protest: Culture, Biography, and Creativity in Social Movements.* Chicago and London: University of Chicago Press 1997.

Jasper, James, and J.D. Poulsen. "Recruiting Strangers and Friends: Moral Shocks and Social Networks in Animal Rights and Anti-Nuclear Protest." *Social Problems* 42, no. 4 (1995): 493–512.

Jay, Martin. *Downcast Eyes: The Denigration of Vision in Twentieth-Century French Thought.* Berkeley: University of California Press 1993.

Jenkins, Barbara. "Toronto's Cultural Renaissance." *Canadian Journal of Communication* 30, no. 2 (2005): 169–86.

Jessup, Lynda. "Bushwhackers in the Gallery: Antimodernism and the Group of Seven." In *Antimodernism and Artistic Experience: Policing the Boundaries of Modernity*, edited by Lynda Jessup, 130–52. Toronto, University of Toronto Press 2000.

Johnson, Lorraine. "Introduction." In *Suggestive Poses: Artists and Critics Respond to Censorship*, edited by Lorraine Johnson, 5–7. Toronto: Toronto Photographers Workshop and Riverbank Press 1997.

– ed. *Suggestive Poses: Artists and Critics Respond to Censorship.* Toronto: Toronto Photographers Workshop and Riverbank Press 1997.

Johnston, Jude. "V.A.L. at V.A.G." *Fuse Magazine* (spring 1984): 275.

Jones, Jonathan. "Slick Art Sponsorship: Why Shouldn't BP Pour Oil Money into the Tate?" *Guardian*, 19 December 2011.

Jordan, John. "The Art of Necessity: The Subversive Imagination of Anti-Road Protest and Reclaim the Streets." In *DIY Culture: Party and Protest in Nineties Britain*, edited by George McKay, 129–51. London and New York: Verso 1998.

Jordan, John, and Jennifer Whitney. "Resistance Is the Secret of Joy." *New Internationalist* 138 (September 2001): https://newint.org/features/2001/09/05/secret.

Jordan, Tim. *Activism! Direct Action, Hacktivism and the Future of Society.* London: Reaktion Books 2012.

Justice, Daniel Heath. *Our Fire Survives the Storm: A Cherokee Literary History.* Minneapolis, University of Minnesota Press 2006.

Kamping-Carder, Leigh. "At the Gastown Riot." *The Walrus*, 12 July 2009: https://thewalrus.ca/at-the-gastown-riot.

Kane, Laura. "Occupy Vancouver Camps Out at Art Gallery." *Vancouver Sun*, 17 October 2011.

Karp, Ivan, and Corinne A. Kratz. "The Interrogative Museum." In *Museum as Process: Translating Local and Global Knowledges*, edited by Raymond Silverman, 279–98. London: Routledge 2015.

Karp, Ivan, and Steven D. Lavine, eds. *Exhibiting Cultures: The Poetics and Politics of Museum Display.* Washington and London: Smithsonian Institution Press 1991.

Katz-Rosene, Ryan. "The Rise of Reactionary Environmentalism in the Tar Sands." In *A Line in the Tar Sands: Struggles for Environmental Justice*, edited by Joshua Kahn Russell, Stephen d'Arcy, Tony Weis, and Toban Black, 24–43. Oakland: PM Press 2014.

Kay, Barbara. "Ottawa Sex Exhibition Is an Issue of Waste, Not Prudery." *National Post*, 20 May 2012.

Kay, Jonathan. "Every Identity-Politics Activist Known to Humanity Is Attacking Canada's Human Rights Museum." *National Post*, 21 September 2014.
– "The Problem with Richard Florida." *National Post*, 10 March 2009, A15.
Kearney, Cathy. "Vancouver Real Estate Magnate Donates $12 Million in Art to the National Gallery of Canada." CBC News, 10 May, 2017.
Keller, James. "Art Gallery Expected to Continue Protest Tradition." Canadian Press/CTV, 7 January 2010: http://www.ctvolympics.ca/about-vancouver/news/newsid=25009.html.
Kelly, Deirdre. "Banned Work Takes to the Street: Maxi-Pad Robe Deemed 'Offensive.'" *Globe and Mail*, 30 September 1999.
Kenneally, Rhona Richman, and Johanne Sloan, eds. *Expo 67: Not Just a Souvenir*. Toronto: University of Toronto Press 2010.
Kennedy, Randy. "Two Groups Scuffle amid Art inside a Minneapolis Museum." *New York Times*, 27 February 2017.
Kershaw, Baz. "Ecoactivist Performance: The Environment as Partner in Protest?" *TDR* 46, no. 1 (spring 2002): 118–30.
Kester, Grant. *Conversation Pieces: Community and Communication in Modern Art*. Los Angeles: University of California Press 2004.
– *The One and the Many: Contemporary Collaborative Art in a Global Context*. San Diego: Duke University Press 2011.
Khan, Sheema. "We Sell the Charter to Muslim Countries – Let's Apply It Here." *Globe and Mail*, 4 May 2005, A25.
Kilibarda, Konstantin. "Lessons from #Occupy in Canada: Contesting Space, Settler Consciousness and Erasures within the 99%." *Journal of Critical Globalisation Studies* 5 (2012): 24–41.

Killy, George. "Message from the Chair 2003." In *Annual Report 2003*, 4–5. Vancouver: Vancouver Art Gallery 2003.
– "Message from the Chair 2004." In *Annual Report 2004*. Vancouver: Vancouver Art Gallery 2004.
– "Message from the Chair 2005." In *Annual Report 2005*. Vancouver: Vancouver Art Gallery 2005.
Kines, Lindsay. "Royal BC Museum Aims to Preserve a Montage of Tent-City Life." *Victoria Times Colonist*, 10 August 2016: https://www.timescolonist.com/news/local/royal-b-c-museum-aims-to-preserve-a-montage-of-tent-city-life-1.2319714.
Kinew, Wab. "Human Rights Museum Needs to Act on First Nations Right to Water." *CBC News*, 10 July 2014): http://www.cbc.ca/news/indigenous/human-rights-museum-needs-to-act-on-first-nations-right-to-water-1.2703052.
Kino, Carol. "Welcome to the Museum of My Stuff." *New York Times*, 18 February 2007.
Kino-nda-niimi Collective. *The Winter We Danced: Voices from the Past, the Future, and the Idle No More Movement*. Winnipeg: ARP Books 2014.
Kirbyson, Geoff. "Rights Museum Seen as Crucial." *Winnipeg Free Press*, 16 May 2006, 6.
Klanten, Robert, Matthias Hubner, and Alain Bieber, eds. *Art and Agenda: Political Art and Activism*. Berlin: Gestalten Verlag 2011.
Klein, Naomi. "The Bonding Properties of Tear Gas." www.naomiklein.org, 25 April 2001. Accessed 14 September 2015: http://www.naomiklein.org/articles/2001/04/bonding-properties-tear-gas.
– "Canada's Founding Myths Hold Us Back from Addressing Climate Change." *Globe and Mail*, 23 September 2016.
– "Dancing the World into Being: A Conversation with Idle No More's Leanne Simpson."

Yes Magazine, 5 March 2013: http://www.yesmagazine.org/peace-justice/dancing-the-world-into-being-a-conversation-with-idle-no-more-leanne-simpson.
– *This Changes Everything: Capitalism vs. the Climate*. Toronto: Knopf Canada 2014.
Klepac, Walter. "The Art of Dissent." *Canadian Forum* 56, no. 669 (March 1977): 5–8.
Knelman, Martin. "Holocaust Memorial in Ottawa Corrects 70-Year Mistake." *Toronto Star*, 14 May 2014.
– "Museum Caught in Backlash," *Toronto Star*, 25 April 2005, AO3.
Koenig, Peter. "Creative Industries: The Cool Economy; Is Chris Smith More Vital Than Gordon Brown?" *Independent*, 15 February 1998: http://www.independent.co.uk/news/business/creative-industries-the-cool-economy-is-chris-smith-more-vital-than-gordon-brown-1144798.html.
Koutsoukis, Jason. "The Night When Tahrir Square Exploded in Joy." *Sydney Morning Herald*, 13 February 2011.
Krauss, Rosalind. "The Cultural Logic of the Late Capitalist Museum." *October* 54 (autumn 1990): 3–17.
Kreps, Christina. "Museum Anthropology in the Age of Engagement." Unpublished paper presented and circulated at Museum Futures, Montreal, 2017.
Kritzwiser, Kay. "Another Age of Revolution." *Globe and Mail*, 29 March 1975.
– "Are Museums the Next Target for Youth?" *Globe and Mail*, 7 February 1970.
Kunzig, Robert. "The Canadian Oil Boom." *National Geographic*, March 2009: http://ngm.nationalgeographic.com/2009/03/canadian-oil-sands/kunzig-text.
Kuus, Merje. "Cosmopolitan Militarism? Spaces of NATO Expansion." *Environment and Planning A* 41 (2009): 545–62.

Labossiere, Robert. "Guest Post: Bartels vs. Rennie and the Vancouver Art Gallery." *View on Canadian Art*, 27 August 2012: http://viewoncanadianart.com/2012/08/27/guest-post-bartels-vs-rennie-and-the-vancouver-art-gallery.
Laboucan-Massimo, Melina. "Awaiting Justice: The Ceaseless Struggle of the Lubicon Cree." In *A Line in the Tar Sands: Struggles for Environmental Justice*, edited by Joshua Kahn Russell, Stephen d'Arcy, Tony Weis, and Toban Black, 91–6. Oakland: PM Press 2014.
Lacy, Suzanne. *New Genre Public Art*. Seattle: Bay Press 1994.
Laghi, Brian, and Jeff Sallotalan Freeman. "Bush Gets Along Nicely with Martin and the Protests ... " *Globe and Mail*, 1 December 2004.
Lalakenis/All Directions: A Journey of Truth and Unity. (16 January–17 April 2016): http://belkin.ubc.ca/exhibitions/lalakenis-all-directions-journey-of-truth-and-unity.
Lamoureux, Mack. "How 4Chan's Worst Trolls Pulled Off the Heist of the Century." *Vice*, 11 March 2017: https://www.vice.com/en_us/article/d7eddj/4chan-does-first-good-thing-pulls-off-the-heist-of-the-century1.
Lannon, Valerie. "From the Red Power Movement to Idle No More." *socialist.ca*, 23 August 2013: http://www.socialist.ca/node/1872.
Lash, Scott, and Celia Lury. *Global Culture Industry: The Mediation of Things*. Cambridge, UK: Polity 2007.
Lauder, Adam. "Slasher Mary." *Canadian Art* 33, no. 3 (fall 2016): 60–1.
Laurence, Robin. "Iconic Artists Together at Last." *Georgia Straight*, 13–20 June 2002, 65, 76.
Lawlor, Allison. "Museum Backpedals, Will Show Arab Art." *Globe and Mail*, 28 September 2001.
Lazzarato, Maurizio. "Immaterial Labour." In *Radical Thought in Italy*, edited by Paolo

Virno and Michael Hardt, translated by Paul Colilli and Ed Emory, 132–46. Minneapolis: University of Minnesota Press 1996.
– "The Misfortunes of the 'Artistic Critique' and of Cultural Employment." In *Critique of Creativity: Precarity, Subjectivity and Resistance in the "Creative Industries,"* edited by Gerald Raunig, Gene Ray, and Ulf Wuggenig, 41–56. London: Mayfly 2011.
Leahy, Stephen. "Canada's Environmental Activists Seen as 'Threat to National Security.'" *Guardian*, 14 February 2013.
Le Bon, Gustave. *The Crowd: A Study of the Popular Mind*, 2nd edition. Dunwoody, GA: N.S. Berg 1968.
Lederman, Marsha. "Artists to Have Say in Gallery's New Home." *Globe and Mail*, 13 December 2012.
– "Big Name Artists Square Off over the Vancouver Art Gallery." *Globe and Mail*, 13 October 2012.
– "Building a Mystery: Vancouver Art Gallery to Finally Reveal Its Long-Delayed New Expansion Design." *Globe and Mail*, 26 September 2015.
– "D'Arcy Levesque: The Man Who Holds the Purse Strings for Enbridge's Support for the Arts." *Globe and Mail*, 10 July 2012.
– "Is No News Good News for the New Vancouver Art Gallery Building?" *Globe and* Mail, 30 March 2017.
– "Three History-Making Exhibitions of Indigenous Art and Culture Open in BC." *Globe and Mail*, 25 April 2018: https://www.theglobeandmail.com/arts/art-and-architecture/article-three-history-making-exhibitions-of-indigenous-art-and-culture-open-in.
Lee, Betty. "The Year of the Miracles at AGO." *Globe and Mail*, 26 September 1970: 25.
Léger, Marc. "Afterthoughts on Engaged Art Practice: ATSA and the State of Emergency." *Art Journal* 70, no. 2 (summer 2011): 50–65.
– "The Non-Productive Role of the Artist: The Creative Industries in Canada." *Third Text* 24, no. 5 (2010): 557–70.
Lehrer, Erica. "Thinking through the Canadian Museum for Human Rights." *American Quarterly* 67, no. 4 (December 2015): 1195–216.
Lehrer, Erica, and Cynthia Milton. "Introduction: Witnesses to Witnessing." In *Curating Difficult Knowledge: Violent Pasts in Public Places*, 1–22. New York: Palgrave, 2013.
LeMenager, Stephanie. *Living Oil: Petroleum Culture in the American Century*. Oxford: Oxford University Press 2014.
Lett, Dan. "Measured Museum Debate Welcome." *Winnipeg Free Press*, 6 September 2011.
Levin, Laura, and Kim Solga, "Building Utopia: Performance and the Fantasy of Urban Renewal in Contemporary Toronto." *TDR: The Drama Review* 53, no. 3 (fall 2009): 37–53.
Lewis, John. *Walking with the Wind: A Memoir of the Movement*. New York: Simon and Schuster 2015.
Ley, David. "Artists, Aestheticisation and the Field of Gentrification." *Urban Studies* 40, no. 12 (2003): 2527–44.
Liberate Tate. "Confronting the Institution in Performance: Liberate Tate's Hidden Figures." *Performance Research* 20, no. 4 (2015): 78–84.
Libin, Kevin. "Climate 'Debt' Comes Due." *National Post*, 10 October 2009, A1.
Linenthal, Edward T., and Tom Englehardt, eds. *History Wars: The Enola Gay and Other Battles for the American Past*. New York: Metropolitan Books 1996.
Linsley, Johanna. "How to Write Protest." *activate* 1, no. 1 (spring 2011): 1–14: http://

www.thisisactivate.net/thisisac_roeham/wp-content/uploads/2011/05/Linsley-How-to-Write-Protest.pdf.

Lippard, Lucy. "Biting the Hand: Artists and Museums in New York since 1969." In *Alternative Art New York*, edited by Julie Ault. Minneapolis: University of Minnesota Press 2002.

– *Undermining: A Wild Ride through Land Use, Politics, and Art in the Changing West*. London and New York: New Press 2014.

Littman, Sol. "Controversy at the McMichael Gallery." *Canadian Forum* LXL, no. 716 (March 1982): 20–1, 29.

Livingstone, Phaedra. "Controversy as Catalyst: Administrative Framing, Public Perception, and the Late-Twentieth-Century Exhibitionary Complex in Canada." In *Museums and the Past: Constructing Historical Consciousness*, edited by Viviane Gosselin and Phaedra Livingstone, 181–205. Vancouver: UBC Press 2016.

Loewe, Sebastian. "Basically Ignore the Exhibition." *Field* 2 (fall 2015). http://field-journal.com/issue-2/loewe-2.

Logan, Tricia. "National Memory and Museums: Remembering Settler Colonial Genocide of Indigenous Peoples in Canada." In *Remembering Genocide*, edited by Nigel Eltringham and Pam Maclean, 112–30. London and New York: Routledge 2014.

Lonetree, Amy. *Decolonizing Museums: Representing Native America in National and Tribal Museums*. Chapel Hill: University of North Carolina Press 2012.

Lord, Barry. "Memo." Lord Cultural Resources (12 December 2012): https://www.theglobeandmail.com/news/british-columbia/article6588427.ece/BINARY/Lord+Cultural+Resources+analysis+of+VAG+multi-site+proposal.

Lord, Gail Dexter. "The 'Bilbao Effect': From Poor Port to Must-See City." *The Art Newspaper* 184 (October 2007): http://www.lord.ca/Media/TheArtNewspaper32-33 Museums.pdf.

Lord Cultural Resources. *National Aboriginal Art Gallery*. (2005): https://www.lord.ca/projects/project-experience/national-aboriginal-art-gallery.

Lou, Ethan, and Alistair Sharp. "Canada Oil Pipeline Spills 200,000 Liters on Aboriginal Land." *Reuters*, 23 January 2017: http://www.reuters.com/article/us-canada-pipeline-leak/canada-oil-pipeline-spills-200000-liters-on-aboriginal-land-idUSKBN1572UJ.

LSE Library Services. "The Women's Library Suffrage Collection," VADS: http://www.vads.ac.uk/collections/WLS.html.

Luke, Timothy. *Museum Politics: Power Plays at the Exhibition*. Minneapolis: University of Minnesota Press 2002.

– "Nuclear Reactions: The (Re)Presentation of Hiroshima at the National Air and Space Museum." In *Museums and Their Communities*, edited by Sheila Watson, 197–212. London and New York: Routledge 2007.

Lyons, Steve. "*Disobedient Objects*: Towards a Museum Insurgency." *Journal of Curatorial Studies* 7, no. 1 (2018): 2–31.

– "Life and Times of Woodward's." *Vancouver Sun*, 20 September 2002, A5.

– "Old Lady of Hastings a Rich Part of City's Lore." *Vancouver Sun*, 20 September 2002, A4.

MacAndrew, Barbara. "Native Art Honoured at Festival." *Globe and Mail*, 23 June 1997.

McAree, J.V. "Modernist Art Regarded as Racket." *Globe and Mail*, 28 March 1940, 6.

McArthur, Greg, Kate Taylor, and Jacquie McNish. "Crystal Myths: Behind the ROM's Philanthropic Façade." *Globe and Mail*, 27 March 2015.

McCarthy, Pearl. "Art and Artists: This Argument Shows a Need for Freedom." *Globe and Mail*, 6 September 1958, 16.

– “Art Criticism Vigorously Defended by Massey.” *Globe and Mail*, 1 October 1949, 5.
McClellan, Andrew. *The Art Museum from Boullée to Bilbao*. Oakland: University of California Press 2008.
McCracken, Krista. “Archives as Activism.” *Activehistory.ca*, 10 April 2017: http://activehistory.ca/2017/04/archives-as-activism.
– “Ten Books to Contextualize Reconciliation in Archives, Museums and Public History.” *Activehistory.ca*, 17 October 2016: http://activehistory.ca/2016/10/ten-books-to-contextualize-reconciliation-in-archives-museums-and-public-history.
McCready, A.L. “Tie a Yellow Ribbon ’Round Public Discourse, National Identity and the War: Neoliberal Militarization and the Yellow Ribbon Campaign in Canada.” *Topia* 23/24 (2010): 28–51.
MacDonald, George F. “Museum of Human Rights.” *Globe and Mail*, 23 January 1999, D6.
MacDonald, Sharon. “Museums, National, Postnational and Transcultural Identities.” *Museum and Society* 1, no. 1 (2003): 1–16.
– *The Politics of Display: Museums, Science, Culture*. London and New York: Routledge 1998.
MacDonald, Sharon, and Gordon Fyfe, eds. *Theorizing Museums*. London: Blackwell 1996.
McDowell, Adam. “New Spot to Park the Carrs; Vancouver Renos; Gallery Hopes for Visionary Architect.” *National Post*, 7 July 2008, AL3.
McGuinty, David. “Portrait Gallery Move Paints a Grim Picture.” *Ottawa Citizen*, 9 December 2006, B7.
McKay, George. DIY *Culture: Party & Protest in Nineties Britain*. London and New York: Verso 1998.
McKay, Ian, and Jamie Swift. *Warrior Nation: Rebranding Canada in an Age of Anxiety*. Toronto: Between the Lines 2012.
McKee, Yates. *Strike Art: Contemporary Art and the Post-Occupy Condition*. London and New York: Verso 2016.
Mackey, Eva. *The House of Difference: Cultural Politics and National Identity in Canada*. Toronto: University of Toronto Press 2002.
Mackie, John. “It’s Vancouver, but Not as We Know It; Our City Would Have Looked Very Different Had These Plans Gone Ahead.” *Vancouver Sun*, 31 May 2008, F1.
Mclean, Archie. “Protesting ‘Tourists’ Want Albertans to Care about Climate.” *Edmonton Journal*, 6 October 2009, A2.
McLean, Fiona. “Museums and the Construction of National Identity: A Review.” *International Journal of Heritage Studies* 3, no. 4 (1998): 244–52.
Maclean’s. “The Gentrification War in East Vancouver.” (2 April 2003): http://www.macleans.ca/news/canada/violent-protesters-go-off-menu.
McLellan, L. Hudson. “Contemporary Settler Colonialism: Media Framing of Indigenous Collective Action in Elsipogtog, Mi’kma’ki.” Honours thesis, Dalhousie University, 20 April 2015.
MacLeod, Cameron. “W2 Arts Hub Locked out of Woodward’s.” *24hrs/Vancouver*, 20 December 2012: http://vancouver.24hrs.ca/2012/12/19/W2-arts-hub-locked-out-of-Woodward%27s.
Macleod, Suzanne. “Civil Disobedience and Political Agitation: The Art Museum as a Site of Protest in the Early Twentieth Century.” *Museum and Society* 5.1 (July 2006): 44–57.
– “Introduction.” In *Reshaping Museum Space: Architecture, Design, Exhibitions*, edited by Suzanne Macleod, 1–8. New York and London: Routledge 2005.

– “Rethinking Museum Architecture: Towards a Site-Specific History of Production and Use.” In *Reshaping Museum Space: Architecture, Design, Exhibitions*, edited by Suzanne Macleod, 9–25. New York and London: Routledge 2005.
McLoughlin, Moira. *Museums and the Representation of Native Canadians: Negotiating the Borders of Culture*. New York: Taylor and Francis 1999.
McMartin, Pete. “Woodward’s Opens Door to Cutting-Edge Condo Living.” *Vancouver Sun*, 8 April 2006.
MacMillan, Margaret. *The Uses and Abuses of History*. ebook. Toronto: Penguin Canada 2008.
– “Memory Fails: Whom Should We Trust to Tell Us the Truth about the Past.” *National Post*, 12 April 2008, A22.
McNally, David. *Another World Is Possible: Globalization and Anti-Capitalism*. Winnipeg: Arbeiter Ring 2002.
McQuaig, Linda. “Canadian ‘Peacekeeping’ Troops in Afghanistan: Keep Pearson Out of It.” *Toronto Star*, 5 February 2008.
McRae, Don. “CRA Audits of Charities Look Fair but Feel Foul.” *Toronto Star*, 5 April 2015.
McRobbie, Angela. *Be Creative: Making a Living in the New Culture Industries*. London: Polity 2016.
– “‘Everyone Is Creative’: Artists as New Economy Pioneers?” *Open Democracy*, 29 August 2001: http://www.opendemocracy.net/node/652.
– “Re-thinking Creative Economy as Radical Social Enterprise.” *Angela McRobbie: Sociology of Culture*, 18 November 2010: http://www.variant.org.uk/pdfs/issue41/amcrobbie41.pdf.

McSheffrey, Elizabeth. “Trudeau Says Pipelines Will Pay for Canada’s Transition to a Green Economy.” *National Observer*, 2 March 2016): https://www.nationalobserver.com/2016/03/02/news/trudeau-says-pipelines-will-pay-canadas-transition-green-economy.
McTavish, Lianne. “The Torrington Gopher Hole Museum: A Model Institution.” In *Museums and the Past: Constructing Historical Consciousness*, edited by Viviane Gosselin and Phaedra Livingstone, 60–77. Vancouver: UBC Press 2016.
McTavish, Lianne, and Susan Ashley, Heather Igloliorte, Andrea Terry, and Kirsty Robertson. “Critical Museum Theory/Museum Studies in Canada: A Dialogue.” *Acadiensis* 46, no. 2 (2017): 223–41.
Maharawal, Manissa McCleave. “Occupy Wall Street and a Radical Politics of Inclusion.” *The Sociological Quarterly* 54 no. 2 (spring 2013): 177–81.
Mahoney, Jill. “Angry Ranchers Protest Oil Law: Alberta Legislation a Profit Killer, Farmers Say.” *Globe and Mail*, 20 May 1999.
– “Kyoto Protest Angers Klein.” *Globe and Mail*, 12 April 2002.
Margolis, Michael, ed. *Free Expression, Public Support, and Censorship: Examining Government’s Role in the Arts in Canada and the United States*. Lanham, NY, and London: University Press of America 1994.
Maloney, S. Timothy. “The Canadian Commitment to Culture.” In *Report of the Working Group of Cultural Policy for the 21st Century*, 20–9. Ottawa: Canadian Conference of the Arts 1999.
Markusoff, Jason. “Energy Exports Generated Revenues of $125 Billion in 2008.” *Calgary Herald*, 17 January 2008, A1.
Marriott, James. “A Social Licence to Operate.” In *Not If But When: Culture beyond Oil*,

edited by Jo Clarke, Mel Evans, Hayley Newman, Kevin Smith, and Glen Tarman, np. London: Platform/Liberate Tate 2011.
Marshal, Alex. "A Museum Held a Show of Protest Art. Then the Artists Protested the Museum." *New York Times*, 3 August 2018: https://www.nytimes.com/2018/08/03/arts/design/design-museum-london-shepard-fairey.html.
Marshall, Clem. "Paternalism Promotes Racism at ROM." *Globe and Mail*, 21 April 1990, D7.
Martin, Lee Ann. "The Politics of Inclusion and Exclusion: Contemporary Native Art and Public Art Museums in Canada." Report presented to the Canada Council, 1991.
Martin, Reinhold. "Public and Common(s)." *Places*, January 2013: https://placesjournal.org/article/public-and-commons/?gclid=CMSr2NGvhtUCFRhLDQod9TADBg.
Martin, Robert. "Will Downtown Progress Kill Toronto's Chinatown?" *Globe and Mail*, 10 November 1972, 29.
Mathiesen, Karl. "Anti-Fossil Fuel Activists Stage Louvre Oil Slick." *Climate Home News*, 3 July 2017: http://www.climatechangenews.com/2017/03/07/anti-fossil-fuel-activists-stage-louvre-oil-slick.
Matthews, Bebeto. "Occupy Wall Street Becomes Highly Collectible." *USA Today*, 24 December 2011: http://usatoday30.usatoday.com/news/nation/story/2011-12-24/occupy-wall-street/52213044/1.
Mays, John Bentley. "Anti-Censorship Protest Grows." *Globe and Mail*, 15 June 1984.
– "Anti-porn Bill C-54 'Must be Amended.'" *Globe and Mail*, 16 December 1987, C5.
Mendoza, Gian-Paolo. "Kinder Morgan Donation Scholarships Refused by Kwantlen Students." *CBC News*, 26 June 2015: http://www.cbc.ca/news/canada/british-columbia/kinder-morgan-donation-scholarships-refused-by-kwantlen-students-1.3129523.

Meskimmon, Marsha. *Contemporary Art and the Cosmopolitan Imagination*. London and New York: Routledge 2011.
Message, Kylie. *Museums and Social Activism: Engaged Protest*. London and New York: Routledge 2013.
– *The Disobedient Museum: Writing at the Edge*. London and New York: Routledge 2017.
Metcalfe, Robin. "The Wardens of Memory." In *Suggestive Poses: Artists and Critics Respond to Censorship*, edited by Lorraine Johnson, 29–42. Toronto: Toronto Photographers Workshop and Riverbank Press 1997.
Miller, Phil. "Signs of the Times as Museum Gathers Placards from Recent Protests." *The Sunday Herald Scotland*, 25 April 2017: http://www.heraldscotland.com/news/15243818.Signs_of_the_times_as_museum_gathers_placards_from_recent_protests.
Miller, Toby, and George Yúdice. *Cultural Policy*. London: Sage 2002.
Mills, Jeanette C. "The Meares Island Controversy and Joe David: Art in Support of a Cause." *American Indian Art Magazine* 14.4 (autumn 1989): 60–9.
Milne, Heather. "Human Rights and/or Market Logic: Neoliberalism, Difficult Knowledge, and the Canadian Museum for Human Rights." *Review of Education, Pedagogy, and Cultural Studies* 37, nos. 2–3 (2015): 106–23.
Min, Christa, ed. *Vancouver Matters*. Vancouver: Blueimprint 2009.
Mitchell, Katherine. "Global Diasporas and Traditional Towns: Chinese Transnational Migration and the Redevelopment of Vancouver's Chinatown." *International Journal for the Study of Traditional Environments* 11, no. 2 (spring 2000): 7–18.
Mitchell, W.J.T., Bernard E. Harcourt, and Michael Taussig. "Image, Space, Revolution: The Arts of Occupation." In *Occupy: Three Inquiries in Disobedience*, edited by W.J.T.

Mitchell, Bernard E. Harcourt, and Michael Taussig, ebook, np. Chicago: University of Chicago Press 2013.
– *Occupy: Three Inquiries in Disobedience*. ebook. Chicago: University of Chicago Press 2013.
MOA. "Cedar Man." Item Number: Nb11.368 from the MOA: https://www.rrncommunity.org/items/25620.
Modest, Wayne. "Keynote." Museum Futures: Inaugural Conference for the Council for Museum Anthropology. Montreal, 24–7 May 2017.
Modigliani, Leah. *Engendering an Avant-Garde: The Unsettled Landscapes of Vancouver Photoconceptualism*. Manchester: Manchester University Press 2018.
Mogel, Lize. "Model Cities." In *Momentarily: Learning from Mega-Events*, edited by Bik Van der Pol, Alissa Firth-Eagland, and Urban Subjects, 71–8. Vancouver: Western Front 2010: http://www.urbansubjects.org/images/learning_from_vancouver/Momentarily%20Learning%20from%20Mega-Events.pdf.
Monaghan, Jeffrey, and Kevin Walby. "Making up 'Terror Identities': Security Intelligence, Canada's Integrated Threat Assessment Centre and Social Movement Suppression." *Policing and Society* 22, no. 2 (2012): 133–51.
Monbiot, George. "Please, Canada, Clean Up Your Act." *Globe and Mail*, 30 November 2009, A13.
Montpetit, Isabelle. "Rights Set in Constitution, Defined by Judges." CBC *News*, 26 May 2011: http://www.cbc.ca/news/canada/rights-set-in-constitution-defined-by-judges-1.1097012.
Moore, Alan W. "A Brief Genealogy of Social Sculpture." *Journal of Aesthetics and Protest*, nd: http://www.joaap.org/webonly/moore.htm.

Moore, Charles W. "Air Show Censorship Soars over the Top." *Telegraph-Journal*, 14 September 2006, A7.
Moreton-Robinson, Aileen. *The White Possessive: Property, Power, and Indigenous Sovereignty.* Minneapolis: University of Minnesota Press 2015.
Moriyama, Raymond. *In Search of a Soul: Designing and Realizing the New Canadian War Museum*. Vancouver: Douglas and McIntyre 2006.
Morrow, Shayne. "Two Major Artworks Continue to Inspire." *Globe and Mail*, 25 April 2014.
Mosby, Ian. "Colonial Science: Nutrition Research and Human Biomedical Experimentation in Aboriginal Communities and Residential Schools, 1942–1952." *Histoire Sociale/Social History* 46, no. 91 (May 2013): 145–72.
Moses, Dirk A. "Protecting Human Rights and Preventing Genocide: The Canadian Museum for Human Rights and the Will to Intervene." In *The Idea of a Human Rights Museum*, edited by Karen Busby, Adam Muller, and Andrew Woolford, 40–69. Winnipeg: University of Manitoba Press 2015.
Moussa, Ahlia. "Point of Origin: The Global Positioning of Recent Vancouver Art." MA thesis, Western University, 2011.
MOV. "City on Edge: A Century of Vancouver Activism." *Museum of Vancouver*: http://www.museumofvancouver.ca/exhibitions/exhibit/city-edge-century-vancouver-activism.
MOVments. *Museum of Vancouver blog*: http://www.museumofvancouver.ca/programs/blog.
Mulgrew, Ian. "A Long Battle to Avoid Scars." *Globe and Mail*, 8 August 1984.
– "Unfriendly Crowds Mar BC Visit: Called Liar by Indians, Trudeau Stalks Off." *Globe and Mail*, 24 November 1981.

Mumford, Gwilym. "Shia LaBoeuf's Trump Art Project Shut Down One Day after Moving to Liverpool." *Guardian*, 24 March 2017.
Murphy, Jacqueline Shea. "Gathering from within: Indigenous Nationhood and Tanya Lukin Linklater's *Woman and Water*." *Theatre Research International* 35, no. 2 (2010): 165–71.
Murphy, Timothy S., and Abdul-Karim Mustapha. *Resistance in Practice: The Philosophy of Antonio Negri*. London and Ann Arbor, MI: Pluto Press 2005.
MuseumNext. "Should Museums Be Activist?" *museumnext.com* (accessed 13 September 2017): https://www.museumnext.com/2017/04/should-museums-be-activists.
Museums Association. "Do Sponsorship Protests Damage Relations with Sponsors and Philanthropists?" *museumsassociation.org*, 23 May 2017: http://www.museumsassociation.org/museums-journal/comment/24052017-do-sponsorship-protests-damage-relations-with-sponsors-and-philanthropists.
Nancy, Jean-Luc. *The Inoperative Community*. Minneapolis: University of Minnesota Press 1991.
Nanopolitics Group. "Nanopolitics: A First Outline of Our Experiments in Movement." *Lateral* 1, no. 1 (2012): http://lateral.culturalstudiesassociation.org/issue1/content/nanopolitics.html.
National Arts Centre. "2014 Governor General's Performing Arts Awards Gala." (2014): https://nac-cna.ca/en/event/8470.
Natural History Museum. "Exhibition of Fossil Fuel Industry Greenwashing in Science Museums." (29 April 2015): http://thenaturalhistorymuseum.org/exhibition-on-fossil-fuel-industry-greenwashing-in-science-museums-2.
– "Our Letter Has Gone Viral." (25 March 2015): http://thenaturalhistorymuseum.org/our-letter-has-gone-viral.

Natural Resources Canada. "Media Room: An Open Letter from the Honourable Joe Oliver." (9 January 2012): http://www.nrcan.gc.ca/media-room/news-release/2012/1/1909.
Nayeri, Farah. "Anti-BP Activists Stage Nude Lie-in, Pour Oil at Tate Britain." *Bloomberg*, 20 April 2011: http://www.bloomberg.com/news/articles/2011-04-20/anti-bp-activists-stage-nude-lie-in-pour-oil-at-tate-on-spill-anniversary
Nead, Lynda. *The Female Nude: Art, Obscenity, and Sexuality*. London and New York: Routledge 1992.
Neale, Jonathan. *You Are the G8, We Are the 6 Billion: The Truth behind the Genoa Protests*. London: Vision Paperbacks 2002.
Neufeld, Joshua. "Sucked Dry." *The Walrus*, 23 February 2015: https://thewalrus.ca/sucked-dry.
Newberry Library. "Building a Living Archive of Modern Protest." *newberry.org*, January 2017: https://www.newberry.org/building-living-archive-modern-protest.
Newell, Jennifer, Libby Robin, and Kirsten Wehner, eds. *Curating the Future: Museums, Communities and Climate Change*. London and New York: Routledge 2017.
Newhouse, Victoria. *Towards a New Museum*, 2nd edition. New York: Monacelli Press 2005.
Nikiforuk, Andrew. "Opinion: Understanding Harper's Evangelical Mission." *The Tyee*, 26 March 2012: http://thetyee.ca/Opinion/2012/03/26/Harper-Evangelical-Mission.
– "Secret Memo Casts Doubt on Feds' Claims for Science Library Closures." *The Tyee*, 30 December 2013: http://thetyee.ca/News/2013/12/30/Harper-Library-Closures.
No Goldcorp at SFU. "Demands." *No Goldcorp at SFU*: http://nogoldcorpsfu.wordpress.com.

Nochlin, Linda. "Issues and Commentary: In the Wake of the 'Sensation' Uproar." *Art in America* 87, no. 12 (1999): 37.
Nope to Arms. "From Nope to Hope." *Nope to Arms*: https://nopetoarms.org.
Not An Alternative. "Institutional Liberation." *e-flux* 77 (November 2016): http://www.e-flux.com/journal/77/76215/institutional-liberation.
– "Interview with the Natural History Museum." (18 December 2015): http://notanalternative.org/2015/12/18/the-natural-history-museum-interview.
Notes from Nowhere, ed. "Carnival: Resistance Is the Secret of Joy." In *We Are Everywhere: The Irresistible Rise of Global Anti-capitalism*. London: Verso Books 2003.
Nova Scotia. "Gallery Expands into Southwest." *Nova Scotia Government*, 28 May 1999: https://novascotia.ca/news/release/?id=19990528009.
Nowell, Iris. *Joyce Wieland: A Life in Art*. Toronto: ECW Press 2001.
O'Brian, Melanie. *Vancouver Art and Economies*. Vancouver: Arsenal Pulp Press 2007.
Occupy Museums. http://www.occupymuseums.org.
Off, Carol. *The Ghosts of Medak Pocket: The Story of Canada's Secret War*. Toronto: Random House Canada 2004.
Oleksijczuk, Denise. "Haunted Spaces." In *Stan Douglas: Every Building on 100 West Hastings*, edited by Reid Shier, 96–117. Vancouver: Contemporary Art Gallery and Arsenal Pulp Press 2002, 2005.
Oliphant, Elayne. "Il n'y a pas de 'Potentially Hot Issues': Paradoxes of Displaying *Lands within Me* at the Canadian Museum of Civilization Following 9.11." MA thesis, Department of Political Economy, Carleton University, 2005.
O'Neill, Susan. "What a Riot." *Bizbash.com*, 3 April 2009. Accessed 14 September 2015: http://www.bizbash.com/toronto/content/editorial/15014_a_g_o_adopts_massive_uprising_theme_with_mock_protests_riot_police.php.
Oosterom, Nelle. "Harper Vows Winnipeg Showpiece Will Be a National Institution." *Edmonton Journal*, 21 April 2007, A2.
Orpana, Jennifer. "Transformation AGO: It's What's Inside That Counts." *Fuse Magazine* (spring 2009): 6–11.
Ostaman, Jacob, in conversation with Leanne Simpson. "We're Protecting, Not Protesting." In *This Is an Honour Song: Twenty Years since the Blockades*, 223–8. Winnipeg: Arbeiter Ring Press 2010.
Palmater, Pam. "Canada 150 Is a Celebration of Indigenous Genocide." *Now Magazine*, 29 March 2017: https://nowtoronto.com/news/canada-s-150th-a-celebration-of-indigenous-genocide.
– "Feathers versus Guns: The Throne Speech and Canada's War with Mi'kmaw Nation." *Rabble.ca*, 18 October 2013: http://rabble.ca/blogs/bloggers/pamela-palmater/2013/10/feathers-versus-guns-throne-speech-and-canadas-war-mikmaw-nat.
Palmer, Bryan. *Canada's 1960s: The Ironies of Identity in a Rebellious Era*. Toronto: University of Toronto Press 2009.
Parliament of Canada. "Bill C-42: An Act to Amend the Museums Act." (22 February 2008): https://lop.parl.ca/About/Parliament/LegislativeSummaries/bills_ls.asp?lang=E&ls=c42&Parl=39&Ses=2&source=library_prb.
Paul, Alexandra. "Where Are the Children Buried?" *Winnipeg Free Press*, 19 February 2011.
Paul, Catherine. *Poetry in the Museums of Modernism*. Ann Arbor: University of Michigan Press 2002.
PBS News Hour. "Museums Are Curating an Era of Social Movements in Real Time."

PBS *News Hour*, 24 November 2018: https://www.pbs.org/newshour/show/museums-are-curating-an-era-of-social-movements-in-real-time.
Pearson, Matthew. "Artists' Group Wants NAC to Drop Enbridge." *Ottawa Citizen*, 27 January 2011.
Peck, Jamie. *Neoliberal Urbanism: Artful Alternatives?* Lecture. Vancouver: SFU Vancity Office of Community Engagement (12 November 2013): https://www.youtube.com/watch?v=Wak7IO3V9jQ.
– "Struggling with the Creative Class." *International Journal of Urban and Regional Research* 29, no. 4 (December 2005): 740–70.
Perfitt, Katie. "Museum of History Needs to Cut Ties with Big Oil." *Ottawa Citizen*, 29 March 2017.
Perreault, Kelsey. "Remembrance as Presence: Promoting Learning from Difficult Knowledge at the Canadian Museum for Human Rights." MA thesis, Western University, 2017.
Perry, Adele. *Aqueduct: Colonialism, Resources, and the Histories We Remember*. Winnipeg: ARP Books, 2016.
Phillips, Ruth. "APEC at the Museum of Anthropology: The Politics of Site and the Poetics of Sight Bite." *Ethnos: Journal of Anthropology* 65, no. 2 (2000): 172–94.
– "APEC at the Museum of Anthropology: The Politics of Site and the Poetics of Sight Bite." In *Imagining Resistance: Visual Culture and Activism in Canada*, edited by Keri Cronin and Kirsty Robertson, 171–92. Waterloo: Wilfrid Laurier Press 2011.
– "Beyond Difficult Histories: First Nations, the Right to Culture, and the Obligation of Redress." In *The Idea of a Human Rights Museum*, edited by Kathy Busby, Adam Muller, and Andrew Woodford, 296–321. Winnipeg: University of Manitoba Press 2015.
– "The Museum of Art-Thropology: Twenty-First Century Imbroglios." *RES: Anthropology and Aesthetics* 52 (autumn 2007): 8–19.

– *Museum Pieces: Toward the Indigenization of Canadian Museums*. Kingston and Montreal. McGill-Queen's University Press 2011.
– "Re-placing Objects: Historical Practices for the Second Museum Age." *Canadian Historical Review* 86, no. 1 (March 2005): 83–110.
Pignare, Philippe, and Isabelle Stengers. *Capitalist Sorcery: Breaking the Spell*. New York: Palgrave 2011.
Pinto, Meg. "Pamela Masik and the *Forgotten* Exhibition: Controversy and Cancellation at the Museum of Anthropology." *Museum Anthropology* 36, no. 1 (2013): 4–17.
Pinto, Nick. "In Dishonor of Columbus: Protesters Shroud Obscenely Racist Statue at AMNH." *Village Voice*, 11 October 2016: https://www.villagevoice.com/2016/10/11/in-dishonor-of-columbus-day-protesters-shroud-obscenely-racist-statue-at-amnh.
Platform London. "Infographic: Culture Clash, Arts & Oil Money." *Platform: Arts Activism, Education, Research*, 26 April 2014: http://platformlondon.org/p-publications/artoilinfographic.
– "Legal Oil, Ethical Oil and Profiteering in the Niger Delta and the Canadian North." *Platform: Arts Activism, Education, Research*, 30 January 2012: http://platformlondon.org/2012/01/30/legal-oil-ethical-oil-and-profiteering-in-the-niger-delta-and-the-canadian-north.
– "An Open Letter in Support of the Tar Sands Blockade." *Platform: Arts Activism, Education, Research*, 6 October 2012: http://platformlondon.org/2012/10/06/thirty-national-international-groups-call-for-support-of-tar-sands-blockade.
– "Social License: Complicity in the Age of Extraction." *Platform: Arts Activism, Education, Research*, 15 March 2012: http://platformlondon.org/p-article/social-licence-complicity-in-the-age-of-extraction.

Platt, Susan Noyes, and Peter Selz. *Art and Politics Now: Cultural Activism in a Time of Crisis*. New York: Midmarch Arts Press 2011.
Plum Creative. "Canadian Museum for Human Rights." (2014): https://vimeo.com/92563401.
Poirier, Patricia. "Museum Says No to Band over Boycott of Exhibition." *Globe and Mail*, 29 October 1987.
Polletta, Francesca. *It Was Like a Fever: Storytelling in Protest and Politics*. Chicago: University of Chicago Press 2006.
Postmedia News. "Trudeau Says First Nations 'Don't Have a Veto' over Energy Projects." *Financial Post*, 20 December 2016.
Powless. "Museums Tar Sands Funding Pollutes Snow Exhibit, Says Snowperson." *Ecology Ottawa*, 6 December 2013: https://ecologyottawa.ca/2013/12/06/museums-tar-sands-funding-pollutes-snow-exhibit-says-snowperson.
Preston, Jen. "Neoliberal Settler Colonialism, Canada and the Tar Sands." *Race and Class* 55, no. 2 (2013), 42–59.
Professional Institute of the Public Service of Canada. "Two Wrongs Don't Make It Right." (25 November 2002): www.pipsc.ca.
Protestcamp. "Protest Camps and White Cubes." *protestcamps.com*. 28 September 2012: https://protestcamps.com/2012/09/28/793.
Protevi, John. *Political Affect: Connecting the Social and the Somatic*. Minneapolis: University of Minnesota Press 2006.
Proudfoot, Jesse. "The Derelict, the Deserving Poor, and the *Lumpen*: A History of the Politics of Representation in the Downtown Eastside." In *Stan Douglas:* Abbott & Cordova, *7 August 1971*, 88–107. Vancouver: Arsenal Pulp Press 2011.

Proudfoot, Shannon. "War Vets Want Action after Revelers Urinate on National War Memorial." *Edmonton Journal*, 3 July 2006, A5.
Proulx, Craig. "Colonizing Surveillance: Canada Constructs an Indigenous Terror Threat." *Anthropologica* 56, no. 1 (2014): 83–100.
Pue, W. Wesley, ed. *Pepper in Our Eyes: The APEC Affair*. Vancouver: UBC Press 2000.
Pullen, Kelly. "The Plutocrats' Playground: Inside Hilary and Galen Weston's Exclusive Enclave of Palatial Vacation Homes." *Toronto Life*, 28 November 2013: http://www.torontolife.com/informer/features/2013/11/28/hilary-and-halen-weston-multimillion-dollar-vacation-homes/5.
Purdie, Jamie. "Artists Protest Firm's Sponsorship of Exhibit." *Globe and Mail*, 10 February 1976.
Quinn, Ellis. "Marchers Slam War in Iraq." *Globe and Mail*, 21 March 2005, A8.
Rabinovitch, Victor. *Public History and the Bomber Command Controversy*. Gatineau. (2008, 1–5): http://www.chashcacommittees-comitesa.ca/public_history/Victor%20Rabinovitch%20CHA%202008.pdf.
Rabson, Mia. "Human Rights Museum Budget Already Short." *Winnipeg Free Press*, 16 May 2009, A3.
Raj, Althia. "Nicole Eaton: Green Charities Using Foreign Cash to Fight Oil Sands Development." *Huffington Post*, 28 February 2012: http://www.huffingtonpost.ca/2012/02/28/nicole-eaton-green-charity-oil-sands-canada_n_1307440.html.
Rancière, Jacques. *The Emancipated Spectator*. London: Verso 2011.
Rancière, Jacques, and Steve Corcoran. *Dissensus: On Politics and Aesthetics*. London and New York: Continuum 2010.
Raunig, Gerald. "The Monster Precariat." *eipcp*, 3 October 2007: http://translate.eipcp.net/strands/02/raunig-strands02en#redir.

Raunig, Gerald, and Aileen Derieg. *Art and Revolution: Transversal Activism in the Long Twentieth Century*. Los Angeles and Cambridge, MA: Semiotexte; Distributed by the MIT Press 2007.

Razack, Sherene H. *Dark Threats and White Knights: The Somalia Affair, Peacekeeping, and the New Imperialism*. Toronto: University of Toronto Press 2004.

– "Gendered Racial Violence and Spatialized Justice: The Murder of Pamela George." In *Race, Space, and the Law: Unmapping a White Settler Society*, edited by Sherene H. Razack, 121–56. Toronto: Between the Lines 2002.

Rea, Naomi. "The British Museum Wants to Borrow That 'Baby Trump' Balloon – But It's Got Competition." *Artnet news*, 19 July 2018: https://news.artnet.com/art-world/museums-trump-baby-balloon-1320611.

Recollet, Karyn. "Glyphing Decolonial Love through Urban Flash Mobbing and Walking with Our Sisters." *Curriculum Inquiry* 45, no. 1 (2015): 129–45.

Rectanus, Mark W. *Culture Incorporated: Museums, Artists, and Corporate Sponsorships*. Minneapolis: University of Minnesota Press 2002.

Redsky, Erwin. "Statement by Chief Erwin Redsky on the Occasion of the Visit of Prime Minister Justin Trudeau to Shoal Lake 40 First Nation." (28 April 2016): http://www.sl40.ca/Microsoft%20Word%20-%20Statement%20by%20Chief%20Redsky%20-%20PM%20Visit.docx.pdf.

Reed, Thomas Vernon. *The Art of Protest: Culture and Activism from the Civil Rights Movement to the Streets of Seattle*. Minneapolis: University of Minnesota Press 2005.

Reguly, Eric, and Jane Taber. "How US Pranksters Hoaxed the World at Canada's Expense." *Globe and Mail*, 15 December 2009, A15.

Reily, Susan. "Opinion: Why Are Our Museums So Bland?" *Ottawa Citizen*, 7 December 1996, D1.

Rennie, Bob. "Bob Rennie Reflects on a Labour of Love and Building a Legacy in Art." BC *Business*, 2 December 2009: https://www.bcbusiness.ca/bob-rennie-and-contemporary-art-test-of-time.

Renzetti, Elizabeth. "Artists Will Act Up in Days of Action." *Globe and Mail*, 23 October 1996.

Retort and Iain A. Boal. *Afflicted Powers: Capital and Spectacle in a New Age of War*. London and New York: Verso 2005.

Richer, Shawna. "Opponents, Supporters Greet Bush in Halifax," *Globe and Mail*, 2 December 2004, A13.

Right Side of History. "Canadian Museum of History AGM Flooded with Message to Cut CAPP." (24 April 2017): http://rightsideofhistory.ca/agm.

Rights Action. "Petition the Canadian Museum for Human Rights." (2014): http://myemail.constantcontact.com/Petition-The-Canadian-Museum-for-Human-Rights—Remove-Hudbay-Minerals-from-Museum-of-Human-Rights.html?soid=1103480765269&aid=hQ4lcA_dkt8.

Rivers, Khelsilem. "Why Is Big Oil Funding Reconciliation Week Events in Vancouver?" *rabble.ca*, 19 September 2013: http://rabble.ca/news/2013/09/why-big-oil-funding-reconciliation-week-events-vancouver.

Ro, Christine. "A BP Oil Protest Spills through the British Museum's Protest Exhibition." *Hyperallergic*, 29 October 2018: https://hyperallergic.com/468466/a-bp-oil-protest-spills-through-the-british-museums-protest-exhibition.

Robertson, Clive. *Policy Matters: Administrations of Art and Culture*. Toronto: YYZ Books 2006.

Robertson, Kirsty. "Capitalist Cocktails and Moscow Mules: The Art World and Global Justice Protest." *Globalizations* 8, no. 4 (2011): 473–86.
– "Crude Culture: Canada and Creative Industries." *Fuse Magazine* (spring 2008): 12–21.
– "'This Is What Democracy Looks Like?' Or, the Art of Opposition." In *Transnationalism, Activism Art*, edited by Kit Dobson and Áine McGlynn. Toronto: University of Toronto Press 2012.
Robertson, Kirsty, with Sarah Smith, Stephanie Anderson, Elizabeth Diggon, and Ahlia Moussa. "More a Diplomatic Than an Aesthetic Event: Canada, Brazil and Cultural Exchange." *Journal of Canadian Studies* 47 (January 2014): 1–29.
Robertson, Kirsty, and Keri Cronin, eds. *Imagining Resistance: Visual Culture and Activism in Canada*. Waterloo: Wilfrid Laurier Press 2011.
Rochon, Lisa. "Asper's Dream Will Be a Sci-Fi Castle." *Globe and Mail*, 16 April 2005, R7.
Rogoff, Irit. "Hit and Run: Museums and Cultural Difference." *Art Journal* 61, no. 3 (2002): 63–73.
– "What Is a Theorist?" In *The State of Art Criticism*, edited by James Elkins, 97–110. New York and London: Routledge 2008.
Rogoff, Irit, and Daniel J. Sherman, eds. *Museum Culture: Histories, Discourses, Spectacles*. Minneapolis: University of Minnesota Press 1994.
Rollason, Kevin. "Rights Museum Needs $45M." *Winnipeg Free Press*, 27 May 2009, B1.
Rosenfeld, Kathryn. "This Is Not an Essay on Political Art." *In These Times*, 15 September 2003: http://inthesetimes.com/article/105.
Rosler, Martha. "The Artistic Mode of Revolution: From Gentrification to Occupation." *e-flux* 33 (March 2012): http://www.e-flux.com/journal/the-artistic-mode-of-revolution-from-gentrification-to-occupation.

– "Culture Class: Art, Creativity, Urbanism, Part 1." *e-flux* 21 (December 2010): http://www.e-flux.com/journal/21/67676/culture-class-art-creativity-urbanism-part-i.
– "Culture Class: Art, Creativity, Urbanism, Part 2." *e-flux* 23 (March 2011): http://www.e-flux.com/journal/23/67813/culture-class-art-creativity-urbanism-part-ii.
Ross, Andrew, ed. *The Gulf: High Culture/Hard Labor*. New York: OR Books 2015.
– *Nice Work If You Can Get It: Life and Labor in Precarious Times*. New York: New York University Press 2009.
Ross, Cathy. "Occupy Collecting." *History Workshop Journal* 75 (2013): 236–46.
Ross, Val. "Coming to a Town near You: National Museums." *Globe and Mail*, 20 December 2006, R1.
– "Fighting Words Rile Historians." *Globe and Mail*, 29 August 2007.
– "Museum Faces a Second Offensive." *Globe and Mail*, 19 July 2007.
– "Museums in Waiting." *Globe and Mail*, 6 March 2007.
Rothfield, Lawrence. *Unsettling "Sensation": Arts Policy Lessons from the Brooklyn Museum of Art Controversy*. Rutgers: Rutgers University Press 2001.
Rowland, Robin. "Protecting Canada's Lakes, Rivers: 2012 Media Fail." *Huffington Post*, 25 February 2013: http://www.huffingtonpost.ca/robin-rowland/navigable-waters-protection-act-media-fail-idle-no-more_b_2356595.html.
Royal Ontario Museum. "Museums and Climate Change: Two Easy Steps and One Provocative Move." *rom.on.ca*: http://www.rom.on.ca/en/blog/museums-and-climate-change-two-easy-steps-and-one-provocative-move.
– "Of Africa." *rom.on.ca*: https://www.rom.on.ca/en/of-africa.
Rugoff, Ralph. "Baja to Vancouver: The West Coast and Contemporary Art." In *Baja to Vancouver: The West Coast and Contemporary Art*, 12–19. San Francisco: CCA Wattis Institute for Contemporary Art 2003.

Rustin, Susanna. "Tate and Oil: Does the Art World Need to Come Clean about Sponsorship?" *Guardian*, 8 October 2014.
Rutherford, Scott. "Canada's Other Red Scare: Rights, Decolonization, and Indigenous Political Protest in the Global Sixties." PhD dissertation, Queen's University, Kingston, 2011.
Ryan, Charlotte. "As Protesters Take On the Tate, Is the Fear of Demonstrations Causing Galleries to Take Fewer Risks?" *New Statesman*, 15 June 2016: http://www.newstatesman.com/politics/feminism/2016/06/tate-modern-protesters-call-cuban-artists-work-be-displayed-0.
Ryan, Lisa. "Museums across the World Are Collecting Women's March Signs." *The Cut*, 22 January 2017: http://nymag.com/thecut/2017/01/museums-across-the-world-are-collecting-womens-march-signs.html.
Sacco, Pier Luigi, with Bob Williams and Elvy Del Bianco. *The Power of the Arts in Vancouver: Creating a Great City*. Vancouver: Vancity 2007: http://www.theholmteam.ca/votewendy/media/PowerOfTheArts.pdf.
Samson, John K. "Vampire Alberta Blues." *Winter Wheat* (ANTI-records), 2016.
Samtani, Hiten. "The Anarchivists: Who Owns the Occupy Wall Street Narrative?" *Brooklyn Ink*, 26 December 2017: http://brooklynink.org/2011/12/26/39230-the-anarchivists-who-owns-the-occupy-wall-street-narrative.
Samyn, Paul. "Ottawa Not Likely to Fund Winnipeg Human Rights Museum." *Calgary Herald*, 6 November 2004, A10.
Sandell, Richard, Jocelyn Dodd, and Rosemarie Garland-Thomson, eds. *Re-presenting Disability: Activism and Agency in the Museum*. New York and London: Routledge 2010.
Sandell, Richard, and Eithne Nightingale. "Introduction." In *Museums, Equality and Social Justice*, edited by Richard Sandell and Eithne Nightingale, 1–10. New York and London: Routledge 2012.
Sanders, Douglas E. "The Indian Lobby and the Canadian Constitution, 1978–82." In *Indigenous Peoples and the Nation State*, edited by Noel Dyck, 151–89. St John's: Institute of Social and Economic Research, Memorial University of Newfoundland 1985.
Sanger, Penny. "Marching to the Museum." *Globe and Mail*, 19 March 2005, A18.
Sarty, Roger. "The Nationalization of Military History: Scholarship, Politics and the Canadian War Museum." In *Canadas of the Mind: The Making and Unmaking of Canadian Nationalisms in the Twentieth Century*, edited by Norman Hillmer and Adam Chapnick, 110–32. Montreal and Kingston: McGill-Queen's University Press 2007.
Sassen, Saskia. *Cities in a World Economy*, 3rd edition. Thousand Oaks, CA: Pine Forge Press 2006.
– "The Global City: Introducing a Concept." *The Brown Journal of World Affairs* 11, no. 2 (winter/spring 2005): 27–43.
Schechner, Richard. *The Future of Ritual: Writings on Culture and Performance*. London and New York: Routledge 1993.
Schechter, Fran. "Slut Nation: Anatomy of a Protest." *Now Magazine*, 10 December 2014: https://nowtoronto.com/art-and-books/art/slut-nation-anatomy-of-a-protest.
Schildkrout, Enid. "Ambiguous Messages and Ironic Twists: *Into the Heart of Africa* and the Other Museum." *Museum Anthropology* 15, no. 2 (May 1991): 16–23.
Schmidt, Andrea. "Indigenous Canadian Fracking Protesters Refuse to Back Down." *Al Jazeera*, 2 December 2013.
Scott, Andrea K. "New York Museums Signal Their Resistance to Trump." *The New Yorker*, 17 February 2017: http://www.newyorker.com/culture/cultural-comment/new-york-museums-signal-their-resistance.

Scott, Michael. "Art of Protest: Making an Exhibition of Yourself." *Vancouver Sun*, 22 June 2002, H6.

– "Campbell Protesters Disrupt VAG Exhibition Opening." *Vancouver Sun*, 16 June 2002.

Searle, Adrian. "Schlock and Awe." *Guardian*, 5 October 2006.

Serafini, Paula. *Performance Action: The Politics of Activism*. ebook. London and New York: Routledge 2018.

Sharma, Karen. "Governing Difficult Knowledge: The Canadian Museum for Human Rights and Its Publics." *Review of Education, Pedagogy, and Cultural Studies* 37, nos. 2–3 (2015): 184–206.

Shaw, Christopher A. *Five Ring Circus: Myths and Realities of the Olympic Games*. Gabriola Island: New Society Publishers 2008.

Shelton, Anthony. "Critical Museology: A Manifesto." *Museum Worlds: Advances in Research* 1 (2013): 7–23.

Sherlock, Tracy. "Vancouver Developer Donates $7 Million to New Emily Carr University." *Vancouver Sun*, 2 May 2014: http://www.vancouversun.com/entertainment/Vancouver+developer+donates+million+Emily+Carr+University/9801071/story.html.

Shier, Reid. "Introduction." In *Stan Douglas: Every Building on 100 West Hastings*, 10–17. Vancouver: Contemporary Art Gallery and Arsenal Pulp Press 2002.

Shilton, Katie, and Ramesh Srinivasan. "Counterpoint: Participatory Appraisal and Arrangement for Multicultural Archival Collections." *Archivaria* 63 (spring 2007): 87–101.

Shlegel, Amy. "My Lai: We Lie They Die." *Third Text* 9, no. 31 (1995): 47–66.

Sholette, Gregory. *Dark Matter: Art and Politics in the Age of Enterprise Culture*. New York: Pluto Press 2011.

– *Delirium and Resistance: Activist Art and the Crisis of Capitalism*. New York: Pluto Press 2017.

– "Merciless Aesthetic: Activist Art as the Return of Institutional Critique. A Response to Boris Groys." *Field* 4 (spring 2016): http://field-journal.com/issue-4/merciless-aesthetic-activist-art-as-the-return-of-institutional-critique-a-response-to-boris-groys.

Sholette, Gregory, and Nato Thompson. *The Interventionists: Users' Manual for the Creative Disruption of Everyday Life*. Cambridge: MIT Press 2006.

Shore, Forest and Beyond: Art from the Audain Collection. Vancouver Art Gallery: 29 October 2011 to 29 January 2012.

Shrivastava, Meenal, and Lorna Stefanick. "Framing the Debate on Democracy and Governance in an Oil Exporting Economy." In *Alberta Oil and the Decline of Democracy in Canada*, edited by Meenal Shrivastava and Lorna Stefanick, 3–28. Athabaska: Athabaska Press 2015.

Siemiatycki, Elliot, Thomas Hutton, and Trevor Barnes. "Trouble in Paradise: Resilience and Vancouver's Second Life in the 'New Economy.'" *Urban Geography* 37, no. 2 (2016): 183–201.

Simpson, Leanne Betasamosake. "Aambe! Maajaadaa! (What #IdleNoMore Means to Me)." *Decolonization: Indigeneity, Education and Society*, 21 December 2012: https://decolonization.wordpress.com/2012/12/21/aambe-maajaadaa-what-idlenomore-means-to-me.

– *As We Have Always Done: Indigenous Freedom through Radical Resistance*. Minneapolis: University of Minnesota Press 2017.

– *Dancing on Our Turtle's Back: Stories of Nishnaabeg Re-creation, Resurgence and a New Emergence*. Winnipeg: ARP Books 2011.

Simpson, Leanne Betasamosake, and Kiera Ladner, eds. *This Is an Honour Song: Twenty Years since the Blockades*. Winnipeg: ARP Books 2010.
Simpson, Jeffrey. "When It Comes to Climate Change, We're Still Emitting Hot Air." *Globe and Mail*, 8 July 2009, A15.
Singh, Anita. "V&A Director Fights Back against 'Art Washing' Claims as He Refuses to Take Down Controversial Venice Exhibit." *The Telegraph*, 29 May 2018: https://www.telegraph.co.uk/news/2018/05/29/va-curator-fights-back-against-art-washing-claims-refuses-take.
Sirove, Taryn. *Ruling Out Art: Media Art Meets Law in Ontario's Censor Wars*. Vancouver: UBC Press forthcoming 2019.
Slaney, Frances M. "Harper's History Museum Betrays First Nations." *CAUT Bulletin*, February 2014: https://bulletin-archives.caut.ca/bulletin/articles/2014/02/harper-s-history-museum-betrays-first-nations.
Sloan, Johanne. "Joyce Wieland at the Border: Nationalism, the New Left, and the Question of Political Art in Canada, circa 1971." *Journal of Canadian Art History* 26 (fall 2005): 81–104.
– "Urban Art Histories (in Canada)." In *Narratives Unfolding: National Art Histories in an Unfinished World*, edited by Martha Langford, 271–87. Montreal and Kingston: McGill-Queen's University Press 2017.
Smith, Charlie. "Bob Rennie Condemns Vancouver Art Gallery Consultants' Response to His Proposal." *Georgia Straight*, 20 December 2012.
Smith, Joanna. "Museum of History to Exclude Winnipeg General Strike Exhibit." *Toronto Star*, 22 May 2015: http://www.thestar.com/news/canada/2015/05/22/museum-of-history-to-dismantle-winnipeg-general-strike-exhibit.html.
Smith, Jordan. "Reinventing Canada: Stephen Harper's Conservative Revolution." *World Affairs*, March/April 2012: http://www.worldaffairsjournal.org/article/reinventing-canada-stephen-harper%E2%80%99s-conservative-revolution.
Smith, Lyn. *Voices against War: A Century of Protest*. Edinburgh and London: Mainstream Publishing 2010.
Smith, Neil, and Jeff Derksen. "Urban Regeneration: Gentrification as Global Urban Strategy." In *Stan Douglas: Every Building on 100 West Hastings*, 62–95. Vancouver: Contemporary Art Gallery and Arsenal Pulp Press 2002.
Smith, Sarah E.K. *Art and the Invention of North America*. Vancouver: UBC Press, forthcoming.
Spence, Rachel. "Who Funds the Arts and Why We Should Care." *Financial Times*, 19 September 2014.
Spring, Christopher. "Art, Resistance and Remembrance: A Bicentenary at the British Museum." In *Representing Enslavement and Abolition in Museums: Ambiguous Engagements*, edited by Laurajane Smith, Geoffrey Cubitt, Ross Wilson, and Kalliopi Fouseki, 193–212. London and New York: Routledge 2011.
Staff Writer. "Imperial Donation Inspires New Art Gallery Exhibit." *Blackburn News*, 24 March 2017: http://blackburnnews.com/sarnia/sarnia-news/2017/03/24/imperial-donation-inspires-new-art-gallery-exhibit.
Stallabrass, Julian. *Art Incorporated: The Story of Contemporary Art*. Oxford: Oxford University Press 2004.
– "The Politics of the Political Catalogue Essay." In *Villa Lituania: Nomeda & Gediminas Urbonas*. Lithuanian Pavilion, 52nd International Art Exhibition, La Biennale di Venezia, 68–78. Berlin: Sternberg Press 2008.

Stanners, Sarah. "Adopting Moore and Modernity in Toronto: Controversy, Reputation and Intervention on Display." In *Sculpture and the Museum*, edited by Christopher R. Marshall, 73–93. London: Ashgate 2011.
Statistics Canada. *Median Total Income*. (2017): http://www.statcan.gc.ca/tables-tableaux/sum-som/l01/cst01/famil107a-eng.htm.
Steel, Patrick. "Polish Supreme Court to Rule on Future of Museum of the Second World War." *Museums Association News*, 28 March 2017: http://www.museumsassociation.org/museums-journal/news/28032017-museum-of-the-second-world-war-gdansk-poland.
Steffenhagen, Janet. "Injunction Sought to Evict Activists." *Vancouver Sun*, 16 September 2002, B1.
Steinhauer, Jillian. "Anti-Fascists Clash with White Nationalists at the Minneapolis Institute of Art." *Hyperallergic*, 28 February 2017: https://hyperallergic.com/361809/anti-fascists-clash-with-white-nationalists-at-the-minneapolis-institute-of-art.
Stewart, Michael. "No Fun? No Point: Vancouver's Political Boredom." *Rabble.ca*, 13 May 2003: http://rabble.ca/blogs/bloggers/michael-stewart/2013/05/no-fun-no-point-vancouvers-political-boredom.
Steyerl, Hito. "A Thing Like You and Me." *eflux* 15 (April 2010): http://www.e-flux.com/journal/a-thing-like-you-and-me.
Stimson, Blake, and Gregory Sholette, eds. *Collectivism after Modernism: The Art of Social Imagination after 1945*. Minneapolis: University Of Minnesota Press 2007.
Studio Voltaire. *The Neo Naturists*. (2016): http://www.studiovoltaire.org/wp-content/uploads/2016/04/160630-neo_naturists_third_draft.pdf.
Subcommittee on Veterans Affairs of the Standing Senate Committee on National Security and Defence. *An Enduring Controversy: The Strategic Bombing Campaign Display in the Canadian War Museum*. Ottawa: Parliament of Canada (June 2007): http://www.parl.gc.ca/Content/SEN/Committee/391/defe/rep/rep16jun07-e.htm.
Sullivan, Paul. "Home at the Woodward's Squat." *Globe and Mail*, 30 October 2002, A21.
Sutton, Benjamin. "May Day Occupation at Guggenheim Closes Museum." *Hyperallergic*, 1 May 2015: http://hyperallergic.com/203794/breaking-may-day-occupation-at-guggenheim-closes-museum-guggoccupied.
Swann, Peter. "Stage for Protest." *Globe and Mail*, 8 June 1970.
– "Where Were They?" *Globe and Mail*, 16 May 1994.
Sweeney, Shelley. "Lady Sings the Blues: The Public Funding of Archives, Libraries, and Museums in Canada." In *Better off Forgetting? Essays on Archives, Public Policy, and Collective Memory*, edited by Cheryl Avery and Mona Holmlund, 17–38. Toronto: University of Toronto Press 2010.
Szeman, Imre. "Out with the New." In *Negotiations in a Vacant Lot: Studying the Visual in Canada*, edited by Lynda Jessup, Erin Morton, and Kirsty Robertson. Montreal and Kingston: McGill-Queen's University Press 2014.
Taber, Jane, and Gloria Galloway. "War of 1812 Fund Adds to Harper's Patriotic Initiatives." *Globe and Mail*, 28 September 2011.
Tait, Carrie. "Ottawa Launches Alberta Counterterrorism Unit." *Globe and Mail*, 6 June 2012.
Tam (Bends Towards Justice). "Dear White Protesters." *Bends Towards Justice*, 9 December 2014: http://bendstowardjustice.tumblr.com/post/104742740875/dear-white-protestors. Accessed 11 September 2017.
Tancons, Claire. "Keynote: Flesh as Object in Circum-Atlantic Performance: A Critique of the Exhibitionary Complex." In *Animate Entities: Objects in Performance*. Toronto: Jackman Institute for the Humanities 18 March 2016.

– and Krista Thompson, eds. *EN MAS': Carnival and Performance Art of the Caribbean*: http://curatorsintl.org/special-projects/en-mas.
Tator, Carol, Frances Henry, and Winston Mattis. *Challenging Racism in the Arts: Case Studies of Controversy and Conflict*. Toronto: University of Toronto Press 1998.
Taussig, Michael. "I'm So Angry I Made a Sign." In *Occupy: Three Inquiries in Disobedience*, edited by W.J.T. Mitchell, Bernard E. Harcourt, and Michael Taussig, ebook, np. Chicago: University of Chicago Press, 2013.
Taylor, Diana. "The Politics of Passion." *Dissidence* 10, no. 12 (2013): http://webcache.googleusercontent.com/search?q=cache:BcoFtiv4roYJ:hemisphericinstitute.org/hemi/en/e-misferica-102/taylor+&cd=1&hl=en&ct=clnk&gl=ca.
Taylor, Drew Hayden. "Why First Nations People Can't Just Move." *TVO*, 20 April 2016: https://tvo.org/article/current-affairs/shared-values/why-first-nations-people-cant-just-move.
Taylor, Lesley Ciarula. "Who Are the Yes Men and Why Did They Punk Canada at Copenhagen?" *Toronto Star*, 15 December 2009.
Taylor, Noel. "Portrait Gallery a Capital Idea." *Ottawa Citizen*, 6 August 2007, C4.
Tayler, Theresa. "EnCana in Talks for National Gallery." *Calgary Herald*, 6 December 2006, A1.
Teitel, Emma. "Anti-Mask Legislation Defies Logic." *Maclean's*, 18 May 2012: http://www2.macleans.ca/author/eteitel.
The Beat. "Thanks but No Tanks: Haida Gwaii Museum." (8 June 2013): http://www.coastalartbeat.ca/thanks-but-no-tanks-haida-gwaii-museum/.
The Globe. "An Architect's Protest." 8 April 1910.
– "Art Cross-Section of Canadian Life Is Fresh and Vital." 8 March 1930.
– "Canadian Artists Protest Actions, National Gallery: 118 Sign Petition." 9 December 1932.
– "Exhibition of Canadian Art at National Gallery, Ottawa." 6 August 1932.
– "'Group of Seven Art' to Be Hung Again at Art Gallery: Retrospective Arouses Keen Interest." 14 May 1936.
– "Marred by Pink and Green Hair, He Pays Respects to Group." 20 February 1936.
– "Old Style Art Is Exemplified at Exhibit." 23 November 1935.
– "Suffragettes Foiled by London Police." 25 May 1914.
The Polygon. *Funding from All Levels of Government Paves the Way for Construction of New Polygon Gallery*. (31 July 2015): http://newhome.presentationhousegallery.org/funding-from-all-levels-of-government-paves-the-way-for-construction-of-new-polygon-gallery.
Thiverge, Jennifer. "Exhibiting Dark Heritage: Representations of Community Voice in the War Museum." In *Adult Education, Museums and Art Galleries: Animating Social, Cultural and Institutional Change*, edited by Darlene E. Clover, 153–64. Rotterdam: Sense Publishers 2016.
Thom, Ian, and Grant Arnold, eds. *Shore, Forest and Beyond: Art from the Audain Collection*. Toronto: Douglas and McIntyre 2011.
Thompson, Nato. *Living as Form: Socially Engaged Art from 1991–2011*. Cambridge, MA: MIT Press 2011.
– *Seeing Power: Art and Activism in the Twenty-First Century*. New York: Melville House Press 2015.
Thomson, Stephen. "MOV of Vancouver Mulls Moving into VAG Building." *Georgia Straight*, 25 April 2013.
Todd, Douglas. "War and Peace: New War Museum Tells of Our Bravery, but Gives Short Shrift to Pacifism." *Edmonton Journal*, 6 July 2005, A15.

Todd, Zoe. "Fish, Kin and Hope: Tending to Water Violations in amiskwaciwâskahikan and Treaty Six Territory." *Afterall: A Journal of Art, Context and Inquiry* 43 (spring /summer 2017): http://www.journals.uchicago.edu/doi/abs/10.1086/692559.

Toledano. "How Activists Shut Down the Enbridge Line 9 Pipeline Hearings." *Vice*, 21 October 2013: https://www.vice.com/en_ca/article/xdm593/how-activists-shut-down-the-enbridge-line-9-pipeline-hearings.

Toler, Lindsay. "Missouri History Museum Collects Ferguson Protest Artifacts, Wants Your Donations." *Riverfront Times*, 21 January 2015: https://www.riverfronttimes.com/newsblog/2015/01/21/missouri-history-museum-collects-ferguson-protest-artifacts-wants-your-donations.

Tonner, Mark. "Latte Leftists Not Helping Homeless." *Province*, 27 October 2002, A22.

Toronto Star. "Canada the Ant at Climate Conference Picnic." 8 December 2009, B2.

– "Canada's Role Constructive in Copenhagen." 17 December 2009, A22.

Toronto Ward Museum. "Our Living History." (May 2017): http://www.wardmuseum.ca/thewardourlivinghistory.

Torrevillas, Phylicia. "Tent City Poses Danger to Art Collection: City." *Metro News Vancouver*, 18–20 November 2011, 6.

Tosone, Austen, "Get to Know 'An Incomplete History of Protest' at the Whitney." *Nylon.com*, 17 August 2017: https://nylon.com/articles/incomplete-history-of-protest-curator-interview.

Troian, Martha. "Copper Broken on Parliament Hill in First Nations Shaming Ceremony." CBC *News*, 29 July 2014: http://www.cbc.ca/beta/news/indigenous/copper-broken-on-parliament-hill-in-first-nations-shaming-ceremony-1.2719175.

Truth and Reconciliation Commission of Canada. *Calls to Action*. Winnipeg: Truth and Reconciliation Commission of Canada 2015.

Tsing, Anna Lowenhaupt. *Friction: An Ethnography of Global Connection*. Princeton: Princeton University Press 2004.

Tuck, Eve, and Wayne Yang. "Decolonization Is Not a Metaphor." *Decolonization: Indigeneity, Education & Society* 1, no. 1 (2012): 1–40.

Tucker-Abramson, Myra. "Spectacle Capitalism: Expo 86, the Olympics, and Public Education." In *Momentarily: Learning from Mega-Events*, edited by Bik Van der Pol, Alissa Firth-Eagland, and Urban Subjects, 58–63. Vancouver: Western Front 2010: http://www.urbansubjects.org/images/learning_from_vancouver/Momentarily%20Learning%20from%20Mega-Events.pdf.

Tuer, Dot. "Is It Still Privileged Art? The Politics of Class and Collaboration in the Art Practice of Carol Condé and Karl Beveridge." In *But Is It Art? The Spirit of Art as Activism*, edited by Nina Felshin. Seattle: Bay Press 1995.

turions, cheyanne. "Decolonization, Reconciliation, and the Extra-Rational Potential of the Arts." *Artseverywhere*, 23 March 2016: http://artseverywhere.ca/2016/03/23/1218.

– "How Not to Install Indigenous Art as a Feminist." In *Desire Change: Contemporary Feminist Art in Canada*, edited by Heather Davis, 242–56. Montreal: McGill-Queen's University Press 2017.

– "Thinking Again about Artist-Run Culture." *cheyanne turions's blog*, 14 October 2014: https://cheyanneturions.wordpress.com/2014/10/14/thinking-again-about-artist-run-culture.

Turk, James L. "Whose History on Display at New Museum?" *Toronto Star*, 9 December 2012.

Turner, Michael, and Melanie O'Brian. "Melanie O'Brian's View on Vancouver." *Canadian Art*, 5 September 2013: http://canadianart.ca/features/melanie-obrian/#sthash.4fV55RIN.dpuf.

Turner, Victor. *The Ritual Process: Structure and Anti-Structure*. Piscataway, NJ: Aldine Transaction 1995.

UK Department for Culture, Media, and Sport. *Creative Industries Mapping Document*. London: UK Government 1998: http://webarchive.nationalarchives.gov.uk/+/http://www.culture.gov.uk/reference_library/publications/4740.aspx.

Ukemonde. "Press Release." (3 August 1999): http://www.ukemonde.com/muser press1.html.

UPI Archives. "Indians Left the Museum of Anthropology at the University." (21 November 1981): http://www.upi.com/Archives/1981/11/21/Indians-left-the-museum-of-anthropology-at-the-University/9891375166800.

Urban Subjects. *602:000: Works on Housing*. (2011): http://www.urbansubjects.org/602000_works_on_housing.html#.

Valpy, Michael. "Police Do Better at Second Protest." *Globe and Mail*, 22 June 1988.

Van der Pol, Bik, and Urban Subjects. "In Dialogue." In *Momentarily: Learning from Mega-Events*, edited by Bik Van der Pol, Alissa Firth-Eagland, and Urban Subjects, 32–8. Vancouver: Western Front 2010: http://www.urbansubjects.org/images/learning_from_vancouver/Momentarily%20Learning%20from%20Mega-Events.pdf.

Vancouver Anarchist Online Archive. "Great Depression Radical History of Vancouver." (October 2009): https://vanarchive.wordpress.com/2009/10/20/great-depression-radical-history-of-vancouver.

Vancouver Art Gallery. "The Conceptual Design of the New Vancouver Art Gallery." *Vancouver Art Gallery website*: https://www.vanartgallery.bc.ca/future.html.

– *Master Planning Summary: A New Threshold*. Vancouver: Vancouver Art Gallery April 2005.

– *Strategic Plan 2002–2004*. Vancouver: Vancouver Art Gallery 2001.

– *Strategic Plan 2003–2006*. Vancouver: Vancouver Art Gallery 2002.

– *Strategic Plan 2007–2010*. Vancouver: Vancouver Art Gallery 2006.

Vancouver Courier. "Occupiers Vow to Stay on Vancouver Art Gallery Lawn." (16 October 2011): http://www.vancourier.com/news/occupiers-vow-to-stay-on-vancouver-art-gallery-lawn-1.379893.

Vancouver Magazine. "The Philanthropist." (1 March 2009): http://vanmag.com/uncategorized/the-philanthropist.

Vancouver Sun. "The Show Should Go On." 28 September 2001, A14.

Varga, Vincent. "Sightings." *Vernissage* (spring 2002): 22.

Vargas, Lance. "Baja to Vancouver Exhibits a Creative Cultural Corridor." In *La Jolla Light* nd, np. *Carr, O'Keefe, Kahlo: Places of Their Own*, 15 June–15 September 2002, VAG Exhibition Files, Library Press Clippings File.

Vartanian, Hrag. "Art Protest Groups Join Forces for Guerrilla Ribbon Cutting at New Whitney Museum." *Hyperallergic*, 15 April 2015: http://hyperallergic.com/199269/art-protest-groups-join-forces-for-guerrilla-ribbon-cutting-of-new-whitney-museum.

Vecsey, Christopher. "Grassy Narrows Reserve: Mercury Pollution, Social Disruption, and Natural Resources, a Question of Autonomy." *American Indian Quarterly* 11, no. 4 (1987): 287–314.

Vendeville, Geoffrey. "Protesters March on Queens Park over Mercury Poisoning in Grassy Narrows First Nation." *Toronto Star*, 7 July 2016.

Veterans Affairs Canada. "National Aboriginal Veterans Monument." (2016): http://www.veterans.gc.ca/eng/remembrance/memorials/canada/national-aboriginal-veterans-monument.

Vice Staff. "Canada's Waterless Communities: Shoal Lake 40." (2 October 2015): https://www.vice.com/en_ca/article/wd74qn/canadas-waterless-community-shoal-lake-40.

– "Drag the Red: Meet the Volunteers Searching for Bodies in Winnipeg's Red River." (10 September 2015): https://www.vice.com/en_ca/article/dp5dnv/drag-the-red.

Victoria and Albert Museum. *Rapid Response Collecting*. (2014): http://www.vam.ac.uk/content/articles/r/rapid-response-collecting.

Vinnick, Jeff, and Rafal Gerszak. "The Collector vs. the Director: Bob Rennie and the VAG." *Globe and Mail*, 11 August 2012.

Virno, Paolo. *Grammar of the Multitude: For an Analysis of Contemporary Forms of Life*. Translated by Isabella Bertoletti, James Cascaito, and Andrea Casson. Los Angeles: Semiotext(e) 2004.

Virno, Paolo, and Michael Hardt. *Radical Thought in Italy*, vol. 7. Minneapolis: University of Minnesota Press 1996.

Vishmidt, Marina. "Precarious Straits." *Mute* 1, no. 29, *The Precarious Issue* (2005): 93–5.

Vogel, Vanessa M.L. "The Glenbow Controversy and the Exhibition of North American Art." *Museum Anthropology* 14, no. 4 (1990): 7–11.

Vyhnak, Carola. "Once upon a City: Taking Aim at the Archer." *thestar.com*, 20 October 2016: https://www.thestar.com/yourtoronto/once-upon-a-city-archives/2016/10/20/once-upon-a-city-taking-aim-at-the-archer.html.

Walcott, Rinaldo. "Lament for a Nation: The Racial Geography of the Oh! Canada Project." *Fuse Magazine* 19 (1996): 15–23.

Walia, Harsha. "Decolonizing Together: Moving beyond a Politics of Solidarity toward a Practice of Decolonization." *Briarpatch*, 1 January 2012: https://briarpatchmagazine.com/articles/view/decolonizing-together

Wall, Karen. "Sharpest Knives in the Drawer: Culture at the Intersection of Oil and the State." In *Alberta Oil and the Decline of Democracy in Canada*, edited by Meenal Shrivastava and Lorna Stefanick, 333–61. Athabaska: Athabaska Press 2015.

Wallace, Mike. "The Battle of the *Enola Gay*." In *Mickey Mouse History and Other Essays on American Memory*, 269–318. Philadelphia: Temple University Press 1996.

Wallis, Brian. "The Art of Big Business." *Art in America* 74 (June 1986): 28–32.

– "Selling Nations: International Exhibitions and Cultural Diplomacy." In *Museum Culture: Histories, Discourses, Spectacles*, edited by Irit Rogoff and Daniel Sherman, 221–40. Minneapolis: University of Minnesota Press 1994.

Ward, Dennis. "Shoal Lake First Nation Residents Weep as Ottawa Balks at Funding Construction" *APTN*, 25 June 2015: http://aptnnews.ca/2015/06/25/shoal-lake-first-nation-residents-weep-as-ottawa-balks-at-funding-road-construction.

– "What's in a Name?" *APTN*, 20 December 2016: http://aptnnews.ca/2016/12/20/whats-in-a-name-manitoba-government-staying-clear-of-freedom-road-for-now.

Ward, John. "War Museum, Vets Reach Compromise." *Toronto Star*, 10 October 2007.

Warsza, Joanna, ed. *I Can't Work Like This: A Reader on Recent Boycotts and Contemporary Art*. Berlin: Sternberg Press 2017.

Watson, Albert. "Developers Build up Public Art." *Globe and Mail*, 13 January 2004, B13.

Watson, Scott. "'Pornography Disguised as Art': Some Recent Episodes Concerning Censorship and the Visual Arts in Canada." In *Interpreting Censorship in Canada*, edited by Klaus Petersen and Allan C. Hutchinson, 221–40. Toronto: University of Toronto Press 1999.

– "Urban Renewal: Ghost Traps, Collage, Condos, and Squats – Vancouver Art in the 1960s." In *Intertidal: Vancouver Art and Artists*, 31–50. Vancouver: Morris and Helen Belkin Art Gallery, UBC 2005.
Watson, Scott, and Lorna Brown, eds. "Introduction." In *Lalakenis/All Directions: A Journey of Truth and Unity*, 13–17. Vancouver: Morris and Helen Belkin Art Gallery, UBC 2014.
Weaver, Andrew. "Consider Environment When Voting." *Star-Phoenix*, 9 October 2008, A12.
Weinstein, Tamar. *You Should Have Stayed at Home*. Toronto: CBC 2011.
Welch, Mary Agnes. "CMHR No Conversation Starter." *Winnipeg Free Press*, 3 December 2014.
– "CMHR Rejects 'Genocide' for Native Policies." *Winnipeg Free Press*, 26 July 2013.
Werb, Jessica. "Vancouver Concert Hall and Theatre Society Envisions Hall beneath VAG Plaza." *Georgia Straight*, 4 March 2011.
Wherry, Aaron. "What He Was Talking about When He Talked about Colonialism." *Maclean's*, 1 October 2009: http://www.macleans.ca/uncategorized/what-he-was-talking-about-when-he-talked-about-colonialism.
Whitaker, Reg, Gregory S. Kealey, and Andrew Parnaby. *Secret Service: Political Policing in Canada from the Fenians to Fortress America*. Toronto: University of Toronto Press 2012.
White, Micah. *The End of Protest: A New Playbook for Revolution*. Toronto: Knopf Canada 2016.
Whitelaw, Anne. "Placing Aboriginal Art at the National Gallery of Canada." *Canadian Journal of Communications, Special Issue on Culture, Heritage and Art* 31, no. 1 (2006): 197–214.

Whitworth, Sandra. "Militarized Masculinities and the Politics of Peacekeeping: The Canadian Case." In *Critical Security Studies and World Politics*, edited by Ken Booth, 89–106. Boulder, CO: Lynne Rienner Publishers 2005.
Whyte, Murray. "AGO: Massive Downer." *Toronto Star blog*, April 2009: http://thestar.blogs.com/untitled/2009/04/ago-massive-downer.html.
– "Anatomy of a Protest: Wendy Coburn and the Mechanics of Slutwalk." *Toronto Star*, 18 January 2015.
– "Canada Revisited at the Art Gallery of Ontario." *Toronto Star*, 3 July 2017: https://www.thestar.com/entertainment/visualarts/2017/07/03/canada-revisited-at-the-art-gallery-of-ontario.html.
– "'Of Africa' at the ROM Aims to Repair Old Wounds." *Toronto Star*, 23 October 2014: http://www.thestar.com/entertainment/visualarts/2014/10/23/of_africa_at_the_rom_aims_to_repair_old_wounds.html.
Wiebe, Lindsey. "Digging up Dirt on Museum: 2008 Search for Artifacts at The Forks 'a Tragedy.'" *Winnipeg Free Press*, 16 June 2009.
Wilkes, Rima, Catherine Corrigall-Brown, and Danielle Ricard. "Nationalism and Media Coverage of Indigenous People's Collective Action in Canada." *American Indian Culture and Research Journal* 34, no. 4 (2010): 41–59.
Wilkin, Karen, and Roald Nasgaard. *Changing Visions: The Canadian Landscape*. Toronto: Art Gallery of Ontario 1976 (1989).
Williams, Caleb. "The Transformation of the Museum into a Zone of Hot Topicality and Tabbo Representation: The Endorsement/Interrogation Response Syndrome." In *Hot Topics, Public Culture, Museums*, edited by Fiona Cameron and Lynda Kelly, 18–34. Newcastle upon Tyne: Cambridge Scholars Press 2010.

Williams, Carol. "A Working Chronology of Feminist Cultural Activities and Events in Vancouver, 1970–1990." In *Vancouver Anthology*, 2nd edition, edited by Stan Douglas, 173–216. Vancouver: Talon Books 2009.
Williams, Kristian. "The Politics of Denunciation." *TowardsFreedom.com*, 20 February 2014: http://towardfreedom.com/29-archives/activism/3455-the-politics-of-denunciation.
Wilson, Jordan. "'Belongings' in *c̓əsnaʔəm: the city before the city*." IPinch: *Intellectual Property Issues in Cultural Heritage: Theory, Practice, Policy, Ethics*, 27 January 2016: https://www.sfu.ca/ipinch/outputs/blog/citybeforecitybelongings.
Wilson, Sheena, Adam Carlson, and Imre Szeman, eds. *Petrocultures: Oil, Politics, Culture*. Kingston and Montreal: McGill-Queen's University Press 2017.
Wilson-Goldie, Kaelen. "On Bandwagons." *Frieze* 142: https://frieze.com/article/bandwagons.
Windsor Star. "Pranksters Say Canada Wiping Out Websites." 8 January 2010, A8.
Withey, Elizabeth. "Art Gallery of Alberta Timeline." *Edmonton Journal*, 27 January 2010.
Withrow, William J. "To Herald the Opening of a Magnificent New Canadian Wing." *Globe and Mail*, 24 September 1977, D2.
Witt, Andrew. "Splendour without Diminishment." *The Mainlander*, 11 June 2017): http://themainlander.com/2017/06/11/splendour-without-diminishment.
– "The Vancouver Art Gallery and the Eviction of a Political Idea – Part I." *The Mainlander*, 13 July 2013: http://themainlander.com/2013/07/13/the-vancouver-art-gallery-and-the-eviction-of-a-political-idea-part-i.
– "The Vancouver Art Gallery and the Eviction of a Political Idea – Part II." *The Mainlander*, 28 July 2013: http://themainlander.com/2013/07/28/the-vancouver-art-gallery-and-the-eviction-of-a-political-idea-part-ii.

Wodtke, Larissa. "A Lovely Building for Difficult Knowledge: The Architecture of the Canadian Museum for Human Rights." *Review of Education, Pedagogy, and Cultural Studies* 37, no. 2–3 (2015): 207–26.
Wolfe, Patrick. "Settler Colonialism and the Elimination of the Native." *Journal of Genocide Research* 8, no. 4 (2006): 387–409.
Wood, Kelly. "The Vancouver Carts: A Memoire." In *The Vancouver Carts: Photographs by Kelly Wood*, 7–11. London: Black Dog Publishing 2016.
Woods, Allan. "Liberals Add New $9 Billion." *Gazette*, 23 November 2005, A1.
Woodward's Anti-Poverty Coalition. *Community News* 10 (3 February 2002).
Worth, Jess. "Getting Europe Out of the Tar Sands: The Rise of the UK Tar Sands Network." In *A Line in the Tar Sands: Struggles for Environmental Justice*, edited by Joshua Kahn Russell, Stephen d'Arcy, Tony Weis, and Toban Black, 186–95. Oakland: M Press 2014.
Wrightson, Kelsey R. "The Limits of Recognition: *The Spirit Sings*, Canadian Museums and the Colonial Politics of Recognition." *Museum Anthropology* 40, no. 1 (March 2017): 36–51.
Wu, Chin-Tao. *Privatising Culture: Corporate Art Intervention since the 1980s*. London: Verso 2003.
Wulwik, Lisa. "Squatting as an Organizing Tool." *Woodsquat (West Coast Line)* 37, nos. 2–3 (2003–04): 18–19.
Wysote, Travis. "Risk Your Life Accessing the Museum: The Canadian Museum for Human Rights and the Question of Indigenous Genocides." MA thesis, Concordia University, 2015.
X, Andrew. "Give Up Activism." *Do or Die* 9 (1999): 160–6.

Yaffe, Barbara. "Does Enbridge Donate to Ethical Oil?" *Vancouver Sun*, 20 February 2012.
– "Tories May Be Close to Mood of Populace on Climate Change." *Vancouver Sun*, 15 December 2009, B1.
Yang, Guobin. "Achieving Emotion in Collective Action: Emotional Processes and Movement Mobilization in the 1989 Chinese Student Movement." *Sociological Quarterly* 41, no. 4 (2000): 593–614.
Yates, Kieran. "Artist Stan Douglas: Why I Restaged the London Riots." *Guardian*, 25 October 2017: https://www.theguardian.com/artanddesign/2017/oct/25/artist-stan-douglas-2011-london-riots.
Yates, McKee. "The Arts of Occupation." *The Nation*, 11 December 2011: http://www.thenation.com/article/165094/arts-occupation#axzz2Zmk3jK3r.
Yedlin, Deborah. "Weak Climate Deal; Canada Missing in Action." *Times-Colonist*, 22 December 2009, A12.
Yes Men. "About." http://theyesmen.org/index.php/about.
York, Geoffrey. "Shoe Museum Not Apartheid Issue, Aldermen Told." *Globe and Mail*, 13 February 1986.
Yoshida, Adam. "Protesters Pose Threat." *Province*, 19 September 2002, A19.
Young, Carey. *Incorporated*. London: Film and Video Umbrella 2002.
Yúdice, George. *The Expediency of Culture: Uses of Culture in the Global Era*. Durham and London: Duke University Press 2003.
Yuen, Eddie, Daniel Burton-Rose, and George N. Katsiaficas. *Confronting Capitalism: Dispatches from a Global Movement*. Brooklyn and Berkeley: Soft Skull Press 2003.
Yuen, Eddie, George Katsiaficas, and Daniel Burton Rose, eds., *The Battle of Seattle: The New Challenge to Capitalist Globalization*. New York: Soft Skull Press 2001.

Zacharias, Yvonne, with file from Lindsay Kines. "Protesters Camp at Woodward's Door." *Vancouver Sun*, 23 September 2002, B1.
Zardini, Mirko. *It's All Happening So Fast: A Counter-History of the Modern Canadian Environment*. Heijningen, Netherlands: Jap Sam Books 2017.
Zemans, Joyce. "How Far Will the Rust Spread." In *Free Expression, Public Support, and Censorship: Examining Government's Role in the Arts in Canada and the United States*, edited by Michael Margolis, 87–97. Lanham, NY, and London: University Press of America 1994.
Zolberg, Vera. "Museums as Contested Sites of Remembrance: The Enola Gay Affair." In *Theorizing Museums*, edited by Sharon Macdonald and Gordon Fyfe, 69–82. Oxford: Blackwell 1996.
Zorach, Rebecca. "Art and Soul: An Experimental Friendship between the Street and a Museum." *Art Journal* 70, no. 2 (summer 2011): 66–87.

Index

1%, 16–17, 82, 102, 243, 247, 333n117
1st Canadian Parachute Battalion Association, 130
1867 (CMH), 211
350.org, 184, 215–18
420 sit-in, 329n29
9/11, xii, 120, 122, 124–5, 140, 142
99%, 243, 247

Aariak, Eva, 203
Abbot & Cordova (Douglas), 263–5
Aboriginal Healing Foundation, 161
Abu Ghraib, 124
activist art, 19, 180, 271. *See also* art activism; political art
ACT UP, 102
affect, xiv, 123–4; and art, 19; of protest, 180, 278n16, 278n23; theory, 283n92. *See also* emotional habitus; tear gas epiphany
Afghanistan War, 124–6, 140, 154, 200
Africa, 63–4, 200, 292n135. See also *Into the Heart of Africa*
African Americans, xv, 45. See also *Harlem on My Mind* (Met); Smithsonian National Museum of African American History and Culture
African Canadians, 63, 65–6, 136, 292n135. *See also* Coalition for the Truth About Africa (CFTA); *Into the Heart of Africa*
Aga Khan Museum (Toronto), 80
agents provocateurs, 316n4. *See also* police
Agitprop! (Brooklyn Museum), 298n40
AIDS activism, 102. *See also* ACT UP
Air Force Association of Canada, 136
Akiwenzie, Alec, 54
Akwesasne Warrior Society, 66
Akyeaw, Yaw Oluwasanjo, 66
Alberta, 73; battle over the tar sands, 202–3; climate change policy, 219, 221; oil culture of, 193–4, 200–5; oil sponsorships in, 193; pipelines, 201; pollution, 197–8; Smithsonian folklife display, 199–200, 322n106. *See also* Art Gallery of Alberta; tar sands
Alberta Ballet, 193
Alberta Crafts Council, 199
Alberta Theatre Projects, 193
Alcan, 317n6(6)
Alexander Docks (Winnipeg), 145–6
Allward, Walter Seymour, 131
alterglobalization movement, xi, 14–16, 188, 277n6, 281n63
alt-right, 279n25
Amaya, Mario, 33
American Alliance of Museums, 188–9
American Association of Museums, 44, 287n29
American Indian Movement (AIM), 45, 53, 95, 289n75
American Museum of Natural History (New York), 42, 313n64, 327n230
Ames, Michael, 59, 71–4
Amnesty International, 269

anarchism, xiv, 3–4, 243, 262, 285n11; Anarchist Archive, 300n98; horizontalism of, 14. *See also* squats
Anatomy of a Protest (Coburn), 178–81, 317n6 (interstice 5), 317n9 (interstice 5)
Andy Warhol Gang, 225
Anicinabe Park (Kenora), 106
Anishinaabe, 104, 154, 171
anti-abortion movement, xv, 93, 146, 169, 229
anti-Americanism, 31, 33, 47, 304n37
anti-capitalism: and Canadian nationalism, 47–8; parody of, 4; protests, 14–15, 28, 57, 76, 229, 247
anti-catalogue (MOMA), 288n53
antifa, 267
anti-globalization. *See* alterglobalization movement
anti-logging protests, 93, 200, 300n79, 317n6(6)
anti-pipeline activism, 184–5, 191
anti-poverty activism, 225–6, 330n45. *See also* homelessness
Anti-Poverty Committee, 262–3
anti-racism movement, xii, 16, 93, 229
Anti-Reed Campaign (ARC), 104, 106–7. See also *Changing Visions: The Canadian Landscape* (AGO); Reed Paper
Anti-Terrorism Act, xii
anti-war movement, xi, 27, 42, 47, 129; in the Canadian War Museum, 86, 129, 307n103–307n104; in *Canvas of War*, 119; protests, 125–6; and the Warrior Nation, 123
APEC. *See* Asia-Pacific Economic Cooperation (APEC) meeting
Arab-Canadian community, 142–4
Arab Spring, xii, 15–16, 243
The Archer (Moore), 46
architecture: of ceremonial spaces, 111; of museums, 39–40, 71, 83–4, 114, 168, 253, 295n190, 303n17, 307n110; renovations, 76, 78–84, 230, 297n10; in Vancouver, 242. *See also* Art Gallery of Ontario (AGO); Bilbao effect; Canadian Museum for Human Rights; Canadian War Museum; Creative Cities; Royal Ontario Museum (ROM); starchitects; Vancouverism
archives, 84, 88; community-based, 100; and corporate sponsorship, 97; digital, 101; hidden collections, 214–15; neutrality of, 11, 102; political collections, 76–7, 268–71; protest, 28, 91–2, 187, 300n98; racism in, 302n126; rebel, 300n89. *See also* Art Gallery of Ontario (AGO); Interference Archive; Political Art Documentation/Distribution; protest ephemera; Simon Fraser University; Society of American Archivists; UBC Museum of Anthropology
Archuar Indigenous Community, 197
Arctic, 203
Arendt, Hannah, 229, 244
Armenian-Canadian Community, 151
Arone, Shidane, 117, 119. *See also* Somalia Affair
art activism, 19, 184–5; in Canada, 191, 198, 213; impact of, 217, 222. *See also* Liberate Tate; Not An Alternative; participatory art; performance art; site-specific art; social art
art criticism, 20–1, 23, 26, 90, 326n225
Art for an Oil-Free Coast (Calgary City Hall), 195
Art Gallery of Alberta, 80, 193, 195, 256
Art Gallery of Nova Scotia, 80
Art Gallery of Ontario (AGO), 5–6; archives, 33, 36, 91–2; Canadian art wing of, 36; contemporary art in, 46–7, 49–50; Creative Minds symposium, 204; curator hiring, 31–6, 47, 285n13; exhibitions, 23, 68–9, 88, 288n52; funding of, 35–6; fundraisers for, 3–4; Henry Moore at, 286n22; layoffs at, 83; protests against, 48, 51, 68, 104–7; protests at, 43, 56, 279n10; protests by, 57; as racist, 36; renovation of, 80–1, 114, 242, 254, 256, 335n192; Zacks wing, 35. See also *Changing Visions*; *Every.Now.Then*; Henry Moore Sculpture Centre; *It's Still Privileged Art* (Condé and Beveridge); "Massive Uprising"; Wattenmaker, Richard
art history, 6, 26; Canadian, 47, 54–5, 104; on museums, 21; of Vancouver, 235. *See also* visual culture studies
Artifact 671B (Belmore), 61
Art Institute of Chicago, 239
artist-run centres, 29, 58, 285n140; censorship protests, 57; private funding, 239–40; radical, 295n191
artists: and censorship, 57–8, 67; and creative industries, 12, 14, 20, 232–3, 238, 280n44, 282n70; and the Culture Wars, 284n137; and gentrification, 18, 82, 239–40, 246, 256; museum activism of, 188–91, 195, 216, 254, 287n29; and the museums system, xvi, 16, 43, 45, 47–52, 55, 85, 287n21; and nation, 24; political organizing of, 31, 41, 104–6, 142–3, 218n27, 280n33, 290n91. *See also* Art Workers' Coalition; Canadian Artists' Representation (CAR); creative workers; entrepreneurs
Artists' Protest Committee, 45
"Artists' Tower of Protest," 45
Art & Language group, 290n91
art market, 49–51, 82, 223, 233, 238, 246
Art Museum at the University of Toronto, 179
Art Not Oil, 222, 271, 317n10, 319n46

artscanada, 27
Arts Council England, 22
arts funding: cuts to, 56, 68, 82, 116–17, 193; and museums, 69–70, 256; by oil companies, 211; public, 13, 25, 82–3, 188, 241, 257. *See also* Canada, federal government
Art Strike Against Racism, Sexism, Repression and War, 20
Art Workers' Coalition, 16, 34, 45, 51–2, 279n15, 290n91
Asher, Michael, 216
Asia-Pacific, 201, 207, 236, 242
Asia-Pacific Economic Cooperation (APEC) meeting, 28, 93–5, 102, 268–71, 328n12. *See also* UBC Museum of Anthropology
Aslop, Will, 80
Asper, David, 311n13
Asper, Gail, 160, 169, 311n13
Asper, Israel, 118, 148–54, 256. *See also* Canadian Museum for Human Rights
Asper Foundation, 149, 153–4
Assembly of First Nations, 61, 157, 163
Assembly of Manitoba Chiefs, 151
Asubpeeschoseewagong First Nation, 51, 104, 106. See also *Changing Visions: The Canadian Landscape* (AGO); Grassy Narrows; mercury poisoning; Reed Paper
Athabasca Chipewyan First Nation, 189–90, 201
Athabasca River, 200
Attawapiskat First Nation, 324n152
Audain, Michael, 239, 243–5, 251–2, 255, 332n83. *See also* Michael Audain Foundation; Polygon Gallery; Polygon Homes; real estate developers
Audain Art Museum (Whistler), 252
Audain Gallery at SFU, 239
austerity, 15–16, 247, 256, 282n70
Australia, 10, 40, 159, 280n33, 303n14
authoritative institutions, 25, 29, 295n190; and activists, 85–6, 95, 189; collecting policies, 97, 101, 300n89; and colonization, 157–8; consumption of culture in, 140; and controversies, 42; core myths of, 90, 92; display practices of, 13, 86; elitism of, 16, 39, 43, 77; Indigenous critique of, 147; intersectionality in, 327n230; museums as, 69, 81; political art in, 294n185; and political context, 268; power of, 218; and resistance, 29. *See also* artists; museum collections; museum display; museum exhibitions; protest ephemera; universal survey museums
Awalaskensis I, 326n205
Awalaskensis II: Journey of Truth and Unity, 213–15, 326n205

Baffin Island, 73
Baja to Vancouver (VAG), 235
band councils, 210, 289n76
Banff, Alberta, 256
Banff Centre for the Arts, 320n55
Bartels, Kathleen, 224–5, 232, 241, 251–2, 255. *See also* Vancouver Art Gallery
Bata Shoe museum, 56, 124
Battle for Seattle, xiii, 14–15, 277n12
Baxter, Iain, 104
Beaverbrook Art Gallery (Fredericton), 57
Beaverbrook Collection of War Art (CWM), 119, 132
Bechara, Soha, 142
Belcourt, Christi, 204
Bella Coola, BC, 73
Belmore, Rebecca, 29, 61, 297n13, 314n103. See also *Artifact 671B*; *Traces*
Benner, Tom, 104
Bennett, Bill, 73
Berlant, Lauren, 123, 246
Berlin Biennale 7, 16, 18
Bernier, Serge, 135
Beveridge, Karl, 29, 49–50, 56, 288n52, 288n53; on CAR, 34; and CARFAC, 286n15; political organizing of, 290n91. *See also* Condé, Carole; Independent Artists' Union
Bilbao effect, 78–84, 116, 169, 240, 243. *See also* Creative Cities; tourism
BIPOC activism, 58, 77, 285n13, 332n93. *See also* African Canadians; Black artists; Indigenous peoples
Bird, Kate, 259
"Birthmark" (Liberate Tate), 186
Bishopsgate Institute, 98
Black Action Defense Committee, 66
Black artists, 45, 52
Black Bloc, 180
Black Emergency Cultural Coalition, 45, 293n164
Black Lives Matter, xii, 16; collecting from, 97, 301n106; online, 101; at the Smithsonian, 282n87; Toronto, 23
Black Power movement, 45
blockades, xiii, 156; artefacts from, 91, 102, 303n28; at Elsipogtog, 209; Grassy Narrows, 107; as Indigenous resistance, 184, 206, 247. *See also* Kanehsatà:ke Resistance
blockbuster exhibitions, 84, 86, 118, 255. *See also* museum exhibitions
Bogusky, Alf, 241
boil-water advisories, 90, 146, 172, 175. *See also* Shoal Lake 40 First Nation
Bomber Command, 133, 137, 305n44, 309n160. *See also* Canadian War Museum; *The Valour and the Horror*

Borduas, Paul-Émile, 35
Bourdieu, Pierre, 123
Bourriaud, Nicolas, 14
Boutin-Sweet, Marjolaine, 212
boycotts, 40, 75; of 2014 Sydney Biennale, 280n33; of the Canadian War Museum, 131, 134, 308n114; moving beyond, 157–8; of *Spirit Sings*, 58–9, 60–1, 63, 76–7, 192, 212, 290n108
BP or Not BP, 85–6, 186; actions, 317n25; objectives of, 319n46; "Stolen Goods" tour, 327n230; strategies of, 187, 216
Brantford, Ontario, 53
Brazil, 317n27
Britain. *See* United Kingdom
British Columbia: arts funding, 332n83; government of, 225–7, 240–1, 254–5; homelessness in, 98; Indigenous title, 329n30, 333n127; Japanese internment camps in, 124; protests in, 73, 76, 93–5; resource development, 300n79; tanker traffic, 218. *See also* Campbell, Gordon; Clark, Christy
British Council, 232–6
British Museum, 40, 65; collecting protest material, 97–8; contemporary art, 80; exhibition protests, 85, 186; sponsorship of, 317n1; "Stolen Goods" tour, 327n230. See also *I Object*; *Sunken Cities*
British Petroleum (BP): in London, 201; protests against, 85, 182–3, 185–7; sponsorships of, 8, 21, 317n1, 317n26; tar sands operations, 190. *See also* BP or Not BP; corporate and private sponsorships; Liberate Tate; oil industry; Tate Museum
Brooks, Sharon, 67
Brown, Jim, 32–3
Brown, Kyle, 130–2. *See also* Somalia Affair
Brown, Lorna, 238
Brown, Mike, xv
Buehrle, Emil G., 67, 294n173
Bureau of Indian Affairs (US), 95
Burnaby, BC, 94, 201, 322n110
Busby, Cathy, 213
Bush, George W. (President), 125
Bush, Jack, 104
Butler, Judith, xiv–xv, 123

Cairo, xiii, 85
Calatrava, Santiago, 78
Calgary, Alberta, 58, 153, 193, 195, 312n40. *See also* Glenbow Museum; *Spirit Sings: Artistic Traditions of Canada's First Peoples*
Calgary Olympics, 58–9, 212, 290n108. See also *Spirit Sings: Artistic Traditions of Canada's First Peoples*
Cameron, Duncan, 36, 43–5, 49–52, 59, 287n29, 332n91
Campaign for Nuclear Disarmament, 97
Campbell, Gordon (Premier), 225–6, 230, 236, 239, 262, 329n28
Camp for Climate Action, 189–90
Canada: broken treaties, 213–14; constitution of, 72–3; creative industries in, 12; environment, 184, 205–10, 216, 327n1; extraction economy, 184, 194, 199, 203; history of resistance, 264; human rights in, 151–2, 156; military conflict, 306n72; and museum displays, 5, 22, 24–5, 90, 294n185, 326n196; oil culture of, 199–205, 208, 210, 216, 323n143; racism in, 267; as a settler nation, 9, 23, 25, 35, 54, 63, 88–9, 154, 159, 212; sponsorships of museums and galleries, 190–1, 317n5(6); suppression of protests, 5. *See also* Canada, federal government; Canada 150; colonialism; colonization; peacekeeping; petroculture; petrostate; settler nationalism; Warrior Nation
Canada, federal government: 1969 White Paper, 289n75, 295n7; APEC meeting, 269; climate change policy, 219–21; as employer, 115; funding for the arts and museums, 97, 116–17, 121–2, 124, 149, 152–3, 167–8, 254, 304n32, 332n83; genocides recognized by, 163; heritage and museums policy, 6, 25–6, 58, 153–4, 211; and Indigenous peoples, 147, 157, 174, 176–7, 209, 290n109, 298n52; and the oil lobby, 212; residential schools apology and settlement, 161–2, 313n82; sponsorship regulations, 320n59. *See also* Canada 150; Canadian Broadcasting Corporation (CBC); Conservative Party of Canada; Department of Communications; Department of Indian and Northern Affairs; Environment Canada; Fisheries and Oceans Canada; Harper, Stephen; Liberal Party of Canada; National Research Council of Canada; residential schools; Senate of Canada; Trudeau, Justin; Trudeau, Pierre
Canada 150, 23, 88–9, 211–12, 284n119
Canada Council, 56, 116, 121–2
Canada House (London), 190
Canada Revenue Agency (CRA), 208
Canadian Airborne Division, 117. *See also* Canadian military forces; Somalia Affair
Canadian Anthropology Society, 211
Canadian Archaeological Association, 212
Canadian Art, 35–6, 41, 47, 285n13
Canadian Artists' Representation (CAR): curator hiring, 31, 34–6; protests by, 47, 51, 104–5; radicalization of artists, 58; success of, 52
Canadian Association of Petroleum Producers (CAPP), 193, 196–9, 211–13, 215–16,

325n172. *See also* corporate and private sponsorships; *Energy: Power to Choose* (CSTM); oil industry
Canadian Association of University Teachers, 211
Canadian Broadcasting Corporation (CBC), 35, 56, 116, 133, 138, 304n32. *See also* media; *The Valour and the Horror*
Canadian Conference of the Arts, 43, 70
Canadian Ethnology Society (CESCE), 60
Canadian Forum, 27
Canadian Historical Association, 211–12
Canadian International Development Agency, 261
Canadian Lesbian and Gay Archives, 300n98
Canadian military forces: in Afghanistan, 124; budget cuts, 117; history, 118, 120, 211, 306n72; and Indigenous resistance, 66, 168; marginalized members of, 305n48; policy, 126–7; public interest in, 116, 121–2. *See also* Canadian Airborne Division; Canadian War Museum; military; new warriors; peacekeeping; Somalia Affair; veterans; Warrior Nation
Canadian Museum for Human Rights: and activism, 168–70; architecture of, 80–1, 170–1, 175, 227, 314n108; Content Advisory Committee, 160–2; cost of, 254, 312n31, 335n192; critiques of, 166–8; decolonization of, 147–8, 155–60, 176–7; display strategies of, 84, 86–7, 162, 165–6, 268, 314n103; founding of, 118, 148–55; fundraising for, 82–3, 153, 256; Grassy Narrows exhibition, 303n28; hydroelectricity supply, 315n137; Idle No More, 206; as a national museum, 75, 160–1, 211; opening of, 145–6, 310n6(5); and Shoal Lake 40, 147, 170–6; sponsorship of, 198; use of "genocide," 163–6, 311n16, 314n101. *See also* genocide; human rights; Indigenous Perspectives Gallery; media; Murray, Stuart; Museum of Canadian Human Rights Violations; national museums; residential schools; Shoal Lake 40 First Nation
Canadian Museum of Civilization: architecture of, 80, 303n17; collecting practices, 54; exhibitions, 61, 86, 118–23, 158, 294n183, 294n185, 306n74, 310n4 (interstice 4); Idle No More, 206; name change, 167, 211; as a national museum, 121; oil sponsorship, 197; protests against, 142–4; state functions at, 125; support for CWM, 124; trustees of, 136. *See also* Canadian Museum of History; *INDIGENA*; *Lands Within Me: Expressions by Canadian Artists of Arab Origin*
Canadian Museum of History: architecture of, 80; benefit to oil companies, 218; collections, 54, 90–1, 95–6, 101, 300n76; establishment of, 167, 210–12; exhibitions, 89–90, 211, 325n191, 325n193–325n194, 326n196; Indigenous actions at, 326n218; as a national museum, 75; protest archives, 92–3; sponsorship of, 184, 197, 212–16, 325n172. *See also* Canadian Museum of Civilization
Canadian Museum of History Crown corporation, 112
Canadian Museum of Nature, 197, 321n92
Canadian Museums Association, 61, 157, 217, 298n52. *See also* Task Force on Museums and First Peoples
Canadian Science and Technology Museum (CSTM), 195–7, 320n77. *See also* Canadian Association of Petroleum Producers; *Energy: Power to Choose*; Imperial Oil
Canadian Security Intelligence Service (CSIS), 207, 226, 329n21
Canadian War Museum: anti-war activism in, 86; architecture of, 80, 129–30, 307n110; bombing exhibition, 112–13, 131, 308n118; campaign for a new building, 116–18, 124, 304n29, 304n30; Canadian Experience Galleries, 127–30; collections, 92, 118–19, 305n49, 307n103, 307n113, 308n114; content decisions, 305n44; and the contestation over Canadian history, 139–41; and Creative Cities rhetoric, 113–16; Holocaust memorial at, 118, 137, 148, 304n42, 311n11; on Japanese internments, 309n161; as national museum, 121; Passing the Torch campaign, 121–2, 124, 151, 311n14; press coverage of, 125–6; reviews of, 128–9; Senate subcommittee hearings on, 137–8; veterans' protest of, 128–36, 138–9, 176. *See also* Bomber Command; Canadian military forces; media; new warriors; veterans; Warrior Nation
Canadian Women's Movement Collection (University of Ottawa), 300n98
Cannizzo, Jeanne, 63–5, 292n135. See also *Into the Heart of Africa*
Canvas Georgia, 253
Canvas of War, 119–23, 138, 305n48, 308n116. *See also* Canadian Museum of Civilization; Canadian War Museum; media
Canwest Global Communications and Media Corporation, 118, 149–50, 311n13. *See also* Asper, Israel
Cape Breton, 203
capitalism, 17; and assimilation of Indigenous peoples, 210; imposition of, 155; and museums, 18, 79, 189; new, 12; protests against, 14, 42; struggle against, 19. *See also* anticapitalism; neoliberalism

Cardinal, Douglas, 80, 303n17
Cardinal-Schubert, Joane, 29
CARFAC, 52, 56, 286n15. *See also* Canadian Artists' Representation
Carnegie Community Action Project (CCAP), 261
CARO (CAR Ontario), 106
Carr, Emily, 35, 223–4
Carr, O'Keefe, Kahlo: Place of Their Own (VAG), 223–7, 230–1, 331n71; opening, 328n12; protests at, 239, 262, 329n28. *See also* Vancouver Art Gallery
A Cause for Celebration? First Things First (Themuseum), 23. *See also* Canada 150
Cedar Man (David), 93
censorship, xvi, 57–8, 67–8. *See also* pornography and obscenity legislation
Chadderton, Cliff, 118, 131, 134. *See also* veterans
Chambers, Jack, 47, 104–5
Changing Visions: The Canadian Landscape (AGO), 51, 55, 104–7, 285n1
Charter of Rights and Freedoms, 74, 149, 151–2
Chenhall object classification system, 91, 299n65
Chiapas, Mexico, 15
child welfare system, 164
Chile, 148
Chilliwack Indian Council, 73
China, 255. *See also* China National Offshore Oil Corporation (CNOOC); National Museum of China
China National Offshore Oil Corporation (CNOOC), 193, 255–6
Chipewyan Prairie Dene First Nation, 201
Chrétien, Jean (Prime Minister), 306n70
Christian, Wayne (Chief), 296n11
citizenship, 68, 77, 111–12; active, 84; and museums, 166–7, 210, 216; and oil, 200
City on Edge: A Century of Vancouver Activism (MOV), 86, 258–60
civil rights movement, xiii–xiv; in Canada, 42, 305n57; collecting from, 95; in museums, 45; occupations, 247
Clandestine Insurgent Rebel Clown Army, 187–8
Clark, Christy (Premier), 248
Clark, Paraskeva, 299n71
class: activism, 280n44; and art, 35; and museums, 91, 189; and Occupy Wall Street, 245; and protest, xiv; and real estate development, 239, 265; and tourism, 78; warfare, 43–4, 226, 267; working, 36, 280n44. *See also* creative class; labour
Clayoquot Sound, 94–5. *See also* anti-logging protests
Clearsky, Murray, 163
Clifford, James, 39, 71. *See also* contact zones
climate change, xii, 16; action on, 8, 202, 221–2; in Canada, 327n1; and censoring, 183; documenting of, 205; exhibitions on, 86; as human rights issue, 164; impact of, 199; and museums, 218, 317n9(6), 327n229; and museums sponsorship, 196, 215–16; policy, 203; protests, 169, 185, 189, 219–22, 318n31; and tar sands extraction, 200. *See also* media
Climate Debt Agents, 220
climate jihadist, 207
Clinton, Bill (President), 269–70
Coalition for the Truth About Africa (CFTA), 64–6, 136, 139, 292n135, 292n144, 319n47. See also *Into the Heart of Africa*
Coalition to Oppose the Arms Trade, 129
Coast Salish, 93, 247–8
Coburn, Wendy, 178–81, 317n6 (interstice 5), 317n9 (interstice 5). See also *Anatomy of a Protest*
Cockburn, Bruce, 129
collective effervescence (Durkheim), xiv
Collis, Stephen, 244, 248–9
Collison, Nika, 218
colonialism, 25; in the Canadian Museum for Human Rights, 164; and infrastructure projects, 319n45; and museums, 42, 66, 158–9; protests against, 47; and recognition of Indigenous peoples, 62. *See also* colonization; settler colonialism
colonization: of Africa, 64; in Canada, 284n119; fight against, 334n140; role of museums in, 68–9, 158–9; wealth derived from, 111. *See also* colonialism; decolonization; Indigenous land; settler colonialism
Colville, Alex, 104
Comfort, Charles, 290n107
Committee to Strengthen Canadian Culture, 31–6, 285n11
communitas (Taylor), xiv
Concord Pacific, 245, 333n127. *See also* real estate developers
Condé, Carole, 29, 49–50, 56, 288n52, 288n53; political organizing of, 290n91. *See also* Beveridge, Karl; Independent Artists' Union
condominiums, 237–8, 262. *See also* gentrification; real estate; real estate developers; Vancouverism
Confederation Centre (PEI), 290n107
Confused: Sexual Views (VAG), 55, 241, 290n105
Conservative Party of Canada, 174; attack on scientists and the environmental movement, 205–10; embrace of the Warrior Nation, 126;

heritage policy, 211; and human rights museum, 152–3; ideology, 167–8; new warriors, 140. *See also* Harper, Stephen; Jobs and Growth Act
Constitution Act, 1982, 74, 295n7, 295n10
Constitutional Express, 73. *See also* Constitution Act, 1982
contact zones (Clifford), 25, 39, 71
contemporary art, 21, 27; activism, 19; in Canada, 24; controversies, 29; as critique, 297n13; market, 78–80; in museums, 35, 45–6, 51; private collections, 239; Vancouver scene, 27, 228, 230, 232–6, 330n50. *See also* activist art; artists; contemporary art galleries
contemporary art galleries, 50–1, 55, 80, 216, 253
Contemporary Photography from the Collection of the National Film Board, 56
Cool Britannia, 232
COP 15 (Copenhagen), 219–22, 327n1, 327n7. *See also* climate change
COP 21 (Paris), 222. *See also* climate change; Paris Climate Accord
Copenhagen, Denmark, 219–22. *See also* COP 15
Copenhagen Centre for Contemporary Art, 222
Copper-Breaking Ceremony, 213–15, 217–18, 326n205. See also *Awalaskensis II: Journey of Truth and Unity*, Dick, Beau
Copps, Sheila, 124, 306n70
Coreth, Mark, 221
corporate and private sponsorships: of the arts, 27, 80; Canadian context of protests against, 192–3, 216, 318n31; of *Changing Visions*, 104–7; and collecting from social movements, 97; of museum building/renovations, 82; of museums, 7, 25, 77, 317n5(6); need for, 69, 90; protests against, 10, 23, 28, 39, 60–1, 67, 182–3, 191, 210–18, 280n33; of public institutions, 17, 151, 185–9, 211; reversal of, 50, 68; support for, 21–2; UK protests against, 185–7. *See also* Asper, Israel; British Petroleum (BP); Canadian Association of Petroleum Producers (CAPP); greenwashing; Imperial Oil; naming rights; oil industry; Petro-Canada; Shell Oil; Transfield; Vale
corporate creativity, 79
Cotter, Holland, 17–18
Coulthard, Glen, 62, 202, 204, 284n127
Council of Canadians, 197–8, 215–16
counterpublics, 187–8, 229
Cranmer-Webster, Gloria, 158
Creative Cities, 5, 11–12; artists in, 246; and museum building, 78, 114–16, 139–40; museums' role in, 29, 70, 77; and Occupy Wall Street, 246; Ottawa as, 116; over-enthusiasm for, 256; struggles with, 247; and the VAG's strategic plan, 242–3; Vancouver as, 228, 231–3, 238–9, 245, 252. *See also* Bilbao effect; creative class; creative industries; Florida, Richard; neoliberalism; Ottawa; Vancouver, BC
creative class, 12, 78, 115–16, 239, 251. *See also* corporate creativity; Creative Cities; creative industries; creative workers; entrepreneurs; Florida, Richard; labour
creative industries, 4, 11; Bilbao effect on, 78; critique of, 20, 281n63, 330n49; defence as, 140; demise of, 282n70; and the global economy, 15; jobs in, 238, 246; literature, 26; and museums, 24–5; in Ottawa, xi, 115–16, 140; resistance to, 14, 16; rhetoric, 12, 23; in Vancouver, 232–3; work in, 12. *See also* artists; capitalism; Creative Cities; creative class; defence industry; entrepreneurs; finance industry; knowledge economy; neoliberalism; new economy; post-industrial economy; UK Mapping Document on the Creative Industries
creative workers, 115–16, 232–3, 247, 257. *See also* artists; entrepreneurs; knowledge workers; labour
critical museology, 67, 71, 292n135. *See also* curatorial studies; difficult knowledge; museum studies
Croatia, 119, 140, 305n46. *See also* Medak Pocket; peacekeeping
The Crossroads: The End of World War II, the Atomic Bomb, and the Origins of the Cold War (Smithsonian), 113, 135, 138, 307n112
cruel optimism (Berlant), 246
Cullen, Maurice, 119
cultural appropriation, 22–3, 29, 63
cultural nationalism, 36, 47, 51, 106
Culture Wars, 58, 284n137
curatorial studies, 26. *See also* reflexive curating
curators, 20; activist, 77; and activists, 271–2; collection activities of, 95–8; on collections policies, 91–2; concerns of, 22; expertise of, 138; Indigenous, 157–8, 162, 164–5, 191; lay-offs of, 83; and sponsors, 197. *See also* archives; museum collections; museum display; museum exhibitions
Curnoe, Greg, 35, 104–5, 285n11, 288n48

Danson, Barney, 122
da Silva, Judy, 104, 107
David, Joe, 93
David Suzuki Foundation, 208
Dead Horse and Rider in a Trench (Cullen), 119
decolonization, 313n73; of archives, 100–1; of

land, 107; of museums, 10, 23, 159–60, 166–7, 176–7, 218, 295n190; and oil, 209; and the politics of recognition, 77; processes of, 25, 206. *See also* Idle No More; Indigenization; Indigenous land; reconciliation
Decolonize This Place, 216, 313n64, 318n31, 327n230
Deepwater Horizon, 182
defence industry, 26, 67, 85, 115–16, 140
Delgamuukw v. British Columbia (SSC), 329n30
Democracy Street (MOA), 93, 268–70
DePape, Brigette, xiii
Department of Canadian Heritage, 117, 124, 153, 211, 254; cuts to, 167; human rights museum proposal, 149
Department of Communications, 61
Department of Defence, 135
Department of Indian and Northern Affairs, 53, 74
Derksen, Jeff, 236
Design Museum, 85–6, 98
Desmond, Viola, 305n57
Detroit, Michigan, 201
Diaguita Huascoaltinos Indigenous and Agricultural Community, 197
Dick, Beau, 93, 185, 213–15, 217. See also *Awalaskensis II*; Copper-Breaking Ceremony
difficult knowledge, 17–18, 22, 146, 152, 165, 177. *See also* critical museology
digital activism, 101, 206, 267. *See also* social media
direct action, xii, 28, 191, 209, 222
disobedient museum, 26, 280n28
disobedient objects, 90, 91
Disobedient Objects (Victoria and Albert), 18–19, 85–6
divestment, 184, 216
Documenta 13, 16, 18
Douglas, Stan, 233, 240–1, 261, 263–5, 337n23, 337n25. See also *Abbot & Cordova*
Douglas, Thomas (Lord Selkirk), 154
Doukhobors, 57
Downtown Eastside Residents Association (DERA), 261–2
drone warfare, xii
Drowning Sailor (Nichols), 119
Drury, Ivan, 226, 262
Dryden Chemical, 51, 103–4. *See also* Grassy Narrows; Reed Paper
Duhamel, Karine, 175, 314n108

East Timor Alert Network, 269
Ecology Ottawa, 197
Economopolous, Beka, 272. *See also* Not An Alternative
Edinburgh, UK, 97–8
Edmonton, Alberta, 56, 104, 106, 194, 200, 312n40
Egypt, 85, 243
Eke, Bright Ugochukwu, 222
Elizabeth A. Sackler Center for Feminist Art at the Brooklyn Museum, 298n40
Elsipogtog, NB, 208–9, 325n172
Emily Carr University, 239
Emin, Tracey, 233
emotional habitus, 123–4, 307n105. *See also* affect
Enbridge Inc., 193, 218; Line 6B, 202; Line 9, 201, 320n60; sponsorships of, 195, 323n120. *See also* corporate and private sponsorships; Northern Gateway; oil industry
EnCana Corporation, 153, 193, 196, 200, 312n40. *See also* corporate and private sponsorships; oil industry
Energy: Power to Choose (CSTM), 195–7, 199, 320n77, 321n82, 321n84. *See also* Canadian Association of Petroleum Producers (CAPP); Canadian Science and Technology Museum; corporate and private sponsorships; Imperial Oil
English-Wabigoon river system, 51, 103–4, 106, 302n18. See also *Changing Visions: The Canadian Landscape*; Grassy Narrows; mercury poisoning
Engstrom, Mark, 66
En Mas': Carnival and Performance Art of the Caribbean, 19
Enola Gay (airplane), 135
Enola Gay (Smithsonian). See *The Crossroads: The End of World War II, the Atomic Bomb, and the Origins of the Cold War*
entrepreneurs, 12, 79, 203, 232. *See also* artists; creative industries; creative workers
environmental justice activism: in Canada, 184, 200; and Indigenous peoples, 10, 104, 107; privilege of, 191; protests, 14–15, 21, 28, 51, 93, 219–22, 288n48; and sovereignty, 204–5; targeting of, 195, 205–10, 324n165. *See also* BP or Not BP; climate change; Liberate Tate; oil industry; resource extraction
Environmental Liberation Front, 324n160
Environment Canada, 205, 220–1
Epcor Centre (Calgary), 195
Equiterre, 220–1
Erasmus, George, 157
Erickson, Arthur, 71–2, 80
ethical oil, 202, 323n120
Every.Now.Then (AGO), 23, 86
experience economy, 12–13. *See also* performance art; social art

Experience Music Project (EMP), 79
Experimental Lakes Area, 205
Expo 67, 52. *See also* Indians of Canada Pavilion
Expo Rail, 153
Exxon, 321n87

Falun Gong, 229
Favro, Murray, 105–6
Federation of International Human Rights Museums, 311n12
feminism, 93, 169, 223–6, 288n48, 317n6. *See also* Elizabeth A. Sackler Center for Feminist Art at the Brooklyn Museum; gender; women's rights and suffrage
Ferguson, Missouri, xv
Film Museum (New York), 279n25
finance industry, 4, 11, 15, 236, 238. *See also* creative industries
First Nations: alliance with CFTA, 66; burial grounds, 54; contemporary art, 158; drinking water, 172, 315n135; history, 167, 325n194; and museums, 52, 55, 58–9, 60–1, 88–9, 212–14, 268; political actions of, 28, 72–4, 91, 208–9, 259; and racism, 146; soldiers, 120, 122; ways of knowing, 177, 192. *See also* Assembly of First Nations; Indigenous peoples; Inuit; land claims; Métis; reconciliation
First Nations Property Ownership Initiative (FNPOI), 205–6, 323n146. *See also* Indian Act
First World War. *See* World War I
First World War Canadian War Memorials Fund, 119
Fisher, Noah, 16–18. *See also* Occupy Museums
Fisheries and Oceans Canada, 205
Flaherty, Jim, 208
Flanagan, Tom, 206
flash mob, 221
Floor Burger (Oldenburg), 46, 48
Florida, Richard, 12, 70; Creative Cities, 231–3, 236; creative class, 78; creative industries, 246; mea culpa, 256; on Ottawa, 115
Fluxus, 188
Fontaine, Phil, 163
Fontaine, Tina, 145, 310n1, 310n6(5). *See also* Missing and Murdered Indigenous Women
Forbidden City, 8
Forbidden City (VAG), 193, 255
Forgotten (MOA), 75
For Those Who Cannot Speak: The Land, the Water, the Animals and the Future Generations (Myre), 299n59
Fort McKay First Nation, 201
Fort McMurray, Alberta, 193, 201, 323n143
Fort McMurray No. 468 First Nation, 201
For What? (Varley), 119
fossil fuel industry. *See* oil industry
Foster, Norman, 78, 312n40
fracking, 208, 319n51
Fraser, Andrea, 82, 216
Fraser, Nancy, 229
Fredericton, NB, 57
Freedom Road, 172–5, 177, 316n145, 316n154. *See also* Shoal Lake 40 First Nation
Free Grassy Narrows, 107
free speech, 29, 227, 264, 267, 319n44
free trade, 47, 281n65. *See also* neoliberalism
Free Trade Area of the Americas, xiii, 224, 328n12
from shangri-la to shangri-la (Lum), 234–5
Front de libération du Québec (FLQ), 47, 288n47
fundraising: for the arts, 4; for the CMHR, 149, 151, 153, 155, 159; and exhibition space, 151; and museum building, 82–3; for the new VAG, 251, 253–6. *See also* arts funding; blockbuster exhibitions; corporate and private sponsorships; "Massive Uprising"
Fuse Magazine, 27
The Future Starts Now (Victoria and Albert), 86

G7/G8, 15, 57, 70, 95, 100, 282n66
G20, 5, 57, 162, 180–1, 279n10, 282n66
Galbraith, John Kenneth, 133
Gander, NFL, 125
Gdansk, Poland, 303n13
Gehry, Frank, 3–4, 78–80, 297n7. *See also* Bilbao effect
gender, xiv, 223, 225
General Idea, 29
Genoa, Italy, 328n12
genocide, 84; admission of, 313n82; cultural, 149, 311n16; of Indigenous peoples, 158, 284n119; and Occupy, 247; use of term, 147, 163–6, 177, 315n115. *See also* Canadian Museum for Human Rights
gentrification: and artists, 239, 246; and condos, 237–8; and museums, 12, 18, 27, 36, 81–2, 301n111; and Occupy Vancouver, 244; of Occupy Wall Street, 334n144; protest against, xii, 28, 39, 245, 250–1; of Vancouver, 228, 230–1, 234, 256, 262, 265, 337n23. *See also* condominiums; real estate; urban regeneration
George, Dudley, 54
"The Gift" (Liberate Tate), 186–7
Giindajin Haawasti Guujaaw, 213
Gingrich, Newt, 135, 138
Gledhill, Jim, 96–8, 100–1
Glenbow Museum (Calgary), 9, 58–63, 290n108; archives, 321n87; and arts funding,

116–17; collecting of protest ephemera, 95, 100; defence of, 74; sponsorship of, 184, 191–2. *See also* Lubicon Lake First Nation; *Spirit Sings: Artistic Traditions of Canada's First Peoples*; Task Force on Museums and First Peoples
global economic crisis 2008, xii, 15–16, 79, 83, 167, 256. *See also* arts funding; creative industries
globalization, 24–5, 155, 236. *See also* alterglobalization movement
global justice movement, 229, 328n12
Goldcorp, 337n16. *See also* SFU Goldcorp Centre for the Arts
Goldman, Emma, 278n23
Gosselin, Viviane, 259
Gough, Ashlie, 248
Governor General's Performing Arts Awards, 193
Graham, Rodney, 233
Granatstein, J.L., 118, 120, 128, 138; on the CMHR, 152, 160–1; on peacekeeping, 304n37. *See also* Canadian War Museum; new warriors; Warrior Nation
Grassy Narrows, xiv, 51, 103–7, 303n28. *See also* Asubpeeschoseewagong First Nation; Canadian Museum for Human Rights; *Changing Visions: The Canadian Landscape*
Great Recession. *See* global economic crisis 2008
greenhouse gases. *See* climate change
Greenpeace, 190, 207, 219, 221, 319n39, 330n57
Greenwald, Dara, 100
greenwashing, 8, 182, 185, 210; through museums, 210, 255; through sponsorships, 211, 218. *See also* corporate and private sponsorships; oil industry
Greer, Germaine, 169
Griffiths Rankin Cook Architects, 124
Grimsby, Ontario, 53–4
Grindon, Gavin, 19, 85
Groce, Nancy, 199–200, 322n106
Gros-Louis, Michel, 54
Group of Seven, 35, 41–3, 89, 119, 305n49
Guatemala, 165
Guerrilla Art Action Group, 45
Guerrilla Girls, 225–6
Guerts, Joe, 138
Guggenheim: Abu Dhabi, 16, 187, 318n29; Bilbao, 78; New York, 20, 80, 187, 297n7. *See also* Bilbao effect
Guilbeault, Steven, 220–1
G.U.L.F., 183
Gulf Labor, 10, 16–17, 187
Haake, Hans, 216, 317n6(6)
Habermas, Jürgen, 229
Hadid, Zaha, 78
Hage, Rawi, 143
Haida Gwaii Museum and Heritage Centre, 93, 215, 218
Haida Nation, 61, 74, 213. *See also* Giindajin Haawasti Guujaaw; Haida Gwaii Museum and Heritage Centre
Haley Sharpe, 127, 130
Halifax, NS, 73, 125
Hall, Faron, 310n1
Hamilton, Duncan, 221
Hammond, Lorne (Dr), 91, 94–5, 98–9, 102
Hardt, Michael, 229–30
Hari Krishnas, 229
Harlem on My Mind (Met), 45, 293n164
Harper, Stephen (Prime Minister), 89; anti-climate agenda, 205–10, 219; embrace of new warriors, 126; government of, 154, 161; heritage policy, 167–8, 211; and the oil industry, 200, 203; residential schools apology, 162, 213, 313n82; support for CMHR, 152–3. *See also* Canada, federal government; Conservative Party of Canada; Jobs and Growth Act
Harris, Arthur "Bomber," 133
Harris, Mike (Premier), 68
Harrison, Julia, 61, 192, 291n124
Hart, Jim, 300n80
Hassan, Jamelie, 29
Haw, Brian, 282n90
Heiltsuk Cultural Education Centre, 215
Henry Moore Sculpture Centre, 35
Hereditary Chiefs, 289n76
Herzog & de Meuron, 253
He Will Not Divide Us (LeBoeuf), 279n25
Hill, Tom, 53
Hiroshima, 135, 303n14
Hirst, Damien, 233
Holocaust, 118, 150, 154, 161, 163. *See also* Canadian Museum for Human Rights; Canadian War Museum; genocide; Holocaust memorials
Holocaust memorials: at the CMHR, 148–50, 155, 161, 309n160, 311n11; at the CWM, 118, 137, 305n44, 309n160; in Ottawa, 305n43. *See also* Canadian Museum for Human Rights; Canadian War Museum; United States Memorial Holocaust Museum
Holodomor, 150, 155, 163, 315n115. *See also* genocide
homelessness, 22, 27, 98; and Occupy Wall Street, 334n144; protests, 318n31; in Vancouver, 230, 244–7, 257, 262–3, 333n128. *See also* gentrification; INTent City (Victoria);

Occupy Homes; Occupy Vancouver; real estate; Vancouver, BC
homophobia, 267
Hope to Nope: Graphics and Politics 2008–2018 (Design Museum), 85–6. See also *Nope to Hope* (Brixton)
Hopkins, Candice, 214
Hopkins, Owen, 98
Hudbay Minerals, 198
Hudson's Bay Company, 155
Human Cost (Liberate Tate), 183, 186
human rights: abuses in Canada, 156; call to action, 168–70, 177; Canada's promotion of, 200; education, 151; and extraction industries, 197–8; of Indigenous peoples, 171–4; liberal-order framework of, 150–2; museology, 280n26; politics of, 154; and tourism, 168. *See also* Canadian Museum for Human Rights; Charter of Rights and Freedoms; United Nations
Human Rights Tribunal, 170
Human Rights Watch, 129, 174
Humphrey, John, 148, 151
Hunter, Andrew, 285n13

Ice Bear (Hamilton), 221
identity politics, 39, 155, 170
Idle No More: actions, xiii, 326n218; CMHR vigil, 146, 169; collecting from, 101; Copper-Breaking Ceremony, 326n205; emergence of, xii, 16, 173, 206–7, 324n156; exhibition, 90
Illuminator, 187, 318n30
immigration, 10, 118, 120, 159; opposition to, 247, 267
imperialism, 16, 35, 63, 204, 247
Imperial Oil, 191, 196–7, 321n84, 321n85, 321n87. *See also* climate change; corporate and private sponsorships; *Energy: Power to Choose* (CSTM); oil industry
Imperial War Museum (UK), 125, 303n14, 307n104
An Incomplete History of Protest: Selections from the Whitney Collection, 1940–2017, 86
Independent Artists' Union (IAU), 55, 56, 67
Indian Act, 156, 167, 171, 205, 323n146. *See also* treaties
Indians of Canada Pavilion, 52–3, 288n53
INDIGENA (CMC), 158, 294n183, 294n185
Indigenization, 155–60, 164, 313n73. *See also* decolonization
Indigenous art, 60–1, 166. *See also* Indigenous artists
Indigenous artists, 51, 104, 158, 194, 282n78. *See also* Indigenous art
Indigenous communities: collecting from, 91; duty to consult with, 209; human remains belonging to, 289n76; museum responsibilities to, 61; and the oil industry, 194, 218; reconciliation with, 298n52; support for Lubicon Cree, 60; work with museums, xvi. *See also* First Nations; Indigenous peoples; Inuit; Métis
Indigenous Environmental Network, 189
Indigenous land: battle for, 316n141; colonization of, 247, 319n45; and pipelines, 216–17; protections for, 209; as resource frontier, 203–4. *See also* land claims; land protectors; water protectors
Indigenous peoples: activism, 58–9, 277n5, 289n75; appropriation from, 22–3, 29; assimilation of, 295n7; collecting from, 53–5, 100–1, 300n98; colonization of, 158, 280n31; continuity and resurgence of, 89, 267; engagement with museums, 9–10, 23, 29, 147, 150, 157–62, 191; and genocide, 163–5; government experiments on, 163–4; and human rights, 149, 151, 156; and the nation state, 111–12; and the oil industry, 204; and oral history, 89; and the politics of recognition, 25, 62, 72, 77, 216, 284n127; representation in museums, 7, 24, 52, 61–2, 68–9, 74–5, 85; resistance of, 16, 25, 77, 88, 91, 184; rights of, 28, 72–4, 172, 214, 259, 295n10, 296n11; self-determination and sovereignty of, 10, 90, 162, 166–8, 206, 209, 216, 218; systemic exclusion of, 171–2, 285n13. *See also* First Nations; Indigenous communities; Indigenous land; Inuit; land claims; land protectors; Métis; racism; reconciliation; residential schools; Shoal Lake 40 First Nation; *Spirit Sings: Artistic Traditions of Canada's First Peoples*; Task Force on Museums and First Peoples; treaties; water protectors
Indigenous Perspectives Gallery, 170, 176. *See also* Canadian Museum for Human Rights
Indonesia, 85, 203
inequality, 247; economic, 16, 247, 251, 333n117; and museums, 22, 79, 224; social, 21, 117
Institute of Contemporary Art (London), 232
Insurrectionary Anarchists of the Coast Salish Territories (IAOfCST), 225
intellectual property (IP), 11–12
INTent City (Victoria), 98
Interfaith Coalition against Hate Art, 68
Interference Archive (New York), 100
International Council of Museums (ICOM), 24, 60
International Monetary Fund (IMF), 15
International Workers of the World, 264, 279n25

interrogative museum, 83–4, 89
intersectionality, 10, 58, 66, 213, 327n230
The Interventionists (MASS MOCA), 298n37
Into the Heart of Africa (ROM), 9–11, 22, 27, 58, 63–6; apology for, 293n168; archive, 92; curation of, 292n135; marketing of, 292n140; outcome of protests against, 67–8; press coverage of, 293n157, 293n164; protesters of, 134; ROM's response to protest, 136. *See also* Coalition for the Truth About Africa (CFTA); media; Royal Ontario Museum
Inuit, 28, 72, 88, 147, 177; in Quebec, 51; representation in museums, 89. *See also* First Nations; Indigenous peoples; Métis
Inuit Centre (WAG), 256
I Object (British Museum), 85–6
Ipperwash, Ontario, 54
Iraq War, 14, 124–6
Isaac, Richard, 289n76
Isaac Gallery, 34
Islamophobia, 267
Israel, 142, 149–50, 152
It's All Happening So Fast, 86
It's Still Privileged Art (Condé and Beveridge), 49–50, 288n52

J18 Carnival Against Capital, 14
J20 Art Strike, 20
Jacks, David, 170
Jackson, A.Y., 35
James Bay hydroelectric project, 51
Janus Museum Consultants Ltd, 43
Japan, 135
Japanese internment camps, 124, 139, 151, 309n161
Jewish-Canadian community, 118, 151, 304n42
Jewish Museum (Berlin), 303n14, 304n19
Jobs and Growth Act, 205

Kahlo, Frida, 223–6. See also *Carr, O'Keefe, Kahlo: Place of Their Own* (VAG)
Kahnawake, 60
Kalamazoo River, Michigan, 202
Kanehsatà:ke Resistance, 54, 66, 91, 168, 289n85
Kantor, Istvan, 29
Kaouk, Aida, 143, 310n10
Karasawa, Yoshiko, 244–5
Kay, Diamond Darryl, 178–80
Kay Llinagaay, 93, 215
Kearns, Gertrude, 130–2
Kenora, Ontario, 106
Kerr, Clark, 287n36
Keystone XL pipeline, 201, 208
Kigali Genocide Memorial (Rwanda), 303n14
Kinder Morgan, 255, 322n110, 336n203
Kingston, Ontario, 54, 126
Kitchener, Ontario, 88
Kitimat, BC, 191, 201, 203
Klein, Naomi, xiv, 203–4
Klein, Ralph (Premier), 199
knowledge economy, 25, 246. *See also* creative industries
knowledge workers, 5, 12. *See also* creative industries; creative workers
Koch, David, 8, 183, 187, 189. *See also* Koch Industries
Koch Industries, 8, 187
Koolhaas, Rem, 78
Kwakwaka'wakw, 93, 185
Kwantlen Polytechnic University, 336n203
Kyoto Protocol, 219, 222, 327n1, 327n4

Laboeuf, Shia, 279n25
labour: affective, xi, 12; alienated, 12; of art, 20; big, 14; exploitation of, 15; in extraction industries, 197, 199–200; flexibility, 79; intellectual, 115; at museums and galleries, 187, 294n186; post-Fordist, 246, 281n63; precarious, 12, 16, 232–3, 247, 280n44; protests, 42, 229, 240–1, 318n29; records, 182. *See also* class; creative class; creative workers; knowledge workers
Lac Mégantic, Quebec, 202
Lalakensis/All Directions, 86, 326n205
Lamanna, Carmen, 106
Lambeth, Michel, 32–3, 35
land claims, 28, 61–3; archives, 300n98; and human rights, 156; ignoring of, 162; legal basis of, 295n10; of the Lubicon Cree, 191–2, 290n109, 291n117; and museums, 67, 159, 218; and sponsorship protests, 218; suppression of, 210. *See also* Indigenous land; Indigenous peoples; land protectors; treaties
land protectors, xvi–xvii, 10, 28, 51, 168; and climate change, 222; strategies of, 184; targeting of, 205, 210; threats to, 208–10. *See also* Indigenous land; water protectors
Land Spirit Power (NGC), 158, 294n183
Lands within Me: Expressions by Canadian Artists of Arab Origin (CMC), 142–4, 306n74. *See also* media
Langer, Eli, 67
Larwill Park, 243, 252–3, 255, 333n115. *See also* Vancouver Art Gallery
Law Commission of Canada, 205
Layton, Jack, 57
Lebanon, 142
LeBon, Gustav, xiv, 278n16
Leonardo, 85. *See also* defence industry

Leong, Oei Hong, 255
Les Automatistes, 287n20
"Les casseroles," 87, 298n49. *See also* Maple Spring
Levant, Ezra, 202
Levi-Perf, Susan, 209
Levy, Moe, 151
Lewis, John, xiii
Liberal Party of Canada, 116, 139, 161, 174, 212. *See also* Canada, federal government; Trudeau, Justin; Trudeau, Pierre
Liberate Tate, 10–11, 182–3, 195; actions of, 185–7, 319n46; cooperation with Canadian groups, 208; oil industry in London, 201; privilege of, 191; strategies of, 187–8, 193, 216, 326n225; work with Indigenous peoples, 190. *See also* "Birthmark"; British Petroleum; "The Gift"; *Human Cost*; oil industry; Tate Museum
Liberty Park. *See* Zucotti Park
Libeskind, Daniel, 78, 80, 83, 304n19
Library and Archives Canada, 167
Linklater, Tanya Lukin, 205
Lippard, Lucy, 8, 28
Logan, Tricia, 150, 157, 164
London, Ontario, 47, 285n11
London, UK: creative industries in, 115, 233; museums of, 7–8, 82, 85–6, 96–102, 232, 253, 307n104; oil industry in, 201; protests in, 14, 40, 182–3, 190, 282n90, 337n25; public institutions, 216, 230. *See also* Institute of Contemporary Art; Museum of London; National Gallery; Occupy London; Tate Museum; Trafalgar Square; Victoria and Albert
Lord Cultural Resources, 212, 252, 305n43
Los Angeles County Art Museum, 45
Los Angeles MOCA, 298n46
Louvre (Musée du), 44, 65, 111, 186, 222
Lubicon Lake First Nation, 58–63; boycott of *Spirit Sings*, 212, 291n117; land claim of, 76–7, 218, 290n109, 319n51; oil sponsorship action, 189–92. *See also* Glenbow Museum; Ominayak, Bernard; *Spirit Sings: Artistic Traditions of Canada's First Peoples*
Lum, Ken, 234–5
Lummi Nation, 327n230

McAdam, Sylvia, 206
McCord Museum (Montreal), 59, 291n112
MacDonald, George, 148
Macdonald, John A. (Prime Minister), 54
McDonough, Alexa, 143
Mackenzie, Robin, 105–6
McKibben, Bill, 215–16
McLean, Sheelah, 206
McMichael Canadian Art Collection, 223, 287n15
McRae, John, 122
Madonna, 223
Mallard, Derrick, 94
Mall of America, 206, 324n156
Malzen, Jerry, 33
Manhattan project, 135
Manitoba, 151
Manitoba Hydro, 315n137
Manson, Paul, 133
Manuel, George, 73
Mao Zedong Mausoleum, 8
Maple Spring, xii, 92, 100, 298n49. *See also* "Les casseroles"
Mar, Gary, 199
Marks, Laura U., 143
Marshall, Clement, 65
Marskell, David, 23
Masik, Pamela, 75
Massey, Vincent, 42, 121
Massey Commission, 42, 121, 305n50
"Massive Uprising," 3–5
MASS MOCA, 78, 80, 298n37
Matchee, Clayton, 130–2. *See also* Somalia Affair
material culture: of activism, xvi, 70, 76–7, 91–102; colonial, 160; display of, 18–19, 63, 67, 86, 90; Indigenous, 157–8. *See also* archives; museum collections; protest ephemera
May 1968, 280n44
Mayo, Edith, 95
Meares Island, 93, 300n79. *See also* anti-logging protests
Meat Dress (Sterbak), 294n186
Medak Pocket, 305n46. *See also* Croatia; peacekeeping
media: as allies, 112–13; anti-sponsorship coverage, 189; arts debates in, 42; Canadian War Museum coverage, 125–6, 134, 138–9, 141, 308n120; *Canvas of War* coverage, 120–1; climate coverage, 220, 222; CMHR coverage, 150–1, 155, 163, 169–70, 173; corporate control of, 149–50; coverage of museums building, 114; coverage of protests, 33, 41, 43, 225–6, 293n157, 293n164, 308n120; *Into the Heart of Africa* coverage, 63, 65–6; *Lands within Me* coverage, 143; and Occupy Vancouver, 247, 249; oil industry coverage, 194, 199; portrayal of Afghan war, 124; reporting on Indigenous actions, 73–4, 325n185; reporting on museum controversies, 9, 29, 40; role in protests, 40; sources, 6; *Spirit Sings* coverage, 61; US control of, 35; Woodsquat coverage, 262–3

memes, 101
Mercer Union Gallery (Toronto), 67
mercury poisoning, 51, 103, 106–7
Métis, 28, 72, 74, 88; in Fort McMurray area, 201, 322n112; heritage sites, 167; interventions in museums, 89, 147; material culture, 89; resistance, 155; ways of knowing, 177. *See also* First Nations; Indigenous peoples; Inuit
Metropolitan Museum (New York), 8, 18, 187; and nation, 111; protest against, 45, 293n164; sponsorship of, 183. See also *Harlem on My Mind* (Met)
Michael Audain Foundation, 239, 244. *See also* Audain, Michael
Middle East, 142, 200, 310n10, 318n29
Mikisew Cree First Nation, 201
Mikisew Cree First Nation v. Canada, 325n181
Mi'kmaq, 208–9
militant research, 29
militarization, 123–4, 244
military: artists, 307n113; Indonesian, 85; investment in, 27; in museums, 89, 112–13, 125, 128; research and development, 26; surveillance, 210; US, 45. *See also* Canadian military forces; defence industry; militarization; Warrior Nation
Minamata disease. *See* mercury poisoning
Mining Watch, 197
Minneapolis Institute of Art, 279n25
Missing and Murdered Indigenous Women (MMIW), 75, 145–6, 156, 310n2; and the CMHR, 164–5, 310n6(5). *See also* Fontaine, Tina
mob mentality, xiv, 278n16
modernist art, 41–2, 46–7, 78
Mohawk Warriors, 66, 168
Molesworth, Helen, 298n46
Monbiot, George, 327n7
Montebello, Quebec, 179
Montreal, Quebec: museum building in, 80, 256; Occupy, 230; pipelines, 201; student protests, 87, 100, 298n49. *See also* Maple Spring; McCord Museum; Montreal Museum of Fine Arts
Montreal Museum of Fine Arts, 67, 193
Moore, Henry, 35, 46, 286n22
Moriyama, Raymond, 124, 129–30, 306n70
Moriyama and Teshima Architects, 124, 129
multiculturalism, 23, 87, 89, 139, 144, 167
Murray, Stuart, 160, 163–4, 314n101
Musée des Civilisations (Quebec), 92
Museu de Arte Moderna (Rio de Janeiro), 317n27
Museum and Galleries Act (UK), 186–7
museum anthropology, 6, 26
museum audiences/visitors: and citizenship, 111–12; education of, 220, 295n190; engagement of, 13, 98, 159, 165, 168; expectations of, 22; experiences of, 90, 129, 163; Indigenous, 156; priority to, 21, 84; and protesters, 229; as white, 64
museum boards of trustees: AGO, 35–6; and artists, 246; interests of, 90; interventions of, 162; profiteering of, 82; protests against, 136, 294n186; ROM, 65; VAG, 242, 252; and Vietnam War, 51–2
museum collections: abandonment of, 13; changes to, 10, 294n185; colonial, 7, 217; of contemporary material culture, 76–7, 91, 298n34; decolonization of, 23, 25; human remains in, 54, 60, 158; of Indigenous activism, 54–5; Indigenous interventions into, 157, 296n24; limitations of, 91; opening of, 295n190; permanent, 87–8; practices, 53, 60, 84–5, 215, 282n78; protests against, 8, 10; and treaties, 218. *See also* archives; protest ephemera
museum controversies, 9–10, 28–9, 67, 284n137, 294n186, 320n77; about appropriation, 23; and change, 177, 211; about exhibition content, 22, 46, 89, 113, 130–9, 160, 173
museum display, 10; of ceremonial objects, 60; community input on, 291n121; decolonization of, 159–60; Indigenous intervention into, 157; and Indigenous relations, 296n24; of political material culture, 76–7, 298n34; practices, 84; storytelling, 165; used as protest strategy, 189. *See also* museum collections; museum exhibitions
museum exhibitions: of activist art, 271–2, 298n46; about activist movements, 77, 85–91; and archives, 26; change to, 294n185; decolonization of, 23; design of, 128; dialogue-based, 84; framing of, 292n135; interrogative, 89; narratives of, 25; permanent, 86–91, 102; power of, 18; protests against, 8, 28; racism in, 293n168; space, 151; spaces, 85. *See also* blockbuster exhibitions; museum display
MuseumNext USA, 22
Museum of Anthropology (MOA). *See* UBC Museum of Anthropology
Museum of Canadian Human Rights Violations (MCHRV), 100, 173, 175, 189. *See also* Shoal Lake 40 First Nation
Museum of London, 96–8, 100–2, 282n90. *See also* Gledhill, Jim
Museum of Memory and Human Rights (Chile), 148, 303n14
Museum of Modern Art (MOMA), 18, 20, 45;

board of trustees, 51–2; collections processes, 26; engagement with protest, 52; library, 301n118; political topics in, 268. *See also* Political Art Documentation/Distribution
Museum of Oil (Greenpeace), 319n39
Museum of the American Indian (New York), 291n117
Museum of the Second World War (Gdansk), 303n13
Museum of Vancouver, 26, 86–7, 93–4, 235, 253, 331n62. See also *City on Edge: A Century of Vancouver Activism*; protest ephemera
museum representation, 10, 23; identity, 39; of Indigenous peoples, 24, 52, 68; minority artists, 52. *See also* cultural appropriation; Indigenous peoples
Museums Act, 121, 153, 211
Museums Assistance Program, 153–4
Museums Association, 21–2
museum storage, 10, 95, 121, 214
museum studies, 7–8, 17–18, 21; canon, 43, 67, 279n12; and contentious politics, 24; critical, 26, 28, 58, 292n135; disobedient museum, 26, 280n28; national themes in, 111. *See also* Cameron, Duncan; critical museology; difficult knowledge; museum anthropology; Phillips, Ruth
Musqueam Cultural Education and Resource Centre, 215
Musqueam Nation, 71, 75, 257, 268–9
Myre, Nadia, 299n59

Nagasaki, Japan, 135
naming rights, 82–3, 251, 331n82. *See also* corporate and private sponsorships
Nasgaard, Roald, 34
National Arts Centre, 116, 195
National Association of Japanese Canadians, 139, 309n161
National Cambodian Heritage Museum and Killing Fields, 303n14
National Capital Commission, 122
National Council of Veterans Associations, 118, 134. *See also* Chadderton, Cliff
National Film Board, 56–7, 116
National Gallery (UK), 7–8, 40, 230
National Gallery of Canada, 29; architecture, 80, 303n17; cultural brokering of, 41–2; exhibitions, 158, 294n183; funding of, 70; fundraising, 312n43; Indigenous art in, 299n59; power of, 218; protests of, 67; rehanging of permanent collection, 89–90, 299n71; Rennie Gallery, 239, 331n82; sponsorship of, 317n6 (6); war art collection, 305n49. See also *For Those Who Cannot Speak: The Land, the Water, the Animals and the Future Generations*; Group of Seven; *Land Spirit Power* (NGC); *Voice of Fire*
national identity, 167; museums as representatives of, 112, 115, 130, 144, 155, 167, 211; and oil, 200, 203. *See also* citizenship; national museums; settler nationalism
National Indian Brotherhood, 104
nationalism: and oil, 202–3; parochial, 89, 247; progressive, 31, 51–3; and racism, 304n36; and war, 124. *See also* cultural nationalism; petroculture; settler nationalism
National Museum of Canada, 57
National Museum of China, 8
National Museum of Man, 41. *See also* Canadian Museum of Civilization; Canadian Museum of History
national museums of Canada, 75, 112, 115, 304n30; arm's-length from government, 138–9; and citizenship, 166–7; CMHR as, 155, 160–1; decentralization of, 148, 153–4; funding of, 116, 152, 254; fundraising for, 312n43; legislation, 236. *See also* authoritative institutions; Canadian Museum for Human Rights; Canadian Museum of Civilization; Canadian Museum of History; Canadian Museum of History Crown corporation; Canadian Science and Technology Museum; Expo Rail; Museums Act; National Gallery of Canada; National Portrait Gallery; Pier 21 Immigration Museum
National Portrait Gallery (Canada), 153, 166, 312n40
National Portrait Gallery (UK), 40, 317n1
National Research Council of Canada, 205
National Round Table on Environment and Economy, 205
National War Memorial (Ottawa), 122, 306n59, 307n107
nation-building, 25, 89–90; culture and, 305n50; museums and, 75, 88–90, 112, 295n190; and oil, 323n143; war and, 116, 120. *See also* Canadian War Museum; citizenship; settler colonialism; settler nationalism
Nations of Warriors, 54. *See also* "Walk of the Living Dead"
nation state, 35, 111, 205. *See also* Canada, federal government
Natural History Museum (Ottawa), 80
natural history museums, 11, 13, 187, 189
Navigable Waters Protection Act, 205, 323n144
Neal, Marlon, 293n161
Neel, David, 290n107

Negri, Antonio, 229–30
neoliberalism, 15, 281n65; and the arts, 12–13; and global cities, 82, 236; and museums, 76–7, 84, 114–16, 154; and Occupy Wall Street, 246; and philanthropy, 149; protest against, 15, 70, 247, 262; and public institutions, 20; in Vancouver, 226–7, 230, 237–41. *See also* capitalism; creative industries; globalization
Neo-Naturists, 317n20
Neutral Nation, 53
New Brunswick, 208–9
New Democratic Party, 57, 143, 212, 221, 285n11
new economy, xi, 12–13, 79, 232–3. *See also* creative industries
New Glasgow, NS, 305n57
New Left, 47, 51
Newman, Barnett, 29, 41, 294n186
new warriors, 120, 122–4, 140, 305n46. *See also* Warrior Nation
New York City: art market, 82; cultural funding in, 297n7; exhibitions/collections of protest ephemera from, 86, 96, 100, 298n46; Occupy Wall Street, 243, 245–6; oil industry in, 201–2; protests in, 7, 45, 52, 290n91, 318n31, 327n230. *See also* 9/11; Art Workers' Coalition; Guggenheim; Metropolitan Museum; Museum of Modern Art; Natural History Museum; Occupy Wall Street; Whitney Museum of American Art
New York Historical Society, 97
New Zealand, 159
Nichols, Jack, 119
Nisga'a Museum/Hli Goothl Wilp-Adokshl Nisga'a, 215
Noble, Sara, 178–80
Nope to Arms Collective, 86. See also *Nope to Hope* (Brixton)
Nope to Hope (Brixton), 86. See also *Hope to Nope*
North American Free Trade Agreement (NAFTA), 224–5, 328n12
North American Leaders' summit, 179
Northern Gateway pipeline, 195, 201
North Vancouver, BC, 239
Not An Alternative, 10, 24, 183, 318n31; Natural History Museum of, 188–9; open letter to museums, 187; on the role of museums, 272; strategies of, 188–9, 216–17
Notes from Nowhere, xiii
nuclear arms race, 135
Nunavut, 203
Nuu-chah-nulth, 93, 300n79

occupations, xiii, 16, 95, 106; of occupied land, 257; by the Occupy movement, 230, 243–51; by Shoal Lake 40, 173; of the UBC MOA, 55, 72–3, 268; of the Vancouver Post Office/Gallery, 7, 92, 94, 253. *See also* Occupy Vancouver; Occupy Wall Street
occupycondos, 250
Occupy Debt, 52
Occupy Faith, 318n31
Occupy Homes, 318n31
Occupy London, 84, 96–8, 102
Occupy Museums, 10–11, 16–17, 183, 333n116; activism of, 18; and creative industries rhetoric, 25; oil sponsorship actions, 187
Occupy Oakland, 334n143
Occupy the Pipeline, 187
Occupy Vancouver, 27, 228, 230–1; archiving of, 96, 333n120; as art, 250; city response to, 246–8; contradictions of, 247–8, 251, 257; organization of, 243–4, 265; VAG response to, 248–50
Occupy Wall Street, xii, 15–16, 230, 243; archives working group, 99–100, 102, 271; contradictions of, 247; and creative industries, 23; material culture of, 77, 96–7, 101; participants in, 245–6; as public art, 335n165; race and power in, 334n142, 334n144. *See also* Occupy Debt; Occupy Homes; Occupy Museums; Zucotti Park
Oda, Bev, 153
Oerlikon, 67, 294n173
Of Africa (ROM), 67
oil industry, xvi; and culture, 199–205, 208; greenwashing of, 203, 210; and Indigenous communities, 192, 218; in museums, 85–6; protests against, xii, 8, 10, 185–9, 216; research, 115; and sponsorships, 16, 27, 58–9, 62, 182–5, 191, 200, 210–18, 222, 317n5(6); sponsorships of Canadian museums, 184, 192–8, 211–16; threats to, 206–7. *See also* Alberta; British Petroleum; Canadian Association of Petroleum Producers; corporate and private sponsorship; Enbridge Inc.; Petro-Canada; petroculture; Shell Oil; Suncor; tar sands
oil sands. *See* tar sands
Oil Sands Discovery Centre, 193, 321n85, 323n143
Ojibway Warriors Society, 106
Oka Crisis. *See* Kanehsatà:ke Resistance
O'Keefe, Georgia, 223–4
Oldenburg, Claes, 46, 48
Oliver, Joe, 207–8
Ominayak, Bernard, 58
O'Neill, Mark, 128, 140, 212–13, 216
Onley, Toni, 104
Ontario, 54, 211; art scene, 31; arts funding, 35,

83; censorship protests, 57; Days of Action, 68; Ministry of Natural Resources, 103; "ring of fire," 203. *See also* Ontario Film Review Board; Queen's Park
Ontario College of Art and Design, 80
Ontario Film Review Board, 57
Open Casket (Schutz), 298n45
oral history, 89, 102
organized crime, 208
Origin Studios, 127
Other Sights art collective, 238, 331n74
Ottawa, Ontario, 42, 73, 193, 213; as a Creative City, 114–15, 140; museum building in, 256

Painters Eleven, 287n20
Palestine, 142, 149–50, 169
Palmater, Pam, 209
Pankhurst, Emmeline, 7, 41
Paris Climate Accord, 222
Parks Canada, 167
participatory art, 12–14, 19, 23, 189. *See also* performance art; performative protest; site-specific art; social art
Passionate Eye: Impressionist and Other Master Paintings (Montreal), 67
Patriot Act, xii
patriotism, 123, 138, 211
Peabody Museum of Archaeology and Ethnology (Harvard), 291n117
peacekeeping, 25, 117, 124; Croatia mission, 119; and human rights, 149, 151–2, 200; monument to, 122; narrative of, 120, 123, 125–6, 139, 304n37; in the new CWM, 128–9; and racism, 304n36; veterans of, 140
Pembina Foundation, 208
People for the Ethical Treatment of Animals (PETA), 8
People's Exhibition of Barrick (Mining Watch), 197
performance art, 13, 19, 213, 217, 250, 326n225. *See also* participatory art; site-specific art; social art; Yes Men
performative protest, 4, 10, 16, 18, 23, 62
Petro-Canada, 194, 200
petroculture, 199
petro-state, 25, 194
Petroushka (Clark), 299n71
Phillips, Ruth, 9–10, 42, 111, 157, 159; on decolonization of museums, 52–3, 159–60, 166–7, 295n190; as director of the MOA, 268; on *Spirit Sings*, 58, 60–1, 291n118, 294n183
Piano, Renzo, 78
Pickton, Robert, 331n71
Pier 21 Immigration Museum, 125, 153
Pimicikamak Cree First Nation, 315n137
Pink Bloc, 187–8
pipelines: and colonialism, 319n45; as environmentally friendly, 203; on Indigenous land, 212, 216–18; protests against, 94, 170, 184–91, 195, 200–1, 208, 322n110; and sponsorships, 255, 320n60, 3336n203. *See also* Keystone XL; Northern Gateway; TransMountain pipeline
Platform, 190, 208, 216
Point, Steven, 73
Poitras, Jane Ash, 290n107
Polaris Institute, 197
police: and the homeless, 248, 262–3; at museums, 3–4, 40, 56–7, 64, 169–70, 188, 225–7; at protests, xii, 5, 62, 226; response to protests, 68, 139, 178–81, 268–9; and tar sands opposition, 200, 207, 210, 324n165; violence, xv, 10, 65–6, 264–5, 282n87, 293n161, 299n71, 329n31, 335n168. *See also* agents provocateurs; security forces; surveillance
political art, 17, 19–20, 233; exhibitions of, 49–51, 85–6, 90, 294n185. *See also* activist art; *It's Still Privileged Art* (Condé and Beveridge)
Political Art Documentation/Distribution (PAD/D), 100, 288n53, 301n118
political correctness, 120, 123, 136, 140, 160–1
pollution, 104, 170, 208; art response, 222; and corporate sponsorship, 182–3; and the tar sands, 199–200, 321n85, 321n87. *See also* greenwashing
Polygon Gallery, 239, 332n83
Polygon Homes, 239, 244, 332n83
Pootlas, Archie, 74
pornography and obscenity legislation, 57–8, 67. *See also* censorship
Port Elizabeth, South Africa, 7, 279n16
Portland Hotel Society, 262–3
postcolonialism, 23, 42, 295n190
post-Fordism, 12–13, 246
post-industrial economy, 4, 11, 15. *See also* creative industries
potlatch, 157
Povarchook, Jillian, 93
poverty, 10; activism, 225–6, 230, 262–3, 279n16, 330n45; and Indigenous disenfranchisement, 157, 192. *See also* homelessness
Pratt, Christopher, 104
Pratt, Mary Louise, 71
precarity, 225, 246–7, 280n44. *See also* labour
Predock, Antoine, 154, 172–3
Prentice, Jim, 220
Presentation House, 239
Preserving Our Heritage: A Working Conference for Museums and First Peoples (1989), 157
press. *See* media

Prince of Wales Northern Heritage Centre (Yellowknife), 313n68
private collectors, 235, 239, 246, 255; oil companies as, 194–5. *See also* Audain, Michael; private galleries; Rennie, Bob
private galleries, 82, 150
Project Ploughshares, 129
Prom Arts, 154
Protestbarrick.net, 197
protest ephemera, 26–7; anti-war, 307n104; collecting policies, 95–6; collection of, 76–7, 92–102, 235, 253, 268, 284n133, 301n110; exhibitions of, 85–6, 272, 298n37; in museum archives, 27, 40, 70, 91–102. *See also* Museum of Vancouver; rapid response collecting; UBC Museum of Anthropology
public art, 239
public–private partnerships, 27, 149–50, 152–5, 239–40, 256
public space, xiii, 229–31, 262; museums as, 21, 69, 78; and Occupy, 243. *See also* counterpublics; public sphere; ritual
public sphere, 77, 82, 101, 207, 229–30, 267
pussy hats, 97, 101

Quartier des spectacles (Montreal), 80
406 Quebec, 54, 60, 66, 179, 202; anti-conscription in, 129; and the Constitution Act, 74; independence movement, 47, 68, 93; James Bay hydro project in, 51; museums funding, 242; student protests, 92, 100, 298n49. *See also* Maple Spring
Quebec City, xiii, xix, 92, 256, 328n12
Quebec student strike. *See* Maple Spring
Queen's Museum, 20, 298n46
Queen's Park, 54; protests at, 107

Rabinovitch, Victor, 136, 138, 144, 310n4
race, xiv, 28, 36, 42, 67. *See also* racism
racism, 63–4, 117, 267; anti-Arab, 143; anti-Indigenous, 284n119, 323n146; anti-Japanese, 309n161; environmental, 206; in museums, 66, 68; and peacekeeping, 304n36; and policing, 319n47; protest against, xii, xv, 10, 16, 106; systemic, 146, 175
Raging Grannies, 129, 269
Raicovich, Laura, 298n46
Randall Stout Architects, 256
RAND Corporation, 45
rapid response collecting, 96, 98, 271
Rat Life and Diet (Wieland), 48
RCMP Heritage Centre (Regina), 80
reactionary environmentalism, 202, 204–5
Reagan, Ronald (President), 287n36
real estate, 27; and art, 237–40; development, 231–2; and Occupy Vancouver, 244; in Vancouver, 228, 236, 252, 256–7. *See also* Canvas Georgia; condominiums; Vancouver, BC; Woodward's Department Store
real estate developers, 239–40; as art collectors, 235, 244–5, 256; and the arts, 239–40, 246; at the Olympics, 330n44; power of, 253, 262, 265. *See also* Audain, Michael; Concord Pacific; condominiums; Reliance Properties; Rennie, Bob
reconciliation, 25, 313n73, 314n102; museums as sites of, 88, 159, 164, 257, 298n52, 311n11; and the oil industry, 194, 209; opposition to, 267; work of, 175. *See also* decolonization; Indigenization; Truth and Reconciliation Commission of Canada (TRC)
Red River, 145
Red River Colony, 155
Redsky, Erwin (Chief), 172, 174–5. *See also* Shoal Lake 40 First Nation
Reed Paper, 51, 103–7
reflexive curating, 63, 89
refugees, 118, 169, 267
Refus Global, 287n23
Regina, Saskatchewan, 80, 206
Reid, Bill, 61
Reitzenstein, Reinhard, 105–6
relational aesthetics (Bourriaud), 14
Reliance Properties, 239
Rennie, Bob, 239, 250–2, 255, 331n82. *See also* condominiums; real estate developers; Vancouver Art Gallery
Rennie Marketing Systems, 239
repatriation of objects, xvi, 10, 60–1, 89, 157–8, 319n46; Indigenous advocacy for, 52, 88, 289n75. *See also* Indigenous communities; Indigenous peoples; reconciliation
Research Centre for Material Culture (Tropenmuseum), 6
residential schools, 54, 88; apology for, 162, 164, 173, 213; CMHR treatment of, 156, 161–5; and the extraction industry, 194; human rights abuses of, 149, 151, 157; TRC report on, 147. *See also* Truth and Reconciliation Commission of Canada (TRC)
resource extraction, 16, 26, 85–6; abuses of, 197; art responses to, 317n6(6); and assimilation of Indigenous peoples, 210; and Canadian culture, 192–3, 216; and colonialism, 319n45; dangers of, 191; immediacy of, 202, 217; and land, 184; opposition to, 106, 202; and settler nationalism, 203–4; sponsorships, 198. *See also* oil industry
resource frontiers, 203–4. *See also* resource extraction; settler colonialism

RETHINK: *Contemporary Art and Climate Change* (Copenhagen Centre for Contemporary Art), 221–2
Re-Visions (Banff Centre), 320n55
Richardson, Mary, 7, 41
Rickford, Greg, 174
Rights Action, 198
Rising Tide UK, 317n10
ritual, 77, 111–12, 129–30, 210, 216
Rivers, Khelsilem, 194
Roach, Charles, 66
Roberts, Amy, 99–100
Roberts, Goodridge, 104
Robertson, Gregor, 246–7
Rockefeller, Nelson, 45
Rockefeller Collection of American Art, 288n53
Rokeby Venus (Velazquez), 7, 41
Rombout, Luke, 241
The Rooms (St John's, NL), 80, 256
Rosler, Martha, 245–6
Royal Alberta Museum, 193, 256
Royal BC Museum, 91–2, 94–5, 98–9, 102. *See also* Hammond, Lorne
Royal Canadian Academy of Arts, 41, 43
Royal Canadian Legion, 124, 129, 134, 136, 138
Royal Canadian Mounted Police, 207–9. *See also* police; security forces
Royal Commission on Aboriginal Peoples (RCAP), 158
Royal Commission on National Development in the Arts, Letters, and Sciences. *See* Massey Commission
Royal Ontario Museum (ROM), 9–10; apology for *Into the Heart of Africa*, 293n168; board of trustees of, 65, 289n87; and climate change, 327n229; collecting practices of, 53–4, 92; contemporary art in, 80; fundraising, 83; protests against, 57, 60–1, 63–6, 68, 176, 293n155, 319n47; protests at, 43, 63, 287n36; renovation of, 80–1, 114, 242, 254, 256, 335n192. See also *Into the Heart of Africa*; *Of Africa*
Royal Opera House, 317n1
Royal Proclamation, 326n218
Royal Tyrrell Museum (Alberta), 68, 320n68
Rumsfeld, Donald, 139
R v. Sparrow, 209
Rwanda, 140, 163. *See also* Kigali Genocide Memorial (Rwanda)

Sacco, Pier Luigi, 233
Safdie, Moshe, 80, 303n17
Sagkeen First Nation, 145
Salloum, Jayce, 142–4
salvage paradigm, 52, 157
Sandell, Richard, 9, 21
Sanger, Penny, 125
Saraceno, Tomás, 222
Sarnia, Ontario, 201
Saskatoon, Saskatchewan, 256
Sault Ste Marie, Ontario, 73
Schnitger, Lara, 317n8 (interstice 5)
Schutz, Dana, 298n45
Science Museum (London), 98, 183
Seattle, Washington, xiii, 14, 79, 277n12. *See also* Battle for Seattle; Experience Music Project (EMP)
Second World War. *See* World War II
security forces, xii–xiii, 4; and environmentalists, 207, 209–10, 221; at museums, 64, 73, 85, 144, 226, 318n25; transparency of, 179; violence of, 184, 188. *See also* Canadian Security Intelligence Service; police; Royal Canadian Mounted Police; surveillance
Seidl, Joan, 228–9
Senate of Canada, 113, 309n160; investigation of charity funding, 208; subcommittee on Holocaust memorial, 118; subcommittee on Veterans' Affairs, 137–9, 141, 303n12, 304n42. *See also* Canada, federal government
Seneca, 53
Serrano, Andres, 68
settler colonialism, 280n31; and archives, 100–1; effects of, 146; histories of, 212; in museums, 157, 176, 215, 218; and Occupy, 247; opposition to, 206; politics of recognition, 25, 77, 216; and resource extraction, 184, 204–5, 210; traumas of, 162, 208–9. *See also* Canada; nation-building; residential schools; settler nationalism; settlers
settler nationalism, xvi; among Canadian artists, 31, 34–5; in museums, 39, 88; narratives of, 122, 139, 144; and resource extraction, 204, 210. *See also* Canada; nationalism; settler colonialism; settlers
settlers, 55, 160; as allies, 88, 173, 334n140; artists, 51; and land, 204, 280n31; moves to innocence, 77, 176–7. *See also* settler colonialism; settler nationalism
SFU Goldcorp Centre for the Arts, 263, 337n16. *See also* Woodward's Department Store
Shell Oil, 221; drilling on Indigenous land, 58, 218; sponsorships of, 62, 183–4, 191–2, 212. See also *Spirit Sings: Artistic Traditions of Canada's First Peoples*
Shoal Lake 40 First Nation, 27; and the CMHR, 146–7, 160, 169–76; community archiving, 100; road access to, 310n5(5), 316n141, 316n154; Road to Freedom campaign, 174. *See*

also Canadian Museum for Human Rights; Museum of Canadian Human Rights Violations
Shore, Forest and Beyond: Art from the Audain Collection (VAG), 244
Sierra Club, 195–6
Simon Fraser University: archives and special collections, 96, 243–4, 300n98, 333n120; as real estate developer, 239, 265, 337n17. *See also* SFU Goldcorp Centre for the Arts; Woodward's Department Store
Simpson, Leanne Betasamosake, 210
site-specific art, 234, 250. *See also* participatory art; performance art; social art
Six Nations, 53, 60–1, 289n76
Sixties Scoop, 156
Skidegate, BC, 93, 215
skinheads, 229
Skorton, David J., 18
slavery, 148, 161, 247
Slut Walk, 178–9
Smithsonian, 18; collecting of protest ephemera, 95–6; exhibitions, 113; Folklife Festival, 199–200, 322n106; and the National Mall, 230; protests at, 8, 189, 319n47. See also *The Crossroads: The End of World War II, the Atomic Bomb, and the Origins of the Cold War*
Smithsonian History and Technology Museum, 95
Smithsonian National Air and Space Museum, 135
Smithsonian National Museum of African American History and Culture, 18, 97, 282n87
Smithsonian National Museum of American History, 26
Snow, Michael, 47, 104–5
social art, 12–14, 19, 283n92. *See also* participatory art; site-specific art
social media, xii, 6, 40, 206, 213, 267, 328n4. *See also* digital activism; memes; Twitter
social movements, xiv–xvi, 6, 10, 15; archiving of, 26, 77, 100–2, 300n98; and art, 14, 19, 216; culture of, 283n96. *See also* Occupy Wall Street; political art; social art
social movement studies, 6, 278n16
social movement theory, 26, 278n16
Society of American Archivists, 101
Solidarity Coalition, 240–1
Somalia Affair, 121–2
South Africa, 7, 56
South America, 200
Southbank Centre, 183
Southern Chiefs Organization, 163
Southwest Energy, 208–9
Sparrow, Gail, 268–9
special interest groups, 134, 136, 140–1, 160, 207–8, 306n84
Spectra Energy, 187
Spence, Theresa (Chief), 324n152
Spirit Sings: Artistic Traditions of Canada's First Peoples (Glenbow), 9–11, 22, 27; boycott of, 58–63, 212, 217–18, 290n108, 291n117; defence of, 74, 134; marketing of, 292n140; outcome of protests against, 67–8, 76–7, 84, 157, 291n118, 320n55; sponsorship of, 184, 191–2. *See also* boycotts; Glenbow Museum; Lubicon Lake First Nation; Shell Oil; Task Force on Museums and First Peoples
sponsorship. *See* corporate and private sponsorships
Squamish-Lil'wat Cultural Centre, 215
Squamish Nation, 257
squats, 101, 234–5, 243; in Vancouver, xii, 245, 262–3, 330n57. *See also* Woodsquat
standpoint politics, 9, 47, 58, 101, 235
staples theory, 204. *See also* resource frontiers
starchitects, 3, 12, 124, 149, 154, 240; and the new economy, 79. *See also* architecture; Bilbao effect; Creative Cities
Statistics Canada, 205
Statoil, 183, 190, 193, 317n27, 319n44
Stelmach, Ed (Premier), 221
Sterbak, Jana, 294n186
Stopp Oljesponsing av Norsk Kulturliv, 317n27
Stout, Randall, 80
Students for a Free Tibet, 269
Suffragette City (Schnitger), 317n8 (interstice 5)
suffragists, 7, 40–1. *See also* women's rights and suffrage
Suncor, 193, 200. *See also* oil industry
Sunken Cities (British Museum), 186
surveillance, xv, 101, 208–10, 324n165. *See also* police; security forces
Suzuki, David, 327n229
Swann, Peter, 43–5, 47–8, 52, 65, 287n29, 289n87
Sydney Biennale 2014, 280n33
synchronic museum, 78
Syncrude Canada Ltd., 193–5, 320n68

T'aaw, 93, 213–15. See also *Awalaskensis II: Journey of Truth and Unity*; Copper-Breaking Ceremony; Dick, Beau
Tahrir Square, xiii, 243
Take Back the Night, 229
Taliban, 154
Talisman Energy Inc., 197
tar sands, 107, 320n68, 321n85; culture of,

199–205; investment in, 187, 193, 255, 319n44; lobbying for, 323n120; representation in exhibitions, 196–7; resistance to, 190, 210, 213; in US perspective, 323n143. *See also* oil industry; petroculture
Taskforce on Military History Museums Collections in Canada, 304n30
Task Force on Museums and First Peoples, 10, 61–2, 68; backtracking on, 167–8, 212; outcomes of, 76–7, 157–8, 160–1, 164–5. See also *Spirit Sings: Artistic Traditions of Canada's First Peoples*
Tate Museum, 8, 239, 282n90; Modern, 80, 186, 232, 253; and oil sponsorship, 182–3, 185, 201, 318n26; sponsorship protests, 186–8, 195, 216. *See also* Liberate Tate
Tea Party, 96
tear gas, xiii–xiv, 168, 277n6
tear gas epiphany, xii–xiii, xv–xvi, 277n6; in the archive, 102; fragility of, 180–1; joy of, 191; in museums, 18–19
Telefilm Canada, 116
temporary autonomous zones, 188
terrorism, 202, 207–9, 324n165. *See also* climate jihadist
terrorist attacks, xii, 120. *See also* 9/11
Texas, 201, 255
Thanks But No Tanks (Haida Gwaii Museum), 218
Themuseum (Kitchener, Ontario), 23, 88
This Is Not an Exhibition (MOA), 268
Thomas, Jacob (Chief), 60
Thomas-Muller, Clayton, 189, 216
Thompson, Nato, 298n37
Thomson, Tom, 35
Thunder Bay Art Gallery, 61
Tiananmen Square, 8
Tichkowsky, Kyla, 95
Tides Canada, 208
tobacco industry, 85–6, 320n59
Toronto, Ontario, 12, 33, 286n22; Black community, 64–6, 68; cultural establishment of, 4, 42; Idle No More in, 206; museum building in, 256; police, 178–81, 293n161; protests in, 5, 32, 56, 107. *See also* Art Gallery of Ontario; G20; Royal Ontario Museum
Toronto Police Accountability Coalition, 179
Torrington (Alberta) Gopher Museum, 6, 8
tourism, 112, 155, 226; global cities, 5, 233, 236; and museums, 24, 78, 116, 168, 177; in Vancouver, 229, 240, 243
Traces (Belmore), 297n13, 314n103
Trade Routes, 154
Trafalgar Square, 8, 190, 230
Transfield, 280n33
TransMountain pipeline, 201, 255, 322n110, 336n203
trans-rights activism, 169
treaties, 72–3, 89, 167, 322n112; honouring of, 216–17; rights, 171, 191–2, 209, 295n7, 295n10, 323n146. *See also* Indian Act
Treaty 1, 147
Treaty 8, 191, 322n112
Trudeau, Justin, 174–5, 190, 203, 209, 327n2
Trudeau, Pierre, 47, 72–4, 149, 289n75, 296n11
True Patriot Love/Veritable Amour Patriotique (Wieland; NGC), 288n48
Trump, Donald, 20, 97–8, 267
Trump Baby, 97–9, 301n109
Truth and Reconciliation Commission of Canada (TRC), 88, 147, 161–2, 298n52; calls to action, 160; recommendations for museums, 158; revelations of, 164. *See also* reconciliation; residential schools
Tsleil-Waututh Nation, 257
turions, cheyanne, 162, 218, 285n140
Tushingham, Douglas, 53
Twitter, 101, 220, 267, 328n4. *See also* social media

UBC Museum of Anthropology, 28, 80; encouragement of protests, 176–7; exhibitions, 215, 310n7; occupation of, 55, 59, 71–5, 296n17; protest collection of, 93, 268–71; relationship with Indigenous peoples, 296n24
UK Mapping Document on the Creative Industries, 11–12, 14, 78, 121
Ukrainian Canadian Civil Liberties Association, 150
Ukrainian-Canadian community, 150–1, 157, 315n115
Ukrainian Canadian Congress, 150
UK Tar Sands Network, 190
U'Mista Cultural Centre, 25
Underground Railway, 150
Union of BC Indian Chiefs, 73–4, 296n11, 300n98
United Kingdom, xiv, 22, 72–3; and the creative industries, 12, 15, 232–3; exhibitions on protest movements, 85–6; museum boards in, 16; museum sponsorship in, 21, 182–5, 255, 297n10; protests in, xi, 16, 43, 185–7, 327n230; role of museums in, 41. *See also* UK Mapping Document on the Creative Industries
United Nations, 148, 156, 219; Declaration of Human Rights, 151; Declaration on the Rights of Indigenous Peoples (UNDRIP), 88, 158, 209. *See also* COP 15; COP 21

United States, xi, xii, 16; assimilationist policies, 157; Congress, 135; Culture Wars, 58; draft dodgers, 129; exhibitions on protest movements, 85–6; funding for culture, 297n7; as imperial power, 35, 48; museum boards in, 16; museum protests in, 10, 34, 44–5, 51, 327n230; museums in, 20, 23, 112, 294n185; oil market, 201; oil sponsorship in, 187–9, 336n203; Second World War generation, 135. *See also* Vietnam War
United States Memorial Holocaust Museum, 20, 148, 268, 303n14, 311n9, 315n111
United Technologies, 67
universal survey museums, 6, 80, 111–12, 129–30. *See also* authoritative institutions
University of Alberta Museum, 193
University of British Columbia (UBC), 28, 71, 75; Occupy Archive, 300n98; protest events, 94, 268, 290n107; as real estate developer, 337n17
University of Victoria, 94, 300n98
urban regeneration, 155, 168, 240. *See also* Bilbao effect; gentrification
Urban Subjects, 231
Urquhart, Tony, 104

V&A. *See* Victoria and Albert
The Valour and the Horror, 133, 308n119, 309n160
Vancouver, BC: art scene, 27, 232–5, 246, 252, 331n82, 332n93; as a creative city, 232–3, 237–40; development of, 329n31, 330n56; Downtown Eastside, 75, 237, 239, 245, 261–5, 331n71; Gastown Riot, 264, 337n23; as a global city, 241; homelessness in, 225, 230–1, 244–5, 262–3, 331n70; pipelines in, 201; as post-national, 236; protest material culture, 93–4, 229, 235; protests in, 73, 227–9, 264, 328n12, 333n127; public space, 230; Strathcona neighbourhood, 86. *See also* Burnaby, BC; gentrification; real estate; real estate developers; Vancouver Art Gallery; Vancouverism; Vancouver Olympics
Vancouver Anti-Poverty Committee, 225–6, 262–3
Vancouver Area Network of Drug Users (VANDU), 261
Vancouver Art Gallery: collection, 94; and contemporary art, 233–4, 330n50, 332n99; funding of, 82–3, 236, 335n194, 336n200; new building, 239–43, 251–7, 333n114, 335n192; occupation of, 7, 42, 92; oil sponsorship, 193, 255–6; protests against, 55, 68; as site for protests, 8, 28, 223–32, 244, 248–9, 253–60, 287n21, 329n28, 329n31, 332n91. *See also* Bartels, Kathleen; Canvas Georgia; fundraising; gentrification; Larwill Park; Occupy Vancouver; real estate; real estate developers; Vancouver, BC
Vancouver Artists' League, 55
Vancouverism, 238, 240
Vancouver Olympics, 93, 230, 257; housing squat, 245; as real estate deal, 330n44; sponsors of, 333n127
Vancouver Post Office, 92, 94, 329n31
Vancouver School, 238
Varley, F.H., 119
veterans: activism, 27, 76, 112–13, 116; fundraising, 151, 311n14; opening of the new CWM, 113; opposition to Holocaust memorial, 118, 304n42; protest of CWM display, 130–4, 136–8; as special interest group, 140–1; US, 135. *See also* Canadian War Museum
Victoria, BC, 93, 98
Victoria and Albert, 18–19, 85–6, 96, 301n111
Victory of Samothrace, 186, 222
Vietnam War: and museums, 51–2; protests against, 45, 48, 95, 129, 228, 279n15, 285n11, 288n48
Vimy Ridge, 121–2, 126, 131
Vision Vancouver, 330n45
visual culture studies, 28, 42, 58. *See also* art history; museum studies
Voice of Fire (Newman), 41, 294n186
Voice of Women, The, 43

W2 Community Media Arts, 265
W.A.G.E., 52
Walia, Harsha, 10
"Walk of the Living Dead," 54
Wall, Jeff, 233
Wallace, Ian, 29
wampum, 89
Wanderingspirit, Alvin, 59
War on Terror, 124
war art, 116, 118–19, 132. *See also* Beaverbrook Collection of War Art; Canadian War Museum; *Canvas of War*; War Art program
War Art program, 121, 308n114, 308n116
Ware, Syrus Marcus, 23
War Measures Act, 47
war museums, 11, 130, 303n14. *See also* Canadian War Museum; Imperial War Museum
War of 1812, 120, 126, 167, 325n190, 325n191
Warrior Nation, 25; and human rights, 149, 151–2; in museums, 89, 125–6, 128–32, 200, 325n191; narrative of, 120–4, 139, 307n105; protests against, 124. *See also* Canadian military forces; new warriors
warrior societies, 66, 206–7

Washington Consensus, 281n65. *See also* neoliberalism
water protectors, xvi–xvii, 10, 28, 51, 168; and climate change, 222; strategies of, 184; threats to, 205, 208. *See also* land protectors
Waters, Moya, 73
Watson, Scott, 215
Wattenmaker, Richard, 31–4, 47, 51, 106
welfare state, 13, 257, 281n65
Wendat, 54
West Coast Environmental Law, 208
Western Front artist-run centre, 57
Weyerhauser, 104
White Dog Reserve, 103
white supremacy, xii, 267
Whitney Biennale, 16, 82, 298n45
Whitney Museum of American Art, 18, 26; engagement with protests, 52; exhibition of protest ephemera, 86; protests at, 187, 288n53; and race, 45. See also *An Incomplete History of Protest: Selections from the Whitney Collection, 1940–2017*
Widgington, Dave, 100
Wieland, Joyce, 36, 47–8, 104–5, 286n23, 288n48, 302n15
Wilson, Fred, 216
Wilson, Nina, 206
Windsor, Ontario, 54, 106, 201
Winnipeg, Manitoba, 145–6, 154–5, 312n35, 313n52; and the CMHR, 151–2, 177; demonstrations in, 73; Indigenous population of, 147; municipal water system, 146, 171–2, 315n134; and Shoal Lake 40, 174. *See also* Alexander Docks (Winnipeg); Canadian Museum for Human Rights; Shoal Lake 40 First Nation; Treaty 1
Winnipeg Art Gallery, 256
Winnipeg General Strike, 86, 325n193
Withrow, William, 46
Women Opposed to Political Intimidation, 269
Women's March 2017, 77, 97, 101. *See also* pussy hats
women's rights and suffrage, 42, 45, 100, 152
Wong, Paul, 55, 241, 290n105. See also *Confused: Sexual Views* (VAG)
Woodland Cultural Centre, 53, 61
Woodsquat, 245, 262–5, 331n71
Woodward's Department Store, 239, 261, 264–5, 331n81, 337n23. *See also* Woodsquat
World Bank, 70
World Trade Organization (WTO), xiii, 15, 70
World War I, 119–21, 129
World War II, 112, 119–21, 130, 133, 136–7. *See also* Bomber Command; Japanese internment camps
World Wildlife Fund, 221
Wounded Knee, South Dakota, 106

Ya Basta!, 187–8
Yee, Jessica, 247
Yellowknife, NWT, 313n68
Yes Men, 190, 220–2, 327n12
Young British Artists (YBAs), 233
YouTube, 179

Zapatista uprising, 15, 328n12
Zucotti Park, 96, 243, 245–6